Foreword

From a bracing walk across the hills and tarns of The Lake District to a relaxing weekend spent discovering the unspoilt hamlets of East Anglia, nothing quite matches getting off the beaten track and exploring Britain's areas of outstanding beauty.

Each month, *Country Living Magazine* celebrates the richness and diversity of our countryside with features on rural Britain and the traditions that have their roots there. So it is with great pleasure that I introduce you to the *Country Living Magazine Guide to Rural England* series. Packed with information about unusual and unique aspects of our countryside, the guides will point both fair-weather and intrepid travellers in the right direction.

Each chapter provides a fascinating tour of the West Country area, with insights into local heritage and history and easy-to-read facts on a wealth of places to visit, stay, eat, drink and shop.

I hope that this guide will help make your visit a rewarding and stimulating experience and that you will return inspired, refreshed and ready to head off on your next countryside adventure.

Susy Smith

Susy Smith
Editor, Country Living magazine

PS To subscribe to *Country Living Magazine* each month, call 01858 438844

Introduction

This is the 3rd edition of the *Country Living Guide to Rural England - The West Country* and we are sure that it will be as popular as its predecessors. Regular readers will note that the page layouts have been attractively redesigned and that we have provided more information on the places, people, and activities covered. Also, in the introduction to each village or town we have summarized and categorized the main attractions to be found there which makes it easier for readers to plan their visit. David Gerrard, a very experienced travel writer has, of course, completely updated the contents of the guide and ensured that it is packed with vivid descriptions, historical stories, amusing anecdotes and interesting facts on hundreds of places in Cornwall, Devon, Dorset and Somerset

The coloured advertising panels within each chapter provide further information on places to see, stay, eat, drink, shop and even exercise! We have also selected a number of walks from walkingworld.com (full details of this website may be found to the rear of the guide) which we highly recommend if you wish to appreciate fully the beauty and charm of the varied rural landscapes and coastlines of the West Country.

The guide however is not simply an "armchair tour". Its prime aim is to encourage the reader to visit the places described and discover much more about the wonderful towns, villages and countryside of the West Country. In this respect we would like to thank all the Tourist Information Centres who helped us to provide you with up-to-date information. Whether you decide to explore this region by wheeled transport or on foot we are sure you will find it a very uplifting experience.

We are always interested in receiving comments on places covered (or not covered) in our guides so please do not hesitate to use the reader reaction forms provided at the rear of this guide to give us your considered comments. This will help us refine and improve the content of the next edition. We also welcome any general comments which will help improve the overall presentation of the guides themselves.

For more information on the full range of travel guides published by Travel Publishing please refer to the order form at the rear of this guide or log on to our website (see below).

Travel Publishing

Did you know that you can also search our website for details of thousands of places to see, stay, eat or drink throughout Britain and Ireland? Our site has become increasingly popular and now receives over 160,000 hits per day. Try it!

website: www.travelpublishing.co.uk

Contents

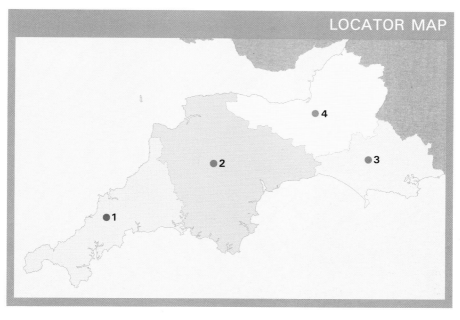

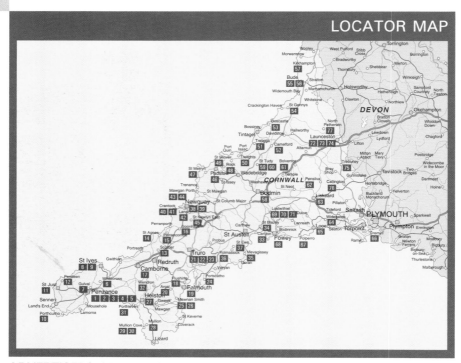

LOCATOR MAP

ADVERTISERS AND PLACES OF INTEREST

🏠 historic building   🏛 museum   🏛 historic site   🌿 scenic attraction   🌱 flora and fauna

1 Cornwall

"I like Cornwall very much. It is not England," wrote DH Lawrence. That was more than 80 years ago but the ancient Duchy of Cornwall remains stubbornly distinct from the rest of England, not just in its dramatic and spectacular scenery, but in its strong Celtic heritage. The landscape is dotted with ancient monuments, crosses and holy wells, and ancient legends – especially those relating to King Arthur and the Knights of the Round Table – appear to have been hot-wired into the Cornish psyche.

Cornish people have been recognised as a separate identity by the Commission for

St Michaels Mount

🎭 stories and anecdotes   🐦 famous people   🎨 art and craft   🎟 entertainment and sport   🚶 walks

Racial Equality and they have their own distinctive and attractive dialect. According to the Cornish Language Board, around 2,600 people still speak Kernuack, the original language of the peninsula. A firm in Helston occasionally publishes books in the ancient language and Kernuack has been recognised as a living language by the European Commission. Elements of Kernuack still survive in the names of Cornish places and people – as Sir Walter Scott put it: *By Tre-, Pol- and Pen- , You shall know all true Cornishmen.*

Kingsand across Cawsand Bay

One simple fact about the county helps to explain its distinct character. Wherever you are in Cornwall, you are never more than 20 miles from the sea. Maritime trade started early here – in the days of King Solomon, the Cornish people were already trading tin with the Phoenicians. Cornish eyes, it seems, were always turned seawards rather than inland, and the people's cultural affinity was with the Celtic diaspora of Ireland and Brittany rather than their mainland neighbours.

Porthleven Harbour

Added to this cultural separation was the county's physical distance from major centres of population. Even today, Cornwall's population of around 500,000 is less than that of the city of Bristol. There's not a single mile of motorway within its boundaries and long stretches of the main through route, the A30 from Penzance to London, are still single carriageway.

It was this isolation – and the luminous light of the area – that attracted major artists to the little seaside resort of St Ives which now boasts a world-class art gallery in the Tate St Ives. More recently, an abandoned china clay pit has been transformed into what has been described as the Eighth Wonder of the World, the inspired – and phenomenally successful – Eden Project whose enormous bio-spheres celebrate the complex relationship between plants, people and resources.

Elsewhere, the county boasts the third largest natural harbour in the world, Falmouth; acres of glorious gardens such as the Lost Gardens of Heligan; King Arthur's legendary fortress at Tintagel, and other medieval castles at St Mawes, Falmouth and St Michael's Mount; the wonderful Elizabethan mansion of Prideaux Place at Padstow; and, of course, Land's End where the granite bulwark overlooks the Atlantic waters beneath which lies the legendary Land of Lyonesse.

Penzance

Penzance's famous promenade, the longest in Cornwall, runs from the open air art deco-style Jubilee Swimming Pool around the broad curve of Mount's Bay. Just along from the Jubilee Pool are the harbour and docks, still busy with fishing and pleasure boats. The town's main street is Market Jew Street, a busy shopping area that leads gently uphill to the handsome classical building of the **Market House** (1836). In front of this domed structure stands a statue to Penzance's most famous son, Sir Humphry Davy, the scientist best remembered for inventing the miners' safety lamp. Born in a nearby street, Davy was one of the foremost chemists of the 19th century and, along with his contribution to miners' safety, he also founded both the Athenaeum Club and London Zoo.

Leading downhill from the Market House is the town's most interesting area, Chapel Street. Along this thoroughfare stands the exotic **Egyptian House**, created from two cottages in the 1830s by John Lavin, to entice customers into his shop. Although the designer of the magnificent façade is unknown, it is believed to have been inspired by the Egyptian Hall in Piccadilly, London. Opposite this splendid building stands the Union Hotel, whose Georgian façade hides an

THE PENZANCE ART GALLERY / PZAG INTERNATIONAL FINE ARTS

1 East Terrace, Penzance, Cornwall TR18 2DT
4 New Street, Penzance, Cornwall TR18 2LZ
Tel: 01736 332999
website: www.thepenzanceartgallery.com

Penzance is known as "The Gateway to Penwith" – the peninsula that leads down to Land's End. On the south coast of the peninsula, Newlyn formed as an art colony from 1873 when J. Henry Martin took up residence there. On the north coast, the Atlantic Coast colony of St Ives formed following JM Whistler's visit in 1883. What drew artists here in the past was the light, and the colour that created form and which continues to draw artists today.

So Penzance was an appropriate location for artists Melanie Anne Camp CWS and Vaughan Warren RAS to open the **Penzance Art Gallery** in August 2004. "The work The Penzance Art Gallery represents" they say, " is an expression of that tradition reaffirming the influence of the area upon contemporary British painting".

In addition to their own paintings the gallery showcases the work of many leading artists. Among them are Ben Gunn, Nicholas St John Rosse, David Penhale, Gillian Hobbs, John O'Carroll, Raymund Rogers RAS, John Blight CWS, Carl and Ralf Thorgood, Mark Bennett RAS and Brian and Cynthia Austen.

The Gallery also exhibits works by the sculptors Michael Chaikin, Bas Roscoe and Chris Holmes, and the photographers Peter Crumpler, Selina Bates and Keith Spurgin.

The Gallery website occupies five floors with paintings displayed on the ground floor; prints on the first floor; photography on the second; books and poetry (Melanie is also an accomplished poet) on the third; sculpture and woodwork on the fourth and jewellery on the top floor.

During the summer months, the gallery hosts a variety of demonstration and tutorials with experienced artists conducting seminars on topics such as life drawing, still life drawing and the techniques of the masters. Full details can be found on the gallery's website. The gallery is open Wed-Sat, 11am until 4pm all year.

🏛 historic building   🏛 museum   🏛 historic site   🏞 scenic attraction   🌱 flora and fauna

LEATHER CRAFTS

24 Causewayhead, Penzance, Cornwall TR18 2SP
Tel: 01736 367200
website: ww.bulldogbelts.co.uk

John Grey established **Bulldog Belts** as a manufacturer of leather belts to the wholesale trade back in 1968 in St Ives. He subsequently moved to Penzance in 2002 where he has continued to manufacture hand-tooled leather goods using the best English cowhide. He currently makes shoulder bags, belts and small leather goods featuring his own designs, Celtic patterns and oak leaf tooling. He also carries a wide range of motorcycle gear, toolrolls, belts, pouches and jackets. One of his earliest products was guitar straps which were used by major stars such as Mike Oldfield, Spandau Ballet, the Cliff Richard band and Duran Duran.

impressive Elizabethan interior. From here was made the first announcement in mainland England of the victory of Trafalgar and the death of Lord Nelson. Chapel Street was also the childhood home of Marie Branwell, the mother of the Brontë sisters.

For centuries, a remote market town that made its living from fishing, mining and smuggling, Penzance today is popular with holidaymakers as well as being the ferry port for the Isles of Scilly. Along with its near neighbours, Newlyn and Mousehole, Penzance

JUST CORNISH

65 Causeway Head, Penzance, Cornwall TR18 2SR
Tel: 01736 331616
e-mail: milo@justcornish.com
website: www.justcornish.com

For a special memento of a holiday in Cornwall, a visit to **Just Cornish** is strongly recommended. Here, owner Milo Perrin has put together a fascinating collection of contemporary arts, crafts and giftware, every piece of which has been proudly made in Cornwall. There's a wide selection of paintings by local artists such as Sarah Vivian, Izumi Omori, Jo Poore and Nick Smith, photography by Philip Trevenen and Andrew Ray as well as a huge choice of CDs and DVDs by Cornish musicians and film makers. In the books department you'll find over 700 titles – if it is published in Cornwall it will almost certainly be here.

The book stock includes the most comprehensive selection of Cornish language material to be found anywhere - full details can be found on the Just Cornish website. In the clothing area there are fishermen's smocks and "chunky" jumpers, T-shirts, etc all with a Cornish provenance, tartan bandanas, scarves and ties, and some genuine surfwear. The gifts ranges from calendars and candles to satellite maps of the local area and collections from St Justin pewter and South Crofty tin. There's also a great natural cosmetics range, including the internationally renowned Spezia Organic Care. Just Cornish also has a branch in the gallery hotspot of St Just in Penwith - where you'll find about 13 galleries in a town of 3000 people. Look out for the "Just Arts" leaflet for details on these.

HARBOUR CRYSTALS

69 Causewayhead, Penzance,
Cornwall TR18 2SR
Tel: 01736 874455
e-mail: sales@harbourcrystals.com
website: www.harbourcrystals.com

Combining a Shop and Complementary Therapy Centre, a visit to Harbour Crystals can offer you a deep sense of relaxation, relief from a nagging health complaint, as well as a pleasure of beautiful and unusual gifts and jewellery. The founder, Helen Stone, is an experienced practitioner in many forms of Complementary Therapy. Discovering she was a natural healer many years ago Helen now practises Reflexology, Hopi Ear Candling, Crystal Healing, Tachyon Healing, Indian Head Massage, Tai Chi and Chi Kung Classes, and has recently become a Reiki Master. Helen takes great pleasure in restoring harmony and balance in peoples lives and says "my aim is to help people to get to the cause of their illness and not just treat their symptoms".

Helen works alongside several other practitioners in the Complementary Therapy Centre who provide a varied selection of beauty and holistic treatments to cover the body from head to toe. All treatments are carried out in a peaceful environment with calming music to heighten the relaxing atmosphere if required.

Stress relief is one of the main concerns so come along and try something new like Ionic Detoxing, Bowen Technique, Chavutti Thai Massage, Aromatherapy Massage, Reiki Healing, Indian Head Massage or one of the many beauty treatments which are holistic in their approach. Helen says "these therapies are gentle but powerful" and adds "we like to create an environment that provides an optimum situation for the body to heal itself".

The shop offers an extensive collection of crystals both natural and polished. The crystals are carefully hand picked by Helen from specialist suppliers around the world. Crystals are alive and vibrate, just like ourselves and our environment, they help us to establish harmony and balance.

Helen sells a wide range of Fair Trade silver and gemstone jewellery, which is high quality with very unusual yet beautiful gemstones. Making some of the jewellery herself, Helen takes orders for bespoke items. The extensive range of gifts includes lamps, clocks, vases, candle holders, carvings, aromatherapy products, candles, cards, music cd's and much more. Many of the items can be purchased through the website.

🏛 historic building   🏛 museum   🏛 historic site   ⌣ scenic attraction   ❧ flora and fauna

was sacked by the Spanish in 1595. Having supported the Royalist cause during the Civil War, it suffered the same fate again less than 60 years later. A major port in the 19th century for the export of tin, the fortunes of Penzance were transformed by the railway's arrival in 1859. Not only could the direct despatch of early flowers, vegetables and locally caught fish to the rest of Britain be undertaken but the influx of holidaymakers boosted the town's fledgling tourist industry.

Penzance celebrates its long-standing links with the sea at the **Maritime Museum** which houses a fascinating collection of artefacts that illustrate the ferocity of the waters along this stretch of coast. Down at the harbour, at the **Trinity House Lighthouse Centre**, the story of lighthouse keeping is told. Opened by

Prince Andrew in 1991, the centre has assembled what is the probably the largest and finest collection of lighthouse equipment in the world. Visitors can operate the 100-year-old equipment, blast off a foghorn or just sit back and watch a video about the history of the lighthouse.

Elsewhere in Penzance, local history and the work of the Newlyn School of artists can be seen at the recently refurbished **Penlee House Art Gallery and Museum**. The county's long association with the mining industry is highlighted at the **Cornwall Geological Museum** which has some intriguing fossil displays. Just to the northwest of the town, and close to the village of Madron, lie **Trengwainton Gardens**, the National Trust-owned woodland gardens that

HARDY EXOTICS NURSERY

Gilly Lane, Whitecross, nr Penzance, Cornwall TR20 8BZ
Tel: 01736 740660   Fax: 01736 741101
e-mail: contact@hardyexotics.co.uk
website: www.hardyexotics.co.uk

In 1986 Clive Shilton and his wife Julie moved from London to establish **Hardy Exotics Nursery**. Now, 20 years later, it is one of the best known nurseries in the country for its collection of wonderfully distinctive and exciting plants. More than 1,500 different species of exotic plants are grown here specifically for cool temperate climates. While this south-western tip of Cornwall is noted for its mild climate, most of the plants here are able to thrive in carefully chosen locations all over the United Kingdom. A wander around this fascinating nursery is educational to gardener and non-gardener alike and provides a feast for the eye.

Most of the plants are very strong visually and may well bring back memories of holidays much further afield than Cornwall. Each plant is given a hardiness rating which describes its ability to survive cold weather. This is a great aid in choosing the best plants to create a desert, tropical rainforest or oasis in a British urban garden. Whether it is small plants for the conservatory or large trees to create architectural interest, Hardy Exotics Nursery is just the place. With their mail order service throughout the UK, everyone can benefit from the amazing range of plants here. If the name Shilton rings any bells with visitors then it is likely they remember Clive's other great success - as a fashion designer of hand-made shoes and accessories in the 1970s and 1980s. This career culminated in his creation of the wedding slippers of Diana, Princess of Wales.

🎭 stories and anecdotes   🦅 famous people   🎨 art and craft   🎵 entertainment and sport   🚶 walks

CORNISH LILIES

Top Orchard Nurseries, Gulval, Penzance,
Cornwall TR18 3BG
Tel: 01736 332300
e-mail: info@cornishlilies.co.uk
website: www.cornishlilies.co.uk

Based in the tranquil village of Gulval near Penzance, **Cornish Lilies** is run by a family that has been farming and growing flowers for four generation. The surrounding area has often been called the "Golden Mile" because of the richness of the soil and of the phenomenal crops it produces. Cornish Lilies are no exception – they have extraordinary stem strength and amazing bud counts. The company has been growing lilies on its 15-acre site for more than 10 years, selling to local florists including their own "Buds to Bloom" business as well as wholesalers across the country.

However, recent customer awareness of the importance of buying from and supporting English producers has led to the company sending its superb lily bouquets by mail order. They make wonderful gifts and also add a little bit of luxury to your own home.

Cornish Lilies specialise in three groups of the lilium family. The Oriental Lilies have an outstanding perfume and come in many shades of whites and pinks, either pure, mixed or speckled. The most commonly known variety is Stargazer. Longiflorum Lilies create a striking impression with their wonderfully scented white trumpets, simple purity and elegance. The Asiatic Lilies come in an immense range of colours, sometimes two-toned or speckled. Occasionally they can be faintly scented.

Cornish Lilies, stunning bouquets are sent in bud to ensure that the recipient can enjoy their maximum life. They are carefully gift-wrapped with complementing foliage. They are dressed with cellophane, tissue, a large bow and flower food and then secured firmly into a specially designed box. If you are sending them as a gift, your message is handwritten for a personal touch on a decorative card which also includes care instructions and helpful tips. Orders can be made by phone or online and Cornish Lilies can also provide appropriate flowers for all occasions, including weddings and funerals. If you are visiting personally, Cornish Lilies is easily found about halfway between Gulval church and the heliport, and has its own ample parking area.

🏚 historic building   🏛 museum   🏛 historic site   ⊕ scenic attraction   🌱 flora and fauna

are known for their spring flowering shrubs, their exotic trees and the walled garden that contains plants that cannot be grown in the open anywhere else in the country. The walled garden was built in the early 19th century by the then owner Sir Rose Price, the son of a wealthy Jamaican sugar planter.

Around Penzance

ZENNOR

5½ miles N of Penzance on the B3306

🏛 Wayside Folk Museum

🏚 Chysauster Ancient Village

This delightful ancient village, situated between moorland and coastal cliffs, shows evidence of Bronze Age settlers. It also has a 12th century church, famous for its carved bench end depicting a mermaid holding a comb and mirror. A local legend tells of a mysterious young maiden who was drawn to the church by the beautiful singing of a chorister, the churchwarden's son Matthew Trewhella. An enchanting singer herself, the maiden lured Matthew down to nearby Pendour Cove where he disappeared. On warm summer evenings, it is said that their voices can be heard rising from the waves. By the porch in the church is a memorial to John Davey, who died in 1891, stating that he was the last person to have any great knowledge of the native Cornish language Kernuack. It is said that he remained familiar with the language by speaking it to his cat. There has recently been a revival of interest in Kernuack, and visitors to Cornwall who chance upon a Kernuack speaker might impress him by asking, "Plema'n diwotti?" and with any luck being directed to the nearest pub. Another useful entry in the Cornish

phrasebook is, "Fatell yu an pastyon yn gwerthji ma? A wrons I ri dhymn drog goans?", which means, "What are the pasties like in this shop? Will they give me indigestion?"

For an insight into the history of Zennor and the surrounding area, the **Wayside Folk Museum** is a unique private museum, founded in 1935, that covers every aspect of life in Zennor and district from 3000BC to the 1930s. On display are waterwheels, a millhouse, a wheelwright and blacksmith's premises, a miller's cottage with kitchen and parlour, and exhibits on tin mining. Tin mining is also referred to in the name of the local inn, The Tinners. DH Lawrence spent many hours at this pub while living in the village with his wife Frieda during World War I. It was during his stay here, under police surveillance, that Lawrence wrote *Women in Love*. However, his pacifist tendencies and Frieda's German heritage (her cousin was the flying ace the Red Baron von Richthofen) caused them to be 'moved on' in October 1917. Lawrence refers to the episode in his semi-autobiographical novel *Kangaroo* (1923).

To the southeast of the village lies the Neolithic chamber tomb, Zennor Quoit. One of the many ancient monuments in the area, the tomb has a huge capstone that was once supported on five broad uprights.

A couple of miles to the south of Zennor, on a windy hillside, lies **Chysauster Ancient Village**, a Romano-Cornish village, built around 2,000 years ago, which has one of the oldest identifiable streets in the country. The site was only discovered during archaeological excavations in the 1860s but the villagers here were farmers, as cattle sheds have been unearthed. They also worked tin beside the nearby stream. Their housing consisted of

🎭 stories and anecdotes   🕊 famous people   🎨 art and craft   ✏ entertainment and sport   🚶 walks

stone-walled homesteads, each with an open central courtyard surrounded by several circular living rooms topped with thatch or turf.

ST IVES
7 miles NE of Penzance on the A3074

- Tate St Ives Gallery
- St Ives Museum
- Barbara Hepworth Sculpture Garden
- Carbis Bay

This lovely old fishing town with its maze of narrow streets and picturesque harbour, has been showered with various awards in the last couple of years. It won the Gold Award in the international Entente Florale, has made off with more Britain in Bloom top prizes than any other UK town, and a recent University of Surrey survey, using a complex formula to decide which were the best beach destinations globally, placed St Ives at the top of its UK list, and 4th in the world. An organisation called "The Most Beautiful Bays in the World" has declared St Ives Bay one of its select few, on a par with Caribbean, Asian and American beauty spots. Another two of St Ives' five sandy beaches have also qualified for a Blue Flag award.

Culturally, the town is famous worldwide as an artists' colony. They were drawn by the special quality of the light – ultra-violet radiation is greater here than anywhere else in the country. JMW Turner was the first major artist to arrive, in 1811, to be followed in later decades by Whistler, Sickert, McNeill, Munnings, Ben Nicholson, the sculptor Barbara Hepworth and the potter Bernard Leach. Art still dominates and, along with the

THE SLOOP CRAFT CENTRE
St Ives, Cornwall, TR26 1LS
Tel: 01736 796051

Established in 1969, **The Sloop Craft Centre** was the first purpose built craft market in England. Located just 50 yards from the picturesque harbour, behind the Sloop Inn, the Centre is now home to 12 artisans. Amongst those working on the premises is Emma Byron who creates beautiful bespoke jewellery in gold and silver incorporating a variety of stones. Emma works mostly to commission and also offers a repair and alteration service. The Brooks Smith Gallery showcases the work of Rick Smith and Susie Brooks: Rick's paintings are based on illustrative storytelling in gouache on board; Susie makes artist prints using silkscreen and etching.

At Fairyland Bears you'll find Hayley Turner's jointed collector's bears, dragons and other beasties made from hand dyed mohair, vintage velvets and mini-bear fabric. Off The Bitten Track displays the work of Claire Cullen and Daniel Barnard who create contemporary abstract work, quirky installations and sculptural art. Textile artist Claire Louise Butler uses antique fabrics to create hand-stitched dolls, pictures and cards with a feel of days gone by. Also working on site are stained glass artist Deborah Martin, and the St Ives Art Co. which designs and produces canvas rug and tapestry wool kits reflecting the St Ives primitive and naïve artistic style.

---

numerous private galleries, there is the **Tate St Ives Gallery**, where the work of 20th century painters and sculptors is permanently on display in a rather austere three-storey building backing directly into the cliff face. Opened in 1993, the gallery offers a unique introduction to contemporary and modern art, and many works can be viewed in the surroundings that inspired them. The Tate also manages the **Barbara Hepworth Sculpture Garden and Museum** at Trewyn Studio, where she both lived and worked until her tragic death in a fire in 1975. Many of her works are exhibited in the Tate St Ives Gallery; still more are dotted around the town.

The original settlement at St Ives takes its name from the 6th century missionary St Ia, who is said to have landed here from Ireland on an ivy leaf. The 15th century parish church bears her name along with those of the two fishermen Apostles, St Peter and St Andrew.

One of the most important pilchard fishing centres in Cornwall until the early 20th century, St Ives holds a record dating back to 1868 for the greatest number of fish caught in a single seine net. Known locally as The Island, St Ives Head is home to a Huer's Hut, from where a lookout would scan the sea looking for shoals of pilchards. A local speciality, heavy or *hevva* cake, was traditionally made for the seiners on their return from fishing. As well as providing shelter for the fishing fleet, the harbour was also developed for exporting locally mined ores and minerals. The town's two industries led the labyrinthine narrow streets to become divided into two

SPARKLES

17 Fore Street, St Ives, Cornwall TR26 1AB
Tel: 01736 795999

Located on the main shopping street of St Ives, **Sparkles** provides an intriguing showcase for the work of local artists and crafts people, many of whom participate in the Made in Cornwall scheme. Amongst the varied items on display are dichroic glass and beadware, beautiful locally made jewellery, home linen and table ware, hand-made carob, and a fascinating selection of shaped driftwood objects. Owner Jo Stokes also stocks the Claremont & May range of home fragrances, the Milano range of Romanian glassware, and the Bioflow range of magnotherapy products.

The beneficial properties of magnets have been known for thousands of years and more than 1.5 million customers have found relief from pain with a Bioflow product. These include bracelets, watch straps, rings, sweatbands, armchair and car seat pads and even buttons. There's a special range of Bioflow products for children and another for animals. The range also includes a device for mobile phones designed to effectively neutralise the potentially damaging frequencies used in cell phones.

communities: *Downalong* where the fishing families lived and *Upalong*, the home of the mining families.

Housed in a building that once belonged to a mine, **St Ives Museum** displays a range of artefacts chronicling the natural, industrial and maritime history of the area. There is also a display dedicated to John Knill, mayor of the

View to Marazion from St Michaels Mount

town in the 18th century. A customs officer by profession, he was also rumoured to be an energetic smuggler. Certainly one of the town's most memorable citizens, he built the Steeple monument to the south of the town to be his mausoleum, but it also served to guide ships carrying contraband safely to the shore. Knill left a bequest to the town so that, every five years, a ceremony would be held when ten girls and two widows would dance around the Steeple.

It is not only artists who have been inspired by the beautiful surroundings of St Ives: Virginia Woolf recaptures the happy mood of the childhood holiday here in her novel *To the Lighthouse*, and Rosamunde Pilcher, famous for her books set in Cornwall, was born near here in 1924.

Just to the southeast of the town, easy to reach on foot and a great favourite with families, lies the sheltered beach of **Carbis Bay**, where various water sports are also available. To the west of St Ives is a wonderful

and remote coastline of coves, cliffs and headland that provides a wealth of wildlife and archaeological interest. Following the network of footpaths from St Ives to Pendeen, walkers can discover small wooded valleys, rich bogs, old industrial remains and prehistoric features such as the cliff castles at Gurnard's Head and Bosigran.

HAYLE
7½ miles NE of Penzance on the B3301

🌿 Paradise Park

Established in the 18th century as an industrial village, Hayle was also a seaport with a harbour in the natural shelter of the Hayle estuary. It was here, in the early 1800s, that the Cornish inventor Richard Trevithick built an early version of the steam locomotive. A short time later, one of the first railways in the world was constructed here to carry tin and copper from Redruth down to the port. With its industrial past, Hayle is not a place naturally associated with cosmetics, but it was

Hayle-born Florence Nightingale Graham who set up her own beauty parlour on New York's Fifth Avenue under the name Elizabeth Arden.

The Hayle estuary and sands around the town are an ornithologist's delight. Some of the world's rarest and most beautiful birds can be seen at **Paradise Park**, a leading conservation zoo located on the southern outskirts of the town. As well as providing a sanctuary for tropical birds and exotic animals, the park also has a huge indoor play centre and a special toddlers area.

Across the estuary lies **Lelant,** a thriving seaport in the Middle Ages that lost its traffic as the estuary silted up. Now a popular holiday village, with a golf course, Lelant is particularly loved by birders, who come to watch the wide variety of wildfowl and waders on the mud and salt flats. Lelant was the birthplace of Rosamunde Pilcher who celebrated her native county in enormously popular novels such as *The Shell Seekers*.

MARAZION
3 miles E of Penzance off the A394

Marazion Marsh   St Michael's Mount

St Michael's Mount Castle

Cornwall's oldest charter town (dating from 1257), Marazion was for many centuries the most important settlement around Mount's Bay. The legacy of this harbour town is its fine old inns and residential houses overlooking the sandy beach. The town is now a windsurfing and sailing centre, but to the northwest is **Marazion Marsh & RSPB Reserve**, an extensive area of wetland and reed beds behind Marazion Beach on the Penzance road. More than 450 plant species have been recorded here, and the reserve is home to many nesting and roosting birds,

including herons, reed and sedge warblers and Cetti's warbler.

Situated a third of a mile offshore, **St Michael's Mount** rises dramatically out of the waters of Mount's Bay. It is connected to Marazion by a cobbled causeway that is exposed at high tide. Inhabited since prehistoric times, this granite rock is named after the Archangel St Michael who, according to legend, appeared to a party of fishermen in a vision in the 5th century. In the 11th century, Edward the Confessor founded a priory on the mount, which had become a place of pilgrimage, in tribute to the famous Benedictine Mont St Michel in Normandy. The remains of these buildings are incorporated into the marvellous **St Michael's Mount Castle** owned by the St Aubyn family from 1660 until 1954, when it was donated to the National Trust. The St Aubyn family remain in residence however, with a 999-year lease. Along with the impressive medieval remains, the castle incorporates architectural styles from the 17th to the 19th century. A fine plaster frieze of 1641 depicting scenes of bear and deer hunting, and some elegant Chippendale furniture are amongst the heritage treasures; a model of the castle made out of discarded champagne corks by the St Aubyn's butler, Henry Lee, amongst the quirkier attractions.

When the present St Aubyn resident, the 4th Lord St Levan, was asked what had been his most significant contribution to the family home, he replied, "The ten tons of manure I had brought to the island." They were used to fertilise the extraordinary maritime garden created in terraces just above the sea. Sub-tropical plants flourish here in abundance and even in winter fuchsias and hydrangeas are still in bloom.

GODOLPHIN CROSS
9 miles E of Penzance off the B3302

🏠 Godolphin House   🏛 Wheal Prosper Mine

To the northwest of the village lies
Godolphin House, an exceptional part
Tudor, part Stuart house that still retains its
original Elizabethan stables. The former home
of the Earls of Godolphin, the house has
many splendid features. However the family,
who made their fortune in mining, are more
interesting; Sidney the poet was killed during
the Civil War while on the side of the king;
Sidney, the 1st earl was a Lord High Treasurer
to both William III and Queen Anne; the 2nd
earl imported the famous Godolphin Arabian,
one of three stallions from which all British
thoroughbreds are descended. While the
house remains in private ownership, the
Godolphin estate is owned by the National
Trust and this historic landscape includes
more than 400 recorded archaeological
features.

To the south of Godolphin lies the hamlet
of Rinsey where evidence of tin mining can
be seen in the restored 19th century engine
house of **Wheal Prosper** and the ruins of the
copper mine, **Wheal Trewavas**. Just to the
west of Rinsey two headlands enclose the mile
long crescent of **Praa Sands**, one of the
finest family beaches in Cornwall. Further
west again lies **Prussia Cove**, a clifftop
settlement, named after a notorious 18th
century smuggler, John Carter, who modelled
himself on Frederick the Great.

NEWLYN
1 mile S of Penzance on the B3315

🏛 Pilchard Works Heritage Museum

🎨 Newlyn Art Gallery

The largest fish landing port in England and
Wales, this town has a long association with
fishing. Its massive jetties, built in the 1880s,
embrace not only the existing 15th century
harbour but also 40 acres of Mount's Bay.
The arrival of the railway in 1859 allowed the
swift transportation of fresh fish and
seafood to London and beyond. Newlyn is
still a base for around 200 vessels. The
Pilchard Works Heritage Museum offers
a unique insight into the fascinating history
of the industry in Cornwall. The company
can speak with authority, as it is the sole
producer and exporter of the county's
traditional salted pilchards. Visitors can see
traditional salt fish processing using ancient
presses that pack the fish into wooden boxes
known as 'coffins'. The museum contains
many paintings, photographs and artefacts
from a bygone age, including Britain's oldest
pilchard net-making machine.

However, it was not fish but the
exceptionally clear natural light that drew
Stanhope Forbes to Newlyn in the 1880s. He
was soon joined by other artists, keen to
experience the joys of painting outside. The
Newlyn School of art was founded with the
help of other artists such as Lamorna Birsh,
Alfred Munnings and Norman Garstin, but to
see their work you have to visit the Penlee
House Gallery in Penzance. The **Newlyn Art
Gallery**, currently closed for major
redevelopment until Spring 2007, will exhibit
a wide variety of work with special emphasis
on the work of local artists, past and present.

MOUSEHOLE
2 miles S of Penzance off the B3315

Mousehole (pronounced 'Mowzel') was
described by Dylan Thomas, who honey-
mooned here in 1937, as "the loveliest
village in England". Still largely unspoilt, it

district and from all over the world.

ST BURYAN

5 miles SW of Penzance on the B3283

🏛 Boscawen-Un Stone Circle

The landscape around this village is dominated by the 14th century tower of one of the finest churches in Cornwall. It also provides a day mark for shipping around Land's End. To the north of St Buryan is the isolated **Boscawen-Un Stone Circle**, whose

Mousehole

fulfils the popular image of what a Cornish fishing village should look like, complete with a picturesque harbour where a small number of fishing boats off-load their daily catch. At the southern end of the quay, rising from the water, is Merlin's Rock. Here the great wizard is supposed to have prophesied:

There shall land on the Rock of Merlin
Those who shall burn Paul, Penzance and Newlyn.

In 1595, four Spanish galleys fulfilled his prophecy.

In winter, the entrance to Mousehole harbour is closed by sturdy wooden beams to keep the force of the sea at bay. In past times, the village has suffered ferocious winter storms and one of these events is commemorated annually shortly before Christmas on "Tom Bawcock's Eve" when a huge fish pie is baked and consumed by the patrons of the Inn on the quayside. This event, which becomes a major village party, attracts visitors from both the surrounding

central standing stone is an attractive leaning pillar of sparkling quartz.

To the southwest and sheltered in a shallow valley is the unspoilt hamlet of Treen. A short walk away is the spectacularly sited Iron Age coastal fort, Tretyn Dinas. Also on this headland lies the famous Logan Rock, a massive 60-ton granite boulder that was once so finely balanced that it could be rocked by hand.

PORTHCURNO

7½ miles SW of Penzance off the B3315

📷 Museum of Submarine Telegraphy

🎭 Minack Theatre

It was from this dramatic cove, protected by Gwennap Head and Cribba Head, that the first telegraph cable was laid in 1870 linking Britain with the rest of the world. The **Museum of Submarine Telegraphy** (see panel on page 18), housed in a secret underground wartime communications centre, explains the technology that has been

🎬 stories and anecdotes   🕊 famous people   🎭 art and craft   🖌 entertainment and sport   🚶 walks

Porthcurno Telegraph Museum

*Eastern House, Porthcurno, Cornwall, TR19 6JX   Tel: 01736 810966   Fax: 01736 811914
website: www.porthcurno.org.uk*

This unique museum stands in the beautiful valley of Porthcurno. The first cable station here was built in 1870, and from that time an increasing number of undersea cables were laid, creating a communications network which

connected the village with remote and exotic parts of the world.

By the start of the Second World War, there were 14 cables and it had become the most important cable station in the world, so it was considered necessary to build bomb-proof tunnels to protect the station from attack. These tunnels now house the major part of the

museum, where regular demonstrations show working telegraph equipment from throughout the era, as well as giving a taste of the social changes that took place.

The sights, sounds and smells here are evocative of times gone by, and there is something to interest every member of the family. There are many hands-on exhibits, as well as special activities for children, a local history exhibition and an exhibition about Brunel.

The museum is open daily throughout the summer, and Friday to Monday in the winter, 10am-5pm, with last admission before 4pm.

developed from Victorian times to the present.

This interesting village is also home to the **Minack Theatre.** This open-air amphitheatre cut into the cliffside looks as if it might have been created by the Romans but in fact it was founded by a very determined lady, Rowena Cade, in the 1930s. Appropriately, with the sea providing a not always serene backdrop, the first play produced here, in 1931, was Shakespeare's *The Tempest.* Since then the Bard's plays have provided the central focus for each season's performances, along with other classics, avant-garde plays and the

perennially popular *Pirates of Penzance.* Daytime visitors can explore the **Rowena Cade Exhibition Centre** which tells the story of how she spent decades developing the 750-seat theatre.

LAND'S END
9 miles SW of Penzance on the A30

Mainland England's most westerly point, Land's End was once a mystical place. Somewhere beyond its craggy cliffs lay the Lost Land of Lyonesse and the stark, treeless surroundings often draped in sea mist spoke eloquently of elemental, hostile forces. Then

in 1982, a London businessman, Peter de Savary, outbid the National Trust to buy the 120-acre site. At the same time he bought the John o'Groats, 874 miles away near the northern tip of Scotland. "Cornwall is a goldmine," he declared and proceeded to make Land's End into a kind of theme park with a huge hotel, amusements complex and car parks. The evocative name still draws many thousands here each year

Notable among the attractions here are an exhibition telling the story of the men of the RNLI and state-of-the-art displays of local tales and legends and the lives of the Cornish farmers and craftsmen. From this headland can be seen Longships Lighthouse, just off shore, and Wolf Rock Lighthouse, seven miles away.

Land's End

SANCREED

3½ miles W of Penzance off the A30

🏛 Carn Euny 🌿 Bartinney Downs

The best example of an ancient Celtic Cross in Cornwall stands nine feet high in the churchyard of 15th century **St Credan's Church**. In the surrounding area are two Bronze Age monuments, the Blind Fiddler and the Two Sisters. Like many Cornish menhirs, they are said to represent humans turned to stone for committing irreligious acts on the Sabbath.

To the southwest of the village is **Carn Euny**, a fascinating Iron Age courtyard farming settlement that was founded around 200BC. By far the most impressive building here is the Fogou which was first discovered by miners in the 19th century and takes its name from the Cornish for 'cave'. This underground chamber was constructed in three separate stages, and the 65ft room was entered by a low 'creep' passage at one end.

Immediately west of Carn Euny is **Bartinney Downs**, a large area of heathland where programmes are in place to preserve both wildlife habitats and archaeological sites and historic features, including old china clay works, abandoned quarries and the ruins of Bartinney Castle.

🎭 stories and anecdotes 🦜 famous people 🎨 art and craft ✒ entertainment and sport 🚶 walks

Bosllow

Distance: *4.0 miles (6.4 kilometres)*

Typical time: *180 mins*

Height gain: *70 metres*

Map: *Explorer 102*

Walk: *www.walkingworld.com ID:1052*

Contributor: *Dennis Blackford*

ACCESS INFORMATION:

From Penzance take the B3311 road to Madron and continue towards Trevowhan. 2½ miles along this road look for the 'Men-an-Tol' studio on your left and park in the parking area on the opposite side of the road. On this road you will pass the ancient healing well just outside Madron and Lanyon Quoit a bit over one mile further on.

From the St Just to St Ives road - turn at Trevowhan (approximately five miles from St Just) onto the Madron road. Approx one mile along this road look for the 'Men-an-Tol' studio on your right.

DESCRIPTION:

This walk takes you up onto Ding Dong Moor and visits ancient stone monuments. The first is The Men-an-Tol which is an ancient healing site about 6,000 years old and where sick or infertile people were passed through the holed stone. Secondly we visit Men Scyfa. This is an inscribed stone marking the grave of a warrior killed near this spot around 500AD. Next we pass the group of stones known as the 'Nine Maidens', which would have been used for various religious rites throughout the year. The age of this stone circle is unknown but is thought to have been redundant by 1250BC. The more modern building of Ding Dong Mine is next, although there has been a mine

here for over 2,000 years and legend has it that the young Jesus was brought here by his uncle Joseph of Arimathea. Finally we visit Lanyon Quoit, a classical monument whose massive stones were erected over 6,000 years ago. Those who are interested can also visit the ancient healing well just outside Madron, where even today hundreds of people tie tokens on the branches (please use biodegradable ones, plastics do not work!)

ADDITIONAL INFORMATION:

This walk is on open moor so be sure to take 'moor care' and wear stout walking shoes and take an extra layer of clothing; a thin waterproof cagoule is most useful to keep out wind or rain. There are many old mine shafts and cave-ins in this area, so keep to the paths and be careful with children and dogs.

FEATURES:

Hills or fells, wildlife, birds, flowers, great views, butterflies, industrial archaeology, moor, ancient monument.

WALK DIRECTIONS:

1 | From the car park go through the gate leading to a farm track.

2 | About one kilometre up the track, go over the small stone bridge and steps signed 'The Men-an-Tol'. After visiting the Men-an-Tol return to the farm track and continue on up the track. The Men-an-Tol is an ancient healing site about 6,000 years old where sick or infertile people were passed through the holed stone.

3 | About another ½km up the track there is a stone stile to the left of a metal gate; this leads to Men Scyfa. This is an inscribed stone marking the grave of a warrior killed near this spot around 500AD. This 1.8-metre stone is

the same height as the warrior, although part is now underground. Return to the track and continue on up.

4 | The track now curves to the left, but you should take the path leading straight on past a ruined building on the left and up to a metal gate. Pass through the gate and follow the path straight on up and over the moor.

5 | The track is well-worn so is easy to follow. Remember that there are many old mine shafts and cave-ins in this area, so keep to the paths and be careful with children and dogs.

6 | The path leads to the ring of standing stones known as the "Nine Maidens". Pass through the circle and follow the path to your right. This will lead past a fenced off mine shaft and go to Ding Dong mine engine house.

7 | Having reached the engine house of Ding Dong Mine and looked around, there are three ways back. The shortest and best route is to walk to the end of the spoil heap in front of the mine and find the well-worn path to the NW of it (right-hand side when facing the heap from the engine house). This path meanders back to the Men-an-Tol, which, although out of sight for most of the way, is in line with the farm on the valley wall roughly midway between the farm on the horizon left and the tor on the right. From the Men-an-Tol, retrace your steps back to the car park. To visit Lanyon Quoit drive towards Madron, where you can also visit the Holy Well and Celtic Chapel.

8 | The second route is very rough going especially in late summer and autumn, due to bracken and brambles. Take the smaller track past the engine house entrance and pass under the wooden pole onto a grassy path. Pass through the gate at the end and follow the field boundary on your left, down to the bottom of the hill and then another field boundary wall on your right as you ascend the hill to Lanyon Quoit. After visiting the Quoit go over the stone stile to the road and turn right to follow the road back to the car park (approx 1 kilometre).

9 | The third route is the longest and has a lot of road walking. Follow the wide farm track past the mine and onto the metalled farm road down to the main road from Madron (approx 1.5 kilometres).

10 | Turn right and follow the road back to the car park (approx 2.5 kilometres), passing Lanyon Quoit on your right about halfway along.

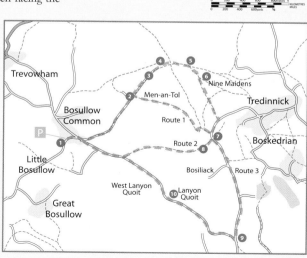

JUST FINE ART

3-4 Market Square, St Just, Penzance,
Cornwall TR19 7HF
Tel: 01736 788869
e-mail: nick@justfineart.net
website: www.justfineart.net

If you are looking for a memory of this beautiful and historic area, then **Just Fine Art** is the place for you. Resident artist Nicholas, shows a large collection of original oil paintings or finely detailed watercolours of the Penwith area, most of which are available as limited edition reproductions.

Other hand picked local artists share the wall space, with their views of this ever popular Cornish landscape. To compliment the paintings they have a selection of ceramics, wood carvings, glass ware, jewellery, bronze sculpture and hand made cards.

Nicholas says his aim is to "provide our patrons with a relaxed but informative atmosphere where they can view some of the best art in comfortable surroundings".

The gallery also offers a fast frame service for those other memories you have picked up along the way. They have a large range of traditional and modern styles to choose from as well as ready made frames in stock. Free quotations available.

Gallery opening times
9.30-5.30 Monday to Saturday.
Additional evening opening through the main season.

ST JUST

7 miles W of Penzance on the A3071

🦶 The Tinners' Way

The westernmost town in mainland Britain, St Just was a copper and tin mining centre and the surrounding area is littered with industrial remains. A narrow road leads from this rather sombre town westwards to Cape Cornwall, the only cape in England, passing the last remains of Cape Cornwall mine – its tall chimney. On the southern side of this headland lies Priest's Cove, a quiet boulder strewn beach while, further along, the South West Coast Path follows the cliff tops. The coastal road from St Just to St Ives, the B3306, is regarded by many as the most spectacular coastal route in England.

St Just marks the start (or the end) of **The Tinners' Way**, an ancient track way between the town and St Ives. The track follows ancient moorland paths that were certainly used more than 2,000 years ago and may originally have been part of a network of paths dating to Neolithic times.

To the northwest of the town lies Botallack, where the remains of Three Crowns Mine stand on the dramatic clifftop. Here, tunnels were cut over half a mile out to sea, under the seabed, to extract rich copper lode.

PENDEEN

8 miles NW of Penzance on the B3306

🏛 Geevor Tin Mine   🏛 Levant Steam Engine

Tin has been mined at Pendeen since

🏛 historic building   🏛 museum   🏛 historic site   🦗 scenic attraction   🌱 flora and fauna

THE GEM & JEWELLERY WORKSHOP

Mining Exhibition and Mineral Shop, St Johns Terrace, Pendeen, Penzance, Cornwall TR19 7DP Tel: 01736 788217

Located on the B3306 coast road between St Ives and Land's End, **The Gem & Jewellery Workshop, Mining Exhibition and Mineral Shop** is a three-in-one attraction. The Gem & Jewellery Workshop was created by Rodney and Maureen Hobbs who came to Pendeen in the heart of the Granite Kingdom many years ago and have developed the workshop into one of the most important heritage attractions in the area. In his workshop, Rodney, a Somerset man and an engineer of great talent in many aspects of craftwork, uses granite, gemstones and silver to produce beautiful jewellery and high quality gifts.

In the adjoining shop, rock and mineral specimens are for sale along with rock tumblers, geology hammers, and books and maps pertaining to the locality and its minerals. While trying hard to offer all the things advertised they reserve the right to change or remove anything without prior notice.

Open 10-5 Easter-Oct, 11-4 Nov-March.(these times may vary).

In the same group of buildings is the Pendeen Mining Exhibition where visitors can trace the history of mine production in the Pendeen area. The workshop and exhibition are open all year, except Sundays, and entrance is free.

---

prehistoric times. At the Geevor Mine, tin was still being extracted until 1985 when the international crash in tin prices sounded its death knell. The mine closed in 1990 but has been preserved as the **Geevor Tin Mine and Heritage Centre**. It not only preserves the mine but offers visitors the chance to experience the claustrophobic conditions of miners underground.

Close by, housed in a tiny building perched high on the cliff, is the National Trust-owned **Levant Steam Engine**, once again producing power. Further to the north, on the slate promontory of Pendeen Watch, stands Pendeen Lighthouse, which has been guiding ships for nearly a century.

Redruth

Carn Brea   Gwennap Pit

Redruth was once the capital of the largest and richest metal mining area in Britain.

The deep mining of copper after the 1730s brought prosperity to the town – at the peak of production in the 1850s, two-thirds of the world's copper came from Cornwall. Some pockets of Victorian, Georgian and earlier buildings bear witness to those days of comparative affluence for some. The miners themselves endured dreadful conditions. Children started work as young as eight and fatal accidents were frequent. The average life span of a miner was less than 40 years. The only memorials they have are the ruined mine

---

GOONEARL COTTAGE GUEST HOUSE

Wheal Rose, Scorrier, Redruth, Cornwall TR16 5DF
Tel: 01209 891571   Fax: 01209 891916
e-mail: goonearl@onetel.com
website: www.goonearlcottage.com

Set in its own lovely grounds and surrounded by open countryside with glorious views across to the North Cornish coast, **Goonearl Cottage Guest House** is one of those places where "you may arrive as strangers but leave as friends". It's the home of Geoff and Sarah West who offer a genuinely friendly Cornish welcome to their guests.

The accommodation here boasts a 4-Diamond rating from the English Tourist Board and have 8 bedrooms which are beautifully decorated and comprehensively equipped. Sarah and Geoff provide a superb English breakfast and also offer evening meals from an extensive menu on weekday evenings.

The guest house is licensed so you can enjoy a drink with your meal. Goonearl Cottage is open all year round and there is ample parking within the grounds. It is within easy reach of the golden sandy beaches of Porthtowan, Portreath and St Agnes, and is just one mile from the A30 which gives easy access to the whole of the county. Newquay, St Ives and the beautiful cathedral city of Truro are just a few miles away and within easy travelling distance are the major attractions of Lands End, Falmouth and the Eden Project.

buildings and chimney stacks dotted across the countryside around Redruth.

On a more cheerful note, Redruth was also the home of the Scottish inventor William Murdock, who is famous for such innovations as coal-gas lighting and vacuum powered tubes. His home was the first private house to have gas lighting installed, in 1792.

Immediately south of the town rises dramatic **Carn Brea**, a granite hill that reaches some 738 feet above sea level and is crowned by a 90-foot monument to Francis Basset, a local, benevolent mine and land owner. Once the site of an early Neolithic settlement, Carn Brea is also home to a small, part-medieval castle and it is still the site of the pagan ritual of the Midsummer Bonfire ceremony.

To the north, along the coast, lie the two thriving holiday centres of Porthtowan and Portreath. Although they developed as a copper mining village and ore exporting port respectively, they are now both the preserve of surfers and families during the summer season.

Just to the southeast of Redruth is the mysterious **Gwennap Pit**, a round, grass-covered amphitheatre, thought to have been created by the collapse of a subterranean mine shaft. Once used as a pit for the staging of cock fights, this curious theatre is sometimes known as the 'Methodist Cathedral' as John Wesley preached here on many occasions. Methodists from all around the world still gather here on Spring Bank Holiday.

Around Redruth

ST AGNES

7 miles NE of Redruth on the B3285

Stippy-Stappy   Blue Hills Tin Streams

St Agnes Parish Museum   Wheal Coates

Once known as the source of the finest tin in Cornwall, this old village still retains many of its original miners' cottages and grander mine owners' houses. Of particular interest is the steeply terraced row of 18th century cottages known as **Stippy-Stappy**. Surrounding the village are the ruins of old mine workings including the clifftop buildings of one of Cornwall's best known mines – **Wheal Coates** (National Trust). The mine operated between 1860 and 1890 and its derelict Engine House is one of the more exceptional landmarks along this stretch of coast. Walkers should beware of the mass of abandoned mine shafts that litter the area but the walk to the remains of Wheal Kitty provides panoramic views over this once industrial area. Visitors coming to this now popular seaside resort can learn more about

the village's heritage through the displays on mining, seafaring and local natural history at the **St Agnes Parish Museum**. Visitors with an interest in learning about the tin production processes should take one of the guided tours around **Blue Hills Tin Streams** at nearby Trevellas where production still continues on a small scale.

Renowned as the birthplace of the Georgian society painter, John Opie, St Agnes was also introduced to thousands through the *Poldark* novels of Winston Graham in which the village appeared as 'St Ann'. From the village a footpath takes walkers out to St

Stippy Stappy, St Agnes

INSPIRED EARTH

54A Vicarage Road, St Agnes, Cornwall TR5 0TQ
Tel: 01872 552022   website: www.inspiredearth.com
e-mail: victoria@inspiredearth.com / sally@inspiredearth.com

Inspired Earth offers customers the chance to view the work of more than 30 artists living and working in Cornwall. Their work covers a very wide range of Art and Craft and includes ceramics by owner Sally Heritage, photography, textiles, wood craft, glass, jewellery, papier mâché, painted furniture and paintings in various mediums. Sally opened the gallery in March 2004 and has since been joined by her daughter Victoria, a textiles artists who specialises in felt. Their – and the other artists' pieces – are complemented by a range of design-led products for the home from innovative companies.

stories and anecdotes   famous people   art and craft   entertainment and sport   walks

LEYCROFT VALLEY HOLIDAYS

Perrancombe, Perranporth, Cornwall TR6 0JQ
Tel: 01872 573044   Fax: 01872 571440
e-mail: info@leycroftvalley.co.uk
website: www.leycroftvalley.co.uk

Situated within easy reach of all the major attractions Cornwall has to offer, **Leycroft Valley Holidays** provide everything you need for a perfect relaxing holiday. Nestling in a beautiful wooded valley, the 29 spaciously appointed self-catering chalets and bungalows are available in a variety of sizes. There are cosy and comfortable studio chalets just for two; and attractive 3-bedroomed bungalows with accommodation for six people. One of the most popular chalets, the Ascot, offers a light and airy atmosphere and pine furnished accommodation for four; there are traditional style European Chalets, some with outdoor hot tubs, also for 4 people, with private patio and terrace; compact Woodland Chalets for 4 and Bredon Bungalows with neat and compact accommodation for four. All the properties are equipped with television, fridge, heating and their own garden area with garden furniture provided.

Close to every chalet is its own allocated parking space. Dogs are welcome and must be kept on leads at all times. There are many footpaths bordering the site and dog owners can use the meadow to exercise their pets.

The reception area has laundry facilities with two washing machines and two tumble driers, a payphone (very few people can receive a mobile phone signal at Leycroft), and a pleasant bar with a terrace and conservatory. The bar serves a good selection of draught lagers and bitters, wines and spirits. At the present time, it doesn't offer a regular food menu but may run barbecues in the high season.

The site is owned and run by the Matthews family who point out that the Valley does not have many of the commercials attractions associated with a larger holiday park, but with miles of tracks and coastal paths to explore, fabulous beaches nearby, and the secluded privacy of the valley to return to after a day of sightseeing, they are sure that Leycroft Valley offers something for everyone.

They also note that most of their chalets have a number of steps leading from the car park to the chalet. The nature of the site means that some have fairly steep paths by which to reach them. If you require something more accessible, just point this out when you make your booking.

🏛 historic building   🏛 museum   🏛 historic site   🍃 scenic attraction   🌿 flora and fauna

Agnes Head and St Agnes Beacon from whose summit may be seen 30 parish churches, both Cornish coasts, part of Devon and, at night, the lights of 12 lighthouses. There are also spectacular views over the old mine workings and also remains from both the Bronze and Iron Ages. Now the home of some rare and localised plants and a wide variety of bird life, this area is criss-crossed by footpaths and is owned by the National Trust.

PENHALLOW
8 miles NE of Redruth on the A3075

Cornish Cyder Farm

Acclaimed by the English Tourist Board as 'The Nation's Favourite Farm Visit', the **Cornish Cyder Farm** just south of Penhallow offers a fully guided tour of the site and orchards. Visitors can sample some of the fruit products made here, including jams,

country wines and cider and traditional scrumpy. The **Cyder Museum** tells the history of cider making through displays of old equipment and artefacts, and the Mowhay Restaurant serves Cornish cream teas and home-made food.

PERRANPORTH
10 miles NE of Redruth on the B3285

Lowender Peran Festival   St Piran's Oratory

This pleasant holiday resort, with its three-mile stretch of golden sand, was at one time a pilchard fishing and mining village that also harboured smuggling gangs. Though little has survived from those days, the small town's Celtic heritage is still remembered during the annual **Lowender Peran Festival** in mid-October which brings all the Celtic nations together through music and dance.

High up in the dunes overlooking Penhale

ON THE TABLE

Goonhavern Garden Centre,
Newquay Road, Goonhavern, Truro,
Cornwall TR4 9QQ
Tel: 01872 571400 Fax: 01872 573183
e-mail: josymons@hotmail.com
website: www.onthetable.org

A top quality farm shop attached to a 200-acre organic farm, **On The Table** was established in December 2005 but has been so successful that its owner, Josephine Symonds, is already planning a major expansion. Josephine and husband Daniel also run the farm, the second generation of his family to do so. Josephine is a qualified butcher and also has three children.

On The Table stocks meats from the farm – the range of gourmet sausages is especially popular – along with eggs and vegetables also from the farm. Also on sale are local cheeses, ice cream, breads, wholefoods, fish and a range of tasty home producedready meals. On The Table also runs a Meat Box scheme that can be distributed throughout the UK.

stories and anecdotes   famous people   art and craft   entertainment and sport   walks

Sands, **St Piran's Oratory**, a ruined 6th or 7th century building constructed on the site of St Piran's grave, lay beneath the sand until it was uncovered in 1835. It's the oldest known church in the south-west but the shifting sands have once again claimed the remains. A simple plaque now marks the burial place of the saint, who is said to have travelled from Ireland to the Cornish coast on a millstone.

ST ALLEN
9½ miles NE of Redruth off the A30

🌿 Chyverton Garden

As with many parts of the country with a Celtic tradition, Cornwall has its own 'little people' – the *piskies*. One legend tells of a boy from St Allen who failed to return home after going out to pick flowers in a nearby wood. His frantic mother began a search and eventually he was found, three days later, dazed but unharmed. All the boy could remember was being led deep into the forest, to a fantastic cave filled with jewels, and being fed the purest honey by the piskies.

Just to the north of St Allen, at the village of Zelah, lies **Chyverton Garden** which is centred around the grand Georgian house of a wealthy local mine owner. The landscaped garden is renowned for its rhododendrons, the first of which were planted in 1890, and its magnolias, camellias and conifers. Admission to the garden is by appointment only.

POOL
2 miles SW of Redruth on the A3047

🏛 Industrial Discovery Centre

🌿 Shire Horse Farm

Now consumed into the Camborne and Redruth conurbation, this village was very much at the heart of Cornwall's mining

industry. The **Cornish Mines and Engines**, owned by the National Trust, shows the two huge engines that were used to pump water from the mines. At the **Industrial Discovery Centre**, the secrets of the county's dramatic heritage are revealed.

Before the days of steam, heavy work was carried out by horses, and the **Shire Horse Farm and Carriage Museum**, at nearby Treskillard, pays a living tribute to these gentle giants. The museum has an interesting collection of private carriages and horse-drawn commercial vehicles, (including the largest collection of horse-drawn omnibuses in the country), farming implements and hand tools from days gone by. There are wheelwright and blacksmith shops, and wagon rides are available.

CAMBORNE
3 miles SW of Redruth on the A3047

🏛 Geological Museum

Once the capital of Cornwall's tin and copper mining area, in the 19th century the land around Camborne was the most intensely mined in the world. In the 1850s, more than 300 mines were producing some two thirds of the world's copper. However, the discovery of extensive mineral deposits in the Americas, South Africa and Australia led to the industry's decline in Cornwall in the early 1900s when it became no longer economically viable. Before the industry took off in the 18th century, Camborne was a small place and the traces of rapid expansion can still be seen in the numerous terraces of 18th and 19th century miners' houses.

As the town's livelihood has depended on mining for several hundred years, it is not surprising that Camborne is home to the world famous School of Mining. Its **Geological Museum** displays rocks and

TRELAWNEY RESTAURANT

109 Trelowarren Street, Camborne,
Cornwall TR14 8AW
Tel: 01209 612078
e-mail: bridgettew1@tiscali.co.uk

Located in the heart of Camborne, the **Trelawney Restaurant** offers traditional home-cooked food in a cosy and relaxed setting. This long established restaurant is owned and run by Bridgette and Andy Evans, a friendly and welcoming couple with extensive experience in the hospitality business. Their evening menu presents a good choice of dishes ranging from starters such as home-made soup of the day or garlic mushrooms; and main courses that include steaks, chicken, pork, lamb and fish dishes along with vegetarian options like the walnut & stilton stuffed mushrooms or Mediterranean vegetables in a rich tomato sauce.

All the food is freshly cooked to order and served with a genuine smile. At lunchtimes, a different menu offers a wide choice of light bites, salads and sandwiches as well as main courses like home-cooked ham, egg and chips, chicken in black bean sauce and home-made beef lasagne. In addition, there are several specials of the day listed on the blackboard. The 30-seat restaurant, which is non-smoking, has a table licence so you can enjoy a drink along with your meal. On Sundays, a hearty roast is served, complete with all the trimmings.

minerals from all over the world. Outside the town's library is a statue to Richard Trevithick, a talented amateur wrestler known as the Cornish Giant, who was responsible for developing the high pressure steam engine, the screw propeller and an early locomotive that predated Stephenson's Rocket by 12 years.

To the northwest of Camborne lies **Godrevy Point**, whose low cliffs mark the northern edge of St Ives Bay, a well-known beauty spot from where seals can be sighted offshore. Just off the point lies **Godrevy Island** with the lighthouse that featured in Virginia Woolf's novel *To the Lighthouse*. Much of the coastline from Godrevy eastwards to Navax Point is owned by the National Trust and the clifftops support some of the botanically richest maritime heath in Europe.

Falmouth

🏰 Pendennis Castle   🌿 Fox Rosehill Garden

🏛 National Maritime Museum Cornwall

Falmouth has grown up around a spectacular deep-water anchorage that is the world's third largest natural harbour – only Sydney and Rio de Janeiro are more extensive. Falmouth lies in Britain's Western Approaches and guards the entrance into Carrick Roads. First settled centuries ago, it was not until the 17th century that the port was properly developed, although Henry VIII, 100 years earlier, sought to defend the harbour from invasion. Standing on a 200ft promontory overlooking the entrance to Carrick Roads, Henry's **Pendennis Castle** (English Heritage) is one of Cornwall's great fortresses. Along with St Mawes Castle on the opposite bank, it has protected Britain's shores from attack ever since its construction. Strengthened further during the threat of a second Spanish Armada, Pendennis was one of the last Royalist strongholds to fall during the Civil War. It remained in use until the end of World War II. Now, through a variety of displays and exhibitions, the 450-year history of the fortress is explained.

During its heyday in the early 19th century, Falmouth was the home of almost 40 packet ships, which carried passengers, cargo and mail to every corner of the globe. The introduction of steam-powered vessels put paid to Falmouth's days as a major port and, by the 1850s, the packet service had moved to Southampton. A charming legacy of the packet ships' prosperous days is **Fox Rosehill Gardens** which is stocked with many exotic plants from around the world brought back by various ships' captains. Blessed by the mild Cornish climate, banana, eucalyptus, bamboos, agaves and a wide variety of palms flourish here – and in many private gardens.

Although the docks continue to be used by merchant shipping, the town's traditional activities are being overtaken by yachting and tourism. Falmouth's nautical and notorious past is revealed at the **National Maritime Museum Cornwall** where the wealth of displays explain the rise in popularity of the town due to the packet ships. The museum's collection includes 120 historic British and international boats as well as contemporary vessels, prototypes and future designs. A great

THE STICKY PRAWN

Flushing Quay, Falmouth, Cornwall TR11 5TY
Tel: 01326 373734   Fax: 01326 373698
e-mail: paullight@hotmail.com

Paul Lightfoot is putting years of international experience in the catering and hospitality business to excellent use at **The Sticky Prawn**, which he has owned and run since 1999. A great favourite with both locals and visitors, it stands on the water's edge, overlooking the River Fal on a jetty built centuries ago by the Dutch. It serves as bar, café and restaurant, open for morning coffee, lunch and dinner. Inside, stone walls, beams and wooden furniture create a friendly, inviting ambience, and when the weather is kind, the outside tables are in great demand. Paul's son Ben is the senior chef.

Not surprisingly, Ben's menu puts the emphasis on fish, landed daily by local boats, but there's no shortage of choice for meat-eaters, with raw materials sourced as far as possible from Cornish suppliers. Oysters, mussels and superb crevettes are always popular among the daily specials, which might also include grilled lemon sole, halibut, medallions of monkfish and sea bass with a red pepper dressing. There are always some imaginative meaty options, and in season nothing can beat a finale of Cornish strawberries with Cornish clotted cream.

Parking is available right outside, but a delightful alternative is to arrive by water taxi – pick-ups can be arranged from various local points.

🏛 historic building   🏛 museum   🏛 historic site   🌿 scenic attraction   🌱 flora and fauna

way to arrive at the museum is to use the Park & Float service, located on the A39 at the northern end of the town, and sail to the museum on a classic ferry.

Pirates and smugglers were also drawn to Falmouth. On **Custom House Quay**, stands an early 19th century brick-built incinerator known as the Queen's Pipe. It was here that contraband tobacco seized by Falmouth's customs men was burnt.

From Falmouth's busy harbour, ferries and cruise boats ply the local waters to St Mawes, Flushing, Truro and other enticing destinations, including whale and dolphin spotting trips.

Falmouth Harbour

GREEN LAWNS HOTEL & GARRAS RESTAURANT

Western Terrace, Falmouth, Cornwall TR11 4QJ
Tel: 01326 312734 Fax: 01236 2114237
e-mail: info@greenlawnshotel.com website: www.greenlawnshotel.com

Surrounded by some of the most stunning scenery in Britain, the **Green Lawns Hotel & Garras Restaurant** provides a beguiling blend of charm and elegance. This privately owned and well-established hotel is affectionately known locally as the "Ivy Hotel" because of its creeper-clad walls. It stands in its own mature grounds overlooking a beautiful lawn with wonderful shrubs and a colourful profusion of flower beds in spring and summer. Inside, everything from the comfortable luxury of the elegant lounge with its open log fire to the immaculate standards of the bedrooms ensures that a stay here will be a memorable one.

A major attraction at the hotel is its famous Garras Restaurant which boasts an RAC Dining Award and serves mouth-watering combinations of succulent meats, full flavoured fish and a colourful array of rich tasting local produce. The outstanding cuisine is complemented by a fine selection of wines and excellent service. The hotel offers a variety of accommodation ranging from a "honeymoon" style 4-poster with sunken spa bath, through the sophisticated charm of the Victorian suite to spacious family rooms. Other amenities include the Garras Leisure Club with its large heated swimming pool, sauna, Jacuzzi spa and mini-gymnasium.

 stories and anecdotes   famous people   art and craft   entertainment and sport   walks

Around Falmouth

MYLOR
2 miles N of Falmouth off the A39

🏛 Celtic Cross

The two attractive villages of Mylor
Churchtown and Mylor Bridge have now
blended into one another as a yachting and
water sports centre. It was at Mylor
Churchtown that the packet ships called and
in the village's ancient churchyard lie the
graves of many sea captains. In the
churchyard, too, by the south porch, stands a
10-foot **Celtic Cross** which is one of the
tallest in Cornwall. A further seven feet of the
cross lies underground. Just to the southwest
lies another popular yachting centre, Flushing,
which was given its distinctive look by Dutch

settlers from Vlissingen who arrived here in
the 17th century.

FEOCK
4 miles N of Falmouth off the B3289

🏛 Smugglers Cottage   🏛 Trelissick

This is one of the prettiest small villages in
Cornwall, and there is a pleasant creekside
walk to the west. This follows the course of
an old tramway, which dates from the time
when this area was a bustling port. To the
south of the village is **Restronguet Point** and
the 17th century Pandora Inn, named after the
ship sent out to capture the mutineers from
the *Bounty*.

From Tolverne, just north of Feock, Allied
troops left for the Normandy coast during the
D-day landings. On the shingle beach the
remains of the concrete honeycombed

ARGAL FARM SHOP
Argal Farm, Argal, Falmouth TR11 5PE
Tel: 01326 373896

For almost 30 years **Argal Farm Shop** has been
selling quality fresh produce, most of it from local
Cornish growers. There are cheeses from a farm just
over a mile down the road, apple juices from another
three miles away, Rodda's Cornish clotted cream,
and potatoes and cauliflowers from the shop's own
farm.

Owner Sam Shaw also tries to stock as much
locally produced organic vegetable and dairy
produce as possible – the organic eggs are
particularly tasty. Even your pets are catered for
with a variety of products that includes locally-
made, preservative-free dog biscuits.

The shop also stocks a range of natural cleaning
and beauty products, none of which has been
tested on animals. Sam operates a delivery service
and will happily make up a "vegetable box" to your
requirements. Located about 2.5 miles from
Falmouth, the shop enjoys a stunning location close
toTrebah Gardens and reservoirs, with lovely walks
all around. Argal Farm Shop is open from 9am to 5.30pm, Monday to Friday; 9.30am to 3.30pm
on Saturday.

🏛 historic building   📷 museum   🏛 historic site   🍃 scenic attraction   🌿 flora and fauna

mattresses can still be seen. While in the area General Eisenhower stayed at **Smugglers Cottage,** a lovely Grade II listed thatched cottage which is now a tearoom. Its owners have amassed a fascinating collection of memorabilia relating to that period.

Close by lies the estate of **Trelissick,** a privately owned 18th century house, surrounded by marvellous gardens and parkland with wonderful views over Carrick Roads. While the house is not open to the public, the estate, which is owned by the National Trust, offers visitors tranquil gardens of exotic plants and the chance to walk the miles of paths through its extensive park and woodland. Various outbuildings have been converted into restaurants, an art and craft gallery and a gift shop.

TRURO
14 miles N of Falmouth on the A39

🏥 Truro Cathedral   🏥 Lemon Street

🏛 Royal Cornwall Museum

This elegant small city at the confluence of three rivers – 'Tri-veru' in Cornish – is the administrative and ecclesiastical centre of Cornwall. It expanded from its ancient roots in medieval times on the prosperity originating from local mineral extractions. It was one of the first towns to be granted the rights of stannary, and several small medieval alleyways act as a reminder of those busy times before the silting up of the river saw Truro decline as a port and be overtaken by Falmouth. It was a fashionable place to rival Bath in the 18th century, and the short-lived

SAFFRON

5 Quay Street, Truro, Cornwall TR1 2HB
Tel: 01872 263771
e-mail: saffronrestaurant@btconnect.com
website: www.saffronrestauranttruro.co.uk

A passion for food and drink led Nik and Traci Tinney to open **Saffron** in January 1999, since when their style of cooking, their eclectic menu and the informal, welcoming ambience have made the restaurant a popular venue for locals and visitors to Truro. In a side street just off the centre, in an old part of town, the cheerful flower-decked frontage promises a warm welcome. Inside, the scene is set by flagstone floors, mirrors and straight-backed chairs set at scrubbed wooden tables. All the dishes are cooked to order from fresh seasonal ingredients, including the best available Cornish produce.

The keen owners offer a menu that keeps an eye on healthy eating. Their menus are excitingly and intriguingly different – tian of spider crab with mango and citrus fruit salsa, for example, turmeric dusted red fish, cauliflower and lentil dhal, yoghurt dressing, or fillet of corned beef with Falmouth Bay oyster, hollandaise sauce. The enjoyment level stays high right to the end with some scrumptious desserts, and the brilliant food is complemented by interesting wines and beers. This child-friendly restaurant is also non-smoking and there's good disabled access.

🎭 stories and anecdotes   🦜 famous people   🎨 art and craft   🎭 entertainment and sport   🚶 walks

Trelissick Gardens

Distance: *4.4 miles (7.0 kilometres)*

Typical time: *180 mins*

Height gain: *50 metres*

Map: *Explorer 105*

Walk: *www.walkingworld.com ID:1513*

Contributor: *Jim Grindle*

ACCESS INFORMATION:

Trelissick is four miles south of Truro on the B3289. Buses T7 and 89B run from Truro where there is a railway station.

DESCRIPTION:

Trelissick House is in an enviable position with rivers on three sides, and this walk will enable you to see all of them - Lamouth Creek to the north; the Fal to the east; and Carrick Roads to the south, all three part of the complex Fal estuary. You begin by entering the park and dropping to the river which is followed through woods to King Harry Ferry. Further woodland paths are succeeded by open views of the estuary before a gentle climb back through the park to the starting point.

ADDITIONAL INFORMATION

The first house was built here in about 1750 and went through many hands with much development of the gardens before they were acquired by the National Trust in 1955. Among the notable restoration by the Trust has been the re-planting of the once famous orchards with many old Cornish varieties of apple . The best place for seeing birds is between Waymarks 6 and 7. Between 7 and 8 is a sizeable Iron Age promontary fort, while at 8 is Roundwood Quay. This was built in the 18th century to ship tin and copper, and in

past days there were buildings for smelting and refining and many wharves. Since 1888 the King Harry Steam Ferry Company has operated a ferry which pulls itself across the Fal by chains but the motive power is now diesel. Between Waymarks 10 and 11 watch for large sea-going vessels at anchor; some are waiting repair, others are more permanently anchored for economic reasons or because they have been impounded by customs for drug smuggling for instance, or are the subject of litigation.

FEATURES:

River, toilets, stately home, National/NTS Trust, wildlife, birds, flowers, great views, butterflies, cafe, gift shop, food shop, good for kids, industrial archaeology, nature trail, restaurant, tea shop, woodland, ancient monument.

WALK DIRECTIONS:

1 | The kiosk is where you pay for car parking. Take the tarmac path next to it - it is signposted 'Woodland Walks.' Go through a gate next to a cattle-grid (Waymark 12) and follow the tarred path to a junction.

2 | Turn right and stay on this driveway until at the edge of a wood you reach another cattle-grid.

3 | Go through the gate at the left of the grid and then turn to the right on a path going uphill. This will bring you to one of the lodge-gates on the estate.

4 | Pass the lodge and go through the green gate. Cross the road and go through the matching gate on the other side. Follow a gravel track which zig-zags downhill, passing a bench on one corner. When it straightens out there is a stream on the left, with pools made for the cultivation of water-cress. In a few metres you meet another track at right-angles.

At this point is a low notice in cast metal with directions - for people going the other way.

5 | Turn left and you will see a footbridge over the stream that you have been following. Cross it, and on the other side the track forks again.

6 | Take the right fork which follows Lamouth Creek which is below you on your right. (When the tide is out this is a good spot for waders and where we saw the egret more than once.) The woods become no more than a strip of trees with a field visible on the left, until you reach the next wood. There is an entrance of kinds here formed from two low stone banks.

7 | There are several unmapped paths here. The simplest way is to take the right fork beyond the entrance. The path goes over the ditch and then straight through the rampart of the Iron Age fort before joining the other track where you turn right. Just before the quay you go down a few steps and emerge into the open.

8 | This is a magical spot and you could spend some time here looking for the remains of the old industries. When you have had enough, retrace your steps over the bridge back to Waymark 5.

9 | Now continue with the river on your left for 1.5km. You will reach a steep flight of steps leading down to the road you crossed earlier. The ferry is just to your left, and opposite is a white house with a flight of steps going up on its right.

10 | This is Bosanko's Cottage. The track that you have been on continues on the far side.

Only one track branches off to the right away from the river and your way is signposted. This is the section where you might see the anchored boats; in fact you are quite likely to hear their auxiliary engines first. The track clears the woods to give beautiful views of the river, much of it used for rehearsing the D-Day landings of 1944. 1.5km from the ferry you leave the woods by a kissing gate.

11 | This is where you re-enter the parkland. Go up the hill with the iron fence on your right and at the top cross the drive which enters Trelissick House. In a few moments you will reach the exit from the car park, recognised by the cattle grid.

12 | Go through the gate on the right to complete the walk.

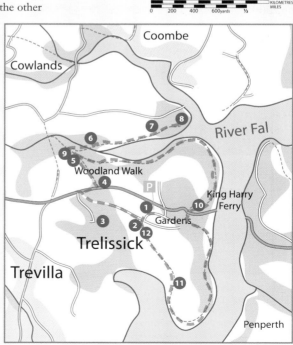

CHARLOTTE'S TEA-HOUSE

Coinage Hall, 1 Boscawen Street, Truro,
Cornwall TR1 2QU
Tel: 01872 263706

Charlotte's tea-house has a superb position on the first floor of the grand old Coinage Hall in the centre of the city. The Hall has a history that goes back to the early 1300s but the present building, which has Grade II listed status, was erected in imposing neo-Gothic style in 1848. It has recently been lovingly restored and now provides a peaceful sanctuary away from the busy streets of the city.

Owners Joan and Mike Pollard have maintained the Victorian ambience of this elegant tearoom with crystal chandeliers, period furniture, waitresses in charming period costume and home-made cakes served on silver-plated cake stands. Teatime treats here include cream teas, Charlotte's speciality high teas, an inviting array of wonderful cakes and a large selection of teas and herbal infusions. No wonder Charlotte's has won the annual Award of Excellence from the Tea Guild every year since 2002. The menu also offers a good choice of light lunches such as potato toasties, omelettes and salads. Charlotte's is open from 10am to 5pm, Monday to Saturday, all year.

VITREOUS CONTEMPORARY ART

7 Mitchell Hill, Truro, Cornwall TR1 1ED
Tel: 01872 274288
e-mail: info@vitreous.biz website: www.vitreous.biz

"The quality of work at **Vitreous Contemporary Art** is astonishing" was the judgement of the *Guardian's* art critic, Rupert Smith. Located just five minutes walk from Truro city centre, Vitreous Contemporary Art is recognised as a serious contemporary art gallery specialising in modern Cornish and southwest artists. The gallery showcases a wide variety of styles and media, and is not confined to any particular genre. As a result of this policy, the gallery has gained a reputation for innovation and diversity and continues to attract many regular visitors and clients.

Since the inception of the gallery, owner Jake Bose has always sought to exhibit high quality fine art with affordable price tags. He achieves this by combining long established artists with new, emerging talent. This broad spectrum means that most exhibitions provide ample choice to both serious collectors as well as new buyers – and, of course, for those who simply wish to look. The gallery runs an extensive exhibition programme of ten shows a year. All details of current exhibitions as well as archival information about previous shows can be found on the gallery's website.

🏛 historic building 🏛 museum 🏛 historic site 🉂 scenic attraction 🌿 flora and fauna

recovery in mineral prices at that time saw the creation of the gracious Georgian streets and houses that are still so attractive today – **Lemon Street** in particular is regarded as one of the finest surviving Georgian streets in the country. Overlooking Lemon Street is a lofty memorial column to the African explorer Richard Lander who was born in Truro and in the 1830s discovered the source of the River Niger.

Truro Cathedral

Nearby is one of the city's most recent developments, **Lemon Quay.** It occupies the site of the original Quay which was covered over in 1923 and still remains beneath the surface. Above it, the pedestrianised piazza is busy with bars, restaurants and cafés, and hosts various events such as the regular French Markets and the popular Made in Cornwall Fairs.

The arrival of the railway in 1859 confirmed Truro's status as a regional capital. In 1877, it became a city in its own right when the diocese of Exeter was divided and Cornwall was granted its own bishop. The foundation stone of **Truro Cathedral** was laid by the future Edward VII in 1880. This splendid Early English style building, with its celebrated Victorian stained glass window, was finally completed in 1910. Its three spires soar high above a city in which high-rise buildings are still very much the exception.

Housed in one of Truro's fine Georgian buildings, the **Royal Cornwall Museum & Art Gallery** covers the history of the county from the Stone Age to the present day. Amongst its treasures are some early Bronze Age collars of beaten gold and the coffin of Ast Tayef Nakht dating from around 675BC, complete with unwrapped mummy. The Art Gallery, one of ten scattered around the city, displays fine art from the Newlyn School to the present day.

The city has two major parks. The larger, Boscawen Park, sits beside the Truro River; Victoria Gardens, originally created to commemorate Queen Victoria's Diamond Jubilee, is filled with exotic trees shrubs and flowers. On Sunday afternoons in the summer, concerts are held here. The park's peaceful atmosphere is occasionally disturbed by a train rumbling over the majestic granite viaduct nearby. Originally built by Isambard Kingdom Brunel but replaced in 1904, the viaduct carries the main line from Paddington to Penzance.

Truro combines a pleasant modern city with an attractive shopping centre with living historic traditions. During Advent, wassailers continue the age-old custom of circulating through the streets, drinking from a decorated wassail bowl and collecting money for charity.

PORTSCATHO

4½ miles NE of Falmouth off the A3078

This pleasant, unspoilt fishing village, with its sandy beach on Gerrans Bay, may appear familiar to anyone who watched the TV drama, *The Camomile Lawn*, for which it provided a scenic a location. To the west, at St Just in Roseland, stands an exquisite 13th century church, surrounded by gardens containing many subtropical trees and shrubs

first planted by the botanist John Treseder at the end of the 19th century.

ST MAWES

2 miles E of Falmouth by ferry, on the A3078

🏛 St Mawes Castle

🏛 St Anthony's Lighthouse

This charming town, a popular and exclusive sailing centre in the shelter of Carrick Roads, is dominated by its artillery fort, **St Mawes Castle**. Built in the 1540s as part of Henry VIII's coastal defences, it is a fine example of Tudor military architecture. The castle's cloverleaf, or trefoil, design ensured that, whatever the direction of an attack, the castle could defend itself. However, a shot was never fired from here in anger and today visitors can

---

THE SEA GARDEN

3 River Street, Portscatho, Truro, Cornwall TR2 5HQ
Tel: 01872 580847

The Sea Garden really is a unique little shop. You'll find this listed Georgian building in a narrow lane that leads down to the seafront of the charming village of Portscatho. Behind the pretty white-washed walls and small-paned windows lies a fascinating collection of decorative antiques, kitchen and garden paraphernalia, second-hand china and glass, distinctive contemporary crafts sourced from all over Britain, and hand-made accessories for the home.

Owner Christine Nullmeyers relishes the challenge of providing year-round inspiration for her customers, whether they be seeking a simple birthday card or a complete wedding list. The Sea Garden also provides the principal outlet for Christine's own works. These include her photographic cards of local Cornish scenes, framed shell collages and striking arrangements of sepia postcards, fragments of letters and old stamps, with delicate handwritten text and pressed plants from her garden. Pretty linen cushions and bags are appliquéd with hand-stitched quotes and vintage patchwork hearts filled with lavender scent the air.

David Montgomery
Country Living Magazine UK

🏛 historic building　📷 museum　🏛 historic site　🗘 scenic attraction　🌱 flora and fauna

look around the Tudor interiors which are in remarkably good condition.

From the town, ferries take passengers across the river to Falmouth and, during the summer, a boat also takes passengers down the river to the remote and unspoilt area of Roseland around St Anthony. From St Anthony Head, the southernmost tip of the Roseland peninsula, there are wonderful views across Carrick Roads. At the foot of the headland lies **St**

St Mawes Castle

Anthony's Lighthouse, built in 1834 to warn sailors off the notorious Manacles rocks. An excellent starting point for a number of coastal walks, St Anthony Head, owned by the National Trust, is also home to the remains of a military battery in use right up until the 1950s.

MAWNAN SMITH
3 miles S of Falmouth off the A39

🌱 Glendurgan Garden 🌱 Trebah Garden

Just to the west of this pretty village lies **Glendurgan Garden**, created in the 1820s in a wonderful wooded valley that drops down to the shores of the Helford estuary. The garden contains many fine trees and exotic plants, and children will enjoy the famous Heade Maze, created in 1833 from laurels, as well as the Giant's Stride – a maypole.

To the southeast, the tower of the 15th century church at Mawnan has been a local landmark for sailors for centuries. An excellent place from which to take in the sweeping coastline, the tower was also used as a lookout post during times of war. Further up Helford Passage is the tiny fishing hamlet of Durgan along with the sub-tropical **Trebah Garden** (see panel on page 41) that has often been dubbed the 'garden of dreams'. On a 25-acre site that falls down to a private beach on the Helford Estuary, the owner at the time Charles Fox set out to create a garden of rare and exotic plants and trees collected from around the world. Reaching maturity in the early 1930s and regarded at the time as one of the most beautiful in England, the garden was sold in 1939. Then began over 40 years of neglect before a massive restoration programme in the 1980s returned it to its original impressive state.

BUDOCK VEAN HOTEL

Helford Passage, Mawnan Smith, Nr Falmouth,
Cornwall TR11 5LG
Tel: 01326 252100   e-mail: relax@budockvean.co.uk
Fax: 01326 250892   website: www.budockvean.co.uk

Nestled in 65 acres of tropical gardens and parkland with private foreshore on the tranquil Helford River– this family-run 4 star hotel includes outstanding leisure facilities and space to relax.

The award-winning restaurant which has a pianist playing each evening has beamed ceilings and a minstrel's gallery over the inglenook fireplace. Head Chef Darren Kelly uses excellent local produce to create imaginative four-course dinners with fresh seafood a speciality.

♦   The golf course has 9-holes and 18-tees. Its overall length is about 2700 yards with three par 3's and one par 5. It was originally designed by James Braid. Golf is free of charge to residents and discounted green fees are available for a large number of nearby courses.

♦   Other sporting facilities include a Snooker room, all-weather tennis courts and a spectacular indoor heated swimming pool, opening out onto the terrace in summer, with its own log fire in the winter months. Our 32 foot Sunseeker motorboat can whisk you to a secluded creek for picnic lunch.

♦   Five lounges, a conservatory and a garden patio ensure there is always a corner to put your feet up and relax with a traditional Cornish Cream Tea.

♦   Situated within about fifty yards of the hotel's front door are the four Budock Vean cottages and lodges accommodating up to eight people. Each has a small private garden, convenient parking, and central heating and includes full use of hotel facilities.

♦   The Natural Health Spa is open 7 days a week and offers treatments dedicated to relaxation, rejuvenation and good health for men and women. Tempting treatments can be found on the extensive brochure including 100% organic Head In Heaven for restoring the body to total harmony or the Elemis Exotic Lime and Ginger Salt Glow to deeply cleanse, polish and soften the body to perfection. The Hydrotherm Essentials Massage takes the body into a deeper state of relaxation, combining warm pads and massage.

♦   Stroll through the valley garden, past ponds and waterfalls to the foreshore sun-lounge. The local ferryboat can take you from our slipway to local waterside pubs in the village of Helford, or Helford passage where sailing and motor boats can be hired.

Budock Vean is centrally located for all the Great Gardens of Cornwall, next door to Trebah and Glendurgan Gardens and opposite the Royal Duchy oyster farm. Explore some of Britain's most dramatic coastline from the wild grandeur of Kynance and the Lizard to the Peace of the Helford itself.

Please contact Reception for a brochure or more information about the Hotel

🏛 historic building   🏛 museum   🏛 historic site   ⚘ scenic attraction   🌿 flora and fauna

Trebah Garden

Mawnan Smith, Nr. Falmouth, Cornwall, TR11 5JZ Tel: 01326 252200 Fax: 01326 250781
e-mail: mail@trebah-garden.co.uk website: www.trebahgarden.co.uk

Trebah is a uniquely beautiful, 26-acre Cornish ravine garden - the wild and magical result of 160 years of inspired and dedicated creation. Glades of sub-tropical ferns and palms mingle with a forest of trees and shrubs in ever-changing colours

Trebah was first planted in the 1840s by Charles Fox, a Quaker landowner and inspired gardener. The rarest and most exotic trees and plants were imported from all over the world to create this lovely garden, and Fox ensured that every last sapling was painstakingly placed for maximum effect -even though he knew he'd never see the garden in its mature splendour.

Subsequent occupants continued his work until WW11, when the house was sold, the estate split up and

and scents, contained beneath a canopy of century-old rhododendrons and magnolias.

A steeply wooded ravine descends 200 feet down to a private secluded beach on the historic Helford River. A stream cascades over waterfalls and meanders through ponds of giant koi carp and exotic water plants before winding through two acres of blue and white hydrangeas and spilling onto the beach.

parts of the garden slowly reverted to nature under a succession of owners.

Then, in 1981, Trebah was bought by the Hibbert family, who began a massive programme to restore the gardens to their Victorian heyday. Trebah opened to the public in 1987 and three years later the family donated the house and garden to the Trebah Garden Trust, a registered charity, to ensure that the garden is preserved for the pleasure of all future generations.

HELFORD

5½ miles SW of Falmouth off the B3293

🚶 Helford River Walk

A picture-postcard village standing on the secluded tree-lined southern banks of the Helford estuary, Helford must have one of

the most attractive settings in the whole of the county. Once the haunt of smugglers who took advantage of the estuary's many isolated creeks and inlets, this is now a popular sailing centre. During the summer, it is linked to **Helford Passage**, on the northern bank, by a ferry that has been in existence since the

🎭 stories and anecdotes   🐦 famous people   🎨 art and craft   🎟 entertainment and sport   🚶 walks

Helford River

landmark for ships attempting to negotiate the treacherous rocks, **The Manacles**, which lie offshore. In the churchyard, there are some 400 graves of those who have fallen victim to the dangerous reef.

Just outside the village a statue commemorates the 500th anniversary of the **Cornish Rebellion**

Middle Ages. The deep tidal creeks in the area have given rise to rumours that this is the home of Morgawr, the legendary Helford monster. The first recorded sighting of Morgawr was in 1926 and ever since there have been numerous people who claim to have seen this 'hideous, hump-backed creature with stumpy horns'.

From the village, the five-mile **Helford River Walk** takes in several isolated hamlets and a 200-year-old fig tree in the churchyard at Manaccan before returning to the tea rooms and pubs of Helford. The rich mud of the Helford River, revealed at low tide, is a wonderful feeding ground for many birds including heron, cormorant and curlew, while the ancient natural woodlands along the shores support a wealth of plants and wildlife.

ST KEVERNE
7 miles SW of Falmouth off the B3293

Something of a focal point on this part of the Lizard Peninsula, the pleasant village of St Keverne is rare in Cornwall in that it has a handsome village square. Its elevated position has led to its church spire being used as a

of 1497, one of whose leaders was a blacksmith from St Keverne, while the church has a plaque in memory of the executed rebel leaders. Although St Keverne has been dominated by the sea for centuries, its agricultural heritage is continued in the ancient custom of 'Crying the Neck'. It was believed that the corn spirit resided in the last wheatsheaf cut, which was plaited and hung over the fireplace until spring.

GWEEK
8 miles SW of Falmouth off the A394

🐦 National Seal Sanctuary

Set at the head of the Helford River, Gweek developed as an important commercial port after Helston harbour became silted in the 13th century. The same fate befell Gweek years later although it retains its links with its maritime past and the old harbour is very much alive with craft shops and small boatyards. Just a short distance from the centre of the village along the north side of the creek, is the **National Seal Sanctuary**, the country's leading marine rescue centre established over 40 years ago. The sanctuary cares for sick, injured and orphaned seals.

🏠 historic building   🏛 museum   🏛 historic site   🌿 scenic attraction   🐦 flora and fauna

Visitors can witness the joyful antics of the seals at feeding time and explore the Woodland Nature Quest around an ancient coppiced wood.

HELSTON
10 miles SW of Falmouth on the A394

🏠 Blue Anchor Inn   🏛 Helston Folk Museum

🌱 Trevarno Estate   🎬 Lady of the Lake

🏛 National Museum of Gardening

🎢 Flambards

Dating back to Roman times, when it was developed as a port, Helston is the westernmost of Cornwall's five medieval stannary towns. During the Middle Ages, tin was brought here for assaying and taxing before being shipped. However, in the 13th century a shingle bar formed across the mouth of the River Cober, cutting off the port's access to the sea. Helston's long history has left it with a legacy of interesting buildings. **The Blue Anchor Inn** was a hostel for monks before becoming an inn during the 15th century. It has its own private brewery, believed to be the oldest in the country. It's at the rear of the inn, next to the old skittle alley, and its beer, 'Spingo', comes in three strengths.

Another hostelry, the 16th century **Angel Hotel** was originally the town house of the Godolphin family and was converted into a hotel in the mid-1700s. Around that time, the Earl of Godolphin provided funds for the parish church to be rebuilt after the previous structure had been struck by lightning and had to be demolished. In the churchyard lies a memorial to Henry Trengrouse, the Helston man who invented the rocket-propelled safety line that has saved so many lives around the British coast. Elsewhere, there are a surprising

number of Georgian, Regency and Victorian buildings, which all help to give Helston a quaint and genteel air. Housed in one of the town's old market halls, close to the classical 19th century **Guildhall**, is the **Helston Folk Museum** (see panel on page 44), which covers many aspects of the town's and the local area's history. The displays range from archaeological finds and mineral specimens to the reconstruction of a blacksmith's shop, an 18th century cider mill and a farm wagon from 1901.

Still very much a market town serving much of the Lizard Peninsula, Helston has managed to escape from the mass tourism that has affected many other Cornish towns. However, the famous **Festival of the Furry**, or Flora Dance, a colourful festival of music and dance, does bring people here in droves. The origins of the name are unknown but it is clear that the festival has connections with ancient pagan spring celebrations as it is held on May 8th. The climax of the celebration is the midday dance when invited participants wearing top hat, tails and dress gowns, weave in and out of shops, houses and gardens.

Just to the northwest of the town lies **Trevarno Estate and Gardens** – "the best excuse anyone could possibly want to go to Cornwall" according to *The Times*. This beautiful estate stocked with many rare shrubs and trees has a long history stretching back to 1296 when Randolphus de Trevarno first gave the land its name. Over the intervening centuries the gardens and grounds have been developed and extended so that, today, Trevarno is known as one of the finest gardens in a county, with a great gardening tradition. The estate's **National Museum of Gardening** complements the grounds and

Helston Museum

Market Place, Helston, Cornwall TR13 8TH
Tel: 01326 564027
e-mail: enquiries@helstonmuseum.org,uk
website: www.kerrierleisure.org.uk

Helston Museum is housed in the former Butter and Meat Markets, and the Drill Hall. All the buildings date from 1837 and are in the heart of the conservation area. The collection relates to local crafts and industries which flourished in the 19th and 20th centuries.

Transport and Trades feature a farm wagon, wagonette, butcher's cart. and an assortment of bicycles, including a tradesman's bicycle and a penny-farthing. An array of tools relating to the wheelwright, cooper and carpenter are also on display.

A **Costume Gallery** was opened three years ago, containing a wide variety of costumes. The gallery is divided into themed areas – in the Men's Cabinet is a variety of items from a sailor's pigtail dating from the early 19th century to a pair of mine captain's trousers. The Ladies Cabinet includes early Victorian footwear and clothing from various periods. The Accessories Cabinet contains items such as muff warmers, bonnets, gloves, etc.

The Loft area incorporates **Home Life, Mining and Quarrying, Sports and Pastimes,** Wartime, **Gardening, Toy Shop** displays and **Cycles** from the penny-farthing to a tradesman's bike.

There is also a new **Early Learning Area**, for the use of accompanied pre-school children.

Role-play workshops take place in the **Victorian Classroom** where the children experience life in a Victorian school (minus the corporal punishment!) and dress in costume of that period.

Regular Art Exhibitions are held in the **Mezzanine Art Gallery**

Opening Hours: Mon-Sat 10am-1pm plus extra hours (10am-4pm) during holiday times.

highlights the ingenuity of gardeners down the ages by the range of gardening implements exhibited. Other attractions here include Soap and Skincare Workshops; a Vintage Soap Museum; adventure play area; a conservatory serving refreshments and a shop.

To the east of the town lies another interesting and award-winning family attraction, **Flambards.** Based around a faithful recreation of a lamp-lit Victorian street, complete with more than 50 shops, it has numerous attractions for all the family. Other exhibits include an undercover life-size re-creation of a World War II blitzed street, an Anderson Shelter and a wartime pub. Wedding Fashions Down the Years features a romantic

🏢 historic building   🏛 museum   🏛 historic site   🌣 scenic attraction   🌿 flora and fauna

assembly of changing styles with a collection of wedding dresses and wedding cakes from 1870 to 1970. Rides and slides keep the youngsters happy and for older children and adults the figure-of-eight karting circuit provides the opportunity to put driving skills to the test.

Close by is the Royal Navy's land and sea rescue headquarters at **Culdrose**, the largest and busiest helicopter base in Europe. Since the base was established here in 1947 as *HMS Seahawk*, it has carried out a great many successful search and rescue operations. There are guided tours and a special viewing area from which the comings and goings of the helicopters can be observed.

Mullion Cove

When the shingle bar formed to the west of the town in the 13th century and dammed the River Cober, it created the largest freshwater lake in Cornwall, **Loe Pool**. This is now owned by the National Trust and is a haven for sea birds as well as waterfowl such as mallard, mute swan, coot, teal and red-necked grebe. A Cornish folk tale links Loe Pool with the Arthurian legend of the **Lady of the Lake** – Tennyson himself favoured this site. As at Bodmin Moor's Dozmary Pool, a hand is said to have risen from the depths of the water to catch the dying King Arthur's sword. Another local story connects Loe Bar with the legendary rogue, Jan Tregeagle, who was set the task of weaving a rope from its sand as a punishment.

MULLION

12 miles SW of Falmouth on the B3296

🐚 Mullion Cove 📡 Guglielmo Marconi

📻 Satellite Earth Station

The largest settlement on the peninsula, Mullion has a 15th century church and a 16th century inn and is an ideal base from which to explore this remarkable part of Cornwall. A mile to the east lies the pretty, weather-worn harbour of **Mullion Cove** (National Trust), and just up the coast is the popular sandy beach of **Poldhu Cove**. It was from the clifftops above the beach in 1901 that the radio pioneer, **Guglielmo Marconi**, transmitted the first wireless message across the Atlantic. His Morse signal, the letter 's' repeated three times, was received in St John's, Newfoundland, quelling the doubts of the many who said that radio waves could not bend round the Earth's curvature. In 1903 Marconi was honoured with a visit by the future King George V and his wife, and in

TRECARNE POTTERY

Meaver Road, Mullion, Cornwall TR12 7DN
Tel: 01326 241294
e-mail: trecarne.pottery@virgin.net
website: trecarnepottery.co.uk

In his workshop at the **Trecarne Pottery**, Michel Roux creates a striking range of decorative and functional pieces. He was born in Aix-en-Provence in France and since his father was an artist he grew up amid paints and canvas. But it was in England, in 1978, that he became fascinated by clay and pottery. A potter friend who had trained at Harrow School of Art gave him some initial tuition before telling Michel "to get on and learn by yourself". Years later, he set up a workshop in the Pyrenees and began successfully selling and exhibiting his work. When his three children moved back to England, Michel decided to come too and in 2003 opened his present workshop.

He is greatly inspired by the natural features of the Lizard peninsula – "by the energy of the Lizard sea and wind, by the amazing colours of the sky and the rocks, and by the local beaches. All my pottery is unique" he says, "I never make the same piece twice. There may be series of cups or bowls, but they will never be identical. My work is stoneware, fired to 1280°C, and is robust enough to be used daily".

JT CRAFTS

Mullion Meadows Craft Centre, Trenance Barton, Mullion,
Helston, Cornwall TR12 7HB
Tel: 01326 240560   e-mail: jtcrafts@fsbdial.co.uk

For more than 12 years now, Julia Trahair has been designing and creating a unique range of domestic items which can be seen at her studio/shop **JT Crafts** just outside the village of Mullion on the road to the Cove. Julia cuts all her own blocks from lino so all the designs are original. She also does all the printing, usually on cotton calico, and the making-up of the articles. Recent additions to her repertoire include a print of a Jacobean tree of life, a series of little money bags decorated with dollar, pound and euro signs, and a case to fit an MP3 player.

Julia's regular items include lavender sachets edged in lace and with a ribbon hanging loop; door signs painted with your choice of pattern; coffee and tea cosies; an AGA mat just the right size to fit the lid of an AGA; baguette and bread bags; aprons for both adults and children; an onion bag that hangs up to dispense onions conveniently; kit and shopping bags, and much more.

Julia offers a catalogue and mail order service and is also happy to accept commissions – just give her a call.

GALLERY ANTHONY

Mullion Meadows Craft Centre, Mullion, Helston, Cornwall TR12 7HB
Tel: 01326 241050
e-mail: info@galleryanthony.co.uk
website: www.galleryanthony.co.uk

Since opening in 2001, **Gallery Anthony** has welcomed increasing numbers of visitors who enjoy the relaxed and friendly atmosphere. The gallery showcases the work of the husband and wife resident artists, Anthony and Marjorie Smith. They work with oriental papers and water soluble media to produce artwork in their unique styles. Anthony's evocative, powerful seascapes and romantic beach scenes hang alongside Marjorie's sculptural, stylised, organic forms that are linked by their use of strong colour.

Both artists are happy to share their techniques with the public and feel it is their mission to share the creative process with as many people as possible. "These days people spend so much money purchasing a house" says Anthony, "and we appreciate their need to get their décor just right. Our commission process meets this need". Three sample paintings are sent to the customer so that they can check the colour, texture and composition in their own home and select the aspects that are most suitable. No deposits are taken and payment for the final painting is only accepted when the customer is completely satisfied.

The gallery is situated on the road leading to Mullion Cove and also shows the work of local crafts people.

1905 a daily news service for ships was inaugurated. In 1910 a message from Poldhu to the *SS Montrose* led to the arrest of the murderer Dr Crippen. A small granite obelisk, the **Marconi Monument**, was unveiled on the site of the wireless station by his daughter after the inventor's death.

Just a couple of miles inland, on the windswept heathland of **Goonhilly Downs**, is a monument to the very latest in telecommunications – the **Satellite Earth Station**. It is the largest such station in the world and there have been few world events that have not been monitored through here since it opened in the 1960s. The guided tour around the station, which takes in all manner of telecommunications including the internet and videophone links, is a fascinating and rewarding experience.

PORTHLEVEN

12 miles SW of Falmouth on the B3304

This pleasant fishing town developed from a small village in the 19th century. In 1811, London industrialists built its three-section harbour to export tin and china clay and import mining machinery, and also to protect the growing fishing fleet. Although this scheme to establish Porthleven as a major tin-exporting centre failed, the inner basin of the harbour can still be sealed off to protect boats from the worst of the southwesterly gales. A number of the town's old industrial buildings have been converted into handsome craft galleries, restaurants and shops, and the charming old harbour is overlooked by an assortment of attractive residential terraces and fishermen's cottages.

📖 stories and anecdotes   🐦 famous people   🎨 art and craft   🎵 entertainment and sport   🚶 walks

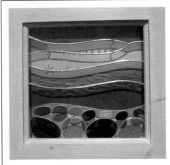

JULIA MILLS GALLERY & WORKSHOP

Fore Street, Porthleven, nr Helston, Cornwall TR13 9HH
Tel: 01326 569340
e-mail: julia@juliamills.wanadoo.co.uk
website: www.juliamillsgallery.co.uk

Just a short distance from the charming old harbour at Porthleven is the **Julia Mills Gallery & Workshop** which has attracted a steadily growing number of visitors since it opened in December 2000. A diverse and ever-changing selection of contemporary art, ceramics, glass, jewellery and sculpture is on display. Julia's own speciality is working with hand-blown glass, creating contemporary panels in a vast range of chiefly pastel colours. Inspired not only by the Cornish landscape but also by Kaffe Fassett (for colour), Jane Ray and Terry Frost, the panels are beautifully produced, very decorative and highly desirable.

Also on display are the works of associate Catherine Hyde whose paintings combine symbolism derived from Greek, Norse, European and Welsh myths. The fish, stag and hare – ancient symbols with multiple layers of meaning – represent wildness, fertility and permanence. Soaring between earth, sea and air, they leap through her landscapes which resound with the profound connection between all living things. Catherine Hyde produces giclee prints from her paintings, printed in limited editions using light fast ink on high-quality acid-free papers.

A popular and attractive town today, Porthleven is gaining a gastronomic reputation on account of the many excellent and tempting restaurants, cafés and inns to be found in such a small area.

LIZARD

14 miles SW of Falmouth on the A3083

🚶 South West Coast Path   🌄 Kynance Cove

Lizard is a place of craft shops, cafés and art galleries and lends its name to the **Lizard Peninsula,** the most southerly point of mainland Britain and also the country's warmest area. Just 14 miles by 14 miles, the peninsula's unique scenery has caused it to be designated an Area of Outstanding Natural Beauty. The **South West Coast Path** follows the coastline, much of which is in the hands of the National Trust, and provides many opportunities for walkers of all abilities. In particular, there is a nine-mile, and sometimes strenuous, walk to Mullion that takes in some of the most spectacular scenery as well as passing lowland Britain's largest National Nature Reserve.

The Lizard is also known for its unique Serpentine rock, a green mineral that became fashionable in the 19th century after Queen Victoria visited Cornwall and ordered many items made from the stone for her house, Osborne, on the Isle of Wight. The village is still the centre for polishing and fashioning the stone into souvenirs and objets d'art.

To the south of the village lies **Lizard Point**, the tip of the peninsula, whose three sides are lashed by waves whatever the season.

🏠 historic building   🏛 museum   🏚 historic site   🌄 scenic attraction   🌱 flora and fauna

The Lizard

There has been a form of lighthouse here since the early 1600s. The present **Lighthouse** was built in 1751 despite protests from locals, who feared that they would lose a regular source of income from looting wrecked ships. It now houses a light that is one of the most powerful in the world.

Just to the northeast of Lizard is the very picturesque fishing village of **Cadgwith,** wedged in a rocky cove with fishing boats drawn up on the beach. With its cluster of pastel coloured thatched cottages and two shingle beaches, it is everyone's idea of a typical Cornish village. Life has not always been so peaceful here as, in the 19th century, this was a busy pilchard fishing centre. In 1904, a record catch of nearly 1.8 million pilchards was landed in just four days! A small fleet of boats still sails from here, though their catch now is mainly lobster, crab, shark and mullet. Nearby is the curiously named Devil's Frying Pan, a collapsed sea cave with a spectacular blow-hole in the cliff.

To the northwest lies the famous beauty spot, **Kynance Cove**, whose marvellous sandy beach and dramatic offshore rock formations have been a favourite destination ever since Prince Albert visited here with his children in 1846. The cove is the site of the largest outcrop of the Lizard Peninsula's curious Serpentine rock and the caves to the west of the cove can be explored, with care, at low tide.

WENDRON
8½ miles W of Falmouth on the B3297

🏛 Poldark Mine Heritage Complex

Close to this bleak village is one of the many mines that have been worked in this area since the 15th century. It has now re-opened as the **Poldark Mine Heritage Complex** , and

📕 stories and anecdotes   🕊 famous people   🎨 art and craft   🎭 entertainment and sport   🚶 walks

VICARAGE FARM SHOP

Viscar, Wendron, Helston, Cornwall TR13 0EJ
Tel/Fax: 01326 340484
e-mail: info@vicaragefarmshop.com
website: www.vicaragefarmshop.com

Vicarage Farm sits high on the hills above Helston where streams gather to run down to Cober and Loe Pool. Here Kim and Gill Courtauld produce meat and poultry to their own, very high standards and sell it in their **Vicarage Farm Shop.** They have stocked Vicarage Farm well: for prime beef, there are Aberdeen Angus cows; the sheep are mainly Suffolk, but they have other more unusual breeds too – badger-faced Welsh mountain, Hebredian and rare Castlemilk Moorit, for example. Some are bred for their fine wools, others for their firm, well-flavoured meat.

Gill and Kim like the old healthy, vigorous breeds so they also keep traditional breeds of pigs for succulent pork; Marans and Khaki Campbell ducks for astonishing eggs, and at Christmas and Easter they produce Broad Breasted White turkeys, for which you should place your orders well in advance. They are proud of their animals, which they tend carefully and well. As Gill says, "We believe that happy, healthy animals taste better!" In addition to their own products, the shop also stocks produce from friends and neighbours including jams, chutneys, fresh vegetables, home baking and bread, smoked cheese and fish, and local pottery and cards.

visitors to this interesting attraction can take an underground tour of the tunnels, see the famous 18th century Poldark village and wander around the machinery exhibits, some of which are in working order. For a small charge, you can also try your hand at panning for real gold.

St Austell

🏵 St Austell Brewery Centre

🏛 Wheal Martyn China Clay Museum

"This strange white world of pyramid and pool," was Daphne du Maurier's response to the bizarre landscape around St Austell. The man ultimately responsible was William Cookworthy, a chemist from Plymouth, who discovered large deposits of kaolin, or china clay here in 1748. Cookworthy realised the importance of the china clay which is a constituent of many products including porcelain, glossy paper, textiles and pharmaceuticals. But for every ton of china clay extracted, another nine tons of spoil is created. Over the years, the waste material from the clay pits to the north and west of the town has been piled up into conical spoil heaps that led to these bare, bleached uplands being nicknamed the **Cornish Alps**. More recently the heaps and disused pits have been landscaped with acid-loving plants, such as rhododendrons, and they now have gently undulating footpaths and nature trails.

Although china clay has dominated St Austell since it was first discovered, and is now Cornwall's largest industry, the town is also the home of another important local

THE CLIFF HEAD HOTEL

Sea Road, Carlyon Bay, nr St Austell,
Cornwall PL25 3RB
Tel: 01726 812345 Fax: 01726 815511
e-mail: info@cliffheadhotel.com
website: www.cliffheadhotel.com

Located in the centre of the Cornish Riviera, **The Cliff Head Hotel** is ideally positioned for exploring Cornwall, the nearby Eden Project, and many attractive fishing villages and gardens. The hotel stands in its own extensive grounds, close to the beach with fine sea views and bracing clifftop walks. Privately owned, the Cliff Head has a warm, relaxed atmosphere and friendly, caring staff who make guests feel genuinely welcome. The hotel has its own popular restaurant offering both table d'hôte and à la carte menus, together with a keenly priced selection of classic and vintage wines from around the world.

Accommodation at the Cliff Head offers en suite bedrooms, all provided with colour TV, telephone, radio and baby listening service; family rooms are also available with a children's room interconnected to the master bedroom. Other amenities include a cocktail bar and lounge, a heated indoor swimming pool and a sauna . The Cliff Head is also a popular venue for weddings, functions and conferences. The Trelawney Suite has its own bar and together with the two acres of delightful gardens stocked with mature trees and shrubs is particularly suited for those all-important wedding photographs.

business – the St Austell Brewery. Founded by Walter Hicks in 1851, the brewery flourished as the town expanded on the prosperity of the kaolin. Still thriving today, it remains a family business. The history of the company and an insight into the brewing process can be found at the informative **St Austell Brewery Visitor Centre**, from where visitors are also taken on a guided tour of the brewery.

Just to the north of the town, in the heart of the Cornish Alps, is Wheal Martyn, an old clay works, now home to the **Wheal Martyn China Clay Museum**. This open air museum tells the 200-year story of the industry in Cornwall through a wide variety of displays. The land around this once busy mine has been replanted and it now has a unique range of habitats. The nature trail through the surrounding countryside offers visitors the

opportunity to discover many different birds, small mammals, plants and insects.

Around St Austell

ST BLAZEY
3½ miles NE of St Austell on the A390

🦜 Eden Project

To the west of the village is the remarkable **Eden Project** which, since its opening in May 2001, has been a huge international success. The project aims to "promote the understanding and responsible management of the vital relationship between plants, people and resources." The brain-child of former record producer Tim Smit, back in 1994, the Project took over an abandoned, 50-metre deep china clay pit which now

🎭 stories and anecdotes   🦅 famous people   🎨 art and craft   🌿 entertainment and sport   🚶 walks

PENARTH GUEST HOUSE

St Austell Road, St Blazey Gate, Par, Cornwall PL24 2EF
Tel: 01726 815165/813332
e-mail: patriciaclarke79@aol.com
website: www.penarthguesthouse.com

Just a three-minute drive (or a pleasant 25-minute walk) from the Eden Project, **Penarth Guest House** is a spacious detached house set in its own grounds on the edge of St Blazey Gate Village. Guests have the use of a comfortable TV lounge and also a covered patio area at the rear of the house. In the spacious dining area, a generous full English breakfast is served and the well-appointed guest bedrooms are all en suite and provided with TV and hospitality tray. Penarth Guest House offers a free station taxi service or budget car hire is available. Graded Three Diamonds by the ETB it is also AA listed.

contains the largest conservatories (biomes) in the world. Three of the world's climate zones (Biomes) have been chosen for interpretation: the Humid Tropics (Rainforests and Tropical Islands) and the Warm Temperate regions (the Mediterranean, South Africa & California) are contained within the two giant conservatories that have already captured the public imagination. The third, or Outdoor Biome, is our own Temperate zone that thrives on the climatic advantages that Cornwall has to offer. A new Education Centre is currently nearing completion as is a covered eating area outside the Biomes where visitors can eat alfresco whatever the weather. Designs for a third 'semi-arid' Biome – part of the original plan for Eden – have been developed and will be the final element of this awe-inspiring enterprise.

CHARLESTOWN

1 mile SE of St Austell off the A390

🏠 Shipwreck & Heritage Centre

🌿 Tregrehan Gardens

This small fishing village, once named West Polmear, was transformed in the 1790s by Charles Rashleigh, a local mine owner, who built a harbour here to support the recently

established china clay industry. Charlestown's harbour declined in the 19th century as other ports, such as Fowey and Plymouth, developed better facilities. However, what has been left is a harbour and village in a Georgian time capsule. As well as providing a permanent berth for square-rigged boats, it is a popular destination with holidaymakers and has been used as the location for TV series such as *Poldark* and *The Onedin Line*. Close to the docks is the **Charlestown Shipwreck and Heritage Centre**. This offers an insight into the town's history, local shipwrecks and the various devices that have been developed over the years for rescuing and recovering those in peril at sea. There are hundreds of artefacts recovered from more than 150 shipwrecks and the many and varied exhibitions reflect village life in Charlestown, its history, shipwrecks and the once thriving China Clay industry. The exhibition shows a tremendous range of maritime history dating back to 1715 and one of the largest underwater diving equipment collections in the country, including various suits used for treasure seeking and naval purposes.

Just to the northeast of Charlestown, close to Tregrehan Mills is **Tregrehan Gardens**,

🏛 historic building   🏠 museum   🏛 historic site   🌄 scenic attraction   🌿 flora and fauna

where visitors can not only see many mature trees from as far afield as North America and Japan but also rhododendrons and a range of Carlyon hybrid camellias. The garden has been created over the years since the early 1800s by the Carlyon family who have lived here since 1565.

MEVAGISSEY

5 miles S of St Austell on the B3273

- 🏛 Mevagissey Folk Museum
- 🚂 World of Model Railways
- 🌱 Lost Gardens of Heligan
- 🌱 Caerhays Castle Gardens

Once aptly known as Porthilly, Mevagissey was renamed in the 14th century after the saints St Meva and St Issey. The largest fishing village in St Austell Bay, Mevagissey was an important centre of the pilchard industry and everyone who lived here was linked in some way with either the fishing boats or processing the catch. This has led to a labyrinth of buildings all within easy reach of the harbour. The Inner Harbour of today dates from the 1770s while the Outer Harbour, built to increase the size of the port, was finally finished at the end of the 19th century.

Housed in a harbour building dating from 1745, the **Mevagissey Folk Museum** has a broad collection of artefacts that includes not only the pilchard industry but agricultural machinery, early photographs of village life and the story of Pears soap – originally created by Cornishman Andrew Pears in the 18th century. Elsewhere around the harbour,

---

MARIE MORRISON DESIGN

19 Church Street, Mevagissey, Cornwall PL26 6DA
Tel: 01726 844487 Fax: 01726 844944
e-mail: info@mariemorrison.co.uk
website: www.mariemorrison.co.uk

Anyone who has visited **Marie Morrison Design** at one of her shops in Mevagissey or Padstow will know that she stocks some of the most innovative, hand-made jewellery to be found. With nearly 30 years experience in designing and retailing jewellery, Marie has drawn on her extensive knowledge to create her latest collection. Last year, she travelled the world sourcing beautiful and unusual gemstones which she has combined with silver to produce a stunning and individual range. Customers can always be sure of purity and quality.

The majority of pieces are 925 sterling silver and are hallmarked at the Edinburgh Assay offices, either with the Marie Morrison hallmark or stamped simply '925' or 'silver'. Necklets and bracelets are tagged with a heart-shaped logo to prove that they are authentic Marie Morrison designs. If you like a particular design but would prefer it in another stone, you'll find that your preference is often available. Similarly, it's possible to purchase earrings or bracelets to match many of the necklaces available. You can see much of the extensive range on Marie's website, a brochure is available, or you can contact her by phone to discuss your requirements.

🎭 stories and anecdotes   🍽 famous people   🎨 art and craft   ✏ entertainment and sport   🚶 walks

visitors can see the fascinating displays and models at the **World of Model Railways Exhibition.** It contains an impressive collection of 2,000 models and a working display featuring more than 30 trains travelling through varied landscapes including town, country, seaside and even an Alpine winter scene. The Mevagissey Aquarium features local sea life and is located in the old Lifeboat House just by the quay.

In the 1750s, when John Wesley first came to Mevagissey to preach, he was greeted with a barrage of rotten eggs and old fish and had to be rescued from the crowd and taken to safety.

To the northwest of Mevagissey are the famous **Lost Gardens of Heligan,** one of the country's most interesting gardens. Originally laid out in 1780, the gardens lay undisturbed, or 'lost', for 70 years before being rediscovered in 1990. The 200-acre estate contains Victorian pleasure grounds with spring-flowering shrubs; a lush 22-acre 'sub-tropical' jungle with exotic foliage; a pioneering wildlife conservation project and woodland and farm walks.

Gorran Haven, to the south of Mevagissey, was once a settlement to rival its neighbour. Those days were long ago and it is now an unspoilt village with a sandy beach, sheltered by **Dodman Point** – a prominent headland where the remains of an Iron Age defensive earthwork can be seen.

To the west of Mevagissey, **Caerhays Castle Gardens** is an informal 60-acre woodland garden on the coast near Porthluney Cove. It was created in the late 1800s by JC Williams who sponsored plant-hunting expeditions to China to stock his grounds. The gardens are best known for their huge Asiatic magnolias which are at their most

KILBOL COUNTRY HOUSE HOTEL

Polmassick, nr Megavissey,
Cornwall PL26 6HA
Tel: 01726 842481　Fax: 01726 844438
e-mail: info@kilbol-hotel.co.uk
website: www.kilbol-hotel.co.uk

Offering tranquil seclusion deep in beautiful countryside, **Kilbol Country House Hotel & Cottages** are within two miles of the Lost Gardens of Heligan, and close to the Eden Project and the fishing village of Mevagissey. Once part of the great Mount Edgcumbe estate, Kilbol became a hotel in the 1960s and since 1992 has been owned and run by Jenny and Tony Woollam who have carried out extensive refurbishment and upgrading whilst retaining the charm of its 16th century origins.

Beamed ceilings, cottage style windows and an inglenook fireplace give great character to the main hotel building which has ten en suite double or twin rooms and one suite of rooms, all with remote control TV, direct dial telephones, hairdryer, hospitality tray and complimentary toiletries. Every room enjoys a garden view; some also have a ground floor patio or first floor balcony. The hotel's kitchen offers the freshest local produce, all cooked by AGA, with the emphasis on classic traditional British fare. Other amenities include a 16th century lounge bar, conservatory, 15-metre outdoor swimming pool, croquet and riverside walks. For those who prefer self-catering, Kilbol has two cottages, one 16th century rebuilt in 1996, the other purpose-built in 1997.

🏯 historic building　🏛 museum　🏛 historic site　🐉 scenic attraction　🌱 flora and fauna

LOBBS FARM SHOP

Heligan, St Ewe, nr St Austell, Cornwall PL26 6EN
Tel: 01726 844411
website: www.lobbsfarmshop.com

Located next to the famous Lost Gardens of Heligan, **Lobbs Farm Shop** is stocked with an abundance of the very best produce of Cornwall and the West Country, and was acclaimed as the Local Retail Outlet of the Year, 2005.

The farmshop butchery provides an outlet for the Lobb family's own home-produced beef and lamb which comes from farm animals grazing ancient pastures where wild flowers and grasses ideal for butterflies and other insects flourish and form the essence of the natural food chain. The meat has been well hung, is of the highest quality, succulent and full of flavour, and is prepared to customers' requirements by experienced butchers. Locally-sourced bacon, pork, poultry and game, plus the Lobbs own home-made award-winning sausages and burgers are also available. The delicatessen is packed with local cheeses, cold meats,

olives and pâtés, along with fresh home-grown fruit and vegetables. You'll also find an extensive range of West Country chocolates, ice cream, alcohol, soft drinks, preserves and pickles to choose from. Also on site is the Heligan Countryside Barn which features displays on the Lobbs traditional Cornish farm, together with interactive computer displays depicting farmlife and wildlife.

---

magnificent in March and April. The castle itself was built in the gothic style by John Nash between 1805 and 1807, and is open for conducted tours on certain days.

PROBUS

8 miles SW of St Austell off the A390

 Trewithen House & Gardens

This large village is noted for having the tallest parish church tower in the county. Built of granite in the 16th century and richly decorated, it stands 124 feet high.

Just west of the village is **Trewithen House and Gardens**. The early Georgian house, whose name literally means 'house of the trees', stands in glorious woods and parkland and has gardens containing many

rare species laid out in the early 20th century by George Johnstone. Of particular note are the magnificent collections of camellias, rhododendrons and magnolias.

To the southeast lies **Tregony**, a small village that was an important river port long before Truro and Falmouth were developed; it is often called the 'Gateway to the Roseland Peninsula'. This indented tongue of land, which forms the eastern margin of the Fal estuary, is always known by its Cornish name **Carrick Roads**. It has a network of footpaths that take in not only the craggy cliffs with their nesting seabirds but also the grasslands dotted with wildflowers and the ruined military fortresses that go back to the time of the Armada and beyond.

Roundhouses at Veryan

VERYAN

13 miles SW of St Austell off the A3078

🏠 Roundhouses

Set within a wooded hollow, this charming village is famous for the five **Roundhouses**

that lie at its entrance. Built in the early 19th century for the daughters of the local vicar, the cottages' circular shape was believed to protect the residents from evil as there are no corners in which the Devil can hide.

Eastwards, on the coast, is the unspoilt fishing village of **Portloe** whose tiny harbour is completely overshadowed by steep cliffs. To the south lies **Carne Beacon**, one of the largest Bronze Age burial mounds in the country.

Newquay

🎭 Huer's Hut   🐾 Trenance Leisure Park

🐦 Newquay Zoo   🐦 Blue Reef Aquarium

🐾 Water World   🏛 Tunnels Through Time

🐾 Holywell Bay Fun Park

Washed by the warm waters of the Gulf Stream, Newquay is an ancient settlement.

THE NEW HARBOUR RESTAURANT

The Old Boat House, South Quay Hill, Newquay Harbour, Cornwall TR7 1HR
Tel: 01637 874062   website: www.finnscafe.co.uk

The New Harbour Restaurant occupies a superb position in a former boathouse overlooking busy Newquay Harbour - a wonderful setting in which to enjoy "the essence of Cornish life on a plate". Owner Cassandra Langwith believes in simple, clean tastes and in offering a stress free approach to dining. Just settle down in the alfresco area, sipping on a cocktail and watching the world go by on the beach below – fishermen going about their daily tasks, seals playing on the beach. Meanwhile, the excellent team of chefs will prepare your meal in the stage-lit barbecue kitchen.

Naturally, fresh fish dishes take pride of place on the menu here – you can actually watch the fishermen bringing their catch to the kitchen – but there's also a good selection of meat, vegetarian and children's dishes. To complement your meal there's an excellent selection of wines and traditional cocktails. And you don't need to worry about the dress code: "Wear anything you like" says Cassandra, "you're on the beach!" The restaurant is open from 10.30am until late, daily during the summer season; and from Wednesday to Sunday during the winter.

🏠 historic building   🏛 museum   🏛 historic site   🝐 scenic attraction   🐦 flora and fauna

There is evidence of an Iron Age coastal fort among the cliffs and caves of **Porth Island** – the outcrop connected to the mainland by an elegant suspended footbridge. For centuries, the harbour lay at the heart of this once important pilchard fishing village. The town takes its name from the 'New Kaye' that was built in the mid-15th century by the villagers who wanted to protect the inlet here. On Towan Headland, the **Huer's Hut** can still be seen; this was where the Huer would scan the sea looking for shoals of red pilchards. Once spotted, he would cry "hevva" to alert the fishing crews and then guide them to the shoals using a pair of bats known as 'bushes'. As the fishing industry declined, Newquay became a major port for both china clay and mineral exports. However, today, its beautiful rocky coastline and acres of golden sands has seen it develop into a popular seaside resort, famed throughout the world for its surfing.

Fistral Beach faces the Atlantic head on, so when the wind is coming from the south-west the waves arrive after an unbroken 3,000-mile run – a worthy challenge for the top national and international surf riders. By contrast, the sheltered beaches at Towan, Great Western and Tolcarne provide a gentle start for beginners on belly-boards.

Although there is some Regency architecture in Newquay, the rise of the town's fortunes in the 19th century saw a rapid expansion and many of the large Victorian hotels and residential houses still remain. The **Trenance Heritage Cottages**, Newquay's oldest dwellings were built in the 1700s but have stood empty since 2002. The local council, which owns the cottages, is currently developing plans for their restoration.

Newquay is a traditional English resort and boasts a wide variety of attractions in and

LUSTY GLAZE RESTAURANT

Lusty Glaze Beach, Lusty Glaze Road, Newquay, Cornwall TR7 3AE
Tel: 01637 879709
e-mail: info@lustyrestaurant.com
website: www.lustyrestaurant.com

Providing the ultimate beachside dining experience, the **Lusty Glaze Restaurant & Bar** is situated in a secluded, sandy cove on the north Cornish coast with stunning sea views and magnificent sunsets. The combination of idyllic setting, great food and laid-back atmosphere provides a truly unique dining experience.

The menu, designed by acclaimed chef Nick Hodges, offers modern British cuisine with a strong Mediterranean influence. The emphasis is on quality – fresh ingredients, all cooked to order, enjoyed in an environment where you can just sit back and take in the view. Fish and seafood dishes are obvious favourites, but the chefs also prepare a range of land-sourced options, such as char-grilled escalopes of beef fillet with blue cheese, air-dried tomatoes and rocket. As well as offering a full sit-down dining experience, the kitchen crew at Lusty Glaze also serve up a range of Cornish 'tapas'. Bar snacks are also available during the day to satisfy the hungers of the obsessed winter surfer, brave coastal walker or the adventure enthusiast.

CRANTOCK BAY HOTEL

Crantock, Cornwall TR8 5SE
Tel: 01637 830229   Fax: 01637 831111
e-mail: nina@crantockbayhotel.co.uk
website: www.crantockbayhotel.com

Since 1950, Tony and Nina Eyles's family have owned and run the **Crantock Bay Hotel** which enjoys one of the most spectacular settings in Cornwall. Tony's grandparents first visited the Bay in 1933 and fell in love with the sheer magic of the glorious beach, mild climate, cliff walks and beautiful wild flowers. "We feel hugely privileged to live on a National Trust headland" says Tony, "and excited to be so close to the Eden Project and the famous Lost Gardens of Heligan which is just one of more than 90 beautiful Cornish gardens open to the public".

The hotel has great appeal to family members of all ages and has been welcoming some family groups for more than 50 years. Open for ten months of the year, the hotel also offers a wide choice of Special Interest Breaks including bridge, walking, painting, garden appreciation, spa and yoga and digital photography.

The spacious public rooms command breathtaking sea views and provide a choice of comfortable lounge areas. The private garden with its sheltered sunbathing leads directly to the South West Coast Footpath, and on over the rocks to the wide sands of the National Trust beach of Crantock Bay. With more than a mile of golden sands, rock pools and caves to explore, this really is a paradise for beach lovers and surfers alike.

Another major attraction of the hotel is its excellent cuisine. Head Chef Angus McNair takes great pride in researching and selecting high quality West Country produce for his kitchen. This includes the freshest fish from Newlyn, Crantock Bay shellfish, locally reared beef from Bodmin, local cheeses, specially made Crantock Bay sausages, plus herbs and vegetables grown less than half a mile from the hotel. The evening meal is a very special part of the day with a 4-course dinner menu featuring numerous dishes prepared by the award-winning team, along with special dishes for the "little adults" in your family!

Naturally, the accommodation at Crantock Bay maintains the same high standards evident throughout the hotel. Most of the bedrooms enjoy those spectacular sea views where, if you are lucky, you may see a pod of dolphins swimming across the bay. All 32 bedrooms are en suite with bath and shower, and provided with remote control colour TV, direct dial telephone, radio/alarm, complimentary toiletries, hairdryer and hospitality tray.

around the town. **Trenance Leisure Park** offers 26 acres of indoor and outdoor including bowling, boating, horse-riding, pitch & putt, crazy golf, horse-riding, ramp sports and a miniature railway. Also within the park is **Newquay Zoo** where conservation, education and entertainment go hand in hand, hundreds of animals can be seen in sub-tropical lakeside gardens. Siberian lynx are amongst the stars of the show but amongst the other residents are African lions, red pandas, sloths, tapirs, capybara and many more. Nearby, at the indoor **Water World** complex, the whole family can enjoy a range of pools and water activities in a tropical climate.

Crantock Beach, Newquay

In Towan Bay, the **Blue Reef Aquarium** is home to a huge variety of Cornish and tropical species including octopi, giant crabs, clownfish, lobsters and many more. Some of them can be seen as you stroll among the

CRANTOCK GALLERY

Langurroc Road, Crantock, Cornwall TR8 5RB
Tel: 01637 830212
e-mail: marionrowlanduk@yahoo.co.uk
website: crantockgallery.co.uk

Located next door to the Old Albion Inn in the picturesque village of Crantock, the purpose built **Crantock Gallery** was founded in 1994 and provides a showcase for original watercolours and prints by the artist Marion Rowland. Trained in art and design, Marion specialises in local views and wildlife, inspired by the beautiful scenery in Cornwall and a love of wildlife. She paints in a realistic, highly detailed style with some paintings taking months to complete.

Marion also paints commissioned paintings of much loved pets, people, houses and other subjects for which she has become much in demand.

Her many clients include the National trust and the Bradford exchange plate collectors company. Marion's paintings have been exhibited several times at the Mall Galleries in London and her work was shortlisted for the Daily Mail "Not the Turner Prize" awards. Some examples of her distinctive works can be seen on her website. Crantock Gallery is open every day from 10am to 5pm, from April to October; during the winter months please phone as times vary.

📖 stories and anecdotes 　🦅 famous people 　🎨 art and craft 　✏ entertainment and sport 　🚶 walks

colourful denizens of a coral reef through a spectacular underwater tunnel. There are more than 30 living displays including some graceful sharks and rays.

The characters and events that have shaped the history of this part of Cornwall can be discovered at **Tunnels Through Time**: more than 70 realistic life-size figures set in carefully constructed tableaux bring the days of smugglers and highwaymen, plague victims and miners, King Arthur and Merlin vividly to life. The scariest part is the Dungeon of Despair, where visitors can hear the screams of prisoners being tortured in the name of old-time 'justice'.

To the southwest of Newquay's famous beaches, Towan Beach and Fistral Beach, between the headlands of Pentire East and Pentire West, lies the quieter **Gannel**, home to notable populations of waders and wildfowl, which feed off the mudflats and saltings. Just a short distance further on is the pretty hamlet of Holywell with its attractive beach, towering sand dunes and **Holywell Bay Fun Park** offering a whole range of activities for young and old.

Around Newquay

ST COLUMB MAJOR
7 miles E of Newquay off the A39

🐚 Hurling the Silver Ball   🏰 Castle-an-Dinas

🐦 Cornish Birds of Prey Centre

Once in the running for consideration as the site of Cornwall's cathedral, this small town has an unusually large and flamboyant parish church with monumental brasses to the

---

TREVILLEY FARM SHOP

Trevilley Farm Lane, Lane, Newquay,
Cornwall TR8 4PX
Tel/Fax: 01637 872310

Situated about a quarter of a mile from the main Newquay to Penzance road, Trevilley Farm has been worked by Keith Barrett's family for four generations. The farm is a mix of beef, sheep and arable, with the animals providing most of the meats on sale at **Trevilley Farm Shop**, a lively place where Cornish conviviality can be found in abundance. One of the shop's Saturday specialities is its "Proper Job Cornish Pasties" which are handmade – "the way they have been by my family for generations," says Keith's wife, Gill. During the week, the shop's kitchen produces a steady stream of breads, cakes, pies and ready meals, using Cornish produce wherever possible.

In addition to the wonderful pasties and baked goods, the shop sells a huge range of Cornish products – just about every conceivable edible produce can be found here, including around 50 different kinds of Cornish cheeses.

You can be sure of a real Cornish welcome, and some 'Proper Job' food at Trevilley Farm Shop at any time of the year, Monday - Saturday from 9.30am-5.30pm.

🏛 historic building   🏛 museum   🏛 historic site   🍃 scenic attraction   🌾 flora and fauna

influential Arundell. In the 14th century Sir John Arundell was responsible for the town receiving its market charter. In 1850 the town's officials constructed a bishop's palace in anticipation of the county's cathedral being built here. Now called the **Old Rectory**, it retains much of its grandeur though it does not play host to its originally intended guests.

Twice a year, the town plays host to **Hurling the Silver Ball**, a medieval game once common throughout Cornwall but now only played in St Columb and St Ives. It is played on Shrove Tuesday and then again on the Saturday 11 days later. The game involves two teams of several hundred people (the 'townsmen' and the 'countrymen') who endeavour to carry a silver ball made of apple wood to goals set two miles apart.

A couple of miles south-east of St Columb Major, on Castle Downs, are the remains of a massive Iron Age hill fort. **Castle-an-Dinas** was a major defence of the Dumnonia tribe, who occupied this area around the 2nd century BC. The earthwork ramparts enclose an area of over six acres, and anyone climbing to the gorse-covered remains will be rewarded with panoramic views over the leafy Vale of Mawgan to the northwest and the unearthly landscape created by china clay extraction to the south.

To the northeast of St Columb Major, at Winnards Perch, is the **Cornish Birds of Prey Centre** where visitors can see more than 50 hawks, falcons and buzzards fly freely during demonstrations. There are also waterfowl, ducks, pheasants, peacocks, emus, rheas, kookaburras, fallow deer, dwarf zebus

🕮 stories and anecdotes   🕊 famous people   ✎ art and craft   ✐ entertainment and sport   🚶 walks

THE BEDRUTHAN STEPS HOTEL

Mawgan Porth, Cornwall TR8 4BU
Tel: 01637 860555
Reservations: 01637 860860
e-mail: office@bedruthan.com
website: www.bedruthan.com

The Bedruthan Steps Hotel is the place to escape to, slow to Cornwall's pace and find yourself lulled into serenity by the sea. This family-run hotel has been cherished and nurtured over 40 years to give guests memorable holidays on the unique North Cornish coast. Bedruthan will help you to find hidden Cornwall and discover why so many people are inspired by the natural landscapes of the county all year round. You can stroll on the beaches, feeling sand between your toes; watch autumn storms from deep within a comfortable sofa beside a crackling log fire – you have the freedom to be as energetic or as lazy as you please.

The hotel takes food very seriously. Its Indigo Bay table d'hôte and à la carte restaurants offer the finest of Cornish seafood, cheese and local produce. For a very special evening, try the Indigo Bay à la carte option relaxing in sumptuous suede chairs, with candles highlighting the crisp white linen and sparkling glasses. And family meals here are relaxed happy affairs – the staff are a friendly crowd who enjoy looking after their guests and love life. For guests without children, the hotel provides tranquil and peaceful dining.

"Deep squashy comfort is what Bedruthan bedrooms are about" say the owners. The bedrooms are simple and contemporary, reflecting the hotel architecture and beach side setting. Huge comfortable beds, generous soft towels and all that would expect to find in a relaxed seaside hotel are provided. Spectacular views over the sea and generous armchairs to curl up in come with every sea-facing room. There are also two bedroom suites offering plenty of space for families to spread themselves out.

Outside, there are pools of sun-flecked water to idle beside, surrounded by exotic gardens of agapanthus, palms and tamarisk. A secluded bubbling hydro-spa overlooks the gardens and there are shallow pools for water babies to splash around and learn in whilst parents watch, perhaps with a drink in hand. And on the coolest days, there are indoor pool and hydro spas that are always warm and inviting.

The hotel also offers a purpose built, comprehensively equipped conference and event centre that can accommodate up to 200 guests. All rooms have natural light and sea views, and full technical support is provided.

🏛 historic building   🏛 museum   🏛 historic site   🍃 scenic attraction   🌿 flora and fauna

and Shetland ponies. Also in the centre are three well-stocked fishing lakes, a tearoom and gift shop.

INDIAN QUEENS
8 miles E of Newquay off the A30

🐦 Screech Owl Sanctuary

Close to an area dominated by china clay quarries, this chiefly Victorian village is home to the **Screech Owl Sanctuary**, just to the northeast. A rehabilitation, conservation and education centre, the sanctuary has the largest collection of owls in the southwest of England – more than 170 owls of 46 different species. As well as offering visitors the chance to see hand-tame owls at close quarters, the centre runs courses on owl welfare; Harry Potter would approve.

KESTLE MILL
3m SE of Newquay on the A3058

🐦 DairyLand Farm World   🏛 Trerice

🏛 Lawnmower Museum

Just to the south of Kestle Mill is a family attraction that has seen more than two million visitors since opening in 1975. **DairyLand Farm World** is a working dairy farm where visitors can see the 140 cows being milked to music; try their hand at milking a life-size model cow; explore the nature trail and look around the Heritage Centre and Alternative Energy Centre.

Hidden away in the country lanes two miles west of Kestle Mill is the delightful small Elizabethan manor house, **Trerice** (National Trust). A real architectural gem, it was built in 1571 for the influential Arundell family. As well as the hint of Dutch styling in the gables and the beautiful window in the Great Hall with 576 small panes of 16th century glass, Trerice is noted for its huge, ornate fireplaces, elaborate plasterwork and fine English oak

and walnut furniture. Several rooms contain superb English and Oriental porcelain, and among the more esoteric collections are clocks and drinking glasses. There are portraits by the renowned Cornish painter John Opie and an unusual set of early wooden skittles. Within the charming grounds, a small barn houses the **Lawnmower Museum** which traces the history of the lawnmower and contains more than 100 machines.

ST NEWLYN EAST
5 miles S of Newquay off the A3075

🍃 Lappa Valley Steam Railway

🏛 East Wheal Rose mine

A mile or so south of this sizeable village is the **Lappa Valley Steam Railway**. This narrow gauge railway (15 inch gauge) was opened in 1849 as a mineral line from Newquay, to East Wheal Rose and later became part of Great Western Railway's Newquay to Chacewater branch line. This line closed in 1963 but part of the track was re-opened in 1974 as a narrow gauge railway. Two steam locos, Muffin and Zebedee, work the line, running from Benny Halt on a two mile return journey to East Wheal Rose. The railway is open from the beginning of April to the end of September and runs between 7 and 11 trains a day, depending on the season.

At the northern terminus of the line are the imposing engine house and chimney stack of **East Wheal Rose** mine, Cornwall's richest lead mine that was the scene, in 1846, of the county's worst mining disaster. Following a flash flood caused by a sudden, unexpected cloudburst 39 miners were drowned. The village cockpit, where cockfighting had taken place for centuries, was restored as a memorial to the dead; the mine was re-opened a year after the tragedy but closed for good in 1885.

Lappa Valley Steam Railway

St Newlyn East, Nr Newquay, Cornwall TR8 5HZ
Tel: 01872 510317
website: www.lappavalley.co.uk

Lappa Valley Steam Railway is one of the
most popular attractions in the whole
county, offering a great day out for
families. The centrepiece is the 15" gauge
steam railway that runs through beautiful
countryside from Benny Halt to East Wheal
Rose, but there are two other, tinier
railways, one of them featuring a miniature
Intercity 125. The site provides a good
habitat for wildlife, and other attractions
include nature trails, woodland walks, a
nine-hole golf course, a boating lake, a
brick path maze, play areas, coffee and
gift shops and old mine engine house.

Wadebridge

🐾 Cornwall Folk Festival   🎿 Camel Trail

📷 John Betjeman Centre

Standing at the historic lowest bridging point
on the River Camel, this ancient port and busy
market town is now a popular holiday centre
which is not only attractive but also is
renowned for its craftware. Linking the north
and south coasts of Cornwall and the
moorland with the sea, Wadebridge has always
been a bustling place and its establishment as a
trading centre began in earnest in the 15th
century. The Rev Lovibond, the vicar of St
Petroc's, was looking for a means of
conveying his flock of sheep safely across the
river and in the 1460s he built the 320-feet-
long and now 14-arched bridge which can still
be seen today. One of the longest bridges in
Cornwall, it originally had 17 arches and it is
said that this bridge, nicknamed the **Bridge
on Wool**, was constructed on bridge piers that
were sunk on a foundation of woolsacks. The

bridge still carries the main road that links the
town's two ancient parishes.

With a permanent river crossing there was a
steady growth in trade through the town and
its port but the arrival of the railway in the
19th century saw Wadebridge really thrive. As
a result, much of the town's architecture dates
from the Victorian era. Wadebridge maintains
its links with farming and each June to the
west of the town centre the **Royal Cornwall
Agricultural Show** is held. Another popular
annual event is the **Cornwall Folk Festival**, a
feast of dance, music and fun that takes place
over the August Bank Holiday weekend. The
town's former railway station is now home to
the **John Betjeman Centre**, dedicated to the
life and work of the much-loved Poet
Laureate. Among the tributes and intimate
artefacts on display are the poet's desk, his
chair and drafts of his books.

Although the railway line, which opened in
1899, closed in the 1960s, a stretch of the
trackbed has been used to create the superb

🏛 historic building   📷 museum   🏚 historic site   🌊 scenic attraction   🌿 flora and fauna

Camel Trail, a 17-mile traffic-free footpath and cycleway that leads up into the foothills of Bodmin Moor to the east and westwards, along the River Camel, to Padstow.

John Betjeman Centre, Wadebridge

Just to the west of Wadebridge, close to the hamlet of **St Breock**, stands **St Breock Downs Monolith**, a striking Bronze Age longstone that is also known as the Men Gurta (the Stone of Waiting). Other prehistoric remains, such as the Nine Maidens stone row, can also be found on St Breock Downs.

Around Wadebridge

PENCARROW
4 miles SE of Wadebridge off the A389

 Pencarrow

A fine Georgian country house completed in 1775, **Pencarrow** is the home of the Molesworth-St Aubyn family with a Grade II* listed garden containing more than 600 varieties of rhododendron, along with rock and woodland gardens. A notable feature is the avenue of araucaria whose English name is said to have originated at Pencarrow in 1834 when a guest examined the prickly leaves and declared, "It would puzzle a monkey!" During the season, the gardens are open daily, and guided tours of the house with its superb collections of paintings, furniture, porcelain and antique dolls are available Sunday to Thursday.

PORTHCOTHAN
8 miles W of Wadebridge on the B3276

🐚 Trevose Head   🐚 Bedruthan Steps

This tiny village overlooks a deep, square, sheltered cove, with a sandy beach, which was once the haunt of smugglers but today is just one part of a stretch of coastline owned by the National Trust. A footpath over the southern headland leads to **Porth Mear**, another secluded cove beyond which, on a low plateau, is a prehistoric earthwork of banks and ditches. Further south again lie the **Bedruthan Steps** (not National Trust) a curious beach rock formation that is best viewed from the grassy clifftops. The giant slate rocks have been eroded over the centuries and their uniform shape has caused them, according to local legend, to be thought of as the stepping stone used by the Cornish giant Bedruthan.

To the north, the South West Coast Path leads walkers around **Constantine Bay** and past a succession of sandy beaches which are ideal for surfing, but unfortunately the strong currents along this stretch make swimming hazardous. Beyond Constantine Bay lies the remote headland of **Trevose Head** from where there are wonderful views down the coast, taking in bay after bay. At the tip of the headland stands Trevose Lighthouse, which has been warning mariners away from its sheer granite cliffs since 1847 with a beam that, today, can be seen up to 27 miles away.

PADSTOW
6 miles W of Wadebridge on the A389

🏃 Saints Way   🦞 National Lobster Hatchery

🏛 Raleigh Cottage   🕮 Charles Dickens

🦋 May Day   🏛 Prideaux Place

Padstow's sheltered position, on the western side of the Camel estuary, has made it a welcome haven for vessels for centuries and the area has been settled by many different people over the years, including the prehistoric Beaker folk, Romans, Celtic saints and marauding Vikings. Originally named Petroc-stow, it was here that the Welsh missionary St Petroc landed in the 6th century and, before moving on to Bodmin Moor to continue his missionary work, founded a Celtic Minster. Beginning at the door of the town's 13th century parish Church of St Petroc, the **Saints' Way** is a 30-mile footpath that follows the route taken by travellers and pilgrims crossing Cornwall on their way from Brittany to Ireland.

The silting up of the River Camel in the 19th century and the evocatively named Doom Bar, which restricts entry into the estuary mouth, put paid to Padstow's hopes of continuing as a major port.

THE PADSTOW MUSSEL CO.
9 Market Square, Padstow, Cornwall PL28 8AH
Tel: 01841 533111
website: www.thepadstowmusselco.co.uk

Launched by cornish artist and designer Susie Ray, the **Padstow Mussel Co** provides a unique range of lifestyle products inspired by the county. The unusual and beautifully made products, which include the unique Cornish Pebble Range, bone china, table mats, tea towels, fine art prints and original gift cards and paperware are only available in the shop, which nestles in the heart of Padstow, or at the company's on-line shop. Everything the company sells has been created by Susie herself or is made from her own designs by local craftspeople. "Padstow Mussel is about creating a range of products that have Cornwall at their heart." says Susie, "items that are meant to be enjoyed, are interesting, stylish, beautifully made and that people just can't get anywhere else."

Susie draws inspiration for her products from the beaches, coves, rock pools and sand dunes around Padstow. One of the most unusual ranges is the Cornish Pebble range. Based on pebbles borrowed from a Cornish beach, Susie worked with a local pottery to develop a completely new technique to create the beautiful and unique range which includes a wine cooler, vases, plates, goblets and salt and pepper shaker.

🏛 historic building   🏛 museum   🏚 historic site   🝔 scenic attraction   🌿 flora and fauna

Today the harbour still teems with people and the influence of the sea is never far away. Since 1975, Padstow has been closely linked with the famous chef, restaurateur and ardent promoter of seafood, Rick Stein, whose empire now includes a seafood restaurant, a bistro café, a seafront delicatessen, fish & chip shop, a cooking school, accommodation and even a gift shop.

Padstow

More seafood is on display at the **National Lobster Hatchery** on South Quay. In 2005, the Hatchery released more than 15,000 juvenile lobsters into the sea – for just £1 you can adopt one of them, name it and receive a certificate and information pack. There's also a gift shop area with sea-life related goods and a range of books about marine life and Cornwall.

The Hatchery is close to the harbour which remains the town's focal point. Here can be found many of Padstow's older buildings including **Raleigh Cottage**, where Sir Walter Raleigh lived while he was Warden of Cornwall, and the tiny **Harbour Cottage**.

As well as the annual Fish and Ships Festival, Padstow continues to celebrate **May Day** in a traditional manner that has it roots back in pagan times. Beginning at midnight on the eve of May Day and lasting throughout the next day, the townsfolk sing in the new morning and then follow the 'Obby 'Oss through the town until midnight when the 'Obby 'Oss dies.

IVY HOUSE RESTAURANT

The Ivy House Restaurant, Treveglos,
St Merryn, Padstow, Cornwall PL28 8NB
Tel: 01841 520623

The Ivy House Restaurant occupies a charming old house which is, appropriately, smothered in creeper. The restaurant is well-established and having delighted local gourmets for more than 25 years it has a reputation for excellent, freshly prepared dishes based as much as possible on locally sourced produce. As well as serving appetising food, which is all cook on traditional Agas, Ivy House also offers comfortable accommodation in three attractively furnished and decorated rooms, all with en suite facilities.

🎭 stories and anecdotes   🦅 famous people   🎨 art and craft   🎵 entertainment and sport   🚶 walks

DI'S DAIRY AND PANTRY

Rock Road, Rock, Wadebridge,
Cornwall PL27 6NW
Tel: 01208 863531
Fax: 01208 869035
e-mail: sales@disdairyandpantry.co.uk
website: www.disdairyandpantry.co.uk

In his *Food Heroes Guide* Rick Stein described **Di's Dairy and Pantry** as "a paradise for food lovers"; "an amazing place" said Martyn Harris in the *Daily Telegraph*; and it has also been acclaimed as the "Food Lovers Temple of the West". Located in the centre of Rock on the North Cornish Coast, Di's can provide everything to make your every meal an easy, yet memorable experience.

The home baking on offer includes lemon drizzle and chocolate banana cakes; lemon meringue pies, cheese cakes, fruit pies and crumbles. Amongst the wide range of home-made savouries you'll find chicken & mushroom and steak & kidney pies; pasta bakes and pasties; and lasagne. Then there are the cheeses – more than 100 English and Continental varieties, including local cheeses and local organic brie.

Other local products include several varieties of Cornish butter, Helsett Farm Ice Cream from Boscastle, clotted cream, preserves, chutneys and honey.

The choice is extended further by the selection of cold meats and charcuterie, upmarket tinned goods, an interesting range of wines, as well as fresh ground coffee and specialist teas.

Di's Pantry is a great place to browse, or you can do the same on its website and order by e-mail. Rock itself is popular because of its long stretches of golden sandy beaches and it's also well-known as a major watersports centre.

There are some high class shops, the renowned St Enodoc golf club and, for a pleasant excursion, the Black Tor passenger ferry runs from Rock to Padstow all year round.

It was while visiting Padstow in 1842 that **Charles Dickens** was inspired to write *A Christmas Carol* in which he mentions a lighthouse - the one at Trevose Head. His good friend, Dr Miles Marley, whose son, Dr Henry Marley, practised in Padstow for 51 years, provided the surname for Scrooge's partner, Jacob. Dr Henry Marley died in 1908, at the age of 76, at his home in Mellingey, at nearby St Issey and his funeral took place in the local parish church.

On the northern outskirts of the town and built on the site of St Petroc's monastery lies **Prideaux Place**, a magnificent Elizabethan mansion which has been the home of the ancient Cornish Prideaux-Brune family for more than 400 years. Along with family portraits and memorabilia the house is home to many artefacts that tell of the history of this area and the country. The mansion is surrounded by glorious gardens and parkland overlooking the Camel estuary that were laid out in Capability Brown style in the 18th century.

POLZEATH AND NEW POLZEATH
6 miles NW of Wadebridge off the B3314

🏛 Rumps Cliff Castle   🏚 Church of St Enadoc

🐦 Sir John Betjeman

Surfers and holidaymakers flock to these two small resorts as the broad west-facing beach is not only ideal for surf, but the fine sands, caves and tidal rock pools make it a fascinating place for children. This was also a place much loved by Sir John Betjeman. To the north of the villages is a beautiful coastal path that takes in the cliffs and farmland of Pentire Point and Rumps Point – where stands

---

PORTEATH BEE CENTRE

St Minver, Wadebridge, Cornwall PL27 6RA
Tel: 01208 863718 Fax: 01208 862192
e-mail: porteathbecentre@aol.com
website: www.porteathbeecentre.co.uk

Since 1988 Eddie and Heather have been producing superior quality honey here at **Portreath Bee Centre**, which is situated six miles from Wadebridge just off the B3314 - follow the brown signs.

The shop offers a wide range of excellent products (including several different honeys - clear, set, creamed, chunky, cut comb and heather), honey and beeswax natural skincare products and beeswax soaps. In addition there is a range of traditional beeswax furniture and leather polishes, water-proofer for boots and shoes and a delightful array of pure beeswax candles, both rolled and moulded.They also make delicious fudge, honey marmalades, jams and honey mustards and sell gifts and bee supplies. There is also a Winnie the Pooh corner for children and collectors.

Upstairs, morning coffee, light lunches and delicious Cornish cream teas are served in the Bee Hive Tea Room, and between April and October a living bee exhibition, with bees behind glass and an educational video, tells you about the life of the bee.

Rumps Cliff Castle, an Iron Age fortification where the remains of four defensive ramparts can still be seen. The area is known for its wild tamarisk, an elegant flowering shrub that is more commonly found around the shores of the Mediterranean Sea. In the 1930s, Pentire Head was saved from commercial development by local fund raisers who bought the land and donated it to the National Trust.

This stretch of dramatic coastline that runs round to **Port Quin** includes sheltered bays and coves, ancient field patterns, old lead mines and Iron Age defensive earthworks. It is ideal walking country, and there are numerous footpaths taking walkers on circular routes that incorporate both coastal countryside and farmland.

The tiny hamlet of Port Quin suffered greatly when the railways took away the slate trade from its once busy quay and the demise was so swift that, at one time, outsiders thought that the entire population had been washed away by a great storm. Overlooking the now re-populated hamlet is Doyden Castle, a squat 19th century castellated folly that is now a holiday home.

To the southwest of Polzeath lies the delightful **Church of St Enodoc**, a Norman building that has, on several occasions, been virtually submerged by windblown sand. At these times the congregation would enter through an opening in the roof. The sand was finally cleared away in the 1860s when the church was restored, and the bell in the tower, which came from an Italian ship wrecked nearby, was installed in 1875. The beautiful churchyard contains many graves of shipwrecked mariners but what draws many people to this quiet place is the grave of the poet **Sir John Betjeman,** who is buried here along with his parents. Betjeman spent many of his childhood holidays in the villages and coves around the Camel Estuary, and his affection for the local people and places was the inspiration for many of his works. The church is reached across a golf course that is regarded as one of the most scenic links courses in the country.

Tintagel

🏛 Tintagel Castle   🏛 Old Post Office
🏛 King Arthur's Great Hall   ♤ Rocky Valley
♤ Bossiney Haven

The romantic remains of **Tintagel Castle** (English Heritage), set on a wild and windswept headland that juts out into the Atlantic, are many people's image of Cornwall. Throughout the year, many come to clamber up the wooden stairway to **The Island** to see the castle that legend claims was the birthplace of King Arthur. If the great king was born at this spot, it was certainly not in this castle which was built in the 12th century. But in 1998 the discovery of a 6th century slate bearing the Latin inscription 'Artognov' – which translates as the ancient British name for Arthur – renewed the belief that Tintagel was Arthur's home.

The legends were first written down by Geoffrey of Monmouth in the mid-1100s and over the years were re-worked by many other writers, notably Sir Thomas Malory's *Morte d'Arthur* of around 1450, and Tennyson's epic poem *Idylls of the King* in 1859.

Tintagel village, of course, owes a lot to its Arthurian connections, so souvenir and 'themed' shops have proliferated along its main street. You might prefer to pass on the 'genuine Excaliburgers' on offer in one pub, but an oddity worth visiting is **King Arthur's Great Hall**. It was built in 1933 of Cornish granite by a group calling themselves the Knights of King Arthur. They furnished the vast halls with a Round Table and seventy-two stained glass windows depicting their coats of arms and some of their adventures.

However, there is more to Tintagel than King Arthur. In the High Street, is the weather-beaten **Old Post Office** – a 14th century small manor house that first became a post office in the 19th century. Purchased by the National Trust in 1903 for £100, the building is set within an enchanting cottage garden and still has its original stone-paved medieval hall and ancient fireplace along with the ground-floor office of the former postmistress.

To the north of the village lies the mile-long **Rocky Valley**, a curious rock-strewn cleft in the landscape which has a character all of its own. In the wooded upper reaches can be found the impressive 40-foot waterfall known as **St Nectan's Kieve**. This was named after the Celtic hermit whose cell is believed to have stood beside the basin, or kieve, at the foot of the cascade. Here, too, can be seen the **Rocky Valley Carvings**, on a rock face behind a ruined building. Though it is suggested that the carvings date from early Christian times, around the same time that St Nectan was living here, it is impossible to be accurate and other suggestions range from the 2nd century BC to the 17th century.

A little further north, and reached by a short

Tintagel Castle

footpath from the village of Bossiney is the beautiful, sheltered beach of **Bossiney Haven**, surrounded by a semi-circle of cliffs. The views from the cliff tops are spectacular but only the fit and agile should attempt to scramble down to the inviting beach below. Inland, at Bossiney Common, the outlines of ancient field patterns, or lynchets, can still be traced.

Around Tintagel

PORT ISAAC
6 miles SW of Tintagel on the B3267

   Tregeare Rounds

   Long Cross Victorian Gardens

A delightful fishing village that has retained much of its ancient charm, Port Isaac has become well-known to viewers of the ITV drama series, *Doc Martin*, for which it provides

  stories and anecdotes   famous people   art and craft   entertainment and sport   walks

Tintagel Castle

Distance: *3.8 miles (6.0 kilometres)*

Typical time: *170 mins*

Height gain: *100 metres*

Map: *Explorer 111*

Walk: *www.walkingworld.com ID:1095*

Contributor: *Dennis Blackford*

ACCESS INFORMATION:

From Tintagel, take the Boscastle road for about 1 km until you come to Bossiney car park on your left. Look for the mast.

DESCRIPTION:

The walk takes us through the village of Tintagel and out along the cliff path to visit the legendary castle of King Arthur and Merlin's Cave. All along the path you will find wonderful views and a wealth of wildlife.

ADDITIONAL INFORMATION

There are toilets at the start point. Toilets, food and drink are available at Tintagel and the castle visitor centre.

FEATURES:

Hills or fells, sea, toilets, castle, National Trust/NTS, wildlife, birds, flowers, great views, butterflies, cafe, gift shop, food shop, public transport, restaurant, tea shop, ancient monument

WALK DIRECTIONS:

1 | After parking in the car park, turn right onto the main road and walk into Tintagel Village, about 0.7 kilometre away.

2 | Walk through the village until reaching the 'no through road' to 'Glebe Cliff' at the side of the 'Cornishman's Inn'. Turn into this road.

3 | Follow this road almost one kilometre down to the car park at the end. Follow the church wall around to the right and on to the coast path. The corner of the road may be cut off by going through the churchyard, which is being kept rough as a nature reserve.

4 | After a few hundred metres you will be looking out over the ruins of the castle. Follow the path down.

5 | When you have reached the paved path to the castle, take the path to your right which zigzags down to the visitor centre. At low tide you can, with care, go to the beach and visit Merlin's Cave. Cross over the little bridge and up the steep flight of steps, or go past the cafe (which is an easier path) to continue on the coast path up the other side of the valley.

6 | 200 metres further on after crossing a little wooden bridge, the path branches and you can go left or right; left goes up onto the point of

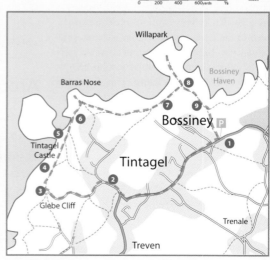

'Barras Nose' and is well worth the detour for a spectacular view over the cove and the castle. Continue on the coast path.

7 | About 1 km further on and you pass through a gate which will lead you to the headland known as 'Willapark'.

8 | After the path passes through the gap in the wall it branches. Left takes you out onto the point and is a very pleasant place to visit and relax before finishing your walk. After visiting the point, return to this junction and continue on the path to the right of the gap, which will take you down into the valley.

9 | Steps up the other side of the valley bring you to a stone stile. Cross the stile down to the track. Turn right to return to the starting point. Alternatively, turn left down into the secluded cove of Bossiney Haven, which is popular for swimming at low tide (the sand is covered at high tide).

the major location as 'Port Wenn'. The town is surrounded by open countryside, Heritage Coast and an Area of Outstanding Natural Beauty. A busy port since the Middle Ages, during its heyday in the 19th century, fish along with cargoes of stone, coal, timber and pottery were loaded and unloaded on Port Isaac's quayside. Following the arrival of the railways, pilchards were landed here in great numbers, gutted and processed in the village's many fish cellars before being packed off to London and beyond by train. The centre of this conservation village is concentrated around the protected harbour where old fish cellars and fishermen's cottages line the narrow alleys and 'opes' that wend their way down to the coast.

Just to the east lies **Port Gaverne**, another busy 19th century fishing port where, in one

season, more than 1,000 tons of pilchards were landed and processed in the village's fish cellars or 'pilchard palaces'. Today, most of the large stone buildings, including some of the old fish cellars, have been converted into holiday accommodation. Tourism has prospered as the village has one of the safest beaches along the North Cornwall coast.

Just inland from the village can be found the double ramparts of **Tregeare Rounds**. This Celtic hill fort was excavated in 1904. Among the finds uncovered were pottery fragments thought to be more than 2,000 years old. It is believed to be the Castle Terrible in Thomas Malory's 15th century epic, *Morte D'Arthur*. Here Uther Pendragon laid siege and killed the Earl of Cornwall because he had fallen in love with the earl's beautiful wife, Igerna.

Just over a mile inland, close to the village of Trelights, lies the only public garden along this stretch of North Cornwall coast – **Long Cross Victorian Gardens**, a real garden lover's delight. Located next to the Long Cross Hotel (see panel on page 74), the gardens' imaginative planting and superb panoramic views make it a very special place. Other attractions here include a secret garden and a fascinating Victorian maze.

DELABOLE
3 miles S of Tintagel on the B3314

Gaia Energy Centre

Delabole Slate Quarry

Home to the most famous slate quarry in Cornwall, Delabole is almost literally built of slate. It has been used here for houses, walls, steps and the church. The high quality dark blue slate has been quarried here uninterrupted since Tudor times and it is known that, in around 2000BC Beaker Folk

stories and anecdotes 　 famous people 　 art and craft 　 entertainment and sport 　 walks

LONG CROSS HOTEL & VICTORIAN GARDENS

Trelights, Port Isaac, Cornwall PL29 3TF
Tel: 01208 880243
website: www.portisaac.com

An elegant country house hotel and the only public gardens in North Cornwall comprise the twin attractions of the **Long Cross Hotel & Victorian Gardens**. The hotel was originally built as a Victorian gentleman's residence and later converted to an hotel. Purchased by James and Sharon Bishop in January 2005, the hotel has been beautifully refurbished with all the rooms receiving brand new bathrooms and interior design. Some of the rooms have glorious sea-views and many have the generous proportions, high ceilings and detailed features so favoured by the Victorians. The hotel has 14 recently refurbished elegant bedrooms all with private bathrooms, central heating, colour TV and tea/coffee making facilities. Many of the rooms have panoramic views. The Long Cross is able to cater for those who are less mobile, with three rooms on the ground floor that are no more than four metres from the car park. The hotel boasts all modern creature comforts along with a stunning new restaurant with terraces taking advantage of the expansive panoramic views.

Set in almost four acres of its own grounds and gardens overlooking the North Cornwall coast between Port Isaac and Port Quin, The Longcross is in the perfect secluded location to enjoy a quiet relaxing break yet is within easy striking distance of some of the area's best attractions. Rock and the Camel Estuary with their associated sailing and watersports and easy ferry access to Padstow, the championship golf course at St. Enodoc, Daymer Bay and Polzeath surfing beaches, historic Port Isaac fishing village, the local market town of Wadebridge with cycle hire for the Camel Trail to Padstow, and the diversity of Bodmin Moor are all within 20 minutes drive. The Eden Project is 40 minutes away; Tate Gallery about an 80-minute drive.

Located adjacent to the hotel are Long Cross Victorian Gardens which were the subject of a TV feature because of their unusual aspects – they were constructed primarily to overcome the difficulties of the local climate. North Cornwall is England's windiest area with strong winds laden with salt even in the summer which results in the garden receiving one hundredweight of salt per acre per year. So most of the shrubs in the garden have shiny or leathery leaves to provide protection against the salt. Plants are available to buy at the gardens, including some of the 18 herbs that grow here.

🏛 historic building   🏛 museum   🏛 historic site   🍃 scenic attraction   🌱 flora and fauna

on Bodmin Moor used slate as baking shelves. The huge crater of **Delabole Slate Quarry** is over half a mile wide and 500 feet deep – making it the largest man-made hole in the country. Although the demand for traditional building materials declined during the 20th century, the quarry is still worked and there are occasional slate splitting demonstrations.

To the southwest of the village lies the first wind farm in Britain, **Delabole Wind Farm**, which became operational in 1991. It produces enough power each year to satisfy more than half the annual demands of both Delabole and Camelford. The tall turbines provide an unusual landmark and at the heart of the farm is the **Gaia Energy Centre** where visitors can learn all about the past, present and future of renewable energy. One of the many striking exhibits is a giant steel and glass waterwheel. The centre has a café and shop, a picnic area and easy access and facilities for disabled visitors.

CAMELFORD
4 miles SE of Tintagel on the A39

🏛 North Cornwall Museum

🏛 British Cycling Museum

This small and historic old market town, on the banks of the River Camel, prospered on the woollen trade. Around its central small square are some pleasant 18th and 19th century houses. The **North Cornwall Museum and Gallery**, housed in a converted coach house, displays aspects of life in this area throughout the 20th century as well as the reconstruction of a 19th century moorland cottage. Just to the north of the town and housed in the former railway station is the **British Cycling Museum**, whose exhibits include more than 400 cycles, an old cycle repair shop, a gallery of

CARADOC OF TREGARDOCK

Treligga, Delabole, North Cornwall PL33 9ED
Tel/Fax: 01840 213300
e-mail: tregardock@hotmail.com website: www.tregardock.com

A beautiful conversion of Grade II listed barns in a romantic coastal setting just north of Port Isaac, **Caradoc of Tregardock** offers a variety of holiday options. The magnificent scenery makes it a popular choice with artists who have the use of a 60ft studio and the Malaysian summerhouse, or can hire the upstairs apartment with its glorious sea views. Painting courses are available with tuition and full accommodation – meals are provided leaving the artist free to paint and work. Groups are free to bring their own tutor if they wish.

There are two well-appointed houses. The main house sleeps eight with four bedrooms, all en suite and with two spacious living rooms with woodburning stoves, fully fitted kitchen areas and French windows opening onto sea views. The second house sleeps four in two bedrooms, and has a bathroom and a charming sitting room with woodburning stove and original high beams. If you want a change from self-catering, meals are available and, for a special occasion perhaps, a private chef can be arranged. Pets are not accepted because of the farm, but owner Janet Cant welcomes babies – high chairs are available. Close by are golf courses, gardens and historic houses, fishing villages, good pubs and restaurants, wonderful beaches and the watersports centres of Rock and Polzeath, Padstow and The Eden Project.

📖 stories and anecdotes   🐦 famous people   🎨 art and craft   🏌 entertainment and sport   🚶 walks

JULIOT'S WELL HOLIDAY PARK

Camelford, North Cornwall PL32 9RG
Tel: 01840 213302   Fax: 01840 212700
e-mail: juliotswell@holidaysincornwall.net

Set in beautiful woodland with extensive views across some of the finest Cornish countryside, **Juliot's Well Holiday Park** continues a tradition that began in medieval times when pilgrims visiting the holy well found a resting place here. Today, the 33 rolling acres of sheltered parkland in an Area of Outstanding Natural Beauty provides visitors with a wide choice of holiday accommodation in peaceful and relaxed surroundings. There are five de luxe two-bedroom stone-built cottages with a maximum capacity of four adults and two children; a choice of spacious de luxe pine cottages added in 2006, all with full central heating, double glazing and their own verandahs; and a wide range of mobile homes with a choice of four, six or eight berths. Motorhomes, tourers and tents are also welcome.

Amenities available to all guests include an outdoor heated swimming pool during the summer months; a large attractive Coach House bar; a restaurant with a range of à la carte dishes; a sun patio for al fresco eating; a tennis court, level playing field and a children's play area; a games room with pool table and machines; a shop providing basic daily essentials, a launderette and public telephone.

framed cycling pictures, an extensive library and a history of cycling from 1818. Close by, on the riverbank at Slaughterbridge, lies a 6th century slab that is said to mark the place where King Arthur fell at the Battle of Camlann in 539AD, defeated by his nephew Mordred. The **Arthurian Centre** houses the Land of Arthur exhibition and also contains an information room (including brass rubbing and a video presentation), a play area, a refreshment area and a shop stocked with Arthurian books and gifts.

BOSCASTLE

3 miles NE of Tintagel on the B3263

📷 Museum of Witchcraft   🖋 Thomas Hardy

On August 16th, 2004, torrential rain fell on the hills above the picturesque fishing village of Boscastle and within hours its main street was filled with a turbulent torrent of water sweeping everything before it towards the sea. Vivid television pictures recorded the dramatic scenes as cars were jostled along like toys on the surging waves, and residents were winched by helicopters from their rooftops. Astonishingly, no-one died and no-one was seriously injured in the calamity, but most of the houses in the path of the flood were rendered uninhabitable. Insurance companies estimated that claims would exceed half a billion pounds.

Before this disaster, Boscastle was best known for its picture-postcard qualities and its associations with the novelist Thomas Hardy. The village stands in a combe at the head of a remarkable S-shaped inlet that shelters it from the Atlantic Ocean. The only natural harbour between Hartland Point and Padstow, Boscastle's inner jetty was built by the renowned Elizabethan, Sir Richard Grenville, when the village was prospering as a fishing, grain and slate port. The outer jetty, or breakwater, dates from the 19th century when Boscastle had grown into a busy commercial port handling coal, timber, slate and china clay. Because of the dangerous harbour entrance, ships were towed into it by rowing boats – a blowhole in the outer harbour still occasionally sends up plumes of spray.

Next to the slipway where the River Valency meets the sea is the **Museum of Witchcraft** (see panel below) which suffered badly in the floods of August 2004. It re-opened the following Easter and once again boasts the world's largest collection of witchcraft related artefacts and regalia. Visitors can also learn all about witches, their lives, their spells, their charms and their curses.

Even before the floods, Boscastle was becoming familiar to viewers of BBC-2's documentary series, *A Seaside Parish,* which followed the arrival of a new vicar, the Revd Christine Musser, in the village and recorded her role in its various activities. The series later detailed the aftermath of the inundation which included visits by Prince Charles and the Revd Musser's fictional TV equivalent, Dawn French's Vicar of Dibley.

Museum of Witchcraft

The Harbour, Boscastle, Cornwall PL35 0HD
Tel: 01840 250111
e-mail: museumwitchcraft@aol.com
website: www.museumofwitchcraft.com

The **Museum of Witchcraft** in Boscastle houses the world's largest collection of witchcraft related artefacts and regalia. The museum has been located in Boscastle for over 40 years and despite severe damage in recent floods, it remains one of Cornwall's most popular museums.

The fascinating displays cover all aspects of witchcraft and include divination, sea witchcraft, spells and charms, modern witchcraft, herbs & healing, ritual magic, satanism and hare & shapeshifting

One exhibit features the burial of Joan Wytte who was born in Bodmin, Cornwall, in 1775 and died of bronchial pneumonia in Bodmin Jail in 1813. She was a renowned clairvoyant and healer but became aggressive and impatient due to an untreated abscess in her tooth and people came to believe she was possessed by the devil. She became

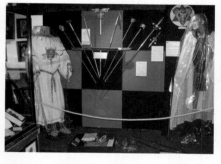

known as 'The Fighting Fairy Woman' and was imprisoned for grievous bodily harm.

Her skeleton came into the possession of the Museum of Witchcraft and was exhibited there for many years. When Graham took over eight years ago he and the museum team believed she deserved a proper burial and Joan was finally laid to rest in 1998.

Among the other artefacts to be seen here are an amazing collection of figures and dolls, carved plates and stones, jewellery, cauldrons, weapons and unpleasant devices used for extracting confessions. A stair lift is available for those with limited mobility.

The spectacular slate headlands on either side of Boscastle's harbour mouth provide some excellent, if rather demanding, walking. This stretch of tortuous coastline is not only of ecological importance but also historic. An Iron Age earthwork can be seen across the promontory at Willapark, and there is a 19th century lookout tower on the summit.

From the village there is a footpath that follows the steep wooded Valency Valley to the hidden hamlet of **St Juliot** which appears as 'Endelstow' in one of **Thomas Hardy**'s novels. As a young architect, Hardy worked on the restoration of the church and it was here, in 1870, that he met his future wife, Emma Gifford, the rector's sister-in-law. Emma later professed that the young architect had already appeared to her in a dream and wrote how, on first meeting him, she was "immediately arrested by his familiar appearance." Much of the couple's courtship took place along this wild stretch of coastline between Boscastle and Crackington Haven. When Emma died more than 40 years later, Hardy returned to St Juliot to erect a memorial to her in the church. Following his death in 1928 a similar memorial was erected to Hardy.

CRACKINGTON HAVEN
7½ miles NE of Tintagel off the B3263

One of the most dramatic places along this remarkable stretch of coastline, this tiny port is overlooked by towering 400-foot cliffs, which make it Cornwall's highest coastal point. The small and narrow sandy cove is approached, by land, down a steep-sided

🏛 historic building   🏛 museum   🏛 historic site   🍃 scenic attraction   🌱 flora and fauna

wooded combe. It is difficult to see how sizeable vessels once landed here to deliver their cargoes of limestone and Welsh coal. Just to the south of Crackington Haven the path leads to a remote beach, curiously named **The Strangles**, where at low tide, large patches of sand are revealed amongst the vicious looking rocks. During one year alone in the 1820s, some 20 ships were said to have come to grief here. The undercurrents are strong and swimming is always unsafe.

Bude

🏃 Bude Canal Trail   🏰 Bude Castle

🏛 Town Museum

A traditional seaside resort with sweeping expanses of sand, rock pools and Atlantic breakers, Bude has plenty to offer holidaymakers and coastal walkers. A popular surfing centre, said to be where British surfing began, the town is a much favoured holiday destination in summer. However, during the winter, gales can turn this into a remote and harsh environment.

The **Bude Canal** was an ambitious project that aimed to connect the Atlantic with the English Channel via the River Tamar. However, the only stretch to be finished was that between Bude and Launceston. It was a remarkable feat of engineering as the sea lock at the entrance to the canal was the only lock even though it ran for 35 miles and rose to a height of 350 feet in six miles. In order to achieve the changes in level a series of inclined planes, or ramps, were used between

🎭 stories and anecdotes   🍵 famous people   🎨 art and craft   🎭 entertainment and sport   🏃 walks

the different levels and a wheeled tub boat was pulled up the ramps on metal rails. It finally closed to commercial craft in 1912 and now only two miles of the canal are passable. The **Bude Canal Trail** follows this tranquil backwater through some wonderfully peaceful and unspoilt countryside.

Close to the entrance to the canal stands **Bude Castle**, an unusually small fortification with no towers or turrets, designed by the local 19th century physician, scientist and inventor, Sir Goldsworthy Gurney. It is now an office building but is particularly interesting because it is thought to be the first building in Britain to be constructed on sand. The castle rests on a concrete raft - a technique developed by Gurney. Among his other

inventions were a steam jet, a musical instrument consisting of glasses played as a piano, and the Bude Light, an intense light obtained by introducing oxygen into the interior flame and using mirrors. He used this to light his own house and also to light the House of Commons, where his invention replaced 280 candles and gave rise to the expression 'in the limelight'. The Bude Light served the House of Commons for 60 years and earned Gurney a knighthood.

To celebrate the new millennium, Carole Vincent and Anthony Fanshawe designed the Bude Light 2000, the first large-scale public sculpture to combine coloured concrete with fibre optic lighting. It stands close to the castle and was officially opened in June 2000 by the

---

SUNRISE

Burn View, Bude, Cornwall EX23 8BY
Tel: 01288 353214
e-mail: sunriseguest@btconnect.com
website: www.sunrise-bude.co.uk

Expect something special, in addition to service with a smile. **Sunrise** is a beautifully refurbished Victorian house combining comfort and style whilst providing 4-Diamond rated en suite accommodation. Ideally located in the heart of the town, Sunrise is just a few moments walk from two Blue Flag beaches, it overlooks the golf course and is close to numerous shops, restaurants and cafés. Open all year, Sunrise has 7 guest bedrooms with a choice of single, twin, double, triple and family rooms. All of them are equipped with TV, video, radio, hairdryer, a well-stocked hospitality tray, toiletries and extras such as wine glasses and a corkscrew. For those who find stairs difficult, there's a double room on the ground floor.

In the morning your hosts, Lesley and Bob Sharrat, will serve you one of their renowned breakfasts with a choice of traditional English, fish, vegetarian or continental, along with an extensive buffet bar of fruits, juices and yoghurts. Home-cooked evening meals are available by arrangement from September to June. Golfers can take advantage of 1, 2 or 3-night golfing breaks with plenty to interest non golfing partners, including surfing, walking, horseriding, swimming, shopping or simply sight-seeing around the beautiful North Cornish coastline.

🏚 historic building   🏛 museum   🏛 historic site   ⛲ scenic attraction   🌱 flora and fauna

Duke of Gloucester.

The history of the town and its canal can be explored in the **Town Museum**, which stands on the canal side in a former blacksmith's forge. The story of Bude and the surrounding area, including shipwrecks, railways, farming and geology, is told

Bude

in a series of vivid displays. One of the high spots in the Bude calendar is the annual jazz festival, held in August and featuring numerous performances, street parades, jazz workshops - even jazz church services.

Around Bude

STRATTON
2 miles NE of Bude on the A39

This ancient market town and one time port is believed to have been founded by the Romans. During the Civil War, the town was a stronghold of the Royalists and their commander, Sir Bevil Grenville, made **The Tree Inn** his centre of operations. In May 1643, at the Battle of Stamford Hill, Grenville led his troops to victory over the Parliamentarians and the dead of both sides were buried in unmarked graves in Stratton churchyard. The battle is re-enacted in mid-May each year. The Tree Inn was also the birthplace of the Cornish giant, Anthony Payne, Sir Bevil's bodyguard who stood over

seven feet tall. They fought together both here and later at Lansdown Hill, near Bath, where Grenville was killed. After helping Grenville's son lead the Royalists to victory, Payne carried his master's body back to Stratton. After the Civil War, Payne continued to live at the Grenville manor house until his death. When he died, the house had to be altered to allow his coffin to pass through the doorway.

LAUNCELLS
2½ miles E of Bude off the A3072

🏛 Church of St Swithin

Set in a delightful wooded combe, the 15th century **Church of St Swithin** was acclaimed by Sir John Betjeman as "the least spoilt church in Cornwall". It is notable for its fine Tudor bench-ends and for 15th century floor tiles made in Barnstaple. In the churchyard is the grave of the remarkable Sir Goldsworthy Gurney (1793-1875) whose inventions included a prototype of incandescent lighting, the high-pressure steam jet, and steam-driven coaches that achieved a steady 15mph.

🎞 stories and anecdotes   🐦 famous people   🎨 art and craft   🎭 entertainment and sport   🚶 walks

BUTTERFLY QUILTERS

Marvic House, Kilkhampton, Bude EX23 9RF
Tel/Fax: 01288 321480
e-mail: butterflyquilters.co.uk
website: www.butterflyquilters.co.uk

Butterfly Quilters offer the opportunity to explore the mystery of patchwork, to create your own family heirloom and at the same time make new friends. Teaching is an important part of Carole Sedgley's business, with small informal workshops available for beginners, intermediate and experienced quilters. In the workshops the instructors focus on old as well as new techniques and students have the choice of working either by hand or machine. Carole has had students arrive without any sewing experience and go on to create their own family heirloom. Butterfly Quilters take great pride in stimulating their students to draw on their own artistic creativity to produce beautiful quilts, handbags, clothing and seasonal projects.

The Studio stocks a range of fabrics from Moda, Red Rooster, Clothworks, JR, Hoffman and many other popular American manufacturers. The showroom also contains a great selection of notions, gifts, quilting kits and patterns, and accessories such as bag handles, mini-irons for pressing seams etc., clover thread cutter pendants, needle threaders and much, much more. The Studio also offers a Long Arm machine quilting service with a range of designs to chose from for people who love to make the quilt tops but do not have the time to quilt.

KILKHAMPTON
4 miles NE of Bude on the A39

The tall and elegant Church of St James contains monuments to the local Grenville family, many of them the work of Michael Chuke, a local man and a pupil of Grinling Gibbons. Equally notable are the magnificent carved bench-ends, and the organ is one played by Henry Purcell when it was installed in Westminster Abbey.

MORWENSTOW
5 miles N of Bude off the A39

🐿 Revd Stephen Hawker   🏚 Rectory

🏚 Hawker's Hut

Used to taking the full brunt of Atlantic storms, this tiny village lies on the harshest stretch of the north Cornwall coast. Although

it can sometimes seem rather storm-lashed, it is a marvellous place from which to watch the changing moods of the ocean. Not surprisingly shipwrecks have been common along this stretch of coast. Many came to grief in storms, but it was not unknown for local criminals to lure unsuspecting ships onto the rocks by lighting lanterns on the cliff tops or the shore.

The village's most renowned inhabitant was its eccentric vicar and poet, the **Reverend Robert Stephen Hawker**, who came here in 1834 and remained among his flock of "smugglers, wreckers and dissenters" until his death in 1875. A colourful figure dressed in a purple frock coat, fisherman's jersey, and fishing boots beneath his cassock, Hawker spent much of his time walking through his beloved countryside. When not walking he could often be found writing verses and smoking, opium by some accounts, in the driftwood hut that he built 17 steps from the top of the precipitous Vicarage Cliff. Now known as **Hawker's Hut**, it is the National Trust's smallest property.

Though a bizarre character, Hawker was also one of the first people to show concern at the number of ships coming to grief along this stretch of coastline. He spent hours monitoring the waves and would often climb down the cliffs to rescue shipwrecked crews or recover the bodies of those who had perished among the waves. After carrying the bodies back to the village he would give them a proper Christian burial. One of the many ships wrecked off Sharpnose headland was the *Caledonia*, whose figurehead stands above the grave of her captain in Morwenstow churchyard.

Hawker's other contribution to Morwenstow was the **Rectory**, which he built at his own expense and to his own design. As individual as the man himself, the chimneys of the house represent the towers of various churches and Oxford colleges; the broad kitchen chimney is in remembrance of his mother. His lasting contribution to the church was to reintroduce the annual Harvest Festival and his most famous poem is the rousing Cornish anthem, *The Song of Western Men*. The National Trust-owned land, between the church and the cliffs, is dedicated to this remarkable man's memory.

To the north of the village is **Welcombe Mouth**, the graveyard of many ships that came to grief on its jagged rocks. Set back from the shore are the **Welcombe and Marsland Valleys** that are now a nature reserve and a haven for butterflies. To the south are the headlands, **Higher** and **Lower**

Sharpnose Points. Rugged rocks, caused by erosion, lie above a boulder-strewn beach, while some of the outcrops of harder rock have begun to form tiny islands.

Bodmin Moor

BODMIN

10 miles SW of Bolventor on the A38

🏛 Castle Canyke 🏚 Bodmin Jail

🎨 Shire Hall Gallery 🏚 Lanhyrdrock House

🚲 Bodmin & Wenford Railway 🚶 Saints' Way

Situated midway between Cornwall's two coasts and at the junction of two ancient trade routes, Bodmin has always been an important town used, particularly, by traders who preferred the overland journey to the sea voyage around Land's End. **Castle Canyke**, to the southeast, was built during the Iron Age to defend this important route. A few centuries later, the Romans erected a fort (one of a string they built to defend strategic river crossings) on a site here above the River Camel. The way-marked footpath, the **Saints' Way**, follows the ancient cross-country route. In the 6th century, St Petroc, one of the most influential of the early Welsh missionary saints, visited Bodmin. In the 10th century, the monastery he had founded at Padstow moved here as a protection against Viking raiders. The town's impressive church is dedicated to the saint and in the churchyard can be found one of the many holy wells in Bodmin – **St Goran's Well** – which dates from the 6th century.

The only market town in Cornwall to appear in the Domesday Book, Bodmin was chiefly an ecclesiastical town until the reign of Henry VIII. However, this did not mean that this was a quiet and peaceful place. During the

🎭 stories and anecdotes 🐦 famous people 🎨 art and craft 🚲 entertainment and sport 🚶 walks

Tudor reign, it was the scene of three uprisings: against the tin levy in 1496, in support of Perkin Warbeck against Henry VII in 1597 and, in 1549, against the imposition of the English Prayer Book. The town's failure to flourish when the railways arrived in Cornwall was due to its decision not to allow the Great Western Railway access to the town centre. Not only did it fail to expand as other towns did but, when Truro became the seat of the new bishopric, Bodmin missed out again.

The Crown Jewels and the Domesday Book were hidden at **Bodmin Jail** during World War I and this former county prison, dating from 1776, is an interesting place to visit. The imposing Shire Hall, built in 1837, served as the County Court until 1988. Now restored (it was officially opened by the Queen in 2000), it brings to life in **The Courtroom Experience** the notorious murder in 1844 of Charlotte Dymond on lonely Bodmin Moor and the trial of Matthew Weeks for the crime. Visitors can participate in the drama of the trial as jurors and enter the chilling holding cells where convicted felons awaited their fate. A second courtroom houses the **Shire Hall Gallery** which hosts a varied programme of Cornish and West County artists and craftspeople, as well as community exhibitions.

Bodmin Town Museum provides an insight into the town's past and that of the surrounding area. Just a short distance from the town centre is **Bodmin Beacon Local Nature Reserve**. From the beacon summit, on which stands the 114-foot Gilbert Memorial, there are splendid views over the

---

BODMIN PLANT & HERB NURSERY

Laveddon Mill, Laninval Hill, Bodmin, Cornwall PL30 5JU
Tel: 01208 72837   Fax: 01208 76491
e-mail: bodminnursery@aol.com
website: www.bodminnursery.co.uk

Located halfway between Bodmin and Lanivet on the A389, **Bodmin Plant & Herb Nursery** is the kind of nursery that you thought no longer existed, offering traditional growing, fresh and healthy plants, a range that surprises and excites, as well as providing friendly advice. This a "proper" nursery specialising in herbs and herbaceous perennials. With hundreds of varieties of herbs and a few thousand flowering perennials, be prepared to lose yourself in a sea of blazing colour and scent.

That's not all – the nursery also offers a wide range of shrubs, grasses, climbers, alpines, marginal and water plants, fruit and ornamental trees, vegetable plants, bedding and hanging baskets. There are even whole areas dedicated to the more specific challenges of shady and ground cover gardening. Originally the site of a water mill dating from the 17th century, there are four acres of plants, all in a lovely countryside setting. The nursery is open every day of the year, from 9am to 6pm from April to October; from 9am to 5pm, November to March; and from 10am to 4pm on Sundays.

🏛 historic building   🏛 museum   🏛 historic site   🐸 scenic attraction   🌿 flora and fauna

town and moor. Also easily reached from Bodmin is the **Camel Trail**, a walking and cycling path along the River Camel to Padstow following the track bed of one of the country's first railways.

Housed in The Keep near the railway station in Bodmin, the **Duke of Cornwall's Light Infantry Regimental Museum** covers the military history of the County Regiment of Cornwall, The Duke of Cornwall's Light Infantry.

Nearby, Bodmin General Station is also the base for the **Bodmin and Wenford Railway,** a former branch line of the Great Western Railway. The line closed to passenger traffic in 1963 but has been splendidly restored. Today, steam locomotives take passengers on a 13-mile round trip along a steeply graded line through beautiful countryside. There are occasional luncheon and dinner specials, and driving instruction is also available.

To the south of the town, near the village of Cutmadoc, stands one of the most fascinating late-19th century houses in England, the spectacular **Lanhydrock House** (National Trust). Surrounded by wonderful formal gardens, woodland and parkland, it originally belonged to Bodmin's Augustinian priory. The extensive estate was bought in 1620 by Sir Richard Robarts (who made his fortune in tin and wool) and his family lived here until the estate was given to the Trust in 1953. Partially destroyed by fire in 1881, this mansion is probably the grandest in Cornwall. Visitors can see that many of the rooms combine the building's original splendour with the latest in Victorian domestic comforts and amenities. One special bedroom belonged to Tommy Agar-Robarts, who was killed at the Battle of Loos in 1915; it contains many of his personal possessions. The grounds are equally magnificent and are known for the fabulous springtime displays of rhododendrons, magnolias and camellias, a superb avenue of ancient beech and sycamore trees, a cob-and-thatch summer house and a photogenic formal garden overlooked by the small estate church of St Hydroc. In the woods are many unusual flowers and ferns as well as owls, woodpeckers and many other birds (see walk on page 86).

Around Bodmin

BLISLAND
5 miles N of Bodmin off the A30

🏛 Church of St Protus

Hidden in a maze of country lanes, this moorland village has a tree-lined village green that has stayed true to its original Saxon layout – an unusual sight on this side of the River Tamar. The part-Norman parish **Church of St Protus and St Hyacinth,** was one of Sir John Betjeman's favourites, described by the poet as "dazzling and amazing". The church was restored with great sensitivity in the 1890s by the architect FC Eden who also designed the sumptuously coloured Gothic screen that dominates the interior.

On the moorland to the north of the village are numerous ancient monuments including the stone circle of Blisland Manor Common and Stipple Stone Henge Monument on Hawkstor Down.

BOLVENTOR
10 miles NE of Bodmin off the A30

🐿 Daphne du Maurier 🏛 Dozmary Pool

🏛 Museum of Smuggling 🐿 Roughtor

🏛 Museum of Curiosity

Right at the heart of Bodmin Moor, this scenic village is the location of the former coaching inn, immortalised by **Daphne du**

🎭 stories and anecdotes 🐿 famous people 🎨 art and craft 🎟 entertainment and sport 🚶 walks

Lanhydrock House

Distance: *4.1 miles (6.5 kilometres)*

Typical time: *150 mins*

Height gain: *115 metres*

Map: *Explorer 107*

Walk: *www.walkingworld.com ID:1514*

Contributor: *Jim Grindle*

ACCESS INFORMATION:

The estate is just under two miles from Bodmin Parkway railway station from which the no. 55 bus runs. It is signposted from the A30, the A38 and the B3268.

DESCRIPTION:

This is an excellent walk for anybody with an interest in natural history. The trees in the parkland have on them over 100 species of lichens and there are also mosses, beetles and birds, including treecreeper, tawny owl, nuthatch and all three British woodpeckers. Nine of the 14 British bats can be found here and there is an abundance of grassland flowers. On the River Fowey are otters and we saw lots of dippers and grey wagtails, more of the latter than I have seen anywhere else. You could spend a long time getting round. The walk is a mixture of woodland and river with a steady climb back up to the house.

ADDITIONAL INFORMATION

The National Trust describes the house as, "One of the most fascinating late 19th century houses in England, full of period atmosphere and the trappings of a high Victorian country house." There is enough time to visit the house and do this walk in a day, but obviously there is a lot to see both indoors and out.

FEATURES:

River, toilets, stately home, National Trust/ NTS, birds, flowers, butterflies, cafe, gift shop, good for kids, nature trail, restaurant, tea shop, woodland.

WALK DIRECTIONS:

1 | From the car park go back to its entrance and look for a path on the left. The low signpost directs you to reception and the house. Just out of sight is a gate giving access to a road. (There are toilets in the car park and a refreshment kiosk with limited opening hours.)

2 | From here you can see the award-winning reception building. Cross the road and pass to the right of it. You do not have to pay if you just intend doing the walk and you will be on a public footpath. Follow the main drive to the gatehouse outside the main house.

3 | Pass the gatehouse and follow the tarmac to the right where you will see a wooden gate in a corner.

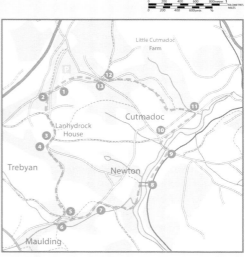

4 | Go through and follow this drive. Don't take any of the smaller paths that join it, including the one immediately to the left behind the gate. You will pass a house with the estate's kitchen gardens and go through a red gate. Almost 1km from this Waymark a track goes off to the right.

5 | Pass by it and where the main track curves right there is another which you also ignore. A few metres past this bend, though, a track joins from the left.

6 | This one you do want. Turn left and pass an old quarry as it leaves the wood to enter meadows. At the entrance to another wood is a gate.

7 | Go through and turn right. The track leads down, with more gates, to the banks of the River Fowey.

8 | Turn left and follow the river until you see a bridge. This is Kathleen Bridge that was built in 1991 by the Royal Engineers. Cross and turn left following the river to an ancient stone bridge.

9 | Once over the bridge turn to the right into the car park and cross to a little footbridge.

10 | Go over the bridge onto Station Drive, a stone track. You will pass a large Giant Redwood just across the stream. Turn right and follow the track for 1km until you see a red, signposted metal gate on your left.

11 | Go through onto a lane and turn left - you will see a similar gate a few metres along on the far side of the road. This gives access to the wood. Turn left on any forks in the path - there are lots of yellow arrows on this stretch - so that you keep to the edge of the wood - you will be able to see the meadows outside for most of the way. When the path levels out it meets a forestry track at right angles. Turn left and follow it until you reach a road.

12 | Cross to the minor road directly opposite. Almost on the corner (on the right) is another of the red gates.

13 | Go through this - a path goes to the left, passing around the edge of a cricket field and then following a wall all the way round to the left to enter the back of the car park.

Maurier in her famous novel, *Jamaica Inn* (1936). During the 18th and 19th centuries this isolated hostelry, on the main route across the bleak moorland, provided an ideal meeting place for smugglers and other outlaws as well as legitimate travellers journeying between Cornwall and the rest of England. Today, as well as providing hospitality, the inn (see panel on page 90) has a **Museum of Smuggling** "devoted to the arts of concealment and evasion" which the arch villain, Demon Davey, the vicar of Altarnum demonstrates with the aid of tableaux; and a room dedicated to the memory of Daphne du Maurier which is full of memorabilia of the writer including her Sheraton writing desk on top of which is a

packet of du Maurier cigarettes named after her father, the actor Gerald du Maurier. There's also a dish of Glacier Mints – Dame Daphne's favourite sweets.

Yet another attraction here is Mr Potter's **Museum of Curiosity**, a fascinating collection gathered by the Victorian taxidermist Walter Potter. Exhibits include the Death and Burial of Cock Robin, Victorian toys and dolls' houses, smoking memorabilia and a variety of strange oddities.

Bodmin Moor, the bleak expanse of moorland surrounding Bolventor, is the smallest of the three great West Country moors and an Area of Outstanding Natural Beauty. Its granite upland is characterised by

HENGAR MANOR COUNTRY PARK

St Tudy, Bodmin, Cornwall PL30 3PL
Tel: 01208 850382 Fax: 01208 850722
e-mail: holidays@hengarmanor.co.uk
website: www.hengarmanor.co.uk

A recent winner of a David Bellamy Silver Conservation Award, the **Hengar Manor Country Park** extends across 35 beautiful acres of landscaped gardens, mature woodland and still-water lakes. Nestling in the heart of the Cornish countryside, the unspoiled 17th century Hengar Manor estate provides the perfect foil to the stresses of modern living.

The park offers a superb range of activities. You can practice your golf on the nine-hole pitch and putt course, enjoy a round of crazy golf or a game of tennis on one of the all-weather courts, try your luck on one of the three private and well-stocked fishing lakes, or just take time out to explore the park and its teeming wildlife. All the equipment you're likely to need can be hired at the Manor. For youngsters, there's a well-equipped woodland adventure playground where they can burn off their excess energy.

Indoors, there's a leisure complex with a pool, waterfall and slide, a separate pool for toddlers and a games room. Or you could indulge yourself in the popular beauty treatment centre with its whirlpool spa and relaxing sauna and steam room. It has a solarium and also offers massage, reflexology and aromatherapy treatments.

During school holiday periods, at various times throughout the day, the Hedgehog Club provides creative activity, music and treasure hunts for children from three to eight years; for older children, the Freddie Fox Club offers supervised tennis, kwik cricket, basketball and other sports. And every evening during the summer months, there's live entertainment to suit every taste.

The Park offers a wide choice of accommodation. There are Scandinavian-style lodges, fully insulated and double-glazed – perfect for all year round holidays. Or you might prefer the Hengar Park bungalows or luxury villas, all set within the bounds of the old apple and cherry orchards. Four properties provide accommodation for between six and ten people. Then there are the 17th century Coach House Cottages with a choice of one, two or three bedrooms. Finally, there are the gracious and elegant Manor House apartments which nestle under the roof of the magnificent 17th century Manor House.

All the properties are comprehensively equipped for a self-catering holiday but if you fancy a meal out, there's an Italian-style restaurant serving home-made pizza and fresh pasta dishes, as well as The Tavern which offers more traditional fare. If you want to eat in but don't want to cook, there's always the popular takeaway service.

🏛 historic building   🏛 museum   🏚 historic site   🍃 scenic attraction   🌿 flora and fauna

POLRODE MILL COTTAGE

Allen Valley, Nr St Tudy, North Cornwall PL30 3NS
Tel: 01208 850203
e-mail: stay@polrodemillcottage.co.uk
website: www.polrodemillcottage.co.uk

Deborah and David welcome you to their tranquil, picturesque country cottage set in three acres of gardens and woodland, in the beautiful Allen Valley. Dating from the 17th century Polrode remains a romantic and charming dwelling offering guests luxurious accommodation in a relaxed environment. Each of the three en suite double rooms is tastefully furnished with period furniture, an antique brass bed and a roll-top bath to pamper yourself. At the end of the day, relax in deep leather chesterfields in the cosy lounge by the log fire.

Eating is an important part of the Polrode experience. Start the day with fresh fruit, homemade preserves and Cornish breakfast including the deepest yellow eggs from their free range hens. The delicious three course dinner menu, changed daily, features the very best of homegrown and local produce. Sample the home-made bread, fish fresh from Cornish waters and venison from local estates. A wide range of wine and spirits are available to complement your meal or relax with in the lounge.

Polrode is an ideal base from which to explore the delights of Cornwall. The enchanting fishing villages of Padstow, Port Isaac and Boscastle are nearby. The Eden Project, the Lost Gardens of Heligan, Lanhydrock, The National Trust Coastline and the mythical castle at Tintagel are just a short drive away. Polrode is a haven for non-smokers.

---

saturated moorland and weather-beaten tors. From here the rivers Inny, Lynher, Fowey, St Neot and De Lank flow to both the north and south coasts of Cornwall. In this wild countryside roams the Beast of Bodmin, an elusive catlike creature which could be an escaped puma or panther – or just another creation of the fertile Cornish imagination.

At 1,377 feet, **Brown Willy** is the highest point of Bodmin Moor, and Cornwall, while, just to the northwest, lies **Roughtor** (pronounced 'row tor' to rhyme with 'now tor'), the moor's second highest point. Standing on National Trust owned land, Roughtor is a magnificent

Bodmin Moor

📖 stories and anecdotes   🦢 famous people   🎨 art and craft   ✐ entertainment and sport   🚶 walks

viewing point and also the site of a memorial to the men of the Wessex Regiment who were killed during World War II.

Throughout this wild and beautiful moor land, there are remains, left behind by earlier occupiers. There are scattered Bronze Age hut circles and field enclosures and Iron Age hill forts. Many villages in and around the moor grew up around the monastic cells of Celtic missionaries and took the names of saints. Others were mining villages where ruined engine houses still stand out against the skyline.

To the south of Bolventor is the mysterious natural tarn, **Dozmary Pool**, a place firmly linked with the legend of King Arthur. Brought here following his final battle at Slaughterbridge, the king lay dying at the water's edge, listening to *"the ripple washing in the reeds, and the wild water lapping on the crag"* as Tennyson described it in his poem *The Passing of Arthur*. Close to death, Arthur asked his friend, Sir Bedivere, to throw his sword Excalibur into the centre of the pool. As the knight did so a lady's arm *"clothed in white samite, mystic, wonderful"* rose from the waters to receive the sword. Dozmary is not the only lake to

Jamaica Inn and Museums

Bolventor, Launceston, Cornwall PL15 7TS Tel: 01566 86250 Fax: 01566 86177
e-mail: enquiry@jamaicainn.co.uk website: www.jamaicainn.co.uk

Built in the mid 18th century to serve travellers making the journey on the new turnpike road between Launceston and Bodmin, **Jamaica Inn** has become one of the best known hostelries in the country if not the world thanks to novelist Daphne du

Maurier. Whilst staying here in the 1920s, she was taken with the romance of the surrounding bleak moorland and fascinated by tales of smugglers and villains who met here.

Today, the inn still serves travellers who can enjoy a drink in the Smugglers

bar, dinner in the du Maurier Restaurant or relax by a roaring log fire before retiring to one of the inn's comfortable guest rooms. However, there is much more here than an atmospheric, 300-year-old inn. Tales of smugglers and the arch villain, Demon Davey, vicar of Altarnun, are told through a theatrical presentation at the Smugglers at Jamaica Inn exhibition whilst more can be learnt of Daphne herself in the Daphne du Maurier Room. Many of her novels are based in Cornwall where she came to live with her husband in the 1930s and the room here is filled with memorabilia including her Sheraton writing desk.

Finally, there is Mr Potter's Museum of Curiosity, a fascinating collection of tableaux created by the Victorian taxidermist, Walter Potter. Visitors can see Steptoe and Son's bear and Walter's first tableau, the Death and Burial of Cock Robin, along with smoking memorabilia, Victorian toys and dolls' houses and some curious oddities.

🏛 historic building   🏛 museum   🏛 historic site   🏞 scenic attraction   🌿 flora and fauna

claim the Lady of the Lake – Loe Pool at Mount's Bay, and Bosherstone and Llyn Llydaw in Wales are also put forward as alternative resting places for Excalibur.

This desolate and isolated place is also linked with Jan Tregeagle, the wicked steward of the Earl of Radnor whose many evil deeds included the murder of the parents of a young child whose estate he wanted. As a punishment, so the story goes, Tregeagle was condemned to spend the rest of time emptying the lake with a leaking limpet shell. His howls of despair are still said to be heard to this day.

By tradition, Dozmary Pool is bottomless, although it did dry up completely during a prolonged drought in 1869. Close by is the county's largest man-made reservoir, **Colliford Lake**. At 1,000 feet above sea level, it is the perfect habitat for long tailed ducks, dippers and grey wagtails, and rare plants such as the heath-spotted and frog orchids.

Wesley Cottage, Trewint

TREWINT
13 miles NE of Bodmin off the A30

🐦 John Wesley   🏚 Wesley Cottage

This handsome village often played host to **John Wesley**, the founder of Methodism, on his preaching tours of Cornwall. One of the villagers, Digory Isbell, built an extension to his house for the use of Wesley and his preachers, and **Wesley Cottage** is open for visits. The rooms, thought to be the smallest Methodist preaching place in the world, have been maintained as they were in the 18th century, and visitors can see the prophets' room and the pilgrims' garden. Digory Isbell and his wife are buried in Trewint churchyard.

ALTARNUN
14 miles NE of Bodmin off the A30

🏚 Cathedral of the Cornish Moors

This moorland village, charmingly situated in a steep-sided valley, is home to a splendid, 15th century parish church that is often referred to as the '**Cathedral of the Cornish Moors**'. Dedicated to St Nonna, the mother of St David of Wales, the church has a 108-feet pinnacled tower that rises high above the river. Inside, it is surprisingly light and airy, with features ranging from Norman times through to 16th century bench end carvings. In the churchyard stands a Celtic cross, thought to date from the time of St Nonna's journey here from Wales in around 527AD. The waters of nearby St Nonna's well were once thought to cure madness. After immersion in the waters, lunatics were carried into the church for mass. The process was repeated until the patient showed signs of recovery.

Just to the northwest, near the peaceful

📖 stories and anecdotes   🐦 famous people   🎨 art and craft   ✐ entertainment and sport   🚶 walks village of St Clether, is another holy well, standing on a bracken-covered shelf above the River Inny beside its 15th century chapel. To the north is **Laneast** where yet another of Bodmin Moor's holy wells is housed in a 16th century building, close to a tall Celtic cross and the village's original Norman church. Laneast was also the birthplace of John Adams, the astronomer who discovered the planet Neptune.

MINIONS
16 miles NE of Bodmin off the B3254

🏠 Minions Heritage Centre   🐾 Golitha Falls

🏛 Hurlers Stone Circle

Boasting the highest pub in Cornwall, this moorland village was a thriving mining centre during the 19th and early 20th centuries with miners and quarrymen extracting granite, copper and lead from the surrounding area. It was also the setting for EV Thompson's historical novel, *Chase the Wind*. One of the now disused mine engine houses has become the **Minions Heritage Centre**. It covers more than 4,000 years of life on the moorland, including the story of mining along with the life and times of much earlier settlers.

Close to the village stands the impressive **Hurlers Stone Circle**. This Bronze Age temple comprising three circles takes its name from the ancient game of hurling, the Celtic form of hockey. Legend has it that the circles were men who were caught playing the game on the Sabbath. As a punishment, they were turned to stone. The **Cheesewring**, a natural pile of granite slabs whose appearance is reminiscent of a cheese press, also lies close to the village. Again, legends have grown up around these stones. One, which is probably true, involves Daniel

Gumb, a local stonecutter who was a great reader and taught himself both mathematics and astronomy. He married a local girl and they supposedly made their home in a cave under the Cheesewring. Before the cave collapsed, numerous intricate carvings could be seen on the walls, including the inscription "D Gumb 1735". Another story tells that the Cheesewring was once the haunt of a Druid who would offer thirsty passers-by a drink from a golden chalice that never ran dry. The discovery at nearby Rillaton Barrow, in 1890, of a ribbed cup of beaten gold lying beside a skeleton gave credence to the story. The chalice, known as the Rillaton Cup, is displayed in the British Museum.

Just to the northeast lies Upton Cross, the home of **Cornish Yarg Cheese**. Made since 1983 in the beautiful Lynher Valley, this famous cheese with its distinctive flavour comes wrapped in nettle leaves. The local delicacy reaches many of the best restaurants and delicatessen counters in the country. Visitors can watch the milking of the dairy herd and the cheesemaking process, follow the pond and woodland trails and enjoy cheese tastings.

South of Minions and not far from the sizeable moorland village of St Cleer, is another holy well, **St Cleer's Holy Well**, also thought to have curative powers. There are several other reminders of the distant past. Dating back to Neolithic times, **Trethevy Quoit** is an impressive enclosed chamber tomb that originally formed the core of a vast earthwork mound. The largest such structure in Cornwall, this quoit is believed to be more than 5,000 years old. Just to the west lies a tall stone cross, **King Doniert's Stone**, erected in memory of King Durngarth, a Cornish king,

Golitha Falls

continued by putting barbed wire around the rectory and patrolling the grounds with a pack of German Shepherd dogs. In response, his flock stayed away from his church and one record in the parish registry reads, "No fog. No wind. No rain. No congregation." Unperturbed, the rector fashioned his own congregation from cardboard, filled the pews and preached on as normal. It would, however, appear that Densham did have a kinder side to his nature, as he built a children's playground in the rectory garden.

To the north and west lie the peaceful backwaters of **Cardinham Woods**, enjoyed by both walkers and cyclists. Acquired by the Forestry Commission in 1922, this attractive and varied woodland is a haven for a wide variety of wildlife as well as producing high quality Douglas Fir for the timber industry. In medieval times, the woods were the location of an important Norman castle belonging to the Cardinham family but all that remains today are an earthwork mound and a few traces of the original keep.

ST NEOT
11 miles E of Bodmin off the A38

📖 St Neot 🏛 Carnglaze Slate Caverns

Once a thriving centre of the woollen industry, St Neot is famous for the splendid 15th century Church of St Anietus and, in particular, its fabulous early 16th century stained glass. Of the many beautiful scenes depicted here, perhaps the most interesting is that of St Neot, the diminutive saint after whom the village is named. Although only 15 inches tall, the saint became famous for his miracles involving animals. One story tells of an exhausted hunted doe, which ran to St Neot's side. A stern look from the saint sent the pursuing hounds back into the forest while

believed to have drowned in the River Fowey in 875AD. Downstream from the Stone the River Fowey descends through dense broadleaved woodland in a delightful series of cascades known as **Golitha Falls**. This outstanding and well-known beauty spot is a National Nature Reserve.

WARLEGGAN
11 miles E of Bodmin off the A38

📖 Revd Frederick Densham

🌿 Cardinham Woods

The remote location of this tiny hamlet has led to it been acknowledged as a haunt of the Cornish 'piskies' but Warleggan's most eccentric inhabitant was undoubtedly **Revd Frederick Densham**, who arrived here in 1931. Immediately alienating his parishioners by closing the Sunday school, Densham

THE INN ON THE HILL

Caradon Hill, Pensilva, Liskeard, Cornwall PL14 5PJ
Tel: 01579 362281   Fax: 01579 363401
e-mail: theinnonthehill@btinternet.com
website: www.theinnonthehill.co.uk

The Inn on the Hill, built in 1850 as a Mine Captains house, is the most wonderful moorland retreat set in 2.5 acres of wooded grounds on the eastern edge of Bodmin Moor. There are no near neighbours or busy roads and being the highest hotel in Cornwall it is surrounded with the peace and tranquillity that you deserve for that special break. There are stunning views from the hotal across the Tamar Valley to Plymouth and Dartmoor beyond, which are some of the most spectacular in the area.

The comfortable accommodation is all en suite and is ideally located for touring Devon and Cornwall with Plymouth, the North Cornwall coast and the Eden Project within easy reach. Being surrounded by Open Access land you can enjoy some wonderful local walks, exploring the ancient and mining heritage of the area.

The cosy comfortable bar is a great place to start your evening before dining in the restaurant on fresh local produce which consists of wholesome and traditional fare. The local real ales and extensive fine wine list can only help to enhance your stay. Guests with limited mobility accommodated. Dogs accepted.

THE COLLECTION

Windsor Place, Liskeard, Cornwall PL14 4BH
Tel/Fax: 01579 343333
e-mail: shop@thecollection-cornwall.co.uk
website: www.thecollection-cornwall.co.uk

Renowned for its 'contemporary style' in the heart of this historic market town, **The Collection** is filled with a fabulous range of goods for you....and your home. The prominent building was originally designed in the 1800's by the town's principal architect, Henry Rice, and now offers a bright and beautiful space for you to shop or browse. One half of the shop dedicates itself to all things **'for you'**:- gorgeous handbags, shoes and body products, ladies and gents gifts and accessories, leather goods and designer jewellery. Complimenting the contemporary style of the shop, is the **'for home'** section which offers a wide range of glassware, home interior accessories and furniture. Gifts for all occasions can be found throughout the store, all lovingly displayed to make your shopping experience a special and relaxing one.

With a background in design and a styling flare, owners Patti & Shaun Donovan, have spent the last five years introducing many international brands and designer products to the region and are on hand to welcome and assist you. Get your purchase gift wrapped 'with compliments', create your wedding list or ask for styling advice for your home. For a wide selection of design-led home interiors, beautiful gifts and personal service, visit The Collection. Open Monday – Saturday 9.30am-6.00pm

🏚 historic building   🏛 museum   🏛 historic site   🐚 scenic attraction   🌱 flora and fauna

the huntsman dropped his bow and became a faithful disciple. Another tale – the one that can be seen in the church window – tells of an angel giving the saint three fish for his well and adding that as long as he only eats one fish a day there will always be fish to eat. Unfortunately, when St Neot fell ill his servant took two fish and prepared them for his master. Horrified, Neot prayed over the meal, ordering the fish be returned to the well and, as they touched the water, they came alive again.

Tied to the tower outside the church is an oak branch that is replaced annually on Oak Apple Day. The ceremony was started by Royalists wishing to give thanks for the oak tree that hid Charles II during his flight from the country.

To the south of St Neot are the **Carnglaze Slate Caverns** where slate for use in the building trade was first quarried in the 14th century. Today, visitors can journey underground and see the large chambers that were once used by smugglers as rum stores and the subterranean lake that is filled with the clearest blue-green water.

LISKEARD

13 miles E of Bodmin on the B3254

🦡 Dobwalls Adventure Park

🐦 Porfell Animal Park 🦆 Looe Valley Line

Situated on the undulating ground between the valleys of the East Looe and Seaton Rivers, this picturesque and lively market town was one of Cornwall's five medieval stannary towns – the others being Bodmin, Lostwithiel, Truro and Helston. The name comes from the Latin for tin, '*stannum*', and these five towns were the only places licensed to weigh and stamp the metal. Liskeard had been a centre for the mining industry for centuries. However, by the 19th century, after the

construction of a canal linking the town with Looe, vast quantities of copper ore and granite joined the cargoes of tin. In the 1850s, the canal was replaced by the Looe Valley branch of the Great Western Railway. An eight-mile long scenic stretch of the **Looe Valley Line** is still open today though the industrial wagons have long since been replaced with passenger carriages.

Although it is a small town, Liskeard does boast some public buildings that act as a reminder of its past importance and prosperity. The **Guildhall** was constructed in 1859 while the **Public Hall**, opened in 1890, is still used as offices of the town council as well as being home to a local **Museum**. Adjacent to the Passmore-Edwards public library stands **Stuart House**, a handsome Jacobean residence where Charles I stayed in 1644 while engaged in a campaign against Cromwell at nearby Lostwithiel. Finally, in Well Street, lies one of Liskeard's most curious features – an arched grotto that marks the site of **Pipe Well**, a medieval spring reputed to have had curative powers.

To the west of Liskeard is an attraction that will please all the family. **Dobwalls Family Adventure Park** has a miniature steam railway based on an old North American railroad, woodland play areas and a restaurant as well as a charming Edwardian countryside museum with a permanent exhibition on the life and works of wildlife artist Archibald Thorburn.

Another top family attraction is **Porfell Animal Land Wildlife Park** at Trecongate. Within its 15 acres of fields bounded by streams and woodland, visitors can meet wallabies, marmosets, lemurs, zebra, meerkats and porcupines; feed the deer, goats, ducks and chickens, just stroll through the woods or relax in the tea room housed in an attractive old barn.

🎭 stories and anecdotes 🌳 famous people 🎨 art and craft 🎢 entertainment and sport 🚶 walks

TREDINNICK FARM SHOP

Widegates, nr Looe, Cornwall PL13 1QL
Tel: 01503 240992
e-mail: combasix@zoom.co.uk

Tredinnick Farm Shop in Widegates is a family run shop situated on the main road between Hessenford and Looe. Open seven days a week all year round, it offers a large range of locally sourced products.

There is a selection of cider, scrumpy and wines along with award-winning ales from local breweries. Cornish bacon and farmhouse sausages, made locally, are a favourite with all of their customers.

Fresh fruit and vegetables are the mainstay of the business, and as well as their daily customers, they also supply many restaurants and guesthouses in the area.

A local wood carver occasionally exhibits his carvings alongside the shops shrubs and plants, of which they carry a small seasonal selection.

THE BYWATER RESTAURANT

Lower Market Street, East Looe, Cornwall PL13 1AX
Tel: 01503 262314
e-mail: contact@thebywater.co.uk
website: www.thebywater.co.uk

Occupying a charming ivy-covered 17th century cottage in a narrow lane between the beach and the quay, **The Bywater Restaurant** is a relaxing yet stylish place in which to enjoy contemporary home-cooked food based on locally sourced, seasonal produce. The menus evolve on a daily basis, making the most of what is fresh and in season that day. Fish is bought directly from the quay and a nearby farm at Trewidland provides the traditionally reared meat for dishes such as Lowertown Farm fillet served with Cornish blue cheese & potato cake, wilted spinach and forest mushroom sauce.

All the food, including bread, pasta and desserts, are hand-made and each meal is freshly prepared to order, just ask if there are any alterations to the menu you would like. To accompany your meal, there's a good choice of wines, ciders and ales. With seating for just 20 people, The Bywater combines 17th century old world charm with clean modern lines. The restaurant is open from 6.30pm, Wednesday to Sunday.

Looe

🏛 Old Guildhall Museum

🚶 Looe Valley Line Footpath

The tidal harbour at Looe, created by the two rivers the East Looe and West Looe, made this an important fishing and sea-faring port from the Middle Ages through to the 19th century. Originally, two separate towns on either side of the estuary, East and West Looe were first connected by a bridge in the early 15th century. In 1883, they were officially incorporated. The present day seven-arched bridge, dating from the 19th century, carries the main road and links the two halves of the town. Something of a jack-of-all-trades, over the years Looe has had a pilchard fishing fleet, it has served the mineral extractors of Bodmin Moor and is has also been the haunt of smugglers. However, it is only the fishing industry that remains from the town's colourful past. Looe is still Cornwall's second most important port with fish auctions taking place at East Looe's busy quayside market on the famous **Banjo Pier**.

Of the two distinct parts, East Looe, with its narrow cobbled streets and twisting alleyways, is the older. Here, housed in one of the town's several 16th century buildings, is the **Old Guildhall Museum**, where can be seen the old magistrates' bench and original cells as well displays detailing much of Looe's history. In 1800, a bathing machine was built overlooking East Looe's sandy beach. After the opening of the Looe Valley Line to passengers in 1879, the development of the twin towns as a holiday resort began. Fortunately, the character of East Looe has been retained while West Looe is, essentially, a residential area.

The Looe Valley Line railway replaced the Liskeard to Looe canal and today the same journey can be made by following the **Looe Valley Line Footpath**. A distance of ten miles, the walk takes in some of Cornwall's most beautiful woodlands as well as the 'Giant's Hedge', a seven-foot earth embankment.

More recently, Looe has established itself as Britain's major shark fishing centre and regularly plays host to an International Sea Angling Festival. Once a refuge for one of Cornwall's most notorious smugglers, Black Joan, **Looe Island**, just off the coast, is now a bird sanctuary. The island was made famous by the Atkins sisters who lived there and featured it in their books, *We Bought an Island* and *Tales from our Cornish Island*.

West Looe

🎞 stories and anecdotes   🐦 famous people   🎨 art and craft   🚴 entertainment and sport   🚶 walks

Around Looe

ST KEYNE
5 miles N of Looe on the B3254

🏛 St Keyne's Well

� Paul Corin's Magnificent Music Machines

Named after one of the daughters of a Welsh king who settled here during the 5th century, St Keyne is home to the famous holy well – **St Keyne's Well** – that lies beneath a great tree about a mile outside the village. Newly married couples came here to drink – the first to taste the waters was said to be the one to wear the trousers in the marriage. Romanticised by the Victorians, the custom is still carried out by newly-weds today.

Though a small village, St Keyne sees many visitors during the year as it is home to **Paul Corin's Magnificent Music Machines**, a wonderful collection that opened in 1967. Housed in the old mill buildings, where Paul was the last miller, this collection of mechanical instruments covers a wide range of sounds and music from classical pieces to musicals, and includes a Wurlitzer from the Regent Cinema, Brighton. Paul's collection has featured on numerous radio and TV programmes. Incidentally, Paul's grandfather was Bransby Williams, the only great star from the Music Hall days to have his own BBC TV show, in the early 1950s.

Just to the south of St Keyne, and in the valley of the East Looe river, is a **Stone Circle** of eight standing quartz stones, said to be older than Stonehenge.

ST GERMANS
7 miles NE of Looe on the B3249

🏛 St German's Church

Before the Anglo Saxon diocese of Cornwall was incorporated with Exeter in 1043, this rural village was a cathedral city and the present **St German's Church** stands on the site of the Saxon cathedral. Dating from Norman times, it was built as the great church for the Augustinian priory founded here in 1162. As well as curiously dissimilar towers dating from the 13th and 15th centuries, the church contains several striking monuments to the Eliot family, including one by Rysbrack commemorating Edward Eliot who died in 1722. Other treasures in the church include a glorious east window with stained glass by Burne-Jones, and an old chair that bears a series of carvings depicting Dando, a 14th century priest from the priory. According to local stories, one Sunday Dando left his prayers to go out hunting with a group of wild friends. At the end of the chase, the priest called for a drink and was handed a richly decorated drinking horn by a stranger on a black horse. While quenching his thirst Dando saw the stranger stealing his game. Despite his calls, the horseman refused to return the game. In a drunken frenzy, Dando swore that he would follow the stranger to Hell in order to retrieve his prizes, whereupon the stranger pulled Dando up onto his horse and rode into the River Lynher. Neither the stranger on the horse nor the priest was ever seen again.

SALTASH
11½ miles NE of Looe on the A38

🏛 Royal Albert Bridge   🌤 Fore Street

A medieval port on the River Tamar, Saltash was once the base for the largest river steamer fleet in the southwest. Today, it remains the 'Gateway to Cornwall' for many holidaymakers who cross the river into Cornwall via one of the town's mighty bridges. Designed by Isambard Kingdom

---

🏛 historic building   🏛 museum   🏛 historic site   🌤 scenic attraction   🌿 flora and fauna

Brunel in 1859, the iron-built **Royal Albert Bridge** carries the railway while, alongside, is the much more slender **Tamar Bridge**, a suspension road bridge that was opened in 1961 replacing a ferry service that had operated since the 13th century.

Though older than Plymouth, on the other side of the Sound, Saltash is now becoming a suburb of its larger neighbour, following the construction of the road bridge. However, Saltash has retained much of its charm and Cornish individuality. There's an impressive 17th century **Guildhouse** which stands on granite pillars and is now home to the town council and tourist information centre. Close by is **Mary Newman's Cottage**, a quaint 15th century building that was the home of Sir Francis Drake's first wife.

An interesting initiative by the local council and traders can be seen in **Fore Street** which served as the main retail hub of the town for many years. But with the growth of out of town shopping, competition from Plymouth and increased use of motor vehicles, shops here were struggling. So it was decided to try and make some of the empty shop-fronts look more appealing. Local artist Emma Spring was commissioned to carry out the work and her colourful murals certainly brighten up this corner of the town.

Royal Albert Bridge, Saltash

TORPOINT
11½ miles E of Looe on the A374

 Antony House

This small town grew up around a ferry service that ran across the **Hamoaze** (as the Tamar estuary is called at this point) to Devonport in the 18th century. From here there are excellent views over the water to the Royal Navy Dockyards and *HMS Raleigh*, the naval training centre for ratings and artificer apprentices. Commissioned in 1940, *HMS Raleigh* is also the home of the Royal Marine Band (Plymouth).

To the north of the town, overlooking the River Lynher as it meets the Tamar, is **Antony House** (National Trust), a superb example of a Queen Anne house. Built of pale silver-grey stone between 1711 and 1721, it has been the ancestral home of the influential Carew family for almost 600 years. It contains a wonderful collection of paintings (many by Sir Joshua Reynolds), tapestries and furniture. Surrounding the house are the gardens and grounds landscaped by Humphry Repton in the late 18th century, including the delightful **Antony Woodland Gardens**, which are at their best in the spring and autumn. The formal gardens contain the National Collection of Day Lilies.

📷 stories and anecdotes   🍴 famous people   ✐ art and craft   🎭 entertainment and sport   🚶 walks

CREMYLL

12½ miles E of Looe on the B3247

🏛 Mount Edgcumbe House   🐾 Rame Head

Linked to Plymouth by a passenger ferry, Cremyll is an excellent place from which to explore **Mount Edgcumbe House**, the 16th century home of the Earls of Mount Edgcumbe. They moved here from Cotehele House after Piers Edgcumbe married Jean Durnford, an heiress with considerable estates including the Cremyll ferry. The gardens here, overlooking Plymouth Sound, have been designated as one of the Great Gardens of Cornwall. The ten acres of grounds feature classical garden houses, statues, follies, an exotic Shell Seat, and the National Camellia Collection.

To the southwest of Cremyll are the two small and attractive villages of **Cawsand** and **Kingsand.** By some administrative quirk, for centuries they were placed in different

Mount Edgcumbe House and Country Park

Cremyll, near Torpoint, Cornwall PL10 1HZ
Tel: 01752 822236 Fax: 01752 822199

Dating back to the mid 16th century, **Mount Edgcumbe House** was built by Sir Richard Edgcumbe of Cotehele in his deer park. A magnificent red sandstone building, of a typical Tudor style, the house has survived today very much intact, despite receiving a direct hit during an air raid in 1941.

Beautifully restored between 1958 and 1964 by the Earl of Mount Edgcumbe, there are many treasures to see within its splendid rooms including paintings by Sir Joshua Reynolds, 16th century tapestries and 18th century Chinese and Plymouth porcelain. Whilst the house is certainly a remarkable place the extensive grounds, including the 800-acre Country Park, draw many to this historic estate. Close to the house is the Earl's Garden which was created in the 18th century and where a whole host of rare and ancient trees can be seen. To the south, and overlooking Plymouth Sound, are the Formal Gardens. Again laid out in the 18th century, over an original 17th century wilderness garden, this is a series of gardens of contrast where the formal beds of the Italian and

French Gardens give way to the irregular pattern of English lawns. There is also the modern addition of a New Zealand garden complete with a geyser.

Beyond, to the north and continuing around the coastline, there is the extensive Country Park which was created in 1971. Visitors are guided through woodland and large lawns beside shingle beaches and around numerous historic forts and follies. The house is open from April to the end of September and, as well as the marvellous sights there is also an information centre, shop and restaurant within the Formal Gardens.

🏛 historic building   🏛 museum   🏛 historic site   🐾 scenic attraction   🌱 flora and fauna

counties: Cornwall and Devon respectively. Though it is hard to believe today, it was from here that one of the largest smuggling fleets in Cornwall operated. At the peak of their activities in the late 18th and early 19th centuries, thousands of barrels of brandy, silk and other contraband were landed here in secret and transported through sleeping villages to avoid the attentions of the revenue men. It was also at **Cawsand Bay** that the Royal Navy fleet used to shelter before the completion of the **Plymouth Breakwater** in 1841, leaving a legacy of a large number of inns that still welcome locals and holidaymakers alike.

Further southwest again and at the southernmost point of Mount Edgcumbe Country Park lies the spectacular **Rame Head**, which guards the entrance into Plymouth Sound. From the 400-foot cliffs there are superb views but this beautiful headland has its own special feature – the ruined 14th century St Michael's Chapel, from which a blazing beacon warned of the coming of the Armada. In the little hamlet of Rame itself is the older Church of St Germanus, which is still lit by candles; for centuries its west tower and spire acted as a landmark for sailors.

The **Eddystone Lighthouse**, which can be seen on a clear day, lies ten miles offshore from Rame Head. It was from here, in July 1588, that the English fleet had their first encounter with the Spanish Armada.

WHITSAND BAY
8 miles E of Looe off the B3247

🐦 Monkey Sanctuary

Running between Rame Head and the hamlet of Portwrinkle, this bay has an impressive stretch of beach that is more a series of coves that one continuous expanse of sand. The seaside village of Portwrinkle developed around its medieval harbour. Further west along the coast, at the coastal village of Murrayton, is the famous **Monkey Sanctuary**, the world's first protected colony of Amazonian woolly monkeys. The sanctuary was set up in 1964 to provide a safe environment for monkeys rescued from zoos or abandoned as pets, and its inhabitants roam freely in the gardens of the outdoor enclosures. Plants for the monkeys to eat are grown in a forest garden, while the Tree Top Café takes care of hungry humans.

POLPERRO
3 miles SW of Looe off the A387

🏛 Museum of Smuggling

Polperro is many people's idea of a typical Cornish fishing village as its steep, narrow streets and alleyways are piled high with fisherman's cottages built around a narrow tidal inlet. All routes in this lovely village seem

Polperro Harbour

JOAN THE WAD

3 Fore Street, Polperro, Cornwall PL13 2QR
Tel/Fax: 01503 272975
e-mail: ruth@foulkes2329.freeserve.co.uk
website: www.joanthewad.co.uk

Feeling down on your luck? Then a visit to **Joan the Wad** is definitely indicated. Joan is Queen of the Cornish piskies and consort to Jack o'Lantern, the only other of the piskie folk known by name. The piskies are the cheery wonder workers of Cornwall and wherever they abide good luck attends. A man who scooped £1.5 million on the football pools attributed his good luck to his Cornish piskie.

At Ruth and Dave Foulkes's unique shop in Polperro, you can acquire Piskies in different forms – figurines, key hangers, door knockers, necklaces, ear-rings and lucky charms. Also replica statues of the original piskie tribe, which can be seen on the outside of the building. Make a wish to the piskies in the wishing well. To keep them company, the shop also stocks a range of magnetic copper bracelets, tankards, clocks and plaques of the green man, and much more. There is also a huge range of silver jewellery including Celtic designs. Cornish piskie with pixies – the latter, says Joan the Wad, "are a Devon race, whereas we consider our influence for the well-being of others to be unsurpassed." Contact Ruth for mail order prices.

to lead down to its beautiful harbour. It is still a busy fishing port, where there is normally an assortment of colourful boats to be seen. For centuries dependent on pilchard fishing for its survival, Polperro also has a long association with smuggling. During the 18th century, the practice was so rife that nearly all of the inhabitants were involved in the shipping, storing or transporting of contraband. To combat this widespread problem, HM Customs and Excise established the first 'preventive station' in Cornwall here in the 1800s. At the **Museum of Smuggling** a whole range of artefacts and memorabilia are used to illustrate the myths and legends surrounding the characters who dodged the government taxes on luxury goods. A model of *Lady Beatrice*, a traditional gaff-rigged fishing boat, can also be seen.

FOWEY

8 miles W of Looe on the A3082

🌿 Fowey Marine Aquarium   🐿 Daphne du Maurier

Guarding the entrance to the river from which it takes is name, Fowey (pronounced Foy – "to rhyme with joy") is a lovely old seafaring town with steep, narrow streets and alleyways leading down to one of the most beautiful natural harbours along the south coast. An important port in the Middle Ages, though it was certainly occupied by the Romans, the town exhibits architectural styles ranging from Elizabethan to Edwardian. As a busy trading port, Fowey also attracted pirates and was the home of the 'Fowey Gallants', who preyed on ships in the Channel and engaged in raids on the French coast. Brought together during the Hundred Years War to fight the French, these local mariners did not disband at the end of the hostilities but continued to terrorise shipping along this stretch of coast and beyond. A devastating raid by the French in 1457, that saw much of Fowey burnt to the ground, was in direct retaliation for attacks made by the Gallants.

Later, in the 19th century, much of the china clay from St Austell was exported through Fowey. It is still a busy place as huge ships continue to call at this deep water harbour alongside fishing boats and pleasure craft. The town's **Museum,** housed in part of the medieval town hall, is an excellent place to discover Fowey's colourful past, from the days of piracy through to the china clay exports of the 19th century. Naturally, there are many inns here including the **King of Prussia,**

named after Frederick the Great whose victories in the Seven Years War made him a popular figure in England; and the **Ship Inn,** originally a town house built by the influential Rashleigh family in 1570.

On the Town Quay, **Fowey Marine Aquarium** contains a collection of fish from the local waters around the town. Sinister conger eels, bass, turbot, mullet and colourful members of the wrasse family are on display, together with an occasional octopus. There's also a range of lobsters and crabs, with a crab touch pool for children.

Fowey has two important literary connections. Sir Arthur Quiller-Couch (or 'Q'), who lived for over 50 years at **The Haven,** on the Esplanade just above the Polruan ferry. Sir Arthur was a Cambridge

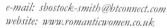

stories and anecdotes   famous people   art and craft   entertainment and sport   walks

professor, sometime Mayor of Fowey, editor of the *Oxford Book of English Verse* and author of several books connected with Fowey – he called it Troy Town. He died in 1944 after being hit by a car and was buried in St Fimbarrus churchyard.

The second literary figure was the novelist **Daphne du Maurier** who lived at Gribbin Head. Each year in mid-May, a general arts and literature festival is held in her memory. A 'tented village' is set up overlooking the picturesque Fowey Estuary and the events include talks by a sparkling mix of star names, guided walks, drama, community events and free entertainment.

To the south of Fowey is Readymoney Cove whose expanse of sand acts as the town's beach. Further along, **St Catherine's Castle** was part of a chain of fortifications built by Henry VIII to protect the harbours along the south coast. From Readymoney Cove the **Coastal Footpath** is clearly marked all the way around to Polkerris and the walk takes in many fine viewpoints as well as the castle and the wonderful daymark on Gribbin Head. The beacon on Gribbin Head was built in 1832 to help seafarers find the approaches into Fowey harbour. But the craggy headland is best known as the home of Daphne du Maurier, who lived at the still private house of Menabilly, which featured as Manderley in her most famous novel *Rebecca* (1938).

Facing St Catherine's Castle across the mouth of the River Fowey and reached by ferry from Fowey, **Polruan** is an impossibly picturesque village. Tiny cottages cling to the steep hillside, threaded with winding steps, alleys and passageways. Life here revolves around the quay where the ferry lands. Beside the harbour, busy with pleasure craft and some industrial vessels, stands the late-15th century **Polruan Blockhouse**, one of a pair of artillery buildings constructed to guard the narrow entrance into Fowey.

Just to the north of Polruan and also facing Fowey lies the pretty hamlet of **Bodinnick** where the actor Gerald du Maurier bought a holiday home beside the landing slip. He named it Ferryside and it was here that his daughter Daphne lived before her marriage

Bodinnick

and where she wrote her first novel *The Loving Spirit*. The house is still owned by the Du Maurier family but not open to the public. If you arrive in Bodinnick by the ferry, you pass the gates to the house as you walk off the landing slip.

Sir Arthur Quiller-Couch is remembered by a monolithic memorial that stands on the coast facing Fowey. It was close to the site of this monument that, in 1644, Charles I narrowly escaped death from a sniper's bullet while making a survey of Cromwell's forces at Fowey. From the Bodinnick ferry there is a delightful walk across mainly National Trust land that leads up to the 'Q' memorial and then back via the Polruan ferry back to Fowey.

GOLANT
8 miles W of Looe off the B3269

Close to this delightful waterside village, which is home to yet another of Cornwall's many holy wells, are the **Castle Dore Earthworks**. This densely overgrown Iron Age lookout point is thought to be the site of King Mark's palace and is therefore linked with the legend of Tristan and Iseult.

Upriver and found in a sleepy creek is the quiet village of **Lerryn** that was once a busy riverside port. Those familiar with Kenneth Grahame's novel, *The Wind in the Willows*, may find the thickly wooded slopes of Lerryn Creek familiar as they are believed to have been the inspiration for the setting of this ever-popular children's story.

LOSTWITHIEL
10 miles NW of Looe on the A390

🏛 Lostwithiel Museum   🏰 Restormel Castle

Nestling in the valley of the River Fowey and surrounded by wooded hills, Lostwithiel's name – which means 'lost in the hills' –

WATTS TRADING

12 Fore Street, Lostwithiel, Cornwall PL22 0BW
Tel/Fax: 01208 872304
website: www.wattstrading.co.uk

The advertising signs in the window of **Watts Trading** were left behind by a previous owner of this handsome Georgian Grade II listed building and are misleading. Today, the shop is stocked with an enormous variety of environmentally friendly products, a reflection of owner Denise Watts's philosophy and lifestyle. Her aim, she says, is "to use products that have not harmed the planet by their production, and that will rot back into the earth when they have reached the end of their useful life".

So you'll find wool and woollen goods made from Cornish sheep and goats; bio-degradable cleaning products; one of the biggest selections of natural brushes in the country; organic pre-packaged food; local and fair trade products, including some very beautiful baskets and bags; and much, much more. The shop also sells the amazing Earthborn claypaint, the only environmental paint sold in the UK with the European eco label.

Visitors and locals alike love the smell and atmosphere of the shop and are intrigued by the curved wall that hides the wonderful staircase. This is a great place to stock up on essential supplies and to buy those special gifts and treats.

📖 stories and anecdotes   🐦 famous people   🎨 art and craft   🎭 entertainment and sport   🚶 walks

HOME STORE

8 Queen Street, Lostwithiel, Cornwall
PL22 0AB
Tel: 01208 873228
e-mail: adavidge@yahoo.com

Occupying the ground floor of a Georgian town house, **Home Store** is the creation of Amanda Davidge who has always had a love of antiques, especially kitchenalia. Having bought and sold at fairs and flea markets for her own collection, she decided in 2004 to open her own shop specialising in kitchen related antiques and collectables. It is decorated with bunting hanging from the ceiling, and old enamel signs and willow heart wreaths hang on the walls. The shop is crammed full of items relating to the home – anything from 1930s enamel bread bins to Victorian pine dressers.

There are kitchen cabinets from the 1940s, and pine kitchen tables are arrayed with a collection of country pottery ranging from old sponge ware to Caroline Zoob mugs. Among the more unusual products are the aprons and peg bags which are hand-made in Cornwall using vintage American fabric. Amanda also stocks these fabrics and can send them through mail order. Outside the shop is an area displaying gardening bygones – Victorian pots, vintage garden tools, herbs and seasonal plants.

THE STUDIO GALLERY

28 Fore Street, Lostwithiel, Cornwall PL22 0BL
Tel: 01208 873313
e-mail: info@constancewoodartist.com
website: www.constancewoodartist.com

The Studio Gallery in Lostwithiel provides a showcase for the work of Constance Wood who is not only an accomplished artist but also makes stylish jewellery and handbags. Constance lives in a house overlooking the rolling Cornish countryside so the sky, land and sea are a constant influence in her work. She is fascinated, she says, by "the way the light reflects and moves across water and hills, dramatic sunsets and fabulous cloud patterns". Her atmospheric works, many of them marine paintings, especially of yacht racing and tall ships, have been exhibited in the UK and in Venice.

The Gallery also exhibits rare lithographic prints from famous artists such as Louis Wain and Margaret Tarrant, and there are fantastic pieces for all ages, like the faery prints, and the classic *Midsummer Night's Dream* prints by Arthur Rackham which are all elegantly mounted and make perfect gifts. So do the exclusive handbags, purses and jewellery created by Constance. "I source unusual vintage or luxurious fabrics for the bags, unusual gemstones for my jewellery, and then design, create, paint, silversmith or sew everything myself." She adds: "I hope you like what I create; it comes from the heart."

perfectly describes its location. This small market town was the 13th century capital of Cornwall. As one of the stannary towns, tin and other raw materials were brought here for assaying and onward transportation until the mining activity cause the quay to silt up and the port moved further down river.

Lostwithiel was also a major crossing point on the River Fowey and the bridge seen today was completed in Tudor times. Beside the riverbank lies the tranquil **Coulson Park**, named after the American millionaire, Nathaniel Coulson, who grew up in Lostwithiel. On the opposite bank of the river from the town lies **Bonconnoc Estate**, the home of the Pitt family who gave Britain two Prime Ministers: William Pitt the Elder and his son, William Pitt the Younger.

Throughout the town there are reminders to Lostwithiel's once important status including the remains of the 13th century **Great Hall**, which served as the stannary offices, and the early 18th century **Guild Hall**. Built by Richard, Lord Edgcumbe, this building is now occupied by the **Lostwithiel Museum** (free). It tells the story of this interesting town as well as displaying photographs of everyday life from the late 1800s to the present day.

Lostwithiel's strategic position as a riverside port and crossing place, led to the construction of **Restormel Castle** upstream from the town high on a mound overlooking the wooded Fowey valley. The Black Prince stayed here in 1354 and 1365 but following the loss of Gascony soon afterwards, most of the contents of any value were removed and the castle was left to fall into ruin. In summer, the site is one of the best picnic spots in Cornwall, boasting stunning views of the peaceful surrounding countryside.

LANREATH
5½ miles NW of Looe off the B3359

🏛 Lanreath Folk & Farm Museum

This pretty village of traditional cob cottages is home to the **Lanreath Folk and Farm Museum**, found in Lanreath's old tithe barn. There are numerous vintage exhibits here, many of which can be touched, including old agricultural implements, mill workings, engines, tractors, a traditional farmhouse kitchen and a bric-a-brac shop. Craft workshops and a pets' corner complete the museum.

Launceston

🏛 St Mary Magdalene Church

🏛 Launceston Castle   🚂 Launceston Steam Railway

🚶 Tamar Valley Discovery Trail

Situated on the eastern edge of Bodmin Moor close to the county border with Devon, Launceston (pronounced locally Lawnson) is one of Cornwall's most pleasant inland towns and was a particular favourite of Sir John Betjeman. The capital of Cornwall until 1838, it guarded the main overland route into the county. Shortly after the Norman Conquest, William I's half-brother, Robert of Mortain, built the massive **Launceston Castle** overlooking the River Kensey. Visited by the Black Prince and seized by Cornish rebels in 1549, the castle changed hands twice during the Civil War before becoming an assize court and prison. George Fox, the founder of the Society of Friends was detained here in 1656. The court was famous for imprisoning and executing 'on the nod'. Although now in ruins, the 12-foot thick walls of the keep and tower can still be seen.

🎭 stories and anecdotes   🐦 famous people   🎨 art and craft   ✒ entertainment and sport   🚶 walks

VG.DELI.CO

6-8 Church Street, Launceston, Cornwall PL15 8AP
Tel/Fax: 01566 779494
e-mail: vgdelico@tiscali.co.uk
website: vghampers.co.uk

Located in the heart of Launceston, opposite the 16th century St Mary's Church, **vg.deli.co** has gone from strength to strength since Victoria Goach first opened here in October 2000. Before that, Victoria had spent the previous 15 years working in the catering industry and the wine trade. Many of the products on sale in her delicatessen are sourced in the South West, including no fewer than 25 cheeses from Cornwall, as well as locally produced chocolates, organic vegetables, soft drinks, wine, cider and beer. But you'll also find regional products from around the UK, items from Italy, Spain, France, South America and Asia.

Wherever possible, Victoria selects Fair Trade and organic products. The shop also sells ready meals made with finest local ingredients, along with sandwiches, savoury tarts and cakes which are freshly made on the premises each day. Victoria also provides outside catering for offices and private parties, and if you can't get to the shop, you can order hampers either by phone or through the website. The hampers are packed full of either Cornish goodies, organic delicacies or 'foodies' favourites.

MAGNIFFYSCENT

Unit 7, White Hart Arcade, Launceston,
Cornwall PL15 8AA
Tel/Fax: 01566 779671
e-mail: tremac915@aol.com

Established in 2001, **Magniffyscent** provides its customers with a wide range of environmentally friendly aromatherapy and other products. Owner Cath Tremain has gathered together a huge selection that includes the Meadowsweet range which, for example, always uses glass containers since these can be recycled.

Their ingredients are obtained from natural sources such as herbs and plants which are of course bio-degradable. They do not test their products on animals and all their literature is printed on paper supplied by a company which plants three trees for every one it cuts down.

Magniffyscent also stocks B Natural Skincare products which are hand-made by a family business in Bodmin which has a similar policy to Meadowsweet. Their extensive range includes beeswax creams and salves, lavender-based cleansers, creams and moisturisers, and a wide variety of other creams, oils, balms and moisturisers. Also available Essential Oils and oil-based products (bath bombs, salts etc), gift ideas including crystals, range of imported candles from Austria, relaxation music CDs from New World Music.

The most striking building in the town however is **St Mary Magdalene Church**. Its walls of sturdy Cornish granite are covered with delicate carvings that include angels, roses, pomegranates and heraldic emblems. The church was built by a local landowner, Sir Henry Trecarrel, in the early 1500s. He had started building a manor house nearby when both his beloved wife and infant son died within days of each other. Overwhelmed with grief, Sir Henry abandoned the manor house and devoted the rest of his life to building this magnificent church in their memory.

Launceston Castle

stories and anecdotes   famous people   art and craft   entertainment and sport   walks

Elsewhere in the town, the streets around the castle are filled with handsome buildings including the impressive **Lawrence House** that was built in 1753 for a wealthy local lawyer. Given to the National Trust to help preserve the character of the street, the house is home to a **Museum**, which dedicates its numerous displays to the history of the area. To the west of the town and running through the beautiful Kensey Valley, the **Launceston Steam Railway** takes visitors on a nostalgic and scenic journey back in time. Travelling in either open or closed carriages, passengers can enjoy a round trip along five miles of narrow-gauge track to Newmills and back. The locomotives used to haul the trains were built in the 1880s and 1890s by the famous Hunslet Engine Company of Leeds and once worked on the slate carrying lines high in the mountains of North Wales.

Launceston is also the start, or the finish, of the **Tamar Valley Discovery Trail**, a 30-mile footpath from here to Plymouth that takes in many of the villages scattered along the Cornwall-Devon border. Passing through old mining country, past market gardens and through ancient river ports, walkers of the trail will also see the wealth of bird, plant and wildlife that the varying habitats along the way support. In 1995, the Tamar Valley was designated an Area of Outstanding Natural Beauty.

Around Launceston

GUNNISLAKE
10 miles SE of Launceston on the A390

Often referred to as the first village in Cornwall, it was here in the 1520s that Sir

LAKESIDE GALLERY

nr Treburley, Launceston,
Cornwall PL15 9NW
Tel/Fax: 01579 370760
e-mail: roger@lakeside-gallery.com
website: www.lakeside-gallery.com

Artists Linda and Roger Garland have spent the past 20 years sympathetically renovating a Cornish barn complex to create a home, art gallery and holiday cottages. Lakeside Gallery & Cottages are located in a peaceful pastoral setting between Dartmoor and Bodmin Moor near the Tamar Valley. The Garlands personally make all visitors welcome. The gallery was established in 1989 with the primary aim of promoting book illustration as a serious art form to a wider audience. Lakeside Gallery has gained a reputation for showing quality artwork and features work by both artists and their son, Seth. Permanently on show is the Tolkien Collection, more that 70 paintings and drawings commissioned by the original publishers for many of JRR Tolkien's titles including *The Lord of the Rings*. In the main gallery, many original drawings and prints for other projects and private work are exhibited.

The renovated cottages on the 70-acre estate are available for holiday letting from April to October. 'Shirebourne' which sleeps three, and Brandywine (sleeps four) are in a separate wing and form two well-appointed units. Short breaks and weekend bookings accepted.

🏢 historic building   🏛 museum   🏛 historic site   🔾 scenic attraction   🌱 flora and fauna

Piers Edgcumbe built the **New Bridge** over the River Tamar that continues to serve as one of the major gateways into the county. In fact, this 180-foot-long granite structure remained the lowest crossing of the river by road right up until the 1960s when the massive suspension bridge linking Saltash with Plymouth was opened. The 16th century bridge meant that this charming village also had an important strategic value. During the Civil War, it was the centre of bitter fighting. In the 18th and 19th centuries the village came alive with mining. Though the mines have closed some of the mine buildings have been immortalised by Turner in his great painting, *Crossing the Brook*, that also captures Gunnislake's famous bridge. The River Tamar is tidal as far as the weir upstream near Newbridge and salmon fishermen continue to come to Gunnislake, as they have done since medieval times, to catch the fish as they travel up river to their spawning grounds.

Cotehele House

CALSTOCK
12 miles SE of Launceston off the A390

🏠 Cotehele House

Well known for its splendid views of the Tamar Valley, the origins of the village go back beyond the Romans. As well as being settled by Romans in search of tin, at the time of the Domesday Book the manor of Calstock was owned by Asgar the Saxon. The village was an important river port in the 19th century when vast quantities of tin, granite and copper ore were brought here for loading on to barges to be transported down the Tamar to the coast. In the countryside surrounding Calstock the remains of old mine workings, along with the spoil heaps, can still be seen along with the remains of the village's boat-building industry. The decline of Calstock as a port came with the construction of the huge **Railway Viaduct**, which carries the Tamar Valley Line southwards to Plymouth. Completed in 1908, this giant 12-arched viaduct, the first in the country to be constructed of concrete blocks, stands 120 feet above the river. Probably one of Britain's most picturesque branch lines, the **Tamar Valley Line** can still be taken down to the coast. Though the river has lost most of its commercial traffic, it is a starting point for Tamar River canoe expeditions.

Just to the southwest of the village lies one of the best preserved medieval estates in the

LOUIS' TEA ROOMS

*Kit Hill Approach Road, Callington,
Cornwall PL17 8AX
Tel: 01579 389223*

At 800ft above sea level, **Louis' Tea Rooms** must be one of the loftiest in the land. Perched on the south side of Kit Hill, the tea rooms command unspoilt views over the Tamar Valley all the way to Plymouth, the sea and even beyond on a good day. Kit Hill itself was presented to the people of Cornwall by Prince Charles, Duke of Cornwall, to commemorate the birth of his first son, Prince William. It is now a 400-acre countryside park within whose boundaries at least 18 Neolithic burial mounds have been identified.

Husband and wife team Rich and Cath Roche took over the tea rooms in 2005 and offer an appetising and extensive menu. Naturally, cornish cream teas and the home-made cakes are very popular but you'll also find a choice of all day breakfasts, including vegetarian versions; main meals such as steak & ale pudding or home-made macaroni cheese; salads, jacket potatoes, burgers, freshly prepared sandwiches, and light bites such as cheese on toast. At Sunday lunchtime, a delicious roast dinner is served, with a nut roast available as a vegetarian alternative. All the meat served is British, and wherever possible local products are used.

The Tamar Otter Sanctuary

*North Petherwin, Nr Launceston,
Cornwall PL15 8GW Tel: 01566 785646*

A branch of the famous Otter Trust, the **Tamar Otter Sanctuary** is dedicated to breeding otters for release into the wild to save the species from extinction in lowland England. Visitors can watch the otters at play and in their breeding dens (holts), and see orphaned cubs in the rehabilitation centre. Also here are a dormouse conservation project, a visitor centre, refreshment and gift shop, lakes with waterfowl and an area of woodland where fallow and Muntjac deer roam freely. Pheasants, peacocks and wallabies can also be seen at the sanctuary, which is located at North Petherwin five miles northwest of Launceston off the B3254 Bude road.

🏛 historic building   🏛 museum   🏛 historic site   🔶 scenic attraction   🌱 flora and fauna

Trust). Mainly built between 1485 and 1539, this low granite fortified manor house was the principal home of the Edgcumbe family until the mid-16th century when they moved their main residence to Mount Edgcumbe. Along with its Great Tudor Hall, fabulous Flemish and Mortlake tapestries and period furniture, the house incorporates some charming features such as the secret spy-hole in the Great Hall and a tower clock with a bell but no face or hands. Surrounding the house are, firstly, the grounds, containing exotic and tender plants that thrive in the mild valley climate and beyond that the estate with its ancient network of pathways that allow exploration of the valley.

The River Tamar runs through the estate and close to an old cider house and mill is **Cotehele Quay**, a busy river port in Victorian times. The quay buildings now house an outstation of the National Maritime Museum, an art and craft gallery and a licensed tea room. The restored Tamar sailing barge *Shamrock* is moored alongside the museum.

CALLINGTON
9½ miles S of Launceston on the A388

Situated on the fertile land between the rivers Tamar and Lynher, Callington is now rich fruit growing country. During the 19th century, the surrounding landscape was very different as it was alive with frantic mining activity. The area's heritage, landscape and character are

depicted on many of the walls of the town's buildings, thanks to the interesting and unusual **Mural Project**.

About a mile outside the town, **Dupath Holy Well** is enclosed in a fine granite building of 1510. The water in the basin was believed to cure whooping cough.

Overlooking the River Lynher, southwest of this old market town, lies **Cadsonbury Hillfort** – a massive Iron Age bank and ditch that are thought to be the remains of a local chief's home. To the northeast lies **Kit Hill**, now a country park, where a 19th century chimney stack built to serve one of the area's mines adds a further 80 feet to the hill's summit.

NORTH PETHERWIN
5 miles NW of Launceston off the B3254

🐾 Tamar Otter Sanctuary

Found above the River Ottery, this village is home to the **Tamar Otter Sanctuary** (see panel opposite) a branch of the famous Otter Trust, dedicated to breeding young otters for release into the wild to prevent the species from becoming extinct in lowland England. Visitors can watch the otters playing in large natural enclosures, see them in their breeding dens, or holts, and watch the orphans in the rehabilitation centre. Also here are a dormouse conservation project, refreshment and gift shop, lakes with waterfowl and an area of woodland where fallow and Muntjac deer roam freely.

2 | Devon

Asked to describe the "ideal" English countryside, many people would conjure up a landscape of green rolling hills, of bright, fresh streams tumbling through wooded valleys, of white thatched cottages clustering around a venerable church, with a picturesque inn nestling beside it. Devon, of course, but only part of it. The whole of the Dartmoor National Park lies within its boundaries, a huge area of dome-shaped granite where the most frequently seen living creatures are the famous Dartmoor ponies which have roamed here since at least the 10th century.

Haytor Rocks, Dartmoor

The moor is notorious for its abundant rainfall – an annual average of 60 inches, twice as much as falls on Torbay, a few miles to the east. In some of the more exposed westerly fringes, an annual rainfall of 100 inches is common. In prehistoric times the climate was much drier and warmer. The moor then was dotted with settlements and this Bronze Age population left behind them a rich legacy of stone circles, menhirs, burial chambers, and single, double or even triple rows of stones. The row of 150 stones on Stall Moor above Burrator Reservoir is believed to be the longest prehistoric stone row in the world.

Then there's the busy port of Plymouth with its proud maritime history and associations with Sir Francis Drake and the Pilgrim Fathers. The rugged coastline to the north contrasts with the almost Mediterranean character of Torbay – the "English Riviera". There are hundreds of picture postcard villages, of which Clovelly and Inner Hope are perhaps the most famous, and scores of delightful small towns such as Salcombe, Totnes and Dartmouth.

The county also boasts some outstanding buildings. The Gothic masterpiece of Exeter Cathedral has been described as "one of the supreme architectural pleasures of England", and it was a 14th century Bishop of Exeter who built the glorious parish church of Ottery St Mary. The sumptuous mansion of Saltram House near Plymouth contains fine work by Robert Adam, Sir Joshua Reynolds and Thomas Chippendale, while Buckland Abbey is famed as the home of the Drake family and their most famous son, Sir Francis. Arlington Court is notable for the eclectic collections amassed by its last owner, Rosalie Chichester, during the course of a long life, and the now redundant church at Parracombe is a "time warp" building still just as it was in the 18th century.

Part of Devon's enormous charm derives from the fact that it is so lightly populated. Just over a million people, roughly equivalent to the population of Birmingham, occupy the third largest county in England, some 670,000 acres in all. And most of those million people live in towns and resorts along its coastline, leaving huge tracts of countryside where the villages, the lanes and byways are still magically peaceful.

LOCATOR MAP

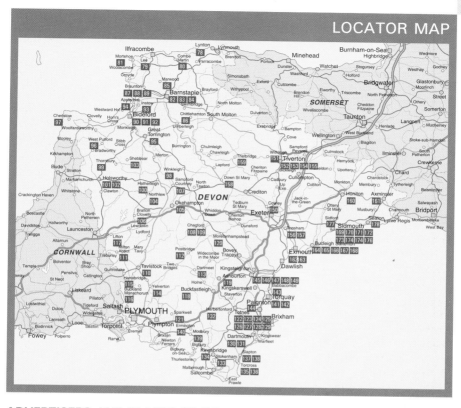

ADVERTISERS AND PLACES OF INTEREST

Continued Overleaf

🎭 stories and anecdotes   🐦 famous people   🎨 art and craft   🎢 entertainment and sport   🚶 walks

🏠 historic building   🏛 museum   🏚 historic site   🌿 scenic attraction   🌱 flora and fauna

Lynton

Lynton and Lynmouth, though often mentioned in the same breath, are very different in character. Lynton is the younger of the two settlements and sits atop a great cliff 600ft high; Lynmouth, far below, clusters around the junction of the East and West Lyn rivers just before they reach the sea.

Lynton is a bright and breezy village, its houses and terraces mostly Victorian. The **Exmoor Museum**, housed in a restored 16th century house, has an interesting collection of the tools and products of bygone local craftsmen and other exhibits relating to the area.

If you are visiting Lynton in August, you won't be able to avoid the odd characters standing in gardens and doorways, sitting on roofs or shinning up drainpipes. Don't worry – they are just participating in the **Lynton & Lynmouth Scarecrow Festival,** a popular event that has become the largest and longest running such festival in the West Country.

To the west of Lynton, about a mile or so along a minor road, is one of the most remarkable natural features in Devon, the **Valley of the Rocks.** When the poet Robert Southey visited the area in 1800, he was most impressed by this natural gorge *"covered with huge stones...the very bones and skeletons of the earth; rock reeling upon rock, stone piled upon stone, a huge terrific mass"*. In *Lorna Doone*, the author RD Blackmore transforms the site into the

"Devil's Cheesering" where Jan Ridd visits Mother Meldrun who is sheltering under "eaves of lichened rock". And it was after walking along the clifftop path, more than 1,300ft above the sea, in company with William Wordsworth and his sister Dorothy, that S.T. Coleridge was inspired to write his immortal *Rime of the Ancient Mariner*.

An unusual attraction in the valley is its herd of feral goats, introduced here in the 1970s. A good time to see them is in January when the nannies give birth to their kids.

LYNMOUTH
1 mile E of Lynton on the A39

🐾 Lynmouth Pottery   🍃 Watersmeet

🐾 Exmoor Brass Rubbing Centre

Lynton is connected to its sister-village Lynmouth by an ingenious cliff railway which, when it opened on Easter Monday 1890, was the first of its kind in Britain. A gift from Sir George Newnes, the publisher and newspaper tycoon, the railway is powered by water, or rather by two 700-gallon water tanks, one at each end of the 450ft track. When the tank at the top is filled, and the one at the bottom emptied, the brakes are released and the two passenger carriages change place.

For centuries, the people of Lynmouth subsisted on agriculture and fishing, especially herring fishing and curing. By good fortune, just as the herring

shoals were moving away to new waters, the North Devon coast benefited from the two new enthusiasms for "romantic" scenery and sea bathing. Coleridge and Wordsworth arrived here on a walking tour in the 1790s, Shelley wrote fondly of his visit in 1812, and it was Robert Southey, later Poet Laureate, who first used the designation "the English Switzerland" to describe the dramatic scenery of the area. The painter Gainsborough had already described it as "the most delightful place for a landscape painter this country can boast". One of the most picturesque villages in Devon, Lynmouth also has a tiny harbour surrounded by lofty wooded hills, a curious Rhenish Tower on the pier, and do seek out Mars Hill, an eye-ravishing row of thatched cottages.

Understandably, this lovely setting acts as a magnet for artists and craftspeople. People like Peter Allen, for example, whose

Lynmouth Harbour

Lynmouth Pottery is very much a pottery with a difference. For one thing, it's a working pottery and one of the few places where you can try out your own skills at the potter's wheel. (Children too are encouraged to have a go). If you're not totally ashamed of the result, Peter Allen will then fire the finished item and post it on to you. Many a visitor to Lynmouth Pottery has discovered an unsuspected talent for turning slippery clay into a quite presentable decorative piece. More hands-on experience is offered at the **Exmoor Brass Rubbing and Hobby Craft Centre** on Watersmeet Road. The first collection of brass rubbings was made by a man named Craven Ord between 1790 and 1830. His collection is now housed in the British Museum but because of his method – pouring printer's ink into the engraved lines and then pressing a sheet of damp tissue paper on the brass – the results are often very poor. It was the Victorians who developed a process using heelball (shoemaker's black wax) and white paper that is still in use today. The Centre provides all the necessary materials and friendly instruction.

If you continue along Watersmeet Road you will come to the popular beauty spot of **Watersmeet,** where the East Lyn river and Hoar Oak Water come together. An 1832 fishing lodge, Watersmeet House, stands close by. A National Trust property, it is open during the season as a café, shop and information centre where you can pick up leaflets detailing some beautiful circular walks, starting here, along the East Lyn valley and to Hoar Oak Water.

Lynmouth's setting beside its twin rivers is undeniably beautiful, but it has also proved to be tragically vulnerable. On the night of August 16th, 1952, a cloudburst over Exmoor deposited nine inches of rain onto an already saturated moor. In the darkness, the normally placid East and West Lyn rivers became raging cataracts and burst their banks. Sweeping tree trunks and boulders along with it, the torrent smashed its way through the village, destroying dozens of houses and leaving 34 people dead. That night saw many freak storms across southern England, but none had matched the ferocity of the deluge that engulfed this pretty little village. The Flood Memorial Hall has an exhibition that details the events of that terrible night.

An earlier exceptional storm, in 1899, involved the Lynmouth lifeboat in a tale of epic endurance. A full-rigged ship, the *Forest Hall,* was in difficulties off Porlock, but the storm was so violent it was impossible to launch the lifeboat at Lynmouth. Instead, the crewmen dragged their three-and-a-half ton boat, the *Louisa,* the 13 miles across the moor. Along the way they had to negotiate Countisbury Hill, with a gradient of 1,000ft over two miles, before dropping down to Porlock Weir where the *Louisa* was successfully launched and every crew member of the stricken ship was saved.

Ilfracombe

⚲ Landmark Theatre		🏛 Chapel of St Nicholas	
🏛 Tunnel Baths		🐦 Ilfracombe Aquarium	
🏛 Old Corn Mill		🏛 Chambercombe Manor	

Like Barnstaple, Ilfracombe takes its floral decorations very seriously – during the 1990s the town was a consistent winner of the Britain in Bloom Competition. Between June and October the town goes "blooming mad" with streets, parks and hotels awash with flowers. Ilfracombe also promotes itself as a

"Festival Town" offering a wide variety of events. They include a Victorian Celebration in mid-June when local people don period costumes. A grand costume ball and a fireworks display all add to the fun. There's the National Youth Arts Festival in July, a Fishing Festival in early August, a Carnival Procession later that month, and many more.

A fairly recent addition to the town's amenities is **The Landmark Theatre**, a striking building with what look like two gleaming white truncated cooling towers as its main feature. This multi-purpose arts centre has a 480-seat theatre, cinema screening facilities, a spacious display area and a café-bar with a sunny, sea facing terrace.

With a population of around 11,000, Ilfracombe is the largest seaside resort on the North Devon coast. Up until 1800, however, it was just a small fishing and market town relying entirely on the sea both for its living and as its principal means of communication. The boundaries of the old town are marked by a sheltered natural harbour to the north, and, half-a-mile away to the south, a part-Norman parish church boasting one of the finest medieval waggon roofs in the West Country.

The entrance to Ilfracombe harbour is guarded by Lantern Hill, a steep-sided conical rock which is crowned by the restored medieval **Chapel of St Nicholas**. For centuries, this highly conspicuous former fishermen's chapel has doubled as a lighthouse, the light being placed in a lantern at the western end of the building. St Nicholas must surely be the only ecclesiastical building in the country to be managed by the local Rotary Club – it was they who raised the funds for its restoration. From the chapel's hilltop setting there are superb views of Ilfracombe,

its busy harbour and the craggy North Devon coastline.

Like so many west country resorts, Ilfracombe developed in response to the early-19th century craze for sea bathing and sea water therapies. The **Tunnel Baths,** with their extravagant Doric façade, were opened in Bath Place in 1836, by which time a number of elegant residential terraces had been built on the hillside to the south of the old town.

The arrival of the railway in 1874 brought an even larger influx of visitors to Ilfracombe. Much of the town's architecture, which could best be described as "decorated Victorian vernacular", dates from this period, the new streets spreading inland in steeply undulating rows. Around the same time the harbour was enlarged to cope with the paddle steamers bringing in tourists from Bristol and South Wales. Today, visitors can take advantage of regular sailings from that harbour to Lundy Island, as well as cruises along the spectacular Exmoor coast.

Standing beside the harbour is the **Ilfracombe Aquarium,** housed in the former lifeboat house. It contains an impressive collection of both freshwater and marine species in carefully re-created natural habitats. Worth a visit is the fun fish retail area here.

For walkers, the **South West Coast Path** from Ilfracombe provides some spectacular scenery, whether going west to Capstone Point, or east to Hillsborough Hill.

Just to the east of Ilfracombe, at Hele Bay, **The Old Corn Mill & Pottery** is unique in North Devon. Dating back to the 16th century, the mill has been lovingly restored from near dereliction and is now producing 100% wholemeal stone-ground flour for sale. In Robin Gray's pottery, you can watch him in action at the potter's wheel and try your own

THE OLD SCHOOLROOM GIFT & CRAFT SHOP

Lee, nr Ilfracombe, Devon EX34 8LW
Tel: 01271 864141

Situated next to the church and just a few minutes walk from scenic Lee Bay, The Old Schoolroom Gift & Craft Shop occupies a sturdy Victorian building with plenty of space to display Carol Porton's intriguing selection of gifts and crafts.
An ideal place to browse while seeking out your holiday gifts, the shop offers a wide selection that includes jewellery, glassware, pottery, cards, local scenes, fudge and biscuits. The shop is open every day from early April to late October, fromm 11am to 5pm, Sunday to Friday, and from 2pm to 5pm on Saturday.

skill in fashioning slippery clay into a more-or-less recognisable object. If you really want to keep the result, the pottery will fire and glaze it, and post it on to you.

Half a mile or so south of the mill, set in a secluded valley, **Chambercombe Manor** is an 11th century mansion which was first recorded in the Domesday Book. Visitors have access to eight rooms displaying period furniture from Elizabethan to Victorian times, can peek into the claustrophobic Priest's Hole, and test their sensitivity to the spectral presences reputed to inhabit the Haunted Room. The Coat of Arms bedroom was once occupied by Lady Jane Grey and it is her family's arms that are displayed above the fireplace. Outside, the four acres of beautiful grounds contain wildfowl ponds, a bird sanctuary and an arboretum.

Chambercombe Manor

Combe Martin, Devon EX34 9RJ
Tel: 01271 862624

Although the manor here was mentioned in the Domesday Book, the present **Chambercombe Manor** was not built until the 12th century and it still retains much of its medieval charm and character today. When, exactly, it fell from being a manor house to a farmhouse is unknown but fortunately such features as its plaster frieze and barrel ceiling in on the bedrooms can still be seen. Displaying period furniture from Elizabethan times up to the Victorian era, this is a delightful house that allows visitors to soak up the atmosphere of what was also a family home. Along with the Great Hall, there is the private chapel of the Champernon family, the manor's first owners, an old kitchen and the Coat of Arms bedroom that was once occupied by Lady Jane Grey and it is the Grey coat of arms, who were descendants of the Champernons, that is depicted above the fireplace. Meanwhile, outside there is a paved courtyard, with ornamental ponds, a delightful garden of lawns, shrubbery and herbaceous borders, and a water garden beyond which lie the extensive grounds that take in the peaceful, secluded wooded valley in which the manor house is situated.

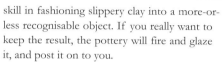 stories and anecdotes 🍂 famous people 🎨 art and craft 🎭 entertainment and sport 🚶 walks

South West Coast Path and Woody Bay

Distance: *6.0 miles (9.7 kilometres)*

Typical time: *180 mins*

Height gain: *200 metres*

Map: *Outdoor Leisure 9*

Walk: *www.walkingworld.com ID:309*

Contributor: *Bryan Cath*

ACCESS INFORMATION:

From the Ilfracombe direction go towards Combe Martin on the A399, continuing through Combe Martin and on up the winding road until it eventually straightens out. After a while the first turning on your left comes up, signposted to Hunters Inn. Take this road and keep on it all the way to Hunters Inn. Park in the car park opposite the toilets. From other directions, pick up the A399 Ilfracombe to South Molton road, and Hunters Inn is signed off this road above Combe Martin.

DESCRIPTION:

This walk will take you along a section of the South West Coast Path that is often considered to be one of the most scenic sections of its whole 630 miles. It starts by following the old coaching road giving easy walking and amazing views. On reaching the aptly-named Woody Bay, clothed mainly in sessile oak, you return via the lower coast path, locally known as the 'goat path', being narrow and closer to the sea and cliffs. You pass by one of the highest waterfalls along this section of the coast, overlook a rock arch and generally experience some wonderful coastal scenery.

FEATURES:

River, sea, pub, toilets, National Trust/ NTS, wildlife, birds, flowers, great views.

WALK DIRECTIONS:

1 | Having parked in the car park opposite the toilets and National Trust shop, walk back towards the Hunters Inn and take the road on the right of the inn, continuing ahead when the road turns right up the hill.

2 | Go through the facing gate and follow the sign to Woody Bay 2.75 miles, on the wider track ahead.

3 | This climb brings you above Heddon's Mouth, with glorious views over the valley.

4 | Follow this track all the way to Woody Bay, with wonderful coastal views, to reach the gate by a hairpin bend.

5 | Follow the road down, following the left-hand fork to the car park.

6 | Have a look at the National Trust information board on the area, then continue down the hill to the small road that goes hard back on the left down through the woods,

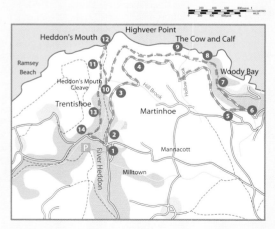

signposted to Martinhoe Manor. Follow this down through the woods, past Wringapeak House to the hairpin bend and carry on straight ahead over the stile, signposted Coastpath to Hunters Inn.

7 | Follow the sign to Hunters Inn, up through the woods, with views on your right (leaves permitting) of Lee Abbey and the Valley of Rocks, with Foreland Point lighthouse flashing in the distance.

8 | Carry on and over the stile, now being wary of the drop on your right!

9 | Soon you come to a high waterfall in a lovely valley. Carry on out to the point; a pause to look at the rock arch and surrounding scenery is most rewarding. Carry on up between the heather, around the next rocky point to more spectacular cliff scenery. Continue round the next two rocky points and down into the Heddon Valley.

10 | When the path reaches the Heddon Valley path, turn hard right and walk down by the river to Heddon's Mouth.

11 | Cross the bridge by the picnic area and continue down to reach the beach.

12 | Having visited the beach and newly-restored limekiln, return to the picnic area by the bridge and continue across it, with the river on your left. In a while ignore the path going down to your left.

13 | Pass through the gate and continue ahead, ignoring the signpost to Combe Martin up to the right, instead continuing along the level path.

14 | On reaching the gate by the road, pass through and turn left to follow the small road over the bridge and on back to Hunters Inn. Be aware of cars, particularly on the narrow bends.

BERRYNARBOR
3 miles E of Ilfracombe off the A399

🏠 St Peter's Church   🏠 Watermouth Castle

Nestling in a steep-sided combe, Berrynarbor is a wonderfully unspoilt village set around **St Peter's Church** which, with its 96ft high tower, is one of the grandest churches in North Devon. Inside, there's an interesting collection of monuments, many of them memorials of the Berry family, once the owners of the nearby 15th century manor house which later became the village school.

On the coast here is the pretty cove of Watermouth and the Victorian folly, **Watermouth Castle,** which has been transformed into a family theme park. In the castle's great hall, there's a collection of suits of armour and visitors can enjoy mechanical music demonstrations. Elsewhere, there are displays on Victorian life, antique pier machines, a room devoted to model railways and, down in the depths of the dungeon labyrinths, fairy tales come to life.

COMBE MARTIN
4 miles E of Ilfracombe on the A399

🏛 Combe Martin Museum   🐾 Exmoor Zoological Park

🐾 Wildlife & Dinosaur Park   🏠 Pack o' Cards Inn

Just a short distance from Berrynarbor, on the other side of the River Umber, is another popular resort, Combe Martin. There's a good sandy beach here and a short walk will take you to one of the secluded bays. An added attraction, especially for children, is the large number of rock pools amongst the bays. In the village itself, the main street is more than two miles long, reputed to be the longest in the country and featuring a wide selection of inns, cafés and shops. As well as the **Combe Martin Museum**, there is also the **Wildlife**

and Dinosaur Park where life-sized animated dinosaurs lurk in the woods. The 25-acre site also shelters 250 species of real animals, including a large and lively collection of apes and monkeys. Within the park are animal handling areas, an "Earthquake Ride", a dinosaur museum and oriental gardens. There's an otter pool and daily sea lion shows and falconry displays, and if you book ahead you can experience the unique thrill of swimming with the sea lions.

Combe Martin

A remarkable architectural curiosity in the village itself is **The Pack o' Cards Inn**, built by Squire George Ley in the early 18th century with the proceeds of a highly successful evening at the card table. This Grade II listed building represents a pack of cards with four decks, or floors, 13 rooms, and a total of 52 windows. Inside there are many features representing the cards in each suit.

About five miles to the east of Arlington Court, **Exmoor Zoological Park** is home to more than 170 species of unusual and exotic animals and birds. The residents of the 12 acres of gardens here range from pygmy marmosets to tarantulas, from penguins to catybara. Children can enjoy close encounters with many of the more cuddly animals, there are informative talks by the keepers but, as at any zoo, the most magnetic visitor attraction is the feeding time for the various animals.

PARRACOMBE

13 miles SE of Ilfracombe off the A39

🏛 Church of St Petrock

The redundant **Church of St Petrock** is

notable for its marvellously unspoilt interior, complete with 15th century benches, 17th century box pews, a Georgian pulpit and a perfectly preserved musician's gallery. Perhaps most striking of all is the unique gated screen between the chancel and the nave which bears a huge tympanum painted with the royal arms, the Lord's Prayer, the Creed and the Ten Commandments. We owe the church's survival to John Ruskin who led the protests against its intended demolition in 1879 after another church was built lower down the hill.

The Exmoor National Park features hog-backed hills where rivers fall 1,500ft in less than four miles. The views are entrancing, preparing the traveller for the quite astonishing loveliness of those inseparable twins, Lynton and Lynmouth, just a few miles further on.

MORTEHOE

4 miles W of Ilfracombe off the B3343

🌳 Barricane Beach

Mortehoe is the most north-westerly village in Devon and its name, meaning "raggy stump", reflects the rugged character of the Morte peninsula. In this pretty stone-built village Mortehoe's part-Norman church is certainly

SHORE & MOOR

1 The Crescent, Mortehoe, North Devon EX34 7DX
Tel: 01271 870346
e-mail: graham@yeo9001.fsworld.co.uk

Located in the picturesque coastal village of Mortehoe, surrounded by beautiful National Trust land, Shore & Moor is a small and unique shop offering a wide range of unusual gifts, jewellery, local hand-thrown pottery and framed photographic prints of scenes of the lovely countryside around Mortehoe and Woolacombe. Shore & Moor also stocks a selection of cards and limited edition prints with a country theme by acclaimed artists Emma Ball and Alex Clark. Open every day, Shore & Moor also provides a bespoke framing service.

worth a visit. It's a small cruciform building with a 15th-century open-timbered wagon roof, an interesting early 14th century table tomb, a bell in the tower which may be the oldest in Devon, and a wonderful series of grotesquely carved Tudor bench ends. The church is also notable for the large mosaic of 1905 which fills the chancel arch. Designed by Selwyn Image, the Slade Professor of Art at Oxford, the mosaic was created by the same craftsmen who did the mosaics in St Paul's Cathedral.

A short walk from Mortehoe village leads you to the dramatic coastline, mortally dangerous to ships, but with exhilarating views across to Lundy Island. Much of this clifftop area is in the guardianship of the National Trust which also protects nearby **Barricane Beach** (remarkable for being formed almost entirely of sea shells washed here from the Caribbean), and the three-mile stretch of Woolacombe Sands.

WOOLACOMBE

7 miles SW of Ilfracombe on the B3343

🖉 Once Upon a Time

The wonderful stretch of golden sands at Woolacombe is justifiably regarded as the finest beach in North Devon. This favoured

resort lies between two dramatic headlands, both of which are now in the care of the National Trust. The sands and rock pools lying between these two outcrops are a delight for children, (along with the swing boats and donkey rides), and surfers revel in the monster waves rolling in from the Atlantic.

Back in the early 1800s, Woolacombe was little more than a hamlet whose few residents sustained a precarious livelihood by fishing. Then, suddenly, the leisured classes were seized by the craze for sea bathing initiated by George III at Weymouth and enthusiastically endorsed by his successor George IV at Brighton. Inspired by the economic success of those south coast towns, the two families who owned most of the land around Woolacombe, the Fortescues and the Chichesters, began constructing villas and hotels in the Regency style, elegant buildings which still endow the town with a very special charm and character. Many friends of the Fortescue and Chichester families regarded their initiative as a suicidally rash enterprise. Woolacombe was so remote and the roads of North Devon at that time still so primitive, little more than cart tracks. "Who," they asked, "would undertake such an arduous journey?" During the first few years only a

🎞 stories and anecdotes   🦃 famous people   🖉 art and craft   🖉 entertainment and sport   🦌 walks

trickle of well-to-do visitors in search of a novel (and comparatively inexpensive resort) found their way to Woolacombe. But their word of mouth recommendations soon ensured a steady flow of tourists, a flow which has swelled to a flood over subsequent years.

Just outside the town, **Once Upon a Time** provides a huge variety of entertainment for younger children, - indoor and outdoor play areas, crazy golf, a young scientist's room, children's driving school, train rides, animated fairy tales, an ocean of plastic balls to play through in the Wild Boar Adventure Trail, and much more.

Barnstaple

🏛 Pannier Market	🏛 St Ann's Chapel
🏛 Queen Anne's Walk	🏛 Railway Museum

Barnstaple enjoys a superb location at the head of the Taw estuary, at the furthest point downstream where it was possible to ford the river. The first bridge across the Taw was built in the late 1200s, but the present impressive structure, 700ft long with 16 arches, dates from about 1450 although it has been altered and widened many times.

Visitors will immediately realise that Barnstaple takes its floral decorations very seriously. The town began its association with the Britain in Bloom movement in 1991 and just five years later crowned its efforts by winning the Gold award for the "Prettiest Floral Town in Europe" in the Entente Florale Competition. Wherever you turn you may well find a magnificent display, - a haycart full of flowers outside the police station and civic centre, for example, a giant postage stamp modelled in blossoming plants outside the Post Office, or a stunning model of a train

(again, all created in flowers) at the entrance to the railway station.

The town's love of floral exuberance may be one of its most endearing features but Barnstaple is also the administrative and commercial capital of the region, a pre-eminence it already enjoyed when the Domesday Book recorded the town as one of only four boroughs in the county. Back then, in 1086, Barnstaple had its own mint and, already, a regular market. More than nine centuries later, the town still hosts produce markets every Tuesday and Friday, but the **Pannier Market** is open every weekday. This huge, glass-roofed building covering some 45,000 square feet was built in 1855 and its grandiose architecture resembles that of a major Victorian railway station, (London's St Pancras springs to mind). The Market takes it name from the pannier baskets, (two wicker baskets connected by a leather strap draped across the back of a donkey, pony or horse), in which country people in those days would carry their fruit and vegetables to town.

Just across the road from the Pannier Market is **Butchers Row,** a quaint line of booth-like Victorian shops built mostly of wood and with brightly painted wooden canopies. When they were built, back in 1855, they were occupied exclusively by butchers, but now you'll find a much wider variety of goods on sale – seaweed amongst them. Every week during the summer season at least 300lbs of this succulent algae are sold, most of it ending up as a breakfast dish, served with bacon and an egg on top.

In Barnstaple's High Street stands the rather austere **Guildhall,** built in the Grecian style in 1826 and now housing some interesting civic memorabilia – portraits, municipal regalia and silverware – which are occasionally on display.

Nearby, the **Church of St Peter and St Paul** dates back to the early 1300s. After having its spire twisted by a lightning strike in 1810, it suffered even more badly later that century under the heavy hand of the Victorian restorer, Sir Gilbert Scott. Much more appealing are the charming 17th century **Horwood's Almshouses** nearby, and the 15th century **St Anne's Chapel** which served for many years as the town's Grammar School. During the late 17th century John Gay, author of *The Beggar's Opera,* was numbered amongst its pupils. The town has other literary associations. William Shakespeare visited in 1605 and it was the sight of its narrow streets bustling with traders that inspired him to write *The Merchant of Venice.* The diarist Samuel Pepys married a 15-year-old Barnstaple girl in 1655.

As at Tiverton, the 17th century well-to-do residents of Barnstaple were given to charitable endowments. As well as Thomas Horwood's almshouses, Messrs. Paige and Penrose both bequeathed substantial funds for almshouses, and in 1659 Thomas' wife, Alice, paid for the building in Church Lane of a school for "20 poor maids". It is now a coffee house.

A slightly later building of distinction is **Queen Anne's Walk**, a colonnaded arcade with some lavish ornamentation and surmounted by a large statue of the Queen herself. Opened in 1708, it was used by the Barnstaple wool merchants who accepted that any verbal bargain they agreed over the Tome Stone was legally binding. The building stands on the old town quay from which, in 1588,

FOUR SEASONS RESTAURANT

27 Boutport Street, Barnstaple,
Devon EX31 1RP
Tel: 01271 325531

Although David Ker and Pat Holden only opened their Four Seasons Restaurant in February 2006, they have already established a reputation for quality cuisine served in a relaxed and friendly atmosphere. The fact that between them they have some 50 years experience in the hospitality business no doubt has something to do with their success. Everything served here is homemade with dishes based on fresh local produce – the vegetables, for example, come from the nearby Pannier Market.

Amongst the starters you'll find Exmoor Game Paté, West Country Mussels, local smoked salmon, and hand-picked Brixham Crab. The main courses offer a selection of Devonshire-sourced dishes – fillet of beef, rack of lamb, duck or corn-fed chicken – along with Cornish monkfish and other fish dishes. And if you prefer a savoury to finish your meal, just choose from the range of West Country cheeses on offer. Vegetarian options are available and if you have any special dietary needs, just let your waiter know. The Four Seasons also provides a full outside catering service.

🎬 stories and anecdotes   🍴 famous people   🎨 art and craft   🏆 entertainment and sport   🚶 walks

five ships set sail to join Drake's fleet against the Armada. The building is now home to the **Barnstaple Heritage Centre** where more can be found out about this ancient town and one of its .most enduring industries, pottery which has been made here continuously since the 13th century. As in those days, local Fremington red clay is used.

Another interesting museum has the unusual distinction of being housed in a former signal box. The **Lynton and Barnstaple Railway Museum** records the history of the narrow-gauge railway that ran between Barnstaple to Lynton from 1898 to 1935. Barnstaple is also the northern terminus of the **Tarka Line**, a lovely 39-mile route that follows the gentle river valleys of the Yeo and the Taw where Tarka the Otter had his home. The railway is actually the main line route to Exeter but has been renamed in honour of one of the area's major visitor attractions.

Walkers along the Tarka Trail will know Barnstaple well as the crossover point in this figure-of-eight long-distance footpath. Inspired by Henry Williamson's celebrated story of *Tarka the Otter*, the 180-mile trail wanders through a delightful variety of Devon scenery – tranquil countryside, wooded river valleys, rugged moorland, and a stretch of the North Devon coast, with part of the route taking in the Tarka Line railway in order to get the best views of the locations described in the novel.

COOL CALM COLLECTED

Mermaid Walk, 130 Boutport Street, Barnstaple, Devon EX31 1TD
Tel: 01271 859356
e-mail: info@coolcalmcollected.net
website: www.coolcalmcollected.net

Three elegant rooms stocked with divine interior "must-haves" – that's what you will find at **Cool Calm Collected**, the creation of Andrew Short and David Thompson. Both worked in the film industry, David as a chief hair designer whose credits include an Oscar nomination for his work as chief hair designer on *Titanic*. Alongside his film career, he has always had a love for interior design. As well as renovating and designing his own homes, he has advised on projects as diverse as a seaside cottage and a Docklands penthouse.

Andrew's background is in costume for the film industry and the theatre, where he worked as a freelance costumier for the National Theatre and the Royal Opera House amongst others. Both dreamed of moving away from London to start afresh in the country, a dream which has now become a reality. "We've had such fantastic fun putting the collection together," they say. "We've sourced things from all over Europe: Linum from Sweden, Greengate from Denmark, gifts from Paris and Amsterdam, lots of lovely goodies from England and Scotland and a stunningly designed range of cookware by Nigella Lawson". All are new in town and many are exclusive to the shop.

🏨 historic building   🏛 museum   🏛 historic site   🜄 scenic attraction   🌱 flora and fauna

ART STORE

21 Joy Street, Barnstaple, Devon EX31 1BS
Tel: 01271 346426
e-mail: gerry@artstore.co.uk
website: www.artstoregallery.co.uk

Located just off Barnstaple's main shopping area, Green Lanes, Art Store is also close to the famous Butcher's Row and Pannier Market. Owner Gerry Fry has worked the art publishing industry for more than 10 years and specialises in the buying and selling of original and limited edition art. The Art Store also sells a wide selection of open edition contemporary prints and art cards, and showcases the work of local artists.

The Gallery has a large glass frontage enabling a good display of the works available and the interior has an extensive wall area for hanging as well as free-standing browsers.

The Art Store offers a comprehensive framing service provided by Tony Toop who has several years experience and is Guild Commended. Customers can see him at work in the designated area screened off by a glass partition.

Around Barnstaple

MUDDIFORD

4 miles N of Barnstaple on the B3230

🌿 Marwood Hill Gardens

From Barnstaple to Ilfracombe, the B3230 winds through a pretty valley, passing along the way through attractive little villages. Despite the rather unappealing name, Muddiford is one of them. The village really did get its name from the "muddy ford" by which medieval travellers used to cross the river here.

About two miles southwest of Muddiford, **Marwood Hill Gardens** (see panel on page 130) offers visitors some 18 acres of trees and shrubs, many of them rare and unusual. The collection was started more than half a century ago and now includes an enormous number and variety of plants. The three lakes, linked by the largest bog garden in the West Country, are busy with ducks and multi-coloured carp. From spring, when camellias and magnolias are in bloom, through to the brilliant hues of autumn, the gardens provide a continuous spectacle of colour. The gardens are home to the national collections of astilbe, iris and tulbaghia.

ARLINGTON

6 miles NE of Barnstaple on the A39

🏛 Arlington Court

Arlington Court is an imposing National Trust property which was home to the Chichester family from 1534 until the last

---

🎭 stories and anecdotes   🦜 famous people   🎨 art and craft   🎶 entertainment and sport   🥾 walks

MARWOOD HILL GARDENS

Marwood, nr Barnstaple,
North Devon EX31 4EB
Tel: 01271 342528
e-mail:
marwoodhillgardens@netbreeze.co.uk

When Dr Jimmy Smart came to Marwood Hill in 1949 the estate contained a Georgian house and a completely neglected garden consisting of the Walled Garden and its immediate surround. There was no tree or shrub of merit and many diseased bushes, espalier and cordon apple trees. More than half a century later, **Marwood Hill Gardens** has developed into one of the country's most delightful and important botanical centres.

Over the years many new areas have been planted and new features added such as the Folly and the Scented Arbour. Today, with many genera planted in close association – eucalyptus, betula, sorbus and so on – and most plants clearly labelled, there is something of a botanic garden about Marwood Hill. In 1969, a stream was dammed to make two lakes, one with an island in its centre which features a graceful statue of a mother and two children. At the same time, a greenhouse was built inside the walled garden. This holds a collection of camellias that are at their best in March; the large outdoor collection flowers in April. Earlier in the year, masses of snowdrops welcome the early spring, soon followed by daffodils and bluebells.

During March and April the large collection of magnolias is at its best and, together with rhododendrons and cherry blossom, create a riot of colour for Easter time. In May, the alpines and early-flowering herbaceous plants come into bloom. Around the lakes and streams, drifts of colourful primulas are starting to give several months of colour. A large bog garden linked to the lakes is a haven for moisture-loving plants such as astilbes, iris, hostas and ligularias. A large pergola is covered with wisteria, roses and clematis.

During the summer months, the areas around the walled garden are a mass of colourful blooms and the walls are draped with clematis. As autumn approaches, the hardy cyclamen around the bases of the trees start to produce their pink and white flowers while, above, the autumn tints of the trees' leaves provide one last flourish of colour.

Marwood Hill is home to the national collections of iris, tulbaghia and astilbe, the latter being one of the biggest collections in the world. The three lakes are home to many ducks and large fish, and within the walled garden is a plant centre where plants propagated and grown here can be bought. Please ring for further details and opening times.

🏠 historic building 🏛 museum 🏚 historic site ♨ scenic attraction 🌱 flora and fauna

owner, Rosalie Chichester, died childless in 1949. (Sir Francis Chichester, famous as an aviation pioneer and as the first solo round-the-world sailor, was born two miles away at Shirwell). The present house was built in 1822 to an unambitious design by the Barnstaple architect, Thomas Lee, and extended some 40 years later by Sir Bruce

Arlington Court

Chichester who also added the handsome stable block. When he died in 1881, he left the house and its 2,775-acre park to his daughter Rosalie, along with a staggering mountain of debts. Only 15 years old when she inherited the estate, Rosalie managed to keep it intact and stayed on at Arlington Court until her death at the age of 83.

The interior today is really a museum reflecting Rosalie's varied interests. There are displays of her collections of porcelain, pewter, shells, snuff boxes, and more than a hundred model ships, some made by French soldiers captured during the Napoleonic wars.

Intriguingly, Rosalie never saw the most valuable work of art amongst her possessions. After her death, a watercolour by William Blake was discovered on top of a wardrobe where it had lain forgotten for over 100 years. It is now on display in the white drawing room.

During her lifetime, Rosalie Chichester transformed the grounds of Arlington Court into something of a nature reserve. She ordered the building of an eight-mile long perimeter fence to protect the native wildfowl and heron populations. The Shetland ponies

and Jacob sheep grazing the fields today are descendants of those introduced by Rosalie. Another of her eclectic interests is evident in the 18th century stable block which houses a unique collection of horse-drawn carriages she saved from destruction.

LANDKEY
2 miles SE of Barnstaple off the A361

Landkey boasts a fine church with some impressive memorials (well worth visiting) and also the distinction of being the only village bearing this name in Britain. Historians believe that it is derived from *Lan*, the Celtic word for a church, and the saint to which it was dedicated, Kea. An enduring legend claims that St Kea rowed over from Wales with his personal cow on board determined to convert the pagans of north Devon to Christianity. Sadly, these benighted people were not persuaded by his eloquence, so they chopped off his head. Not many public speakers could cope with that kind of negative response, but St Kea calmly retrieved his severed head and continued, head in hand, to preach the Gospel for many years.

🎭 stories and anecdotes   🐲 famous people   🎨 art and craft   🎵 entertainment and sport   🚶 walks

SWIMBRIDGE
5 miles SE of Barnstaple on the A361

Revd "Jack" Russell   Church of St James

For almost half a century from 1833 this attractive village was the home of the **Rev. John "Jack" Russell,** the celebrated hunting parson and breeder of the first Jack Russell terriers. A larger than life character, he was an enthusiastic master of foxhounds and when his Bishop censured him for pursuing such an unseemly sport for a man of the cloth, he transferred the pack into his wife's name and continued his frequent sorties. He was still riding to hounds in his late 70s and when he died in 1880 at the age of 87 hundreds of people attended his funeral. Russell was buried in the churchyard of St James', the church where he had been a diligent pastor. He was gratefully remembered for his brief sermons, delivered as his groom waited by the porch with his horse saddled and ready.

Mostly 15th century, the **Church of St James** is one of Devon's outstanding churches, distinctive from outside because of its unusual lead-covered spire. Inside, there is a wealth of ecclesiastical treasures: a richly carved rood screen spanning both the nave and the aisles, an extraordinary 18th century font cover in the shape of an elongated octagonal "cupboard", a fine 15th century stone pulpit supported by a tall pedestal and carved with the figures of saints and angels, and a wonderful nave roof with protective angels gazing down. Collectors of unusual epitaphs will savour the punning lines inscribed on a monument here to John Rosier, a lawyer who died in 1658:

> *Lo, with a Warrant sealed by God's decree*
> *Death his grim Seargant hath arrested me*
> *No bayle was to be given, no law could save*
> *My body from the prison of the grave.*

The village itself has some elegant Georgian houses and a pub which in 1962 was renamed after Swimbridge's most famous resident. Jack Russell societies from around the world frequently hold their meetings here.

COBBATON
6 miles SE of Barnstaple off the A377

Cobbaton Combat Collection

The hamlet of Cobbaton is home to the largest private collection of military vehicles and wartime memorabilia in the southwest. Owner Preston Isaac started the **Cobbaton**

Cobbaton Combat Collection

Chittlehampton, near Umberleigh, Devon EX37 9RZ
Tel: 01769 540740 Fax: 01769540141
e-mail: info@cobbatoncombat.co.uk
website: www.cobbatoncombat.co.uk

A private museum that was the result of one man's lifetime of collecting anything relating to World War II, Cobbaton Combat Collection has two hangars that house over 50 mainly British vehicles, including fully equipped tanks, all displayed in combat condition. Along with hardware, from mortar shells and machine guns to ration books and gas masks, visitors can find refreshment at the NAAFI canteen truck whilst, outside in the children's play area, there is a Sherman tank. Open daily from April to October and weekdays in the winter.

historic building   museum   historic site   scenic attraction   flora and fauna

Combat Collection (see panel opposite) as a hobby but admits that "it got out of hand!" His schoolboy's box of treasures has grown to comprise more than 50 World War II military vehicles, including tanks and artillery, along with thousands of smaller items. For visitors' convenience, a NAAFI truck is on duty to provide snacks and drinks.

BISHOPS TAWTON
2 miles S of Barnstaple on the A377

Bishop's Tawton takes its name from the River Taw and the medieval Bishop's Palace that stood here until the reign of Henry VIII and of which a few fragments still stand. The village today is not over-endowed with listed buildings but it can boast a very unusual one, a sociable three-seater outside lavatory which has been accorded Grade II Listed status. This amenity has not been used for 40 years or more (and the brambles which have invaded it would make it rather uncomfortable to do so) but it still looks perfectly serviceable.

ATHERINGTON
7 miles S of Barnstaple on the B3217

St Mary's Church

A landmark for miles around, **St Mary's Church** stands in the picturesque square of this hilltop village and is notable for a feature which is unique in Devon – a lavishly carved and alarmingly top-heavy rood loft. Created by two carvers from Chittlehampton in the 1530s, it is an exceptionally fine example of their craft. The church also contains striking effigies of Sir John Wilmington, who died in 1349, and his wife; a window of medieval glass; and well-preserved brasses of Sir John Basset, (died 1529), his two wives and 12 children.

HIGH BICKINGTON
8 miles S of Barnstaple on the B3217

Two miles south of Atherington is another hilltop village. Standing at almost 600ft above sea level, the village commands excellent views in all directions. It boasts a fine 16th century inn, The George, which is set amongst a delightful group of thatched cottages, and a parish church dating back to the 1100s which is renowned for its exceptional collection of carved bench and pew ends. There are around 70 of them in all: some are Gothic (characterised by fine tracery); others are Renaissance (characterised by rounded figures). More recent carving on the choir stalls depicts an appealing collection of animals and birds.

BRAUNTON
6 miles NW of Barnstaple on the A361

Braunton Great Field

Braunton claims the rather odd distinction of being the largest village in Devon. It is certainly a sizeable community, spreading along both sides of the River Caen, with some handsome Georgian houses and a substantial church reflecting Braunton's relative importance in medieval times. The church is dedicated to St Brannoc, a Celtic saint who arrived here from Wales in the 6th century. It's said that his bones lie beneath the altar of the present 13th century church, a story which may well be true since the building stands on the site of a Saxon predecessor. What is certainly true is that the church contains some of the finest 16th century carved pews to be found anywhere in England. Many of the carvings depict pigs, a clear allusion to the ancient tradition that St Brannoc was instructed in a dream to build a church where

WILLOWFIELD LAKE COTTAGES

Gallowell Lane, Braunton Burrows, Braunton ,
North Devon EX33 2NX
Tel: 01271 814346
e-mail relax@willowfieldlake.com
website www.willowfieldlake.com

Willowfield Lake Cottages enjoy a superb location within Braunton Burrows Nature Reserve with 5 miles of golden sands and surf nearby. The cottages are set amidst mature trees and shrubs and are surrounded by 12 acres of pastureland, where mown paths meander through wildflower meadows to picnic areas and a tranquil and picturesque lake, which is stocked to satisfy the most ambitious coarse fisherman. There are mature stocks of carp, up to 25lbs, tench up to 8lbs, and roach up to 1.5lbs. Warm summer evenings can be enjoyed rowing peacefully across the water while the children will find adventure amongst the trees, in the fort and play area. The grounds provide plenty of open space for ball games. Giant chess is also available.

Perfect for family holidays, Willowfield Lake offers a great range of facilities. In addition to the lake there is an indoor heated swimming pool, with a shallow end, changing, w/c and showers, sun bed and a hot tub. The games room offers table tennis, pool and table football, plus an enclosed toddlers' area. Willowfield Lake is an ideal location for walking and cycling, being 1.5 miles from the Tarka Trail which follows the estuary as far as Torrington.

The tastefully furnished cluster of single storey cottages can accommodate from 2 up to 5 guests, and all enjoy soothing views of unspoilt countryside. They are comprehensively equipped including widescreen TVs with digital freeview, and DVD players, and either have their own garden or a shared one.

The Nature Reserve designated as a UNESCO Biosphere, covers more than 1000 acres of one of Britain's finest sand dune areas. The marram grass covered dunes shelter rare toadflax, sea stock and marsh orchids. A half-hour walk (or a 5 minute drive) brings you to the famous Saunton Sands beach, where huge Atlantic rollers create some of the best surfing in the world. Saunton also boasts a championship links golf course.

Just 2 miles inland is Braunton, which also has good pubs and shops, excellent restaurants to suit all tastes and pockets, and a locally renowned art gallery and craft centre. Nearby are the

pretty thatched villages of Croyde and Georgeham, both of which have good inns and restaurants. Just 7 miles away is the lovely old market town of Barnstaple, winner of "Britain in Bloom" in Europe. Further a field you can explore the delights of the National Trust properties of Arlington Court, Lundy Island and Heddon Valley. The RHS garden at Rosemoor and Dr Smart's garden at Marwood are other places of interest to visit.

INSPIRATIONS

2 Cedar House, Caen Street, Braunton,
Devon EX33 1AH
Tel: 01271 816428

Cheryl Swan, the owner of **Inspirations**, has been working with flowers since she was 13 years old and her experience and flair are clearly evident in the beautiful floral arrangements she creates. Cheryl took over the business here at the end of 2005 and has made sure that all her flowers are sourced locally for freshness and quality. In addition to the fresh and dried flowers on sale in her shop, Cheryl creates flower arrangements, bouquets and other items for all kinds of occasions, or as gifts. A local delivery service is available.

he came across a sow and her litter of seven pigs. Arriving in North Devon the saint happily discovered this very scene at the spot where Braunton's church now stands.

There is further evidence of Saxon occupation of this area to be found in **Braunton Great Field**, just to the southwest of the village. This is one of very few remaining examples of the Saxon open-field strip system still being actively farmed in Britain. Around 350 acres in total, the field was originally divided into around 700 half-

AZURE APPLIED ARTS & GIFTS

Exeter Road, Braunton, Devon EX33 2JL
Tel: 01271 816004
e-mail: azuregifts@aol.com
website: www.azuregifts.co.uk

Located in the centre of Braunton, **Azure Applied Arts & Gifts** offers a real treasure trove of giftware with such a variety of stock you can be sure of finding whatever you are looking for, and if you're not sure what you are looking for, this is the place to come for inspiration.

Owner Sharon Walker studied Design at university and has put together a wonderful collection of attractively displayed items of style and quality that includes fashion jewellery, elegant glassware, cuddly toys, ceramics and much, much more.

Leading ranges such as Kit Heath, AG Silver, Balagan, Jellycat, Berni Parker Cards, Juicy Lucy, Raff Photography and SGW cards are all represented here, along with many unusual items and works of art. In fact, there's something here that will solve every gift problem or to brighten up your own home decor.

Friendly and knowledgeable staff add to the pleasure of shopping here and as an extra bonus there's free parking on the road outside.

stories and anecdotes   famous people   art and craft   entertainment and sport   walks

acre strips, each of them a furlong (220yds) long, and 11yds wide. Each strip was separated by an unploughed "landshare" about one foot wide. Throughout the centuries, many of the strips have changed hands and been combined, so that now only about 200 individual ones remain.

CROYDE
9 miles NW of Barnstaple on the B3231

🐾 Braunton Burrows 🐾 Baggy Point

Croyde is renowned for its excellent beach with, just around the headland, another three-mile stretch of sands at Saunton Sands, one of the most glorious, family-friendly sandy beaches in the West Country. The sands are backed by 1,000 acres of dunes known as **Braunton Burrows.** The southern part of this wide expanse is a designated nature reserve noted for its fluctuating population of migrant birds as well as rare flowers and insects.

Also noted for its abundant wildlife is **Baggy Point,** just northwest of Croyde. This headland of Devonian rock (so named because the rock was first identified in this county) is a popular nesting place for seabirds, including herring gull, fulmar, shag and cormorant. Grey seals can often be seen from here.

Running northwestwards from the cliffs is a shoal known as Baggy Leap. In 1799, *HMS Weazle* was driven onto the shoal during a gale and all 106 souls on board perished.

GEORGEHAM
9 miles NW of Barnstaple off the B3231

🐦 Henry Williamson

It was here that **Henry Williamson** settled in 1921 and where he wrote his most famous novel, *Tarka the Otter,* which was published in 1927. 'Tarka' lived in the land between the Taw and Torridge rivers and many of the small villages and settlements feature in the story. The writer lived a very simple life in a wooden hut that he built himself. After World War II, he farmed for a while in Norfolk but returned to Georgeham where he died in 1947. He is buried in the graveyard of St George's Church.

Bideford

🏛 Pannier Market 🏛 Royal Hotel

🏛 Burton Museum 🐾 Lundy Island

Dubbed the "Little White Town" by Charles Kingsley, this attractive town set beside the River Torridge was once the third busiest port in Britain. The first bridge across the shallow neck of the Torridge estuary was built around 1300 to link Bideford with its aptly-named satellite village, East-the-Water.

Croyde

🏛 historic building 🏛 museum 🏛 historic site 🐾 scenic attraction 🐾 flora and fauna

That bridge must have been very impressive for its time. It was 670ft long, and built of massive oak lintels of varying length which created a series of irregular arches between 12 and 25ft apart. These erratic dimensions were preserved when the bridge was rebuilt in stone around 1460, (the old bridge was used as scaffolding), and despite widening during the 1920s they persist to this day. Unusually, Bideford Bridge is managed by an ancient corporation of trustees, known as *feoffees,* whose income, derived from property in the town, not only pays for the upkeep of the bridge but also supports local charities and good causes. A high-level bridge a mile or so downstream, opened in 1987, has relieved some of the traffic congestion and also provides panoramic views of the town and the Torridge estuary.

Bideford received its Market Charter from Henry III in 1272, (on May 25th to be precise) and markets still take place every Tuesday and Saturday. Since 1883 they have been held in the splendid **Pannier Market** building, reckoned to be one of the best surviving examples of a Victorian covered market. Along with local produce, there's a huge selection of gifts, crafts, and handmade goods on offer: "Everything from Antiques to Aromatherapy!"

Devon ports seemed to specialise in particular commodities. At Bideford it was tobacco from the North American colonies which brought almost two centuries of prosperity until the American War of Independence shut off supplies. Evidence of this golden age can still be seen in the opulent merchants' residences in Bridgeland Street,

ALTARED ST8

4 Grenville Street, Bideford, Devon EX39 2EA
Tel: 01237 421506
Mobile: 07779 610449 / 07739 397900
e-mail: mandmrunes@aol.com
website: www.mandmrunes.co.uk

Altared St8 started life as a market stall in nearby Barnstaple but such was the interest in their wares, Mel and Myrna Bushell soon moved to their present shop close to Bideford Market. Mel has been interested in New Age philosophies for some 20 years and is knowledgeable in many areas; Myrna is a trained Stress Consultant and Aromatherapist. Altared St8 sells a wide range of New Age and pagan products including incenses, essential oils, candles, witches, dragons, Tarot cards, jewellery, specialist teas and infusions plus some homemade products – runes, wands, soaps, creams and lotions. Mel performs rune readings daily in the shop and Myrna offers aromatherapy massage.

The shop also sells a wide range of different types of ornaments, not just those of pagan interest. It also stocks dream catchers, Native American items, Chinese items, Buddhas, books, clothing and unusual and interesting gift items. There are also paintings and crafts from local artists, an extensive selection of role-playing games, card and trading games, and strategy games. "Our stock is ever-changing," says Mel, "and we strive to find something different that other shops don't have."

stories and anecdotes   famous people   art and craft   entertainment and sport   walks

PANACHE INTERIORS

20 Chingswell Street, Bideford, Devon EX39 2NF
Tel: 01237 429101

After working in the industry for several years, Joanne Wade achieved her great ambition of opening her own soft furnishing business. At **Panache Interiors** in Bideford's town centre, this lively young woman provides customers with a huge choice of fabrics, wallpapers and interior accessories such as occasional furniture, lighting, pictures, throws and cushions. The stylish items come from leading suppliers such as Colefax & Fowler, Jane Churchill, Osborne & Little, Liberty, Sanderson, Sibona, Bombay Duck and Au Maison.

    The large open plan display area is crowded with every possible accessory for the home, anything from candles to curtain rails, from tassels to tie-backs. Knowledgeable friendly staff are on hand to advise and assist you if required. Joanne also provides a made to measure service for curtains, blinds, loose covers and other soft furnishings, and is happy to undertake complete interior design commissions. Such is the success of her business, Joanne is planning to move to more spacious premises in the near future.

THE DANCING OTTER

Art Deco & Antiques, 1 North Road, Bideford,
Devon EX39 2NW
Tel: 01237 477706
e-mail: dancingotter@btinternet.com
website: www.dancingotterdirect.co.uk

Located at the very top of North Road, just beyond Bideford's main shopping run, **The Dancing Otter** specialises in a wide range of Art Deco, antiques and twentieth century design. This family run business has 25 years experience in collecting, buying and selling Art Deco and other 20th century pieces from some of the finest designers and manufacturers.

    Examples of the Dancing Otter's stock include Shelley, Moorcroft, Susie Cooper, Clarice Cliff and Doulton ceramics, and the shop also stocks a number of bronze and Spelter figures along with lighting, chrome and other metal items, and some interesting jewellery that would make great gifts. "As a client orientated business we rely on personal recommendation and repeat purchases," says owner David Hardy, "in particular from visitors who we have met face to face at the Dancing Otter Art Deco & Antiques. By finding out our client's particular areas of interest, we tailor our stock purchases from the UK, France and the USA to meet this profile."

🏛 historic building   🏛 museum   🏛 historic site   ⛰ scenic attraction   🌿 flora and fauna

and most strikingly in the **Royal Hotel** in East-the-Water, a former merchant's house of 1688 with a pair of little-seen plasterwork ceilings which are perhaps the finest and most extravagant examples of their kind in Devon.

It was while he was staying at the Royal Hotel that Charles Kingsley penned most of *Westward Ho!* A quarter of a million words long, the novel was completed in just seven months. There's a statue of Kingsley, looking suitably literary, on Bideford Quay. Broad and tree-lined, the Quay stands at the foot of the narrow maze of lanes which formed the old seaport.

Just round the corner from the Quay, on the edge of Victoria Park, is the **Burton Museum & Art Gallery**, opened in 1994. The museum contains some interesting curios such as Bideford harvest jugs of the late 1700s, and model ships in carved bone made by French prisoners during the Napoleonic wars. The gallery has frequently changing exhibitions with subjects ranging from automata to kites, quilts to dinosaurs, as well as paintings by well-known North Devon artists. Starting at the Burton Gallery, guided walks around the town are available.

One excursion from Bideford that should not be missed is the day trip to **Lundy Island** on the supply boat, the *MS Oldenburg*. Lundy is a huge lump of granite rock, three miles long and half a mile wide, with sheer cliffs rising 500ft above the shore. Its name derives from the Norse *lunde ey*, meaning puffin island, and these attractive birds with their multi-coloured beaks are still in residence, along with many other species. More than 400 different birds have been spotted on Lundy, and you might also spot one of the indigenous black rats which have survived only at this isolated spot. The island has a ruined castle, a church, a pub, a shop selling souvenirs and the famous

stamps. There's even an hotel, but if you hope to stay overnight you must book well ahead.

Around Bideford

WESTWARD HO!
2 miles NW of Bideford on the B3236

🐦 Northam Burrows Country Park

🖉 Pot Walloping Festival

Is there any other place in the world that has been named after a popular novel? Following the huge success in 1855 of Charles Kingsley's tale of Elizabethan derring-do, a company was formed to develop this spectacular site with its rocky cliffs and two miles of sandy beach. The early years were troubled. A powerful storm washed away the newly-built pier and most of the houses. When Rudyard Kipling came here in 1874 as a pupil at the United Services College he described the place as "twelve bleak houses by the shore". Today Westward Ho! is a busy holiday resort well worth visiting for its two miles of golden sands, recently awarded a Blue Flag, and the nearby **Northam Burrows Country Park,** almost 1,000 acres of grazed burrows rich in flora, fauna and migratory birds, and offering tremendous views across Bideford Bay.

An unusual event at Westward Ho! is the **Pot Walloping Festival** which takes place in late spring. Local people and visitors join together to throw pebbles which have been dislodged by winter storms back onto the famous ridge, after which pots of a different kind also get a walloping.

NORTHAM
2 miles N of Bideford on the A386

🏛 Bloody Corner

Northam is said to have been where Hubba

WATERSIDE GALLERY

2 Marine Terrace, Instow, Bideford,
Devon EX39 4HZ
Tel/Fax: 01271 860786
e-mail: jmj@watersideart.co.uk
website: www.watersideart.co.uk

The seaside village of Instow, between Barnstaple and Bideford, enjoys glorious views across the Torridge Estuary to the old fishing community of Appledore. The **Waterside Gallery** occupies a superb position on the quayside at Instow, its large windows overlooking the water.

The Gallery showcases work by leading local artists, potters and craftsmen of the South West and also stages occasional exhibitions of individual artist's work – details can be found on the Gallery's website or if you wish to be included in its mailing list just let owner Judith James know.

Examples of work by artists such as Colin Albrook, Tony Williams and Mary Tozer; pottery by Geoff Ambler, Phillip and Frannie Leach can also be seen on the website.

GALLERIE MARIN

31 Market Street, Appledore, Devon EX39 1PP
Tel: 01237 473679 Fax: 01237 421655
e-mail: galleriemarine@btopenworld.com

It was back in 1972 that Audrey Hinks opened Gallerie Marin with a collection of 26 paintings, all by Mark Myers who would later become the President of the Royal Society of Marine Artists. Audrey's passion for marine art has its roots in her childhood when her father worked as a designer for a shipbuilding company. "One of my earliest memories," she says, "is going around the shipyard with him and climbing over boats in various stages of construction." She later followed in her father's footsteps and joined him in the drawing-office.

Having looked at boats all her life, Audrey instinctively knows if a painting is right or not. The main theme is predominantly marine. Artists currently exhibiting with the gallery include Mark R Myers PPRSMA, David Brackman, Tim Thompson, Jenny Morgan, Bill Mearns ASMA, Steven Thor Johanneson RSMA and Michael Lees.

The paintings are displayed in a delightful cottage in a quiet lane just 100 yards from the waterfront. Slate floors, wooden beams and a vintage Bodley stove in the fireplace all add to the charm.

'Mist on the Hills'
by Michael Lees

 historic building   museum   historic site   scenic attraction   flora and fauna

the Dane attacked Devon and was repelled by either Alfred the Great or the Earl of Devon. Another tale recounts that in 1069AD, three years after King Harold had been slain at the Battle of Hastings, his three sons landed at Northam in an attempt to regain their father's throne. They came from Ireland with an invasion force of more than 60 ships but their rebellion was mercilessly suppressed at a site just to the south of the town. To this day, it is known as **Bloody Corner**.

APPLEDORE

3 miles N of Bideford on the A386

🏛 North Devon Maritime Museum

✿ Appledore Visual Arts Festival

Overlooking the Taw-Torridge estuary, Appledore is a delightful old-world fishing village of narrow winding lanes and sturdy fishermen's cottages from the 18th and 19th centuries. All types of fishing can be arranged here and you can even go crabbing from the quayside. The streets of the old quarter are too narrow for cars although not, it seems, for the occasional small fishing boat which is pulled up from the harbour and parked between the buildings.

It seems appropriate that the **North Devon Maritime Museum** should be located in this truly nautical setting. Housed in a former ship-owner's residence, the museum contains a wealth of seafaring memorabilia, a photographic exhibit detailing the military exercises around the estuary in preparation for the D-Day landings during World War II, a reconstructed Victorian kitchen, and much more.

A stroll along Bude Street is recommended. Art and craft galleries have gathered here amongst the Georgian style "Captains" houses, and it's particularly colourful during

the **Appledore Visual Arts Festival** in late May-early June when one of the many events is a door decorating competition.

GREAT TORRINGTON

7 miles SE of Bideford on the A386

🏛 Church of St Michael   ✿ Dartington Crystal

🦋 May Fair   🌿 Rosemoor Garden

A good place to start exploring Great Torrington is at **Castle Hill** which commands grand views along the valley of the River Torridge. (There's no view of the castle: that was demolished as long ago as 1228: its site is now a bowling green). On the opposite bank of the river is the hamlet of Taddiport where the tiny 14th century church by the bridge was originally the chapel of a leper hospital: its inmates were not permitted to cross over into Torrington itself.

Not many churches in England have been blown up by gunpowder. That was the fate however of the original **Church of St Michael and All Angels.** It happened during the Civil War when General Fairfax captured the town on February 16th, 1645. His Royalist prisoners were bundled into the church which they had been using as an arsenal. In the darkness, the 80 barrels of gunpowder stored there were somehow set alight and in the huge explosion that followed the church was demolished, 200 men lost their lives, and Fairfax himself narrowly escaped death. The present spacious church was built five years later, one of very few in the country erected during the Commonwealth years.

Today, the town's leading tourist attraction is **Dartington Crystal** where visitors can see skilled craftsmen blowing and shaping the crystal, follow the history of glass-making from the Egyptians to the present day, watch a video presentation, and browse amongst some

10,000 square feet of displays. The enterprise was set up in the 1960s by the Dartington Hall Trust to provide employment in an area of rural depopulation: today, the beautifully designed handmade crystal is exported to more than 50 countries around the world.

Torrington's **May Fair** is still an important event in the local calendar, and has been since 1554. On the first Thursday in May, a Queen is crowned, there is maypole dancing in the High Street, and a banner proclaims the greeting *"Us be plazed to zee 'ee"*.

About a mile south of Great Torrington, the Royal Horticultural Society's **Rosemoor Garden** occupies a breathtaking setting in the Torridge Valley. The 40-acre site includes mature planting in Lady Anne Palmer's magnificent garden and arboretum; a winding rocky gorge with bamboos and ferns beside the stream, and a more formal area which contains one of the longest herbaceous borders in the country. There are trails for children, a picnic area and an award-winning Visitor Centre with a licensed restaurant, plant centre and shop.

MONKLEIGH
5 miles S of Bideford on the A388

Monkleigh parish church contains a striking monument, an ornate canopied tomb containing the remains of Sir William Hankford who was Lord Chief Justice of England in the early 1400s. He lived at nearby Annery Park and the story goes that having been troubled by poachers Sir William instructed his gamekeeper to shoot anyone he found in the park at night. The gamekeeper did indeed see a figure passing through the park, fired and discovered to his horror that he had killed his master.

RHS Garden Rosemoor

Rosemoor, Great Torrington, Devon EX38 8PH
Tel: 01805 624067
website: www.rhs.org.uk

The Royal Horticultural Society Garden Rosemoor is acclaimed by gardeners throughout the world, but visitors do not have to be keen gardeners to appreciate the beauty and diversity of Rosemoor. Whatever the season, the garden is a unique and enchanting place that people return to time and time again. Situated on the west-facing slopes of the

beautiful Torridge Valley, Rosemoor has become one of the jewels in the West Country crown. Generously donated to the Society by Lady Anne Palmer in 1988, Rosemoor is now established as a garden of national importance, famous for its variety and planting.

To Lady Anne's collection of rare and interesting plants a wide range of varied features have been added. They include a formal garden, where the object is to show an enormous selection of plants and planting schemes, and a series of individual gardens such as the renowned Rose Gardens, Foliage Garden and the Cottage, Square and Spiral Gardens, and the Winter Garden with stunning effects in the colder months. All this, a lake, a bamboo and fern planted rock gully, an Arboretum and three new Model Gardens, as well as a marvellous Fruit and Vegetable Garden, make a visit to Rosemoor essential.

🏛 historic building   🏛 museum   🏛 historic site   ♨ scenic attraction   🌿 flora and fauna

WEARE GIFFARD
5 miles S of Bideford off the A386

🏠 Weare Giffard Hall

This appealing village claims to be the longest riverside village in England, straggling for almost two miles along the banks of the Torridge. Weare Giffard (pronounced *Jiffard*) has a charm all its own, suspended in time it seems to belong to the more peaceful days of half a century ago. The villagers have even refused to have full street lighting installed, so avoiding the "street furniture" that blemishes so many attractive places.

Another attraction in the village is a fine old 15th century manor house, **Weare Giffard Hall**. Although its outer walls were partially demolished during the Civil War, the splendid gatehouse with its mighty doors and guardian lions has survived. Inside, the main hall has a magnificent hammer-beam roof, and several of the other rooms are lined with Tudor and Jacobean oak panelling. For centuries, the house was the home of the Fortescue family and in the nearby church there is an interesting "family tree" with portraits of past Fortescues carved in stone.

WOOLFARDISWORTHY
11 miles SW of Bideford off the A39

🐾 Milky Way Adventure Park

Naturally, you don't pronounce Woolfardisworthy the way it looks. The correct pronunciation is *Woolsery*. The extraordinary name goes back to Saxon times

GNOME RESERVE & WILD FLOWER GARDEN

West Putford, nr Bradworthy,
North Devon EX22 7XE
Tel: 01409 241435
website: www.gnomereserve.co.uk

If you go down to the woods today – near West Putford, that is – you're sure of a big surprise. No Teddy Bears but more than 1,000 gnomes and pixies all resident in four enchanted acres. Here the little people can be observed in their natural habitat pursuing their traditional activities of fishing, sitting on toadstools, partying and smoking. **The Gnome Reserve & Wild Flower Garden** was established in 1978 by the Atkin family and has become one of North Devon's most popular visitor attractions.

Gnome hats and fishing rods are loaned free of charge so that you can mingle amongst the gnomes as one of them; you can see the Gnome Airport, step into the Gnome Seaside, sit at the seat in the centre of the Circle of Imagination or watch the Gnome Motor Bike Scramble. There's a collection of rare antique gnomes and if you'd like to adopt a gnome for your house or garden, the Pixie Kiln produces a wonderful range of characters, each individually modelled by Ann Atkin, a graduate of the Royal Academy of Arts. Part of the site is devoted to a colourful wildflower garden which has 250 labelled species and was commended by the Royal Horticultural Society as one of the best in the country.

📖 stories and anecdotes 🌿 famous people 🎨 art and craft 🐾 entertainment and sport 🚶 walks

when the land was owned by Wulfheard who established a *worthig*, or homestead, here.

A mile or so north of the village, alongside the A39, is another family entertainment complex, the **Milky Way Adventure Park**. The park includes a huge indoor play area (for both children and adults) where you can test your archery and laser target shooting skills, a Pets Corner where children are encouraged to cuddle the animals, a Bird of Prey Centre, a Sheep Dog Training and Breeding Centre, "Toddler Town" - a safe play area for very young children, a Sports Hall, a miniature railway, and a "Time Warp Adventure Zone".

CLOVELLY
12 miles SW of Bideford off the A39

🖼 Kingsley Exhibition   🏠 Fisherman's Cottage

🎨 Clovelly Pottery

Even if you've never been to Devon, you must have heard of this unbelievably quaint and picturesque village that tumbles down a steep hillside in terraced levels. Almost every whitewashed and flower-strewn cottage is worthy of its own picture postcard and from the sheltered little harbour there is an enchanting view of this unique place. One reason Clovelly is so unspoilt is that the village has belonged to the Rous family since 1738 and they have ensured that it has been spared such modern defacements as telegraph poles and "street furniture".

The only access to the beach and the beautifully restored 14th century quay is on foot or by donkey, although there is a Land Rover service from the Red Lion Hotel for those who can't face the climb back up the hill. The only other forms of transport are the sledges which are used to deliver weekly supplies. During the summer months there are regular boat trips around the bay, and the *Jessica Hettie* travels daily to Lundy Island with timings that allow passengers to spend some six hours there, watching the seals and abundant wildlife.

Clovelly

🏠 historic building   🖼 museum   🏛 historic site   🐸 scenic attraction   🌱 flora and fauna

The Clovelly Pottery, opened in 1992, displays an extensive range of items made by Cornish and Devon potters. In the nearby workshop, for a small fee, you can try your own hand at throwing a pot.

This captivating village has some strong literary connections. It features as "Steepway" in the story *A Message from the Sea* by Dickens and Wilkie Collins. Charles Kingsley (*The Water Babies; Westward Ho!*) was at school here in the 1820s and the **Kingsley Exhibition** explores his links with the village. Next door, the **Fisherman's Cottage** provides an insight into what life was like here about 80 years ago. And the award-winning Visitor Centre has an audio-visual show narrating the development of Clovelly from around 2000BC to the present day.

HARTLAND
15 miles SW of Bideford on the B3248

🏛 Church of St Nectan   ⛰ Hartland Point

🏛 Hartland Abbey   🔯 Hartland Pottery

This pleasant village with its narrow streets and small square was once larger and more important than Bideford. Hartland was a royal possession from the time of King Alfred until William the Conqueror and continued to be a busy centre right up to the 19th century. It was at its most prosperous in the 1700s and some fine Georgian buildings survive from that period. But the most striking building is the parish **Church of St Nectan** which stands about 1.5 miles west of the village. This is another of Devon's "must-see" churches. The exterior is impressive enough with its 128ft

---

CHERISTOW HOLIDAY COTTAGES & RESTAURANT

Cheristow Farmhouse, Cheristow, Hartland, North Devon EX39 6DA
Tel/Fax: 01237 441522
e-mail: info@cheristow-cottages.co.uk
website: www.cheristow-cottages.co.uk

Set on the Hartland Peninsula, an Area of Outstanding Natural Beauty, **Cheristow Holiday Cottages** are ideally located for walking the beautiful South West Coastal Path. They are a short walk from the beaches and rock pools of Berry Bay and Blackpool which are ideal for children. Tucked away down a quiet country lane, the five centrally heated cottages have been converted from old stone farm buildings dating back to at least the 18th century. Buzzard Cottage sleeps two; Bond, Shippon and Well cottages each sleep four plus cot; and Furze Cottage can accommodate five/six plus cot. All the cottages are full of charm and character and have been attractively furnished and decorated. Bed linen, duvets, towels, tea towels, fuel, logs etc are provided.

Shared amenities include a sauna and spa; children's play area; washing and drying facilities and an onsite restaurant. Baby sitting service is available and pets are welcome. The village of Hartland is within walking distance through ancient woods and has a variety of shops, including general store/off licences, craft shops, pubs, vet, doctor and a post office/newsagenta post office/newsagent.

📖 stories and anecdotes   🐦 famous people   🔯 art and craft   🎭 entertainment and sport   🚶 walks

high tower, but it is the glorious 15th century screen inside which makes this church one of the most visited in the county. A masterpiece of the medieval woodcarvers' art, its elegant arches are topped by four exquisitely fretted bands of intricate designs. The arches are delicately painted, reminding one yet again how colourful English churches used to be before the vandalism of the Puritan years.

In the churchyard is the grave of Allen Lane who, in 1935, revolutionised publishing by his introduction of Penguin Books, paperback books which were sold at sixpence (2.5p) each.

Back in Hartland village, anyone interested in attractive stoneware will want to visit the **Hartland Pottery** in North Street. Here you can watch Clive C. Pearson and his team involved in the various processes of making their oven to table ware. Functional oil lamps are a popular item, and Clive's own favourite pieces are Chun-glazed, a particularly lovely deep blue glaze that originated during the Sung Dynasty, 960-1279AD.

From the village, follow the signs to **Hartland Abbey.** Founded in 1157, the abbey was closed down in 1539 by Henry VIII who gave the building and its wide estates to William Abbott, Sergeant of the Royal wine cellars. His descendants still live here. The house was partly rebuilt in the mid-18th century in the style known as Strawberry Hill Gothic, and in the 1850s the architect George Gilbert Scott added a front hall and entrance. The abbey's owner, Sir George Stucley, had recently visited the Alhambra Palace in Spain which he much admired. He asked Scott to design something in that style and the result is the elegant Alhambra Corridor with a blue vaulted ceiling with white stencilled patterns. The

abbey has a choice collection of pictures, porcelain and furniture acquired over many generations and, in the former Servants' Hall, a unique exhibition of documents dating from 1160. There's also a fascinating Victorian and Edwardian photographic exhibition which includes many early photographs.

A mile further west is **Hartland Quay**. Exposed to all the wrath of Atlantic storms, it seems an inhospitable place for ships, but it was a busy landing-place from its building in 1566 until the sea finally overwhelmed it in 1893. Several of the old buildings have been converted into a comfortable hotel; another is now a museum recording the many wrecks that have littered this jagged coastline.

About three miles to the north of the Quay, reached by winding country lanes, is **Hartland Point.** On Ptolemy's map of Britain in Roman times, he names it the "Promontory of Hercules", a fitting name for this fearsome stretch of upended rocks rising at right angles to the sea. There are breathtaking sea and coast views and a lighthouse built in 1874.

South Molton

🐾 Quince Honey Farm

This pleasant old market town, thankfully now bypassed by the A361 North Devon link road, has been a focus of the local agriculture-based economy since Saxon times, and in common with many such towns throughout Devon was a centre of the wool trade in the late Middle Ages.

In the heart of the old town lies Broad Street, so broad as to be almost a square, and distinguished by some handsome Georgian

Thatched Cottage, North Molton

were extracted from the hills above the town and transported down the valley of the River Mole and on to the sea at Barnstaple. Evidence of abandoned mine workings are still visible around the town as well as remains of the old Mole Valley tramway.

and Victorian civic architecture. Among the noteworthy buildings to be found here are the **Market Hall and Assembly Rooms,** the eccentric **Medical Hall** with its iron balcony and four Ionic columns, and the **Guildhall** of 1743 which overhangs the pavement in a series of arches.

Just to the north of South Molton is **Quince Honey Farm** where the mysterious process of honey-making is explained in a series of displays and demonstrations.

Around South Molton

NORTH MOLTON
3 miles NE of South Molton off the A399 or A361

🏠 Church of All Saints

Tucked away in the foothills of Exmoor, North Molton was once a busy wool and mining town. At intervals from Elizabethan times until the late 1800s, copper and iron

North Molton's 15th century parish **Church of All Saints** reflects the small town's former industrial importance. It's a striking building with a high clerestory and a 100ft pinnacled tower which seems rather grand for this rather remote community. Several notable features have survived. There's a part-medieval "wine-glass" pulpit complete with sounding board and trumpeting angel, a rood screen, some fine Jacobean panelling, and an extraordinary 17th century alabaster monument to Sir Amyas Bampfylde depicting the reclining knight with his wife Elizabeth reading a book and their 12 sons and five daughters kneeling nearby. The figures are delightfully executed, especially the small girl with plump cheeks holding an apple and gazing wide-eyed at her eldest sister.

Also interesting is the church clock which was purchased in 1564 for the then exorbitant price of £16.14s 4d. However, it proved to be a sound investment since it remained in working order for 370 years before its bells chimed for the last time in 1934.

🎬 stories and anecdotes   🐦 famous people   🎨 art and craft   🎭 entertainment and sport   🚶 walks

Just to the west of the church is a fine 16th century house, Court Barton (private). The iconoclastic biographer and critic Lytton Strachey (1880-1932) stayed here with a reading party in 1908. It seems that the eminent writer greatly enjoyed his stay, reporting enthusiastically on the area's "mild tranquillities", and a way of life which encompassed "a surplusage of beef and Devonshire cream,.....a village shop with bulls'-eyes,.....more cream and then more beef and then somnolence".

MOLLAND
6 miles E of South Molton off the A361

🏛 St Mary's Church

Hidden away in a maze of lanes skittering across the foothills of Exmoor, Molland is one of Devon's "must-visit" villages for anyone interested in wonderfully unspoilt churches. Following the sale of the village in the early 1600s, **St Mary's Church** stood within the estates of the Courtenay family. During and following the Commonwealth years, the Courtenays remained staunch Catholics and showed no interest in restoring or modernising the Protestant parish church. So today you will still find a Georgian screen and tiers of box-pews, whitewashed walls, an elaborate three-decker pulpit crowned by a trumpeting angel and a colourful Royal Arms blazoned with the name of its painter, Rowlands. Despite their Catholic principles, three late-17th and early-18th century members of the Courtenay family are commemorated by some typically flamboyant monuments of the time. Also within Molland parish lies Great Champson, the farm where in the 18th century the Quartly family introduced and developed their celebrated breed of red North Devon cattle.

WEST ANSTEY
9 miles E of South Molton off the B3227

🚶 Two Moors Walk

The tiny hamlet of West Anstey lies just a mile or so from the Somerset border. **The Two Moors Way** passes by just a little to the east and the slopes on which the hamlet stands continue to rise up to the wilds of Exmoor. Despite being so small, West Anstey nevertheless has its own church, which boasts a fine Norman font and an arcade from the 1200s but is mostly 14th century. The area around West Anstey is one of the emptiest parts of Devon – grand open country dotted with just the occasional farm or a tiny cluster of cottages dotting the landscape.

BISHOP'S NYMPTON
3 miles SE of South Molton off the A361

🎨 Lady Pollard

Bishop's Nympton, King's Nympton, George Nympton, as well as several Nymets, all take the Nympton or Nymet element of their names from the River Yeo which in Saxon and earlier times was known as the Nymet, meaning "river at a holy place". Bishop's Nympton has a long sloping main street, lined with thatched cottages, and a 15th century church whose lofty, well-proportioned tower is considered one of the most beautiful in Devon. For many years the church had a stained glass window erected in Tudor times at the expense of **Lady Pollard,** wife of Sir Lewis, an eminent judge and leading resident of the village. Sir Lewis told the author of *The Worthies of Devon*, John Prince, that he was away on business in London at the time and the details of the design were entrusted to his wife. At the time Sir Lewis left for town, he and his wife already had 21 children, 11 sons and 10 daughters. "But his lady caused one more child than she then had to be set there: presuming that, usually conceiving at her husband's coming home, she should have another. Which, inserted in expectation, came to pass in reality". The oddest thing about the story is that Lady Pollard not only correctly predicted the forthcoming child, but also its sex.

CHULMLEIGH
8 miles S of South Molton off the A377

🌱 Eggesford Forest

With its narrow cobbled lanes, courtyards and quiet squares, Chulmleigh is a delight to explore. Sprawled across the hills above the leafy valley of the Little Dart river, it is one of several attractive small towns in mid-Devon which prospered from the wool trade in the Middle Ages and then declined into sleepy, unspoilt communities. Chulmleigh's prosperity lasted longer than most since it was on the old wagon route to Barnstaple but in 1830 one of the newfangled turnpike roads was constructed along the Taw valley, siphoning off most of its trade. A quarter of a century later the Exeter to Barnstaple railway was built along the same route, the final straw for Chulmleigh as a trade centre. But this charming small town has been left with many original thatched cob cottages which cluster around a fine 15th century church noted for its lofty pinnacled tower and, inside, a wondrously carved rood screen that extends 50ft across the nave and aisles.

To the south of Chulmleigh is **Eggesford Forest** where, in 1919, the newly-formed Forestry Commission planted its first tree. This event is commemorated by a stone unveiled by the Queen in 1956. The stone also marks the planting of more than one million

acres of trees by the Commission. There are two walks through the forest, each about one mile long, which provide visitors with the opportunity of seeing the red deer that live here.

LAPFORD
12 miles S of South Molton on the A377

Remarkably, this small community still has its own railway station. Passenger numbers have been much augmented since British Rail's rather prosaic "Exeter to Barnstaple route" was re-christened as the "**Tarka Line**". The original name may have been lacklustre but the 39-mile journey itself has always been delightful as it winds slowly along the gentle river valleys of the Yeo and the Taw.

Lapford stands high above the River Yeo, its hilltop church a famous local landmark for generations: *"when yew sees Lapford church yew knaws where yew'm be"*. It's well worth a visit since the 15th century rood screen inside is regarded as one of the most exquisitely fashioned in the country. There are five bands of the most delicate carving at the top and above them rise modern figures of the Holy Family, (Jesus, Mary and John), surmounted by the original ornamental ceiling with its carved angels gazing down from the nave roof.

WINKLEIGH
12 miles SW of South Molton on the A3124

This attractive village with its open views across to Dartmoor is believed to have been a beacon station in prehistoric times. When the Normans arrived they built two small castles, one at each end of the village. They were probably intended as bases for hunting in the nearby park – the only Devon park to be mentioned in the Domesday Book. For centuries Winkleigh was an important local

---

🎬 stories and anecdotes   🦜 famous people   🎨 art and craft   ✒ entertainment and sport   🚶 walks

WINKLEIGH CIDER COMPANY

Western Barn, Hatherleigh Road, Winkleigh,
Devon EX19 8AP
Tel: 01837 682896 Tel/Fax: 01837 83560

Part of Devon's heritage, **Winkleigh Cider Company** has been producing the county's favourite drink at Western Barn since 1916. The Barn is surrounded by lovely countryside with many old established orchards that supply the company with all its apples.

The apples are pressed here on site during October and November – if you are visiting at that time, you are welcome to watch the process of cider-making. Supervising this centuries old procedure is David Bridgman who has more than 30 years experience in creating great ciders and has named his cider after his mentor, Sam Inch.

There's a full range of ciders, catering for all different tastes – Sam's Dry, Medium and Sweet, plus a selection of Autumn Scrumpies. One of the most popular blends is Sam's Poudhouse, a smooth, dry keg cider. Visitors can sample the ciders before deciding which they prefer. The shop also sells real ales, locally-made wine, Natural Devon Farm pressed apple juice and a range of gifts and souvenirs.

The shop is open from 9am to 5.30pm, (1pm on Sunday), every day of the year except Christmas Day.

trading centre with its own market, fair and borough court. Today, it's a peaceful little place with thatched cottages nestling up to the mainly 15th century church which has a richly carved and painted wagon roof where 70 golden-winged angels stand guard over the nave.

DOLTON
12 miles SW of South Molton on the B3217

Dolton clusters around its parish church of St Edmund's which boasts a real treasure, a Saxon font more than 1,000 years old. Its intricate carvings depict a fantastic menagerie of winged dragons and writhing serpents, with yet more dragons emerging from the upturned face of a man. Their relevance to the Christian message may be a little obscure but there's no denying their powerful impact.

This little village, together with its even tinier neighbour, Dowland, seem unlikely candidates to host an international arts festival but each year, during May and June, performers, artists and visitors seek out these two small communities in the heart of Devon.

MEETH
14 miles SW of South Molton on the A386

🜨 Tarka Walkway

A mile or so north of Hatherleigh, the A386 crosses the River Torridge and a couple of miles further is the pleasant little village of Meeth whose Old English name means "the meeting of the streams". Indeed, a small brook runs down the hillside into the Torridge. From the early 1700s, Meeth and the surrounding area was noted for its "pipe" and

🏛 historic building 🏛 museum ⬚ historic site 🝆 scenic attraction 🌿 flora and fauna

"ball clay" products, generically known as pottery clay. There are still extensive clay works to the northwest of the village.

But for cyclists and walkers Meeth is much better known as the southern terminus of the **Tarka Trail Cycle / Walkway** which runs northwards through Bideford and Barnstaple.

NORTH TAWTON
16 miles SW of South Molton off the A3072 or A3124

Well-known nowadays to travellers along the Tarka Trail, the small market town of North Tawton was once an important borough governed by a portreeve, an official who was elected each year until the end of the 19th century. This scattered rural community prospered in medieval times but the decline of the local textile industry in the late 1700s dealt a blow from which it never really recovered, - the population today is still less than it was in 1750. The little town also suffered badly from the ravages of a series of fires which destroyed most of the older and more interesting buildings. However, a few survivors can still be found, most notably Broad Hall (private) which dates back to the 15th century.

In a field close to the town is **Bathe Pool,** a grassy hollow that is said to fill with water at times of national crises or when a prominent person is about to die. The pool reportedly filled at the time of the death of Nelson, the Duke of Wellington and Edward VII, and also just before the outbreak of World War I.

HATHERLEIGH
17 miles SW of South Molton on the A386

🦃 Abbeyford Woods 🎨 Hatherleigh Pottery

This medieval market town, which still holds its market every Tuesday, has been popular for many years as a holiday base for fishermen trying their luck on the nearby River Torridge and its tributary which runs alongside the small town.

A good starting point for an exploration of Hatherleigh is the **Tarka Country Information Point** at Hatherleigh Pottery *(see panel on page ????)* where there are exhibits detailing the life and countryside in and around this 1,000-year-old town and you can also pick up leaflets to guide you around Hatherleigh's narrow streets.

Hatherleigh was owned by Tavistock Abbey from the late 900s until the Dissolution of the Monasteries in the 1540s and the picturesquely thatched George Hotel is believed to have been built around 1450 as the abbot's court house. The London Inn also dates from around that time and the Old Church House is thought to be even older.

The town would have possessed an even finer stock of early buildings were it not for a devastating fire in 1840 which destroyed much of the old centre. Fortunately, the 15th century church of St John the Baptist escaped the flames. Set high above the Lew valley, the church's red sandstone walls and sturdy tower still provide a striking focus for this pleasant rural community. Although the church survived the great fire of 1840, a century-and-a-half later hurricane force winds, generated during the storms of January 1990, swashed against its spindly tower and tossed it through the roof of the nave. Thankfully, nobody was in the church at the time.

Until 1966, the Okehampton to Bude railway ran through Hatherleigh. In that year it was closed as part of the notorious "Beeching Cuts". Dr Richard Beeching, a successful businessman until then in the employ of the multi-national company ICI, was appointed in

WOODACOTT HOLIDAY PARK

Woodacott, Thornbury, nr Holsworthy,
Devon EX22 7BT
Tel: 01409 261162
e-mail: slecomberwoodacott@yahoo.co.uk
website: www.woodacottholidaypark.co.uk

Set amongst picturesque valleys and rolling hills in the heart of rural Devon, Woodacott Holiday Park has just about everything you need for a great holiday. For anglers, there are two beautiful lakes which are ideally suited to both seasoned professionals and younger anglers. It is stocked with carp ranging up to 30lbs and tench up to 8lbs, as well as rudd, roach, bream and perch. Both lakes play host to a large variety of wildlife – moorhens, ducks, geese and other birds.

There is a shop in the reception from which you can buy tackle and bait and, in nearby Bude, an angling and camping store for a more comprehensive selection.

If you prefer more energetic activity, the Park has a Leisure Club with a heated indoor swimming pool with Jaccuzi and sauna. Expert swimming tuition is available for both adults and children. The leisure centre also has a well-equipped gymnasium and a snack bar serving food and drinks all day. The Leisure Club is open all day, every day and is available to both residents and nonresidents.

The Park offers a choice of accommodation. There are three holiday bungalows available to rent, each having two bedrooms, one with a double bed, the other with two singles. A Z-bed can be provided, as can cots and high chairs. The fully equipped kitchens have oven/hobs, microwave fridges and all utensils for cooking and cleaning. Bathrooms have shower baths and the spacious lounges are provided with colour TV sets. Bed linen is provided and beds are made ready for your arrival. Each bungalow has outside storage for fishing equipment and a garden/patio area. The charge for fishing in the Park's lakes – just 100 yards away – is included in the cost of the bungalow.

Caravaners will find plenty of hard standing pitches when they arrive, all with electric hook-ups and with plenty of space for an awning. Toilets and shower rooms are available together with water taps and waste disposal.

In the surrounding area there are many exciting and enjoyable attractions such as the Big Sheep - Killarney Springs and The Milky Way, as well as Land's End and the stunning beaches of Bude to name but a few.

HATHERLEIGH POTTERY

20 Market Street, Hatherleigh, Devon EX20 3JP
Tel: 01837 810624
e-mail: hatherleighpots@aol.com
website: www.hatherleighpottery.co.uk

Located in a delightful and secluded cobbled courtyard off Market Street, **Hatherleigh Pottery** is owned and run by Jane Payne who has been a keen potter for more than 40 years. After retiring from teaching, she took a four-year course in ceramics and subsequently bought the pottery. Jane specialises in hand-thrown, practical domestic stoneware – jugs, mugs, bowls, dishes and the like. Much of her work is sgraffito decorated and her use of a wide range of glazes brings colour and variety to her wares. All Jane's pottery is trade-marked with a small fish imprinted near the base.

The light and airy showrooms at the Pottery also feature work by other craftspeople such as Michael Taylor, a local potter who shows mugs, vases and casseroles in a style that makes an interesting contrast with Jane's work. Also on display are Jane Ritchie's ranges of shoulder bags and handbags, all delightfully designed and beautifully made in rich, colourful textiles; and Gill Salway's original prints using a variety of techniques. The Pottery is open from Easter to New Year, Monday to Saturday, from 10am-5pm.

1963 by Prime Minister Harold Macmillan, to sort out what the Conservative government of the day regarded as the mess created by the Labour party's nationalisation of the railways in 1948. Naturally, Dr Beeching's solution was to close every mile of line that did not produce a paper profit. The last train on the Hatherleigh to Bude line, a prized local amenity, steamed its way into Cornwall on May 16th, 1966, then to a siding, and then to rust. Long stretches of the old track bed of the railway now provide some attractive walking.

There's more good walking at **Abbeyford Woods,** about a mile to the east of the village, with a particularly lovely stretch running alongside the River Okement.

Holsworthy

🍃 St Peter's Fair

Wednesday is a good day to visit Holsworthy. That's when this little town, just four miles from the Cornish border, holds its weekly market. This is very much the traditional kind of street market, serving a large area of the surrounding countryside and with locally-produced fresh cream, butter, cheese, and vegetables all on sale. The town gets even livelier in early July when it gives itself over to the amusements of the three-day-long **St Peter's Fair.** The Fair opens with the curious old custom of the Pretty Maid Ceremony. Back in 1841, a Holsworthy merchant bequeathed a legacy to provide a small

📖 stories and anecdotes 🍃 famous people 🌿 art and craft 🍃 entertainment and sport 🏃 walks

Holsworthy Museum

Manor Offices, Holsworthy, Devon EX22 6DJ
Tel: 01409 259337
e-mail: holsworthy@devonmuseums.net   website: www.devonmuseums.net

Housed in an 18th century parsonage, this small museum gives you an insight into

Holsworthy's heritage and traditions.
Various themed displays cover the town,
local railway, agriculture, trades and the
World Wars. Researchers into family and
local history may view, by prior
arrangement, a selection of local parish
registers on microfiche, IGI fiche and
Census data as well as information held in
the Local History unit. The museum is run
entirely by volunteers and is dependent on
donations, a small entrance fee and
support from local Councils. Open February
to December. Groups can visit at other
times by arrangement.

GALLOSEK ARTS

Gallosek House, Pins Park, Holsworthy, Devon EX22 6HY
Tel/Fax: 01409 259353
Mob: 07854114462/07870892986
e-mail: michelle.nixonwelburn12@btinternet.com
website: www.gallosekholidays.com

Whatever kind of West Country holiday you are looking for, you will
find something that appeals within the huge range of possibilities
offered by **Gallosek Arts**. The accommodation extends from two
stars to five stars and the varied array of properties includes
charming country cottages, bed & breakfast establishments, seaside
and rural country inns, magnificent manors, quaint old farmhouses,
lodges, chalets and caravans, and even camping. The standards
throughout are of the highest, tariffs are highly competitive and the
service is excellent. There are properties available all across Devon,
Cornwall and central South Coast regions as well as Brittany, France
and other Meditterean destinations. The off peak mini-breaks
represent extraordinarily good value for money.

    The company also offers a choice of art courses to suit all
budgets and which are tailored appropriately for beginners,
intermediary and advanced participants. Each person receives
comprehensive one-to-one tutoring in small groups of up to six
persons, and the courses run for either three days or two days
with one day courses also available. The course facilities are
always close to where you choose to stay and have been specially
furnished and fitted to provide a truly fulfilling experience.

🏛 historic building   🏛 museum   🏚 historic site   🝓 scenic attraction   🌿 flora and fauna

payment each year to a local spinster, under the age of 30 and noted for her good looks, demure manner and regular attendance at church. Rather surprisingly, in view of the last two requirements, the bequest still finds a suitable recipient each year.

Holsworthy's most striking architectural features are the two Victorian viaducts that once carried the railway line to Bude. The viaducts stride high above the southern edge of the town and, since they now form part of a footpath along the old track, it's possible to walk across them for some stunning views of the area.

An interesting feature in the parish church is an organ built in 1668 by Renatus Hunt for All Saints Church, Chelsea. In 1723, it was declared worn out but was nevertheless purchased by a Bideford church. There it gave good service for some 140 years before it was written off once again. Removed to Holsworthy, it has been here ever since.

The area around Holsworthy is particularly popular with cyclists. There are three clearly-designated routes starting and finishing in the town, and it also lies on the **West Country Way**, a 250-mile cycle route from Padstow to Bristol and Bath which opened in the spring of 1997.

Around Holsworthy

SHEBBEAR
7 miles NE of Holsworthy off the A388

🏠 Devils Stone

This attractive village is set around a spacious square laid out in the Saxon manner with a church at one end and a hostelry at the other. Lying in a hollow just outside St Michael's

THE DEVIL'S STONE INN
Shebbear, Devon EX21 5RV
Tel: 01409 281210
website: www.devilsstone.com

The attractive village of Shebbear is set around a spacious square with its church at one end and **The Devil's Stone Inn** at the other. Nearby, beneath an ancient oak tree is the huge boulder, weighing about a ton, from which the inn takes its name. According to one legend, it was dropped by the Devil while descending from heaven to hell. Every November 5th, the bell-ringers of the village 'fire' all the church bells and then turn the Stone over with crowbars "to keep the Devil away for another year".

A board in Stephen and Christine Hurst's delightful 16th century inn tells the full story; another certifies that the inn has qualified as one of the 12 most haunted pubs in Britain. It must also rate as one of the most lively, with pool, darts and skittles available, and the local football and cricket teams making the inn their base. There are real ales on tap and a good choice of wholesome and appetising fare. The inn also has eight comfortable guest bedrooms, all recently refurbished, all en suite and all equipped with colour TV.

🎭 stories and anecdotes   🦜 famous people   ✍ art and craft   🎵 entertainment and sport   🏃 walks

churchyard is a huge lump of rock, weighing about a ton, which is known as the **Devil's Stone.** According to local legend, the boulder was placed here by Old Nick who challenged the villagers to move it, threatening that disaster would strike if they could not. Every year since then, on November 5th (a date established long before the Gunpowder Plot of 1605), a curious ceremony has taken place. After sounding a peal of bells, the bell ringers come out of the church and set about the stone with sticks and crowbars. Once they have successfully turned the stone over, they return in triumph to the bell tower to sound a second peal. The story is recounted in greater detail in the village hostelry, The Devils Stone Inn.

SHEEPWASH
9 miles E of Holsworthy off the A3072 or A386

Sheepwash is yet another Devon community to have been devastated by fire. The conflagration here occurred in 1742 and the destruction was so great that for more than 10 years the village was completely deserted. Slowly, the villagers returned, built new houses in stone, and today if you want the essence of Devon distilled into one location, then the village square at Sheepwash is just about perfect. Along one side stands the famous Half Moon Inn, renowned amongst fishermen; on another, the old church tower rises above pink-washed thatched cottages, while in the centre, cherry trees shelter the ancient village pump.

Just south of the village, the minor road crosses the River Torridge and there's a rather heartening story about the bridge here. Until well into the 1600s, the only way of crossing the river was by means of stepping stones. One day, when the river was in full spate, a young man attempting to return to the village was swept away and drowned. His father, John Tusbury, was grief-stricken but responded to the tragedy by providing money to build a bridge. He also donated sufficient funds for it to be maintained by establishing the Bridgeland Trust and stipulating that any surplus income should be used to help in the upkeep of the church and chapel. The Trust is still in operation and nowadays also funds outings for village children and pensioners.

NORTHLEW
10 miles SE of Holsworthy off the A3072 or A3079

As at Sheepwash, the thatched cottages and houses stand around a large central square which is dominated by a charming 15th century church standing on the hilltop above the River Lew. The church is noted for its Norman remains and the exceptional (mainly Tudor) woodwork in the roof, bench ends and screen. Also of interest is one of the stained glass windows which features four saints. St Thomas, to whom the church is dedicated, is shown holding a model of the church; St Augustine, the first Archbishop of Canterbury, holds the priory gateway, while St Joseph carries the Holy Grail and the staff which grew into the famous Glastonbury thorn tree. The fourth figure is simply clad in a brown habit and carries a bishop's crozier and a spade. This is St Brannock who is credited with being the first man to cultivate the wild lands of this area by clearing woodland and ploughing and could therefore be regarded as the patron saint of farmers.

CLAWTON
3 miles S of Holsworthy, on the A388

A good indication of the mildness of the Devon climate is the number of vineyards which have been established over the last 30

THE MULE COMPANY

Church Gate Farm, Northlew, nr Okehampton, Devon EX20 3NJ
Tel: 01409 221331   Fax: 01409 221183
e-mail: info@themulecompany.co.uk
website: www.themulecompany.co.uk

A family business established in 1982, **The Mule Company** offers a wide range of extremely comfortable slip-on footwear, all of the highest quality and finished to exacting standards.

Styles range from mules with a single piece leather upper, through two-tone styles to the Aztec and Floral options which are individually hand finished with superb designs in specialist leather paint.

A warm welcome awaits you at Church Gate Farm should you wish to make a purchase or view the entire range(please phone first to make an appointment). The Mules are also available via mail order on their secure internet site. You can even send them a sample of the colour you want and they will do their best to replicate it.

The company aims to supply you with the perfect fitting shoe, so if you have 'problem feet' or you are unsure of your foot size you can send them your 'foot profile' by getting someone to draw around your foot on a piece of paper. The company will then use this profile to despatch the correct size.

years or so. **Clawford Vineyard** in the valley of the River Claw is a good example. Set in more than 78 acres of vines and orchards, the vineyard's owners welcome visitors to sample their home-grown wines and ciders, and in the autumn to watch that year's vintage being produced.

In and Around Dartmoor

OKEHAMPTON

🏰 Okehampton Castle   🏛 Museum of Dartmoor Life

🚂 Dartmoor Railway

The old travel-writer's cliché of a "county of contrasts" can't be avoided when describing the landscape around Okehampton. To the north and west, the puckered green hills of North Devon roll away to the coast; to the south, lie the wildest stretches of Dartmoor with the great peaks of **High Willhays** and **Yes Tor** rising to more than 2,000ft. At this height they are, officially, mountains but quite puny compared with their original altitude: geologists believe that at one time the surface of Dartmoor stood at 15,000ft above sea level. Countless centuries of erosion have reduced it to a plateau of whale-backed granite ridges with an average height of around 1,200ft. After so many millions of years of erosion, the moor has become strewn with fragments of surface granite, or moorstone. It was because of this ready-to-use stone that Dartmoor became one of the

🎭 stories and anecdotes   🐦 famous people   🎨 art and craft   🎵 entertainment and sport   🚶 walks

most populous areas of early Britain, its inhabitants using the easily quarried granite to create their stone rows, circles, and burial chambers. Stone was also used to build their distinctive hut-circles of which there are more than 1,500 scattered across the moor.

From Celtic times Okehampton has occupied an important position on the main route to Cornwall. Romantically sited atop a wooded hill and dominating the surrounding valley of the River Okement are the remains of **Okehampton Castle** (EH). This is the largest medieval castle in Devon and the ruins are still mightily impressive even though the castle was dismantled on the orders of Henry VIII after its owner, the Earl of Devon, was convicted of treason.

A good place to start a tour of the town is the **Museum of Dartmoor Life,** housed in a former mill with a restored water wheel outside. In the surrounding courtyard, you will also find the Dartmoor National Park Visitor Centre, craft and gift shops, and a tea-room. Amongst the town's interesting buildings are the 15th century **Chapel of Ease,** and the **Town Hall**, a striking three-storey building erected in 1685 as a private house and converted to its current use in the 1820s. And don't miss the wonderful Victorian arcade within the shopping centre which is reminiscent of London's Burlington Arcade.

Okehampton is also the hub of the **Dartmoor Railway,** part of the former Southern Railway main line from London to Plymouth and Cornwall. This was once the route of the famous Atlantic Coast Express and the Devon Belle Pullman. Okehampton Station has been restored to its 1950s

TEAZLES

44 Red Lion Yard, Okehampton,
Devon EX20 1AW
Tel: 01837 54352

Teazles was established in 1999 by Jean Swift, a lady with many years experience in the womens clothing business. Her shop, located in the heart of this historic old town, offers a wide range of womens' wear – anything from casual to classic. The business has gone from strength to strength and was nominated as one of the top six shops in the country for customer service in the *Drapers Record* Awards.

The service certainly is outstanding, and the atmosphere relaxed and friendly with comfortable armchairs to sink into and magazines to browse through. "We love trading in this old market town," says Jean. "It has a lovely atmosphere and plenty for the visitor to see and do." There's a park, leisure centre, good eating places, lively pubs, two rivers and the largest medieval castle in Devon.

🏛 historic building   🏛 museum   🏛 historic site   Ꮺ scenic attraction   🌿 flora and fauna

EVERSFIELD MANOR

Bratton Clovelly, Okehampton, Devon EX4 4JF
Tel: 01837 871400 Fax: 01837 871114
e-mail: charlottereynolds@eversfieldmanor.co.uk
website: www.eversfieldorganic.co.uk

Nestling deep in the heart of the beautiful Devon countryside on the edge of Dartmoor National Park, **Eversfield Manor** is an 850-acre organic farm estate offering luxurious self-catering chalet style accommodation at Eversfield Lodge, as well as organised rough shooting days, conference facilities and activity breaks. The award-winning organic meat raised on the farm is sold throughout the UK by mail order. Eversfield Lodge offers groups of friends and families a high standard of accommodation in eight en suite twin or double-bedded rooms. Guests can relax in the comfortable living room which commands majestic views across Dartmoor; French doors open onto a terrace which leads down to the landscaped gardens.

The Lodge has a games room with a full sized pool table and a splendid granite open fireplace. There is a spacious, modern and well-equipped kitchen and a dining room that provides an elegant setting for evening meals around the large refectory table. Meals can be provided, using organic produce from the estate and other local organic producers. The Lodge is close to some of the best walking country in England; horse riding, cycling, watersports, fishing and golf are all available nearby. Clay pigeon shooting is available on the estate, whilst more experienced guns are invited to organise a day's shooting with Mark Bury, the land owner.

---

appearance, complete with buffet and licensed bar. Sampford Courtenay Station, 3.5 miles to the east was re-opened in 2004 and provides access to pleasant walking routes, including the Devon Heartlands Way footpath. To the west, Meldon Quarry Station is the highest station in southern England. It has two visitor centres, a buffet with licensed bar, a picnic area and a spectacular verandah giving wonderful views of Dartmoor's highest tors and the Meldon Reservoir dam.

SAMPFORD COURTENAY
5 miles NE of Okehampton

A charming and unspoilt village with a fine medieval church, Sampford Courtenay is notable for its picturesque assortment of cottages, many of them thatched and built of cob. This local building material is created by mixing well-sieved mud with straw. This is then built up in sections. It was the local tradition to limewash the outside of the cottages at Whitsuntide, a process that helps to preserve the cob. This simple material is surprisingly durable and will last indefinitely provided it has a "ggod hat", that is, if the thatched roof is well looked after. Another unusual feature of the village is that every road out of it is marked by a medieval stone cross.

This peaceful and pretty village was the unlikely setting for the start of the Prayer Book Revolt of 1549. It was originally initiated as a protest against Edward VI's introduction of an English prayer book, but when the undisciplined countrymen marched on Exeter, it degenerated into a frenzy of looting and

---

📖 stories and anecdotes   🦜 famous people   ✏️ art and craft   🍴 entertainment and sport   🚶 walks

LOWER TRECOTT FARM

Sampford Courtenay, Okehampton, Devon EX20 2TD
Tel: 01837 880118

Bed & breakfast guests arriving at Lower Trecott Farm are greeted by owner Nicky Craig with a warm welcome and a cream tea. This delightful Grade II listed farmhouse has thick walls built of traditional Devon cob and a charming interior featuring oak beams, inglenook fireplaces, bread ovens and a cross-passage. The house stands on a two-acre smallholding which is home to a variety of hens and a small flock of sheep. Guests are welcome to use and enjoy the evolving garden with its natural spring-fed pond. Inside, the guest lounge has colour TV, a wood-burning stove and a good selection of books and games.

The accommodation boasts a four-Diamonds Silver rating and comprises one family suite, one double and one twin room. All are provided with hairdryer, radio/alarm, dressing gown and hospitality tray. Breakfast here is a real treat, based on local produce and the farm's own free range eggs. No evening meal is provided but there are good eating places nearby. A small fully equipped kitchen is available for the use of guests, as well as laundry facilities and a microwave convection oven. Children are welcome – a cot, high chair, playpen and babysitting service are all available.

---

violence. Confronted by an army led by Lord Russell, the rioters were soon overwhelmed and several unfortunate ringleaders executed.

STICKLEPATH

2 miles E of Okehampton off the A30

🏛 Museum of Waterpower

The little village of Sticklepath boasts one of the most interesting exhibits of industrial archaeology in Devon. **The Museum of Waterpower** (National Trust) is housed in the Finch Foundry which from 1814 to 1960 was renowned for producing the finest sharp-edged tools in the West Country. The three massive waterwheels are now working again, driving the ancient machinery, and pounding rhythms of the steam hammer and rushing

water vividly evoke that age of noisy toil.

SOUTH ZEAL

4 miles E of Okehampton off the A30

South Zeal is yet another of the many Devon villages which have good reason to be grateful for the major road-building undertakings of the 1970s. The village sits astride what used to be the main road from Exeter to Launceston and the Cornwall coast, a road which as late as 1975 was still laughably designated on maps of the time as a "Trunk (major) Road". The "Trunk Road" was actually little more than a country lane but it was also the only route available for many thousands of holiday-makers making their way to the Cornish resorts. Today, the village is bypassed by the A30 dual carriageway.

🏚 historic building   🏛 museum   🏛 historic site   ⌬ scenic attraction   🌿 flora and fauna

Isolated in the middle of the broad main street stand a simple medieval market cross and St Mary's chapel, rebuilt in 1713. To the south of the village rises the great granite hump of Dartmoor. On its flanks, for the few years between 1901-9, the villagers of South Zeal found sorely needed employment in a short-lived copper mine.

WHIDDON DOWN
7 miles E of Okehampton off the A30

🏛 Spinsters Rock

About a mile south of the village stands the **Spinsters' Rock**, the best surviving chambered tomb in the whole of Devon. According to legend, three spinsters erected the dolmen one morning before breakfast, an impressive feat since the capstone, supported by just three uprights seven feet high, weighs 16 tons.

BELSTONE
2 miles SE of Okehampton off the A30

🏛 Nine Stones

Surrounded by the magnificent scenery of the Dartmoor National Park, Belstone is a picturesque village with a triangular village green, complete with stocks and a stone commemorating the coronation of George V, and a church dating back to the 13th century.

A path from Belstone village leads up to the ancient standing stone circle known as the **Nine Stones,** although there are actually well over a dozen of them. Local folklore asserts that these stones under Belstone Tor were formed when a group of maidens was discovered dancing on the Sabbath and turned to stone. The problem with this story is that the stone circle was in place long before the arrival of Christianity in England. It is also claimed that the mysterious stones change

position when the clock strikes noon. What is certain is that the view across mid-Devon from this site is quite breathtaking.

Another path from Belstone leads south to a spot on the northern edge of Dartmoor when the ashes of the Poet Laureate, Ted Hughes, were scattered and where a granite stone was placed to his memory.

For lovers of solitude, this is memorable country, unforgettably evoked by Sir Arthur Conan Doyle in *The Hound of the Baskervilles.* Recalling the villain's fate in that book, walkers should beware of the notorious "feather beds" – deep bogs signalled by a quaking cover of brilliant green moss.

DREWSTEIGNTON
10 miles SE of Okehampton off the A30

🏛 Castle Drogo

This appealing village stands on a ridge overlooking the valley of the River Teign and the celebrated beauty spot near the 400-year-old Fingle Bridge. Thatched cottages and a medieval church stand grouped around a square, very picturesque and much photographed. To the south of the village, Prestonbury Castle and Cranbrook Castle are not castles at all but Iron Age hilltop fortresses. **Castle Drogo** (National Trust) on the other hand, looks every inch the medieval castle but in fact was constructed between 1911 and 1930 – the last castle to be built in England. Occupying a spectacular site on a rocky outcrop with commanding views over Dartmoor, it was built to a design by Lutyens for the self-made millionaire Sir Julius Drewe on land once owned by his Norman ancestor, Drogo de Teigne. Surrounding Sir Julius's dream home is an impressive garden which displays colour and interest all year round.

🎭 stories and anecdotes   🦜 famous people   🎨 art and craft   🎭 entertainment and sport   🚶 walks

CHAGFORD

10 miles SE of Okehampton off the A382

An ancient settlement and Stannary town, Chagford lies in a beautiful setting between the pleasant wooded valley of the North Teign river and the stark grandeur of the high moor. In the centre of the town stands the former **Market House**, a charming octagonal building erected in 1862. Around the square are some old style family shops providing interesting shopping

St Michael's Church, mostly 15th century, has an elaborate monument to Sir John Wyddon who died in 1575. But the church is better known because of the tragic death of one of his descendants here in October 1641. Mary Whiddon was shot at the altar by a jilted lover as she was being married, an incident that is said to have inspired R.D. Blackmore's *Lorna Doone*. Her tombstone bears the inscription "Behold a Matron yet a Maid". Her ghost is thought to haunt Whiddon Park Guest House and a young woman dressed in black appeared there on the morning of a wedding reception due to take place later that day.

The famous Dartmoor guide, James Perrot, lived in Chagford between 1854 and 1895, and is buried in St Michael's churchyard. It was he who noted that some of the farms around Chagford had no wheeled vehicles as late as 1830. On the other hand, Perrot lived to see the town install electric street lighting in 1891 making Chagford one of the first communities west of London to possess this amenity.

It was Perrot also who began the curious

GODOLPHIN FINE ART

11 The Square, Chagford,
Devon TQ13 8AE
Tel: 01647 433999
website: www.godolphinfineart.com

Located in Chagford's historic square, **Godolphin Fine Art** specialises in original watercolour and oil paintings from the 18th century to the present day. There is always a varied and interesting selection of paintings on display by highly regarded internationally renowned artists. Visitors are welcome to enjoy browsing amongst the enticing display which includes a good range of high quality oak and country furniture from the 17th to the early 19th centuries.

The gallery is open all year from 10.30am until 5.30pm, Sundays 11am until 5pm, Thursdays by appointment. A full colour catalogue is available on request and you can view some of the paintings available for sale by visiting the gallery's website.

'On the moors, Nr Belstone, Dartmoor'
F J Widgery 1861-1942 - Watercolour & Gouache 20x30"

'On the River Dart at Dittisham, Devon'
Warren Williams A.R.C.A 1863-1918 - Watercolour 23x34"

🏦 historic building   📷 museum   🏛 historic site   🌿 scenic attraction   🌿 flora and fauna

BLUE ZOO

38 The Square, Chagford, Devon TQ13 8AB
Tel: 01647 432950
e-mail: louise@tryptych.co.uk
website: www.bluezoo.uk.com

Louise McCarthy, the owner of **Blue Zoo**, likes to think of her establishment as a "one stop shop for a present or something for your home, where you may go in to buy a vase but come out with a necklace, perfumery, a bag, a Cath Kidston notebook, a light fitting, a blanket etc., etc." Louise has a background of working in the fashion section at Liberty in Regent Street and moved into contract interior design some 18 years ago. She prides herself on offering unusual products at a good price, working heavily with colour and bringing a personal and friendly touch to the business. Her interior design service includes fabrics and soft furnishings, a wide range of styles of furniture, pictures, wallpaper, lighting and other accessories to give distinction to your home.

Inside the double-fronted shop, white and black walls provide a perfect background for displaying the wide range of colourful items. There are white display units with beautiful wavy-edged oak tops and large drum shades in black and white silk suspended from the ceiling. In the design office at the rear of the shop, customers can browse through pattern books from companies such as Designers Guild, Osborne & Little, Romo and others.

practice of letterbox stamp collecting. He installed the first letterbox at Carnmere Pool near the heart of the moor so his Victorian clients could send postcards home, stamped to prove they had been there. Today, there are hundreds of such letterboxes scattered all over Dartmoor.

To the west of Chagford, an exceptionally pleasant lane leads upstream from Chagford Bridge through the wooded valley of the North Teign river. (For 1.5 miles of its length, this lane is joined by the Two Moors Way, the long-distance footpath which runs all the way from Ivybridge on the southern edge of Dartmoor to the Bristol Channel coast.) A rock beside the river known as the **Holed Stone** has a large round cavity. If you climb through this, local people assure you, a host of afflictions from rheumatism to infertility will be cured.

The land to the south of Chagford rises abruptly towards Kestor Rock and Shovel Down, the sites of impressive Bronze Age settlements and, a little further on, the imposing Long Stone stands at the point where the parishes of Gidleigh and Chagford end and Duchy of Cornwall land begins.

LYDFORD
8 miles SW of Okehampton off the A386

🏰 Lydford Castle   🌊 Lydford Gorge

In Saxon times, there were just four royal boroughs in Devon: Exeter, Barnstaple, Totnes and, astonishingly, Lydford which is now a pleasant small town still occupying the same strategic position on the River Lyd

Lydford Gorge

died in 1802. The inscription includes the statement that George's life had been *Wound up in hope of being taken in hand by his Maker and of being thoroughly cleansed and repaired and set going in the world to come.*

To the southwest of the village, the valley of the River Lyd suddenly narrows to form the 1.5 mile long **Lydford Gorge** (NT), one of Devon's most spectacular natural features. Visitors can follow the riverside path to the Devil's Cauldron, or wander along the two-mile walk to the White Lady, a narrow 100ft high waterfall. Back in the 17th century, the then remote Lydford Gorge provided a secure refuge for a band of brigands who called themselves the Gubbinses. Their leader was a certain Roger Rowle, (dubbed the "Robin Hood of the West"), whose exploits are recounted in Charles Kingsley's novel *Westward Ho!*

which made it so important in those days. In the 11th century, the Normans built a fortification here which was superseded 100 years later by the present **Lydford Castle**, an austere stone fortress which for generations served the independent tin miners of Dartmoor as both a court and a prison. The justice meted out here was notoriously arbitrary. William Browne of Tavistock (1590-1643) observed:

I oft have heard of Lydford law,
How in the morn they hang and draw
And sit in judgement after.

Lydford parish is the largest in England, encompassing the whole of the Forest of Dartmoor, and for many centuries the dead were brought down from the moor along the ancient Lych Way for burial in St Petroc's churchyard. A tombstone near the porch bears a lengthy and laboriously humorous epitaph to the local watchmaker, George Routleigh, who

Tavistock

🖉 **Goose Fair**

This handsome old town is one of Devon's four stannary towns, so named from the Latin word for tin – *stannum*. These towns – the others are Ashburton, Chagford and Plympton – were the only places licensed to weigh and stamp the metal extracted from the moor.

For most of its recorded history, Tavistock has had only two owners. Tavistock Abbey and the Russell family. The Benedictine abbey was founded here, beside the River Tavy, in

🏛 historic building   🏛 museum   🏛 historic site   ᐯ scenic attraction   🌱 flora and fauna

around 974, close to a Saxon stockade or *stoc*, now incorporated into the town's name. The town grew up around the abbey and, following the discovery of tin on the nearby moors in the 12th century, both flourished.

Then, in 1539, Henry VIII closed the Abbey and sold the building, along with its vast estates to John Russell whose family, as Earls and Dukes of Bedford, owned most of the town until 1911. The present town centre is essentially the creation of the Russell family, who after virtually obliterating the once-glorious abbey, created a completely new town plan. Later, in the 1840s, Francis the 7th Duke diverted some of the profits from his copper mines to build the imposing **Guildhall** and several other civic buildings. He also remodelled the Bedford Hotel, and constructed a model estate of artisans' cottages on the western side of the town. A statue of the duke stands in Bedford Square while, at the western entrance to the town, there is a statue of Sir Francis Drake who is believed to have been born at nearby Crowndale.

One of the legacies of the abbey is the annual three-day fair, granted in 1105, which has now evolved into **Goose Fair**, a wonderful traditional street fair held on the second Wednesday in October. Tavistock was also permitted to hold a weekly market which, more than 900 years later, still takes place every Friday in the Pannier Market, a building that was another gift to the town from the 7th duke. There's also an antiques and crafts market on Tuesdays, and a Victorian market

SOUTH WEST CRAFTS

Church Lane, Tavistock, Devon PL19 8AA
Tel: *01822 612689*
e-mail: *enquiry@southwestcrafts.co.uk*
website: *www.southwestcrafts.co.uk*

Located beside the church in the heart of the market town of Tavistock you will find the South West Crafts gallery, owned by Jon Hosking. Jon studied art & ceramics at Southend college of art & design and ran a successful wooden games business for two years in London before moving to the west country to start a family.

Jon was inspired so much by the local crafts in Devon and Cornwall he decided to start up a South West Crafts Gallery to promote quality crafts from local craftspeople. The website was the first venture which started in 1999 to help local craftspeople promote their work on the internet, then the Gallery in July 2004, originally located on the edge of Tavistock's famous Pannier Market and now moved to Church Lane in 2006 to a much larger gallery space allowing for more local quality work to be displayed in a wonderfully tranquil and tasteful setting.

Visitors to the gallery will find a wide selection of skilfully produced crafts from of over 50 makers from throughout the South West, some designer-craftsmen of national and international repute, with an ever changing selection from jewellers, ceramicists, woodturners to sculptors, glass blowers and metalworkers all at very reasonable prices.

⚑ stories and anecdotes   🐦 famous people   ✏ art and craft   ✐ entertainment and sport   🚶 walks

BEERA FARMHOUSE

Milton Abbot, Tavistock, Devon PL19 8PL
Tel/Fax: 01822 870216
e-mail:hilary.tucker@farming.co.uk
website: www.beera-farm.co.uk

Set in the heart of the wonderfully peaceful Tamar valley – a designated Area of Outstanding Natural Beauty – Beera Farmhouse is a traditional stone-built Victorian farmhouse in the middle of an 180-acre working beef and sheep farm. This unspoilt area contains a wealth of flora and fauna, and you may be fortunate enough to catch a glimpse of an otter or kingfisher down by the river, or a deer coming out of the wood to graze. There's a spacioius garden with extensive views across to Cornwall where guests can sit and relax. Guests also have the use of a comfortable lounge with an open log fire, TV, video, piano and a selection of board games and books. On arrival, your host Hilary Tucker serves a delicious home-baked traditional cream tea here.

There are three guest bedrooms, all en suite and tastefully decorated with Laura Ashley and Dorma furnishings, and generously equipped with colour TV, clock/radio and hospitality tray complete with home-made biscuits. Children are very welcome – a cot, linen and high chair are available, and there's also a fridge for baby milk and food. Please note that Beera Farmhouse is a non-smoking establishment.

---

on Wednesdays when many of the stallholders appear in period costume.

Around Tavistock

BRENT TOR
4½ miles N of Tavistock off the A386

🏛 Church of St Michael of the Rocks

Brent Tor, a 1,100ft-high volcanic plug that rears up from the surrounding countryside is one of the most striking sights in the whole of Dartmoor. The **Church of St Michael of the Rocks** stands on the top of it. The fourth smallest complete church in England, St Michael's is only 15 feet wide and 37 feet long and has walls only 10 feet high but three feet

thick. Constructed of stone that was quarried from the rock beneath, the church is surrounded by a steep churchyard that contains a surprising number of graves considering its precarious and seemingly soil-less position. Sometimes lost in cloud, the scramble to the summit of Brent Tor is rewarded on a clear day with magnificent views of Dartmoor, Bodmin Moor and the sea at Plymouth Sound.

LEWDOWN
8 miles N of Tavistock off the A30

🏛 Revd. Sabine Baring-Gould

The completion of a bypass in the early 1990s takes the main road between Exeter and Launceston away from the centre of this

🏛 historic building   🏛 museum   🏛 historic site   🔾 scenic attraction   🌿 flora and fauna

village, making Lewdown a much quieter and more enjoyable place to visit. The village lies within the parish of Lewtrenchard, whose rector for 43 years, between 1881 and 1924, was the **Revd Sabine Baring-Gould**. Best known as the composer of the hymn, *Onward, Christian Soldiers*, Baring-Gould was also a prolific writer. He regularly produced two or three books a year – novels, historical works such as *Curious Myths of the Middle Ages*, and books on Devon legends and folklore. Baring-Gould nevertheless found time to restore St Peter's Church. His most remarkable success was the creation of a replica of a medieval screen that his grandfather, also a rector here, had destroyed. The grandson found enough pieces remaining for the replica to be made. It is very impressive with an elaborate canopied loft decorated with paintings of 23 saints.

The Revd. Sabine scandalised Victorian society by marrying a Lancashire mill girl but the union proved to be a happy one and they had a huge family. One local story tells how, one day, emerging from his study, the rector saw a little girl coming down the stairs. "You look nice, my dear, in your pretty frock," he said, vaguely remembering that a children's party was under way. "Whose little girl are you?" "Yours, papa," she answered and burst into tears.

MARY TAVY
3 miles NE of Tavistock on the A386

🏠 Wheal Betsy

The twin villages of Mary Tavy and Peter Tavy lie on opposite banks of the River Tavy and each takes its name from the saint of its parish church. Roughly twice the size of its east bank twin, Mary Tavy stands in the heart of Dartmoor's former mining area. Just to the north of the village, lies a survivor from those

days. **Wheal Betsy**, a restored pumping engine house, was once part of the Prince Arthur Consols mine that produced lead, silver and zinc. In the village, the grave of William Crossing, the historian of the moor whose magisterial guide first published in the early 1900s is still in print, can be found in the churchyard. Crossing moved to Peter Tavy in 1909 and described it as "a quiet little place, with a church embosomed by trees, a chapel, a school and a small inn". Inside the impressive medieval church there is a poignant memorial to the five daughters of a 17th century rector. The oldest of them was less than a year when she died:

*They breathed awhile and looked the world about
And, like newly-lighted candles, soon went out.*

POSTBRIDGE
14 miles NE of Tavistock on the B3212

🏠 Clapper Bridge   📷 Warren House Inn

In prehistoric times, the area around Postbridge was the "metropolis" of Dartmoor as the wealth of Bronze Age remains bears witness. Today, the village is best known for its **Clapper Bridge** which probably dates back to the 13th century and is the best preserved of all the Devon clapper bridges. Spanning the East Dart River, the bridge is a model of medieval minimalist construction with just three huge slabs of granite laid across solid stone piers. Not wide enough for wheeled traffic, the bridge would originally have been used by pack horses following the post road from Exeter into Cornwall.

Two miles along the road to Moretonhampstead, **Warren House Inn** claims to be the third highest tavern in England. It used to stand on the other side of the road but in 1845 a fire destroyed that building. According to tradition, when the

📷 stories and anecdotes   🦜 famous people   🎨 art and craft   ✍ entertainment and sport   🚶 walks

POWDERMILLS POTTERY

Postbridge, Dartmoor, Devon PL20 6SP
Tel: 01822 880263
e-mail: joss@powdermillspottery.com
website: www.powdermillspottery.com

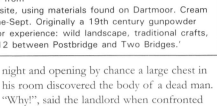

Powdermills gathers the work of Dartmoor's finest
craftspeople. The result is a range of useful things for the
home, beautifully made by individual craft-makers from
clay, wood, willow, and more. Pots are made on site, using materials found on Dartmoor. Cream
teas are served in the courtyard at weekends June-Sept. Originally a 19th century gunpowder
factory, Powdermills offers the complete Dartmoor experience: wild landscape, traditional crafts,
history and clotted cream. Find them on the B3212 between Postbridge and Two Bridges.'

present inn was built its landlord carried some
still-smouldering turves across the road to the
hearth of his new hostelry and that fire has
been burning ever since. It's a pleasant enough
sight in summer and must have been even
more welcome in the winter of 1963. In that
year, the Warren House Inn was cut off by
heavy snow drifts some 20ft deep for almost
three months and supplies had to be flown in
by helicopter. Such a remote inn naturally
generates some good tales. Like the one about
the traveller who stayed here one winter's

night and opening by chance a large chest in
his room discovered the body of a dead man.
"Why!", said the landlord when confronted
with the deceased, "tis only feyther! 'Twas too
cold to take 'un to the buryin', so mother
salted 'un down!"

PRINCETOWN
9 miles E of Tavistock on the B3212

🏛 **Dartmoor Prison Heritage Centre**

Princetown, best known for its forbidding
prison, stands 1,400ft above sea level in
an area of the moor which is notorious
for its atrocious climate. It gets doused
with 80 to 100 inches of rain a year,
more than three times the average for
Exeter which is less than 20 miles away.

That a settlement should be located
here at all was the brainchild of one
man, Sir Thomas Tyrwhitt, the owner
of a local granite quarry. He proposed
that a special prison should be built
here to house the thousands of troops
captured during the Napoleonic wars
who were becoming too numerous and
unruly for the prison ships moored in
Plymouth Sound. The work was
completed in 1809 by the prisoners
themselves using granite from Sir

Postbridge

🏛 historic building   🏛 museum   🏛 historic site   🝆 scenic attraction   🌱 flora and fauna

Thomas' quarry. Paid at the rate of sixpence (2.5p) a day, they also built the main east-west road across the moor which is now the B3212, and the famous Devonport leat which supplied water to the dockyard there. Yet another of their constructions was the nearby Church of St Mary, a charmless building in whose churchyard stands a tall granite cross in memory of all those prisoners whose bodies lie in unmarked graves. (The mortality rate of the inmates in the early 1800s was 50%). Since around 1900, prisoners' graves have been marked just with their initials and date of death. The lines of small stones are a gloomy sight.

At one time the prison held as many as 9,000 French and, later, American inmates but by 1816, with the cessation of hostilities, the prison became redundant and was closed. Princetown virtually collapsed as a result and it wasn't until 1823 that its granite quarries were given a new lease of life with the building of the horse-drawn Dartmoor Railway, another of Sir Thomas Tyrwhitt's initiatives. The prison was eventually re-opened for long-serving convicts in 1850 and since then it has been considerably enlarged and upgraded. It is currently in use as a medium security prison with around 250 inmates. The **Dartmoor Prison Heritage Centre** has exhibits detailing the history of the institution.

Also in the town is the National Park's **Moorland Visitors' Centre** which contains some excellent and informative displays about the moor, and also stocks a wide range of books, maps and leaflets. The centre is housed in the former Duchy Hotel where Sir Arthur Conan Doyle stayed while writing some chapters of *The Hound of the Baskervilles,* much of which is set in Dartmoor.

DARTMEET
13 miles E of Tavistock off the B3357

Dartmeet is a picturesque spot where the boulder-strewn East and West Dart rivers join together. At their junction, a single-span packhorse bridge was built in the 1400s; its remains can still be seen just upstream from the more modern road bridge.

Dartmeet

Rising in the boggy plateau of north Dartmoor, the Dart and its tributaries drain a huge area of the moor. The river then flows for 46 miles before entering the sea at Dartmouth.

In the days when the tin mines were working, this area was extremely isolated, lacking even a burial ground of its own. Local people had to carry their dead across the moor to Lydford –

PIXIELAND-DARTMOOR

Dartmeet, Princeton, Devon PL20 6SG
Tel: 01364 631412
e-mail: keith@pixieland.co.uk
website: www.pixieland.co.uk

A whole extended family of gnomes is scattered around the garden, colourful fleeces are displayed along the garden railings – such is the approach to Pixieland-Dartmoor at Dartmeet. Situated in the heart of Dartmoor's rugged countryside, Pixieland's superb range of handmade garden ornaments, sheepsking rugs, gifts and collectables has been attracting customers since 1947.Pixieland is also famous for its handmade concrete garden ornaments, most of which are made on the premises and it also specialises in West Country sheepskin products with one of the largest ranges of sheepskin rugs to be found in the South West. Other sheepskin products on sale include sheepskin cushion covers, special rugs for babies, mittens, gloves, a remarkable range of sheepskin hats and more than 20 different styles of sheepskin slippers and moccasins.

   The shop also stocks a wide variety of local products: Devon farm fudge, Burt's handmade crisps from Kingsbridge, Luscombe soft drinks from Buckfastleigh, and a tempting selection of local jams, honeys, chutneys and preserves. Other items on sale include locally-made rocking horses, the Country Artists ranges of Tuskers Elephants and Butterfly Fairiesr. Prints of Dartmoor ponies- now officially a vulnerable breed – are on sale and the real animals can be seen at nearby Brimpts Farm.

"Eight miles in fair weather, and 15 in foul". In good weather, this is grand walking country with a choice of exploring the higher moor, dotted with a wealth of prehistoric remains, or following the lovely riverside and woodland path that leads to the famous Clapper Bridge near Postbridge, about five miles upstream.

   To the east of Dartmeet, and hidden among bracken and gorse, is the **Coffin Stone**, a large boulder on which it was customary for the bearers to rest the body while making the moorland crossing. A cross and the deceased's initials were carved into the stone while the bearers had some liquid refreshment and got back their breath before continuing on their journey.

YELVERTON
5 miles SE of Tavistock on the A386

In prehistoric times, the area around Yelverton must have been quite heavily populated to judge by the extraordinary concentration of stone circles and rows, hut and cairn circles, and burial chambers. The B3212 to Princeton passes through this once-populous stretch of moorland, part of which is now submerged beneath **Burrator Reservoir**.

   Situated just inside the Dartmoor National Park, Yelverton itself is a large village with broad-verged streets which has caused it to be described as "rather like a thriving racecourse". The village is centuries old but, curiously enough, is one of very few in the

HARRABEER COUNTRY HOUSE HOTEL

Harrowbeer Lane, Yelverton, Devon PL20 6EA
Tel: 01822 853302
e-mail: reception@harrabeer.co.uk
website: www.harrabeer.co.uk

Haarabeer Country House Hotel is a small and very friendly family-run hotel which was a recent top 20 finalist for the prestigious AA Landlady of the Year Award. Michael and Amanda Willats offer a choice of accommodation to their guests. Bed & breakfast guests stay in the handsome old Devon longhouse which has five twin or double bedrooms, all with en suite or private bathroom facilities and all equipped with TV, telephone and hospitality tray. If you want to really treat yourselves, book the Master Bedroom, a beautifully appointed, spacious room overlooking Dartmoor. Extras here include a video, DVD player, and trouser press. Breakfast is served in the attractive restaurant where you can also order dinner for that evening if you wish. Guests have the use of a gracious sitting room, there's a bar with an open fire for cooler evenings, and a pretty, secluded garden for warmer days.

If you prefer self-catering, there are two well-appointed suites available in a tastefully converted barn. Each suite can accommodate up to five people.

OVERCOMBE GUEST HOUSE

Old Station Road, Horrabridge, Yelverton, Devon PL20 7RA
Tel: 01822 853501 Fax: 01822 853602
e-mail: enquiries@overcombehotel.co.uk
website: www.overcombehotel.co.uk

Located within Dartmoor National Park and backing onto Roborough Downs where Dartmoor ponies roam freely, **Overcombe Guest House** is a popular licensed environmentally aware establishment offering quality facilities and a personal service in a relaxed homely atmosphere. Arriving guests are greeted with complimentary tea or coffee, possibly accompanied by homemade cake. Your hosts, David and John, provide a substantial breakfast based on local produce such as Cornish dry cured bacon, Devon sausages and free range eggs from a nearby farm. The dining room has a small bar and a comfortable sitting area in which to relax, chat or watch TV.

Overcombe has eight guest bedrooms, all en suite, with two on the ground floor, one of which has been specially adapted for the less mobile visitor. All rooms have comfortable beds and are equipped with colour TV, alarm clock, hair dryer and complimentary refreshment tray. Some rooms enjoy beautiful views overlooking the Walkham Valley and the delightful village of Horrabridge which has two welcoming hostelries serving varied menus. And just four miles away is the ancient stannary town of Tavistock with its regular pannier market, abbey ruins and river and canal walks.

📖 stories and anecdotes   🐦 famous people   🎨 art and craft   🎭 entertainment and sport   🚶 walks

country to have had its name bestowed by the Board of Directors of a railway company. When the Great Western Railway opened a station here in 1859 the village was officially known as Elfordtown. The story goes that the London-based surveyors interpreted the Devon pronunciation of Elfordtown as Yelverton. So that was the name blazoned on the station signboard, and the name by which the village has been known ever since.

BUCKLAND MONACHORUM
5 miles S of Tavistock off the A386

🏛 Buckland Abbey   🌿 The Garden House

Tucked away in a secluded valley above the River Tavy, **Buckland Abbey** (National Trust) was founded in 1278 by Amicia, Countess of Devon, but became better known as the home of Sir Francis Drake. Drake purchased the former abbey in 1581 from his fellow-warrior (and part-time pirate), Sir Richard Grenville, whose exploits in his little ship, *Revenge* were almost as colourful as those of Drake himself. The house remained in the Drake family until 1947 when it was acquired by the National Trust. Of the many exhibits at the abbey, Drake's Drum takes pride of place – according to legend, the drum will sound whenever England is in peril. The drum was brought back to England by Drake's brother, Thomas, who was with the great seafarer when he died on the Spanish Main in 1596.

The Garden House

Buckland Monachorum, Yelverton, Devon, PL20 7LQ.
Tel: 01822 854769 Fax: 01822 855358
website: www.thegardenhouse.org.uk

The Garden House is centred on an enchanting Walled Garden created by the plantsman Lionel Fortescue and his wife Katharine around the romantic ruins of a medieval vicarage. Lionel's successor Keith Wiley extended the garden into new areas such as the South African Garden, the Acer Glade, the Bulb Meadow and the Cretan Cottage Garden, creating vistas of stunning colour from Spring until Autumn in a pioneering naturalistic style inspired by great natural landscapes of the world.

Now Head Gardener Matt Bishop is caring for this legacy, refurbishing some of the historic planting and developing exciting new designs to provide year-round colour – all with the aim of maintaining a reputation for excellence and innovation stretching back more than half a century.

🏛 historic building   🏛 museum   🏛 historic site   🞶 scenic attraction   🌿 flora and fauna

(Rather ignominiously, of dysentery). Elsewhere at the abbey, visitors can see a magnificent 14th century tithe barn, 154ft long, housing an interesting collection of carts and carriages; a craft workshop and a herb garden.

In the village itself, on the site of a medieval vicarage, **The Garden House** (see panel opposite) is surrounded by a delightful garden created after World War II by Lionel Fortescue, a retired schoolmaster.

GULWORTHY
2 miles SW of Tavistock on the A390

This little village lies at the heart of an area that, in the mid-1880s, had a world wide reputation. A quarter of the world's supply of copper was extracted from this part of Devon and, more alarmingly, so was half of the world's requirements for arsenic. Mining for copper in this area has long been abandoned, due to the discovery of cheaper sources around the world, particularly in South America. Gulworthy's arsenic has also gone out of fashion as an agent of murder.

BERE ALSTON
5 miles SW of Tavistock on the B3257

🏛 Morwellham Quay

For centuries, Bere Alston was a thriving little port on the River Tamar from whence the products of Dartmoor's tin mines were transported around the world. All that commercial activity has long since gone but the river here is still busy with the to-ings and fro-ings of sleek pleasure craft. Just a few miles upstream from Bere Alston is one of the county's most popular visitor attractions, **Morwellham Quay**. In 1980 it was a ghost

town with the Tamar valley breezes whistling through its abandoned buildings. Now restored, this historic site faithfully recreates the busy atmosphere of the 1850s when half the world's copper came through this tiny harbour. Visitors can journey through the mines on a riverside tramway, and another highlight is the restored Tamar ketch *Garlandstone*. Although Morwellham lies some 20 miles upstream from Plymouth, the Tamar river at this point was deep enough for 300-ton ships to load up with the precious minerals. Once known as the Devon Klondyke, Morwellham suffered a catastrophic decline when cheaper sources of copper were discovered in South America.

The quayside inn has also been restored. It was here that the dockside labourers used to meet for ale, food and the latest news of the ships that sailed from Morwellham. In those days, the news was chalked up on a blackboard and it still is. Though out of date, the stories nonetheless remain intriguing.

LIFTON
9 miles NW of Tavistock on the A30

🏛 Dingles Steam Village

Situated on the banks of the River Lyd, Lifton was, in medieval times, an important centre of the wool trade. Dartmoor sheep tend to have rather coarse fleeces, due to the cold pastureland, so the weavers of Lifton petitioned Henry VII, "by reason of the grossness and stubbornness of their district" to allow them to mix as much lambs' wool and flock with their wool "as may be required to work it".

Just to the east of Lifton is **Dingles Steam Village** where visitors can see one of the best

THE ARUNDELL ARMS

Lifton, Devon PL16 0AA
Tel: 01566 784666   Fax: 01566 784494
e-mail: reservations@arundellarms.com
website: www.arundellarms.com

When Anne Voss-Bark bought **The Arundell Arms** in 1961 she had little experience in the hotel trade and even less of fishing. An established fishing inn, The Arundell Arms 45 years ago was not the luxurious place it is today. There was just one private bathroom for the 17 guest rooms, a temperamental boiler, no hotel bar and the police station, complete with cells, stood on the other side of the car park. How times have changed! Anne, a winner of the Woman Hotelier of the Year Award and a fly fisher of high renown, has turned the inn into one of the best hotels in the West Country, known throughout England for the superb fishing along the stretches of river that it owns. Further recognition came with the hotel's César Award for "Sporting Hotel of the Year 2006".

Built on a site that dates back to Saxon times, the hotel was once a coaching inn on the main route from London through the West Country to Penzance. It has been renovated and refurbished over the years but great care has been taken to ensure that the traditional atmosphere of a country house is preserved, whilst the standard of accommodation throughout is sumptuous. The cosy and intimate lounge is ideal for relaxing and there's also a popular bar. The bedrooms, all with private bathrooms, are perfect with everything provided to ensure that guests enjoy a peaceful night's sleep. Many of the 21 bedrooms have been recently

completely – and attractively – refurbished to designs by Anne Voss-Bark and interior designer Roz Clarke.

The elegant dining room is the perfect setting for some of the best food the West Country has to offer. Led by Head Chef Steven Pidgeon, the team conjures up a fabulous dinner menu each evening. Wherever possible, the meat, fish, cheese and vegetables are all sourced locally and, naturally, the seasonal availability of produce is reflected in the menus.

The superb hospitality undoubtedly draws people to The Arundell Arms time and time again, but it is the sports, particularly the fishing, that have made it such a favourite. Salmon, sea trout and brown trout abound in the hotel's 20 miles of rivers, managed by the hotel's river keeper and instructor, Roy Buckingham. Other activities such as horse riding and shooting can also be arranged and, of course, there is always the beauty of the surrounding countryside to explore.

🏚 historic building   🏛 museum   🏛 historic site   ♧ scenic attraction   ❦ flora and fauna

working steam collections in the country including traction engines, steam rollers, fairground attractions and vintage machinery. There's also a collection of vintage road signs, play areas for children, a gift shop, café and riverside walks.

Ivybridge

🚶 Two Moors Way

The original bridge over the Erme at Ivybridge was just wide enough for a single packhorse and the 13th century crossing that replaced it is still very narrow. When the railway arrived here in 1848, Brunel constructed an impressive viaduct over the Erme valley. It was made of wood, however, so that too was replaced in 1895 by an equally imposing stone structure. The town grew rapidly in the 1860s when a quality paper-making mill was established to make good use of the waters of the Erme and more recently Ivybridge has continued to grow as a commuter town for Plymouth.

Serious walkers will know Ivybridge as the southern starting point of the **Two Moors Way**, the spectacular but gruelling 103-mile path across both Dartmoor and Exmoor, finishing at Barnstaple. The trek begins with a stiff 1,000ft climb up Butterdon Hill, just outside Ivybridge – and that's the easy bit!

SOUTH BRENT
5 miles NE of Ivybridge off the A38

Standing on the southern flank of Dartmoor, just within the National Park, South Brent is a sizeable village of some 3,000 souls. It has a 13th century church with a massive Norman tower, set beside the River Avon, which was once the main church for a large part of the South Hams as well as a considerable area of Dartmoor. Alongside the River Avon are some attractive old textile mills recalling the days when South Brent was an important centre for the production of woollens. In Victorian times, one of the mills was managed by William Crossing whose famous *Crossing's Guide to Dartmoor* provides a fascinating picture of life on the moor in the late 1800s.

In the days of stagecoach travel the town was a lively place with two "posting houses" servicing the competing coaches. It was said that four horses could be changed in 45 seconds and a full-course meal served in 20 minutes. The most famous of the coaches, the *Quicksilver*, left Plymouth at 8.30 in the evening and arrived in London at 4 o'clock the following afternoon – a remarkable average speed of 11 mph, *including* stops.

BUCKFASTLEIGH
9 miles NE of Ivybridge off the A38

🖉 South Devon Railway   🏛 Valiant Soldier Museum
🦋 Buckfast Butterflies & Dartmoor Otter Sanctuary
🖉 Pennywell   🖋 Robert Herrick

A former wool town on the banks of the River Mardle. Several old mill buildings still stand and the large houses of their former owners lie on the outskirts. A unique insight into the lives of local folk is provided by an old inn that has been restored and now houses the **Valiant Soldier Museum and Heritage Centre.** When the Valiant Soldier pub was closed in the 1960s, everything was left in place – even the money in the till. Rediscovered years later, this life-size time capsule features period public and lounge bars as well as domestic rooms including the kitchen, scullery, parlour and bedrooms.

Buckfastleigh is the western terminus and headquarters of the **South Devon Railway**, (formerly known as the Primrose Line), whose

🎭 stories and anecdotes   🐦 famous people   🖌 art and craft   🖉 entertainment and sport   🚶 walks

steam trains ply the seven-mile route along the lovely Dart Valley to and from Totnes. The Dart is a fast flowing salmon river and its banks abound with herons, swans, kingfishers, badgers and foxes. The company also offers a combined River Rail ticket so that visitors can travel in one direction by train and return by boat. The railway runs regular services during the season with the journey taking about 25 minutes each way.

Another popular attraction close to the town is the **Buckfast Butterflies & Dartmoor Otter Sanctuary** where a specially designed tropical rain forest habitat has been created for the exotic butterflies. There's an underwater viewing area and both the butterflies and otters can be photographed, with the otters' thrice-daily feeding times providing some excellent photo-opportunities.

A couple of miles south of Buckfastleigh, **Pennywell** is a spacious all-weather family attraction which offers a wide variety of entertainments and activities. Winner of the West Country "England for Excellence" award in 1999, Pennywell also boasts the UK's longest gravity go-kart ride and promises that their hands-on activities provide something new every half hour.

Another mile or so south, the little church of Dean Prior stands beside the A38. The

The Valiant Soldier

79 Fore Street, Buckfastleigh, Devon TQ11 0BS
Tel: 01364 644522

The **Valiant Soldier** is an amazing place. It's a time-capsule, a building shut up and left for over 30 years. There's nowhere else quite like it anywhere - it is truly unique. It used to be an ordinary pub -now it's an extraordinary family attraction. The Valiant Soldier was a village inn for more than two centuries. It closed in the 1960s - and time stood still. Furniture, pub artefacts and domestic items were simply left where they stood as the last customer walked out.

Now the former pub has been turned into a fascinating place to visit. The authentic period bars are filled with the atmosphere of a working-man's pub during the '40s and '50s. The kitchen and scullery give an insight into domestic life. Upstairs there's more - a parlour and bedroom, plus a re-creation of the attic as it was when it was re-discovered.

Do you remember when a pint of mild cost 1s 4d? Do you remember the Second World War and the years just afterwards? If you do you'll enjoy the Valiant Soldier. Perhaps you'll recognize some of the thousands of items on the shelves and in the cupboards. If you don't remember those times, go and take a look into the past. Plus - there's a little modem technology to add an extra dimension to your visit.

🏢 historic building   🏛 museum   🏛 historic site   🐊 scenic attraction   🌿 flora and fauna

vicar here at the time of the Restoration was the poet and staunch royalist, **Robert Herrick** (1591-1674). Herrick's best known lines are probably the opening of "To the Virgins, to make Much of Time":

> *Gather ye rosebuds while ye may,*
> *Old Time is still a-flying*
> *And this same flower that smiles today*
> *Tomorrow will be dying.*

Herrick apparently found rural Devon rather dull and much preferred London where he had a mistress 27 years his junior. Perhaps to brighten up the monotony of his Devonshire existence, he had a pet pig which he took for walks and trained to drink beer from a tankard. Herrick died in 1674 and was buried in the churchyard where a simple stone marks his assumed last resting place.

BUCKFAST
10 miles NE of Ivybridge off the A38

 Buckfast Abbey

Dominating this small market town is **Buckfast Abbey,** a Benedictine monastery built in the Norman and Gothic style between 1907 and 1938. If you've ever wondered how many people it takes to construct an abbey, the astonishing answer at Buckfast is just six. Only one of the monks, Brother Peter, had any knowledge of building so he had to check every stone that went into the fabric. A photographic exhibition at the abbey records the painstaking process that stretched over 30 years. Another monk, Brother Adam, became celebrated as the bee-keeper whose busy charges produced the renowned Buckfast Abbey honey. The abbey gift shop also sells the famous Buckfast

Tonic Wine, recordings of the abbey choristers and a wide range of religious items, pottery, cards and gifts.

CORNWOOD
3 miles NW of Ivybridge off the A38

Cornwood is a pleasant village on the River Yealm, a good base from which to seek out the many Bronze Age and industrial remains scattered across the moor. One of the most remarkable sights in Dartmoor is the double line of stones set up on Stall Moor during the Bronze Age. One line is almost 550yds long; the other begins with a stone circle and crosses the River Erme before ending at a burial chamber some two miles distant. There are no roads to these extraordinary constructions, they can only be reached on foot.

Buckfast Abbey

If you approach Dartmoor from the south, off the A38, Cornwood is the last village you will find before the moors begin in earnest. Strike due north from here and you will have to cross some 15 miles of spectacular moorland before you see another inhabited place. (Her Majesty's Prison at Princetown, as it happens.)

Bovey Tracy

🏛 Riverside Mill 🐦 Becky Falls

This ancient market town takes its name from the River Bovey and the de Tracy family who received the manor from William the Conqueror. The best-known member of the family is Sir William Tracy, one of the four knights who murdered Thomas à Becket in Canterbury Cathedral. To expiate his crime, Sir William is said to have endowed a church here, dedicated to St Thomas. That building was destroyed by fire and the present church is 15th century with a 14th century tower. Its most glorious possession is a beautifully carved screen of 1427, a gift to the church from Lady Margaret Beaufort, the new owner of the manor and the mother of King Henry VII.

Bovey Tracy, unlike so many Devon towns and villages, has never suffered a major fire. This is perhaps just as well since its fire-fighting facilities until recent times were decidedly limited. In 1920, for example, the town did have an engine, and five volunteers to man it, but no horses to draw it. The parish council in that year issued a notice advising "all or any persons requiring the Fire Brigade with Engine that they must take the responsibility of sending a Pair of Horses for the purpose of conveying the Engine to and from the Scene of the Fire".

For such a small town, Bovey Tracy is remarkably well-supplied with shops as well as the **Riverside Mill** which is run by the Devon Guild of Craftsmen. The Guild presents changing craft exhibitions and demonstrations and the mill also contains a Museum of Craftsmanship, a study centre and a shop.

Walkers will enjoy the footpath that passes through the town and follows the track bed of the former railway from Moretonhampstead to Newton Abbot, which runs alongside the River Bovey for part of its length

Just to the north of Bovey Tracy is **Parke,** formerly the estate of the Tracy family but now owned by the National Trust and leased to the Dartmoor National Park as its headquarters. There are interpretive displays on all aspects of the moor; attractive grounds, in which there is a Rare Breeds Farm; and copious information is available. The centre can also provide details of the many nature trails, woodland and riverside walks in the area, including one to the famous **Becky Falls** where the Becka Brook makes a sudden 70ft drop.

ILSINGTON
3 miles SW of Bovey Tracey off the B3387

Like so many Dartmoor communities, Ilsington was once an important centre of the wool industry. At the heart of the village is a characteristic trio of late medieval buildings – church, church house and inn. The interior of St Michael's Church is well worth seeing with its impressive array of arched beams and roof timbers which seem to hang in mid-air above the nave. The medieval pew ends are thought to be the only ones in Devon carved with the distinctive "poppy head" design; there's also a mid-14th century effigy of a woman; and an elaborately carved 16th century rood screen.

Entry to the churchyard is by way of an

unusual lych gate with an upper storey which once served as the village schoolroom. The present structure is actually a replica of the original medieval gate which apparently collapsed when someone slammed the gate too energetically. The nearby church house, dating back to the 1500s, is now sub-divided into residential dwellings known as St Michael's Cottages.

This small village was the birthplace of the Jacobean dramatist John Ford (1586-1639) whose most successful play, *Tis Pity She's A Whore* (1633), is still occasionally revived.

Ilsington is a sizeable parish and includes the three well-known tors of Rippon, Saddle and Haytor Rocks. The latter is perhaps the most dramatic, especially when approached from the west along the B3387, and with a

height of almost 1,500ft provides a popular challenge for rock climbers.

In the early 1800s, the shallow valley to the north of Haytor Rocks was riddled with quarries which supplied granite for such well-known buildings as London Bridge, the National Gallery and the British Museum.

ASHBURTON
7 miles SW of Bovey Tracey off the A38

🏛 Ashburton Museum

This appealing little town lies just inside the boundary of the Dartmoor National Park, surrounded by lovely hills and with the River Ashburn splashing through the town centre. Municipal history goes back a long way here, to 821AD in fact, when the town elected its first Portreeve, the Saxon equivalent of a mayor. The

---

SARA'S LAVENDER BOX
26a North Street, Ashburton, Devon TQ13 7QD
Tel: 01364 654854 website: www.ashburton.org/directory/ saraslavenderbox

Sara's Lavender Box is situated in the ancient stannery town of Ashburton, which is also known as the 'gateway to the moor'. The shop is enchanting with lots of original stone features and character. The stock includes a wide selection of country emporium gifts ranging from shabby chic furniture to luxurious handmade soaps, a large selection from 'Nougat of London' which are bath and body products scented with jasmine and tuber rose, Shaker style home decor, country quilts with matching linen hangers and wash bags. The baby corner has 'cute factor' with a theme of blue and pink gingham, handmade wrapping paper, tissue box covers, lavender pillows, candles, and truly delightful things.

The stock is constantly changing and there is always something new. There is always a selection of wickedly exotic, fresh, top quality, Dutch flowers and plants and the owners are happy to supply all your needs for your wedding flowers including handmade bead encrusted tiaras, unusual bouquet holders, scented petals for confetti and real decorated horseshoes to bring you good luck on your special day. All funeral tributes can be made ranging from modern to traditional. Why not pop in for a browse.

🎭 stories and anecdotes   🦜 famous people   🎨 art and craft   🎪 entertainment and sport   🚶 walks

Haytor Ramble

Distance: *4.0 miles (6.4 kilometres)*

Typical time: *180 mins*

Height gain: *150 metres*

Map: *Outdoor Leisure 28*

Walk: *www.walkingworld.com ID:1589*

Contributor: *Dennis Blackford*

ACCESS INFORMATION:

On the B3387 Bovey Tracey to Widdecombe road. About 300 metres past the Haytor Vale & Ilsington turning you will pass the bottom car park (tarmac but hot and crowded) where the toilets are. Ignore this car park and continue on for about 200 metres to the middle car park (grass) and park here. There should be buses from Bovey Tracey.

DESCRIPTION:

This circular walk starts at Haytor car park and, after a visit to the scenic quarry with its lake, heads out over the moor to a secret pool that most walkers are unaware of as it is invisible from a distance. From the pool you walk through a gorse and heather part of the moor to Smallacombe Rocks, passing the stone circle sites of ancient round houses. After looking around the rocks with their spectacular outlook you head back towards Haytor and turn onto a Granite Railway to visit a wilder quarry before heading down to Becka Brook (lovely place to picnic). From the stream you return to Haytor by a different route, climbing up over the Tor itself before returning to the starting point.

ADDITIONAL INFORMATION:

Toilets at bottom car park. Ice cream vending van at bottom and top car parks. Park ranger and information at lower car park. This is wild, open moor so care and precautions should be taken. Strong walking boots or shoes, with good tread are strongly recommended. Conditions can change very quickly here so a wind and waterproof extra garment such as a kagoule is also recommended together with a map, compass, water and snack food. Even in mid-summer, it can get very cold on the moor. August and September are possibly the best time to see the gorse and heather in flower.

FEATURES:

Hills or fells, river, toilets, wildlife, birds, flowers, great views, butterflies, industrial archaeology, moor.

WALK DIRECTIONS:

1 | Park in the middle car park which has a firm grass surface and is always far less crowded than the others. Looking across the road, you will see the unmistakable shape of Haytor which can be seen for tens of kilometres in most directions. Leave the car park by the lower of the two entrances and cross the road. After crossing the road, follow the fairly wide path bearing diagonally to the right away from the Tor.

2 | After a few hundred metres, the path widens out and takes you directly to a wooden gate in a wire fence. Go through the gate into the scenic quarry, turn left on the hard dirt path.

3 | After looking around the quarry, follow the path around the left hand edge of the lakes.Follow the path up and over the wooden stile. Continue on the distinct path across the moor for a few hundred metres towards the distant rocky outcrop.

4 | The path crosses the granite railway where you can still see the tracks carved from stone. In the distance you can see the outcrop of

Smallacombe rocks. Do not take the path directly towards the rocks but look for the one diagonally to the right. Follow this path across the moorland (do not follow the railway).

5 | A few hundred metres will suddenly bring you to the secret pool hidden down a fold in the moor. Walk round the left hand edge of the pool and follow the small path through the gorse and heather towards Smallacombe Rocks. As you approach the outcrop, down in the bracken on your left, there are circles of stones with a depression in the centre. These are the remains of ancient roundhouses.

6 | After looking around the rocks and seeing the spectacular views over the valley, turn again towards Haytor and follow the wide path which is fairly clearly visible.

7 | When you reach the railway again, turn right and follow it for about 50 metres until you reach the 'points' in the track. Follow the branch to the right. The track goes downhill for about 800 metres to a rugged quarry with a 'spoil heap' projecting over the valley.

8 | Just before the track appears to end in a pile of rocks, look for a small path down to your right. The first part is a steep scramble down a rocky path (approx five metres) before it becomes a zig-zag path that heads for the trees at the bottom of the valley. Note: If you do not want to attempt this rough section of the walk, retrace your steps out of the quarry until you see the track up to your right and rejoin the walk at waymark 11.

9 | There is another scramble down a rocky path (approx six metres drop) to the lovely Becka Brook which is a great place for a picnic in the shade of the trees and the music of the river. When you have finished here, retrace your steps up the scramble. When you again see the wide path you came down on, look for a smaller branch to your left and follow this path as it winds through the bracken and heather.

10 | The path is not always very definite so aim for the 'big' tree to the left of the rocks. After passing the tree, bear right to pass on the left of the pile of rocks from the quarry. The track ascends here to rejoin the railway at the entrance of the quarry.

11 | After reaching the railway, cross over and follow the wide track up hill, diagonally to your left.

12 | This path will bring you out to the upper railway track. Turn left on it for about 10 metres then turn diagonally right up the side track towards the rocks.

13 | After a few hundred metres, the path heads towards Haytor. Where the path appears to go down a little valley go to the right of the rocks and continue on the path which will again head towards the Tor.

14 | The path disappears in a boulder strewn grassy area. Head towards the massive rock to pass on its right.

15 | Having passed the Tor, bear left around a smaller outcrop of rock to follow the wide track back to the car park.

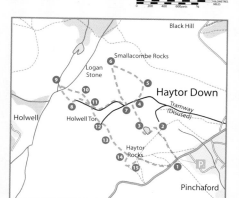

traditional office continues to the present day, although its functions are now purely ceremonial. But each year, on the fourth Tuesday in November, officials gather to appoint not just their Portreeve but also the Ale Tasters, Bread Weighers, Pig Drovers and even a Viewer of Watercourses.

In medieval times, Ashburton's prosperity was based on tin. As one of Devon's four stannary towns, it benefited from the trade generated by the Dartmoor tinners who were obliged to come here to have their metal weighed and stamped, and to pay the duty. Later, the cloth industry was the town's main money-spinner, with several fulling mills along the banks of the Ashburn producing cloth which the East India Company exported to China.

The town is characterised by its many attractive houses and shops, with distinctive slate hung front elevations. Housed in the former home and workshop of a brushmaker, **Ashburton Museum** offers a fascinating

insight into the history of this stannary town as well as the domestic and rural life of Dartmoor down the centuries. The collections include old farming implements, Victorian toys, a model of the old Market Hall and Native American artefacts donated by Paul Endicott, whose parents had left Ashburton for Oklahoma at the beginning of the 1900s.

WIDECOMBE IN THE MOOR
6 miles W of Bovey Tracey off the B3212

🏛 Cathedral of the Moors   🏛 Church House

🍃 Widecombe Fair   🏚 Grimspound

This pleasing village enjoys a lovely setting in the valley of the East Webburn river and its grand old church, with a massive 120ft high granite tower rising against a backdrop of high moorland, has understandably been dubbed the **"Cathedral of the Moors"**. Dedicated to St Pancras, the church was built with funds raised by tin miners in the 14th century, and enlarged during the next two centuries. A panel inside the church records the disastrous events of 21st October 1638. A sizeable congregation had gathered for a service when a bolt of lightning struck the tower, dislodging huge blocks of masonry on to the worshippers. Four were killed and a further 60 badly injured. (Local legend maintains that the Devil had been spotted earlier that day spitting fire and riding an ebony stallion across the moor).

In addition to the church, two other buildings are worth mentioning. Glebe House is a handsome 16th century residence which has since been converted to a shop, and **Church House** is an

Widecombe in the Moor

exceptional colonnaded building which was originally built around 1500 to accommodate those travelling large distances across the moor to attend church services. It was later divided into almshouses then served in succession as a brewery and a school. It is now a National Trust shop and information centre.

The famous **Widecombe Fair** to which Uncle Tom Cobleigh, his boisterous crew and the old grey mare, were making their way is still held here on the second Tuesday in September and although it is no longer an agricultural event, remains a jolly affair. A succession of real-life Tom Cobleighs have lived around Widecombe over the centuries but the song probably refers to a gentleman who died in 1794. An amorous bachelor, this Uncle Tom Cobleigh had a mane of red hair and he refused to maintain any babies that did not display the same characteristic.

From Widecombe, a country lane leads to **Grimspound** which is perhaps the most impressive of all Dartmoor's Bronze Age survivals. This settlement was occupied between 1800BC and 500BC and is remarkably well-preserved. There are 24 hut circles here, some of them reconstructed, and it's still possible to make out the positions of door lintels and stone sleeping shelves. Today, the area around Grimspound is bleak and moody, an atmosphere which recommended itself to Sir Arthur Conan Doyle who had Sherlock Holmes send Dr Watson into hiding here to help solve the case of *The Hound of the Baskervilles*.

LUSTLEIGH
3 miles NW of Bovey Tracey off the A382

Lustleigh is one of Dartmoor's most popular and most photographed villages. Placed at all angles on the hillside, are a ravishing assortment of 15th and 16th century deeply-thatched, colour-washed cottages, picturesquely grouped around the church. Appropriately for such a genuinely olde-worlde village, Lustleigh keeps alive some of the time-honoured traditions of country life, enthusiastically celebrating May Day each year with a procession through the village, dancing round the maypole, and the coronation of a May Queen. From the village there are some delightful walks, especially one that passes through Lustleigh Cleave, a wooded section of the steep-sided Bovey valley. Also close by is the **Becky Falls Woodland Park**, with its waterfalls, rugged landscape and attractions for all the family. Here, too, is **Yarner Wood Nature Reserve**, home to pied flycatchers, wood warblers and redstarts.

NORTH BOVEY
6 miles NW of Bovey Tracey off the B3212

In any discussion about which is the "loveliest village in Devon", North Bovey has to be one of the leading contenders. Set beside the River Bovey, it is quite unspoiled, with thatched cottages grouped around the green, a 15th century church and a delightful old inn, the Ring of Bells, which like many Devon hostelries was originally built, back in the 13th century, as a lodging house for the stonemasons building the church.

MORETONHAMPSTEAD
7 miles NW of Bovey Tracey on the A382

🏛 St Michael's Church   🏛 Almshouses
🐑 Miniature Pony Centre

Moreton, as this little town is known locally, has long claimed the title of "Gateway to east Dartmoor", a rôle in which it was greatly helped by the branch railway from Newton Abbot which operated between 1866 and

GREAT SLONCOMBE FARM

Moretonhampstead, Devon TQ13 8QF
Tel: 01647 440595
e-mail: hmerchant@sloncombe.freeserve.co.uk
website: www.greatsloncombefarm.co.uk

Trudie, Robert and Helen Merchant welcome guests throughout the year at **Great Sloncombe Farm**, a traditional Devon dairy farm set among meadows and woodland in glorious Dartmoor. The three letting bedrooms are in the wonderful 13th century granite and cob farmhouse where oak timbers, granite fireplaces, sloping floors and crooked walls contribute to the old world charm. The traditionally furnished bedrooms – Barley, Clover and Cornflower – all have en suite shower rooms and views of the meadow, and the largest, Cornflower, has a pine four-poster and a separate dressing room.

   The lounge with its beams and brasses is a perfect spot to relax, to plan the day's activities or to enjoy a book or a board game. In the cosy dining room a hearty farmhouse breakfast starts the day. As well as running this delightful bed & breakfast establishment, the Merchants also run Devon Country Carriages which specialises in providing old style transport for weddings. With an equipe of seven horses and six carriages, they also take part in show driving at country shows, and as members of the British Driving Society are about to celebrate the society's 50th anniversary.

1964. This is the gentler part of Dartmoor, with many woods and plantations, and steep-sided river valleys. Within easy reach are picture-postcard villages such as Widecombe in the Moor, striking natural features like Haytor, and the remarkable Bronze Age stone hut-circle at Grimspound.

   The best approach to Moreton is by way of the B3212 from the southwest. From this direction you are greeted with splendid views of the little hilltop town surrounded by fields and with the tower of **St Andrew's Church** piercing the skyline. Built in Dartmoor granite during the early 1400s, the church overlooks the Sentry, or Sanctuary Field, an attractive public park. In the south porch are the tombstones of two French officers who died here as prisoners of war in 1807. At one point

during those years of the Napoleonic Wars, no fewer than 379 French officers were living in Moreton, on parole from the military prison at Princetown. One of them, General Rochambeau, must have sorely tested the patience of local people. Whenever news arrived of a French success, he would don his full-dress uniform and parade through the streets.

   One of the most interesting buildings in Moreton is the row of **Almshouses** in Cross Street. Built in 1637, it is thatched and has a striking arcade supported by sturdy granite columns. The almshouses are now owned by the National Trust but are not open to the public. Just across the road from the almshouses is **Mearsdon Manor Galleries,** the oldest house in Moreton, dating back to

🏛 historic building   🏛 museum   🏛 historic site   🔾 scenic attraction   🌿 flora and fauna the 14th century. The ground floor of the manor is now a very pleasant traditional English tea room. In total contrast, the remaining rooms contain an astonishing array of colourful, exotic artefacts collected by the owner, Elizabeth Prince, on her trips to the Far East. There are Dartmoor-pony-sized wooden horses, Turkish rugs, Chinese lacquered furniture, finely-carved jade – a veritable treasury of Oriental craftsmanship.

Two miles west of Moretonhampstead on the B3212, the **Miniature Pony Centre** is home to miniature ponies, donkeys and other horse breeds, as well as pygmy goats, pigs, lambs and many other animals. There are pony rides for children aged nine and under, a daily birds of prey display, indoor and outdoor play areas and a cafeteria.

Plymouth

- ⯗ Plymouth Hoe   ⯗ The Citadel
- ⯗ Mayflower Steps   ⯗ Eddystone Lighthouse
- ⯗ National Marine Aquarium

With around a quarter of a million inhabitants, Plymouth is now the largest centre of population in the south west peninsula but its development has been comparatively recent. It wasn't until the late 1100s that the harbour was recognised as having any potential as a military and commercial port. Another 300 years passed before it was established as the main base for the English fleet guarding the western channel against a seaborne attack from Spain.

Perhaps the best way of getting to know this historic city is to approach **Plymouth Hoe** on foot from the main shopping area, along the now-pedestrianised Armada Way. It was on the Hoe on Friday, July 19th, 1588,

that one of the most iconic moments in English history took place. Commander of the Fleet, and erstwhile pirate, Sir Francis Drake was playing bowls here when he was informed of the approach of the Spanish Armada. With true British phlegm, Sir Francis completed his game before boarding *The Golden Hind* and sailing off to harass the Spanish fleet. A statue of Sir Francis, striking a splendidly belligerent pose and looking proudly to the horizon, stands on the Hoe which is still an open space, combining the functions of promenade, public park and parade ground.

Just offshore, the striking shape of **Drake's Island** rises like Alcatraz from the deep swirling waters at the mouth of the River Tamar. In its time, this stark fortified islet has been used as a gunpowder repository, (it is said to be riddled with underground tunnels where the powder was stored), a prison, and a youth adventure centre.

Two miles from the Hoe, Plymouth's remarkable **Breakwater** protects the Sound from the destructive effects of the prevailing south-westerly winds. Built by prisoners between 1812 and 1840, this massive mile-long construction required around four million tons of limestone. The surface was finished with enormous dovetailed blocks of stone, and the structure rounded off with a lighthouse at one end.

On a clear day, it's possible to see the famous **Eddystone Lighthouse,** 12miles out in the Channel. The present lighthouse is the fourth to be built here. The first, made of timber, was swept away in a huge storm in 1703 taking with it the man who had built the lighthouse, the ship-owner Winstanley. In 1759, a much more substantial structure of dovetailed granite blacks was built by John

The Hoe, Plymouth

exporting wool and importing wine.

Close by are the **Mayflower Steps** where the Pilgrim Fathers boarded ship for their historic voyage to Massachusetts. The names of the Mayflower's company are listed on a board on nearby Island House, now the tourist information office.

Many other emigrants were to follow in the Pilgrim Fathers' wake, with the result that there are now more than 40 communities named Plymouth scattered across the English-speaking world.

A number of interesting old buildings around the Barbican have survived the ravages of time and the terrible pasting the city received during World War II. **Prysten House,** behind St Andrew's Church, is a 15th century priest's house; the **Elizabethan House** in New Street has a rich display of Elizabethan furniture and furnishings, and the **Merchant's House** in St Andrew's Street, generally regarded as Devon's finest Jacobean building, is crammed full of interesting objects relating to Plymouth's past. A particularly fascinating exhibit in the Merchant's House is the **Park Pharmacy,** a genuine Victorian pharmacy complete with its 1864 fittings and stocked with such preparations as Ipecacuanha Wine ("one to two tablespoonfuls as an emetic") and Tincture of Myrrh and Borax, "for the teeth and gums". Another vintage shop is **Jacka's Bakery** which claims to be the oldest commercial bakery in the country and is reputed to have supplied the *Mayflower* with ship's biscuits.

Smeaton. It stood for 120 years and even then it was not the lighthouse but the rocks on which it stood which began to collapse. The lighthouse was dismantled and re-erected on the Hoe where, as **Smeaton's Tower,** it is one of the city's most popular tourist attractions. From the top, there are good views of Millbay Docks, Plymouth's busy commercial port which was once busy with transatlantic passenger liners. Today, the docks handle a variety of merchant shipping, including the continental ferry services to Brittany and northern Spain. To the east, the view is dominated by **The Citadel,** a massive fortification built by Charles II, ostensibly as a defence against seaborne attack. Perhaps bearing in mind that Plymouth had resisted a four-year siege by his father's troops during the Civil War, Charles' Citadel has a number of gun ports bearing directly on the city. The Citadel is still a military base, but there are guided tours every afternoon from May to September.

Close by the Citadel is Plymouth's oldest quarter, the **Barbican.** Now a lively entertainment area filled with restaurants, pubs, and an innovative small theatre, it was once the main trading area for merchants

Also in the Barbican area is the **National Marine Aquarium**, located on the Fish Quay. State-of-the-art techniques allow visitors to travel through the oceans of the world, dropping from mountains and rivers to the darkest depths of the Atlantic. The virtual reality tour includes encounters with brilliantly coloured fish, seahorses and even Caribbean sharks.

Locally, the Tamar estuary is known as the Hamoaze, (pronounced ham-oys), and it's well worth taking one of the boat trips that leave from the Mayflower Steps. This is certainly the best way to see Devonport Dockyard, while the ferry to Cremyll on the Cornish bank of the Tamar drops off passengers close to Mount Edgcumbe Country Park and the old smuggling village of Cawsand.

The blackest date in Plymouth's history is undoubtedly March 21st, 1941. On that night, the entire centre of the city was razed to the ground by the combined effects of high-explosive and incendiary bombs. More than 1,000 people were killed; another 5000 injured. After the war, the renowned town planner Sir Patrick Abercrombie was commissioned to design a completely new town centre. Much of the rebuilding was carried out in the 1950s, which was not British architecture's golden age, but half a century later the scheme has acquired something of a period charm. Abercrombie's plan included some excellent facilities, like the first-rate **Museum and Art Gallery,** the **Theatre Royal** with its two auditoria, the **Arts Centre**, and the **Pavilions** complex of concert hall, leisure pool and skating rink.

Plymouth's best-known export has to be **Plymouth Gin** which has been produced in the city since1793. At the company's Black Friars Distillery visitors can take a guided tour and learn about the art of making this famous

tipple. In the Refectory Bar here, it is said, the Pilgrim Fathers spent their last night before setting sail in the *Mayflower*. There's also a café and a shop.

Around Plymouth

PLYMPTON
4 miles E of Plymouth on the B3416

🏛 Saltram House

Plympton boasts one of Devon's grandest mansions, **Saltram House** (National Trust). Built during the reign of George II for the Parker family, this sumptuous house occupies a splendid site overlooking the Plym estuary. In the 1760s Robert Adam was called in, at enormous expense, to decorate the dining room and "double cube" saloon, which he accomplished with his usual panache. There are portraits of the Parkers by the locally born artist Sir Joshua Reynolds, and amongst the fine furniture, a magnificent four-poster bed by Thomas Chippendale. Other attractions include the great kitchen with its fascinating assortment of period kitchenware, an orangery in the gardens, and the former chapel, now a gallery displaying the work of West Country artists. Saltram House appeared as Norland House in the 1995 feature film of Jane Austen's *Sense and Sensibility* starring Emma Thompson and Hugh Grant.

SPARKWELL
6 miles E of Plymouth off the B3417

🐦 Dartmoor Wildlife Park

🐦 West Country Falconry Centre

The **Dartmoor Wildlife Park** at Sparkwell provides an excellent family day out, with more than 150 species of animals and birds to see within its 30 acres of beautiful Devon

The Dartmoor Wildlife Park

Sparkwell, Devon PL7 5DG
Tel: 01752 837645

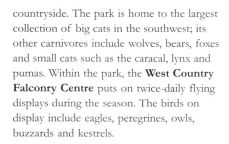

Only five minutes drive from the A38 Devon Expressway, the **Dartmoor Wildlife Park** has been a favourite family attraction for over 35 years, set in 30 acres of beautiful Devon countryside.

The park holds the largest collection of big cats in the south west and other carnivores include wolves, bears, foxes and small cats such as the caracal, lynx and pumas. The Wildlife Park is now the headquarters of the British Big Cat Society and there is a Talk, Touch and Learn all-weather facility.

The West Country Falconry Centre is a large collection of Birds of Prey; there are twice daily flying displays from Easter to the end of October (Fridays excepted) and if you have ever fancied yourself as a falconer there are falconry courses available too. The birds on display include eagles, peregrimes, owls, buzzards, kestrels and many others .

Daily events include the Close Encounters Talks at 2pm and the Big Cat Feeding at 3.30pm. There is also a restaurant, bar and gift shop with a good range of souvenirs.

Don't miss the Annual Classic and Vintage Car and Bike Rally which is held on the second Sunday in September.

countryside. The park is home to the largest collection of big cats in the southwest; its other carnivores include wolves, bears, foxes and small cats such as the caracal, lynx and pumas. Within the park, the **West Country Falconry Centre** puts on twice-daily flying displays during the season. The birds on display include eagles, peregrines, owls, buzzards and kestrels.

TURNCHAPEL
1 mile SE of Plymouth off the A379

Enjoying views across Cattewater to Plymouth, the village of Turnchapel is strung along the waterside. The village was declared a Conservation Area in 1977 and, with its two pubs, church, and waterfront, is a pleasant place to wander around. Nearby, there are ex-

RAF Catalina flying boats to admire; and from Mountbatten Peninsula grand vistas open up over to Plymouth Hoe and Drake's Island. It was at RAF Mountbatten that Lawrence of Arabia served as a humble aircraftman for several years.

A short distance to the south is a stretch of coastline known as **Abraham's Garden**. The story goes that, during the fearful plague of 1665, a number of Spanish slaves were buried here. In their memory, the shrubbery always remains green, even in winter.

WEMBURY
6 miles SE of Plymouth off the A379

Wembury church provides a dramatic landmark as it stands isolated on the edge of the cliff, and the coastal path here provides

🏛 historic building   🏛 museum   🏛 historic site   🌱 scenic attraction   🍃 flora and fauna

spectacular views of the Yealm estuary to the east, and Plymouth Sound to the west. The path is occasionally closed to walkers when the firing range is in use, so look out for the red warning flags. **The Great Mew Stone** stands a mile offshore in Wembury Bay. This lonely islet was inhabited until the 1830s when its last residents, the part-time smuggler Sam Wakeham and his family, gave up the unequal struggle to make a living here. The Mew Stone is now the home of seabirds who surely can't take kindly to its use from time to time by the HMS Cambridge gunnery school on Wembury Point.

NEWTON FERRERS
9 miles SE of Plymouth on the B3186

A picturesque fishing village of whitewashed cottages sloping down to the river, Newton Ferrers is beloved by artists and is also one of the south coast's most popular yachting centres. Part of the village sits beside the River Yealm (pronounced "Yam"), the rest alongside a large creek. When the creek dries out at low tide, it is possible to walk across to Noss Mayo on the southern bank. (When the tide is in, a ferry operates, but only during the season.)

The South Hams

"The frutefullest part of all Devonshire." said an old writer of this favoured tract of land lying south of Dartmoor, bounded by the River Dart to the east and the River Erme to the west. The climate is exceptionally mild, the soil fertile and the pastures well watered. But the rivers that run off Dartmoor to the sea, slicing north-south through the area, created burdensome barriers to communications until fairly recent times. This comparative isolation

kept the region unspoilt but also kept it poor.

There are few towns of any size – only Totnes, Kingsbridge and Modbury really qualify, along with the picturesque ports of Dartmouth and Salcombe. For the rest, the South Hams is a charmed landscape of drowsy villages linked by narrow country lanes running between high banks on which wildflowers flourish: thanks to an enlightened County Council, the verges were never assaulted with massive quantities of herbicides as in other areas.

The area has been known as the South Hams, the 'homesteads south of Dartmoor', since Saxon times, but one town at least claims a history stretching much further back in time. We begin our exploration of the South Hams at Totnes which is the second oldest borough in England. The town sent its first Member of Parliament to London in 1295, and elected the first of its 630-odd Mayors in 1359.

Totnes

🏛 Totnes Castle   🏛 Guildhall   🏠 Bowden House

🏠 Totnes Elizabethan Museum

This captivating little town claims to have been founded by an Ancient Trojan named Brutus in 1200BC. The grandfather of Aeneas, the hero of Virgil's epic poem *The Aeneid,* Brutus sailed up the River Dart, gazed at the fair prospect around him and decided to found the first town in this new country which would take its name, Britain, from his own. The **Brutus Stone,** set in the pavement of the main shopping street, Fore Street, commemorates this stirring incident when both the town and a nation were born.

The first recorded evidence of this town, set on a hill above the highest navigable point

Wembury

Distance: *4.8 miles (7.6 kilometres)*

Typical time: *120 mins*

Height gain: *200 metres*

Map: *Potdoor Leisure 20*

Walk: *www.walkingworld.com ID:2072*

Contributor: *Dave Pawley*

ACCESS INFORMATION:

From the Plymouth direction as you drive into Wembury you will pass the Odd Wheel pub on your right, a few yards along the road turn left and 100 yards on turn left again into Barton Close and at the end of the road are playing fields and a large car park. There are buses from Plymouth bus station to Wembury for those who wish to use public transport.

DESCRIPTION:

A walk with a bit of everything, footpaths through fields, views of Dartmoor at one point, the sea and the lovely river Yealm. It includes a section of the South West Coastal path and even the start of the Devon version of the Coast to Coast path. WThe walk takes you from the large village of Wembury out across fields and roads to high above the river Yealm and a loop down to the very edge of the river and the ferry across it. From there up again to take the coastal path west along to Wembury Beach where there is a church, car park, toilets and a shop and the start of the coast to coast walk. The route is then up a splendid valley and along footpaths and a small amount of road walking to near Knighton before returning to the car park.

ADDITIONAL INFORMATION:

The Great Mewstone Island was once inhabited, if only by a man sent there in isolation for six years as a punishment. There is an excellent signpost right by the beach which indicates just how long the SW coastal path is and the distance of the coast to coast path which runs from Wembury Beach up to Lynmouth in the North. At Waymark 10 the Odd Wheel is well worth a visit and, as with almost all pubs these days, food is served. The Jazz is very good, every Thursday evening.

FEATURES:

Hills or fells, river, sea, pub, toilets, play area, church, wildlife, birds, flowers, great views, food shop.

WALK DIRECTIONS:

1 | Leave the car park at Barton Close near the Odd Wheel public house and follow the track along at the rear of the tennis courts and descend slightly. After a couple of hundred metres you will pass houses to your left. Although the path continues ahead as a lane, there are stone steps to your right up through a hedge leading into a field.

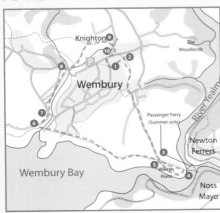

2 | Turn right and walk up the steps and follow the track across a field, through kissing gates and along the side of another field to emerge by a lovely small manor house over a stile onto a road. Follow the road then rough track along south east. After about half a mile you will come to a gate with a house to the left hand side and just beyond the gate there are three tracks, one ahead, one to the left and the other to the right. This walk takes you along all three! First down to the river Yealm before returning back again the coastal path.

3 | Go through the gate and just by the gatehouse turn left and follow the footpath which will loop you right down to the very edge of the very scenic River Yealm. As you descend the views unfold before you. Make your way down an increasingly steep path until you are just above river level where, during the summer months, the passenger ferry departs for the short hop to the other bank.

4 | Continue along the loop, walking to the left of a lovely waterside house and then follow the track back steeply uphill until you reach the gate house /gate again. The main coastal path is off to your left.

5 | Turn left though a gate and onto the coastal path which leads you along overlooking the mouth of the Yealm. Continue along parallel to the mouth of the river below and do not take the track leading inland at a junction. After about a mile you will pass a house on your right. Just beyond the house, turn left and follow the track which descends towards the sea and you will pass a church to your right. Descend to the car park and at the far end make your way down to the beach, passing between a small shop and toilets.

6 | Cross over a small bridge just above the beach. By the signpost turn inland from the coastal path and start the coast to coast walk.

Make your way up a valley. The track leads you up and over a stile to a road after several hundred yards. Turn left on the road and follow it down where you will see another sign guiding you right to continue up the valley.

7 | Turn right onto the track which continues east up the valley. There are two parallel tracks, take the upper one, the lower bridlepath is very, very muddy. The track eventually emerges over a stile and onto a road. Turn left and walk down the road for a hundred yards or more and you will see a sign pointing up by some renovated houses, showing Knighton and Train Road.

8 | Follow the wide track up with a house to your left and right. Just beyond the second house take a narrow track which leads you steeply uphill, not the broader one which is to the left and right. You go up through trees, over a stile and into a field. Continue to walk up the field, heading north east. After passing through two fields you will see a footpath sign to your left. Ignore it and continue ahead. The field is cultivated and the footpath narrow as it levels out. You will reach a gap in the hedge, once a gate was there but not now.

9 | Just beyond the wide gap in the hedge, the path turns slightly right to lead you diagonally across a field as it descends. Again the track is narrow through the cultivated field. At the far corner there is a stile leading out to a narrow lane. Turn right and follow the road which leads you downhill then directly up to the Odd Wheel Pub.

10 | Just beyond the Odd Wheel Pub is the main road you travelled along to reach the car park. Turn right onto the road and a few yards along there is narrow pedestrian only track off to your left which leads you up by a school to your left and directly back into Barton Close and the car park.

SALLY CARR DESIGNS - THE YARN SHOP

31 High Street, Totnes, Devon TQ9 5NP
Tel/Fax: 01803 863060

Right in the heart of old Totnes, occupying an Elizabethan "overhung" building, lies The Yarn Shop, a charming and attractive establishment that is well worth a visit by both knitters and non-knitters alike. With a training in art and design, Sally Carr opened her shop in 1984.

Over the years she has become renowned for only stocking the very best in woollen products as well as offering sound advice and help on any knitting queries. Sally stocks Rowan, Colinette and Sirdar yarns, Debbie Bliss and Noro amongst others, and has a wealth of interesting and imaginative patterns, including her own designs. She also offers a knitting-up service and stocks an extensive range of knitting accessories.

Along with the yarns for which Sally is famous, the shop also sells other unusual and quality items. The glamorous, high quality PILGRIM jewellery from Denmark and semi-precious stones set in silver, complement the

stylish and distinctive Amano clothing from South America. There are numerous other items of similar high quality which would make ideal personal gifts.

on the River Dart, doesn't appear until the mid-10th century when King Edgar established a mint at Totnes. The Saxons already had a castle of sorts here, but the impressive remains of **Totnes Castle** are Norman, built between the 1100s and early 1300s. Towering over the town, it is generally reckoned to be the best-preserved motte and bailey castle in Devon.

A substantial section of Totnes' medieval town wall has also survived. The superb **East Gate**, which straddles the steep main street is part of that wall.

Just a little way down the hill

Totnes Castle

PAPERWORKS

63 High Street, Totnes, Devon TQ9 5PB
Tel: 01803 867009 Fax: 01803 866515
e-mail: shop@paperworkstotnes.com
website: www.paperworkstotnes.com

Unusual and handmade paper and stationery is the speciality of **PaperWorks,** owned and run by partners Heidrun and David Guest. Heidrun is an accomplished artist and the partners design and make many of the cards,books and albums themselves. Their highly successful shop is a paradise for lovers of paper and original design with an amazing range of papers available for all kinds of art, craft and decorative uses.

This unique and fascinating High Street shop, fronted by Heidrun's colourful and often witty window displays, also sells greetings cards, gift wrap and decorated stationery, as well as an extensive selection of paper-related gifts and craft materials. Many of the papers are hand-made; recycled papers are another speciality. PaperWorks also stocks a wide choice of artists' products including pens, pastels and watercolours. This is a place tailor-made for browsing and enjoying the wealth of colour and visual stimulation on offer.

📖 stories and anecdotes   🍄 famous people   🎨 art and craft   🖋 entertainment and sport   🚶 walks

THE CONKER SHOE COMPANY

28 High Street, Totnes, Devon TQ9 5RY
Tel: 01803 862490 Fax: 01803 866457
e-mail: info@conkershoes.com
website: www.conkershoes.com
Partners: Pennie and Simon Gwilt

For more than a quarter of a century The Conker Shoe Co. has enjoyed a well earned reputation for shoemaking excellence and a high standard of customer service. Conker Shoes are produced by hand in the workshops that adjoin the spacious shop situated in the High Street between the Civic Square and the East Gate Arch in the heart of old Totnes. Through the glass doors at the back of the shop customers can see the dedicated Conker team making shoes, 'cordwaining'. The 16th century building is thought at one time to have been used as a theatre.

Originally servicing a niche market with multicoloured shoes, the majority of the 2000 pairs of shoes and boots made each year are just one colour, albeit one of a choice of 50! Conkers' have become synonymous with quality, comfort, durability and renewability, as the shoes are designed to be resoled time after time. With over 30 styles to choose from it's no wonder that they are worn by whole families.

Although many shoes are available off the shelf, most people opt to have a pair tailor made. Shoes prices range from £58 to £145.

The shoes are available from child size 5 through to adult 13 with half sizes and four width fittings as standard, and because most of the shoes are made to your individual requirements it doesn't matter if you have odd sized feet, if both feet fall within the standard sizes you pay the standard price.

For a small supplement people with bunions, narrow heels, high insteps etc can have a bespoke fitting and still enjoy all of the benefits of Conker Shoes. For those with more challenging feet, an appointment only, Made To Measure specialist service is available.

Besides shoes the shop sells high class ladies clothes, a wide range of leather accessories, bags, briefcases, purses belts, glasses cases, along with all manner of leather care products.

For customers not able to visit the shop in person, the company offers a mail order service through its catalogue and website.

from East Gate is the charming **Guildhall** of 1553, a remarkable little building with a granite colonnade. It houses both the Council Chamber (which is still in use) and the underground Town Gaol (which is not). The cells can be visited, as can the elegant Council Chamber with its plaster frieze and the table where Oliver Cromwell sat in 1646.

Almost opposite the Guildhall is another magnificent Elizabethan building, currently occupied by Barclays Bank. It was built in 1585 for Nicholas Ball who had made his fortune from the local pilchard fishery. When he died, his wife Anne married Sir Thomas Bodley and it was the profit from pilchards that funded the world-famous Bodleian Library at Oxford University.

The town's Elizabethan heritage really

comes alive if you are visiting on a Tuesday in summer. You will find yourself stepping into a pageant of Elizabethan colour, for this is when the people of Totnes array themselves in crisp, white ruffs and velvet gowns for a charity market which has raised thousands of pounds for good causes since it began in 1970. In August, the Elizabethan Society organises the **Orange Race** which commemorates a visit to the town by Sir Francis Drake during which he presented "a fair red orange" to a small boy in the street. Today, contestants chase their oranges down the hill.

The parish church of Totnes is **St Mary's.** It was entirely rebuilt in the 15th century when the town's cloth industry was booming – at that time Totnes was second in importance only to Exeter. The church's most glorious

THIS'N'THAT - ANTIQUES, COLLECTABLES & GIFTS
66 High Street, Totnes, Devon TQ9 5SQ
Tel: 01803 868604

This'n'That is a relatively new business, run by husband and wife team Paul and Lesley Loach and situated in 'The Narrows'. This district, nestling at the foot of Totnes' Norman castle, has long been a well kept secret but is now being hailed as a 'must see' part of Totnes - the town described in the British Airways in-flight magazine as, 'One of the 10 funkiest destinations in the world'. Browsers are always made welcome at This'n'That and invariably conversations enter the realms of, "I remember...." as visitors of all ages explore the eclectic mix of old and new. Gifts, jewellery, antiques, 20th century collectables, paintings, books, greetings cards and furniture vie with one another for space.

Carefully selected greetings cards, old toys, books and magazines echo times gone by and bring back memories of homes and holidays. Fashion jewellery complements the textiles to be found alongside vintage dressing tables, chairs and tables. 1950s 'Formica' and 1970s teak, beech and elm display china, glass, linen etc. without the need for conventional retail fittings. Kitchen cabinets from the 1940s frequently house collections from yesteryear to delight and surprise.

New treasures arrive daily and regular passers-by frequently find that the window contents have been changed overnight. Several times each year 'Gallery at This'n'That' events see the display space transformed to accommodate a particular theme. This'n'That is certainly a shop with a difference. Why not visit and find yourself remembering when.....? A look at the website will give you a flavour of the delights in store.

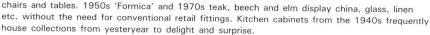
stories and anecdotes   famous people   art and craft   entertainment and sport   walks

IN HOUSE

1 New Walk House, The Plains,
Totnes, Devon, TQ9 5HA
Tel: 01803 865096
Fax: 01803 864552
e-mail: inhouse1@btconnect.com

Stocked with every conceivable item of furnishing, **In House** was established by Pamela Wyles, a lady with an extensive experience in retail management. Her shop occupies two floors with each room laid out in traditional fashion. The upmarket wares on display include soft furnishings, lighting, ceramics, glassware, tables and chairs, cushions of every style and colour, and much more. There are complete bedrooms, dining rooms and kitchens to examine, with friendly staff at hand to answer any questions. In House is located adjacent to the East Quay area of the town with a handy car park close by.

Following the success of In House in Totnes, Pamela has opened a sister establishment in Torquay.

🏭 historic building   🏛 museum   🏚 historic site   🍃 scenic attraction   🌿 flora and fauna

possession is a rood-screen delicately carved in stone from the quarry at Beer.

Close by at 70 Fore Street is the **Totnes Elizabethan Museum**, housed in an attractive half-timbered Elizabethan building whose upper floors overhang the street. One of the fascinating exhibits here honours a distinguished son of Totnes, Charles Babbage (1791-1871) whose 'Analytical Machine' is universally acknowledged as the forerunner of the electronic computer. The museum display records his doomed struggle to perfect such a calculator using only mechanical parts. A little further up the hill, in High Street, the **Butterwalk** and **Poultrywalk** are two ancient covered shopping arcades whose upper storeys rest on pillars of granite, timber or cast iron.

In recent years, Totnes has earned the title of 'Natural Health Capital of the West Country'. The first Natural Health Centre was established here in 1989. Visitors will find specialist shops offering natural medicines, organic food, aromatherapy, relaxation tapes and books on spiritual healing. A variety of craft and antique shops all add to the town's allure for shopaholics.

For centuries, Totnes was a busy river port and down by **Totnes Bridge**, an elegant stone structure of 1828, the quay was lined with warehouses, some of which have survived and been converted into highly desirable flats. Nearby, on the Plains, stands a granite obelisk to the famous explorer William Wills, a native of the town who perished from starvation when attempting to re-cross the Australian

---

VINTAGE LIVING

61 High Street, Totnes, Devon TQ9 5PB
Tel: 01803 863999
website: www.vintageliving.co.uk

Diana Warszawski describes her shop, **Vintage Living**, as her "dream waiting to happen". She left a high-flying London lifestyle for the joys of the West Country in 2003 and now travels more than 20,000 miles a year to source items directly in France, Sweden and Eastern Europe.

Diana's passion for antiques started young – at the tender age of nine she was scouring the antique flea markets near her home in London's Notting Hill.

Now, at Vintage Living, she has created her own unique blend of old and new by mixing mainly antique furniture with country accessories such as birch hearts, Caroline Zoob pottery and fabulous linen lampshades reproduced from 19th century French designs. "I often see customers soaking up the French atmosphere," says Diana, "and listening to the rasping voice of Edith Piaf playing in the background."

The feedback from both locals and tourists has been "phenomenal" with comments such as "I just want to move into your shop" or "It's like walking into *Country Living* magazine". The shop was also voted a "favourite rural shop in the UK" by *The English Home* magazine in September 2005.

📖 stories and anecdotes   🐚 famous people   🎨 art and craft   🎭 entertainment and sport   🚶 walks

FOUR SEASONS GUEST HOUSE

13 Bridgetown, Totnes, Devon TQ9 5AB
Tel: 01803 862146 Fax: 01803 867779
e-mail: ernestecornford@btinternet.co.uk website: www.fourseasonstotnes.com

Located just two minutes from the centre of this picturesque medieval town and within easy reach of the lovely River Dart, **Four Seasons Guest House**, ETB & AA four star registered, is a friendly family-run establishment offering all year round hospitality.

There's a delightful secluded garden where guests can take afternoon tea or just sit and relax, and a comfortable lounge with a fully stocked bar and TV where you can enjoy a drink and a bar snack.

Meals are served in the dining room which offers an excellent choice of cuisine together with fine wines and spirits. The accommodation at the Four Seasons provides a choice of double and twin en suite rooms, plus one single. All guest rooms have shaving point, hair dryer, trouser press, hospitality tray and TV. On the ground floor one twin en suite room is suitable for the partially disabled.

desert with Robert Burke in 1861.

One excursion from Totnes not to be missed is the breathtakingly beautiful river trip to Dartmouth, 12 miles downstream. This stretch of the river has been called the "English Rhine" and the comparison is no exaggeration. The river here is well away from roads, making it an ideal location for seeing wading-birds, herons, cormorants, and even seals. During the summer, there are frequent departures from the quay by the bridge.

Another memorable journey is by steam train along the seven-mile stretch of the **South Devon Railway,** also known as the Primrose Line, which runs through the glorious scenery of the Dart Valley to Buckfastleigh. Most of the locomotives and carriages are genuine Great Western Railway stock and are painted in the GWR's famous chocolate and cream livery.

Even that list of attractions isn't exhaustive. The **Devonshire Collection of Period Costume** is housed in one of the town's most interesting 16th century houses,

Anyone interested in photography will want to visit **Bowden House Photographic Museum,** about a mile south of Totnes. Its vast collection of photographs, photographic bygones, vintage and classic cameras is housed in a grand Tudor and Queen Anne mansion. Bowden House also claims to be seriously haunted. Visitors frequently authenticate sightings of monks, of gentlefolk in 18th century costume, and a pathetic figure known

ALISON WARE

The Coach House, Station Road, Totnes, Devon TQ9 5HW
Tel: 01803 849222 Mobile: 07801 053502 Fax: 01803 813761

Located in Station Street, just off Fore Street, the main shopping area in Totnes, Alison Ware is well worth a visit if you are looking for quality fabrics, soft furnishings and interiors. The extensive stock includes the Biggie Best range of soft furnishings and upholstery, pure silk and faux fur cushions, a large selection of silk flowers and plants, and an exclusive range of leather and nubuck picture frames, lamps and trays. Also exclusive to Alison Ware is a range of bed linen, quilts and continental pillows.

Popular items are the French style cream metal furniture, and the Victorian wirework furniture, shelves, planters, candle sconces and trays. Upholstered furniture and wrought iron beds are another speciality, along with a selection of glassware, candles and tea-lights. Many more home accessories are on display, along with paintings and greetings cards by local artists. Alison Ware also offers a full measuring and making-up service, as well as a gift wrapping service. The shop is open from 10am to 5.30pm, Tuesday to Saturday.

as 'Little Alice'. Needless to say, the Halloween night candlelit tours of the house are extremely popular.

Around Totnes

BERRY POMEROY
2 miles E of Totnes off the A385 or A381

🏛 Berry Pomeroy Castle

For the last 1,000 years this small village has been owned by just two families. The de la Pomerais dynasty arrived with William the Conqueror and held the land for almost 500 years. In the early 1300s they built **Berry Pomeroy Castle** in a superb position on a wooded promontory above the Gatcombe Brook. Substantial remains of the castle still stand, including sections of the curtain wall and the 14th century gatehouse. In 1548 the Pomeroys, as they were now known, sold the estate to Sir Edward Seymour whose sister, Jane, had been the third wife of Henry VIII. Sir Edward built a three-storey Tudor mansion within the medieval fortifications but this too is now a shell. Although the castle is still owned by Sir Edward's descendant, the Duke of Somerset, it is administered by English Heritage and open to the public daily during the season. In the village itself, St Mary's Church contains some interesting monuments to the Pomeroys and Seymours, as well as an outstanding rood screen.

🎬 stories and anecdotes   🍵 famous people   🎨 art and craft   🚲 entertainment and sport   🚶 walks

ASHPRINGTON

2 miles SE of Totnes off the A381

Set in a stunning location above the River Dart, **Sharpham Vineyard and Cheese Dairy** offers two gastronomic experiences. Visitors can sample the international award-winning red and white wines and watch the dairy cheese being made. The entrance fee includes complimentary tastings.

STOKE GABRIEL

5 miles SE of Totnes off the A385

A charming village of narrow lanes and alleys, Stoke Gabriel stands on a hillside above a tidal spur of the River Dart. A weir was built across the neck of the creek in Edwardian times and this traps the water at low tide, giving the village a pleasant lakeside atmosphere. The part-13th century church of St Gabriel has a restored late-medieval pulpit and a truncated screen with some good wainscot paintings. In the churchyard are the rather forlorn remains of an oak tree reputed to be more than 1,500 years old. To the west of the village, a lane leads to the riverside hamlet of Duncannon where, by general consent, the River Dart is at its most lovely.

DITTISHAM

11 miles SE of Totnes off the A3122

🏛 Greenway House

The best way to reach the pretty yachting village of Dittisham is by passenger ferry from Dartmouth. The major attraction here is **Greenway House,** the home of Dame Agatha Christie for the last 30 years of her life. Her daughter now lives there and the house is currently not open to the public, but the lovely gardens overlooking the river are open Wednesday to Saturday inclusive, with gardener's guided walks every Friday. The house itself is expected to open to the public in 2008.

DARTMOUTH

14 miles SE of Totnes on the A3122

🏛 Dartmouth Castle   📷 Dartmouth Museum

🏛 Britannia Royal Naval College

🖉 Dartmouth Regatta

For centuries, this entrancing little town clinging to the sides of a precipitous hill was one of England's principal ports. Millions of casks of French and Spanish wine have been offloaded onto its narrow quays. During the 1100s Crusaders on both the Second and Third Crusades mustered here, and from here they set sail. In its sheltered harbour, Elizabeth's men o'war lay in wait to pick off the stragglers from the Spanish Armada. In 1620, the *Mayflower* put in here for a few days for repairs before hoisting sail on August

Dittisham

20th for Plymouth and then on to the New World where the pilgrims arrived three months later. The quay from which they embarked later became the major location for the BBC-TV series, *The Onedin Line,* and was also seen in the feature film *Sense and Sensibility* starring Emma Thompson and Hugh Grant.

Geoffrey Chaucer visited the town in 1373 in his capacity as Inspector of Customs and is believed to have modelled the Shipman in his *Canterbury Tales* on the character of the then Mayor of Dartmouth, John Hawley. Hawley was an enterprising merchant and seafarer who was also responsible for building the first **Dartmouth Castle** (English Heritage). Dramatically sited, it guards the entrance to the Dart estuary and was one of the first castles specifically designed to make effective use of artillery. In case the castle should prove to be an inadequate deterrent, in times of danger a heavy chain was strung across the harbour to Kingswear Castle on the opposite bank. (Kingswear Castle is now owned by the Landmark Trust and available for holiday rentals.)

There's a striking monumental brass to John Hawley and his two wives in the **Church of St Saviour's**, a part-14th century building against whose wall ships used to tie up before the New Quay was constructed in the late 1500s. Nearby is the **Custom House**, a handsome building of 1739 which has some fine internal plasterwork ceilings.

Also worth seeking out are **The Butterwalk**, a delightful timber-framed arcade dating from 1640 in which the **Dartmouth Museum**

THE DART GALLERY

4 Lower Street, Dartmouth, Devon TQ6 9AJ
Tel: 01803 834923
e-mail: paul.reach@lineone.net
website: www.dart-gallery.com

Located in the charming little port of Dartmouth, the exciting **Dart Gallery** has established a reputation for exhibiting paintings with the widest range of styles, subjects and mediums. The most demanding appreciators of fine art will surely find something of interest here, whether it's a landscape by Dionne Sievewright, Andrew Miller or Martin Procter, portraits by Nicholas St

John-Rosse or Yana Trevail, still life etchings by Emma Davis, watercolours by John Harlow, oils by Tony Amos or sculptures by Rosemary Cook.

At all times, more than 90 new works are on show and the gallery hosts quarterly exhibitions throughout the season. To make contemporary art more affordable, the gallery offers interest free credit with the Own Art scheme. If you love

original art and sculptures the Dart Gallery is a very friendly, informal place to spend half an hour or so just enjoying the view.

⟦R⟧ stories and anecdotes ⟡ famous people ⟡ art and craft ⟡ entertainment and sport ⟡ walks

Dartmouth Museum

The Butterwalk, Duke Street, Dartmouth, Devon TQ6 9PZ
Tel: 01803 832923
e-mail: dartmouth@devonmuseums.net
website: www.devonmuseums.net/dartmouth

People come to Dartmouth today to enjoy the splendour of her scenery, but mariners have been visiting the Dart for centuries because of its sheltered deep water. The Museum has a strong nautical theme with a large collection of models illustrating the developement of ships from early dugouts to 20th century liners and naval craft, and a large collection of photographs and documents maps the history of the ancient town. The Museum is housed in a spectacular Grade I listed building with carved ceilings and wall panels both inside and out.

occupies the ground floor. One of its prize exhibits is the working steam pumping engine built to a revolutionary design by Thomas Newcomen, the celebrated inventor, who was born in Dartmouth in 1663.

Two other buildings in Dartmouth should be mentioned. One is the railway station, possibly the only one in the world which has never seen a train. It was built by the Great Western Railway as the terminus of their line from Torbay and passengers were ferried across to Kingswear where the railway actually ended. The station is now a restaurant. The other buildingof note is the **Britannia Royal Naval College** (guided tours during the season). This sprawling red and white building, built between 1899 and 1905, dominates the northern part of the town as you leave by the A379 towards Kingsbridge.

Near the eastern boundary of the South Hams flows the enchanting River Dart, surely one of the loveliest of English rivers. Rising in the great blanket bog of the moor, the Dart flows for 46 miles and together with its tributaries drains the greater part of Dartmoor. Queen Victoria called the Dart the

"English Rhine", perhaps thinking of the twin castles of Dartmouth and Kingswear that guard its estuary. It was her ancestor, Alfred the Great who developed Dartmouth as a strategic base and the town's long connection with the senior service is reflected in the presence here of the Royal Naval College. The spectacular harbour is still busy with naval vessels, pleasure boats and ferries, and particularly colourful during the June **Carnival** and the **Dartmouth Regatta** in late August.

The most picturesque approach to the town is to drive to Kingswear and then take one of the two car ferries for the 10 minute trip across the river. Parking space in Dartmouth is severely restricted and it is strongly recommended that you make use of the Park & Ride facility located just outside the town on the A3122.

STOKE FLEMING
16 miles SE of Totnes on the A379

🌢 Blackpool Sands

Stoke Fleming is one of the most delightful villages in the South Hams, perched high on the cliffs 300ft above Start Bay and with a

🏛 historic building   🏛 museum   🏛 historic site   🌢 scenic attraction   🌱 flora and fauna

prominent church that has served generations of mariners as a reassuring landmark. Inside is a brass of 1351 which is reckoned to be one of the oldest in Devon and another which commemorates the great-grandfather of the celebrated engineer, Thomas Newcomen. Less than a mile from the village are the misleadingly-named **Blackpool Sands,** a broad crescent of sandy beach overhung by Monterey pines, which boasts a Blue Flag Award for its safe and healthy bathing.

HARBERTON

2 miles SW of Totnes off the A2381

🏛 St Andrew's Church

This delightful village is regarded as absolutely typical of the South Hams, a place where those two traditional centres of English village life, church and inn, sit comfortably almost side by side. **St Andrew's Church,** which is famous for its amazing, fantastically-carved, 15th century altar screen, has been closely linked to the village hostelry for almost 900 years. The inn was originally built to house the masons working on the church around 1100AD. Harberton was then a major centre for church administration and a much more important place than Totnes. The inn became the Chantry House for the monks, the civil servants of their time, and what is now the bar comprised their Great Hall, chapel and workshop where they would congregate for a glass of wine.

In 1327 the Abbot handed the property over to the poor of the parish but it was not until 1950 that it passed out of the Church's

FINE PINE

Woodland Road, Harbertonford, Totnes, Devon TQ9 7SU
Tel: 01803 732465
e-mail: info@fine-pine-antiques.co.uk
website: www.fine-pine-antiques.co.uk

Occupying an old mill building behind the church in Harbertonford village, **Fine Pine** started out some 30 years ago as a simple pine stripping and small-time antique restoration operation. Since then, Nick and Linda Gildersleve have seen their business grow steadily and there are now two floors full of lovingly restored antique pine furniture. The remarkable thing, says Nick, is that most of their clients are loyal local people who made the business the success it is. "We are even getting second generation customers whose parents bought pine furniture from us in the old days and who are now setting up home themselves."

Most of the furniture on display is English, with some Irish and European pieces, all finished to a high standard. There's always a good selection of tables, chairs, wardrobes, cupboards, chests of drawers and many decorative items on display in the recently extended showroom. As Nick says, "The beauty of simple, quality pine furniture such as this is that it blends well with practically any décor." Fine Pine is open from 9.30am to 5pm, Monday to Saturday, and from 11am to 4pm on Sunday.

Dartington

Distance: *4.8 miles (7.5 kilometres)*

Typical time: *120 mins*

Height gain: *65 metres*

Map: *Explorer 110*

Walk: *www.walkingworld.com ID:1782*

Contributor: *Dennis Blackford*

ACCESS INFORMATION:

By car take the A385 from Totnes to Shinners Bridge, turn right at the roundabout for about 100 metres and the Cider Press is clearly marked on your right. Park in the upper 'overflow' car park in the summer or main car parks in winter.

DESCRIPTION:

Starting from the Cider Press Craft Centre walk along a quiet country lane in the Dartington Hall Estate to the gardens of the hall. After an optional look around the hall itself travel down the long, tree lined main drive of the hall with extensive views over the River Dart to the ancient Water Meadow. There

is an optional detour along the river bank to the historic town of Totnes with its castle and museum. Return back along the river bank to the water meadow and follow its side to a woodland track back to the Cider Press.

ADDITIONAL INFORMATION:

Refreshments and toilets at the Cider Press, Dartington Hall and Totnes. The walking is generally good with wide tracks and country roads so is very pushchair friendly.

FEATURES:

River, pub, toilets, museum, church, castle, wildlife, birds, flowers, great views, butterflies, cafe, gift shop, food shop, industrial archaeology, public transport, restaurant, tea shop, woodland.

WALK DIRECTIONS:

1 | From the car parks - leave at the far end and turn left up the path. Cross the road and walk up the lane past the overflow car parks. Follow the country lane to the junction with the access road to Dartington Hall. Turn right along the tarmac footpath on the right hand side of the road.

2 | Where the footpath ends at a large white signpost, go to the right and through the gate into the gardens of Dartington Hall.

3 | Follow the wide drive down through the gardens or detour through any of the woodland paths to the left. Near the end of the drive, look for the wide, paved path on the right leading down to the swan fountain. Follow this path to the end. Turn left along the hedged pavement and then right, through the hedge and along the terrace in front of the buildings. Note: the grass area used to be used for jousting tournaments.

4 | At the end of the terrace, go up the first flight of steps, then turn right down another

flight to the grass. Note: If you wish to look around the buildings or visit the toilets, continue up the steps turning left at the top for 100 metres then left past the restaurant into the quadrangle. Go out through the arched gateway and turn left on the road, then left again along the wide path to pass the tranquil Zen Mediation garden. Go on through the church yard to rejoin the terrace again.

5 | At the bottom of the steps, turn left along the lawn and walk down to its end. Go through the gate at the bottom of the field and turn right onto the tree lined drive following it down to the gate house.

6 | Pass the gatehouse and through the gates to turn left onto the river walk. Follow along the bank of the river. Note: The meadow seen just before the gatehouse is the water meadow and will be the way back to the Cider Press for those who wish to shorten the walk - missing out the river walk and Totnes.

7 | Just past the weir, cross the wooden bridge to follow along the bank of the river. Note: The wide path passing the bridge brings the walker a little outside the top of Totnes.

8 | The river path ends at Brutus Bridge. Go up the steps to the bridge and turn right into the town.

9 | After visiting the town, return along the river, past the gatehouse to the Water Meadow mentioned in Waymark 6 and follow the cycle path along the right hand side of it.

10 | When you see the water mill - either take the wide path along the side of the road, or go up the steps on the woodland path. They join a few hundred metres further along and after passing some old lime kilns, you return to the Cider Press Centre.

hands altogether. During restoration work ancient plaster was removed to reveal massive beams of fluted mellow oak and a fine medieval screen. Other treasures discovered then, and still in place, were a Tudor window frame and a latticed window containing priceless panes of 13th century handmade glass. The inn's ecclesiastical connections are enhanced even more by the old pews from redundant churches which provide some of the seating.

DARTINGTON
2 miles NW of Totnes on the A384

🏛 Dartington Hall   🏛 High Cross House

When Leonard and Dorothy Elmhirst bought **Dartington Hall** and its estate in 1925 the superb Great Hall had stood roofless for more than a century. The buildings surrounding the two large quadrangles laid out in the 1390s by John Holand, Earl of Exeter, were being used as stables, cow houses and hay lofts. The Elmhirsts were idealists and since Dorothy (*née* Whitney) was one of the richest American women of her time, they possessed the resources to put their ideals into practice. They restored the Hall, re-opened it as a progressive school, and set about reviving the local rural economy in line with the ideology of the Indian philosopher, Rabindranath Tagore. The Elmhirsts were closely involved in the creation of the famed Dartington Glass. Sadly, long after their deaths, their school closed in 1995 as a consequence of financial problems and a pornography scandal. But the headmaster's residence, **High Cross House**, a classic Modernist building of the early 1930s has now been converted into an art gallery. Visitors are welcome here and also to wander around the 26-acre gardens surrounding the

THE TRADESMAN'S ARMS

Stokenham, nr Kingsbridge, Devon TQ7 2SZ
Tel: 01548 580313
website: www.thetradesmansarms.com

A detour of a few seconds from the A379 brings visitors to The Tradesman's Arms, a picture postcard inn that has been serving the local community for centuries and has a history going back to 1390. Part thatched, part slate-roofed, the inn is festooned with a wonderfully colourful show of flowers throughout the year, and the bar and dining areas are no less attractive. Gnarled black beams and country-style furniture enhance the appealing olde worlde ambience, and affable hosts Nick and Rebecca make everyone very welcome, young or old, familiar faces or new.

The dishes on the printed menu and specials board are all based on locally sourced produce of the highest quality. Open lunchtime and evenings Mon-Sat and all day on Sundays. Food is served every session (noon-2.30pm and 6.45pm-9.30pm). The splendid food is complimented by fine wines and a choice of 6 real ales, including at least 2 beers from the local South Hams Brewery.

MOYSEYS INTERIORS

16 Fore Street, Kingsbridge, Devon TQ7 1NY
Tel: 01548 852168 Fax: 01548 856478

A family run business, **Moyseys** have been providing a service in Kingsbridge for over 25 years. The new generation, Alice and Roger Honeywill pride themselves on attention to detail, their objective being 'taking more care of your home'. This is a two way project - their knowledge and design abilities helping the customer discover the perfect environment. Their showroom displays an extensive range of fabrics from leading suppliers such as Harlequin, Casamance, Swaffer and Malibar, floor coverings, whether wood, carpets or vinyl, come from The Alternative Flooring

Company, Manx, Karndean Flooring, Westex and Adam.

There's a large range of beds from Sleepeezee, Dorlux and Mansion House; a wide choice of lamps and shades; occasional furniture; cushions and an interesting selection of *objets d'art*. Moyseys also provides a made to measure service for curtains and blinds. All of Moysey's services come with a full and detailed free estimating, measuring and planning service, and the helpful and knowledgeable staff are always happy to give advice on design and colour.

🏛 historic building   🏛 museum   🏛 historic site   ⌘ scenic attraction   🌿 flora and fauna

Hall. There is no charge for entry to the quadrangle and Great Hall, but donations for its upkeep are welcomed. Guided tours are available by appointment.

Dartington Hall hosts more than 100 music performances each year during its International Summer School, a season which attracts musicians and artistes of the highest calibre from all over the world. All year round, even more visitors are attracted to the **Dartington Cider Press Centre,** a huge gallery on the edge of the estate which displays a vast range of craft products – anything from a delicate handmade Christmas or birthday card to a beautifully modelled item of pottery.

Kingsbridge

🏛 Cookworthy Museum of Rural Life

The broad body of water to the south of Kingsbridge is officially known as **Kingsbridge Estuary**, although strictly speaking it is not an estuary at all – no river runs into it – but a ria, or drowned valley. Whatever the correct name, it provides an attractive setting for this busy little town, an agreeable spot in which to spend an hour or two strolling along the quayside or through the narrow alleys off Fore Street bearing such graphic names as Squeezebelly Passage.

In Fore Street is St Edmund's parish church, mostly 13th century, and well known for the rather cynical verse inscribed on the gravestone of Roger Phillips who died in 1798:

Here lie I at the chancel door
Here lie I because I'm poor
The further in the more you pay
Here lie I as warm as they.

Nearby is **The Shambles**, an Elizabethan market arcade whose late-18th century upper floor is supported on six sturdy granite pillars. Above the church, the former Kingsbridge Grammar School, founded in 1670, now houses the **Cookworthy Museum of Rural Life,** named after William Cookworthy who was born at Kingsbridge in 1705. Working as an apothecary at Plymouth, William encountered traders from the Far East who had brought back porcelain from China. English pottery makers despaired of ever producing such delicate cups and plates, but Cookworthy identified the basic ingredient of porcelain as kaolin, huge deposits of which lay in the hills just north of Plymouth. Ever since then, the more common name for kaolin has been China clay.

During the season, a popular excursion from Kingsbridge is the river cruise to Salcombe. Coastal cruises and private charter boats are also available.

TORCROSS
7 miles E of Kingsbridge on the A379

Normally, the four-mile stretch of sand and shingle beach near Torcross is too extensive to ever become crowded but back in 1943 things were very different. The beach had been selected by the Allied Commanders for a "dress rehearsal" of the impending D-Day invasion of Normandy. The area was swarming with troops and because live ammunition was being used in the training exercise, all the local people were evacuated, more than 3,000 of them from seven coastal villages.

Those D-Day preparations are recalled at Torcross where a Sherman tank recovered from the sea in 1984 is on display in the car park. While the exercises were in progress, an

TORCROSS HOTEL APARTMENTS

Torcross, nr Kingsbridge, Devon TQ7 2TQ
Tel: 01548 580206   Fax: 01548 580996
e-mail: enquiries@torcross.com
website: www.torcross.com

Enjoying a superb setting right by the water's edge, **Torcross Apartment Hotel** provides an ideal base for a family holiday by the sea. The handsome late-Victorian building, painted a very cheerful sky blue, has been splendidly converted and modernised to provide a variety of self-catering apartments spread over its three floors. The apartments are furnished to a very high standard and are kept in excellent order. All are comfortably furnished and fully equipped for an independent, go-as-you-please holiday, with a full size cooker, microwave oven, fridge, TV, central heating and fitted carpets. Each apartment has its own external or internal entrance. Options range from

Beachside chalet apartments for two, with patio doors opening on to a terrace; to Coast view apartments sleeping up to seven. Some rooms intercommunicate – perfect for a large family or group of up to 12 people – and a lift is available for elderly or disabled guests.

Shared amenities in the building include a bar and a restaurant serving a full menu at very reasonable prices, including bar snacks, hot beverages and a Sunday roast. A recent addition is a Beauty Treatment Salon offering a range of treatments that include waxing, massage, nail care, make-up, manicure and pedicure. The Salon also has a Far infra-red sauna and a steam room, both with their own CD player and toilet facilities. Coffee, tea and slightly stronger beverages are available to order with your treatments. Currently, plans are under way to introduce a "sun shower" – an upright sunbed. The complex also has its own private car park with an electric security gate, and a launderette.

Bookings are usually taken by the week but outside the peak season short break specials are available, running from Monday afternoon to Friday morning, or from Friday afternoon to Monday morning.

The area surrounding Torcross offers a multitude of attractions. If it's wildlife you'd like to see, the Nature Reserve of Slapton Ley is only a short walk away; or if you have a car, Paignton Zoo or the National Marine Aquarium (England's largest and Europe's deepest) in Plymouth are both well worth a visit. England's highest waterfall at Canonteign and the picturesque Becky Falls are both within easy driving distance. If it's higher octane thrills you're after, there are numerous kart racing circuits and adventure parks in the area catering for the little and big kids alike. A day's paintballing in the South West's largest paintball arena can also be arranged.

THE SEA SHANTY

Torcross, nr Kingsbridge, South Devon TQ7 2TQ
Tel: 01548 580747

"Quality Food at Sensible Prices" is the proud motto of **The Sea Shanty** which has been run in fine style by Les Irons for the past eight years. His stone-built restaurant just a few steps from the beach is open from early in the morning right through to the evening in season, and the day starts with a choice of breakfasts.

Other offerings range from ice creams to daytime snacks, and a children's menu. The Sea Shanty also provides an extensive takeaway service. Family and party bookings are welcome, and the restaurant is a popular choice for private parties and functions; themed menus include traditional, fish and vegetarian.

Torcross came into prominence as one of the allied landing training areas during World War II. A Sherman tank that took part in the preparations was recovered from the sea in 1984 and now stands on display in the village car park.

Today, Torcross is a delightful holiday village with excellent family amenities and a happy, relaxed atmosphere typified by the staff and the customers at The Sea Shanty.

Start Bay, Torcross

enemy E-boat attacked the landing forces and more than 600 Allied servicemen lost their lives. Beside the tank are memorial tablets to the men who died during this little-publicised military tragedy, and to the many who later perished on the Normandy beaches.

SLAPTON

8 miles E of Kingsbridge off the A379

🐦 Slapton Ley Field Study Centre

To the south of Slapton, the A379 runs for 2.5 miles along the top of a remarkable sand and shingle bank which divides the salt water of Start Bay from the fresh water of Slapton Ley, the largest natural lake in Devon. Continually replenished by three small rivers, this shallow body of water is a designated Nature Reserve and home to large

KARIZMA CLOCKS & WATCHES

Meadow Brook, Slapton, Kingsbridge, Devon TQ7 2PU
Tel/Fax: 01548 581388
website: www.karizma-clocks.co.uk

Karizma Clocks was established in June 1996 by the owner, Derek Davies.

Derek started in the clock and watch making trade in August 1968 at a local jewellers in his home town of Oswestry, Shropshire. Having served his five year apprenticeship and becoming a Craft member of the British Horological Institute, Derek stayed in the local firm until his move to Seiko Watches in Maidenhead, Berkshire in 1987.

After nine years, Derek decided that the time was right to use all his collated skills and start up his own business. Initially established in Wokingham, Berkshire, Derek and his wife moved to Slapton, Devon in 2001 along with their four Dalmatian dogs. Karizma Clocks specialises in quality repairs to all types and ages of clocks and watches. Derek also has a small collection of clocks for sale including some ornate French ones.

Derek points out that nowadays, as there are so few qualified Horologists around, it is very difficult for customers to know where to go to have their items repaired properly. If you are one of these people then please give Karizma Clocks a call for a free estimate or even better, call round in person as Derek says, "nothing is too much trouble."

THE TOWER INN

Church Road, Slapton, Devon TQ7 2PN
Tel: 01548 580216
e-mail: towerinn@slapton.org   website: www.thetowerinn.com

Tucked away in the centre of the delightful village of Slapton, **The Tower Inn** has a history that goes back to medieval times. It was originally part of the Collegiate Chantry of St Mary which was founded in 1373 by Sir Guy de Brian, standard bearer to King Edward III. Much of the chantry tower still stands right next to the inn which was itself built around 1347 to house the men working on the chantry buildings. The inn is just bursting with character. You step through the porch into a low-ceilinged, rustic bar with beams and pillars, scrubbed oak tables, church pew seating, log fires, wine-coloured walls, flagstone floors and bare boards.

To the rear of the pub there is a lovely walled garden flanked by the tower. Inside, mine hosts Andrew and Annette Hammett, offer a good selection of freshly prepared and interesting food, either from the lunchtime menu or the separate evening menu when you can dine by candlelight. There's a good range of traditional beers on offer, along with an excellent selection of Old and New World wines. The inn also offers comfortable accommodation in three double rooms, all en suite and equipped with colour TV and hospitality trays.

🏠 historic building   🏛 museum   🏛 historic site   💧 scenic attraction   🌱 flora and fauna numbers of freshwater fish, insects, water-loving plants and native and migrating birds. The **Slapton Ley Field Study Centre**, located in Slapton village, has leaflets detailing the delightful circular nature trails through this fascinating Site of Special Scientific Interest.

An obelisk on the beach near Slapton, presented in 1954 by the US Army authorities to the people of the South Hams, commemorates the period in 1943 when the beach was used by Allied troops as a "dress rehearsal" for the D-Day landings. The story is well told in Leslie Thomas's novel *The Magic Army*.

CHIVELSTONE
7 miles SE of Kingsbridge off the A379

Even in Devon it would be hard to find anywhere further away from the madding crowd than Chivelstone, an unassuming village hidden away in a maze of country lanes in the extreme southwest of the county and well worth seeking out. It's the tranquil rural surroundings that make Chivelstone so appealing but the village also has a fine parish church, the only one in England dedicated to the 4th century pope, St Sylvester. Historically, Sylvester is a misty figure but an old tradition claims that his saintly ministrations cured the Roman emperor, Constantine, of leprosy. Chivelstone church was built at a time (the 15th century) when this disfiguring disease was still common in England: it seems likely the parishioners hoped that by dedicating their church to him, St Sylvester would protect them from the ravages of a deeply feared illness which, once contracted, imposed total social exclusion on its innocent victims.

BEESANDS
8 miles SE of Kingsbridge off the A379

Beesands lies little more than a mile due south of Torcross and can easily be reached on foot along the coast path. By car, a four mile detour is required. If you don't want to walk, it's well worth negotiating the narrow Devon lanes to reach this tiny hamlet, just a single row of old cottages lining the foreshore of Start Bay. Less than 100 years ago, Beesands was a busy little fishing village. There are photographs from the 1920s showing fishermen who have drawn their boats laden with lobster, crab and mullet up the beach virtually to their cottage doors. Sadly, the fishing fleet is no longer operating but the mile-long shingle beach is as appealing as ever.

HALLSANDS
11 miles SE of Kingsbridge off the A379

South of Beesands, the only way to follow the coastline is by a well-trodden footpath. It's part of the South West Coast Path and the route takes you through the ruined village of Hallsands which was almost completely demolished by a violent storm in January 1917. Another mile or so further brings you to the lighthouse at **Start Point,** built in 1836, and open to visitors from Monday to Saturday during daylight hours. And if you want to be able to boast that you once stood at the most southerly point in Devon, continue along the Coast Path for about five miles to **Prawle Point,** an ancient lookout site where today there is a Coastguard Station.

MALBOROUGH
5 miles S of Kingsbridge on the A381

🏠 Yarde

For anyone travelling this corner of the South Hams, the lofty spire of Malborough's 15th century church is a recurrent landmark. It's a broach spire, rising straight out of the low tower. Inside, the church is wonderfully light, so much so that the splendid arcades built in Beer stone seem to glow.

🎭 stories and anecdotes   🐦 famous people   🎨 art and craft   🎭 entertainment and sport   🚶 walks

About half a mile to the east of Malborough, just off the A381, is an outstanding example of a medieval farmhouse. **Yarde** is a Grade I listed manor farm with an Elizabethan bakery and a Queen Anne farmhouse. This is a privately owned working farm but Yarde can be visited on Sunday afternoons from Easter to the end of September, and by groups at any time by arrangement.

SALCOMBE
7 miles S of Kingsbridge, on the A381

🐾 Overbecks   🏛 Salcombe Maritime Museum

Standing at the mouth of the Kingsbridge "estuary", the captivating town of Salcombe enjoys one of the most beautiful natural settings in the country. Sheltered from the prevailing westerly winds by steep hills, it also basks in one of the mildest micro-climates in England. In the terraced gardens rising from the water's edge, it's not unusual to see mimosa, palms, and even orange and lemon trees bearing fruit. The peaceful gardens at **Overbecks** (National Trust), overlooking Salcombe Bar, have an almost Mediterranean character. Otto Overbeck, who lived in the charming Edwardian house here between 1918 and 1937, amassed a wide-ranging collection that includes late-19th century photographs of the area, local shipbuilding tools, model boats, toys and much more.

Like other small South Devon ports, Salcombe developed its own special area of trading. Whilst Dartmouth specialised in French and Spanish wine, at Salcombe high-sailed clippers arrived carrying the first fruits of the pineapple harvest from the West Indies, and oranges from the Azores. That traffic has ceased, but pleasure craft throng the harbour and a small fishing fleet still operates from

Batson Creek, a picturesque location where the fish quay is piled high with lobster creels. The town's seafaring history is interestingly evoked in the **Salcombe Maritime & Local History Museum** in the old Customs House on the quay.

The coastline to the south and west of Salcombe, some of the most magnificent in Britain, is now largely owned by the National Trust. Great slanting slabs of gneiss and schist tower above the sea, making the clifftop walk here both literally and metaphorically breathtaking.

HOPE COVE
6 miles SW of Kingsbridge off the A381

There are two Hopes here: Outer Hope, which is more modern and so gets less attention, and Inner Hope which must be one of the most photographed villages in the country. A picturesque huddle of thatched cottages around a tiny cobbled square, Inner Hope once thrived on pilchard fishing but nowadays only a few fishermen still operate from here, bringing in small catches of lobster and crab.

BANTHAM
6 miles SW of Kingsbridge off the A379

One mile to the north of Thurlestone (as the crow flies) is another fine sandy beach, at Bantham. This small village has a long history since it was a centre of early tin trading between the ancient Britons and the Gauls. By the 8th century, Anglo-Saxons were well-established here, farming the fertile soil. The sea also provided a major source of income in the form of pilchard fishing. Bantham continued to be a busy little port until the early 1900s with sailing barges bringing coal and building stone for the surrounding area.

THURLESTONE

5 miles W of Kingsbridge off the A381

One of the most attractive coastal villages, Thurlestone can boast not just one, but two beaches, separated by a headland. Both beaches are recommended, especially the one to the south with its view of the pierced, or "thyrled", stone, the offshore rock from which the settlement gets its name and which was specifically mentioned in a charter of 846AD. The village itself stands on a long, flat-topped ridge above the beaches and is an attractive mixture of flower-decked cottages, old farm buildings and long-established shops and inns.

BIGBURY ON SEA

10 miles W of Kingsbridge on the B3392

🐾 Burgh Island

This popular family resort has a stretch of National Trust coastline and extensive sands. The most interesting attraction here though is **Burgh Island** which is actually only a part-time island. When the tide is out, it is possible to walk across the sandbar linking it to the mainland. At other times, visitors reach the island by a unique "Sea Tractor", specifically designed for this crossing. It can operate in 7ft of water, in all but the roughest conditions, and it's well worth timing your visit to enjoy this novel experience.

The whole of the 28-acre island, complete with its 14th century Pilchard Inn, was bought in 1929 by the eccentric millionaire Archibald Nettlefold. He built an extravagant Art Deco hotel which attracted such visitors as Noel Coward, the Duke of Windsor and Mrs Wallis Simpson,

and Agatha Christie. The "Queen of Crime" used the island as the setting for two of her novels, *Ten Little Niggers,* (later renamed *And Then There Were None*), and *Evil Under the Sun.* The hotel, which has been described as "a white Art Deco cruise liner beached on dry land" is still in operation, its wonderful 1930s décor meticulously renovated in the 1990s.

AVETON GIFFORD

5 miles NW of Kingsbridge on the A379

Pronounced "Awton Jiffard", this pleasant small village, little more than one main street, had one of the oldest churches in Devon until it was almost completely destroyed by a German bomb in 1943. The modern replacement is surprisingly satisfying. The village's most famous son was born here in 1790, the son of a mason. After learning his father's trade, Robert Macey also studied as an architect. He then walked all the way to London where he successfully established himself and was responsible for designing many hospitals, factories, churches and theatres, of which the most notable were the

Sea Tractor Ferry, Burgh Island

🎭 stories and anecdotes 🐦 famous people 🎨 art and craft ✏️ entertainment and sport 🚶 walks

THE BROWNSTON GALLERY

36 Church Street, Modbury Devon, PL21 OQR
Tel: 01548 831338
e-mail: info@thebrownstongallery.co.uk
website: www.thebrownstongallery.co.uk

This exciting new contemporary art gallery opened in April 2006 in the centre of historic Modbury, South Devon. The Brownston Gallery offers original, high quality, bold contemporary paintings and wall-hung work in all media, and other new work including sculpture, designer jewellery, ceramics and glassware.

A programme of mixed and solo exhibitions throughout the year features a wide range of local, regional and nationally-renowned artists. Original work from leading artists has already included acclaimed Devon-based Kathy Ramsay Carr's contemporary landscapes; Welsh Artist of the Year award-winner Adrian Green's vibrant city interpretations; internationally-renowned Mike Bell's stunning mixed media Northumberland landscapes; local sculptor David Commander's beautiful pieces; and striking oil paintings from emerging Manchester artist Barry Spence.

With a changing programme – and exciting exclusive exhibitions – in our stunning 1300 sq ft gallery, there is outstanding work to be enjoyed all year round.

Paris
Adrian Green
Pen, Ink and Watercolour

Burning Desire
Barry Spence
Oil on Canvas

Kielderwater Rhythms & Reflections
Mike Bell
Mixed Media on Canvas

🏛 historic building   🏛 museum   🏛 historic site   🔱 scenic attraction   🌱 flora and fauna

Adelphi and the Haymarket.

At the southern end of the village, just before the three-quarter-mile long medieval causeway, a lane on the right is signposted to Bigbury. This very narrow road runs right alongside the River Avon and is very beautiful, but be warned – the river is tidal here and when the tide is in the two fords along the way are impassable.

LODDISWELL
3 miles NW of Kingsbridge off the A379

🍇 Loddiswell Vineyard

After the Norman Conquest, Loddiswell became part of the 40,000 acre estate of Judhel of Totnes, a man with an apparently insatiable appetite for salmon. Instead of rent, he stipulated that his tenants should provide

him with a certain number of the noble fish: Loddiswell's contribution was set at 30 salmon a year.

The benign climate of South Devon has encouraged several viticulturists to plant vineyards in the area. The first vines at **Loddiswell Vineyard** were planted in 1977 and since then its wines have been laden with awards from fellow wine-makers and consumer bodies. Visitors are welcome, Monday to Saturday.

MODBURY
9 miles NW of Kingsbridge on the A379

Modbury's main street climbs steeply up the hillside, its pavement raised above street level and stepped. The many Georgian buildings give this little town an air of quiet elegance

📖 stories and anecdotes   🐦 famous people   🎨 art and craft   🎭 entertainment and sport   🚶 walks

IN HOUSE

Unit 3, The Gallery,
Fleetwalk Shopping Centre,
Torquay TQ2 5EH
Tel: 01803 865096
Fax: 01803 864552
e-mail: inhouse1@btconnect.com

Having established a successful **In House** in Totnes, owner Pamela Wyles has now opened a sister establishment in Torquay's Fleetwalk Shopping Centre.

As at Totnes, the store is a showcase for brilliant interior design ideas – anything from contemporary art pieces through ceramics and glassware to the stylish 'Eglo' range of lighting. Pamela is continuously adding to the extensive collection with exciting new products being introduced every couple of weeks or so.

In the well laid out showrooms, a wondrous variety of items are displayed, including ceramics, gifts for the home, and cushions of every style and colour.

and the numerous antique, craft and specialist shops add to its interest. **St George's Church** contains some impressive, if damaged, effigies of the Prideaux and Champernowne families; the White Hart and Assembly Rooms are 18th century, the Exeter Inn even older. Once a coaching inn, this inviting old pub dates back to the 1500s. Modbury's Fair Week in early May is a jolly affair, though perhaps not as riotous as it was in the 19th century when it lasted for nine days and the town's 10 inns stayed open from morning to night.

Torbay

The most extensive conurbation in Devon, Torbay includes the three major towns of Torquay, Paignton and Brixham, strung around the deep indentation of Tor Bay. The excellent beaches and leisure facilities here have made it the county's busiest resort area with a host of indoor and outdoor attractions on offer. Torquay is the more sophisticated of the three, with elegant gardens, excellent shops and a varied nightlife. Paignton prides itself as being "unbeatable for family fun", and Brixham is a completely enchanting fishing town where life revolves around its busy harbour.

If you think Torbay's claim to be "The English Riviera" is a mite presumptuous, just take a look at all those palm trees. You see them everywhere here: not just in public parks and expensively maintained hotel gardens, but also giving a Mediterranean character to town house gardens, and even growing wild. They have become a symbol of the area's identity, blazoned on tourism leaflets, brochures, T-shirts, shop fronts, key-rings and hats.

The first specimen palm trees arrived in Britain in the 1820s and it was soon

discovered that this sub-tropical species took kindly to the genial climate of South Devon. Today, there are literally thousands of them raising their spiky tufted heads above the more familiar foliage of English gardens. To the uninitiated, one palm tree may look much like another, but experts will point out that although the most common variety growing here is Cordyline Australis (imported from New Zealand), there are also Mediterranean Fan Palms, Trachycarpus Fortunei from the Chusan Islands in the East China Sea, and Date Palms from the Canary Islands. The oldest palm tree on record in the area is now over 80 years old and more than 40ft high.

The Mediterranean similarities don't end there. Torquay, like Rome, is set on seven hills and the red-tiled roofs of its Italianate villas, set amongst dark green trees, would look equally at home in some Adriatic resort. The resemblance is so close that in one film in the Roger Moore TV series, *The Saint,* a budget-conscious producer made Torquay double for Monte Carlo.

Torquay

🐦 Edward VII   🏛 Torre Abbey   🐦 Agatha Christie

🏛 Torquay Museum   🏛 Kents Cavern

🏛 Bygones   🌴 Living Coasts

🌴 Occombe Farm Project   ⛲ Cockington Village

🕊 Babbacombe Model Village

In Victorian times, Torquay liked to be known as "The English Naples", a genteel resort of shimmering white villas set amongst dark green trees and spread, like Rome, across seven hills. It was indisputably the West of England's premier resort with imposing hotels like the Imperial and the Grand catering for "people of condition" from across Europe. At

Inner Harbour, Torquay

refurbishment. It is expected to re-open in 2008.

One of the abbey's most popular attractions was the **Agatha Christie Memorial Room** in the Abbot's Tower, which contained fascinating memorabilia loaned by her daughter. Dame Agatha was born in Torquay in 1890 and the town has created an **Agatha Christie Mile** which guides visitors to places of interest that she knew as a girl and young woman growing up in the town.

Torquay Museum also has an interesting exhibition of photographs recording her life, as well as a pictorial record of Torquay over the last 150 years, and displays chronicling the social and natural history of the area. Amongst the museum's other treasures are many items discovered at **Kents Cavern**, an astonishing complex of caves regarded as "one of the most important archaeological sites in Britain". Excavations here in the 1820s revealed a remarkable collection of animal bones – the remains of mammoths, sabre-toothed tigers, grizzly bears, bison, and cave lions. These bones proved to be the dining-room debris of cave dwellers who lived here some 30,000 years ago, the oldest known residents of Europe. The caves are open daily, all year, offering guided tours, a sound and light show, a gift shop and refreshment room.

Another popular attraction is **Bygones** in

one time, the town could boast more royal visitors to the square mile than any other resort in the world. **Edward VII** came here on the royal yacht *Britannia* and anchored in the bay. Each evening he would be discreetly ferried across to a bay beneath the Imperial Hotel and then conducted to the first floor suite where his mistress, Lily Langtry, was waiting.

The town's oldest building is **Torre Abbey,** founded in 1195 but largely remodelled as a Georgian mansion by the Cary family between 1700 and 1750. Within its grounds stand the abbey ruins and the Spanish Barn, a medieval tithe barn so named because 397 prisoners from the Spanish Armada were detained here in 1588. Torre Abbey was sold to Torbay Council in 1930 and, together with its extensive gardens, was open to the public until 2004 when the building was closed for major

🏛 historic building   🏛 museum   🏛 historic site   ᐊ scenic attraction   🌿 flora and fauna

COCKINGTON FORGE GIFTS AND BRASSWARE

Cockington Lane, Cockington, Torquay TQ2 6XA
Tel: 01803 605024
website: www.cockingtonforge.com

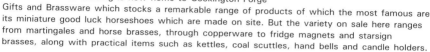

Dating back to the 11th century, Cockington Forge stands at the heart of the impossibly picturesque village of that name. The old thatched building is now home to Cockington Forge Gifts and Brassware which stocks a remarkable range of products of which the most famous are its miniature good luck horseshoes which are made on site. But the variety on sale here ranges from martingales and horse brasses, through copperware to fridge magnets and starsign brasses, along with practical items such as kettles, coal scuttles, hand bells and candle holders.

Fore Street where visitors can wander back in time through a real olde worlde street complete with ironmongers, sweet shop, apothecary's shop, forge – and pub. There are many original Victorian artefacts and other attractions include a giant model railway and railwayana collections; a children's fantasy land; a World War I exhibit, tearoom and shop.

A fairly new attraction is **Living Coasts** which opened in 2003 on Torquay Harbour. It is operated by the same wildlife trust that runs Paignton Zoo and is best described as a coastal zoo which provides a natural habitat for seals, penguins, puffins, auks and sea ducks with the emphasis on the coast and environmental issues. There's a café and a restaurant with grand views across Tor Bay.

Opened in the spring of 2006, the **Occombe Farm Project** is a 150-acre organic demonstration farm and educational venture. It incorporates a nature trail, a working farm, a butcher's, baker's, a shop selling local produce and an educational centre.

Just a mile or so from Torquay town centre is **Cockington Village**, a phenomenally picturesque rural oasis of thatched cottages, a working forge, and the Drum Inn designed by

Sir Edward Lutyens and completed in 1930. From the village there's a pleasant walk through the park to **Cockington Court**, now a Craft Centre and Gallery. Partly Tudor, this stately old manor was for almost three centuries the home of the Mallock family. In the 1930s they formed a trust to preserve "entire and unchanged the ancient amenities and character of the place, and in developing its surroundings to do nothing which may not rather enhance than diminish its attractiveness". The Trust has been spectacularly successful in carrying out their wishes.

About a mile north of Torquay is another village but this village is one-twelfth life size. **Babbacombe Model Village** contains some 400 models, many with sound and animation. Created by Tom Dobbins, a large number of the beautifully crafted models have been given entertaining names: "Shortback & Sydes", the gents' hairdresser, for example, "Walter Wall Carpets" and "Jim Nastik's Health Farm". The site also contains some delightful gardens, including a collection of more than 500 types of dwarf conifer, a 1,000ft model railway, an ornamental lake stocked with koi carp and much more.

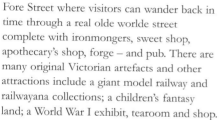

stories and anecdotes   famous people   art and craft   entertainment and sport   walks

Babbacombe Model Village

Hampton Avenue, Babbacombe, Torquay,
Devon TQ1 3LA
Tel: 01803 315315   Fax: 01803 315173
e-mail: mail@model-village.co.uk
website: www.babbacombemodelvillage.co.uk

Why not experience the ever changing miniature world of Babbacombe Model Village. Take time out from the hustle and bustle of every day life and feel on top of the world as you see it recreated in miniature. Thousands of miniature buildings, people and vehicles set in four acres capture the essence of England's past, present and future. It's not just the humour, nor the animation – it has a life of its own.

In 2006 a major new feature will be arriving - **Merrivale Castle** - Towering above a medieval village, Merrivale Castle is a miniature tourist attraction full of visitors enjoying a day out re-living medieval England. The whole scene comes to life with superb animated effects featuring all the bawdy, comic events of old England. Dramatically illuminated at night, part of this feature is the Dastardly Dungeon, where characters are stretched to their limit, and hysterical scenes at the Celebrity Banquet-see who's been invited to the feast. After its popularity in 2005, the fabulous Silvers Circus is returning to town – a unique opportunity to see this amazing animated model of a three-ringed circus. Over 120 animated effects and moving figures.

The village will be open most evenings Easter to September for the evening illuminations and then from 18th Nov to 1st Jan for Winter Wonderland. Balmy Torquay cannot guarantee snow. However, using the craftsmen's endless imagination and creative skills, many features in the gardens will be transformed into magical & nostalgic winter scenes, with miniIlluminations from dusk.

Open all year, and summer evenings until late - times vary so phone or check website for details.

SHALDON
7 miles N of Torquay on the A379

🐾 Shaldon Wildlife Trust

Set on the southern bank of the Teign estuary, Shaldon's Marine Parade provides a grand viewpoint for watching the busy traffic sailing in and out of the river. A goodly number of Regency houses add architectural dignity to the town, a reminder of the era when affluent Londoners, unable to holiday in a Europe dominated by Napoleon, began to discover the gentle charms of south-western England. A more recent attraction for visitors is the **Shaldon Wildlife Trust's** breeding centre for rare small mammals, reptiles and exotic birds, just to the north of the town.

COMBETEIGNHEAD
3 miles N of Torquay off the A380 or A379

🐿 John Keats

Standing across the river from Bishopsteignton, Combeteignhead is a charming village which **John Keats** came to know well when he was staying with his consumptive brother Tom at nearby Teignmouth in 1818. In a letter to his family he often enclosed scraps of "happy doggerel" like this:

Here all the summer I could stay,
For there's Bishop's Teign
And King's Teign
And Coomb at the clear Teign head -
Where close by the stream
You may have your cream
All spread upon Barley bread.

TEIGNMOUTH
9 miles N of Torquay on the A381 & A379

Teignmouth has something of a split personality. On the coastal side is the popular holiday resort with its two miles of sandy beaches, a splendid promenade almost as long, and a pier. There's also a 25ft-high lighthouse which serves no apparent purpose apart from looking rather fetching. The residential area contains much fine Regency and Georgian building. Particularly noteworthy are the **Church of St James** with its striking octagonal tower of 1820, and the former **Assembly Rooms**, a dignified colonnaded building which now houses the Riviera Cinema. Teignmouth's Georgian past is recalled on Wednesdays during the season when local people dress up in 18th century costume.

On the river side of the town is the working port, approached by the narrowest of channels. The currents here are so fast and powerful that no ship enters the harbour without a Trinity House pilot on board. **The Quay** was built in 1821 with granite from the quarries on Haytor Down. This durable stone was in great demand at the time. Amongst the many buildings constructed in Haytor

granite were London Bridge, (the one now relocated to Lake Tahoe in California), and the British Museum. Teignmouth's main export nowadays is potter's clay, extracted from pits beside the River Teign, but boat building also continues, albeit on a small scale.

DAWLISH
12 miles N of Torquay on the A379

🐦 The Lawn 🐦 Dawlish Warren
🏛 Atmospheric Railway

This pretty seaside resort, which boasts one of the safest beaches in England, has the unusual feature of a main railway line separating the town from its sea front. The result is, in fact, much more appealing than it sounds. For one thing, the railway keeps motor traffic away from the beachside, and for another, the low granite viaduct which carries the track has weathered attractively in the century and a half since it was built. The arches under which beach-goers pass create a kind of formal entrance to the beach and the Victorian station has become a visitor attraction in its own right.

By the time Brunel's railway arrived here in 1846, Dawlish was already well-known as a fashionable resort. John Keats, with his convalescent brother, Tom, had visited the town in 1818. The great poet was inspired to pen the less-than-immortal lines:

Over the hill and over the Dale
And over the bourne to Dawlish
Where Gingerbread wives have a scanty sale
And gingerbread nuts are smallish.

Other distinguished visitors included Jane Austen, (one of whose characters cannot understand how one could live anywhere else in Devon but here), and Charles Dickens,

🎬 stories and anecdotes 🐦 famous people 🎨 art and craft 🎭 entertainment and sport 🚶 walks

who, in his novel of the same name has Nicholas Nickleby born at a farm nearby. All of these great literary figures arrived not long after the first houses were built along the Strand. That had happened in 1803. Up until then, Dawlish was just a small settlement beside the River Daw, located about a mile inland in order to be safe from raiders. This is where the 700-year-old church stands, surrounded by a small group of thatched cottages.

At the time of John Keats' visit, the town was being transformed with scores of new villas springing up along the Strand. Earlier improvers had already "beautified" the River Daw, which flows right through the town, by landscaping the stream into a series of shallow waterfalls and surrounding it with attractive gardens like **The Lawn.** Until Regency times, The Lawn had been a swamp populated by

herons, kingfishers and otters. Then in 1808, the developer John Manning filled in the marshy land with earth removed during the construction of Queen Street. Today, both The Lawn and Queen Street still retain the elegance of those early-19th century days.

A couple of miles northeast of the town is **Dawlish Warren,** a mile-long sand spit which almost blocks the mouth of the River Exe. There's a golf course here and also a 55-acre Nature Reserve, home to more than 450 species of flowering plants. For one of them, the Jersey lily, this is its only habitat in mainland England. Guided tours of the Reserve, led by the warden, are available during the season.

Railway enthusiasts will want to travel a couple of miles further to the village of Starcross to see the last surviving relic of Isambard Kingdom Brunel's **Atmospheric Railway.** The great engineer had intended that the stretch of railway between Exeter and Totnes should be powered by a revolutionary new system. The train would be attached to a third rail which in fact was a long vacuum chamber, drawing the carriages along by the effects of air pressure. His visionary plan involved the building of 10 great Italianate engine houses at three mile intervals along the line. Sadly, the project was a failure, partly for financial reasons, but also because the leather seals on the

Dawlish

🏛 historic building 🏛 museum 🏛 historic site 🍃 scenic attraction 🌱 flora and fauna

vacuum pipe were quickly eaten away by the combined forces of rain, salt and hungry rats. The exhibition at Starcross displays a working model, using vacuum cleaners to represent the pumping houses, and volunteers are even propelled up and down the track to demonstrate the viability of the original idea.

Brunel had to fall back on conventional steam engines but the route he engineered from Exeter to Newton Abbot is one of the most scenic in the country, following first the western side of the Exe estuary, then hugging the seaboard from Dawlish Warren to Teignmouth before turning inland along the north bank of the River Teign.

PAIGNTON

3 miles SW of Torquay on the A379

🏛 Oldway Mansion   🐾 Paignton Zoo

🦆 Quaywest   🚂 Paignton & Dartmouth Railway

Today, Torquay merges imperceptibly into Paignton, but in early Victorian times Paignton was just a small farming village, about half a mile inland, noted for its cider and its "very large and sweet flatpole cabbages". The town's two superb sandy beaches, ideal for families with young children, were to change all that. A pier and promenade add to the town's appeal, and throughout the summer season there's a packed programme of specials events, including a Children's Festival in August, fun fairs and various firework displays.

The most interesting building in Paignton is undoubtedly **Oldway Mansion,** built in 1874 for Isaac Singer, the millionaire sewing-machine manufacturer. Isaac died the following year and it was his son, Paris, who gave the great mansion its present exuberant form. Paris added a south side mimicking a music pavilion in the grounds of Versailles, a hallway modelled on the Versailles hall of mirrors, and a sumptuous ballroom where his mistress Isadora Duncan would display the new, fluid kind of dance she had created based on classical mythology. Paris Singer sold the mansion to Paignton Borough Council in 1946 and it is now used as a Civic Centre, but many of the splendid rooms (and the extensive gardens) are open to the public free

Paignton and Dartmouth Steam Railway

Queen's Park Station, Torbay Road, Paignton, Devon TQ4 6AF
Tel : 01803 555872 Fax: 01803 664313
website: paignton-steamrailway.co.uk

The Paignton and Dartmouth Steam Railway from Paignton is the holiday line with steam trains running for seven miles in Great Western tradition along the spectacular Torbay Coast to Churston and through the wooded slopes bordering the Dart estuary to Kingswear. The scenery is superb. Approaching Kingswear is the beautiful River Dart, with its fascinating craft, and on the far side, the old world town of Dartmouth and the famous Britannia Royal Naval College, Butterwalk, Bayards Cove and Dartmouth Castle. Boat train and round robin combined excursions and Riviera Belle Luxury Dining Train are available on selected dates for Sunday lunch and evening dinners.

🎭 stories and anecdotes   🦅 famous people   🎨 art and craft   🎶 entertainment and sport   🚶 walks

of charge and guided tours are available.

An experience not to be missed in Paignton is a trip on the **Paignton and Dartmouth Steam Railway**, a seven mile journey along the lovely Torbay coast and through the wooded slopes bordering the Dart estuary to Kingswear where travellers board a ferry for the ten-minute crossing to Dartmouth. The locomotives and rolling stock all bear the proud chocolate and gold livery of the Great Western Railway, and on certain services you can wine and dine in Pullman style luxury in the "Riviera Belle Dining Train". During the peak season, trains leave every 45 minutes or so.

Another major attraction in the town is **Paignton Zoo**, set in 75 acres of attractive botanical gardens and home to some 300 species of world animals. A registered charity dedicated to protecting the global wildlife heritage, the zoo is particularly concerned with endangered species such as the Asiatic lions and Sumatran tigers which are now provided with their own forest habitat area. Orang utans and gorillas roam freely on large outdoor islands, free from cages. The route of the Jungle Express miniature railway provides good views of these and many other animals.

Located on Goodrington Sands, **Quaywest** claims to be Britain's "biggest, best, wildest and wettest waterpark", with the highest water slides in the country. Other amusements include go-karts, bumper boats, and crazy golf and the site also offers a choice of bars, restaurants and cafés.

BRIXHAM

8 miles S of Torquay on the A3022

🌱 Battery Gardens   ⚜ Revd. Lyte

🌱 Berry Head Country Park

In the 18th century, Brixham was the most profitable fishing port in Britain and fishing is still the most important activity in this engaging little town, although the trawlers now have to pick their way between flotillas of yachts and tour boats. On the quay there are stalls selling freshly caught seafood and around the harbour a maze of narrow streets where you'll find a host of small shops, tearooms and galleries. From the busy harbour, there are regular passenger ferries to Torquay and coastal cruises in the 80-year-old Brixham-built yacht *Vigilance* and other craft.

It was at Brixham that the Prince of Orange landed in 1688 to claim the British throne as William III; an imposing statue of him looks inland from the harbour. And in 1815, all eyes were focussed on the *Bellerophon*, anchored in the bay. On board was Napoleon Buonaparte, getting his only close look at England before transferring to the *Northumberland* and sailing off to his final exile on St Helena.

A short walk from the quay brings you to **Battery Gardens,** so named because an Emergency Coastal Defence Battery was established here in World War II. It is now a Scheduled Monument with many of the buildings and structures from that time still standing. A museum on site tells their story.

Also close to the harbour is All Saints' Church where the **Revd Henry Francis Lyte** was Vicar from 1823 until his death in 1847. During his last illness, the Revd Lyte composed what is perhaps the best known and best loved English hymn – *Abide with me*. The church bells play the tune each evening.

To the west of the town is **Berry Head Country Park** which is noted for its incredible views (on a good day as far as Portland Bill, 46 miles away), its rare plants, (like the white rock-rose), and its colonies of sea birds such as fulmars and kittiwakes

Brixham

nesting in the cliffs. The park also boasts the largest breeding colony of guillemots along the entire Channel coast. A video camera has been installed on the cliffs to relay live close-up pictures of the guillemots and other seabirds. Within the park is a lighthouse which has been called "the highest and lowest lighthouse in Britain". The structure is only 15ft high, but it stands on a 200ft high cliff rising at the most easterly point of Berry Head.

In the town itself, the **Strand Art Gallery** was founded in 1972 and showcases the work of local artists. There are more than 300 original paintings on display and visitors can see the artists at work, either in the gallery or on the slipway outside.

KINGSWEAR
10 miles S of Torquay off the A379

🕊 Coleton Fishacre

Kingswear sits on the steeply rising east bank of the River Dart, looking across to the picturesque panorama of Dartmouth stretched across the hillside on the opposite bank. The town is the terminus for the Paignton and Kingswear steam railway and passengers then join the ferry for the 10-minute crossing to Dartmouth. There's also a vehicle ferry. Above the town stand the

HENRIETTA HENSON

3 Wolborough, Street, Newton Abbot,
Devon TQ12 1JR
Tel: 01626 369131

Readers of Country Living with a discriminating eye for interesting and unusual items of interior décor will find exactly what they want at **Henrietta Henson**'s This intriguing shop is situated near the clock tower in Newton Abbot and on entering this 17th century building, which still has its original fireplace, you may feel as if you are going into your grannys.

Once inside, the shop gives the feel of a French Farmhouse cleverly mixed with a look reminiscent of Old Colonial America. It seems every inch is filled with eye-catching and fabulous items and the relaxed atmosphere encourages you to browse and discover the wealth of classy and chintzy pieces. There is kitchen and tableware, every conceivable kind of soft furnishing for every room in the house, vintage collectables, costume and fashion jewellery, ladies' clothing, quilts and coverings, vintage furniture painted with Farrow & Ball paints and much, much more.

Henrietta herself is an accomplished artist so you will also find a selection of her own striking abstract paintings on sale.

🏛 historic building   🏛 museum   🏛 historic site   🗻 scenic attraction   🌱 flora and fauna

impressive remains of Kingswear Castle which is now owned by the Landmark Trust and has been converted to holiday flats. Together with its twin across the river, Dartmouth Castle, the fortresses guarded the wide estuary of the Dart. If an invasion seemed imminent, a huge chain was strung across the river from Dartmouth as an additional deterrent.

About three miles to the east of Kingswear, **Coleton Fishacre** (NT) is a delightful coastal garden basking in a mild climate which is ideal for growing exotic trees and shrubs. The garden was created between 1925 and 1940 by Lady Dorothy D'Oyly Carte whose grandfather had produced the Gilbert and Sullivan comic operas. Lady Dorothy introduced a wonderfully imaginative variety of plants. The 20-acre site, protected by a deep combe, contains formal gardens, wooded areas with wild flowers, tranquil pools and secret paths weaving in and out of glades.

COMPTON
4 miles W of Torquay off the A381

🏰 Compton Castle

Dominating this small village, **Compton Castle** (NT) dates back to the 1300s and in Elizabethan times was the home of Sir Humphrey Gilbert, Walter Raleigh's half brother and the coloniser of Newfoundland in 1583. Complete with battlements, towers and portcullis, the castle also boasts an impressive Great Hall, a solar and an ancient kitchen. The castle is still occupied by the Gilbert family although owned by the National Trust.

NEWTON ABBOT
7 miles NW of Torquay on the A380

🏰 William III 🏇 Racecourse 🏰 Bradley Manor

🏰 Tuckers Maltings

An ancient market town, Newton Abbot took on a quite different character in the 1850s when the Great Western Railway established its locomotive and carriage repair works here. Neat terraces of artisans' houses were built on the steep hillsides to the south; the more well-to-do lived a little further to the north in Italianate villas around Devon Square and Courtenay Park.

The town's greatest moment of glory was on November 5th, 1688 when William, Prince of Orange, "the glorious defender of the Protestant religion and the liberties of England" was first proclaimed king as **William III.** This climactic moment of

🏛 stories and anecdotes 🦜 famous people 🎨 art and craft 🎭 entertainment and sport 🚶 walks

MAGPIES FOR SOMETHING SPECIAL

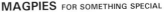

10 Wolborough Street,
Newton Abbot, Devon TQ12 1JR
Tel: 01626 353456
Fax: 01626 335391
e-mail: carol.rick@btopenworld.com
website: www.magpies-gifts.co.uk

Located close to Newton Abbot's famous clock tower, **Magpies** is stocked with a huge variety of gifts and covetable items for the home. Owners Carol and Richard Handley-Collins started the business in 1999 and have gathered together a fascinating collection of distinctive items distributed around the two floors of the shop. There are stylish contemporary gifts which include pictures, frames, lamps, fountains, mirrors, ornaments, glassware, ceramics, jewellery and collectable bears, additionally there are small furnishings, garden ornaments and furniture.

Remember also that Magpies Christmas scene attracts people from miles around and is well worth a visit. Spend

some time browsing through their collection of unusual gifts and sample home made food in THE NEST CAFÉ (see opposite page). With their constantly changing stock no wonder they are called Magpies.

🏛 historic building   🏛 museum   🏛 historic site   🌄 scenic attraction   🌱 flora and fauna

the "Glorious Revolution" took place in front of St Leonard's Church of which only the medieval tower now remains. The new king had landed at Brixham and was on his way to London. Stopping off in Newton Abbot, he stayed at the handsome Jacobean manor, Forde House, which is now used as offices by the District Council.

To the south of the town is a delightful attraction in the shape of the Hedgehog Hospital at Prickly Hill Farm – where else?

On the northern outskirts of the town is **Newton Abbot Racecourse** where National Hunt racing takes place from the autumn through to the spring. For the rest of the year, the site is used for greyhound races, stock car races and country fairs.

On the western edge of the town stands **Bradley Manor** (NT), a notable example of

Stover Country Park, Newton Abbot

medieval domestic architecture. Most of it dates from around 1420 and includes a chapel, Solar, Great Hall and porch. By the mid-1750s this quaint style of architecture was decidedly out of fashion and the building became a farmhouse with poultry occupying the chapel. The house was given to the National Trust in

---

🎭 stories and anecdotes   🐿 famous people   ✏ art and craft   ✐ entertainment and sport   🚶 walks

ST LEONARD'S ANTIQUE & CRAFT CENTRE

Wolborough Street, Newton Abbot, Devon TQ12 1JQ
Tel: 01626 335666

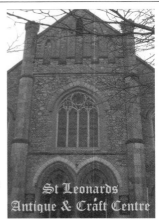

Located close to the town centre, the Victorian church of St Leonard was deconsecrated some years ago and is now home to the **St Leonard's Antique and Craft Centre.** What was formerly the nave is now filled with a wonderful variety of independently owned antique and craft outlets including Tower Clock and Watch Repairs.

There's something for everyone here: period furniture, stripped pine, jewellery, lace, textiles, Art Deco items, silver and plate, kitchenalia, clocks, glassware, china, carpets and rugs, books, cigarette lighters, metal ware, lighting boxes and pictures.

Parking is available adjacent to the Centre.

1938 by the then owner, Mrs AH Woolner. Her family continue to live here and manage the property.

Newton Abbot also boasts the only traditional working malthouse open to the public. **Tuckers Maltings** has been malting in Newton Abbot for more than 100 years and claims to offer the finest selection of bottled beers to be found in Devon. The speciality beer shop is open throughout the year and guided tours of the maltings are available during the summer months.

CHUDLEIGH
14 miles NW of Torquay off the A38

🏠 Ugbrooke House

Activists who oppose the building of new roads will find little sympathy in this former coaching town on what used to be the main thoroughfare between Exeter and Plymouth. By the 1960s, the volume of traffic had reached unbearable levels, especially during the holiday season. Mercifully, the dual carriageway A38 now bypasses the little town and it is once again possible to enjoy Chudleigh's 14th century church, containing some fine memorials to the Courtenay family, and its former Grammar School nearby which was founded in 1668. (It is now a private house). It was at the coaching inn here that William of Orange stayed after his landing at Torbay. From one of its windows, the new king addressed the good people of Chudleigh. The Dutchman's English was so bad however they were unable to understand what he was saying. They cheered him anyway.

Clifford Street is named after Sir Thomas Clifford, Lord Treasurer to Charles II and a member of the king's notorious Cabal, his secretive inner Cabinet. As was the custom then, Sir Thomas used his official position to amass a considerable fortune. This was later put to good use by his grandson who employed Robert Adam and Capability Brown to design **Ugbrooke House and Park,** a couple of miles southwest of Chudleigh and well worth visiting. Dating from the mid-1700s and replacing an early Tudor manor house, Ugbrooke is named after the Ug Brook that flows through the estate and was dammed to create three lakes in the beautifully landscaped grounds. In the 1930s, the 11th Lord Clifford abandoned the estate as he could not afford to live there. During World War II, Ugbrooke was used as a school for evacuated children and as a hostel for Polish soldiers. In the 1950s, some of the ground floor rooms were used to store grain but today the house has been beautifully restored by the present Lord and Lady Clifford. It is noted for its collections of paintings, dolls, military uniforms and furniture.

Exeter & the Exe Valley

Exeter

🏛 Roman Bath House 🏠 Rougemont Castle

🏠 St Peter's Cathedral 🏠 St Nicholas' Priory

🏠 Guildhall 🏠 Tucker's Hall 🖼 Piazza Terracina

🏛 Underground Passages 🖼 Sculpture Walk

🐟 Seahorse Nature Aquarium 🏛 Exeter Ship Canal

A lively and thriving city with a majestic Norman cathedral, many fine old buildings, and a wealth of excellent museums, Exeter's history stretches back for than two millennia. Its present High Street was already in place some 200 years or more before the Romans arrived, part of an ancient ridgeway striking

🎭 stories and anecdotes 🐦 famous people 🎨 art and craft 🏊 entertainment and sport 🚶 walks

across the West Country. The inhabitants then were the Celtish tribe of the Dumnonii and it was they who named the river Eisca, "a river abounding in fish".

Cathedral Close, Exeter

The Romans made Isca their south-western stronghold, surrounding it with a massive defensive wall. Most of that has disappeared, but a spectacular *caldarium,* or **Roman Bath House** was uncovered in the Cathedral Close in 1971.

In the Dark Ages following the Roman withdrawal, the city was a major ecclesiastical centre and in 670AD King Cenwealh founded an abbey on the site of the present cathedral. That, along with the rest of Exeter, was ransacked by the Vikings in the 9th century. They occupied the city twice before King Alfred finally saw them off.

The Normans were next on the scene, although it wasn't until 20 years after the Battle of Hastings that William the Conqueror finally took possession of the city after a siege that lasted 18 days. He ordered the construction of **Rougemont Castle,** the gatehouse and tower of which still stand at the top of Castle Street.

During the following century, the Normans began building **St Peter's Cathedral,** a work not completed until 1206. Half a century later, however, everything except the two sturdy towers was demolished and the present cathedral took shape. These years saw the development of the Decorated style, and Exeter is a sublime example of this appealing form of church architecture. In the 300ft long nave, stone piers rise 60ft and then fan out into sweeping arches. Equally impressive is the west front, a staggering display of more than 60 sculptures, carved between 1327 and 1369. They depict a curious mix of Biblical characters, soldiers, priests and a royal flush of Saxon and Norman kings.

Other treasures include an intricately-carved choir screen from about 1320, an astronomical clock built in 1376 which is one of the oldest timepieces in the world, a minstrels' gallery with a wonderful band of heavenly musicians, a monumental organ, and a colossal throne with a canopy 59ft high, carved in wood for Bishop Stapledon in 1316.

Another strange carving can be found beneath the misericord seats in the choir stalls

---

🏛 historic building   🏛 museum   🏛 historic site   ♧ scenic attraction   ❦ flora and fauna where, amongst other carvings, there is one of an elephant. However, as the carver had no model to work from he has given the animal tusks that look like clubs and rather eccentric feet. It has been suggested that the carving was based on the first elephant to come to Britain as a gift to Henry III in 1253. The carver had probably heard stories of the creature and made up the rest.

In 1941 much of the old part of the city was destroyed by a German air raid and, although the cathedral survived, it was badly damaged. When restoration work began in 1943, a collection of wax models was discovered hidden in a cavity. Including representations of human and animal limbs, the complete figure of a woman and a horse's head, they are thought to have been brought here by pilgrims who would place their wax models on the tomb of Bishop Edmund Lacy. By placing a model of an injured or withered limb on the tomb the pilgrims believed that they would be cured of their affliction.

Such is the grandeur of the cathedral that other ecclesiastical buildings in Exeter tend to get overlooked. But it's well worth seeking out **St Nicholas' Priory**, an exceptional example of a small Norman priory. It is now an interesting museum where visitors can view the original Prior's cell, the 15th century kitchens, and the imposing central hall with a vaulted ceiling and chunky Norman pillars. The church of **St Mary Steps** also repays a visit just to see its beautifully-preserved Norman font, and its ancient "Matthew the Miller" tower clock, named after a medieval miller noted for his undeviating punctuality. The church stands in Stepcote Hill, a narrow cobbled and stepped thoroughfare which until as late as 1778 was the main road into Exeter from the west.

The remarkable **Guildhall** in the High Street has been in use as a Town Hall ever since it was built in 1330, making it one of the oldest municipal buildings in the country. Its great hall was remodelled around 1450, and the Elizabethans added a striking, if rather fussy, portico but the interior is still redolent of the Middle Ages.

Another interesting medieval building is **The Tucker's Hall** in Fore Street, built in 1471 for the Company of Weavers, Fullers and Shearmen. Inside there is some exceptional carved panelling, a collection of rare silver, and a huge pair of fulling shears weighing over 25lbs and almost 4ft long. Nearby Parliament Street claims to be the world's narrowest street.

Exeter's one-time importance as a port is reflected in the dignified **Custom House,** built in 1681, and now the centrepiece of **Exeter Historic Quayside,** a fascinating complex of old warehouses, craft shops, cafés, and the **Seahorse Nature Aquarium** which is specially dedicated to these beautiful and enigmatic creatures. There are riverside walks, river trips, Canadian canoes and cycles for hire, and a passenger ferry across the river to the **Piazza Terracina** which explores five centuries of Exeter's trading connections around the world. The museum contains an extraordinary collection of boats, amongst them an Arab dhow, a reed boat from Lake Titicaca in South America, and a vintage steam launch. A special attraction of the museum is that visitors are positively encouraged to step aboard and explore in detail the many craft on show.

Other excellent museums in the city include the **Royal Albert Memorial Museum** in Queen Street, (local history, archaeology and paintings); the **Devonshire Regiment**

Museum (regimental history); and the **Rougemont House Museum** near the castle which has a copious collection of costumes and lace.

One of the city's most unusual attractions lies beneath its streets: the maze of **Underground Passages** constructed in the 14th and 15th centuries to bring water from springs beyond the city walls. A guided tour of the stone-vaulted caverns is an experience to remember.

Although Exeter is linked to the sea by the River Exe, the 13th century Countess of Devon, with a grudge against the city, built a weir across the river so that boats could sail no further upstream than Topsham. Some 300 years passed before action was taken by the city and the world's first ship canal was constructed to bypass the weir. Originally only three feet deep, this was changed to 14 feet over the years and the **Exeter Ship Canal** continued to be used until the 1970s. However, the M5 motorway, which crosses the canal on a fixed height bridge too low to allow big ships to pass, finally achieved what the Countess of Devon began so many centuries ago.

Exeter University campus is set on a hill overlooking the city, and the grounds, laid out by Robert Veitch in the 1860s, offer superb views of the tors of Dartmoor. The landscape boasts many rare trees and shrubs, and the University has followed Veitch's example by creating many new plantings, including areas devoted entirely to Australasian plants. **Exeter University Sculpture Walk** comprises more

---

BERNAVILLE NURSERIES

Three Horseshoes, Cowley, Exeter,
Devon EX5 5EU
Tel: 01392 851326 Fax: 01392 851553

A fantastic array of trees, shrubs, herbaceous perennials and expertise awaits you at this wonderful family-run nursery. Many of the plants on sale have been grown on site, and if there is something you can't find it can always be sourced for you. Established almost 50 years ago this business has grown steadily but retains its refreshing feeling of friendliness and customer commitment; this has become a local one-stop shop for all your gardening requirements and a lot more besides.

An incredible selection of hard landscaping products is also imaginatively displayed. Fencing, paving, decking, pergolas, sheds, summerhouses, greenhouses, playhouses ...... the list is endless. The newly extended shop area stocks a wide assortment of garden accessories, houseplants, gifts, cards, furniture, bbqs, kitchen ware, clothing, local speciality foods and much, much more. All are beautifully arranged with wonderfully vibrant colour themes changing with the months. Christmas is an especially exciting time in this area, with an incredible selection of decorations, lights and gifts to inspire and excite. Don't forget to leave time for a delicious home cooked lunch or snack at the Lily Pond Restaurant, or try the new mezzanine Coffee Bar. No booking required. Open: Mon-Sat 9am-5.30pm (5pm in winter), Sun 10.30am - 4.30pm. Found on the A377 Crediton road, just outside Exeter, there is plenty of parking and disabled access and facilities.

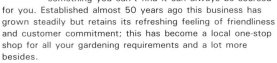
🏛 historic building   🖼 museum   🏛 historic site   ☘ scenic attraction   🌿 flora and fauna

than 20 sculptures, including works by Barbara Hepworth and Henry Moore, set out both in the splendid grounds and within the university buildings.

To the southwest of the city lies the **Devon and Exeter Racecourse**, one

Exeter's Underground Passages

of the most scenic in the country and one that is considered to be Britain's favourite holiday course.

Around Exeter

CADBURY
10 miles N of Exeter off the A3072

🏛 Cadbury Castle 🏚 Fursdon House

To the north of this delightful hamlet is **Cadbury Castle**, actually an Iron Age fort. It was built high on the hilltop, about 700ft above sea level, and it's claimed that the views here are the most extensive in Devon. On a good day Dartmoor and Exmoor are in full view, and the Quantocks and Bodmin Moor can also be seen. A little more than a mile away stands **Fursdon House** which has been lived in by the Fursdon family since around 1260. The varied architecture reflects the many additions made over the centuries. Some fascinating family memorabilia, including old scrapbooks, are on display, there's an excellent collection of 18th century costumes and

textiles, and amongst the family treasures is a letter from Charles I written during the Civil War. Opening times are restricted.

BICKLEIGH
12 miles N of Exeter on the A396

🏚 Bickleigh Castle 🏛 Devon Railway Centre

Running due north from Exeter, the Exe Valley passes through the heart of what is known as "Red Devon". The soil here has a distinctive colour derived from the red Permian rocks that underlie it. Unlike most land in Devon, this is prime agricultural land, fertile, easily-worked and, for some reason, particularly favourable to growing swedes to which it gives a much sought-after flavour.

One of the most charming villages in the Exe Valley is Bickleigh. With its riverside setting and picturesque thatched cottages with lovingly-tended gardens, Bickleigh is one of Devon's most photographed villages. It also boasts two of the area's most popular attractions. Bickleigh Mill has been developed as a craft centre and farm stocked with rare breeds, while across the river is **Bickleigh**

📖 stories and anecdotes 🐦 famous people 🎨 art and craft 🖊 entertainment and sport 🏃 walks

WITHLEIGH NURSERIES

Withleigh, Tiverton, Devon EX16 8JG
Tel: 01884 253351

After discovering Withleigh Nurseries some 4 years ago, Melissa and Terry Watling became regular customers and used to dream of running a nursery like this which enjoys a beautiful location overlooking the Devon countryside. In the autumn of 2005 they were finally able to realise their dream.

Since taking over this long established business they have added to its extensive range of quality plants for the garden. As well as trees, shrubs, grasses and exotics, there's also a wide selection of herbaceous perennials, roses, bedding plants, fruit trees, soft fruits and bare root hedging.

Terry used to own a gardening business before taking over here and brings a great deal of knowledge and experience to the task. He also believes that it is best to concentrate on producing healthy and vigorous plants. So he deliberately hasn't diversified the business into other areas such as a coffee shop, for example. This philosophy is clearly the right one since the Nurseries attracts customers from near and far, including those on holiday. Withleigh Nurseries can be found on the B3137, approximately 3 miles west of Tiverton, on the right hand side just as you enter Withleigh. The nurseries are open from 9am to 5.30pm Monday-Saturday during the summer and 9am to 4.30pm, Tuesday to Saturday in winter .

C9

4 Gold Street, Tiverton, Devon EX16 6PZ
Tel: 01884 251998
e-mail: jill.parr@btinternet.com
website: www.c9gifts.co.uk

Following the success of their **C9** shop in Wellington, Somerset, the mother and daughter team of Jill and Sam Parr have recently opened this sister establishment in Tiverton. C9 is short for Cloud 9 (Worldwide Gifts) Ltd and both shops have adopted the motto "Where Innovation Meets Tradition". They live up to their motto by keeping in touch with new trends whilst ensuring that traditional tastes are never neglected. Since both mother and daughter are involved with choosing and buying the stock, they can make sure that all ages are catered for.

As at their Wellington shop, C9 in Tiverton is a treasure trove of gifts and collectables, gadgets and gizmos, toys and cards and wraps, as well as a traditional sweet shop. Both shops are noted for their range of Ty Beanies and other soft toys by Jellycat and other producers. The Tiverton shop keeps a small range of fancy dress items, and it displays an extensive range of cards for all occasions.

🏠 historic building   🏛 museum   🏛 historic site   ♋ scenic attraction   🌿 flora and fauna

Castle, actually a moated and fortified manor house with an impressive gatehouse dating back to the late 1300s. Even older is the detached chapel which was built in the 11th century. Exhibits include Tudor furniture, (including a massive four-poster), some fine oil paintings, and a Civil War Armoury. The nearby 17th century farmhouse is very atmospheric with its inglenook fireplaces, oak beams and ancient bread ovens. The castle is open daily from the late spring Bank Holiday until the first Sunday in October, and at any time for pre-booked groups.

Railway buffs will enjoy the **Devon Railway Centre** housed in the Victorian station buildings. It has 15 different working model railway layouts and various museum collections, and provides unlimited train rides on two railways. There's also a riverside picnic area, crazy golf and refreshments.

TIVERTON

16 miles N of Exeter on the A396

🏰 Taunton Castle   🏰 St Peter's Church

🏰 St George's Church   🏰 Knightshayes Court

🏛 Museum of Mid-Devon Life

The only town of any size in the Exe valley is Tiverton, originally Twyfyrde, or two fords, for here the Exe is joined by the River Lowman. The town developed around what is now its oldest building, **Tiverton Castle,** built at the command of Henry I in 1106. Unfortunately, the castle found itself on the wrong side during the Civil War. General Fairfax himself was in charge of the successful onslaught in 1645. A few years later Parliament decreed that the castle should be "slighted", destroyed beyond any use as a fortification. Cromwell's troops observed the letter of their instructions, sparing those parts

LANTIC GALLERY

38 Gold Street, Tiverton, Devon EX16 8RP
Tel: 01884 259888   website: www.lanticgallery.co.uk

Open Monday - Friday 10 am-5 pm, Saturday 10 am- 4pm
Lantic Gallery is a new project for Sandra Hare who, after ten years selling clay and potters materials to artists realised that it was cleaner, lighter and much more exciting to sell their finished work. The gallery was opened in 2004 in Tiverton's Gold Street as a platform not only for contemporary ceramic artwork but also paintings, glass and jewellery. There is a gentle emphasis on ceramics, stemming from Sandra's long-term involvement with the business. She is constantly sourcing new work from her native West Country as well as through exhibitions and word of mouth. The excellent selection of saleable work is chosen for its quality, design, imagination and high standard of finish.

In a stylish mixture, well-established names such as Laurel Keeley, John Maltby, Lawson Rudge, Dave Regester and Jenny Southam are shown alongside newer artists including Linda Stevens and Anita Peach. Local work from sculptor Rod Hare, Nancy Wells, Jenny Pitts and Isabel Merrick interpret natural themes whilst Nic Harrison's teapots and dishes are pure tradition. Bronze is introduced with the exquisite animal pieces by both Michael Storey and Paul Jenkins.

Jewellery is a defining feature of the gallery with the unique work of local jewellers Sue Ingrams, Coralie Fish, Trish Thomas and Holly Web proving popular choices. The strawsilk decorated glassware of Margaret Johnson sit along side Jo Downs popular fused glass pieces and make ideal collectable gifts. The Gallery's first exhibition proved a great success; many visitors enjoyed John Hoar's watercolour paintings of the local Exe Valley. Various painters and printmakers are constantly on show including Lester Halhead, Mark Abdey, Mary Sumner and Jo Whiteland. If you add scarves, bags, clocks, mirrors and cards you have a fun and fascinating visit to Lantic Gallery.

🎭 stories and anecdotes   🐦 famous people   🎨 art and craft   🎟 entertainment and sport   🥾 walks

of the castle which had no military significance, and leaving behind them a mutilated, but still substantial, structure.

During the Middle Ages, the citizens of Tiverton seem to have had a very highly-developed sense of civic and social responsibility. Throughout the town's golden age as a wool town, from the late 1400s until it reached its zenith in the 18th century, prosperous wool merchants put their wealth to good use. Around 1613, George Slee built himself a superb Jacobean mansion in St Peter Street, the **Great House,** and in his will bequeathed the huge sum of £500 to establish the **Slee Almshouses** which were duly built right next door. Later almshouses, founded by John Waldron (in Welbrook Street), and John Greenway (in Gold Street) are still in use. As well as funding the almshouse, John Greenway

also devoted another sizeable portion of his fortune to the restoration of **St Peter's Church** in 1517. He added a sumptuous porch and chapel, their outside walls richly decorated with carvings depicting sailing ships of the time.

Peter Blundell chose a different method of demonstrating his beneficence by endowing Tiverton with a school. It was in the **Old Blundell's School** building of 1604, by the Lowman Bridge, that the author R.D. Blackmore received his education. He later used the school as a setting for the first chapter of his novel, *Lorna Doone.* Now a highly-regarded public school, "Blundell's" moved to its present location on the edge of town in 1880.

The **Tiverton Museum of Mid Devon Life** is one of the largest social history

🏠 historic building   🏛 museum   🏚 historic site   🌱 scenic attraction   🌿 flora and fauna

museums in the southwest, containing some 15 galleries in all. It's particularly strong on agriculture – it has a nationally important collection of farm wagons - and the Great Western Railway. One entire gallery is devoted to John Heathcoat's original lace-making machine.

The more one reads of Devon in the early to mid-18th century, the more one becomes convinced that there must have been a serial arsonist abroad. So many Devonshire towns during this period suffered devastating fires. Tiverton's conflagration occurred in 1731, but one happy outcome of the disaster was the building of **St George's Church,** by common consent the finest Georgian church in the county, furnished with elegant period ceilings and galleries.

A quay on the south-eastern edge of Tiverton marks the western end of the Grand Western Canal which was built in the early 1800s with the idea of linking the River Exe to Bridgewater and the Bristol Channel. It was never fully completed and finally closed in 1920. In recent years, an attractive stretch from Tiverton quay to the Somerset border has been restored and provides a pleasant easy walk. Horse-drawn barge trips along the canal are also available.

A few miles north of Tiverton, up the Exe Valley, lies **Knightshayes Court** a striking Victorian Gothic house designed by William Burges in 1869. It remains a rare survivor of his work. The grand and opulent interiors, blending medieval romanticism with lavish Victorian decoration, became too much for

the owner, Sir John Heathcoat-Amory, the lace manufacturer. So he sacked Burges and employed the less imaginative but competent John Diblee Crace. Covered over during the time of the backlash against the High Victorian style, the rooms have been returned to their original grandeur by the National Trust, who were

Knightshayes Court, near Tiverton

given the building by the builder's son in 1973. The house is surrounded by extensive grounds that include a water-lily pond, topiary and some rare shrubs.

BAMPTON
21 miles N of Exeter on the B3190/B3227

🪶 Exmoor Pony Sale

In medieval times Bampton was quite an important centre of the wool trade but it's now best known for its annual **Exmoor Pony Sale,** held in late October. Throughout the rest of the year, though, it's a wonderfully peaceful place with some handsome Georgian cottages and houses, set beside the River Batherm, a tributary of the Exe. To the north of the village, a tree-crowned motte marks the site of Bampton Castle. Bampton's parish church of St Michael and All Angels is popular with collectors of unusual memorials. A stone on the west side of the tower

replicates a memorial of 1776 which records the strange death of the parish clerk's son who was apparently killed by a falling icicle. The inscription is remarkably insensitive and reads: *Bless my I I I I I I (eyes), Here he lies, In a sad pickle, Killed by an icicle.*

BROADCLYST
5½ miles NE of Exeter on the B3181

🏛 Killerton

Just to the north of the village and set within the fertile lands between the Rivers Clyst and Culm, lies the large estate of **Killerton,** centred around the grand 18th century mansion house that was the home of the Acland family. Furnished as a comfortable family home, the house contains a renowned costume collection and a Victorian laundry. While the house provides some interest it is the marvellous grounds laid out by John Veitch in the 1770s that make a visit here special. Veitch introduced many rare trees to the arboretum along with rhododendrons, magnolias and herbaceous borders, and in the parkland are several interesting structures including a 19th century chapel and the Dolbury Iron Age hill fort. Here, too, can be found **Marker's Cottage** dating from the 15th century and containing 16th century paintings, and **Forest Cottage**, originally a gamekeeper's cottage. Circular walks around the grounds and estate provide ample opportunity to discover the wealth of plant, animal and birdlife that thrives in this large estate.

CLYST ST MARY
4 miles E of Exeter on the A376/A3052

 Crealy Park

A couple of miles east of Clyst St Mary is **Crealy Park,** a large all-weather entertainment centre offering a wide range of attractions for children, including the largest indoor PlayZone in the country, bumper boats and go-karts, a farm nursery and pony rides.

TOPSHAM
3 miles SE of Exeter off the A376

It's not surprising to find that the whole of the old town of Topsham has been declared a conservation area. Its narrow streets are lined with fine examples of 17th and 18th century merchants' houses, many built in the Dutch style with curved gable ends, there's a wealth of specialist and antique shops, and some stunning views over the Exe estuary with its extensive reed beds, salt marshes and mud banks. These provide an important winter feeding ground and summer breeding area for birds from all over the world. The estuary is also home to the largest winter flocks of

---

DARTS FARM

Topsham, Nr Exeter, Devon, EX3 0QH
Tel: 01392 878205
e-mail: shop@dartsfarm.co.uk website: www.dartsfarm.co.uk

'I've seen the future of shopping and it's not in London, Manchester or Edinburgh but on a road that runs alongside the Exe Estuary in Devon, a few miles south of Exeter.' The Times.

Darts Farm situated near the historic estuary town of Topsham is fortunate to be situated in a region that is rich in high quality artisan food producers. With all this wonderful local produce on the doorstep and still with their own working farm it's easy to understand why *The Guardian* described Darts Farm as "like finding Selfridges Foodhall dumped in the middle of a field but with affordable prices and all the produce from within a 30 mile radius."

All the fresh food departments have passion and expertise to accompany an incredible range of goods. Visit the deli, the cidermaker, the florist or sample a bit of everything in the restaurant which uses the foodhall as its larder with the chefs preparing fresh dishes everyday letting the good basic ingredients speak for themselves. This philosophy runs throughout Darts Farm whether it be the master butchers – Gerald David and family with their locally reared naturally fed meat or The Fish Shed which only sells locally caught fish straight off day boats, line caught. The choice is yours, either beautiful wet fish to take home and cook or try their famous fish and chips also open in the evenings for takeaway.

Combine all this with the Aga Shop, Fired Earth, Orange Tree and the unusual design-led gifts for the home and garden, children's clothes and toy departments and you will understand why your first visit won't be your last.

REKA DOM

43 The Strand, Topsham, Devon EX3 0AY
Tel: 01392 873385
e-mail: beautifulhouse@hotmail.com

At **Reka Dom**, a delightful 17th century merchant's house with many interesting architectural features, your hosts Richard and Marlene Gardner offer the unusual combination of top quality bed & breakfast accommodation along with the opportunity to experience Reiki therapy. The accommodation comprises three beautifully appointed bedrooms enjoying views over the Exe estuary and the wooded Haldon Hills. *The Woodbury Suite* and *The Tower* both have a double bedroom, small kitchen and bathroom; *The Tower* also has a sitting room which, as one of the highest points in Topsham, commands truly outstanding panoramic views.

A sumptuous breakfast is served in the Blue Room where a log fire crackles in the winter months; a three-course evening meal is also available. Marlene is a fully qualified and insured Reiki Healer, well-versed in this gentle yet powerful complementary therapy. The Reiki holistic approach aims to treat the whole person rather than specific symptoms – "You don't need a spiritual nature or any faith to feel the benefit of healing," says Marlene. Sessions are held by appointment in a quiet calm room overlooking the Exe estuary, a room renowned for its healing and relaxing atmosphere.

avocets in the county. There are walks along the banks of the estuary that lead right from Exeter to the coast at Exmouth.

WOODBURY

7 miles SE of Exeter on the B3179

🍃 Woodbury Common

St Swithin's Church at Woodbury has achieved a rather sad kind of fame because of the Revd. J. Loveband Fulford who in 1846 cut great chunks out of its medieval rood screen so that his parishioners could see him more clearly. Fortunately he left untouched the fine 15th century font made from Beer stone, the Jacobean pulpit, and the interesting memorials.

A mile or so to the east of the village is the famous **Woodbury Common** viewpoint. More than 560ft high, it provides spectacular vistas across the Exe estuary to Dartmoor, and along the south Devon coast. It's easy to understand why an Iron Age tribe chose this spot to build their massive fort whose huge ramparts lie close to the viewpoint.

LYMPSTONE

8 miles SE of Exeter off the A376

Set beside the estuary of the River Exe, Lympstone looks across the water to the impressive outline of Powderham Castle. There's a tiny harbour with a slipway and, on the beach, an Italianate clock tower erected in 1885 by a Mr W. H. Peters in commemoration of his wife, Mary Jane, who was noted for her good works amongst the poor of the village. It's a delight to wander around the old part of Lympstone with its narrow streets, small courts and ancient cottages.

POWDERHAM
7 miles S of Exeter off the A379

 Powderham Castle

Set in a deer park beside the River Exe, **Powderham Castle** has been the home of the Courtenay family, Earls of Devon since 1390. The castle stands in a beautiful setting in an ancient deer park alongside the River Exe and is at the centre of a large traditional estate of about 4,000 acres. The present building is mostly 18th century and contains some fine interiors, a breathtaking Grand Staircase, and historic family portraits – some of them by Sir Joshua Reynolds, a Devon man himself.

KENTON
7 miles S of Exeter on the A379

All Saints Church

Founded in Saxon times, this picturesque village is famed for its glorious 14th century **All Saints Church**. The tower stands over 100ft high and is decorated with a wonderful assortment of ornate carvings. Inside, there is more rich carving in the south porch and in the Beer stone arcades of the nave. The pulpit is a 15th century original which was rescued and restored after it was found in pieces in 1866, and the massive rood screen, one of the finest in Devon, is a magnificent testimony to the 15th century woodcarver's art.

DUNCHIDEOCK
7 miles SW of Exeter off the A30

A beautifully located village, Dunchideock hugs the sides of a deeply-sloping combe. At the northern end, the modest red sandstone church of St Michael has an unusual number of noteworthy internal features. There's a medieval font, a set of carved pew ends and a richly-carved rood screen which at one point

makes a surprising diversion around three sides of an octagonal roof column. Amongst the monuments is one to Major-General Stringer Lawrence, the "Father of the Indian Army", who in 1775 left a legacy of £50,000 to his lifelong friend, Sir Robert Palk. Palk proceeded to build himself a mansion, Haldon House, half a mile to the south, along with a folly in memory of his benefactor. Known locally as Haldon Belvedere, or Lawrence Castle, this tall triangular structure stands on the summit of Haldon Ridge and can be seen for miles around.

CREDITON
8 miles NW of Exeter on the A377

St Boniface   Church of the Holy Cross

Very few Britons have managed to become fully-fledged Saints, so Crediton is rather proud that one of this small and distinguished group, **St Boniface,** was born here in 680AD. The infant was baptised with the name Wynfrith but on becoming a monk he adopted the name Boniface. He rose swiftly through the ranks of the Benedictine Order and in 731 was sent by the Pope to evangelise the Germans. Boniface was remarkably successful, establishing Christianity in several German states. At the age of 71, he was created Archbishop of Mainz but three years later, he and 53 members of his retinue were ambushed and murdered. They were on their way to the great monastery at Fulda in Hesse which Boniface had founded and where he was now laid to rest.

Boniface was greatly revered throughout Germany and a few years later the Pope formally pronounced his sanctification, but it was to be almost 1,200 years before the town of his birth accorded him any recognition. Finally, in 1897, the people of Crediton

J. BULLOCK & SON

Thorne Farm, Down St Mary, Crediton,
Devon EX17 6DU
Tel: 01363 83229   Tel: 01363 85075
e-mail: alig509@hotmail.co.uk

Thorne Farm, near the village of Down St Mary, has been worked by Julie Bullock's family for generations. Trading as **J. Bullock & Son**, Julie and her son Peter have leased the farm shop in the nearby town of Copplestone since 2000 and used it as an outlet for their own farm-produced vegetables and a range of home baking that includes gluten-free products. Recently they acquired the butcher's shop in Lapford (about four miles up the A377). This has its own abattoir which means that animals are less stressed therefore the meat has more flavour and tenderness. Tours of the abattoir can be arranged by appointment.

The Lapford shop now serves as a retail outlet for their farm reared beef – produced from mainly Devon Ruby Reds – and their lamb and pork (occasionally supplemented with locally produced animals). At present, the shop caters to a mostly local trade, but it is gradually broadening its customer base and is currently preparing to offer meat boxes.

THE THELBRIDGE CROSS INN

Thelbridge, nr Witheridge, Crediton,
Mid-Devon EX17 4SQ
Tel: 01884 860316   Fax: 01884 861318
e-mail: reservations@thelbridgexinn.co.uk
website: www.thelbridgexinn.co.uk

A former coaching inn dating back to the 1700s, **The Thelbridge Cross Inn** stands at the heart of a scattered village surrounded by the rolling hills of mid-Devon. Built of cob and stone, with beamed ceilings and open log fires, this fine old hostelry is owned and run by Bill and Ria Ball who have adorned the walls here with photographs and memorabilia from the past. One of the major attractions here is the superb food that brings diners from miles around. The menu offers a wide selection of dishes, many of them traditional English recipes, all home-cooked by chef patronne Ria and her team. In addition to the à la carte restaurant and a daily specials blackboard menu, bar snacks and children's meals are also available. Enjoy your meal either in the non-smoking restaurant or more informally in the bar area.

A fairly recent addition to the inn's amenities is the custom-built Duke's Function Suite, a luxury 120-seater conference and banqueting facility. And if you are planning to stay in this lovely part of the county, the inn has seven double bedrooms, all extremely clean and comfortable, and provided with en suite facilities, colour TV, direct dial telephone and hospitality tray.

installed an east window in the town's grand, cathedral-like **Church of the Holy Cross** depicting events from his life. A few years later, a statue of the saint was erected in the gardens to the west of the church.

The interior of the early 15th century church is especially notable for its monuments which include one to Sir John Sully who fought alongside the Black Prince and lived to the age of 105, and another to Sir William Peryam, a commissioner at the trial of Mary, Queen of Scots. Most impressive of all, though, is the richly ornamented arch in memory of Sir Henry Redvers Buller, commander-in-chief during the Boer War and the hero of the Relief of Ladysmith. Also of interest is the Lady Chapel of 1300 which housed Crediton's famous grammar school from the time of Edward VI until 1859 when it moved to its present site at the western end of the High Street.

East Devon

No less a traveller than Daniel Defoe considered the landscape of East Devon the finest in the world. Acres of rich farmland are watered by the rivers Axe, Otter and Madford, and narrow, winding lanes lead to villages that are as picturesque and interesting as any in England. Steep-sided hills rise towards the coastline where a string of elegant Regency resorts remind the visitor that this part of the coast was one of the earliest to be developed to satisfy the early 19th century craze for sea bathing.

Bounded by the rolling Blackdown Hills to the north, and Lyme Bay to the south, much of the countryside here is designated as of Outstanding Natural Beauty. The best, and for much of the route, the *only* landward way to

explore the glorious East Devon coastline is to follow the South West Coast Path, part of the 600-mile South West Peninsula Coast Path which starts at Minehead in Somerset and ends at Shell Bay in Dorset.

East Devon's most famous son is undoubtedly Sir Walter Raleigh who was born at Hayes Barton near Yettington in 1552 and apparently never lost his soft Devon burr – a regional accent regarded then by 16th century London sophisticates as uncouth and much mocked by Sir Walter's enemies at the court of Elizabeth I. The Raleighs' family pew can still be seen in Yettington parish church. The famous picture by Sir John Everett Millais of *The Boyhood of Raleigh* was painted on the beach at Budleigh Salterton with the artist using his two sons and a local ferryman as the models.

Honiton

🏛 Allhallows Museum   🏛 Thelma Hulbert Gallery
🌿 Dumpdon Hill

Honiton is the "capital" of east Devon, a delightful little town in the valley of the River Otter and the "gateway to the far southwest". It was once a major stopping place on the Fosse Way, the great Roman road that struck diagonally across England from Lincoln to Exeter. Honiton's position on the main traffic artery to Devon and Cornwall brought it considerable prosperity, and its broad, ribbon-like High Street, almost two miles long, testifies to the town's busy past. By the 1960s, this "busyness" had deteriorated into appalling traffic congestion during the holiday season. Fortunately, the construction of a by-pass in the 1970s allowed Honiton to resume its true character as an attractive market town with street market held on the High Street every Tuesday and Saturday.

📖 stories and anecdotes   🐦 famous people   🎨 art and craft   ✏ entertainment and sport   🚶 walks

Surrounded by sheep pastures, Honiton was the first town in Devon to manufacture serge cloth, but the town became much better known for a more delicate material, Honiton lace. Lace-making was introduced to east Devon by Flemish immigrants who arrived here during the early years of the reign of Elizabeth I. It wasn't long before anyone who could afford this costly new material were displaying it lavishly as a signal of their wealth and status. By the end of the 17th century, some 5,000 people were engaged in the lace-making industry, most of them working from their own homes making fine

Copper Castle, Honiton

"bone" lace by hand. Children as young as five were sent to "lace schools" where they received a rudimentary education in the three Rs of Reading, (W)Riting, and (A)Rithmetic, and a far more intensive instruction in the skills of lace-making. Almost wiped out by the arrival of machine-made lace in the late 1700s, the industry was given a new lease of life when Queen Victoria insisted upon Honiton lace for her wedding dress and created a new

Allhallows Museum

High Street, Honiton, Devon EX14 1PG
Tel: 01404 44966

The building housing the museum has a very interesting history. It is the oldest building in Honiton and started its life as part of a chapel, becoming a school before it became a museum. The building dates from before 1327 and was built when the folk from the 'new town' got tired of climbing the hill to St. Michael's. They got permission for a chapel in the centre of town and called it All Saints or Allhallows. The first gallery is the chancel of the chapel, which was shortened last century to make room for St. Paul's, which is just outside.

Fifty years ago the chapel was bought by the townspeople and opened as a museum. It has three galleries, the Murch Gallery, the Nicoll Gallery and the Norman Gallery, in which are housed selections of an extensive lace collection as well as local antiquities. Demonstrations of lacemaking are often a feature.

🏠 historic building   🏛 museum   🏚 historic site   🌀 scenic attraction   🌿 flora and fauna

fashion for lace that persisted throughout the 19th century. The traditional material is still made on a small scale in the town and can be found on sale in local shops, and on display in **Allhallows Museum.** This part-15th century building served as a school for some 300 years but is now an interesting local museum housing a unique collection of traditional lace and also, during the season, giving daily demonstrations of lace making.

Allhallows Schoolroom was one of the few old buildings to survive a series of devastating fires in the mid-1700s. However, that wholesale destruction had the fortunate result that the new buildings were gracious Georgian residences and Honiton still retains the pleasant, unhurried atmosphere of a prosperous 18th century coaching town.

Another building which escaped the flames unscathed was Marwood House (private) in the High Street. It was built in 1619 by the second son of Thomas Marwood, one of Queen Elizabeth's many physicians. Thomas achieved great celebrity when he managed to cure the Earl of Essex after all others had failed. (He received his Devonshire estate as a reward). Thomas was equally successful in preserving his own health, living to the extraordinary age of 105.

Honiton boasts the only public art gallery in East Devon. The **Thelma Hulbert Gallery** occupies Elmfield House, an attractive Grade II listed late Georgian/early-Victorian town house which was the home and studio of the artist Thelma Hulbert (1913-1995). Now owned by East Devon District Council, the gallery has strong links with the Hayward Gallery in London which enables it to exhibit works by artists such as David Hockney, Andy Warhol and Roy Lichenstein.

Some buildings on the outskirts of the town are worth a mention. **St Margaret's Hospital,** to the west, was founded in the middle ages as a refuge for lepers who were denied entry to the town itself. Later, in the 16th century, this attractive thatched building was reconstructed as an almshouse. To the east, an early 19th century toll house known as **Copper Castle** can be seen. The castellated building still retains its original iron toll gates. And just a little further east, on Honiton Hill, stands the massive folly of the **Bishop's Tower,** erected in 1842 and once part of Bishop Edward Copplestone's house.

On the northern edge of Honiton rises the National Trust-owned **Dumpdon Hill,** an 850ft high steep-sided outcrop which is crowned by a sizeable late-Iron Age fort. Both the walk to the summit and the views over the Otter Valley are breathtaking.

DUNKESWELL
5 miles N of Honiton off the A30

🏛 Dunkeswell Abbey

🏛 Dunkeswell Memorial Museum

A pleasant country lane leads past **Dunkeswell Abbey,** of which only the 15th century gatehouse survives, the rest of the site now occupied by a Victorian church of no great charm. A couple of miles further and the road climbs up the hillside to Dunkeswell itself. This little village lies in the heart of the Blackdown Plateau and its main claim to fame is a 900-year-old Norman font in St Nicholas' Church on which is carved a rather crude depiction of an elephant, the earliest known representation of this animal in England. Almost certainly the stonemason had never seen such a beast, but he made almost as good a fist of it as he did with his satirical carvings of a bishop and a doctor. The font was originally located in Dunkeswell Abbey.

To the west of the village, **Dunkeswell Memorial Museum** stands on the site of the only American Navy air base commissioned on British soil during World War II. It is dedicated to the veterans of the US Fleet Air Wing 7 and RAF personnel who served at the base.

DALWOOD
6 miles E of Honiton off the A35

🏚 Loughwood Meeting House　🏚 Shute Barton

🏚 St Michael's Church　🌿 Burrow Farm Gardens

By some administrative freak, until 1842 the little village of Dalwood, despite being completely surrounded by Devon, was actually part of Dorset. Its other main claim to fame is as the home of the **Loughwood Meeting House,** one of the earliest surviving Baptist chapels in the country. When the chapel was built in the 1650s, the site was hidden by dense woodland, for the Baptists were a persecuted sect who could only congregate in out of the way locations. Under its quaint thatched roof, this charming little building contains a simple whitewashed interior with early 18th century pulpits and pews. The chapel was in use until 1833, then languished for many years until it was acquired by the National Trust in 1969. It is now open all year round with admission by voluntary donation.

About three miles south of Dalwood is another National Trust property, **Shute Barton**, an exceptional example of a medieval manor house which dates from the 1380s. Only two wings of the original building have survived, but they include some remarkably impressive features such as the Great Hall with its massive beamed ceiling, and the ancient kitchen with a huge range capable of roasting an ox whole. Entry is by way of a Tudor gatehouse. Shute Barton was owned by the Pole family, a local dynasty which is commemorated by some grand monuments in **St Michael's Church.** Amongst them is an overbearing memorial to Sir William Pole which depicts the Master of the Household to Queen Anne standing on a pedestal dressed in full regalia. More appealing is the 19th century sculptured panel, seven feet high and framed in alabaster, which shows Margaret Pole greeting her three little daughters at the gates of heaven.

Close by are **Burrow Farm Gardens**, beautifully landscaped gardens that provide a peaceful place for a relaxing afternoon's outing as well as plenty of interest for keen gardeners.

AXMINSTER
10 miles E of Honiton on the A35/A358

👤 Thomas Whitty

This little town grew up around the junction of two important Roman roads, the Fosse and the Icknield, and was important in medieval times for its Minster beside the River Axe. Its name has entered the language as the synonym for a very superior kind of floor-covering which first appeared in the early 1750s. Wandering around London's Cheapside market, an Axminster weaver named **Thomas Whitty** was astonished to see a huge Turkish carpet, 12 yards long and 8 yards wide. Returning to the sleepy little market town where he was born, Thomas spent months puzzling over the mechanics of producing such a seamless piece of work. By 1755 he had solved the problem, and on midsummer's day that year the first of these luxurious carpets was revealed to the world. The time and labour involved was so prodigious that the completion of each carpet was celebrated by a procession to St Mary's Church and a ringing peal of bells. Ironically, one distinguished

🏚 historic building　🏛 museum　🏚 historic site　🌿 scenic attraction　🌿 flora and fauna

ACORN OF AXMINSTER

Victoria Place, Axminster, Devon EX13 5NQ
Tel: 01297 33352

Like its sister shop in Lyme Regis, Acorn in Axminster stocks a huge range of presents for all the family, but this shop also features distinctive ranges of solid French oak and English pine furniture with pieces that would add character to any room, and many home accessories to provide that finishing touch.

There is pottery from Emma Bridgewater and Portmeirion. There are also wall clocks, rugs, stationery, toys, toiletries and an amazing selection of cards.

See also Acorn's entry in the Dorset section.

purchaser of an Axminster carpet was the Sultan of Turkey who in 1800 paid the colossal sum of £1,000 for a particularly fine specimen. But the inordinately high labour costs involved in producing such exquisite hand-tufted carpets crippled Whitty's company. In 1835, their looms were sold to a factory at Wilton. That was the end of Axminster's pre-eminence in the market for top-quality carpets, but echoes of those glorious years still reverberate. **St Mary's Church** must be the only house of worship in Christendom whose floor is covered with a richly-woven carpet.

COLYTON

7 miles SE of Honiton off the A3052

🏛 Church of St Andrew

The tramway that starts at Seaton runs by way of Colyford to this ancient and very appealing small town of narrow winding streets and interesting stone houses. Throughout its long history, Colyton has been an important agricultural and commercial centre with its own corn mill, tannery, sawmill and iron foundry.

Many of the older buildings are grouped around the part-Norman **Church of St Andrew,** a striking building with an unusual

15th century octagonal lantern tower, and a Saxon cross brilliantly reconstructed after its broken fragments were retrieved from the tower where they had been used as building material. Nearby is the Vicarage of 1529, and the Old Church House, a part-medieval building enlarged in 1612 and used as a Grammar School until 1928.

OTTERY ST MARY

7m SW of Honiton on the B3177

🏛 Church of St Mary   🐿 Samuel Taylor Coleridge

🏛 Cadhay   🌿 Escot Park

The glory of Ottery St Mary is its magnificent 14th century **Church of St Mary.** From the outside, St Mary's looks part mini-Cathedral, part Oxford college. Both impressions are justified since, when Bishop Grandisson commissioned the building in 1337, he stipulated that it should be modelled on his own cathedral at Exeter. He also wanted it to be "a sanctuary for piety and learning", so accommodation for 40 scholars was provided.

The interior is just as striking. The church's medieval treasures include a brilliantly-coloured altar screen, canopied tombs, and a 14th century astronomical clock showing the moon and the planets which still functions with its original machinery.

🎞 stories and anecdotes   🐿 famous people   ✎ art and craft   ✐ entertainment and sport   🚶 walks

Ottery's Vicar during the mid-18th century was the Rev. John Coleridge whose 13th child became the celebrated poet, **Samuel Taylor Coleridge.** The family home near the church has since been demolished but in one of his poems Samuel recalls

*"my sweet birth-place, and the old church-tower
Whose bells, the poor man's only music, rang
From morn to evening, all the hot Fair-day"*

A bronze plaque in the churchyard wall honours Ottery's most famous son. It shows his profile, menaced by the albatross that features in his best-known poem, *The Ancient Mariner.*

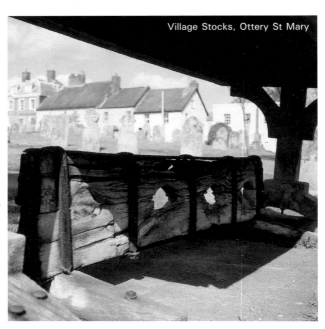
Village Stocks, Ottery St Mary

It's a delight to wander around the narrow, twisting lanes that lead up from the River Otter, admiring the fine Georgian buildings amongst which is an old wool manufactory by the riverside, a dignified example of early industrial architecture.

An especially interesting time to visit Ottery is on the Saturday closest to November 5th. The town's Guy Fawkes celebrations include a time-honoured, if rather alarming, tradition of rolling barrels of flaming tar through the narrow streets.

About a mile northwest of Ottery, **Cadhay** is a beautiful Tudor mansion built around 1550 but incorporating the Great Hall of an earlier mansion built between 1420 and 1470. The house was built for a Lincoln's Inn lawyer, John Haydon, whose great-nephew Robert

Haydon later added the exquisite Long Gallery thus forming a unique and attractive courtyard. Opening times are restricted.

Close by is **Escot Park and Gardens** where visitors can see an arboretum and rose garden along with a collection of wildlife that includes wild boar, pot-bellied pigs, otters and birds of prey.

BLACKBOROUGH
10 miles NW of Honiton off the A373

Most of the villages in this corner of East Devon nestle in the valley bottoms, but Blackborough is an exception, standing high on a ridge of the Blackdown Hills. It's a comparatively new settlement which sprang up when whetstone mining flourished here for a period in the early 1800s. RD Blackmore's novel *Perlycross* presents a vivid picture of life in these makeshift mining camps where the

---

🏠 historic building   🏛 museum   🏛 historic site   🞰 scenic attraction   🌱 flora and fauna

amenities of a comfortable life were few and far between.

UFFCULME
13 miles NW of Honiton off the A38

🏚 Coldharbour Mill

In medieval times, the charming little village of Uffculme, set beside the River Culm, was an important centre for the wool trade. Profits from this booming business helped build the impressive parish church of St Mary around 1450 and to install its splendid rood screen, believed to be the longest in Devon.

Coldharbour Mill, to the west of the village, is one of the few surviving reminders of the county's industrial wool trade. It closed down in 1981 but has since been converted into a Working Wool Museum where visitors can watch the whole process of woollen and worsted manufacture, wander around the carpenter's workshop, a weaver's cottage and the dye room. On most Bank Holidays, the massive 300 horsepower engine in the boiler house is "steamed up"- a spectacular sight. Conducted tours are available and the complex also includes a Mill Shop and a waterside restaurant.

CULMSTOCK
14 miles NW of Honiton on the B3391

🗝 RD Blackmore 🏚 Hemyock Castle

Lovers of **RD Blackmore's** novel *Lorna Doone* will be particularly interested in Culmstock since it was here that the author lived as a boy during the years that his father was the Vicar. One of his playmates in the village was Frederick Temple, another bright boy, and the two friends both went on to Blundell's School at Tiverton where they shared lodgings. Blackmore was to become one of the most successful novelists of his time; Temple entered the church and after several years as Headmaster of Rugby School reached the pinnacle of his profession as Archbishop of Canterbury.

In the centre of the village stands Culmstock's parish church with its famous yew tree growing from the top of the tower. The tree has been growing there for more than 200 years and, despite the fact that its only nourishment is the lime content of the mortar in which it is set, the trunk has now achieved a girth of 18 inches. It's believed that the seed was probably carried up in the mortar used to repair the tower when its spire was demolished in 1776. The church's more traditional kind of treasures include a magnificently embroidered cope of the late 1400s, now preserved in a glass case; a remarkable 14th century tomb rediscovered during restoration in the 19th century; and a richly-coloured memorial window designed by Burne-Jones.

About three miles east of Culmstock is **Hemyock Castle**, built around 1380. Four turrets, a curtain wall, a moat with mallard and moorhen in residence, and a dungeon are all that remains of the Hidon family's sturdy manor house, but it is a peaceful and evocative place. The castle stands behind the church in beautiful grounds and, since it lies close to the head of the lovely Culm valley, is very popular as a picnic spot. Opening times are limited.

The Jurassic Coast

🏃 East Devon Way

The coastal stretch to the east of Exmouth has been named the Jurassic Coast because it was formed during the Jurassic period some 185 million years ago. England's first natural World Heritage Site, the 95 miles of coastline

🎬 stories and anecdotes   🗝 famous people   🎨 art and craft   🏅 entertainment and sport   🏃 walks

from Exmouth to Studland in Dorset is
spectacularly beautiful.

Three river valleys, those of the Axe, the
Sid and the Otter, cut through the hills of east
Devon to meet the sea at Lyme Bay. They
provide the only openings in the magnificent
20-mile long stretch of rugged cliffs and
rocky beaches. Virtually the only settlements
to be found along the seaboard are those
which developed around the mouths of those
rivers: Seaton, Sidmouth and Budleigh
Salterton. The intervening cliffs discouraged
human habitation and even today the only way
to explore most of this part of the coast is on
foot along the magnificent **East Devon Way,**
part of the South West Coast Path. Signposted
by a foxglove, the footpath travels through the
county to Lyme Regis just over the border in
Dorset. Four other circular paths link in with
the East Devon Way providing other options
for walkers to enjoy and explore the quieter
and more remote areas away from this coast.

For centuries the little towns along the
coast subsisted on fishing and farming until
the early 1800s when the Prince Regent's fad
for sea bathing brought an influx of
comparatively affluent visitors in search of
healthy relaxation. Their numbers were
augmented by others whose accustomed

European travels had been rendered
impossible by Napoleon's domination of the
Continent. Between them, they transformed
these modest little towns into fashionable
resorts, imbuing them with an indefinable
"gentility" which still lives on in the elegant
villas, peaceful gardens and wide promenades.

Exmouth

🏠 World of Country Life   🏛 A La Ronde

With its glorious coastal scenery and splendid
beach, Exmouth was one of the earliest
seaside resorts to be developed in Devon,
"the Bath of the West, the resort of the tip-
top of the gentry of the Kingdom". Lady
Byron and Lady Nelson came to stay and
found lodgings in The Beacon, an elegant
Georgian terrace overlooking the Madeira
Walk and Esplanade. This early success
suffered a setback when Brunel routed his
Great Western line along the other side of the
estuary, (incidentally creating one of the most
scenic railway journeys still possible in
England), and it wasn't until a branch line
reached Exmouth in 1861 that business
picked up again. The town isn't just a popular
resort. Exmouth Docks are still busy with

🏛 historic building   🏠 museum   🏛 historic site   🔾 scenic attraction   🌿 flora and fauna

KINGS
Garden & Leisure
Restaurant & Coffee Shop

Family run Garden Centre

*Richard & Niki King welcome you to one of Devon's
leading garden centres and Restaurants. Extensive range
of indoor/outdoor plants, garden furniture, pots,
tools, gift section and much more..!*

the perfect ingredients for a leisurely day out!

Higher Hulham Road • EXMOUTH
Tel: 01395 271911
OPEN: Monday - Saturday 9.00 - 5.30 & Sunday 10.30 - 4.30
FREE PARKING

Parminter who modelled it on the church of San Vitale in Ravenna. Despite its name, the house is not in fact circular but has 16 sides with 20 rooms set around a 45ft high octagon. The sisters lived here in magnificent feminist seclusion, forbidding the presence of any male in their house or its 15 acres of grounds. What, therefore, no gentleman saw during the lifetime of the sisters, was the wonderfully decorated interior that the cousins created. These fabulous rooms, common in Regency times, are rare today. Due to their delicacy, the feather frieze and shell-encrusted gallery can be seen only via closed circuit TV in this National Trust property. Throughout the house the vast collection of pieces that the ladies brought back from their extensive travels is on display.

coasters and in summer a passenger ferry crosses the Exe to Starcross.

Exmouth's major all-weather attraction is **The World of Country Life** which offers an Adventure Exhibition Hall, a collection of vintage cars, a Victorian Street, safari train, pirate ship, pets centre and restaurant.

While in Exmouth, you should make a point of visiting what has been described as "the most unusual house in Britain". **A La Ronde** (National Trust) is a fairy-tale thatched house built in 1765 by the sisters Jane and Mary

East of Exmouth

BUDLEIGH SALTERTON
4 miles E of Exmouth on the B3180

🏛 Fairlynch Museum

With its trim Victorian villas, broad promenade and a spotlessly clean beach flanked by 500ft high red sandstone cliffs,

THE ROWAN TREE

*7 Fore Street, Budleigh Salterton,
East Devon EX9 6NG
Tel: 01395 446066
website: www.rowantreegifts.co.uk*

Located in the charming seaside resort of Budleigh Salterton, **The Rowan Tree** is the perfect place to find that extra special gift, something to decorate your home or just to treat yourself. Owner Karen Ritchie specialises in home and garden gifts and accessories. She stocks everything from quality pottery to greetings cards, designer bags to clocks, pictures to jewellery and a lot more besides.

There are clocks from Roger Lascelles of London; Liz Cox handbags; Jersey Pottery; Burleigh china; colourful cushions from Linum, and a good selection of art prints, notelets and books. The stock is continually changing as Karen is constantly searching for new and exciting items for her loyal customers. And she always ensures that she keeps up-to-date with the latest seasonal collections from top brands such as Cath Kidston and other leading names.

All purchases can be gift-wrapped in tissue and ribbon; handy for those last minute presents or as an extra helping hand before Christmas. Whether you're shopping for presents, searching for quality decorations and ornaments or simply wanting to treat yourself to a special something, The Rowan Tree will have the solution to your needs – and there's a convenient car park situated directly behind the shop.

🏛 historic building   🏛 museum   🏛 historic site   🔱 scenic attraction   🌱 flora and fauna

Budleigh Salterton retains its 19th century atmosphere of a genteel resort. Victorian tourists "of the better sort" noted with approval that the two-mile long beach was of pink shingle rather than sand. (Sand, apparently, attracted the rowdier kind of holiday-maker). The steeply-shelving beach was another deterrent, and the sea here is still a place for paddling rather than swimming.

One famous Victorian visitor was the celebrated artist Sir John Everett Millais who stayed during the summer of 1870 in the curiously-shaped house called **The Octagon.** It was beside the beach here that he

Pebble Beach at Budleigh Salterton

ISCA GALLERY

3 Chapel Street, Budleigh Salterton, East Devon EX9 6LX
Tel: 01395 444193
e-mail: info@iscagallery.co.uk
website: www.iscagallery.co.uk

It's a long way from the jungles of Borneo to the genteel seaside town of Budleigh Salterton but that is the journey that Susanna Lance, owner of the **Isca Gallery**, has made. Susanna was born in Kuching, the capital city of Sarawak, and started her career as a government supervisor helping the indigenous jungle tribes set up co-operatives. She left Malaysia in 1984 with her husband Graham and after working in several countries settled in East Devon in 1988. It was then that she started to develop seriously as an artist, her initial works of the animals and landscapes of Devon proving popular and winning her several prizes at local clubs and exhibitions.

In 1993, Susanna decided to open her own gallery to provide a showcase for her own works and those of other West Country artists. Anything from eight to 15 artists may have their work on show and their paintings, mostly oils, range from local scenes and seascapes to abstract and expressionist works. Business has been brisk with a loyal local clientele as regulars, and many visitors captivated both by the appealing paintings and by Susanna's charming and outgoing personality.

🎭 stories and anecdotes 🦜 famous people 🎨 art and craft ⚽ entertainment and sport 🚶 walks

TOP NOTCH

31 High Street, Budleigh Salterton,
East Devon EX9 6LD
Tel: 01395 444191

Located on the main street of this attractive seaside resort, **Top Notch** offers an enticing range of gifts for all occasions. Owner Paula Broadhurst opened her shop in 1999 and has put together an ever-changing selection of unusual and imaginative pieces with something for every member of the family.

Children will enjoy spending their pocket money, and there are gifts for toddlers to teenagers, from cuddly toys, games, jigsaws and craft kits to trendy jewellery. The Home section displays a choice of white cane furniture, linen baskets, mirrors and wall clocks. There are bathroom accessories and an aromatic range of soaps and toiletries.

Pot pourri, candles, incense and oils fill another corner, and for men there are some exclusive gadgets, key rings, cufflinks and fun gifts. Stylish umbrellas and walking sticks are truly different. Rosina Wachtmeister's porcelain cats are very popular, as are the vases, mugs, brooches and jigsaws in her series.

BADGERS DEN HOLIDAY COTTAGE

Dalbitch Lane, Knowle, Budleigh Salterton,
Devon EX9 7AH
Tel: 01395 443282
e-mail: mandy@adventurearchive.com
website: www.holidaycottagedevon.com

A wonderfully picturesque Grade II listed cottage dating from the 18th century, **Badgers Den Holiday Cottage** stands on the edge of the quiet unspoilt village of Knowle, close to the charming coastal town of Budleigh Salterton. A traditional Devon thatched cottage, it is a non smoking establishment surrounded by beautiful countryside, a number of excellent golf courses, and is just three minutes by car from the beach. Conveniently, there's a pub just 200 yards away. On the ground floor the property has a lounge/dining room, conservatory, kitchen and bathroom; upstairs there are two bedrooms (one double, one twin).

Outside, you have your own secluded garden with patio, garden furniture and barbecue. There's also parking space for two cars. The cottage has gas central heating and is fully equipped with large colour TV, video, radio/CD player, gas fire, electric cooker & gas hob, fridge/freezer, microwave and automatic washing machine. All linen is provided except beach towels. Dogs are welcome. The owners of Badgers Den, Leo and Mandy Dickinson, live in the adjacent Fudge Cottage and extend a warm welcome to their guests. For those actively inclined, there's an abundance of coastal paths such as the spectacular Lyme Bay coastal region or nearby Woodbury Common.

🏠 historic building   🏛 museum   🏛 historic site   🐾 scenic attraction   🌿 flora and fauna

painted his most famous picture *The Boyhood of Raleigh*, using his two sons and a local ferryman as the models. Raleigh's birthplace, Hayes Barton, lies a mile or so inland and remains virtually unchanged.

Found on the town's seafront is **Fairlynch Museum**, one of a very few thatched museums in the country. It houses numerous collections covering all aspects of life through the ages in the lower Otter Valley.

The name Budleigh Salterton derives from the salt pans at the mouth of the River Otter which brought great prosperity to the town during the Middle Ages. The little port was then busy with ships loading salt and wool, but by 1450 the estuary had become blocked by a pebble ridge and the salt pans flooded.

YETTINGTON
7 miles NE of Exmouth off the B3178

Sir Walter Raleigh   Bicton Park

Just to the south of the village of Yettington is Hayes Barton (private), a fine E-shaped Tudor house in which **Sir Walter Raleigh** was born in 1552. The Raleighs' family pew can still be seen in All Saints' Church, dated 1537 and carved with their (now sadly defaced) coat of arms. The church also contains a series of more than 50 16th century bench-ends which were carved by local artisans into weird and imaginative depictions of their various trades.

A mile or so in the other direction is **Bicton Park,** best known for its landscaped gardens which were laid out in the 1730s by Henry Rolle to a plan by André Le Nôtre, the designer of Versailles. There is also a formal Italian garden, a remarkable palm house known as The Dome, a world-renowned collection of pine trees, and a lake complete with an extraordinary summer house, The Hermitage. Its outside walls are covered with

Otterton

The Domesday Book recorded a mill on the River Otter here, almost certainly on the site of the present **Otterton Mill**. This handsome, part-medieval building was restored to working order in the 1970s by Desna Greenhow, a teacher of Medieval Archaeology, and visitors can now buy packs of flour ground by the same methods that were in use long before the compilers of the Domesday Book passed through the village. The site also includes a craft centre, shop and restaurant.

An interesting feature of this village of white thatched cottages is the little stream that runs down Fore Street. At the bottom of the hill, this beck joins the River Otter, which at this point has only a couple of miles to go before it enters the sea near Budleigh Salterton. There's a lovely riverside walk in that direction, and if you go northwards the path stretches even further, to Ottery St Mary some nine or ten miles distant.

thousands of tiny wooden shingles, each one individually pinned on so they look like the scales of an enormous fish. Inside, the floors are made from deer's knucklebones. The Hermitage was built by Lady Louise Rolle in 1839 as an exotic summer-house; any occupation during the winter would have been highly inadvisable since the chimney was made of oak.

OTTERTON
7 miles NE of Exmouth off the B3178

🏛 Otterton Mill

This delightful village has a charming mix of traditional cob and thatch cottages, along with other buildings constructed in the distinctive local red sandstone, amongst them the tower of St Michael's parish church. Nearby stands a manor house which was built in the 11th century as a small priory belonging to Mont St Michel in Normandy. It is now divided into private apartments.

HARPFORD
11 miles NE of Exmouth off the A3052

🐿 Revd Augustus Toplady   🌿 Aylesbeare Common

Attractively located on the east bank of the River Otter with wooded hills behind, Harpford has a 13th century church with an impressive tower and, in its churchyard, a memorial cross to the Revd Augustus Toplady who was vicar of Harpford for a couple of years in the mid-1700s. In 1775 Augustus wrote the hymn *Rock of Ages, cleft for me*, which has proved to be one of the most durable

🏛 historic building   🏛 museum   🏛 historic site   🌾 scenic attraction   🌿 flora and fauna

contributions to English hymnody.

If you cross the footbridge over the river here and follow the path for about a couple of miles you will come to **Aylesbeare Common**, an RSPB sanctuary which is also one of the best stretches of heathland in the area. Bird watchers may be lucky enough to spot a Dartford warbler, stonechats, or tree pipits, and even hear the strange song of the nightjar.

SIDMOUTH
11 miles NE of Exmouth on the A375

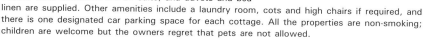 Duke of Kent   Sidmouth Museum

Sidmouth's success, like that of many other English resorts, had much to do with Napoleon Buonaparte. Barred from the Continent and their favoured resorts by the Emperor's conquest of Europe, the leisured classes were forced to find diversion and entertainment within their own island fortress. At the same time, sea bathing had suddenly become fashionable so these years were a boom time for the south coast, even as far west as Sidmouth which until then had been a poverty-stricken village dependent on fishing.

Sidmouth's spectacular position at the mouth of the River Sid, flanked by dramatic red cliffs soaring to over 500ft and with a broad pebbly beach, assured the village's popularity with the newcomers. A grand Esplanade was constructed, lined with handsome Georgian houses, and between 1800 and 1820 Sidmouth's population doubled as the aristocratic and well-to-do

stories and anecdotes   famous people   art and craft   entertainment and sport   walks

THE ROYAL GLEN HOTEL

Glen Road, Sidmouth, Devon EX10 8RW
Tel: 01395 513221/513456 Fax: 01395 514922
e-mail: info@royalglenhotel.co.uk
website: www.royalglenhotel.co.uk

The Royal Glen is an historic Grade I listed building that has been welcoming guests for more than 100 years. Throughout that time it has been run by the same family and is now in the safe hands of Orson and Jean Crane, their daughters Hilary Caldwell and Vivienne Bess, and their loyal staff. But the building has a history going back far beyond its days as a hotel.

Before it became the Royal Glen, the building was known as Woolbrook Cottage; in 1819 it was visited by the Duke and Duchess of Kent with their infant daughter Victoria, later to be Queen.

The room where the Princess stayed is now one of the hotel's 32 very comfortable bedrooms, each of which has its own individual appeal, differing in shape, size and furnishings. All the bedrooms have private bath or shower, TV, radio-alarm clock, telephone and tea-making facilities. The unique oval Drawing Room is a perfect place to relax after a meal, and when the weather is kind the veranda in the secluded garden is a pleasant spot to enjoy a drink.

In Victoria's Restaurant, a tempting table d'hote menu makes excellent use of prime local produce in dishes that offer both traditional and inventive contemporary cuisine. Other eating options include bar snacks (available Monday to Saturday), traditional Sunday lunches, packed lunches and children's high teas.

The Drawing Room, restaurant and TV lounge are non-smoking areas, and smoking is also discouraged in the bedrooms. The hotel's indoor swimming pool - warm in the cooler months and cool in the height of summer - is a great place for working up an appetite or enjoying a relaxing float,

while guests wanting an invigorating dip in the sea have only yards to walk. The Royal Glen has a putting green, while for full-scale golf there are three courses within 10 miles of Sidmouth. Many other sporting activities are available in an around the town, but Sidmouth is also a perfect spot for unwinding and strolling.

🏛 historic building   🏛 museum   🏛 historic site   🝊 scenic attraction   🌱 flora and fauna

built substantial "cottages" in and around the town. Many of these have since been converted into impressive hotels such as the Beach House, painted strawberry pink and white, and the Royal Glen which in the early 19th century was the residence of the royal **Duke of Kent**. The duke came here in 1819 in an attempt to escape his numerous creditors, and it was here that his infant daughter, Princess Victoria, later Queen Victoria, saw the sea for the first time.

Attempting to evade his many creditors, the Duke had his mail directed to Salisbury. Each week he would ride there to collect

Sidmouth

THE DONKEY SANCTUARY

Sidmouth, Devon EX10 0NU
Tel: 01395 578222 Fax: 01395 579266
e-mail: enquiries@thedonkeysanctuary.com
website: thedonkeysanctuary.org.uk

Located just outside Sidmouth, **The Donkey Sanctuary** is home to more than 400 of these engaging animals. Visitors can spend as much time as they wish meeting the donkeys who adore fuss and attention; taking strolls along various field walks, or rambling down to the sea, pausing at the Nature Centre and conservation area on the way. Also on site are restaurant serving snacks and meals, a video room and a rustic picnic barn – bring your own picnic.

Most of the donkeys are elderly and are kept on the farm in order to be close to the veterinary hospital; some of the younger, fitter donkeys are re-homed through the foster scheme. The donkeys remain under the protection of the Donkey Sanctuary and regular home checks are made. Founded in 1969 by Dr Elisabeth Svendsen MBE, the Sanctuary has taken in more than 11,500 donkeys in the UK and Ireland, and also has major overseas projects in Egypt, Ethiopia, India, Kenya, Mexico and Spain. It aims to prevent the suffering of donkeys worldwide through the provision of high quality, professional advice, training and support on donkey welfare. Admission and parking are free, and the site is open 365 days a year, from 9am until dusk.

📖 stories and anecdotes 🐦 famous people 🎨 art and craft 🎸 entertainment and sport 🚶 walks

CHERITON GUEST HOUSE

Vicarage Road, Sidmouth, East Devon EX10 8UQ
Tel/Fax: 01395 513810
website: www.smoothhound.co.uk/hotels/cheritong.html

In their handsome town house backing onto the River Sid, Jane and Rob Speers welcome guests to a relaxing stress-free break from the daily grind. The en suite bedrooms at **Cheriton Guest House** (one of which is on the ground floor) are warm and comfortable, and guests have the use of a very pleasant lounge.

A good breakfast starts the day, and packed lunches and evening meals are available by arrangement. The front of the house is a blaze of colour from seasonal flowers and plants, but the real gem is a lovely secluded rear garden that has several times been a winner in the annual Sidmouth in Bloom contest. Cheriton Guest House, which is open all year round, is a non-smoking establishment.

It's an easy walk to the seafront, either by way of the town centre or along the River Sid which, at a mere four miles long, is one of the shortest in the country. Sidmouth itself has been graced with visits from Jane Austen, William Makepeace Thackeray, Beatrix Potter and the infant Princess Victoria. Today it remains a very attractive spot with its cliffs, broad beach, grand esplanade and dignified Georgian houses – and Cheriton Guest House is an ideal base from which to enjoy it all.

FITZALAN GEMS

Old Fore Street, Sidmouth, East Devon EX10 8LP
Tel: 01395 513501
website: www.sidmouth.ws

Specialising in high quality gold and silver jewellery with semi-precious stones and freshwater pearls, Fitzalan Gems was established in 2000. Many of the beautiful pieces on display have been made on the premises. The shop's huge choice includes silver and gemstone eardrops and necklaces in a wide variety of designs. So if you want something special it may be designed and created within a few days depending on the style and availability of the stones. Amongst the wide range are ready-made, various sized, beautiful gemstone pendants set in hallmarked silver.

Set on the premises are the elegant gemstone ear studs made from solid hallmarked Britannia silver - the specially hardened pins of 99% pure silver make them ideal for most who normally only wear gold.

Gift ideas also include animal carvings from the tiniest to the very individual larger carvings. Rough gemstone specimens as well as polished stones add to the fascination of this shop. Fitzalan Gems is open from 10a.m. -1p.m., and 2p.m. - 5p.m., Monday to Saturday; a mail order service is available.

🏛 historic building   🏛 museum   🏛 historic site   🔱 scenic attraction   🌿 flora and fauna

his letters but in Sidmouth itself he couldn't conceal his delight in his young daughter. He would push Victoria in a little carriage along the mile-long Regency Esplanade, stopping passers-by to tell them to look carefully at the little girl – "for one day she would be their Queen". Half a century later, his daughter presented a stained-glass window to Sidmouth parish church in dutiful memory of her father.

One of the town's early visitors was Jane Austen, who came here on holiday in 1801 and, according to Austen family tradition, fell in love with a clergyman whom she would have married if he had not mysteriously died or disappeared. Later, in the 1830s, William Makepeace Thackeray visited and the town featured as Baymouth in his semi-autobiographical work *Pendennis* (published in 1848). During the Edwardian age, Beatrix Potter was a visitor on several occasions.

A stroll around the town reveals a wealth of attractive Georgian and early-Victorian buildings. Amazingly for such a small town, Sidmouth boasts nearly 500 listed buildings. Curiously, it was the Victorians who let the town down. Despite being the wealthiest nation in the world at that time, with vast resources at its command, its architects seemed incapable of creating architecturally interesting churches and the two 19th century Houses of the Lord they built in Sidmouth display a lamentable lack of inspiration. So ignore them, but it's worth seeking out the curious structure known as the **Old Chancel,** a glorious hotch-potch of styles using bits and pieces salvaged from the old parish church and from just about anywhere else, amongst them a priceless window of medieval stained glass.

SIDMOUTH TRAWLERS

Fisherman's Yard, The Ham, Port Royal, Sidmouth, Devon
Tel: 01395 512714

Tucked away in Fisherman's Yard at the far eastern end of the Esplanade is **Sidmouth Trawlers**, a fishmonger well known in the area for the excellent quality of its locally-caught fish and shellfish. Established in the 1960s by Stan Bagwell, from a long line of fishermen, this family-run business maintains the highest standards in endeavouring to provide for all lovers of seafood a large variety of fish and shellfish sourced from local fishermen.

The family take great pride in the various national craftsmanship awards they have won over the years, and filleting and preparation is all part of the service. No one coming to Sidmouth should miss the opportunity to visit this superb fishmonger's. Insulated packaging is available to take home a selection of the freshest seafood - from brill, Dover sole, mackerel and scallops to freshly cooked lobster and crab - to be found anywhere in the country. A ready-to-eat service is also available for whelks, cockles, mussels, prawns and crabmeat, and generously filled sandwiches are made to order.

PICTURES & PASTIMES

Old Fore Street, Sidmouth,
East Devon EX10 8LP
Tel: 01395 514717
e-mail: graham.lynsey@tiscali.co.uk
website: www.picturesandpastimes.co.uk

The West Country's many professional and
amateur artists are provided with a resource for
all essential and specialist art and craft supplies
at **Pictures & Pastimes**. Lynsey and Graham's
spacious showrooms contain a comprehensive
range of artists' and craftspeople's requirements – everything from Windsor & Newton paints,
Daler Rowney paper and canvasses, artists brushes, through to materials for glass painting,
jewellery making, and clay modelling, and more. Families are catered for with games, jigsaws
and many creativity ideas for all age groups.

Also well worth a visit is **Sidmouth
Museum**, near the sea-front, which provides
a vivid presentation of the Victorian resort,
along with such curiosities as an albatross's
swollen foot once used as a tobacco pouch.
There's also an interesting collection of local
prints, a costume gallery and a display of fine
lace. One of the most striking exhibits in the
museum is the "Long Picture" by Hubert
Cornish which is some 8ft (2.4 metres) long
and depicts the whole of Sidmouth seafront
as it was around 1814.

The town also boasts one of the few public
access observatories in Britain: the **Norman
Lockyer Observatory**. It has a planetarium
and large telescopes, and a radio station
commemorating the contribution of Sir
Ambrose Fleming, a local hero, to the
invention of the radio valve.

Demure though it remains, Sidmouth
undergoes a transformation in the first week of
August each year when it plays host to the
International Folklore, Dance and Song Festival, a
cosmopolitan event which attracts a remarkable
variety of morris dancers, folk singers and even
clog dancers from around the world.

Norman Lockyer Observatory

Sidmouth, Devon EX10 0YQ
Tel: 01395 512096

There are few public access observatories in Britain; the **Norman
Lockyer Observatory** has a planetarium and large telescopes,
including those used to discover helium and establish the sciences
of astrophysics. Lockyer's achievements include the establishment
of meteorology, astro- archaeology, the science journal, *Nature*, the
Science Museum and government departments for Science and
Education. The radio station commemorates the contribution of Sir
Ambrose Fleming, a local hero, to the invention of the radio valve.
Programme of public events available from local tourist offices and libraries, or contact The
Observatory Secretary or phone 01395 512096 for party bookings.

SIDBURY

12 miles NE of Exmouth on the A375

🏰 Sidbury Castle

St Peter & St Giles' church at Sidbury boasts the unique amenity of a Powder Room. In fact, the room over the porch contained not cosmetics, but gunpowder which was stored there by the military during the fearful days when Napoleon was expected to land in England at any moment. The church is also notable for its Saxon crypt, rediscovered during restoration in 1898. It's a rough-walled room just nine feet by 10 located under the chancel floor. Other treasures include a remarkable 500-year-old font with a square iron lock intended to protect the holy water in the basin from witches, and a number of curious carvings on the Norman tower.

Above the village to the southwest stands **Sidbury Castle**, not a castle at all but the site of a hilltop Iron Age fort from which there are some spellbinding views of the coastline extending from Portland Bill to Berry Head.

BRANSCOMBE

14 miles NE of Exmouth off the A3052

🏚 Branscombe Manor Mill

The coastal scenery near Branscombe is some of the finest in the south west with great towers of chalk rising from overgrown landslips. The village is a scattering of farmhouses and cottages with an interesting National Trust property within its boundaries – **Branscombe Manor Mill, Old Bakery and Forge.** Regular demonstrations are held at the Manor Mill which is still in working order. The water-powered mill provided flour

THE SALTY MONK

Church Street, Sidford, nr Sidmouth, East Devon EX10 9QP
Tel: 01395 513174
e-mail: saltymonk@btconnect.com
website: www.saltymonk.biz

Located two miles north of the seafront at Sidmouth, **The Salty Monk** is a delightful restaurant with rooms housed in a 16th century building that was originally used by Benedictine monks on their way to trade salt at Exeter Cathedral. Since 1999 it has been owned and run by Annette and Andy Witheridge who, together with their staff, regale their guests with friendly hospitality, personal service, comfortable accommodation and meals to remember. The owners both cut their culinary teeth in some of the country's finest restaurants. In the light, airy restaurant overlooking the beautiful gardens they serve contemporary English cuisine using top quality ingredients supplied wherever possible from the West Country.

The individually decorated bedrooms are full of the thoughtful extras that make a stay really special, from big fluffy bath sheets and robes to magazines, home-made biscuits and chilled bottled water. Luxury double rooms have either a hydrotherapy spa or power shower, and with two suites, one of which boast a sauna, power shower and bath with super king-sized bed and the other with spa bath and king size water bed, total luxury prevails. The quality of the accommodation and cuisine at The Salty Monk was recognised by a five-Diamonds Gold Award and a two Rosettes rating from the AA for 2005/6.

🖼 stories and anecdotes   🍃 famous people   🎨 art and craft   ✒ entertainment and sport   🚶 walks

for the adjacent bakery which, until 1987, was the last traditional bakery operating in Devon. Its vintage baking equipment has been preserved and the rest of the building is now a tearoom. The Forge is still working and the blacksmith's ironwork is on sale to visitors.

BEER

16 miles NE of Exmouth on the B3174

 Pecorama

Beer

Set between the high white chalk cliffs of Beer Head and Seaton Hole, this picturesque fishing village is best known for the superb white freestone which has been quarried here since Roman times. Much prized for carving, the results can be seen in countless Devon churches, and most notably in the cathedrals at Exeter, Winchester, and St Paul's, as well as at the Tower of London and in Westminster Abbey. Conducted tours around the vast, man-made complex of the **Beer Quarry Caves** leave visitors astonished at the sheer grandeur of the lofty halls, vaulted roofs and massive supporting pillars of natural stone. Not surprisingly, this complex underground network recommended itself to smugglers, amongst them the notorious Jack Rattenbury who was a native of Beer and published his *Memoirs of a Smuggler* in 1837.

A family attraction here is **Pecorama** which has an award-winning miniature railway, spectacular Millennium Gardens, the Peco Model Railway Exhibition, play areas and superb sea views.

SEATON

17 miles NE of Exmouth on the B3172

 Seaton Tramway   South West Coast Path

Set around the mouth of the River Axe, with red cliffs on one side and white cliffs on the other, Seaton was once a quite significant port. By the 16th century, however, the estuary had filled up with stones and pebbles, and it wasn't until moneyed Victorians came and built their villas (and one of the first concrete bridges in the world, in 1877) that Seaton was accorded a new lease of life. The self-confident architecture of those times gives the little town an attractive appearance which is enhanced by its pedestrianised town centre and well-maintained public parks and gardens.

From Seaton, an attractive way of travelling along the Axe Valley is on the **Seaton Tramway,** whose colourful open-topped tramcars trundle through an area famous for its bird life to the villages of Colyford and Colyton. The three-mile route follows the course of the River Axe which is noted for its

 historic building   museum   historic site   scenic attraction   flora and fauna

Seaton Tramway

Harbour Road, Seaton, Devon EX12 2NQ
Tel: 01297 20375
e-mail: info@tram.co.uk
website: www.tram.co.uk

Seaton Tramway operate narrow gauge heritage trams between Seaton, Colyford and Colyton in East Devon's glorious Axe Valley, travelling alongside the River Axe estuary through two nature reserves and giving an unrivalled view of the abundant wading bird life. The coastal resort of Seaton is now a gateway town to the Jurassic Coast, a UNESCO World Heritage Site.

Seaton Tramway is the most recent incarnation of Modern Electric Tramways Ltd, whose origins can be traced to Claude Lane's Lancaster Electrical Company in Barnet, North London, which built battery electric vehicles such as milk floats. However, his passion was trams and the factory helped realise the long held ambition of constructing a 15 inch gauge tram based on one then running on the Llandudno & Colwyn Bay system.

The first tram was completed in 1949, initially featuring at summer events, but with its immediate popularity, the first summer season was booked at St Leonards in Sussex in 1951. Over the following years, more trams were produced to run in more towns and resorts until today,the number of visitors to the tramway stands at over 80,000 per year.

The Tramway runs a number of special trips throughout the year including bird watching trips and Santa Specials. Tram driving lessons are also available for those who would like to try their hand.

abundant wild bird life. Really dedicated tram fans, after a short lesson, are even permitted to take over the driver's seat.

From Seaton, eastwards, the **South West Coast Path** follows the coastline uninterruptedly all the way to Lyme Regis in Dorset. Considered by naturalists as the last and largest wilderness on the southern coast of England, this area of unstable cliffs, wood and scrub is a haven for wildlife.

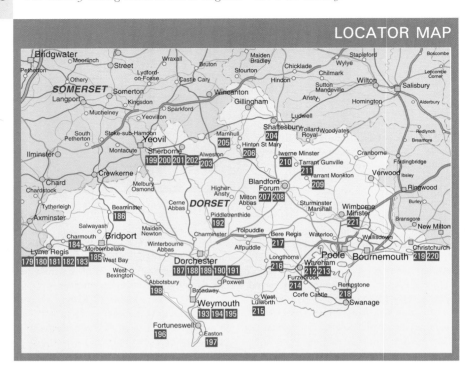

LOCATOR MAP

ADVERTISERS AND PLACES OF INTEREST

🏠 historic building   🏛 museum   🏛 historic site   ⌗ scenic attraction   🌿 flora and fauna

3 | Dorset

"Dorset has no high mountains and no coal. Everything else of beauty and almost everything of utility can be found within its borders." This was Ralph Wightman's introduction to his book about one of England's most enchanting counties. Twenty-five miles of the county's spectacular coastline has been awarded World Heritage Site status by UNESCO for its outstanding geology, an accolade that ranks it alongside the Grand Canyon and the Great Barrier Reef. The glorious coastal scenery includes Lulworth Cove and the strange natural formations of Durdle Door and the 10-mile long stretch of pebbles known as Chesil Beach. South of Weymouth, the Isle of Purbeck – famous for the marble which has been quarried here since Roman times – falls like a tear-drop into the English Channel. To the west is the charming resort town of Lyme Regis, famous for its curved harbour wall, The Cobb, its associations with Jane Austen and for the remarkable fossils discovered in what is now known as the Jurassic Coast.

Inland, gently rolling hills, woodlands and gentle river valleys epitomise the charms of unspoilt rural England. Delightful old market towns like Shaftesbury, Bridport, Blandford Forum and Sherborne have a settled graciousness, while villages such as Milton Abbas, Cranborne and Breamore are almost impossibly picturesque.

The county has more than its fair share of historic castles. Corfe Castle, set high on a hill, is one of the most impressive sights in the southwest; Sherborne Castle was the home of Sir Walter Raleigh and Portland Castle is the best-preserved of Henry VIII's coastal fortresses. Stately homes range from the Tudor gem of Athelhampton House, through the splendour of Kingston Lacy House with its outstanding collection of Old Masters, to Parnham House near Beaminster, a restored Tudor manor house which is now a powerhouse of contemporary craftsmanship. Then there are the magnificent abbeys of Wimborne Minster, Forde and Sherborne, and the fine church at Bere Regis, famed for

🔟 stories and anecdotes   🐦 famous people   🎨 art and craft   🎭 entertainment and sport   🚶 walks

The Cob , Lyme Regis

its superbly carved and painted roof, and the priory at Christchurch with its imposing Norman exterior and wealth of tombs and chantries.

Dorchester, one of England's most appealing county towns, stands at the heart of 'Hardy Country' – most of the scenes in Thomas Hardy's novels are set within a dozen or so miles of the town. Hardy was born in the nearby village of Higher Bockhampton; the humble house where he grew up is open to the public. He spent the last four decades of his life in Dorchester at Max Gate, a modest villa he designed himself which is now a National Trust property. Many of Dorset's most striking features – the Cerne Abbas hill carving of a naked giant, for example – feature in Hardy's novels, either as themselves or lightly disguised.

Lyme Regis

Known as "The Pearl of Dorset", Lyme Regis is a captivating little town enjoying a setting unrivalled in the county, an Area of Outstanding Natural Beauty where the rolling countryside of Dorset plunges to the sea. The town itself is a maze of narrow streets with many charming Georgian and Regency houses, and the picturesque harbour will be familiar to anyone who has seen the film *The French Lieutenant's Woman*, based on the novel by Lyme resident, John Fowles. The scene of a lone woman standing on the wave-lashed Cobb has become one of cinema's most enduring images.

The Cobb, which protects the harbour and the sandy beach with its clear bathing water from south-westerly storms, was first recorded in 1294 but the town itself goes back at least another 500 years to Saxon times when there was a salt works here. A charter granted by Edward I allowed Lyme to add 'Regis' to its name but during the Civil War the town was staunchly anti-royalist, routing the forces of Prince Maurice and killing more than 2,000 of them. Some 40 years later, James, Duke of Monmouth, chose Lyme as his landing place to start the ill-fated rebellion that would end with ferocious reprisals being meted out to the insurgents by the notorious Judge Jeffreys. Happier days arrived in the 18th century when Lyme became a

THE LYME REGIS FOSSIL SHOP

4 Bridge Street, Lyme Regis, Dorset DT7 3QA
Tel: 01299 442088
e-mail: info@fossil-shop.co.uk
website: www.lymeregis.com/lymefossilshop

Established more than 30 years ago, **The Lyme Regis Fossil Shop** stocks a huge variety of local fossils – probably the largest selection in Britain. Their visitors frequently tell them that it has to be the best fossil shop in the UK. The Titchener family are constantly travelling the world to find the best specimen fossils or minerals.

So you'll find a wide choice of amber and copal from the Baltic, Dominican Republic, Columbia and Madagascar, many of them with inclusions of insects. There's also a huge variety of fish plates with specimens originating in America, France, Germany, China, Lebanon and Brazil.

The shop is also well known for its vast range of local fossils with prices ranging from 99p to £1,500. Another interesting fossil available here is the Portland Titanites Gigantus, the largest ammonite in the world, and the very similar Moroccan Agadir ammonites – these range in price from £45 to £400. The shop doesn't confine itself to fossils and minerals. It also sells dinosaur toys, sea shells, carved stone products in soapstone, coal and onyx, as well as jewellery which is mostly handmade with either sterling silver or 9ct and 18ct gold.

COOMBE STREET GALLERY

33 Coombe Street, Lyme Regis, Dorset DT7 3PP
Tel: 01297 444817
website: www.coombestreetgallery.com

Tucked away in a side street behind Broad Street, **Coombe Street Gallery** is definitely worth seeking out for its impressive range of artworks, crafts, jewellery and giftware. Owner Chris Wicking is himself an accomplished photographic artist and his scenes of Lyme Regis and around Lyme Bay have a very distinctive quality. His prints are treated by computer to appear like paintings. It's a fascinating process and the end results are very striking indeed.

Also very eye-catching are the various ethical products such as the wall hangings from Rajasthan, crafts from Morocco, some lovely bags from Kenya and jewellery from around the world, including work by local craftspeople.

A good selection of colourful pottery from the Camphill communities, along with wooden toys and games, and an extensive range of gifts with something to suit everyone. Each year, during the first week of October, Lyme Regis has an Open Studio Event. Chris opens his home and gallery for local artists to exhibit their work.

GINGER BEER

4 Broad Street, Lyme Regis, Dorset DT7 3QD
Tel: 01292 444443
e-mail: gingerbeersw@aol.com
website: www.ginger-beer.biz

If you think your garden could do with something of a makeover, the place to go for some inspiring ideas is **Ginger Beer**. This treasure trove of outdoor living products can be found at the end of Broad Street overlooking the sea front. Owners Dawn Lathey and Nigel and Susie Cole have brought together a fascinating collection of eclectic vintage and new items, largely of a classic design and simple elegance, and all of the highest quality. Their ambition is simple – to ensure that their customers enjoy outside living as much as they do. Items on display range from antique watering cans to the Burgon & Ball range of gardening tools; from croquet and quoits sets to patio furniture and accessories.

The stock isn't confined to gardening items. You'll also find the Sandstorm range of canvas and leather luggage; Lily Flame scented candles which are handmade in Somerset; Burt's traditional beeswax ointments and lip balms; and Luscombe Best Ginger Beer from Buckfastleigh. And once you've thoroughly explored Ginger Beer's varied stock, you could stroll up the street to 'Susie Cole', which specialises in interior decoration and furnishings.

🏠 historic building   🏛 museum   🏛 historic site   🏞 scenic attraction   🌿 flora and fauna

ACORN OF LYME

26 Broad St, Lyme Regis, Dorset DT7 3QE
Tel: 01297 442251

At Acorn you will find a huge range of presents for all the family - "anything from marbles to globes"! There is pottery from Emma Bridgewater and Portmeirion; Bath AquaGlass; Bronte Tweed rugs and wall clocks from Roger Lascelles. There is also stationery, toiletries, home accessories and an amazing selection of cards.

This shop really appeals to all ages, with toys from Devon based House of Marbles; educational books; teddy bears, jigsaws and a wide range of games.

See also Acorn's entry in the Devon section.

fashionable resort, famed for its fresh, clean air. Jane Austen and her family visited in 1803 and part of her novel *Persuasion* is set in the town. The **Jane Austen Garden** commemorates her visit.

A few years after Jane's visit, a 12-year-old girl called Mary Anning was wandering along the shore when she noticed bones protruding from the cliffs. She had discovered the first ichthyosaur to be found in England. Later, as one of the first professional fossil collectors, she also unearthed locally a plesiosaur and a pterodactyl. The six-mile stretch of coastline on either side of Lyme is world famous for its

SUSIE COLE

15 Broad Street, Lyme Regis, Dorset DT7 3QE
Tel: 01297 444933
website: www.susiecole.co.uk

Located in the main shopping street of this charming seaside town, **Susie Cole** is a highly acclaimed interiors and gift shop, overflowing with romance and intrigue. Susie opened the shop in 2003 and has put together an enticing array of products for the home – and for yourself. There are some wonderful leather handbags, briefcases and suitcases from Rome, for example, and some stylish jewellery by both local craftspeople and foreign producers. Or you could indulge yourself with some of the bath gels, hand creams and perfumes from her 'Now and Forever' range.

Amongst items for the home, antique and vintage china features prominently and there are old and new quilts from Denmark, kitchenware, dressing table items and vintage children toys. Susie also stocks a range of painted furniture, old books and the Anzu and Willemien Stevens ranges of greetings cards. And when you finish browsing here, you could just step along the street where you'll find Ginger Beer, which has a brilliant selection of outdoor living and garden products.

stories and anecdotes 🔖 famous people ✏️ art and craft ✒️ entertainment and sport 🚶 walks

fossils and some fine specimens of local discoveries can be seen at the award-winning **Lyme Regis Museum** in Bridge Street and at **Dinosaurland & Fossil Museum** in Coombe Street which also runs guided 'fossil walks' along the beach.

Just around the corner from Dinosaurland, in Mill Lane, you'll find one of the town's most interesting buildings. It was in January 1991 that a group of Lyme Regis residents got together in an effort to save the old **Town Mill** from destruction. There has been a mill on the River Lim in the centre of the town for many centuries, but most of the present buildings date back to the mid-17th century when the mill was rebuilt after being burned down during the Civil War siege of Lyme in 1644. Today, back in full working order, Town Mill is one of Lyme's major attractions, incorporating two Art Galleries which stage a wide range of exhibitions, concerts, poetry readings and other live performances. There is also a stable building which houses craft workshops.

If you enjoy walking, the **South West Coast Path** passes through Lyme: if you follow it eastwards for about five miles it will bring you to **Golden Cap** (617ft), the highest point on the south coast with spectacular views from every vantage point. Or you can just take a pleasant stroll along Marine Parade, a traffic free promenade stretching for about a mile from the Cobb.

For its size, Lyme Regis has an extraordinary range of activities on offer, too many to list here although one must mention the famous week-long **Regatta and Carnival** held in August. Bands play on the Marine Parade, there are displays by Morris Men and folk dancers, and an annual Town Criers Open Championship. Lyme has maintained a town crier for over 1,000 years without a break and the current incumbent in his colourful 18th century costume can be seen and heard throughout the town during the summer months.

CHARMOUTH
2 miles NE of Lyme Regis off the A35

🏛 Charmouth Heritage Coast Centre

What better recommendation could you give the seaside village of Charmouth than the fact that it was Jane Austen's favourite resort? "Sweet and retired" she called it. To quote Arthur Mee, "She loved the splendid sweep of

Golden Cap, Charmouth

🏛 historic building   🏛 museum   🏛 historic site   🍃 scenic attraction   🌿 flora and fauna

Charmouth Heritage Coast Centre

Charmouth Heritage Coast Centre, Lower Sea Lane, Charmouth, Dorset, DT6 6LL
Tel: 01297 560772
e-mail: info@charmouth.org
website: www.charmouth.org

Charmouth Heritage Coast Centre is one of the country's leading coastal geological visitor centres. The Centre's displays introduce the visitor to the amazing geology and fossils of the West Dorset coast. There are fossils for you to look at and touch, interactive fossil identification displays and a "fossil beach" to practice fossil hunting.

Two large aquariums house a variety of local marine life, while a computerised display lets you dive into Lyme Bay and discover the secrets of the underwater world. For a small charge you can visit the Jurassic Theatre and discover "Finding Fossils at Charmouth" or "Secrets of the Sea". A wide selection of books, postcards and gifts are on sale.

The Centre is run by three wardens who organise a series of guided walks throughout the season. As well as the popular fossil hunting walks, there are rockpooling sessions and walks in the local countryside. Details are available from the Centre or from the website.

country all round it, the downs, the valleys, the hills like Golden Cap, and the pageantry of the walk to Lyme Regis." Charmouth remains an attractive little place with a wide main street lined with Regency buildings, and a quiet stretch of sandy beach that gradually merges into shingle. This part of the coast has yielded an amazing variety of fossils, many of which can be seen at the **Charmouth Heritage Coast Centre**. Two large aquariums house a variety of local marine life, while a computerised display enables you to 'dive' into Lyme Bay and explore the secrets of the underwater world. The centre is run by three wardens who, throughout the season, organise a series of guided fossil-hunting walks along this scenic stretch of the Jurassic Coast.

WHITCHURCH CANONICORUM
4 miles NE of Lyme Regis off the A35

⛪ Church of St Candida 👤 St Wite

Clinging to the steep hillside above the valley of the River Char, Whitchurch Canonicorum is notable for its enchanting setting and for its **Church of St Candida and the Holy Cross**. This noble building with its Norman arches and an imposing tower built around 1400 is remarkable for being one of only two churches in England still possessing a shrine to a saint. (The other is that of Edward the Confessor in Westminster Abbey). St Candida was a Saxon woman named Wite – the Anglo-Saxon word for white, which in Latin is Candida. She lived as a hermit but was murdered by a Viking raiding party in AD831.

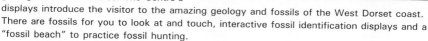 stories and anecdotes 🐟 famous people 🎨 art and craft 🖋 entertainment and sport 🚶 walks

During the Middle Ages a major cult grew up around her memory. A large shrine was built of golden Purbeck stone, its lower level pierced by three large ovals into which the sick and maimed thrust their limbs, their head or even their whole body, in the hope of being cured. The cult of **St Wite** thrived until the Reformation when all such "monuments of feigned miracles" were swept away. That might have been the end of the story of St Wite but during the winter of 1899-1900 the foundations of the church settled and cracked open a 13th century tomb chest. Inside was a lead casket with a Latin inscription stating that "Here rest the relics of St Wite" and inside the casket the bones of a small woman about 40 years old. The shrine still attracts pilgrims today, the donations they leave in the openings beneath the tomb now being devoted to causes which aid health and healing.

BROADWINDSOR

9 miles NE of Lyme Regis on the B3163

Just to the south of this pretty terraced village is a trio of hill forts, Pilsdon Pen, Lambert's Castle and Coney's Castle (all National Trust). They are connected by a network of paths and all provide magnificent views out across Marshwood Vale to the sea. William Wordsworth took a house on Pilsdon Pen for a while and declared that there was no finer view in England.

FORDE ABBEY

11 miles N of Lyme Regis off the B3162

🏠 Forde Abbey

About as far west as you can get in Dorset, **Forde Abbey** enjoys a lovely setting beside the River Axe. Founded as a Cistercian monastery more than 800 years ago, it is now the home of the Roper family. The

abbey church has gone but the monks of those days would still recognise the chapter house, dormitories, kitchen and refectories. The Upper Refectory is particularly striking with its fine timbered roof and carved panelling. After the Dissolution of the Monasteries, the abbot's residence became a private house and was greatly extended in 1649 by Cromwell's Attorney-General, Sir Edmond Prideaux. The mansion's greatest treasures are the superb Mortlake tapestries of around 1630 which are based on cartoons by Raphael and have borders probably designed by Rubens. Gardens extending to 30 acres and with origins in the early 1700s, are landscaped around this enchanting house.

Bridport

🏠 Town Hall　🍺 Purbeck Brewery　👑 Charles II
🏛 Bridport Museum　🏠 Mangerton Mill

With its broad streets, (inherited from the days when they were used for making ropes), Bridport is an appealing little town surrounded by green hills and with a goodly number of 17th and 18th century buildings. Most notable amongst these are the stately Georgian **Town Hall** of 1786, and the pleasing collection of 17th century houses in the street running south from the Town Hall. An even older survivor is the medieval Prior's House. If you visit the town on a Wednesday or Saturday you'll find its three main streets chock-a-block with dozens of stalls participating in the regular Street Market. The Town Council actively encourages local people who produce goods at home and not as part of their regular livelihood to join in. So there's an extraordinary range of artefacts on offer, anything from silk flowers to socks, fossils to fishing tackle. Another popular attraction is **Palmers Brewery** in West Bay Road. Established in 1794, part of the brewery is still thatched. During the season, visitors are welcomed on Tuesdays and Wednesdays for a tour of the historic brewery, the charge for which includes a commemorative certificate and also a glass or two of beer.

The focal point of the town is the oddly-named Bucky Doo Square which has at its centre a magnificent carved centrepiece of Portland and Purbeck stone by a local stone mason, Karl Dixon. The octagonal piece has 8 bas relief panels depicting aspects of the town's past, present and future.

Bridport Museum is good on local history and family records and also has an interesting collection of dolls. You can also learn about two distinguished visitors to the town. One was Joan of Navarre who landed at Bridport in 1403 on her way to become queen to Henry IV; the other, **Charles II** who arrived in the town after his defeat at the Battle of Worcester in 1651. He was fleeing to France, pretending to be the groom in a runaway marriage. As he attended to his horses in the yard of an inn, an ostler approached him saying, "Surely I know you, friend?" The quick-thinking future monarch asked where the ostler had been working before. When he replied "In Exeter," Charles responded "Aye, that is where we must have met." Charles then excused himself and made a speedy departure from the town. If the ostler's memory for faces had been

MOORES DORSET BISCUITS

Morcombelake, Bridport, Dorset DT6 6ES
Tel: 01297 489253 Fax: 01297 489753
website: www.moores-biscuits.co.uk

Moores Dorset Biscuits were a favourite of Thomas Hardy who used to enjoy them in the evening with a slice of Blue Vinny Cheese. They were first produced about 130 years ago at Stoke Mills in west Dorset at the farmhouse of Samuel and Eleanor Moores. Known then as Dorset Knobs, they were baked in the faggot-heated oven after the bread had been made and became the traditional meal for local farm workers at the start of the day. The Moores had 11 children, five of whom became bakers: four of them spread the Dorset Knob tradition around the west Dorset area; one took them to St Louis, Missouri.

Today, the Morcombelake bakery, run by the fourth generation of the family, is the only one still producing these tasty treats. They are still made in the traditional way – each biscuit is individually moulded by hand, has three separate bakings lasting a total of four hours. The whole process takes between 8 and 10 hours. In the 1980s, Dorset Shortbread and Butter Biscuits were introduced, and more recently a wider range of sweet biscuits was added. They are on sale mainly within a 40-mile radius of Morcombelake village.

better, he could have claimed the £1,000 bounty for Charles' capture and subsequent English history would have followed a very different course.

Just to the north of Bridport, **Mangerton Mill** is a working 17th century watermill in a peaceful rural setting. On the same site is a Museum of Rural Bygones, a tea room and craft shop.

In recent years, the area around Bridport has featured extensively in TV chef Hugh Fearnley-Whittingstall's popular "live off the land" cookery series, *Return to River Cottage*.

WEST BAY
1 mile S of Bridport off the A35

 Harbour Life Exhibition

When Bridport's own harbour silted up in the early 1700s, the townspeople built a new one at the mouth of the River Brit and called it West Bay. During the 19th century, hundreds of ships docked here every year, and West Bay had its own shipbuilding industry until 1879. The little town never became a fashionable resort but the beach, backed by 100ft high sandstone cliffs, is much enjoyed by holiday-makers, and there's still a stall at the little harbour where you can treat yourself to a tub of cockles. From the harbour you can take a mackerel boat round the bay or go for the deeper waters in search of cod, conger, skate or pollock – and keep a lookout for one of the friendly dolphins.

Close to the harbour is the Bridport Arms Hotel, an historic old thatched building which in parts dates back as far as the 1500s. The inn's picturesque qualities earned it two rôles in the BBC-TV series *Harbour Lights* starring Nick Berry and Tina Hobky. The inn appeared as both The Piers Hotel and the Bridehaven public house.

The **Harbour Life Exhibition** has exhibitions and displays on the history of this small settlement which is known as the Gateway to the Jurassic Coast – a coast where fossils formed 200 million years ago are continuously being revealed as the cliffs erode.

BEAMINSTER
5 miles N of Bridport on the A3066

 Beaminster Museum   Parnham House

Horn Park Gardens   UK Llamas

In Hardy's novel, when Tess Durbeyville arrives in Beaminster, ("Emminster" in the novel), she finds a delightful little market

West Bay

historic building   museum   historic site   scenic attraction   flora and fauna

town. Visitors today will find that remarkably little has changed. The whole of the town centre is a conservation area and contains an impressive 200 listed buildings. The 17th century almshouse, the majestic church tower in gold-tinted Hamstone, the 16th century Pickwick's Inn, and the charming Market Square with its stone roofed market cross are all much the same as Hardy knew them. What have disappeared are the many small industries that thrived in those days – rope and sailcloth, embroidered buttons, shoes, wrought ironwork and clockmaking were just some of the artefacts produced here. Housed in the former Congregational Chapel of 1749, **Beaminster Museum** displays objects relating to the life of the town from medieval times to the present day

Visitors to Beaminster's imposing 15th century church tend to be overwhelmed by the grandiose, over-lifesize sculptures of the Strode family who lived at **Parnham House**, a gem of Tudor architecture about a mile south of the town. The splendidly restored interior hosts exhibitions of cutting edge contemporary work in glass, wood, textiles and ceramics. The house is now owned by John Makepeace and much of the modern furniture is created by him and his students at the John Makepeace Furniture Workshops that he runs from here. His wife Jennie has undertaken the restoration of the gardens within whose14 acres are some unusual plants, a lake rich in wildlife, delightful woodland walks, children's play area, picnic areas and even a croquet lawn. There's also a licensed tea room and craft shop.

A mile or so to the north of Beaminster, **Horn Park Gardens** are set around a house built in 1910 by a pupil of Sir Edwin Lutyens. The gardens enjoy a magnificent sea view and are full of unusual shrubs and trees, with terraced lawns, lovely herbaceous and rose borders, water gardens and natural wildflower meadows.

For a rather different mode of exploring rural Dorset, drop in at **UK Llamas** just outside the town. Guided llama trekking tours are available and the owners will also modify the tours to suit your individual requirements and pace. A full day's trek starts at approximately 10:30am with a stop for lunch and there's a variety of routes throughout the area.

Mapperton Gardens

Beaminster, Dorset DT8 3NR
Tel: 01308 862645 Fax: 01308 863348
e-mail: office@mapperton.com
website: www.mapperton.com

Two miles from Beaminster, five miles from Bridport, Mapperton Gardens surround a fine Jacobean manor house with stable blocks, a dovecote and its own Church of All Saints. The grounds, which run down a gradually steepening valley, include an orangery and an Italianate formal garden, a 17th century summer house and a wild garden planted in the 1960s. The gardens, which are open to the public from March to October, are a natural choice for film location work, with *Emma* and *Tom Jones* among their credits.

[F] stories and anecdotes   famous people   art and craft   entertainment and sport   walks

MAPPERTON
5 miles NE of Bridport off the A3066

🏛 Mapperton

It's not surprising to find that the house and gardens at **Mapperton** have featured in three three major films – *Tom Jones, Emma* and *Restoration*. Home of the Earl and Countess of Sandwich, this magnificent Jacobean mansion set beside a lake is stunningly photogenic. The Italianate upper gardens contain some impressive topiary, an orangery, dovecote and formal borders descending to fish ponds and shrub gardens. The house stands in an Area of Outstanding Natural Beauty with some glorious views of the Dorset hills. The gardens are open during the season; tours of the house only by appointment.

Dorchester

🏛 Maumbury Rings	🏛 Roman Town House
🏛 Dorset County Museum	🏛 Church of Our Lady
🏛 Tutankhamun Exhibition	🏛 Thomas Hardy
🏛 Terracotta Warrior	🏛 Dinosaur Museum
🏛 Dorset Teddy Bear Museum	🏛 Court & Cells
🏛 The Keep Military Museum	🏛 Max Gate

One of England's most appealing county towns, Dorchester's known history goes back to AD74 when the Romans established a settlement called Durnovaria at a respectful distance from the River Frome. At that time the river was much broader than it is now and prone to flooding. The town's Roman origins are clearly displayed in its street plan, in the

---

COUNTY SHOES

9 Antelope Walk, Dorchester DT1 1BE
Tel: 01305 251555

Located in the centre of Dorchester, in the pedestrianised Antelope Walk, **County Shoes** has been supplying quality footwear to the area for many years. Expanded by Sally King, the shop is as elegant as the extensive range of shoes, boots, trainers and slippers on display. All the leading designers are featured here – Gabor, Van Dal, Rohde, Pikolinos, Josef Seibel, Ecco, Start-Rite and Timberland amongst them. And if you can't find exactly what you are looking for, just ask – Sally and her friendly staff are always helpful and take great care to assist customers in any way they can.

🏛 historic building 🏛 museum 🏛 historic site 🜄 scenic attraction 🌱 flora and fauna

beautiful tree-lined avenues known as The Walks which follow the course of the old Roman walls, at **Maumbury Rings**, an ancient stone circle which the Romans converted into an amphitheatre, and in the well-preserved **Roman Town House** behind County Hall in Colliton Park. As the town's most famous citizen put it, Dorchester "announced old Rome in every street, alley and precinct. It looked Roman, bespoke the art of Rome, concealed dead men of Rome". **Thomas Hardy** was in fact describing 'Casterbridge' in his novel *The Mayor of Casterbridge* but his fictional town is immediately recognisable as Dorchester. One place he describes in great detail is Mayor Trenchard's House, easily identified as what is now Barclays Bank in South Street and bearing a plaque to that effect. Hardy made his home in Dorchester in 1883 and two years later moved into **Max Gate** (National Trust) on the outskirts of the town, a strikingly unlovely 'two up and two down' Victorian villa designed by Hardy himself and built by his brother at a total cost of £450. Here Hardy entertained a roll-call of great names – Robert Louis Stevenson, GB Shaw, Rudyard Kipling and HG Wells amongst many others.

The most accessible introduction to the town and the county can found at the excellent **Dorset County Museum** in High Street West. Designated Best Local History Museum in the 1998 Museum of the Year Awards, the museum houses a comprehensive range of exhibits spanning the centuries, from a Roman sword to a 19th century cheese press, from dinosaur footprints to a stuffed Great Bustard which used to roam the chalk uplands of north Dorset but has been extinct in this country since 1810. Founded in 1846, the museum moved to its present site in 1883,

into purpose-built galleries with lofty arches of fine cast ironwork inspired by the Great Exhibition of 1851 at the Crystal Palace. The building was designed by GR Crickmay, the architect for whom Thomas Hardy worked in 1870. The great poet and novelist is celebrated here in a major exhibit which includes a fascinating reconstruction of his study at Max Gate, his Dorchester home. The room includes the original furnishings, books, pictures and fireplace. In the right hand corner are his musical instruments, and the very pens with which he wrote *Tess of the d'Urbervilles, Jude the Obscure,* and his epic poem, the *Dynasts*. More of his possessions are displayed in the Gallery outside – furniture, his watch, music books, and some of his notebooks. Also honoured in the Writers Gallery is William Barnes, the Dorset dialect poet, scholar and priest, who was also the first secretary of the Dorset Natural History and Archaeological Society which owns and runs the museum.

Just outside the museum stands the **Statue of William Barnes** and, at the junction of High Street West and The Grove, is the **Statue of Thomas Hardy**. There are more statues outside St George's Church, a group of lifesize models by Elizabeth Frink representing Catholic martyrs who were hung, drawn and quartered in the 16th century.

Opposite the County Museum, the Antelope Hotel and the 17th century half-timbered building beside it (now a tea-room) were where Judge Jeffreys (1648-89) tried 340 Dorset men for their part in Monmouth's Rebellion of 1685. As a result of this 'Bloody Assize', 74 men suffered death by being hung, drawn and quartered. A further 175 were transported for life. Jeffreys' ferociousness has been attributed to the agony he suffered from gallstones for which doctors of the time could provide no relief. Ironically, when his patron James II was deposed, Jeffreys himself ended up in the Tower of London where he died. A century and a half after the Bloody Assize, another infamous trial took place in the Old Crown Court nearby. Six farm labourers who later became known as the Tolpuddle Martyrs were condemned to transportation for their part in organising a 'Friendly Society' – the first agricultural trade union. The **Court and Cells** are now open to the public where they are invited to "stand in the dock and sit in the dimly-lit cells...and experience four centuries of gruesome crime and punishment".

There can be few churches in the country with such a bizarre history as that of **Our Lady, Queen of Martyrs, & St Michael**. It was first erected in Wareham, in 1888, by a Roman Catholic sect who called themselves the Passionists, a name derived from their obsession with Christ's passion and death. When they found that few people in Wareham shared their fixation, they had the church moved in 1907, stone by stone to Dorchester where it was re-assembled and then served the Catholic community for almost 70 years. By the mid-1970s the transplanted church had become too small for its burgeoning congregation. The Passionists moved out, ironically taking over an Anglican church whose communicants had become too few to sustain it. A decade later,

---

THE DINOSAUR MUSEUM

Icen Way, Dorchester, Dorset DT1 1EW
Tel: 01305 269880   e-mail: info@thedinosaurmuseum.com
Fax: 01305 268885   website: www.thedinosaurmuseum.com

The only museum on mainland Britain dedicated to dinosaurs, the award-winning **Dinosaur Museum** is a treat, especially for children. The museum combines life-sized reconstructions of dinosaurs with fossils and skeletons to create an exciting hands-on experience. Multimedia displays tell the story of the giant prehistoric animals and their enthralling world millions of years ago. Life-size dinosaur reconstructions, including Tyrannosaurus rex, Stegosaurus and Triceratops, beg to be touched by little hands - that's encouraged.
Open: Daily all year 9.30am-5.30pm (10am-4.30pm in winter)

THE TUTANKHAMUN EXHIBITION

High West Street, Dorchester, Dorset DT1 1UW
Tel: 01305 269571   e-mail: info@tutankhamun-exhibition.co.uk
Fax: 01305 268885   website: www.tutankhamun-exhibition.co.uk

Experience the magnificence and wonder of the world's greatest discovery of ancient treasure. Be there at the discovery, explore the ante-chamber, and witness Howard Carter raising the golden coffins in the burial chamber. Marvel at the superb facsimiles of some of Tutankhamun's greatest golden treasures, including the famous golden funerary mask. Finally view Tutankhamun's mummified body. Featured in numerous television documentaries this internationally renowned exhibition is an amazing experience - spanning time.
Open: Daily all year 9.30am-5.30pm (Winter 10am-5.00pm).

🏛 historic building   🏛 museum   🏛 historic site   🏞 scenic attraction   🌿 flora and fauna

their abandoned church was acquired by an organisation called World Heritage which has transformed its interior into the **Tutankhamun Exhibition**. The life, death and legacy of Tutankhamun is rarely out of the news at present and the exhibition pulls all the various strands of this fascinating tale together. The Exhibition has won international renown and has been featured in most major TV documentaries (see paenl opposite).

Also owned by World Heritage is the **Dinosaur Museum**. Dorchester is just seven miles from Dorset's world famous coastline and in the heart of dinosaur country. The award-winning museum is the only museum on mainland Britain dedicated to dinosaurs (see panel opposite).

Under the same ownership are two more museums. For those who want to get in touch with their softer side a visit to the **Dorset Teddy Bear Museum** is a must. Marvel at the evocative and atmospheric displays of the history of the teddy bear, featuring examples from the very earliest about a century ago up to the present day. Famous bears such as Rupert Bear, Winnie the Pooh, and Paddington are on display, along with bears representing the signs of the zodiac. Many collectors, limited editions, and artists bears are also present. In Teddy Bear House meet Edward Bear and his extended family of human sized teddy bears as they busy themselves or relax around their Edwardian style home. A gem of a museum is **The Terracotta Warriors Museum**. It is the only museum devoted to the terracotta warriors - now regarded as the 8th wonder of the Ancient World - outside China. Featured are unique replicas of the warriors, plus reconstructions of costumes and armour, and multimedia presentations. For further information on these

High West Street, Dorchester

four museums phone 01305 269741.

Also well worth a visit is **The Keep Military Museum** housed in an interesting, renovated Grade II listed building. Audio technology and interactive computerised displays tell the remarkable story of those who have served in the regiments of Dorset and Devon. An additional bonus is the spectacular view from the battlements across the town and surrounding countryside.

Another oddity in the town is an 18th century sign set high up in a wall. It carries the information that Bridport is 15 miles distant and Hyde Park Corner, 120. Apparently, the sign was placed in this position for the convenience of stage-coach drivers, although one would have thought that they, of all people, would have already known the mileage involved.

On the western outskirts of Dorchester, less than a mile from the town centre, is **Poundbury**, the Prince of Wales' controversial experiment in creating a new community based on old principles. The prince wanted to show how traditional quality architecture and modern town planning could combine to create urban life in a rural setting.

📽 stories and anecdotes   🦜 famous people   🎨 art and craft   🎭 entertainment and sport   🚶 walks

One objective was to make it possible for no-one to be more than 10 minutes away from his or her workplace. The enterprise began in 1993 and when completed will consist of four different quarters, each with its own public buildings, shops, pubs, offices and workshops.

The enterprise has attracted much scorn from 'cutting edge' architects who deride the whole concept as 'living in the past' but the traditionally-built properties are much sought after.

THE POET LAUREATE

Pummery Square, Poundbury, Dorchester, Dorset DT1 3GW
Tel: 01305 251511

Named in the memory of Ted Hughes, the poet laureate who died shortly before it opened, **The Poet Laureate** Public House and Restaurant occupies an impressive Georgian-style three-storey building in the centre of Poundbury, the village created on traditional lines by Prince Charles. The prince himself opened this handsome establishment in November 2002. A team of three chefs produce an inviting choice of mostly traditional English fayre – a range of wholesome appetising dishes based on fresh local produce. At lunchtime, there's a choice of a la carte, meals or light bites as well as a selection of vegetarian options.

MAGPIE

2 Wishay Street, Poundbury, Dorchester DT1 3GU
Tel: 01305 265261   Fax: 01305 268890
e-mail: enquiries@mag-pie.co.uk   website: www.mag-pie.co.uk

Stephanie Cooper worked for many years as wardrobe mistress for the Royal Shakespeare Company before changing career in 2003 and opening her unusual gift shop **Magpie** in the village of Poundbury. It was inspired by her travels around the world, especially to Southern Africa and New Zealand from where she imports directly. In addition to these exotic sources, Stephanie also provides a showcase for gifts made in the UK, promoting small companies and hand-made products wherever possible. In the treasure trove of gifts on display is the full range of Burleigh china, St Eval candles, original handknits – including pieces made by Stephanie herself – silver and gemstone jewellery, exquisite baby gifts, organic skincare and a selection of stunning African craft art for which Magpie is the exclusive stockist in the northern hemisphere.

Also on display are soft furnishings, glass, some great cards and items of small furniture. To the rear of the shop, the garden area provides the setting for some striking original sculptures in wood and metal, along with hand-finished granite pieces. Magpie is open from 10am to 5pm, Tuesday to Saturday.

🏛 historic building   🏛 museum   🏚 historic site   ᒫ scenic attraction   🌿 flora and fauna

Around Dorchester

CHARMINSTER
1 mile N of Dorchester on the A52

 Wolfeton House

An attractive town on the River Cerne, Charminster has a 12th century church with an impressive pinnacled tower added in the 1400s. Inside are some striking memorials to the Trenchard family whose noble mansion, **Wolfeton House,** stands on the northern edge of the town. A lovely medieval and Elizabethan manor house, it is surrounded by water meadows near the meeting of the rivers Cerne and Frome. The house contains a great stone staircase, remarkable plaster ceilings, fireplaces and carved oak panelling – all Elizabethan – some good pictures and furniture. Opening times are restricted. There is also a cider house here from which cider can be purchased.

GODMANSTONE
4 miles N of Dorchester on the A352

 Smith's Arms

Dorset can boast many cosy, intimate pubs, but the **Smith's Arms** at Godmanstone is in a class of its own, claiming to be the smallest inn in the country with a frontage just 11 feet wide.

This appealing 14th century thatched building was originally the village smithy and, according to tradition, Charles II happened to stop here to have his horse shod. Feeling thirsty, the king asked for a glass of ale and was not best pleased to be told that as the blacksmith had no licence, no alcoholic drink was available. Invoking the royal prerogative, Charles granted a licence immediately and this tiny hostelry has been licensed ever since. Given the cramped interior, elbow-bending at the Smith's Arms can be a problem at busy times, but fortunately there is a spacious terrace outside.

PIDDLETRENTHIDE
6 miles N of Dorchester on the B3143

Mentioned in the Domesday Book, this village is named after the river beside which it stands and the '30 hides' of land for which it was assessed. A beautiful place in a beautiful location, Piddletrenthide is believed to have been the home of Alfred the Great's brother, Ethelred.

CERNE ABBAS
7 miles N of Dorchester on the A352

 Cerne Abbey   Cerne Abbas Giant

This pretty village beside the River Cerne takes its name from **Cerne Abbey**, formerly a major

---

THE PIDDLE INN

Piddletrenthide, nr Dorchester, Dorset DT2 7QF
Tel: 01300 348468   Fax: 01300 348102
e-mail: piddleinn@aol.com   website: www.piddleinn.co.uk

A wonderful traditional inn offering customers the very best of hospitality, **The Piddle Inn** is located in Thomas Hardy country. The village church, one of the finest in Dorset, is mentioned in the Doomsday Book. However, the inn has found its own fame locally for its wonderful cuisine, all home-cooked and based on local produce with fish and Portland crab specialities of the house. There are four real ales on tap, along with an excellent choice of wines. In good weather, customers can enjoy their refreshments in the patio garden beside a babbling stream. The inn also has three outstanding guest bedrooms with a five-star rating and spacious king size beds.

🎭 stories and anecdotes   🐦 famous people   🎨 art and craft   🏃 entertainment and sport   🚶 walks

Benedictine monastery of which an imposing 15th century gatehouse, a tithe barn of the same period, and a holy well still survive, all well worth seeing. So too are the lofty, airy church with grotesque gargoyles and medieval statues adorning its west tower, and the old Market House on Long Street. In fact, there is much to see in this ancient village where cottages dating back to the 14th century still stand.

But the major visitor attraction is to be found just to the north of the village – the famous **Cerne Abbas Giant** (National Trust), a colossal 180ft-high figure cut into the chalk hillside. He stands brandishing a club, naked and full-frontal, and there can be absolutely no doubt about his maleness. An ancient tradition asserts that any woman wishing to become pregnant should sit, or preferably sleep the night, on the giant's huge erect penis, some 22ft long. The age of this extraordinary carving is hotly disputed but a consensus is emerging that it was originally created by ancient Britons as a fertility symbol and that the giant's club was added by the Romans. (There are clear similarities between the giant and the representation of Hercules on a Roman pavement of AD 191, preserved at Sherborne Castle.) As with all hill-carvings, the best view is from a distance, in this case from a layby on the A352. A curious puzzle remains. The giant's outlines in the chalk need a regular scouring to remove grass and weeds. Should this be neglected, he would soon fade into the hillside. In medieval centuries, such a non-essential task of conservation could only have been authorised by the locally all-powerful Abbots of Cerne. What possible reason did those Christian advocates of chastity have for carefully preserving such a powerful pagan image of virility?

MINTERNE MAGNA
9 miles N of Dorchester, on the A352

🌱 Minterne Gardens

A couple of miles north of the Cerne Giant, Minterne Magna is notable for its parish church, crowded with memorials to Napiers, Churchills and Digbys, the families who once owned the great house here and most of the Minterne valley. The mansion itself, rebuilt in the Arts & Crafts style around 1900 is not open to the public but its splendid **Minterne Gardens** are. The gardens are laid out in a horseshoe below the house and landscaped in the 18th century style of Capability Brown. They contain an important collection of Himalayan rhododendrons and azaleas, along with cherries, maples and many other fine and rare trees. The gardens are open daily from March to early November.

On Batcombe Hill, to the west of the village, stands a stone pillar known as the Cross and Hand which is said to date from the 7th century. Its purpose is unknown but in *Tess of the d'Urbervilles*, Hardy relates the local legend that the pillar marks the grave of a criminal who was tortured and hanged there, and whose mournful ghost appears beside the column from time to time.

STINSFORD
1 mile NE of Dorchester, off the A35

🏛 St Michael's Church

🌱 Kingston Maurward Gardens

It was in **St Michael's Church** at Stinsford that Thomas Hardy was christened and where he attended services for much of his life. He sang hymns to the accompaniment of the village band, (amongst whom were several of his relatives), which played from a gallery at the back of the church. The gallery was demolished in Hardy's lifetime, but many years later he drew a sketch from memory which showed the position of each player and the name of his instrument. A copy of this drawing is on display in the church, alongside a tablet commemorating the Hardys who took part.

Although Thomas Hardy was cremated and his ashes buried in the Poets' Corner of Westminster Abbey, his heart was brought to Stinsford to be interred in a graveyard tomb here. According to a scurrilous local tradition, it is shared with the village cat which had managed to eat the heart before it was buried.

Also buried in the churchyard is the Poet Laureate Cecil Day Lewis (1904-72)

Just to the east of the village, **Kingston Maurward Gardens** are of such historical importance that they are listed on the English Heritage Register of Gardens. The 35 acres of classical 18th century parkland and lawns sweep majestically down to the lake from the stately Georgian house. The formal Edwardian Gardens include a croquet lawn, rose garden, herbaceous borders and a large display of tender perennials, including the National Collection of Penstemons and Salvias. There's also an Animal Park with an interesting collection of unusual breeds, a lovely ornamental lake, nature trails, plant sales and the Old Coach House Restaurant serving morning coffee, lunches and teas.

HIGHER BOCKHAMPTON
2 miles NE of Dorchester off the A35

🏠 Hardy's Cottage   🐿 Thomas Hardy

In the woods above Higher Bockhampton, reached by a series of narrow lanes and a 10-minute walk, is a major shrine for devotees of Thomas Hardy. **Hardy's Cottage** is surrounded by the trees of Puddletown Forest, a setting he evoked so magically in *Under the Greenwood Tree*. The delightful thatched cottage and gardens are now owned by the National Trust and the rooms are furnished much as they would have been when the great novelist was born here in 1840. Visitors can see the very room in which his mother gave birth only to hear her child proclaimed still-born. Fortunately, an observant nurse noticed that the infant was in fact breathing and so ensured that such classics of English literature as *Tess of the*

Hardy's Cottage

d'Urbervilles and *The Return of the Native* saw the light of day. This charming cottage was Hardy's home for the first 22 years of his life until he set off for London to try his luck as an architect. In that profession his record was undistinguished, but in 1871 his first novel, *Desperate Remedies,* was published. An almost farcical melodrama, it gave few signs of the great works that would follow but was sufficiently successful for Hardy to devote himself thereafter to writing full time.

PUDDLETOWN
5 miles NE of Dorchester off the A35

🏛 Athelhampton House

Originally called Piddletown ('piddle' is the Saxon word for 'clear water') the village's name was changed by the sensitive Victorians. It was at Piddletown that Hardy's grandfather and great-grandfather were born. Renamed 'Weatherbury' it features in *Far From the Madding Crowd* as the place where Fanny's coffin was left out in the rain, and Sergeant Troy spends the night in the porch of the church after covering her grave with flowers.

Just to the east of Puddletown, **Athelhampton House** is a delightful, mostly Tudor house surrounded by a series of separate, 'secret' gardens. It's the home of Sir Edward and Lady du Cann and has the lived-in feeling that adds so much interest to historic houses. One of the finest houses in the

county, Athelhampton's most spectacular feature is its magnificent Great Chamber built during the reign of Elizabeth I. In the grounds are topiary pyramids, fountains, the Octagonal Garden designed by Sir Robert Cooke in 1971, and an unusual 15th century circular dovecote. It is almost perfectly preserved, with its 'potence', or revolving ladder used to collect eggs from the topmost nests, still in place and still useable.

MORETON
7 miles E of Dorchester off the B3390

🍃 T.E. Lawrence   🏛 Cloud's Hill

Thomas Hardy may be Dorset's most famous author, but in this small village it is another distinguished writer, (also a scholar, archaeologist and military hero), who is remembered. In 1935 **T.E. Lawrence,** "Lawrence of Arabia", left the RAF where he was known simply as Aircraftsman TE Shaw and retired to a spartan cottage he had bought ten years earlier. It stands alone on the heath

Cloud's Hill, Former Home of T.E. Lawrence

outside Moreton village and here Lawrence lived as a virtual recluse, without cooking facilities and with a sleeping bag as his bed. He was to enjoy this peaceful, if comfortless, retreat for only a few weeks. Lawrence loved speeding along the Dorset lanes on his motorcycle and one sunny spring day his adventurous driving led to a fatal collision with a young cyclist. The King of Iraq and Winston Churchill attended the hero's burial in the graveyard at Moreton and the home Lawrence occupied for such a short time, **Cloud's Hill** (National Trust), is now open to the public.

WINTERBORNE CAME
2 miles SE of Dorchester off the A352

🐦 William Barnes

This tiny hamlet is a place of pilgrimage for admirers of Dorset's second most famous man of letters who is buried in the graveyard here. **William Barnes** was Rector of Winterborne Came from 1862 until his death in 1886 and in the old Rectory (not open to the public) he entertained such luminaries of English literature as Alfred Lord Tennyson and Hardy himself. Although Barnes was highly respected by fellow poets, his pastoral poems written in the distinctive dialect of the county never attracted a wide audience. At their best, though, they are marvellously evocative of the west Dorset countryside:

> *The zwellen downs, wi' chalky tracks*
> *A-climmen up their zunny backs,*
> *Do hide green meads an zedgy brooks...*
> *An' white roads up athirt the hills.*

Winterborne Came's unusual name, incidentally, derives from the fact that in medieval times the village was owned by the Abbey of Caen in France.

OWERMOIGNE
6 miles SE of Dorchester off the A352

🏛 Mill House Cider Museum

🏛 Dorset Collection of Clocks

Just north of the village is a dual attraction in the shape of the **Mill House Cider Museum** and the **Dorset Collection of Clocks**. Housed in a mill that featured in Hardy's *The Distracted Preacher*, the Cider Museum has a collection of 18th and 19th century cider-making mills and presses, reflecting the importance of cider as a main country drink in bygone days. The Collection of Clocks showcases numerous timepieces ranging from longcase clocks to elaborate turret clocks. Visitors get the opportunity to see the intricate movements that are usually hidden away in the large clocks found on churches and public buildings.

MAIDEN CASTLE
2 miles SW of Dorchester off the A35

🏛 Maiden Castle

Maiden Castle is one of the most impressive prehistoric sites in the country. This vast Iron Age fortification covering more than 45 acres dates back some 4,000 years. Its steep earth ramparts, between 60 and 90 feet high, are nearly two miles round and together with the inner walls make a total of five miles of defences. The settlement flourished for 2,000 years until AD44 when its people were defeated by a Roman army under Vespasian. Excavations here in 1937 unearthed a war cemetery containing some 40 bodies, one of which still had a Roman arrowhead embedded in its spine. The Romans occupied the site for some 30 years before moving closer to the River Frome and founding Durnovaria, modern Dorchester. Maiden Castle was never settled again and it is a rather forbidding, treeless place but the extensive views along the Winterborne valley by contrast are delightful.

WINTERBOURNE ABBAS
4 miles W of Dorchester

🏛 Nine Stones

The village of Winterbourne Abbas stands at the head of the Winterborne valley, close to the river which is notable for running only during the winter and becoming a dry ditch in summer. The second part of the name, Abbas, comes from having been owned by the abbots of Cerne. The village is surrounded by ancient barrows, amongst which are the **Nine Stones**, Dorset's best example of a standing stone circle. Not the best location, however. The circle lies beside the busy A35, isolated from the village to the west and surrounded by trees. Despite the constant din of passing traffic, the circle somehow retains an air of tranquillity.

Weymouth

🏛 Timewalk Journey   🖌 Brewers Quay

🏛 Museum of Coastal Defence   🌿 Nothe Gardens

🏠 Nothe Fort   🌿 Lodmoor Country Park

🏛 Deep Sea Adventure   🗺 Model World

No wonder the good citizens of Weymouth erected a **Statue of George III** to mark the 50th year of his reign in 1810. The troubled king had brought great kudos and prosperity to their little seaside resort by coming here to bathe in the sea water. George had been advised that sea-bathing would help cure his 'nervous disorder' so, between 1789 and 1805, he and his royal retinue spent a total of 14 holidays in Weymouth. Fashionable society

naturally followed in his wake and left as its legacy the wonderful seafront of Georgian terraces. Not far away, at the head of King Street, George's granddaughter Victoria is commemorated by a colourful **Jubilee Clock** erected in 1887, the 50th year of her reign.

Nearby, the picturesque harbour is always busy – fishing boats, paddle steamers, pleasure boats, catamarans servicing the Channel Islands and St Malo in France and, if you're lucky, you may even see a Tall Ship or two.

One of the town's premier tourist venues is **Brewers Quay**, an imaginatively redeveloped Victorian brewery offering an enormous diversity of visitor attractions within a labyrinth of paved courtyards and cobbled streets. There are no fewer than 22 different establishments within the complex, ranging from craft shops and restaurants through a fully automated ten pin bowling alley to the **Timewalk Journey** which promises visitors that they will "See, hear and smell over 600 years of Weymouth's spectacular history".

From Brewers Quay, a path leads through **Nothe Gardens** to **Nothe Fort**, built between 1860 and 1872 as part of the defences of the new naval base being established on Portland. Ten huge guns face out to sea; two smaller ones are directed inland. The fort's 70 rooms on three levels now house the **Museum of Coastal Defence** which has many interesting displays illustrating past service life in the fort, history as seen from the Nothe headland, and the part played by the people of Weymouth in World War II. Nothe Fort is owned and operated by the Weymouth Civic Society which also takes care of **Tudor House,** just north of Brewers Quay. One of the town's few remaining Tudor buildings, the house originally stood on the edge of an inlet from the harbour and is

THE CHATSWORTH

14 The Esplanade, Weymouth, Dorset DT4 8EB
Tel: 01305 785012 Fax: 01305 766342
e-mail: stay@thechatsworth.co.uk website: www.thechatsworth.co.uk

Enjoying a superb position on Weymouth's picturesque waterfront, **The Chatsworth** commands wonderful views of the sweeping Georgian Esplanade. Guests can relax with an aperitif on the south-facing terrace, then savour a memorable meal in either the dining room or al fresco on the Sun Terrace. The chef produces interesting dishes using fresh local produce with seafood, naturally, being a speciality of the house. Accommodation ranges from the Panorama Room with the whole of Weymouth Bay as your private view, to balcony rooms overlooking the harbour. All rooms are en suite, and tastefully furnished and decorated.

thought to have been a merchant's house. It's now furnished in the style of an early-17th century middle class home and the guided tour gives some fascinating insights into life in those days.

Only yards from the waters of Weymouth Bay, **Lodmoor Country Park** is another popular attraction. Access to most of the park is free and visitors can take advantage of the many sport and recreation areas, wander

GLENTHORNE

15 Old Castle Road, Weymouth, Dorset DT4 8QB
Tel: 01305 777281
e-mail: info@glenthorne-holidays.co.uk
website: www.glenthorne-holidays.co.uk

Offering both bed & breakfast and self-catering accommodation, **Glenthorne** is beautifully located with magnificent views of the Olympic sailing venue across Castle Cove Bay, with Portland and Chesil Beach on the horizon. The main house was built as a rectory more than 100 years ago and is now the family home of artist Olivia Nurrish. To one side of the house are three apartments, decorated and equipped to a high standard. Within the secluded gardens are many features designed to help you enjoy your stay – a heated swimming pool, summer house, raised decking with fine views, picnic tables, a Wendy house, a trampoline and other play equipment for kids (including four very affectionate cats!)

If you walk to the lower slopes of the garden, there are steps that will take you directly to sheltered and sandy Castle Cove beach with its clean and safe bathing for any age. Inside the house, guests have the use of a large, antique furnished drawing room where they can unwind with a drink by the fire, watch a video or DVD, or browse through a magazine. The three en suite B&B rooms are spacious and elegant, and all enjoy views of either the sea or the garden.

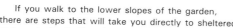
🎭 stories and anecdotes 🐦 famous people 🎨 art and craft 🍃 entertainment and sport 🚶 walks

around the footpaths and nature reserve, or enjoy a picnic or barbecue. Set within the park and surrounded by beautiful gardens complete with a bird aviary, **Model World** is a quite unique attraction which has been more than 25 years in the making. Back in 1972, Colin Sims conceived the idea of creating a model village and during the course of the next nine years constructed hundreds of finely detailed hand-made models from a variety of materials: stone, concrete, specially treated wood and plastics to withstand all kinds of weather. All built to a scale of 1:32 of life size, together the models create a complete world in miniature.

Another major family attraction is **Deep Sea Adventure,** opened in 1988 by Princess Anne, and with two separate attractions under one roof. Deep Sea Adventure tells the story of underwater exploration and marine exploits from the 17th century through to the modern day. This entertaining and educational exhibition fills three floors of an imposing Victorian Grain Warehouse with a wealth of animated and interactive displays recounting compelling tales of shipwreck survival and search & rescue operations, a "Black Hole" in which you can experience what it is like to be a deep sea diver, and a unique display which

tells the epic story of the Titanic in the words of the officers, crew and survivors, along with the original Titanic signals and one of the largest models of the doomed ship in the world. A fairly recent addition to Deep Sea Adventure is Sharky's, a huge, all-weather adventure play area for children of all ages, (with a height limit of 5ft), and with a separate area for toddlers.

OSMINGTON
3 miles NE of Weymouth on the A353

 White Horse   Smugglers Inn

There are several 'White Horses' carved into hillsides around the country, but the **White Horse** near Osmington, apart from being one of the largest, (354ft high and 279ft wide), is the only one which also has a rider. The horse was created in 1807; the rider was added about three years later. Wearing a tall cocked hat and carrying a whip, the horseman represents George III. The king was a frequent visitor to nearby Weymouth and his royal patronage naturally attracted many free-spending courtiers to the town. The town fathers of Weymouth decided to express their appreciation by paying the local militia to add the royal rider. The result was an

Deep Sea Adventure & Sharkey's

9 Custom House Quay, Old Harbour, Weymouth, Dorset DT4 8BG.
Tel: 0871 222 5760

Take a unique journey at the Deep Sea Adventure. Experience one of the worlds foremost Titanic exhibitions and encounter underwater exploration and maritime exploits both past and present. Three floors of this Victorian grain warehouse are devoted to animated and interactive displays, computer games and tales of shipwrecks.

Also under the same roof is Sharkey's, Dorset's premier all weather kids adventure play zone, where children can jump, swing, climb and slide whilst exploring the four floors of safe play areas.

 historic building   museum   historic site   scenic attraction   flora and fauna

unrecognisable, if undoubtedly loyal, tribute to His Majesty. Like all the other White Horses in England, it looks much better when seen from a few miles away; close up, it is meaningless.

A mile south of Osmington, at Osmington Mills, the area's notorious history in trading contraband liquor lingers in the name of The **Smugglers Inn.** Unlike many similarly-named hostelries, this one really was a regular haunt for smugglers. Dating back to the 13th century, this former fisherman's cottage enjoyed a secluded position and the nearby beach provided safe landing. The inn's landlord in the early 1800s was Emmanuel Carless who, together with his French partner, Pierre Latour or 'French Peter', ran a thriving business importing thousands of gallons of brandy each year. Unfortunately, the liquor was so inferior locals refused to drink it and

the spirit had to be carried inland on stage coaches, disguised as luggage, to be distilled again.

ISLE OF PORTLAND
4 miles S of Weymouth, on the A354

🏛 Tout Quarry Sculpture Park   🏰 Portland Castle

🏛 St Andrew's Avalanche Church   🕊 The Fleet

🏞 Chesil Beach   🏛 Portland Museum

Portland is not really an island at all, but a 4.5 mile long peninsula, well known to devotees of shipping forecasts and even more famous for the stone from its quarries. Numerous buildings in London are constructed of Portland stone, amongst them St. Paul's Cathedral, Inigo Jones' Banqueting Hall in Whitehall, and Buckingham Palace. The stone was also favoured by sculptors such as Henry Moore. The quarries still provide the renowned stone and are also used as study centres. In the **Tout Quarry Sculpture Park** some 50 pieces in the local stone are on display – watch out for Anthony Gormley's figure of a man falling down the rock face.

The island's most famous building is **Portland Castle** (English Heritage), one of the finest of Henry VIII's coastal fortresses. Its active role lasted for 500 years, right up to World War II when it provided a D-Day embarkation point for British and American forces. Oliver Cromwell

Portland Bill Lighthouse

🎭 stories and anecdotes   🦅 famous people   🎨 art and craft   🎟 entertainment and sport   🚶 walks

BLUEFISH CAFÉ & RESTAURANT

15-17a Chiswell, Portland, Dorset DT5 1AN
Tel: 01305 822991
e-mail: thebluefish@tesco.net

In 2003 Jo Da Silva, together with her husband Luciano, returned to her home town after some years spent in London and opened the **fully licensed BlueFish Café & Restaurant** in a mid-17th century Portland stone building overlooking Chesil Beach. Luciano is an accomplished cook with some 16 years experience and his menu – which changes every 4 to 6 weeks – offers an enticing mix of classic and modern cuisine, served in a fantastically friendly atmosphere and at affordable prices. "We feel we are putting Portland on the map for great food" says Jo.

A typical evening menu might offer roast quail with sweetcorn & lavender gallette, grapes, thyme and sherry vinegar dressing as a starter; red gurnard with chorizo and baby fennel, crispy polenta, grain mustard sauce & salmon pearls as a main course. There's always a choice of fresh seasonal, fish, meat and vegetarian dishes, and some wonderful desserts – guava bavarois mousse with blackberry tuille and passion fruit, for example. Meals can be enjoyed either inside or, in good weather, at outside tables. The BlueFish is open every weekend, all year round from 9am-3pm for breakfast and lunch, and then 7pm till late for dinner. Seasonal weekly opening hours apply.

WHITE STONES CAFÉ GALLERY

13 Easton Street, Easton, Portland, Dorset DT5 1BS
Tel: 01305 860003   website: www.whitestonescafegallery.com

David Nicholls is both a qualified caterer and a sculptor. At his **White Stones Café Gallery** in the heart of Easton he has combined his two passions into what he describes as "a fusion of food and art" – a space in which to sit and relax, enjoy good food and view high quality art. "I wanted to challenge the expectations of what a gallery space should be" he says, "and break down a few boundaries. Art should be open to all and in a big way I think White Stones achieves this".

In the café, customers can start the day with coffee and fresh baked pastries; drop in for lunch to sample a range of home-made foods; or settle down at teatime to sample the fresh baked cakes. Relax in the comfortable leather sofas and take time to view the excellent art work on display throughout the premises.

A beautiful courtyard garden with seating and sculpture is the perfect place to enjoy breakfast (served all day Sunday) or to relax with a glass of fine wine or bottled beer on a summers evening. White Stones will soon be staging regular musical events, phone or see website for details. Open daily from 9am (10am till 4pm on Sundays).

used the castle as a prison and in Victorian times it was the residence of Portland's governors. Visitors can try on the armour, meet 'Henry VIII' in the Great Hall, and enjoy the special events that are held regularly throughout the year. The battlements overlook superb views of Portland Harbour whose breakwaters were constructed by convict labour to create the second largest man-made harbour in the world. On the highest point of the island is Verne Citadel which was a base for troops defending Portland and Weymouth. It became a prison in 1950.

At Southwell, near the tip of Portland Bill, **St Andrew's Avalanche** church was built in 1879 chiefly as a memorial to those who perished when the clipper *Avalanche* sank off the Portland coast at the beginning of a passage to New Zealand. Also in Southwell is the **Portland Museum** which was founded by the birth control pioneer Marie Stopes who lived on the island. Housed in a charming pair of thatched cottages, the museum tells the story of life on the island from smuggling and shipwrecks to traditions and customs. One of the cottages inspired Thomas Hardy to centre his novel *The Well-Beloved* around it, making it the home of 'Avice', the heroine of the story.

At the southernmost tip of the island, the Bill of Portland, the first lighthouse to be built here is now a base for birdwatchers. The current Portland Bill Lighthouse offers guided tours during the season and also has a visitor centre. Nearby are some particularly fascinating natural features: the tall, upright Pulpit Rock which can be climbed, and some caves to explore.

The Isle provides some good cliff-top walks with grand views of **Chesil Beach**, a vast bank of pebbles worn smooth by the sea

which stretches for some 10 miles to Abbotsbury. Inexplicably, the pebbles are graded in size from west to east. Fishermen reckon they can judge whereabouts on the beach they are landing by the size of the pebbles. In the west they are as small as peas and usually creamy in colour; at Portland they have grown to the size of cooking apples and are more often grey. The long, narrow body of water trapped behind the beach is known as **The Fleet.** It is now a nature reserve and home to a wide variety of waterfowl and plants, as well as fish that can be viewed by taking a trip in a glass-bottomed boat.

CHICKERELL
3 miles NW of Weymouth off the 3157

🌿 Water Gardens

A pretty village of thatched cottages, Chickerell is best known for its **Water Gardens** which were created in 1959 by Norman Bennett. He began by growing water lilies in the disused clay pits of a brickworks and the gardens are now home to the National Collection of Water Lilies. Within the gardens is a museum telling the story of the village which featured in the *Domesday Book*.

PORTESHAM
6 miles NW of Weymouth on the B3157

🏛 Hardy's Monument   🌿 Great Dorset Maize Maze

On the Black Downs northeast of Portesham stands **Hardy's Monument** (National Trust) which commemorates, not Thomas Hardy the great novelist of Wessex, but Sir Thomas Hardy the flag-captain of *HMS Victory* at Trafalgar to whom the dying Lord Nelson spoke the immortal words, "Kiss me, Hardy", (or possibly, "Kismet, Hardy"). Sir Thomas was born in Portesham and, like his novelist namesake, was descended from the Hardys of

🎭 stories and anecdotes   🦜 famous people   🎨 art and craft   ✏ entertainment and sport   🥾 walks

Jersey. After Trafalgar, he escorted Nelson's body back to London and soon afterwards was created a baronet and, eventually, First Sea Lord. Sir Thomas's stunningly graceless memorial has been variously described as a "huge candlestick", a "peppermill", and most accurately as a "factory chimney wearing a crinoline". But if you stand with your back to it, there are grand views over Weymouth Bay.

Just to the east of Portesham, an unusual attraction, the **Great Dorset Maize Maze,** challenges visitors to 'crack' the world-class maze with its fiendishly intricate design. Popular with families, the site also gives youngsters the opportunity to mingle with farm animals, and to have fun on the trampolines and pedal go-carts, or in the indoor fun barns.

ABBOTSBURY
8 miles NW of Weymouth on the B3157

🏛 St Catherine's Chapel   🌱 Abbotsbury Swannery

🏛 Great Abbey Barn

🌱 Abbotsbury Sub-tropical Gardens

Surrounded by hills, picturesque Abbotsbury is one of the county's most popular tourist spots and by any standards one of the loveliest villages in England. Its most striking feature as you approach is the 14th century **St Catherine's Chapel,** perched on the hill-top. Only 45ft by 15ft, it is solidly built to withstand the Channel gales with walls more than four feet thick. St Catherine was believed to be particularly helpful in finding husbands for the unmarried and in medieval times spinsters would climb the hill to her chapel chanting a dialect jingle which

CHAPEL YARD POTTERY

Market Street, Abbotsbury, Dorset DT3 4JR
Tel: 01305 871663/871520
e-mail: lwilson@toucansurf.com
website: www.chapelyard.co.uk

Chapel Yard Pottery stands in the centre of the delightful historic village of Abbotsbury on the World Heritage Jurassic Coastline. It's the workplace of the accomplished potter Richard Wilson whose striking creations add colour and grace to any interior décor. Richard's pots are all hand thrown on a wheel, or slab pressed and cut to shape using a traditional terracotta clay which is then dipped in a white clay slip to give a brighter canvas on which to decorate. With a combination of brushes and slip trailers, he builds up a pattern with coloured slips.

Some designs echo the folds and rhythms of the landscape with colours that reflect the contrast between sea and shore in this part of Dorset. Other patterns are abstract shapes that he discovers within the pots themselves – "form leading to painting," he says. Finally, all his pots are given a transparent glaze and fired to 1,120°C in a gas kiln. The Pottery – where you can watch Richard at work – is open from 9am to 5pm, Tuesday to Saturday; the gallery is also open during these hours.

🏛 historic building   museum   historic site   scenic attraction   🌱 flora and fauna

Abbotsbury Swannery

visitor figures rocket from the end of May to the end of June – the baby swans' hatching season. Quills from the fully-grown swans are still sent to Lloyds of London where they have been used for centuries to write the names of ships lost at sea in their official insurance records. There's also a children's Ugly Duckling Trail and the oldest known duck decoy still working.

Just to the west of the village, **Abbotsbury Sub-Tropical Gardens** enjoy a particularly well-sheltered position and the 20 acres of grounds contain a huge variety of rare and exotic plants and trees. Other attractions include an 18th century walled garden, beautiful lily ponds and a children's play area.

concludes with the words *"Arn-a-one's better than narn-a-one"* – anyone is better than never a one.

Abbotsbury takes its name from the important Benedictine Abbey that once stood here but was comprehensively cannibalised after the Reformation, its stones used to build the attractive cottages that line the village streets. What has survived however is the magnificent **Great Abbey Barn**, 247ft long and 31ft wide, which was built in the 1300s to store the abbey's tithes of wool, grain and other produce. With its thatched roof, stone walls and a mightily impressive entrance it is one of the largest and best-preserved barns in the country.

About a mile south of the village is the famous **Abbotsbury Swannery**, established in Saxon times to provide food for the abbey during the winter months. Up to 600 free-flying swans have made their home here and

Sherborne

🏛 Sherborne Abbey   🏛 Sherborne Old Castle

🏛 Sherborne New Castle   🏛 Sherborne Museum

🏛 Almshouses   🏛 Sandford Orcas Manor House

🏛 Conduit House   🌿 Pageant Gardens

One of the most beautiful towns in England, Sherborne beguiles the visitor with its serene atmosphere of a cathedral city, although it is not a city and its lovely **Abbey** no longer enjoys the status of a cathedral. Back in AD705 though, when it was founded by St Aldhelm, the abbey was the Mother Cathedral

DODGE & SON

28-33 Cheap Street, Sherborne, Dorset DT9 3PU
Tel: 01935 815151   Fax: 01935 818169
e-mail: sales@dodgeandsonantiques.com
website: www.dodgeandson.co.uk

The West Country is famed for its top quality antique dealers but **Dodge & Son** are really in a class of their own. They have been established as antique dealers and interior furnishers since 1918 and they have also built a prestigious reputation as manufacturers of fine English furniture. They have created an exceptional range of top quality traditional reproduction furniture. Each piece is meticulously copied from an original antique, crafted using the finest materials and finished to the most exacting standards. Highly skilled craftsmen produce furniture of distinction in a wide range of designs which can be seen illustrated on their website. This service provides customers with full colour pictures of the many pieces in stock, along with full details of each item.

Alternatively, they can custom-make your furniture in any design, wood, finish and size accordingly to your requirements. Either way they offer expert advice and quality craftsmanship to ensure your needs are met. They will, for example, integrate an order for a complete dining suit ensuring your table, chairs, dressers or other occasional pieces fully complement each other.

Their collection of antique furniture, the largest in the county with more than 500 pieces on display, can be seen in the eight showrooms and gardens at their Sherborne premises and are also available through the internet. A superb range of top quality garden furniture is also on display at the Sherborne premises – everything is made using solid teak which can be polished with oils or left to the weather.

Dodge & Son's Interiors department, also centred in Sherborne, offers a range of custom built sofas and a complete interior service, encompassing carpeting and re-upholstery.

The company is also now able to offer a full interior design service in London for private and corporate clients. The London office is coordinated by Samantha Dodge who trained at the Inchbald School of Interior Design, and worked with Nicola Crawley Interiors of Knightsbridge. The company is able to offer comprehensive design schemes and can coordinate measuring, installation and fitting using our London-based team.

Yet another service offered by Dodge & Son is restoration of every kind – whether major or minor – which is carried out in their on-site workshop in Sherborne.

for the whole of southwest England. Of that original Saxon church only minimal traces remain: most of the present building dates back to the mid-1400s which, by happy chance, was the most glorious period in the history of English ecclesiastical architecture. The intricate tracery of the fan vaulting above the nave of the abbey looks like the supreme culmination of a long-practised art: in fact, it is one of the earliest examples in England. There is much else to admire in this majestic church: 15th century misericords in the choir stalls which range from the sublime, (Christ sitting in majesty on a rainbow), to

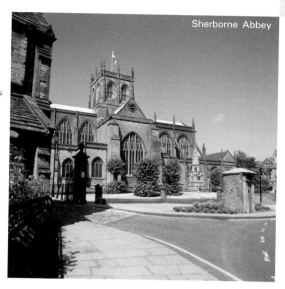

Sherborne Abbey

MELBURY GALLERY

Half Moon Street, Sherborne, Dorset DT9 3LN
Tel/Fax: 01935 814027

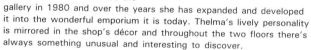

Located in the heart of Sherborne, **Melbury Gallery** is a unique and enchanting shop that stocks a colourful array of clothes, jewellery and accessories, soft furnishings, a distinctive range of lighting, and literally hundreds of gifts.

Thelma Drabik established the gallery in 1980 and over the years she has expanded and developed it into the wonderful emporium it is today. Thelma's lively personality is mirrored in the shop's décor and throughout the two floors there's always something unusual and interesting to discover.

The beautifully made clothes have a style and simplicity that make them suitable for almost any occasion. They include items from such leading designers as Oska, Sahara, Sandwich & Stills, Out of Xile, Flax, Noa Noa, Masai and Adini. To complete the look, the gallery also stocks a range of scarves in a kaleidoscope of colours that blend or contrast with the clothes. The huge range of jewellery provides an extensive choice of necklaces, bracelets, rings and earrings in plain silver and semi precious stones; ideal for day and evening wear, and perfect presents for friends or relations.

Upstairs, customers will find rugs of all shapes and sizes, a huge collection of sumptuous cushions and other larger items for the home. Thelma sources her stock from more than 100 suppliers and the combination of range and quality has gained the Melbury Gallery a large following in Sherborne and for many miles around.

🎬 stories and anecdotes   🐦 famous people   🎨 art and craft   🎵 entertainment and sport   🚶 walks

Sherborne

Distance: *5.0 miles (8.0 kilometres)*

Typical time: *120 mins*

Height gain: *75 metres*

Map: *Explorer 129*

Walk: *www.walkingworld.com ID:582*

Contributor: *Pat Mallet*

Park in Sherborne station car park.

DESCRIPTION:

A delightful walk through fields, woods and farms with views of Sherborne's two famous castles and their lake as well as panoramas of the gentle hills of Dorset. It is mainly undulating countryside with just one short hill.

FEATURES:

Lake/loch, castle, great views

WALK DIRECTIONS:

1 | From the station car park, cross the railway tracks and walk up Gas House Hill to the main road at the top.

2 | From the top of Gas House Hill, turn left at the waymarked path up the gentle slope to the swing-gate at the top.

3 | Follow the well-walked path through the fields with Sherborne Castle and beautiful lake on your left in the distance.

4 | Go through the gate and continue in the same direction, along the path straight ahead. You climb a little here, towards the deer-park at the top of the hill.

5 | Go through the high deer-gate, past a boarded-up thatched gatehouse and on up the hill. Look for the deer in the trees.

6 | Exit the deer park at the top of the hill and follow the path as it goes through the woods

past the overgrown foundations of a World War II army camp. You reach some corrugated iron farm buildings after about ½km.

7 | Turn right in the middle of the group of farm buildings, along a tarmac road. Continue to a small crossroads, about 200m away.

8 | Turn sharp left here so that you are facing a farm cottage up the track. Walk towards the cottage as far as the waymark on the side of the road and there turn right, only about 50 metres. Follow the edge of the field with the fence on your left, to a stile on your left. Climb the stile and follow the path (sometimes muddy) through the trees to another deer-gate.

9 | You are now back in the deer-park. Follow the telegraph poles down the hill towards Pinfold Farm, straight ahead in the valley. Apart from the farm, can you see another building? Keep a straight line for the farm, across a stile and a wooden bridge over the River Yeo. On your left, you may see just the end of the artificial lake created by Capability Brown in the grounds of the castle.

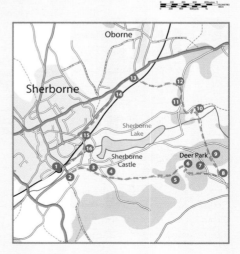

10 | At the waymark on the gate to the left of the main farm buildings, turn left and walk along the farm road for about 100 metres, through another gate with a waymark just beyond on a post on the right. Turn right here and walk through the field towards the two imposing stone gate pillars up the slope.

11 | Walk between the gate pillars and take the second path on the left, through the trees. Immediately turn right and follow a narrow path in the trees, NOT the obvious track which veers left. Follow the path until it reaches a stile, coming out of the woods.

12 | Climb the stile, go straight ahead across the fields towards the railway line, setting your sights on the rail track lights in the distance. The tunnel under the railway line lies to the right of the rail lights. Go through the tunnel, keeping to the right and look for a stile, which at times is hidden behind a farm manure pile.

13 | Climb the stile, go up to the main road and turn left. A detour can be made here to the tiny village of Oborne (signposted from the road).

14 | Walk back towards Sherborne along the main road for a distance of about ¼km, then take the left fork onto the B3145. Continue along the road past the Castleton Waterwheel on the left (sometimes open for tours).

15 | Fork left here towards the castle, cross the bridges over the railway and the River Yeo and see the next waymark on a gate to the right.

16 | Turn through the gate and follow the river back to the station and the car park. As a pleasant extension to the walk, take a stroll through the gardens opposite the station. Veering left, exit the gardens on the north west side, walk up Digby Road to the Abbey (about 200m) and visit this 1,000-year-old church. From there it is a short stroll to the delightful shops and teashops of Sherborne.

the scandalous, (wives beating their husbands); a wealth of elaborate tombs amongst which is a lofty six-poster from Tudor times, a floridly baroque late-17th century memorial to the 3rd Earl of Bristol, and another embellished with horses' heads in a punning tribute to Sir John Horsey who lies below alongside his son.

As well as founding the abbey, St Aldhelm is also credited with establishing Sherborne School which numbered amongst its earliest pupils the two elder brothers of King Alfred, (and possibly Alfred himself). Later alumni include the Poet Laureate Cecil Day-Lewis and the writer David Cornwell, better known as John le Carré, author of *The Spy Who Came in from the Cold* and many other thrillers.

Perhaps the best-known resident of Sherborne however is Sir Walter Raleigh. At a time when he enjoyed the indulgent favour of Elizabeth I he asked for, and was granted, the house and estate of **Sherborne Old Castle** (English Heritage). Sir Walter soon realised that the medieval pile with its starkly basic amenities was quite unsuitable for a courtier of his sophistication and ambition. He built a new castle alongside it, **Sherborne New Castle**, a strange three-storeyed, hexagonal structure which must rate, from the outside, as one of the most badly-designed, most unlikeable mansions to be erected in an age when other Elizabethan architects were creating some of the loveliest buildings in England. Inside Sir Walter's new castle, it is quite a different story: gracious rooms with elaborately-patterned ceilings, portraits of the man who single-handedly began the creation of the British Empire, and huge windows which at the time Sir Walter ordered them proclaimed a clear message that its owner had the wealth to pay the enormous cost of glazing such vast expanses. After Sir Walter's execution, the castle was purchased in 1617 by Sir James Digby and it has remained with his descendants ever since. They added exquisite gardens designed by Capability Brown and in the late 1800s re-decorated the interior in Jacobean style. Amongst the castle's greatest

treasures is the famous painting by Robert Peake depicting Elizabeth I on procession, being carried on a litter and surrounded by a sumptuously dressed retinue. The old cellar of the castle is now a museum housing an eclectic display of items, most gruesome of

SABINS FINE FOODS

5 Hound Street, Sherborne, Dorset DT9 3AB
Tel: 01935 816037
website: www.sabins.co.uk

Recently taken over by Pippa and Dominic Macer, **Sabins Fine Foods** is an outstanding delicatessen offering an enticing variety of top quality produce. Naturally, there's a strong West Country flavour to much of it – Westcombe Cheddar topping the Fennel & Cheese Bake, for example, a range of Dorset Blue Soups, and Childhay Manor ice creams. Sabins was recently listed as No 13 in the Top 50 cheese shops in England and also stocks a wide choice of continental delicacies including fresh pasta from Italy. Home-made treats include fresh bread and baguettes, quiches, canapes and Simmel cake, and Sabins will also cook to order for your own supper dishes.

THE ANTELOPE HOTEL

Greenhill, Sherborne, Dorset DT9 4EP
Tel: 01935 812077   Fax: 01935 816473
e-mail: antelopesherborne@aol.com
website: www.theantelopehotel.co.uk

Located at the top of the beautiful and historic town of Sherborne, **The Antelope Hotel** dates back to 1748 and is the only remaining coaching inn out of the three that once stood on Greenhill. This gracious old hostelry with its elegant public rooms is owned and run by Nick Gregory who prides himself on his hotel's warm and friendly atmosphere. The cuisine here enjoys an excellent reputation – the restaurant is open Tuesday to Saturday evenings and offers an extensive à la carte menu complemented by a comprehensive wine list.

Comfortable accommodation is available in 19 en suite rooms with a mix of singles, doubles, twins and family accommodation. Several of the premier rooms have the added attraction of four-poster beds and antique furnishing, and there is one ground floor room for the disabled. All bedrooms have individually controlled heating, colour TV, radio, direct-dial telephone, hair dryer, trouser press and tea and coffee making facilities. Six of the rooms are equipped with internet access; room service and a laundry service are provided. For larger gatherings, The Thomas Hardy Room is available for banquets and weddings for up to 80 people, as well as for conferences, meetings and small exhibitions.

🏛 historic building   🏛 museum   🏛 historic site   ⌕ scenic attraction   🌿 flora and fauna

which is the skull of a Royalist soldier killed in the seige of 1645. A bullet is still lodged in his eye socket. Sherborne New Castle, incidentally, is one of several locations claiming to be the genuine setting for the old story of Sir Walter enjoying a pipe of tobacco and being doused with a bucket of water by a servant who believed his master was on fire. Sherborne Castle is open from April to October, and also offers visitors an attractive lakeside tearoom, a well-stocked gift shop, and various special events throughout the year.

This appealing small town with a population of around 8,500 has much else to interest the visitor. The **Almshouse of Saints John the Baptist and John the Evangelist**, near the abbey, was founded in 1437 and the original buildings completed in 1448 are still in use as an almshouse, accepting both men and women. The almshouse chapel boasts one of the town's greatest treasures, a late-15th century Flemish altar tryptich which can be viewed on afternoons during the summer. Close by, the **Conduit House** is an attractive small hexagonal building from the early 1500s, originally used as a lavatorium, or washroom, for the abbey monks' ablutions. It was moved here after the Reformation and has served variously as a public fountain and a police phone box. The Conduit House is specifically mentioned in Hardy's *The Woodlanders* as the place where Giles Winterborne, seeking work, stood here in the market place "as he always did at this season of the year, with his specimen apple tree". Another striking building is the former Abbey Gatehouse

MUNDEN HOUSE

Alweston, Sherborne, Dorset DT9 5HU
Tel: 01963 23150
website: www.mundenhouse.demon.co.uk

Munden House is the north Dorset home of Michael and Judith Rust, proprietors of The Green restaurant in Sherborne. The house has been developed over many years from a group of stone cottages whose history stretches back for more than three centuries. Its setting in the Blackmore Vale is spectacular with sweeping views over miles of open farmland. Munden House has been built for comfort. In the breakfast room limestone walls, exposed beams and an inglenook fireplace reveal the long history of the building, while the table settings reflect classical elegance.

Breakfast here is a memorable experience with locally sourced foods from a region famous for the quality of its produce. In the drawing room, large windows, luxurious furniture and a grand piano underline the more modern and relaxed approach to style. Each bedroom tells a different story, with comfort ensured by carefully chosen antique and modern furniture, fittings and decoration. All have en suite showers and baths, direct dial telephones, hair driers, trouser presses and well-equipped hospitality trays. There is also a self-contained studio suite complete with kitchenette for guests seeking a greater degree of privacy.

stories and anecdotes 　　 famous people 　　 art and craft 　　 entertainment and sport 　　 walks

TURNBULLS' DELI

9 High Street, Shaftesbury, Dorset SP7 8HZ
Tel: 01747 853575 Fax: 01747 853576
e-mail: charlie@turnbullandturnbull.co.uk
website: www.turnbulls-deli.co.uk

Charlie Turnbull opened **Turnbulls' Delicatessen & Café** in June 2003 after deciding that accountancy was not as attractive as selling cheese. Already, Turnbulls' is well established as a beacon of excellence and local provender with a friendly, welcoming and decidedly social atmosphere. It's a perfect place to drop in for a bite to eat or to pick up some local delicacies.

The deli specialises in cheese, particularly such local varieties as Ashmore Farmhouse and Dorset Blue Vinney, but you'll also find a great selection of homemade goods such as sweet and savoury tarts, pâtés, hams, dips and pies. Charlotte, the head cook (she doesn't like the term "chef"), is well-known for her signature pie – the Medieval Pork & Apricot. It's simply delicious. The meat counter includes traceable local hams cooked on the premises, along with the best European salamis. The stock includes a wide range of specialities, including several medal winners from the Great Taste Awards, making the deli rich in choice and quality. The staff are friendly and informed, providing superb local and speciality produce with old fashioned service.

In the café, where the main menu is available all day, a favourite is Charlie's Cheese Platter with local seeded bread, Bay Tree caramelised peppers (also local), and Dorset olives. Breakfasts are served until 11am – just try the organic scrambled eggs with Wiltshire smoked trout on a bagel, or with Dorset bacon and toasted Gillingham bread. There's also a daily menu freshly prepared from seasonal and local produce – homemade soups, savoury tarts, risottos and main dishes such as wine-braised sausages with caramelised onion, or 'posh' fish pie. Charlie reckons that the café serves the best coffee in the southwest and also offers a comprehensive range of traditional, herbal and fruit teas. The most popular beverage is the hot chocolate special – with cream, marshmallow and Maltesers. At tea-time, don't miss out on the homemade cakes, cookies, flapjacks and brownies. The scones are fresh every day and the clotted cream comes from farms within five miles of Shaftesbury.

Turnbulls' also offers a range of catering services. They have an extensive choice of dishes that can be ordered for special events or for simply filling your freezer; and a drop-off service where their cooks do all the hard work and prepare anything from canapés to five-course meals, and drop it off into your kitchen for you to finish off.

Turnbulls, is open from 8.45am to 5.30pm, Monday to Saturday.

🏚 historic building   🏛 museum   🏛 historic site   ᙦ scenic attraction   ᙇ flora and fauna

which frames the entrance to Church Lane where the **Sherborne Museum** has a collection of more than 15,000 items relating to local history. Particularly notable are two major photographic collections recording events and people in the town since 1880.

To the south of the town, near the railway station, **Pageant Gardens** were established in 1905 using funds raised by a great pageant of that year celebrating the 1,200th anniversary of the founding of the town by St Aldhelm.

About two miles north of Sherborne, **Sandford Orcas Manor House** is a charming Tudor building with terraced gardens, topiary and herb garden. Since it was built in honey-coloured Ham Hill stone in the 1550s, only three different families have lived here. The present owner, Sir Mervyn Medlycott, whose family has lived here for more than 250 years, personally conducts guided tours that take in the manor's Great Hall, stone newel staircases, huge fireplaces, fine panelling, Jacobean and Queen Anne furniture and family portraits.

MELBURY OSMOND
6 miles SW of Sherborne off the A37

It was in the Church of St Osmund in this pretty village that Thomas Hardy's parents, Jemima Hand and Thomas Hardy, were married in 1839. At the northern end of the footpath through the churchyard is a thatched house where Hardy's mother is thought to have lived as a child. In Hardy's novels the village appears as Great Hintock which provides the setting for *The Woodlanders*. Melbury Osmond is still unspoilt and picturesque with many oak trees – do find time to walk down from the church to the water splash, and beyond to some 17th century thatched stone cottages.

Shaftesbury

🏛 Abbey Museum 🏛 Local History Museum
🔱 Gold Hill ⚜ Shaftesbury Arts Centre
🐏 Dorset Rare Breeds Centre

Set on the side of a hill 700ft high, Shaftesbury was officially founded in 880AD by King Alfred who fortified the town and also built an abbey of which his daughter was first Prioress. A hundred years later, the King Edward who had been murdered by his stepmother at Corfe Castle was buried here and the abbey became a major centre of pilgrimage. A few remains of Shaftesbury Abbey have survived – they can be seen in the walled garden of the **Abbey Museum** which contains many interesting artefacts excavated from the site.

Shaftesbury is a pleasant town to explore on foot. In fact, you *have* to walk if you want to see its most famous sight, **Gold Hill**, a steep, cobbled street, stepped in places and lined with 18th century cottages. Already well-known for its picturesque setting and grand views across the Vale of Blackmoor, Gold Hill became even more famous when it was featured in the classic TV commercial for Hovis. Also located on Gold Hill is the **Shaftesbury Local History Museum** which vividly evokes the story of this ancient market town.

The 17th century Ox House, which is referred to in Thomas Hardy's *Jude the Obscure*, is just one of a number of interesting and historic buildings in the town. Others include the Church of St Peter, the Tudor-style Town Hall dating from the 1820s, and the Grosvenor Hotel, a 400-year-old coaching inn.

Shaftesbury boasts one of the liveliest arts centres in the country, the **Shaftesbury Arts Centre** which, remarkably, is completely

🎭 stories and anecdotes 🦜 famous people ⚜ art and craft 🏅 entertainment and sport 🚶 walks

owned by its membership and administered entirely by volunteers. The results of their efforts are anything but amateur, however. The centre's Drama Group is responsible for three major productions each year, performed in the well-equipped theatre which also serves as a cinema for the centre's Film Society, screening a dozen or more films during the season. One of the most popular features of the centre is its Gallery which is open daily with a regularly changing variety of exhibitions ranging from paintings, etchings and sculpture, to batiks, stained glass, embroideries and quilting.

About three miles northwest of Shaftesbury, the **Dorset Rare Breeds Centre** harbours the county's largest collection of rare and endangered farm animals. They range from knee-high Soay sheep to mighty Suffolk Punch horses weighing a ton or more. All of these native breeds are at great risk and the centre hopes to alert animal lovers to the imminent threat.

Gold Hill, Shaftesbury

Around Shaftesbury

ASHMORE
5 miles SE of Shaftesbury off the B3081

🏛 Compton Abbas Airfield

To the northwest of Ashmore is **Compton Abbas Airfield** which is generally considered to be the most picturesque airfield in the country. It is surrounded by an Area of Outstanding Natural Beauty and 50% of the airfield is organically farmed. One of the most popular displays is the collection of famous aeroplanes, special effects and memorabilia from film and TV productions. For the more adventurous, flights are available with a qualified instructor for a trip over this scenic part of the county; training courses for a full pilot's licence are also conducted here. The airfield hosts regular events throughout the year, including aerobatic displays; there's a shop selling a range of stunt and power kites; a bar and restaurant.

To the west of Ashmore are Fontwell and Melbury Downs, two estates that cover an important stretch of chalk downland that is cut by steep-sided valleys. Both areas are owned by the National Trust and evoke the landscapes described by Thomas Hardy – they are also notable for their population of butterflies.

MARNHULL
7 miles SW of Shaftesbury on the B3092

🏛 Tess's Cottage

The scattered village of Marnhull claims to be the largest parish in England, spread over a substantial area with a circumference of 23 miles. The village itself is well worth exploring for its part-Norman St Gregory's church with a fine 15th century tower,

🏛 historic building   🏛 museum   🏛 historic site   🌄 scenic attraction   🌿 flora and fauna

LOVELLS COURT COUNTRY HOUSE B&B

Burton Street, Marnhull, nr Sturminster Newton, Dorset DT10 1JJ
Tel: 01258 820652
e-mail: maryann.ns@gmail.com   website: www.lovellscourt.co.uk

A large rambling house of character standing at the end of an avenue of chestnut trees, **Lovells Court Country House** enjoys fine views across the Vale of Blackmore and offers all the peace and tranquillity you could wish for. This non-smoking house has three guest bedrooms, all spacious, comfortably furnished in antique pine, and all equipped with colour TV, radio and hospitality tray. Your host, Mary-Ann Newson-Smith, serves a sumptuous breakfast complete with fresh eggs and homemade jams and marmalades. Lovells Court provides an excellent base for exploring Hardy Country and historic towns such as Dorchester and Shaftesbury.

and who knows what you might find along Sodom Lane? This now-prosperous village appears in *Tess of the d'Urbervilles* as 'Marlott', the birthplace of the heroine. The thatched **Tess's Cottage** (private, but visible from the lane) is supposedly the house Hardy had in mind, while the Crown Inn (also thatched) is still recognisable as the "Pure Drop Inn" in the same novel.

STALBRIDGE
9 miles SW of Shaftesbury on the A357

🏠 Market Cross

The 15th century church here has a striking 19th century tower which provides a landmark throughout the Vale of Blackmoor. Perhaps even more impressive is the town's **Market Cross** standing 30ft high and richly carved with scenes of the Crucifixion and Resurrection. Just outside the town, Stalbridge Park (private) sheltered Charles I after his defeat at Marston Moor. The house (now demolished) was built by Richard Boyle, 1st Earl of Cork, and it was here that his 7th son, the celebrated

physicist and chemist Robert Boyle carried out the experiments that eventually led to his formulation of Boyle's Law.

STURMINSTER NEWTON
11 miles SW of Shaftesbury on the A357

🏠 Riverside Villa   🏠 Newton Mill

This unspoilt market town – the 'capital' of the Blackmore Vale – is an essential stop for anyone following in Thomas Hardy's footsteps. It was at Sturminster Newton that

Newton Mill, Sturminster Newton

🎞 stories and anecdotes   🐦 famous people   🎨 art and craft   🎭 entertainment and sport   🚶 walks

STABLE ON THE STOUR

Unit 4, Nicholsons Yard, Hinton St Mary,
Sturminster Newton, Dorset DT10 1LT
Tel: 01258 471110
website: www.stableonthestour.co.uk

Anyone interested in equestrian activities should make their way to **Stable on the Stour**, in the village of Hinton St Mary, where Ruth Harman has gathered together a comprehensive range of stylish accessories for both horse and rider. For horses, there's a huge choice of winter and summer rugs from suppliers such as Rambo, Rhino, Amigo, Masta, Weatherbeeta and William Funnell. The range of bridles, saddles, and bits includes items from Jeffries, Cottage Craft, Wintec, Saracen and James Sterling.

For the rider, there are competition and practical riding clothes from Barbour, TOGGI, Caldene, Equetech, Harry Hall, Shires, Tally Ho and Rectiligne; footwear from TOGGI, Harry Hall, Barbour and Taurus; riding hats from Champion and from Charles Owen to order. Stable on the Stour also stocks a wide selection of casual country clothing to suit all ages and offers a range of services that includes saddle fitting; leatherwork repairs; and rug cleaning, reproofing and repair. A discount is available on all goods to members of the Pony Club and Riding Club, and the shop has gifts for all occasions.

---

he and his first wife Emma had their first real home together. From 1876 until 1878, they lived in "a pretty cottage overlooking the Dorset Stour, called **Riverside Villa**". Here, Hardy wrote *The Return of the Native* and he often referred later to their time at Sturminster Newton in his poems. It was, he said, "our happiest time". The house is not open to the public but is visible from a riverside footpath.

Until Elizabethan times, Sturminster and Newton were separate villages standing on opposite sides of the River Stour. Shortly after the graceful Town Bridge linked the two communities, a mill was built some 250 yards upstream. Once again restored to working order, **Newton Mill** offers guided tours explaining the milling process, and the delightful setting attracts many amateur and professional artists and photographers. Incidentally, the fine old six-arched bridge still bears a rusty metal plaque carrying the dire warning: "Any person wilfully injuring any part of this county bridge will be guilty of felony and upon conviction liable to be transported for life by the court. P. Fooks."

LYDLINCH

13 miles SW of Shaftesbury on the A357

The small hamlet of Lydlinch in the Vale of Blackmore features in a poem by the Dorset dialect poet, William Barnes. He recalls as a young boy hearing the sound of Lydlinch church bells wafting across meadows to his home in nearby Bagber:

Vor Lydlinch bells be good vor sound,
And liked by all the neighbours round.

The five bells he heard still hang in the tower of the 13th century church.

EAST STOUR
4 miles W of Shaftesbury on the A30

🐦 Henry Fielding

East Stour's literary connections are not with Dorset's omnipresent Thomas Hardy but with the man who has been dubbed 'Father of the Novel', **Henry Fielding.** When he was three years old, Fielding's family moved to the Manor House here which stood close to the church. Fielding spent most of his childhood in the village before leaving to study at Eton and Leyden. He then spent a few years in London writing plays before returning to East Stour in 1734 with his new young wife, Charlotte Cradock, who provided the model

for Sophia Western in his most successful novel, *Tom Jones.* By the time that book was published in 1749, Charlotte was dead, Fielding was seriously ill and he was to die just five years later while visiting Lisbon in an attempt to recover his health.

GILLINGHAM
4 miles NW of Shaftesbury on the B3081

🏛 Gillingham Museum

The most northerly town in Dorset, Gillingham was once an important centre for the milling of silk and the manufacture of the distinctive Victorian red-hot bricks. The parish church has a 14th century chancel but the rest of the building, like much of the town, dates from after the arrival of the railway in 1859. **Gillingham Museum** charts the history of the town and the surrounding villages from prehistoric times; an interesting exhibit here is a manual fire engine dating from 1790.

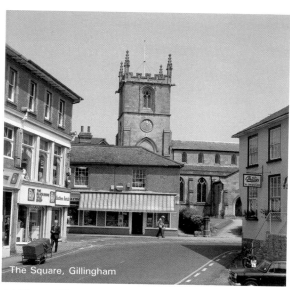
The Square, Gillingham

Blandford Forum

🏛 Church of St Peter & St Paul

🏛 Blandford Museum

🏛 Cavalcade of Costume Museum

🏛 Royal Signals Museum

Blandford Forum, the administrative centre of North Dorset, is beautifully situated along the wooded valley of the River Stour. It's a handsome town, thanks mainly to suffering the trauma of a great fire in 1731. The gracious Georgian buildings erected after that

🎭 stories and anecdotes   🐦 famous people   🎨 art and craft   🎭 entertainment and sport   🚶 walks

THE HAMBLEDON GALLERY

Established more than 40 years ago, this is a small department store with clothes, china, glass, bedding, accessories, toys, rugs, table linen, toiletries, etc. etc.

Clothes by:

Avoca	Fenn Wright & Manson	Mr + Mrs Macleod
Betty Jackson	Great Plains	Saltwater
Clemente	Joyce Ridings	Marion Foale
Cut Loose	Lilith	Orla Kiely
Day **Birger** et Mikkelsen	Marilyn Moore	

"Well worth a detour"
Harpers and Queen

40-44 Salisbury Street, Blandford, Dorset DT11 7PR Tel: 01258 452880

CARRIERES COURTENAY

57 Salisbury Street, Blandford Forum, Dorset DT11 7PX
Tel/Fax: 01258 455221

This well established shop is ablaze with the colours of the most extraordinarily wide selection of fabrics, from well known companies such as Colefax and Fowler, Zoffany and Osborne and Little, and many unusual and less well known brands from around the world. From one cushion to complete houses, the knowledgeable and cheerful team can also show a very comprehensive and up to the minute selection of wallpapers, poles, tracks and interior decoration accessories. In-house workrooms ensure personal attention to detail. The shop is open daily 9am to 4pm, except for Wednesday and Saturday, closing at 11.30am.

conflagration, most of them designed by local architects John and William Bastard, provide the town with a quite unique and soothing sense of architectural harmony. Three important ancient buildings escaped the fire of 1731: the **Ryves Almshouses** of 1682, the **Corn Exchange,** and the splendid 15th century **Old House** in The Close which was built in the Bohemian style to house Protestant refugees from Bohemia. The old parish church did not survive the fire, but its 18th century replacement, the **Church of St Peter & St Paul,** crowned by an unusual cupola, now dominates the market-place. It's well worth stepping inside the church to see the box pews, an organ presented by George III, the massive columns of Portland stone, and the elegant pulpit, designed by Sir Christopher Wren, removed here from St Antholin's Church in the City of London.

In front of the church, the **Fire Monument** (known locally as Bastard's Pump) has a dual purpose – to provide water for fire fighting and as a public drinking fountain. Opposite the church, the **Blandford Museum** features a diorama of the Great Fire along with a wonderful collection of artefacts illustrating many aspects of life in and around Blandford over the years.

Housed in one of the town houses designed by the Bastard brothers, the **Cavalcade of Costume Museum** displays a fantastic collection of costumes from the 1730s through to the 1950s. Originally amassed by the late Mrs Betty Penny, the collection comprises more than 500 items. The museum also has a garden, shop and tea room.

Just outside the town centre, at Blandford Camp, the **Royal Signals Museum** explores the arcane world of military communications with displays featuring spies, codes and code-breaking, the ENIGMA machine, and Dorset's involvement in the preparations for D-Day.

Around Blandford Forum

IWERNE MINSTER
6 miles N of Blandford Forum on the A350

Unusually for Dorset, the church at Iwerne Minster has a spire. It also has one of the few examples of a Victorian church restoration that was actually an improvement. The Lady Chapel here was reconstructed by the architect JL Pearson in elaborate Gothic style,

THE LANGTON ARMS

Tarrant Monkton, nr Blandford,
Dorset DT11 8RX
Tel: 01258 830225 Fax: 01258 830035
website: www.thelangtonarms.co.uk /
www.thestablerestaurant.co.uk

Occupying a peaceful spot next to the church in the centre of Tarrant Monkton village, **The Langton Arms** is wonderfully picturesque with its thatched roof and mellow brick walls. Dating back to the 17th century, this fine old hostelry has been under the caring ownership of Barbara Cossins and her husband, James, a local farmer, since 1992. The inn is well known for its excellent food – based wherever possible on Dorset produce – and its ever-changing selection of real ales. The separate Stables Restaurant is housed in an old converted stable and a conservatory and is open evenings, Wednesday to Saturday, and for Sunday lunch.

The restaurant/conservatory plus the Function Room and Skittles Alley lend themselves very well for wedding receptions and civil ceremonies, birthday and family celebrations, club and social evenings, conferences and small business meetings. The various options are suitable for parties from 12 to 100 people. The inn's picturesque appearance, its attractive grounds and the nearby ford and bridge, have all made it a popular venue for weddings. The inn offers an individual service to suit the needs of each couple and the various rooms or outside marquee enables them to cater for weddings large or small. There is plenty of parking space and good disabled access. The Langton Arms' unique approach to every

wedding includes having their award-winning chef on hand to discuss any special preferences, and the inn also provides a dedicated member of staff to help guide you through your big day.

If you plan to stay in this scenic corner of the county, The Langton Arms has six luxury guest bedrooms built in rustic brick around an attractive courtyard. All are on the ground floor level with their own private entrance and a bay window looking out onto the Dorset countryside. The rooms are furnished to a high standard with full en suite bathrooms, colour TV and hospitality tray. If you prefer self-catering, within a short walk of the inn there's a separate cottage which can sleep up to eight guests.

Tarrant Monkton provides an ideal base for exploring the many attractions of East Dorset – amongst them historic Kingston Lacy House, Wimborne Minster, the New Forest, the ancient cathedral city of Salisbury, and the hilltop market town of Shaftesbury with its Gold Hill made famous by the Hovis adverts.

🏛 historic building   🏛 museum   🏛 historic site   🔾 scenic attraction   🌱 flora and fauna

THE BUTCHER'S SHOP

The Chalk, Iwerne Minster, nr Blandford Forum, Dorset DT11 8NA
Tel/Fax: 01747 811229

The Butcher's Shop in The Chalk, in the heart of the village, is a traditional butcher with a wonderful display of meats and delicatessen products. When Simon Harvell bought the shop in 1982, he was determined to run it in the traditional manner, all but forgotten in an age of uniform supermarket production line meat. Once every town would have had a local butcher's shop like this. Simon knows exactly where all his meat comes from. It is slaughtered locally and Simon ensures that it is properly hung to develop its flavour. White Park beef, Gloucester Old Spot pork, and grass fed Aberdeen Angus beef reared on the Ranston Estate are among the high quality meats that draw people from far beyond Dorset to this tiny village shop.

As well as beef, lamb, pork and bacon, Simon also stocks a range of delicatessen products. You'll find free range eggs, some 40 French cheeses (including un-pasteurised varieties), Italian olive oils and smoked meats and fish, all chosen for taste and quality, and conforming to Simon's exacting standards. This is a shop for people who like to know where their food comes from, and who appreciate the distinctive flavours of natural food.

---

roofed with a stone vault and decorated with intricate floral bosses. The beautiful stained glass is a reproduction of 16th century Flemish glass.

The old village was completely rebuilt in the early 1900s by a very wealthy Lord of the Manor and is notable for its varied cottages all built of red brick.

TARRANT HINTON
5 miles NE of Blandford Forum on the A354

🏛 Great Dorset Steam Fair

This small village is the setting for the **Great Dorset Steam Fair**, held in late-August/early September. Occupying a huge 600-acre site, this is one of the world's largest international steam events, attracting some 200 steam engines and more than 220,000 visitors. The annual extravaganza includes working engine displays, an old-time steam funfair, demonstrations of rural crafts, displays of working Shire horses and live music.

TARRANT GUNVILLE
7 miles NE of Blandford Forum off the A354

A tablet in the church here commemorates the death in 1805 of Thomas Wedgwood, son of the famous potter Josiah. Thomas's own claim to fame is as a pioneer of photography. He treated a sheet of white paper with a solution of nitrate of silver, placed a fern leaf on it and exposed the sheet to the sun. The resulting

HOME FARM TRADITIONAL FOODS

Home Farm Shop, Tarrant Gunville, Blandford Forum,
Dorset DT11 8JW
Tel/Fax: 01258 830083
e-mail: rod@rbelbin.fsnet.co.uk

Marlene Belbin, who runs **Home Farm Traditional Foods** "with a little help from my husband, Rodney" reckons the best thing she can say about the farm shop is that, "it's the kind of shop I regularly use myself." Marlene sold at farmers' markets for some years so she has a good idea of who buys what. As well as their own free range livestock and Marlene's home-cooked meals, practically everything sold here comes from the local area, including some from their own village.

A working farm which has been in the hands of the Belbin family for three generations, Home Farm has its own shorthorn herd, established in 1988, and more recently invested in pigs from which come the sausages freshly made in the farm's own butchery. Cake-making is also done on the premises, "which is just as well," says Marlene, "because they sell like – well – like hot cakes!" Vegetables come fresh each day and the seasonal fruits are also locally grown. Home Farm Shop is open from 9am to 5.30pm, Tuesday to Saturday; and from 10am to 4pm on Sunday. Tea Room open from Easter to October, Tuesday-Sunday, 10am-4pm.

image, according to historians of photography, qualifies as possibly the first photograph ever made.

CHETTLE
7 miles NE of Blandford Forum off the A354

🏠 Chettle House

A picturesque village with a charming manor house, **Chettle House,** designed by Thomas Archer in the English baroque style and completed in 1720. Archer's work includes the north front of Chatsworth and the Church of St John in Smith Square and his buildings are typified by lavish curves, inverted scrolls and their large scale, a style that owed much to the Italian architects Bernini and Borromini. Chettle House was bought in 1846 by the

Castleman family who added an ornate ceiling. The house contains portraits of the Chafin family, earlier owners, and the beautifully laid out gardens include herbaceous border, a rose garden and croquet lawn.

BLANDFORD ST MARY
1 mile SW of Blandford Forum off the A354

🐾 Badger Brewery

The main attraction here is the **Badger Brewery** which was founded at Ansty near Dorchester in 1777 but moved to its present site here beside the River Stour in 1899. The original brewery was founded by Charles Hill, a farmer's son who learnt the brewing art along with farming. The brewery expanded quickly thanks to a contract to supply ale to the Army during the Napoleonic Wars. It is still thriving and visitors can take a tour of the premises.

MILTON ABBAS

6 miles SW of Blandford Forum off the A354

🏛 Abbey Church

This picture postcard village of thatched cottages was created in the 1770s by Joseph Damer, 1st Earl of Dorchester. The earl lived in the converted former abbey from which the village takes its name but he decided to demolish the medieval buildings, and build a more stately mansion surrounded by grounds landscaped by Capability Brown. The earl's ambitious plans required that the small town that had grown up around the abbey would have to go, so more than 100 houses, four pubs, a brewery and a school were razed to the ground. The residents were moved more than a mile away to the present village for which Brown had made the preliminary plans. The earl's new mansion is now a private school and the only part of the abbey that survived is the **Abbey Church** which contains some wonderful Pugin glass and an extraordinary tomb to the earl and his wife Caroline designed by Robert Adam. Exquisitely carved by Agostino Carlini, the monument shows the earl propped up on one elbow gazing out across his beautiful wife.

MILBORNE ST ANDREW

9 miles SW of Blandford Forum on the A354

🎭 John Morton

An attractive village in the valley of a tributary of the River Piddle, Milborne St Andrew was owned in medieval times by the Morton family. One of them gave his name to the expression 'Morton's Fork'. As Lord Chancellor to Henry VII (and Archbishop of

Canterbury), **John Morton** devised a system of parting the rich, and the not-so-rich, from their money. He proposed the thesis that if a man was living in grand style he clearly had money to spare; if he lived frugally, then he obviously kept his wealth hidden away. This ingenious argument became known as Morton's Fork and many a citizen was caught on its vicious prongs. However, the system enriched and delighted the king who made Morton a Cardinal in 1493. Morton spent his remaining years spending lavishly on the building and restoration of churches, most notably in the magnificently carved and painted roof of Bere Regis church.

Wareham

🏛 Church of St Mary   🏛 Wareham Museum
🎐 TE Lawrence Memorial   🎬 Rex Cinema

Situated between the rivers Frome and Piddle, Wareham is an enchanting little town lying within the earthworks of a 10th century encircling wall. Standing close to an inlet of Poole Harbour, Wareham was an important port until the River Frome clogged its approaches with silt. Then, in 1726, a devastating fire consumed the town's timber buildings, a disaster which produced the happy result of a rebuilt town centre rich in handsome Georgian stone-built houses.

Wareham's history goes back much further than those days. Roman conquerors laid out its street plan: a stern grid of roads which faithfully follows the points of the compass. Saxons and Normans helped build the **Church of St Mary**, medieval artists covered its walls with devotional paintings of remarkable quality. It was in the grounds surrounding the church that King Edward was buried in 879AD after his stepmother, Queen

Elfrida, contrived his murder at Corfe Castle. Elfrida added insult to injury by having the late king buried outside the churchyard, in unhallowed ground.

Occupying the 12th century Holy Trinity Church near the quay, the Purbeck Information & Heritage Centre offers copious information about the town; while in East Street, the **Wareham Museum** has some interesting displays and artefacts illustrating the town's history.

In the Saxon St Martin's Church, notable

The Old Granary, Wareham

for its early medieval wall paintings, there's a striking memorial to what appears at first glance to be a medieval crusader dressed in Arab robes, holding an Arab dagger and

YESTERDAYS

13a North Street, Wareham, Dorset BH20 4AB
Tel: 01929 550505
e-mail: yesterdays.collectables@btinternet.com
website: www.yesterdayscollectables.co.uk

Collectables have grown steadily in popularity over the last few years and you'll find an excellent selection of items at **Yesterdays** in Wareham town centre. Joyce Hardie established the business in 1995 and now offers a real treasure trove of pieces that includes a lovely collection of Isle of Wight Glass, Jonathan Harris glass, Okra glass and Roger Cockram Studio Pottery – all of them beautiful and a good investment for the future. There's also a good stock of Poole Pottery from the '50s up to the present day, and lots of interesting pieces of blue and white china. Collectors of Rupert the Bear, Coalport Snowmen, Winnie the Pooh, Beatrix Potter and Winstanley Cats will discover some really special pieces.

Joyce specialises in Dennis China but also in stock are Carltonware, Spode, Border Fine Arts, Cornishware, miniature china and many more unusual pieces, including hand painted china from the 1930s such as Shelley. She has a large collection of honey pots dating mainly from the '30s along with an enticing range of antiques, and if you are looking for a gift Yetserdays cannot fail to please. Yesterdays has gift vouchers available.

🏠 historic building   🏛 museum   🏛 historic site   🔱 scenic attraction   🌿 flora and fauna

THE CREATIVE GALLERY

St John's Hill, Wareham, Dorset BH20 4NB
Tel: 01929 551700
e-mail: gallery@creative-studios.com
website: www.creative-studios.com/gallery

The Creative Gallery in St John's Hill, Wareham features paintings, ceramics and photography by Dorset artists. This is an open studio where you can meet the artists and see them working. It features local contemporary artwork and photography by brothers Cliff and Graham Towler who have a keen interest in nature and all its moods, especially landscapes. Their expressions have been experimented with and cleverly merged with a love of Dorset's Jurassic Coastline to inspire this current collection of works of acrylic and oil on canvas, watercolour and limited edition prints. There are also displays of work by old art school colleagues Jeremy Hammick, Ian Hargreaves and Lance Nation.

Established ceramic artists Andrew Davidson, Rosmarie James, Karen Harrison, Fiona Kelly, Bryony Burn and David Brown display works in stoneware and porcelain, making one off strong sculptural forms with a distinctive variety of glazes, colours and textural surfaces. There are limited edition fine art prints by travel photographer David Jackson, featuring seascapes, landscapes and classic cityscapes from his rapidly expanding west country and worldwide collection, Affinity Image Library (tel: 01929 551555).

Open Monday to Saturday, 10am to 5pm

---

resting his head on a camel's saddle. This is a **memorial to TE Lawrence**, 'Lawrence of Arabia', who is actually buried at Moreton.

Wareham boasts one building that is unique – the privately owned **Rex Cinema** which was built pre-1914 and is the only gas-lit cinema in the country. The original antique carbon arc projectors are still used to show the latest blockbusters.

An even more ancient survival is the custom of the Court Leet. In Norman times these courts were the main judicial institution in many parts of the country. On four evenings in November, strangely dressed men visit the town's inns to check the quality and quantity of the food and ale on offer. The officials include ale-tasters, bread weighers and 'carnisters' who sample the meat. Although they have no powers nowadays, it is a quaint tradition.

ORGANFORD
3 miles N of Wareham off the A35

🌱 Farmer Palmer's

The tiny village of Organford stands on the edge of the tree-covered expanses of Gore Heath. The settlement is so small it doesn't possess either a church or a pub, but it does have a Manor House which enjoys a wonderfully quiet and secluded position surrounded by woods. It's also home to **Farmer Palmer's** countryside theme park where children can feed lambs and goats,

---

📖 stories and anecdotes   🦜 famous people   🎨 art and craft   🎭 entertainment and sport   🚶 walks

watch cows being milked, enjoy a wild trailer ride, drive pedal tractors or work off some energy in the bouncy castles and soft play zone.

FURZEBROOK
4 miles S of Wareham off the A351

🗘 Blue Pool

If you are interested in natural curiosities, follow the brown and white signs for the **Blue Pool**. Here, in what was originally a clay pit, tiny particles of clay in the pool diffract light and create an astonishing illusion of colour, varying from sky blue to deepest azure. There's a tea house, shops and museum here and the tree-lined shore is a popular picnic place.

WORTH MATRAVERS
7 miles SE of Wareham off the B3069

🗠 Benjamin Jesty   🏛 Chapel of St Aldhelm

In the graveyard of St Nicholas' Church is the grave of a local farmer, **Benjamin Jesty,** whose tomb inscription is worth quoting in full: *An upright and honest man, particularly noted for having been the first person known that introduced the Cow Pox by inoculation, and who, from his great strength of mind, made the experiment from the cow on his wife and two sons in the year 1774.* His family's "great strength of mind" might also have been noted since the inoculation was made using a knitting needle. The man usually credited with discovering inoculation, Edward Jenner, didn't make his first successful experiment until 1796 – 22 years after Benjamin's.

THE BLUE POOL
Furzebrook, Wareham, Dorset BH20 5AR
Tel: 01929 551408 Fax: 01929 551404
website: www.bluepooluk.com

Come and relax at Dorset's best kept secret. Visit this unique and tranquil beauty spot set in the midst of the trees and heathland of the magical Isle of Purbeck.

The Blue Pool, once a clay pit and now completely naturalised, is famous for the ever changing colour of its water.

A host of sandy paths lead up to views of the Purbeck Hills or down steps to the waters edge. Enjoy the peace and quiet and finish your visit with a light lunch or a delicious cream tea with homemade scones baked on the premises.

The grounds are open daily from March to November; the Tea House, museum and gift shop from April to October. Dogs on leads welcome. Some facilities for the disabled. Free parking. Head south from Wareham on the A351 Swanage Road and you will see direction signs on the roundabout.

🏛 historic building   🖼 museum   🏛 historic site   🗘 scenic attraction   🌿 flora and fauna

Standing high on the cliffs of St Aldhelm's Head, a couple of miles south of the village and accessible only by a bridleway, the **Chapel of St Aldhelm** stands alone. It is one of the oldest churches in Dorset, a low square building with a fine Norman doorway and one solitary window. Uniquely, the chapel has no east wall as the corners of the walls are aligned to the points of the compass. In its dank, dim interior the stonework is bare of decoration, just a central column from which eight ribs extend to the walls. According to legend, the church was built in 1140 by a local man in memory of his newly-married daughter and her husband. He was watching from this clifftop as the boat in which they were sailing to a new home was caught in a sudden squall and capsized. All on board perished.

WINFRITH NEWBURGH
9 miles SW of Wareham off the A352

🏖 Lulworth Cove 🏖 Durdle Door

🏰 Lulworth Castle

This charming little village stands on a minor road that leads to one of the county's best-known beauty spots, **Lulworth Cove.** An almost perfectly circular bay, the Cove is surrounded by towering 440ft cliffs. Over the centuries, the sea has gnawed away at a weak point in the limestone here, inadvertently creating a breathtakingly beautiful scene. Best to visit out of season, however, as parking places nearby are limited.

About a mile to the west of Lulworth Cove stands another remarkable natural feature which has been sculpted by the sea.

Durdle Door is a magnificent archway carved from the coastal limestone. There's no road to the coast at this point, but you can reach it easily by following the South West Coast Path from Lulworth Cove. Along the way, you will also see another strange outcrop, a forest of tree-stumps which have become fossilised over the centuries.

A couple of miles inland, **Lulworth Castle** (English Heritage) looks enormously impressive from a distance: close-up, you can see how a disastrous fire in 1929 destroyed most of it. Amongst the remains, though, is a curious circular building dating from 1786: the first Roman Catholic church to be established in Britain since Henry VIII's defiance of the Pope in 1534. Sir Thomas Weld was given permission to build this unique church by George III. The king cautiously added the proviso that Sir Thomas' new place of worship should not offend Anglican sensibilities by looking like a church. It

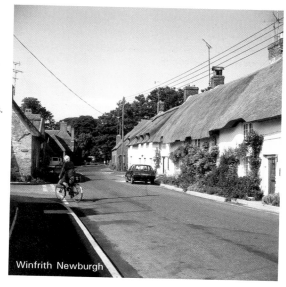

Winfrith Newburgh

📖 stories and anecdotes   🐦 famous people   🎨 art and craft   🎵 entertainment and sport   🚶 walks

CROMWELL HOUSE HOTEL

Lulworth Cove, Dorset BH20 5RJ
Tel: 01929 400253   Fax: 01929 400566
e-mail: catriona@lulworthcove.co.uk
website: www.lulworthcove.co.uk

Standing just 200 yards from Lulworth Cove, the **Cromwell House Hotel** provides guests with spectacular views across the cove and the Stair Hole. Built in the late-Victorian era, this family hotel is owned and personally run by Catriona and Alistair Miller. Together with their small and dedicated staff they have created a relaxed and friendly atmosphere that is reminiscent of a country house. Offering a high standard of luxury and service, there are 18 guest rooms here, along with a self-catering flat and a disabled-friendly ground floor room.

The hotel's reception rooms are spacious and attractive, many of them with glorious views out over the sea, and the Millers pride themselves on the delicious food served in the dining room that faces the terrace and garden. Over the years, Catriona's cuisine has developed a style of its own, based on traditional English cooking but influenced by her years spent abroad. The dishes are freshly prepared from only the finest local ingredients, with lobsters, crabs and scallops from Lulworth Cove's fishermen taking pride of place on the menu. The restaurant also serves a marvellous Dorset Cream Tea served either inside or out on the south-facing patio. Other amenities include a heated outdoor swimming pool during the season.

doesn't, and that's a great part of its appeal. The castle's other attractions include indoor and outdoor children's play areas; an animal farm; pitch & putt; woodland walks; café and shop.

BOVINGTON CAMP
6 miles W of Wareham off the A352

🏛 Tank Museum   🌿 Monkey World

It was at Bovington Camp that TE Lawrence served as a private in the Royal Tank Corps. Today, the camp is home to the **Tank Museum** which has more than 150 armoured vehicles on display dating from World War I to the present day. Audio tours are available, there's a children's play area, restaurant and gift shop, and during the summer tanks take part in live action displays. Also here is **Jumicar**, a children's fun and

educational activity where road awareness skills are taught using real junior sized cars on a mini road layout complete with traffic lights and zebra crossings. Open every weekend and school holiday except December and January.

A very different kind of attraction, to the east of the camp, is **Monkey World** whose 65 acres are home to more than 160 rescued primates. The site also includes the largest children's adventure play area on the south coast, an education centre, woodland walk, pets corner, café, picnic areas and full disabled facilities.

BERE REGIS
7 miles NW of Wareham on the A35

🏠 Church of St John

Most visitors to the **Church of St John** at Bere Regis are attracted by its associations

🏠 historic building   🏛 museum   🏛 historic site   ❦ scenic attraction   🌿 flora and fauna

Monkey World

Longthorns, Wareham, Dorset BH20 6HH
Tel: 01929 462537 Fax: 01929 405414
e-mail: apes@monkeyworld.org
website: www.monkeyworld.co.uk

Welcome to Monkey World Ape Rescue Centre, a unique sanctuary in the heart of the Dorset countryside. This 65-acre woodland park is home to a family of over 160 rescued and endangered apes and monkeys. The park is a haven for 16 different species, where they are free to be themselves in a natural environment and in the company of their own kind. Some have been neglected or kept in unnatural conditions, others have experienced unbelievable cruelty.

Each primate here is a special individual, an important member of the family ... whether they are rescued or part of an international breeding programme for endangered species. Your visit here is important because it helps to protect man's closest living relatives ... for generations to come.

PAMPERED PIGS

Rye Hill Farm, Rye Hill, Bere Regis, Wareham, Dorset BH20 7LP
Tel: 01929 472327
e-mail: pamperedpigs@fsmail.net
website: www.pampered-pigs.co.uk

Meat with real "old-fashioned" flavour is the promise made by **Pampered Pigs,** a traditional farm shop selling its own pork, beef and lamb, along with a wide range of other locally produced meat, organic and GM-free groceries, locally grown fruit and vegetables, dairy products and even some local crafts. Amanda and Kevin Crocker's Rye Hill Farm in the picturesque Bere Valley is home to the beef herd consisting of traditional breeds of Angus and Herefords, crossed with their pedigree British White bull, "The General". This cross of old breeds gives the meat a distinct marbled appearance and hanging the carcasses for three to four weeks before cutting makes the beef wonderfully succulent. The pig herd consisting of traditional English breeds such as British Saddlebacks, Large White, Berkshire and Gloucester Oldspots resides at Tolpuddle in the Piddle Valley.

Over the years, the Crockers have expanded their range of products, including extending the variety of sausages and burgers made on the premises. Their menagerie of small animals has also grown and now includes rabbits, guinea pigs, pygmy goats, two miniature Shetland ponies as well as the more usual farmyard animals. Open 10am to 4pm Monday, 8.30am to 6pm, Tuesday to Friday; 9am to 5pm on Saturday; and 10am to 1pm on Sunday. Guided Farm Walks available on prior booking. School parties welcome.

📖 stories and anecdotes 🐒 famous people 🎨 art and craft ✍ entertainment and sport 🚶 walks

with Hardy's *Tess of the D'Urbervilles*. They come to see the crumbling tombs of the once-powerful Turberville family whose name Hardy adapted for his novel. It was outside the church, beneath the Turberville window, that Hardy had the homeless Tess and her family set up their four-poster bed. A poignant fictional scene,

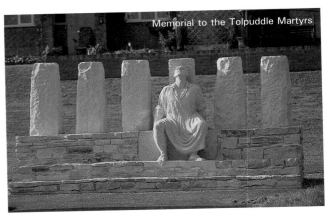

Memorial to the Tolpuddle Martyrs

but the church itself is definitely worth visiting for its unique and magnificent carved and painted wooden roof. Large figures of the 12 Apostles (all in Tudor dress) jut out horizontally from the wall and there are a number of humorous carvings depicting men suffering the discomforts of toothache and over-indulgence. There's also a carving of Cardinal Morton who had this splendid roof installed in 1497. The church's history goes back much farther than that. In Saxon times, Queen Elfrida came here to spend the remainder of her days in penitence for her part in the murder of young King Edward at Corfe Castle in 979. Further evidence of the church's great age is the fact that around 1190 King John paid for the pillars of the nave to be "restored".

TOLPUDDLE
11 miles NW of Wareham on the A35

🏛 Martyr's Museum

The small village of Tolpuddle is a peaceful little place today but in the early 19th century, Tolpuddle was far sleepier than it is now. Not the kind of place you would expect to foment a social revolution, but it was here that six ill-

paid agricultural labourers helped lay the foundations of the British Trade Union Movement. In 1833, they formed a "confederation" in an attempt to have their subsistence wages improved. The full rigour of the landowner-friendly law of the time was immediately invoked. All six were found guilty of taking illegal oaths and sentenced to transportation to Australia for seven years. Even the judge in their case was forced to say that it was not for anything they had done, or intended to do, that he passed such a sentence, but "as an example to others". Rather surprisingly, public opinion sided with the illegal "confederation". Vigorous and sustained protests eventually forced the government to pardon the men after they had served three years of their sentence. They all returned safely to England, honoured ever afterwards in Trade Union hagiography as the "Tolpuddle Martyrs". The **Martyrs' Museum** at Tolpuddle tells an inspiring story, but it's depressing to realise that the 7-shilling (35p) weekly payment those farm-workers were protesting against actually had more buying power in the 1830s than the current legally-enforced minimum wage.

Swanage

- Durlston Country Park
- Swanage Railway
- Town Hall
- King Alfred Column
- Great Globe
- Studland Bay

Picturesquely set beside a broad, gently curving bay with fine, clear sands and beautiful surrounding countryside, Swanage is understandably popular as a family holiday resort. A winner of Southern England in Bloom, the town takes great pride in the spectacular floral displays in its parks and gardens, and its other awards include the prestigious European Blue Flag for its unpolluted waters, and the Tidy Britain Group's "Seaside Award". Swanage offers its visitors all the facilities necessary for a traditional seaside holiday, including boat-trips, (with sightings of bottle-nosed dolphins if you're lucky), water-sports, sea angling and an attractive, old-fashioned pier and bandstand. The Mowlem Theatre provides a seasonal programme of films, shows and plays, and on Sunday afternoons the Recreation Ground resounds to the strains of a brass band. On the clifftops, **Durlston Country Park** covers some 260 acres of delightful countryside; on the front, the Beach Gardens offer tennis, bowls and putting, or you can just rent a beach hut or bungalow and relax. One attraction not to be missed is a ride on the **Swanage Railway** along which magnificent steam locomotives of the old Southern Railway transport passengers some six miles through lovely Dorset countryside to Norden, just north of Corfe Castle.

In the town itself, the **Town Hall** is worth seeing for its ornate façade, the work of Christopher Wren. Wren didn't build it for Swanage, however. It was originally part of Mercers Hall in Cheapside, London. When the Mercers Hall was being demolished, a Swanage man named George Burt scavenged the fine frontage and rebuilt it here. He also brought the graceful little Clock Tower which stands near the pier but once used to adorn the Surrey end of London Bridge; a gateway from Hyde Park for his own house; and cast-iron columns and railings from Billingsgate Market. No wonder older residents of the town refer to Swanage as "Little London".

There is, however, one monument that is purely Swanage – the **King Alfred Column** on the seafront. This commemorates the king's victory here over a Danish fleet in 877AD. The column is topped by cannonballs that would have been of great assistance to Alfred had they been invented at the time.

Collectors of curiosities will want to make their way to Tilly Whim Hill, just south of Swanage, which is also well-known for its murky caves. High above the caves stands the **Great Globe,** a huge round stone, some 10 feet in diameter and weighing 40 tons, its surface sculpted with all the countries of the world. At its base, stone slabs are inscribed with quotations from the Old Testament psalms, Shakespeare and other poets. They include moral injunctions such as, "Let prudence direct you, temperance chasten you, fortitude support you", and the information that, "if a globe representing the sun were constructed on the same scale, it would measure some 1,090 feet across".

A couple of miles north of Swanage, **Studland Bay** offers a lovely three-mile stretch of sandy beach, part of it clearly designated as an exclusive resort for nudists only.

stories and anecdotes   famous people   art and craft   entertainment and sport   walks

LANGTON MATRAVERS
2 miles W of Swanage, on the B3069

🏛 Purbeck Stone Industry Museum

🌿 Putlake Adventure Farm

Before tourism, the main industry around
Swanage was quarrying the famous Purbeck
stone that has been used in countless
churches, cathedrals and fine houses around
the country. **The Purbeck Stone Industry
Museum** at Langton Matravers tells the story
of Purbeck Marble, a handsome and durable
material which was already being cut and
polished back in Roman times. This sizeable
village is also home to **Putlake Adventure
Farm** where visitors are encouraged to make
contact with a variety of friendly animals,
bottle feed the lambs, or have a go at milking
cows. There are pony and trailer rides, picnic
and play areas, a farm trail, gift shop and tea
room.

CORFE CASTLE
5 miles NW of Swanage on the A351

🏛 Corfe Castle   🌿 Model Village

One of the grandest sights in the country is
the impressive ruin of **Corfe Castle** (National
Trust) standing high on a hill and dominating
the attractive grey stone village below. Once
the most impregnable fortress in the land,
Corfe dates back to the days of William the
Conqueror, with later additions by King John
and Edward I. The dastardly John threw 22
French knights into the castle dungeons and
left them to starve to death. Later, Edward II
was imprisoned here before being sent to
Berkeley Castle and his horrible murder.

Corfe Castle remained important right up
until the days of the Civil War when it
successfully withstood two sieges before it fell
into Parliamentary hands through treachery. A
month later, Parliament ordered the castle to
be 'slighted' – rendered
militarily useless.

Although Corfe now stands
in splendid ruin, you can see a
smaller, intact version at the
Model Village in West Street.
This superbly accurate replica
is built from the same Purbeck
stone as the real thing and the
details of the miniature
medieval folk going about
their daily business are
wonderful. Surrounded by
lovely gardens, this intriguing
display is well worth a visit.
You might also want to
explore the local museum
which is housed in the smallest
Town Hall building in the
country.

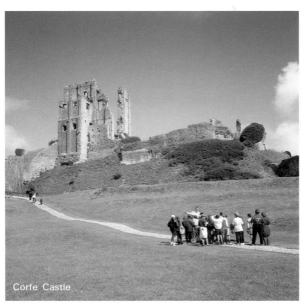
Corfe Castle

🏛 historic building   🏛 museum   🏛 historic site   ⌘ scenic attraction   🌿 flora and fauna

REMPSTONE STABLES

*Rempstone, Corfe Castle, Wareham,
Dorset BH20 5JQ*
Tel: 01929 480490   Mobile: 07967 397743
website: www.rempstonestables.co.uk

Rempstone Stables is located in the beautiful countryside of the Isle of Purbeck with a variety of riding experiences available right on its doorstep. There are beach rides on the two-mile long sweep of golden sands at Studland Bay; routes across the vast heathland; and trips through the varied forest where deer are never far from sight – whatever your preference, Peter Nemitz and his staff will tailor their packages to suit you. All rides are escorted by friendly, helpful staff and all riders are welcome, whether beginners or experienced.

Come on your own or as part of a group; come during the day or in the evening – whatever your requirements, the staff will be glad to help. The stables has weight carrying mounts, and also has horses and ponies for sale. Such is the service at Rempstone that many riders return time and time again – and if you are looking for accommodation in this glorious part of the county, the Stables can also arrange that for you. The stables can be found on the B3351 between Corfe Castle and Studland at the CGPS signpost.

NORDEN

7 miles NW of Swanage, on the A351

🌿 Swanage Railway

About half a mile north of Corfe Castle, Norden Station is the northern terminus of the **Swanage Railway** and there's a regular bus service from the station to the castle. The hamlet of Norden itself is actually another mile further to the northeast, a delightful place surrounded by pine trees and heathland.

Bournemouth

🏛 Pier   🏛 Russell-Cotes Art Gallery & Museum

🏛 St Peter's Church   🌿 Bournemouth Eye

🏛 Casa Magni Shelley Museum   🐚 Oceanarium

🏛 Rothesay Museum   🏛 Teddy Bear Museum

🏛 Bournemouth Aviation Museum

🌿 Alice in Wonderland Family Park

It's been calculated that Bournemouth has "more nightclubs than Soho" as well as a huge range of hotels, shops, bars, restaurants and entertainment venues. The town also supports two symphony orchestras. In July 2005, in the hope of attracting more of Britain's 250,000 surfers to the town, Bournemouth council announced the construction of a 1,600ft-long artificial reef capable of producing breakers up to 16ft high. Beach users will also benefit as the reef will create a peaceful lagoon.

Already, some 5.5 million visitors each year are attracted to this cosmopolitan town which has been voted the greenest and cleanest resort in the UK – there are more than 2,000

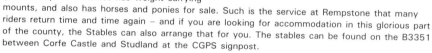

🎭 stories and anecdotes   🗣 famous people   🎨 art and craft   🌿 entertainment and sport   🚶 walks

acres of Victorian parks and gardens, and the town centre streets are washed and scrubbed every morning.

Two hundred years ago, the tiny village of Bourne was a mere satellite of the bustling port of Poole, a few miles to the west. The empty coastline was ideal for smugglers and Revenue men were regularly posted here to patrol the area. One of them, Louis Tregonwell, was enchanted by Bourne's glorious setting at the head of three deep valleys, or chines. He and his wife bought land here, built themselves a house and planted the valleys with the pines that give the present-day town its distinctive appearance. Throughout Victorian times, Bournemouth, as it became known, grew steadily and the prosperous new residents beautified their adopted town with wide boulevards, grand parks, and public buildings, creating a Garden City by the Sea.

They also built a splendid **Pier** (1855) and, around the same time, **St Peter's Church** which is much visited for its superb carved alabaster by Thomas Earp, and the tomb in which Mary Shelley, the author of *Frankenstein*, is buried along with the heart of her poet-husband, Percy Bysshe Shelley. The **Casa Magni Shelley Museum**, in Shelley House where the poet's son lived from 1849 to 1889, is the only one in the world entirely devoted

to Shelley's life and works. Other museums include the **Russell-Cotes Art Gallery & Museum**, based on the collection of the globe-trotting Sir Merton Russell-Cotes; the **Rothesay Museum** which follows a mainly nautical theme but also has a display of more than 300 vintage typewriters; the **Teddy Bear Museum** in the Expocentre; and, north of the town, the **Bournemouth Aviation Museum** at Bournemouth International Airport, home to a collection of vintage jet aircraft – including the last flying Sea Fury fighter – which are flown on a regular basis.

Opposite the airport and set in seven acres of landscaped grounds, the **Alice in Wonderland Family Park** is designed for children aged 2-12 and offers a wide variety of rides and attractions, a huge Alice Maze, indoor play centre, and a daily panto-style Storyline. As you might expect in such a

Bournemouth Pier

🏛 historic building   🏛 museum   🏛 historic site   ☘ scenic attraction   🌿 flora and fauna

popular resort, every conceivable kind of sport and recreation facility is available: anything from surfboarding to paragliding, from symphony concerts to international golf tournaments.

Back in town, the **Oceanarium**, located alongside the Pier, explores the wonders of the natural world beneath the surface of seas, lakes and rivers. Displays include life under the Amazon, the Caribbean and the lagoons of Hawaii. A popular feature here is Turtle Beach, home to rescued green turtles.

And if you're looking for a novel experience, and a really spectacular aerial view of the town and coastline, **Bournemouth Eye,** in the Lower Gardens near the pier, offers day or night ascents in a tethered balloon which rises up to 500ft.

Around Bournemouth

CHRISTCHURCH
5 miles E of Bournemouth on the A35

- Blue Plaques Millennium Trail
- Double Dykes
- Christchurch Priory
- Christchurch Castle
- St Michael's Loft Museum
- Place Mill
- Red House Museum
- Museum of Electricity

An excellent way of exploring Christchurch is to follow the **Blue Plaques Millennium Trail** which commemorates sites around the town from Neolithic times to the 20th century. A booklet detailing this trip through time is available from the tourist information centre in the High Street.

Pride of place on the trail goes to

LE STUDIO
61 The High Street, Christchurch, Dorset BH23 1AS
Tel: 01202 482021
website: www.le-studio.co.uk

Occupying an enviable position on Christchurch High Street, just a stone's throw from the beautiful 900-year-old Priory, **Le Studio** has been established for more than 20 years, selling a wide range of gifts and artwork. Artworks cover the walls and include prints and originals by local artists, large landscape photographic prints, and contemporary prints. Le Studio works in partnership with a long-established and experienced framer and can frame anything from a treasured photograph to a football shirt.

The choice of gifts is just as extensive as the range of artworks. Owners Jocelyn and Stuart Britton have gathered together an enticing selection that includes classic and contemporary jewellery, Cmielow Porcelain, Silver Scenes, AE Williams pewterware, Isle of Wight Glass, and

pieces from Poole Pottery. Also on display are christening and wedding gifts, lead crystal and bone china, and a huge range of stylish photo frames. Le Studio also stocks a large selection of maritime gift items, especially in the summer.

stories and anecdotes   famous people   art and craft   entertainment and sport   walks

Hengistbury Head

Distance: *3.8 miles (6.0 kilometres)*

Typical time: *95 mins*

Height gain: *35 metres*

Map: *Outdoor Leisure 22*

Walk: *www.walkingworld.com ID:719*

Contributor: *Peter Salenieks*

ACCESS INFORMATION:

Cars can be parked in Hengistbury Head Car Park. This is approached from the A35, turning south onto the B3059 and then east onto the Broadway to the west of Tuckton. Hengistbury Head is also accessible by bus during the summer months. Open Top Coastal Service 12 runs between Sandbanks and Christchurch Quay from 28 May to 30 September. It is possible to shorten the walk by catching the Land Train which runs between the Ranger Office and Sandspit. Whilst the service is operating, land trains run from 10am to 4pm. For a longer day, consider combining this walk with a ferry boat trip from Sandspit to Mudeford Quay.

DESCRIPTION:

Hengistbury Head has witnessed 11,000 years of human history, including a Stone Age camp on Warren Hill, an Iron Age port and 18th century quarrying. Nowadays it is a popular tourist spot, including a Local Nature Reserve which is home to a variety of birds, insects and small mammals.

This walk starts at the Ranger Office and Land Train terminus. There are good views of Christchurch Harbour and Christchurch Priory. In clear weather, the Purbecks can be seen across Poole Bay, with the Needles and the Isle of Wight lying to the south-east. The walk reaches the southern tip of Hengistbury Head, before descending to the beach. The return passes Holloway's Dock, a SSSI. The walk includes a short, optional detour to the wildlife pond in the quarry. A cafe and toilets are situated at the end of the walk.

FEATURES:

Sea, toilets, wildlife, birds, great views, nature trail, ancient monument

WALK DIRECTIONS:

1 | Start with the Ranger Office and Land Train terminus behind you and walk about 50 metres east along the tarmac road, until you reach a junction with the track just before the Double Dikes. Bear right (south) and go along the track, which runs parallel to the Double Dikes, until you reach the seaward end of the dikes.

2 | Turn left (east) at the seaward end of the Double Dikes and walk along a tarmac path that goes along the clifftop towards Hengistbury Head. The path takes you towards Warren Hill, passing Barn Field and two paths on your left. Ascend steadily, keeping the wildlife pond on your right, to reach the triangulation pillar on top of Warren Hill.

3 | Continue east along a gravel track, passing a toposcope to reach the coastguard lookout station.

4 | The track continues beside the coastguard lookout station, passing a path junction on the left, to reach a crossroads. Ahead, the Isle of Wight can be seen in the distance.

5 | Turn right at the crossroads and follow the track along the clifftop, passing the southern end of the wildlife pond in the old quarry on your left. The track takes you to the southern tip of Hengistbury Head, before turning north-east to reach broad steps that lead down to the beach. There are several seats where you can sit and admire the view.

6 | Descend the steps and bear left to pick up a broad path which leads inland from the beach

huts at Sandspit. Follow the broad path about 100 metres north-west from the beach huts, until you reach the road.

7 | Turn right (east) and follow the road towards Sandspit. Pass the Land Train terminus and the pontoon for the ferry boat to Mudeford Quay on your left. When you reach The Hut Cafe, cross between it and the beach office to reach the seaward side of Sandspit and walk north towards the end of the spit, where Avon Run marks the outflow from Christchurch Harbour into the sea. Do not enter the water as there are very strong currents.

8 | Retrace your route from Avon Run to Waymark 7 and go west along the road, passing Holloway's Dock (a Site of Special Scientific Interest) on your right. Pass a track on your left before entering woodland and continue until you see a wooded track on your left which leads gently uphill.

9 | Follow the track uphill for about 50 metres to reach the wildlife pond (this detour can be omitted if you are short of time). Retrace your route back to the road and turn left. Walk about a kilometre west to reach the Land Train terminus and Ranger Office.

10 | The walk ends at the Ranger Office and Land Train terminus. There are toilets and you can buy snacks at the Hungry Hiker Cafe.

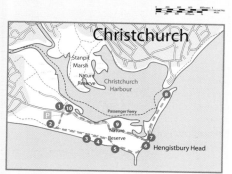

Christchurch

Christchurch Priory, a magnificent building begun in 1094 and reputedly the longest parish church in England, extending for 311ft. It has an impressive Norman nave, some superb medieval carving, and a vast 14th century stone reredos with a Tree of Jesse. Other treasures include the magnificent Salisbury Chantry, some fine misericords and, in the beautiful Lady Chapel, a pendant vault believed to be the earliest of its kind in the country. From the Lady Chapel, a stairway of 75 steps leads to St Michael's Loft, originally a school for novice monks and later a grammar school for boys. It now houses **St Michael's Loft Museum** which tells something of the long history of the priory. Another stairway – a spiral one of 176 steps – winds its way up the tower of the church; from the top there are extensive views out over the town and harbour.

Just north of the priory are the remains of **Christchurch Castle**, built in the late 11th century and slighted (rendered militarily useless) after the Civil War. The site here contains the Constable's Hall which boasts the oldest Norman chimney in Britain, constructed around 1150.

Other nearby attractions include the **Red House Museum & Gardens** which is housed in a former Georgian workhouse and provides some interesting local history as well as a peaceful enclave in the heart of the town; and the **Museum of Electricity**, which occupies a stately Edwardian power station and has something for everyone – from dozens of early domestic appliances to a pair of boot warmers.

On Town Quay, at the meeting of the rivers Stour and Avon, is **Place Mill** which dates back to Anglo-Saxon times and was mentioned in the Domesday Book. The mill

Christchurch

this otherwise built-up stretch of coastline.

Not far from Double Dykes, in 1910, Britain's first air show took place. It was attended by some of the greatest names of early aviation, amongst them Wilbur Wright, Blériot, and the Hon. Charles Rolls (of Rolls-Royce fame) who was killed when his plane crashed at this event.

has been restored and although it is unable to grind corn, you can still see the wheel turning when tidal conditions are right. The body of the mill is now an art gallery with changing exhibitions by local artists, interesting displays of artefacts, and a gift shop.

To the south of Christchurch are the ancient ditches known as **Double Dykes**, an area that offers great walking along with superb views. The dykes cut across the heathland of **Hengistbury Head** which forms the southern side of the town's large natural harbour. The headland is now a nature reserve, one of the few uninhabited parts of

MUDEFORD
7 miles E of Bournemouth off the A337

Standing at the entrance to Christchurch Harbour, Mudeford has a picturesque quay with piles of lobster pots, a fresh fish stall, fishermens' cottages and an old inn. It is still the centre of the local fishing industry and the quay provides a great vantage point for watching yachts and windsurfers as they come up "The Run" into the harbour. The beach here is clean and sandy with a lifeguard service during the summer months when beach huts, deck chairs and canoes can all be

The Museum of Electricity

The Old Power Station, Bargates, Christchurch, Dorset BH23 1QE
Tel: 01202 480467   Fax: 01202 480468

Only five minutes walk from the centre of Christchurch, in the setting of a genuine Edwardian Power Station, the **Museum of Electricity** is a must for all ages. Everything here is electric, from an old Bournemouth tram to a pair of boot warmers! There really is something to interest everyone, with hands-on exhibits and the demonstrations for children tie in with the national curriculum. Car parking is free on site and picnic tables are available.

🏛 historic building   📷 museum   🏛 historic site   🍃 scenic attraction   🌿 flora and fauna

hired, and ferry services cross the harbour to Mudeford Sandbank. Day cruises to the Needles and Yarmouth on the Isle of Wight are also available.

HIGHCLIFFE
9 miles E of Bournemouth on the A337

🏛 Highcliffe Castle

The most easterly community in Dorset, Highcliffe has a fine beach and views of the eastern tip of the Isle of Wight. The bustling village centre hosts a Friday market but the major attraction here is **Highcliffe Castle** (English Heritage), an imposing mansion of gleaming white stone originally built between 1831 and 1835. It was damaged by fire in the 1960s but the exterior was restored in the 1990s although most of the interior remains unrepaired. Guided tours are available every Tuesday afternoon during the summer; the grounds, visitor centre, galleries and gift shop are open all year round.

POOLE
4 miles W of Bournemouth, on the A35/A350

🏛 Waterfront Museum 🎨 Poole Pottery

🌿 Compton Acres 🚶 Brownsea Island

Once the largest settlement in Dorset, Poole is now a pleasant, bustling port. Its huge natural harbour, actually a drowned river valley, has a shoreline of some 50 miles and is the most extensive anchorage in Europe with a history going back well beyond Roman times. A 33ft long Logboat, hollowed from a giant oak tree and dating back to around 295 BC, has been found off Brownsea Island, the largest of several islands dotting the harbour. Poole's extensive sandy beaches boast more Blue Flag awards than any other UK strand, and every Thursday evening in August there's a beach party with sports, calypso bands, barbecues and a spectacular firework finale.

The Quay is a great place to relax with a drink and watch people "just messing about in boats" or participating in one of the many watersports available. Nearby is the **Waterfront Museum**, which celebrates 2,000 years of maritime heritage, and the internationally famed **Poole Pottery** which has been producing high-quality pottery for more than 125 years. Its visitor centre stands on the site of the old factory. Here, visitors can watch a 12-minute video summarising two millennia of ceramic production, see the age-old processes under way, and children can have a

Highcliffe Castle

📖 stories and anecdotes 🐦 famous people 🎨 art and craft 🖌 entertainment and sport 🚶 walks

go themselves at this tricky craft. The Pottery Shop offers factory-direct prices and special savings on seconds, there are superb displays of the Pottery's distinctively designed creations, and a brasserie and bar overlooking the harbour.

Poole is well-provided with public parks offering a wide range of activities, and the town also boasts one of the county's great gardens, **Compton Acres,** which was created in the 1920s by Thomas William Simpson who spent the equivalent of £10 million in today's money. Amongst its varied themed areas, which include a lovely Italian Garden, the Japanese Garden enjoys an especially fine reputation. Japanese architects and workmen were brought over to England to create what is reputed to be the only completely genuine Japanese Garden in Europe, an idyllic setting in which only the most troubled spirit could not find solace. Magnificent sculptures enhance the grounds which also contain restaurants, a delicatessen, model railway exhibition and shops. From the Colonnade viewpoint there are grand views over Poole Harbour to the Purbeck hills beyond.

From Poole Quay there are regular cruises along the coast and ferries to **Brownsea Island** (National Trust), where there are quiet beaches with safe bathing. Visitors can wander through 500 acres of heath and woodland which provide one of the few remaining refuges for Britain's native red squirrel. In 1907, General Robert Baden-Powell carried out an experiment on the island to test his idea of teaching boys from all social classes the scouting skills he had refined during the Boer Wars. Just 20 boys attended that first camp: in its heyday during the 1930s, the world-wide Scouting Movement numbered some 16 million members in more than 120 countries.

CORFE MULLEN
7 miles NW of Bournemouth off the A31

With a population of more than 10,000, Corfe Mullen has a good claim to be the largest village in the country. Much of it is modern housing for commuters to Poole and Bournemouth but the old village beside the River Stour has retained its charm. The ancient mill, mentioned in the Domesday Book, has had its wheel rebuilt and is turning once again, albeit inside a glass case at the centre of a tearoom. There's a medieval church whose first rector, Walter the Clerk, was installed in 1162; a delightful 300-year-old manor house (private); and a traditional pub with a flagstone floor in one of the bars.

WIMBORNE MINSTER
7 miles NW of Bournemouth on the A349/A31

🏛 Wimborne Minster   🌿 Knoll Gardens & Nursery

🏛 Wimborne Model Town   🏛 Stapehill Abbey

🌿 Honeybrook Country Park   🏛 Kingston Lacy

🏛 Verwood Heathland Heritage Centre

🏛 Museum of East Dorset Life

Happily, the A31 now by-passes this beguiling old market town set amongst meadows beside the rivers Stour and Allen. The glory of the town is **Wimborne Minster** which, in 2005, celebrated 1300 years of ministry. It's a distinctive building of multi-coloured stone boasting some of the finest Norman architecture in the county and is also notable for its 14th century astronomical clock, and the 'Quarterjack', a life-sized figure of a grenadier from the Napoleonic wars, which strikes the quarter hours on his bells. Inside, the unique Chained Library, founded in 1686, contains more than 240 books, amongst them a 14th century manuscript on vellum.

🏛 historic building   🏛 museum   🏛 historic site   🌿 scenic attraction   🌿 flora and fauna

In the High Street, the Priest's House is a lovely Elizabethan house set amidst beautiful gardens. It houses the **Museum of East Dorset Life** which recreates 400 years of history in a series of rooms where the decoration and furnishings follow the changing fashions between Jacobean and Victorian times. There's also an archaeology gallery with hands-on activities, a Gallery of Childhood, delightful walled garden and summer tea room.

In King Street you can see Wimborne as it was in the early 1950s – but at one tenth the size. **Wimborne Model Town** presents a meticulous miniature version of the town, complete with an Old English fair and a working small-scale model railway. Also in the heart of the town, **Verwood Heathland Heritage Centre** has permanent displays of the local Verwood pottery industry. The centre occupies a former pottery drying shed and visitors may get the opportunity to throw a pot or two themselves.

On the outskirts of Wimborne, **Honeybrook Country Park** has a family yard with lots of pure breed animals, dray and pony

Wimborne Minster Model Town

King Street, Wimborne Minster,
Dorset BH21 1DY
Tel: 01202 881924
e-mail: info@wimborne-modeltown.com
website: www.wimborne-modeltown.com

Built well over 50 years ago, the superb 1/ 10th scale models continue to surprise and amaze visitors from all over the world with their superb quality and realism. You can get really close up and even touch the buildings, checking out the minute detail of over 100 shop window displays. Created to capture the essence of a typical market town of rural England during the 1950s, the Model Town provides the visitor with a unique experience which will live long and fondly in the memory.

Discover the newly designed and built interactive Model Train and Tram working layout, all set within a room themed as a 1950s railway station waiting room. A new addition to the Model Town is the Sunflower Garden Putting Lawn where you can have fun and enjoy the challenge. Look out for the many special events hosted throughout the season including the spectacular and enchanting Candlelight Evenings in August.

A full range of refreshments are available from the tea rooms, much of which is fresh mouth-watering, homemade fayre. The grown ups can relax and enjoy their cream teas while the children play happily close-by . Wendy Street is designated a safe play area for younger visitors, whilst bargain hunters will enjoy checking out the Gift Shop, which is full of unusual and interesting items.

The Model Town is open every day from 24th March through to 29th October, including School Half-Term Holiday.

rides, an adventure playground, a period farmhouse, a natural maze, river and countryside walks, tea room and picnic areas. The park also hosts events such as country sports days, tug-of-war competitions, beer tasting and barn dances.

A mile or so northwest of Wimborne, **Kingston Lacy** (National Trust) is an imposing 17th century mansion which has been the home of the Bankes family for more than 300 years and exerts an irresistible attraction for anyone who loves the paintings of such Old Masters as Brueghel, Titian, Rubens and Van Dyck. Apart from those owned by the queen, the pictures on display here are generally acknowledged by experts as forming the finest private collection in the country. Kingston Lacy's fabulous gilded-leather Spanish Room and elegant Grand Saloon, both with lavishly decorated ceilings, and a fascinating exhibit of Egyptian artefacts dating back to 3000 BC, all add to the interest of a visit. Outside, you can wander through 250 acres of wooded parkland which contains a genuine Egyptian obelisk of c.150BC and is also home to a herd of splendid Red Devon cattle. A new addition in 2005 was the Edwardian Japanese Tea Garden which follows traditional Japanese design with features such as a waiting pavilion, a dry stream raked with gravel, and a thatched tea house. Also within the grounds of the Kingston Lacy estate are Badbury Rings, an Iron Age hill fort reputedly

Wimborne Minster

the site of a great campaign by King Arthur.

A couple of miles to the east of Wimborne, **Stapehill Abbey** was built in the early 1800s as a Cistercian nunnery providing a peaceful place for retreat and contemplation. Visitors can enjoy the serenity of the restored Nuns' Chapel, stroll around the cloisters and enjoy the glorious award-winning gardens. Inside, there are reconstructions of a Victorian parlour, kitchen and washroom, and an outstanding Countryside Museum recording rural life in the area. Stapehill is also home to a group of working craftspeople, special events are held throughout the year, and the site also contains a licensed coffee shop and picnic areas.

Just to the east of Stapehill are **Knoll Gardens & Nursery** whose gardens were planted some 30 years ago and are famous for the mature trees and shrubs that provide a wealth of colour throughout the seasons. The gardens specialise in grasses and perennials but in all there are more than 6,000 plant species, including many fine trees. Tumbling waterfalls and ponds in an informal English setting add to the appeal.

HORTON
12 miles NW of Bournemouth off the B3078

Just outside the village stands Horton Tower (private), a six-storey triangular folly built in the mid-1700s by Humphrey Sturt, the lord of the manor, as an observatory from which he could watch the movement of deer. The tower appeared in the film *Far From the Madding Crowd*.

WIMBORNE ST GILES
15 miles NW of Bournemouth off the B3081

🏛 Church of St Giles

A pretty village set beside the River Allen, Wimborne St Giles is notable for its **Church of St Giles**. It was rebuilt after a fire by the distinguished architect Sir Ninian Comper who also contributed the fine stained glass. Also worth seeing are the marvellous monuments, notably to Sir Anthony Ashley and to the 7th Earl of Shaftesbury (who is even more memorably honoured by the statue of Eros in Piccadilly Circus).

VERWOOD
12 miles N of Bournemouth on the B3081

🐎 Dorset Heavy Horse Centre

Just north of Verwood village, **The Dorset Heavy Horse Centre** offers a real hands-on experience with these mighty beasts. You can drive a horse and wagon, or a vintage tractor, or have a go at logging or ploughing with the heavy horses. Suitable for all ages and weather conditions, the centre also has a display of gypsy caravans, animal feeding and handling, pedal tractors and go carts, a straw slide barn and a resident menagerie of donkeys, llamas,

kune kune pigs, miniature ponies and pigmy goats. There's also a café, picnic area and gift shop.

CRANBORNE
15 miles N of Bournemouth on the B3078

🏛 Church of St Mary   🏛 Cranborne Manor

🏛 Edmonsham House & Gardens

A picturesque village in a glorious setting, Cranborne sits on the banks of the River Crane with a fine church and manor house creating a charming picture of a traditional English village. The large and imposing **Church of St Mary** is notable for its Norman doorway, 13th century nave, and exquisite 14th century wall-paintings. **Cranborne Manor** was built in Tudor and Jacobean times and acquired by Robert Cecil, Elizabeth I's Chief Minister, and is lived in today by his descendant, Viscount Cranborne. The house is not open to the public but visitors can explore the gardens on Wednesdays during the season, and the Cranborne Manor Garden Centre, which specialises in old fashioned roses, is open all year. The present manor house stands on the site of a royal hunting lodge built by King John for his hunting forays in Cranborne Chase. Much of the huge forest has disappeared but detached areas of woodland have survived and provide some splendid walks.

To the south of the village lies **Edmonsham House & Gardens,** a superb Tudor manor house with Georgian additions that has been owned by the same family since the 1500s. Guided tours of the house are conducted by the owner; the grounds contain a walled organic garden, a six-acre garden with unusual trees and spring bulbs, and a stable block that is a fine example of Victorian architecture.

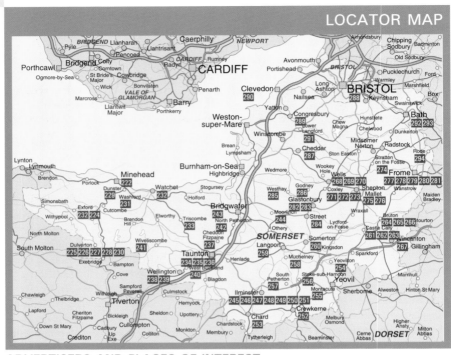

ADVERTISERS AND PLACES OF INTEREST

🏛 historic building   🏛 museum   🏛 historic site   ♨ scenic attraction   🌱 flora and fauna

4|Somerset

Was Cadbury Castle really King Arthur's Camelot? Did Joseph of Arimathea really walk through England's green and pleasant land to plant a thorn from Christ's crown of thorns at Glastonbury, where it blossomed once a year on the day of Christ's resurrection? Was it really at Athelney that King Alfred, deep in thought, allowed the cakes to burn? Myth and legend seem to be as integral to Somerset as its cider orchards and Cheddar cheese, its free-roaming ponies on Exmoor and the olde-worlde pubs with their skittle alleys.

Many literary luminaries found inspiration here. Exmoor provided the setting for RD Blackmore's great historical romance *Lorna Doone*; Wordsworth and Coleridge both lived in the county for several years and it was during their countless walks over the Somerset hills that they fashioned their *Lyrical Ballads*, a new kind of plain speaking verse that inspired the Romantic Revolution. Tennyson was a frequent visitor to the county and it was for his Clevedon friend, Arthur Hallam, that he spent 17 years perfecting his great lyrical poem *In Memoriam*.

Hallam was a member of the Elton family whose great house, Clevedon Court, is just one of many fine mansions within the county borders. Others include the late-medieval stone manor house of Lytes Cary, the Palladian Hatch Court and the exquisite Montacute House, built in the late 16th

🎭 stories and anecdotes   🐦 famous people   🎨 art and craft   🎟 entertainment and sport   🥾 walks

Glastonbury Tor

century for Elizabeth I's Master of the Rolls. The fine houses are sometimes overshadowed by their gardens. There are some splendid examples here particularly those, such as Barrington Court, Hestercombe Gardens and Tintinhull House Gardens, that were planted, or influenced, by the early-20th century landscape gardener, Gertrude Jekyll.

A wealth of prehistoric remains have been found within the county, but two of the area's most popular and famous attractions are both natural – Cheddar Gorge and the caves at Wookey Hole. With cliffs over 400 feet high on either side of the road that runs through the bottom of the gorge, Cheddar is indeed a spectacular sight, while the caves at Wookey Hole, from which the River Axe emerges, are

famous for their echos and for their fantastic stalagmite and stalactite formations.

Somerset also contains the smallest city in England, Wells. It is also one of the country's most delightful cities, clustered around its superb cathedral. This magnificent building boasts a truly wonderful Astronomical Clock which was installed in the 14th century and is still functioning perfectly.

To the north of the Mendip Hill lies the city of Bath, which in the 18th century became the most fashionable spa town in the country. Some 1,600 years earlier, it was equally fashionable among the Romans. Close by is the West Country's largest city, Bristol, Sir John Betjeman's favourite English city which, he asserted, had "the finest architectural heritage of any city outside London".

Minehead

🐦 North Hill Nature Reserve ⬙ Somerwest World

⬙ West Somerset Railway

Award-winning floral displays and gardens, a tree-lined avenue leading to a recently constructed promenade and a sandy beach, a wide range of shops, pubs, restaurants and open-air cafes, and an extensive choice of family attractions and amusements – Minehead has everything you expect of a successful English seaside resort. There are still thatched cottages in the picturesque Higher Town and the unspoilt acres of the Exmoor National Park stretch away to the west and south.

Despite sounding like a product of the industrial age, Minehead is an attractive and popular seaside town, lying at the foot of the wooded promontory known as North Hill. It is one of the oldest settlements in Somerset. A busy Bristol Channel port since the time of the Celts, the old harbour lies in the lee of North Hill, making it one of the safest landing places in the West Country. At one time, ships arrived here with wool and livestock from Ireland, crops from the plantations of Virginia, coal from the South Wales valleys and day trippers from Cardiff and Bristol. The merchants and paddle steamers have gone and nowadays the harbour is the peaceful haunt of sailing dinghies and pleasure craft.

There is a good view of the old port from the **North Hill Nature Reserve** and a three-mile-walk starting near the lifeboat station on the harbour side is an excellent way to explore this area of Minehead and its surroundings. The 14th century parish Church of St Michael stands in a prominent position below

North Hill. For centuries, a light was kept burning in its tower to help guide ships into the harbour. Inside, the church contains a number of unusual features, including a rare medieval prayer book, or missal, which once belonged to Richard Fitzjames, a local vicar who went on to become Bishop of London in 1506.

The decline of Minehead as a port was offset by its gradual expansion as a seaside resort and the town went to great lengths to attract a suitably respectable clientele. So much so, in fact, that there was a local bylaw in force until 1890 that forbad anyone over 10 years of age from swimming in the sea "except from a bathing machine, tent or other effective screen". The arrival of the

Minehead

West Somerset Railway

*The Railway Station, Minehead,
Somerset TA24 5BG Tel: 01643 704996
website: www.west-somerset-railway.co.uk*

Why not unwind as the steam trains of
the West Somerset Railway take you
on a leisurely 20-mile journey between
Bishops Lydeard (near Taunton) and
Minehead, taking in the sights, sounds
and even the unique smells of the golden age of rail travel? As your train makes its way
along, the glorious Somerset countryside offers constantly changing views through the
windows. The intimacy of the Quantock Hills country, Exmoor in the distance and
views from the Exmoor coast across the sea to South Wales all feature at different
times. Ten stations, lovingly restored and maintained by volunteers offer a whole range
of things to do.

railway in 1874 failed to trigger the rapid
expansion experienced by some other
seaside resorts. Nevertheless, during World
War I, Minehead was able to provide an
escape from the ravages of war at timeless
establishments like the Strand Hotel, where
guests were entertained by such stars as
Anna Pavolva and Gladys Cooper. Changes
to Minehead over the years have been
gradual but the most momentous change
came in 1962 when Billy Butlin opened a
holiday camp at the eastern end of the
esplanade. Now updated , this popular
attraction has done much to transform
present-day Minehead into an all round
family resort.

The town is also the northern terminus of
the **West Somerset Railway** (see panel
above), the privately-owned steam railway that
runs for 20 miles between the resort and
Bishop's Lydeard, just northwest of Taunton.
Vintage locomotives up to 80 years old
trundle along the route that follows the coast
as far as Blue Anchor, which has a station next

to the beach and a small Great Western
Railway museum, then on to Watchet which
has a Victorian station with a small gift shop.
The route then turns inland and travels
through peaceful countryside to Bishop's
Lydeard.

Around Minehead

SELWORTHY
3 miles W of Minehead off the A39

🌱 Horner & Dunkery National Nature Reserve

This picturesque and much photographed
village is situated on the side of a wooded hill.
Just to the northwest lies **Selworthy Beacon**,
one of the highest points on the vast
Holnicote Estate. Covering some 12,500 acres
of Exmoor National Park, it includes a four-
mile stretch of coastline between Minehead
and Porlock Weir. There are few estates in the
country that offer such a variety of landscape.
There are north-facing cliffs along the coast,
traditional villages and hamlets of cottages

🏛 historic building   🖼 museum   🏛 historic site   🌾 scenic attraction   🌱 flora and fauna

and farms and the **Horner and Dunkery National Nature Reserve** where **Dunkery Beacon**, the highest point on Exmoor, rises to 1,700 feet. Virtually the full length of the Horner Water lies within the estate, from its source on the high moorland to the sea at Bossington Beach, one of the best examples of a shingle storm beach in the country. The whole area is noted for its diversity of wildlife and the many rare plant species to be found.

This National Trust-owned estate has more than 100 miles of footpaths through fields, moors and villages for walkers to enjoy while the South West Coast Path curves inland at Hurlstone Point to avoid landslips in the soft Foreland sandstone. Among the settlements in the estate is the village of Selworthy created by Sir Thomas Dyke-Acland to house his estate workers. West of this model village is another estate village, Allerford, which has an elegant twin-arched packhorse bridge. In Allerford's old school is a

Museum dedicated to the rural life of West Somerset. Among its many imaginatively presented displays are a Victorian kitchen, a laundry and dairy, and an old school room complete with desks, books and children's toys.

PORLOCK
7 miles W of Minehead off the A39

🏠 Dovery Manor 🗻 Porlock Hill

An ancient settlement once frequented by Saxon kings, in recent decades Porlock has become a popular riding and holiday centre. The village is filled with lovely old buildings, most notably the 15th century

Dovery Manor with its striking traceried hall window and the largely 13th century parish church that lost the top section of its spire during a thunderstorm in the 17th century. Porlock has the feel of a community at the end of the world as it lies at the foot of **Porlock Hill**, a notorious incline where the road rises 1,350 feet in less than three miles, with a gradient of 1 in 4 in places.

PORLOCK WEIR
9 miles W of Minehead off the A39

🏠 Culborne Church

Today this hamlet has a small tide-affected harbour full of pleasure craft but Porlock Weir was once an important seaport. The Danes sacked it on a number of occasions in the 10th century. In 1052, Harold, the future king of England, landed here from Ireland to begin a short-lived career that ended at the Battle of Hastings in 1066. A pleasant and picturesque

Porlock Weir

🎬 stories and anecdotes 🦅 famous people 🎨 art and craft ✒ entertainment and sport 🚶 walks

PUT YOUR FEET UP AT THE
EXMOOR WHITE HORSE

After an exhilarating day spent exploring the spectacular beauty that is Exmoor, there is nothing quite like kicking your boots off and enjoying some special Exmoor Hospitality at the Exmoor White Horse Inn. You can relax with a drink beside one of our real log fires, savour our delicious local Fayre and unwind for the night in one of our 28 sumptuous rooms, each with a character of its own.

Try your hand at something new, we can arrange organised walks, red deer spotting, Exmoor safaris, fly fishing tuition, horse riding, mountain biking and clay shooting. At the end of the day, when you have discovered the best of Exmoor, all you need to do is let us take care of you in true Westcountry style.

Exford, Exmoor National Park, West Somerset. TA24 7PY.
Tel: (01643) 831229 Fax: (01643) 831246
E: info@exmoor-whitehorse.co.uk
W: www.exmoor-whitehorse.co.uk

EXMOOR WHITE HORSE
Truly the Heart of Exmoor

🏠 historic building   🏛 museum   🏚 historic site   ♧ scenic attraction   🌱 flora and fauna

WHITE HORSE GALLERY

The Exmoor White Horse Inn, Exford,
Exmoor National Park, Somerset TA24 7PY
Tel: 01643 831229
website: www.peterhendrie.co.uk

Renowned photographer Peter Hendrie exhibits his photographs both in his gallery and throughout the inn, including the bedrooms, restaurant and bar. He specialises in creative landscape photographs of Exmoor and North Devon and has many exclusive images from around the world. Peter has also produced calanders, greetings cards and two books, on Exmoor and North Devon. He can often be found in his gallery for a chat or you can preview a collection of his work by visiting his website.

place, Porlock Weir offers a number of interesting attractions, including a working blacksmith's forge and museum and a glass studio where visitors can see lead crystal being made in the traditional manner. A short distance offshore a **Submerged Forest**, a relic of the Ice Age, can be seen at low tide.

From Porlock Weir an attractive one-and-a-half-mile walk leads up through walnut and oak to **Culbone Church**, arguably the smallest church in regular use in England, and certainly one of the most picturesque. A true hidden treasure, measuring only 33 feet by 14 feet, this superb part-Norman building is set in a wooded combe that once supported a small charcoal burning community and was at other times home to French prisoners and lepers.

OARE
11 miles W of Minehead off the A39

🐿 RD Blackmore

Set deep in a secluded valley, Oare is one of the highlights for pilgrims following the Lorna Doone Trail. According to **RD Blackmore's** novel, it was in the narrow little 15th century church here that his heroine was shot at the wedding altar by the villainous Carver Doone. Blackmore knew the church well since his

grandfather was rector here in the mid-1800s.

LISCOMBE
13 miles SW of Minehead off the B3223

🏛 Tarr Steps

Just west of the moorland village of Liscombe is an extraordinary survival from prehistoric times. **Tarr Steps** is the longest clapper bridge anywhere in the world, its huge stone slabs supported by low stone pillars extending 180ft across the River Barle. It's a mystery where the stones slabs came from since there are no similar rocks anywhere near. Geologists believe they were probably left here by retreating glaciers at the close of the Ice Age.

WINSFORD
7 miles S of Minehead off the A396

One of the prettiest villages in Exmoor, with picturesque cottages, a ford and no fewer than seven bridges, including an old packhorse bridge. On a rise to the west of the village stands the medieval church with a handsome tall tower that dominates both the village and the surrounding area. This idyllic spot was the birthplace of the firebrand Ernest Bevin, founder of the Transport &

📖 stories and anecdotes 🐿 famous people 🎨 art and craft ✐ entertainment and sport 🚶 walks

Wimbleball Lake

Distance: *4.4 miles (7.0 kilometres)*

Typical time: *105 mins*

Height gain: *200 metres*

Map: *Outdoor Leisure 9 Exmoor*

Walk: *www.walkingworld.com ID:1346*

Contributor: *Paul Edney*

Pay and Display car park at the South West Lakes Trust site off the A396 Minehead to Tiverton Road.

The only road walking, a short section on a quiet lane, is got out of the way at the start. Be sure to leave time for a refreshing pot of tea here after your walk but please note the seasonal opening times. You are soon off the road and gain an impressive view of Wimbleball dam as you round a corner. You can also now see Haddon Hill above you. Once through a short section of Haddon Wood and out on to the open heath the views all around but especially behind you over Wimbleball Lake are superb and get even better as you gain height. Take plenty of breaks to admire these views up to the triangulation point.

This is the highest part of the walk. The descent is gentle at first with the views over the lake on your left as you cross the heath. When you leave the heath and go downhill through the trees the going becomes steeper but nowhere is it uncomfortably so. This short section of woodland is quite open and gives a good opportunity for bird spotting. Through the trees and you are now almost at the lake

and will stay in contact with it nearly all the way back to the car park.

Once over the dam the path stays close to the lakeside and heads back to the sailing club adjacent to the start. This path comprises a mixture of woodland and open grassland with an occasional wooden bench on which to sit and look across the water before that pot of tea from the cafe in the car park.

Tea shop, picnic tables, grass play area, toilets, phone and children's play area at the start. Toilets at the Haddon Hill car park just off route at waypoint 7.

Lake/loch, toilets, play area, birds, great views, cafe

1 | Leave the car park by the gate to the left of the tearoom back onto the road and turn left. At the sailing club sign, 200 metres up the road, keep straight on up the No Through Road.

2 | At the sharp left-hand bend take the track on the right past the farm buildings, through a gate and down a paved track.

3 | At the Y junction go through the left-hand gate and down the concrete road towards the dam. When you reach the dam turn right across the dam wall. Once over the dam go right at the T-junction signed Bury '2½ miles'.

4 | After about 150 metres, take the steep steps in a gap in the wall on the left signed 'Footpath to Haddon Hill'.

5 | The path through the trees ends at a stile over a wire fence. Over the stile turn right on the wide gravel path for 10 metres then take

the faint path on the left onto the heath land. Head up the hill following the faint path. At times there are choices of paths but it does not really matter which ones you choose as long as you continue to head up, zig zagging towards the highest point in front of you where you will find the Hadborough triangulation point.

6 | The triangulation point is set back beyond the main path, crossing in front of you, in a patch of heather and gorse bushes. Turn left here and follow the wide path gently down hill across the heath with superb views of Wimbleball Lake on your left.

7 | Pass Haddon Hill car park and toilets on your right, keeping ahead on the main path until you reach the tarmacked road. Cross here onto the path. After only about 20 metres turn left at this faint cross-roads. The path heads down hill, initially alongside gorse bushes, narrow at first then opening up slightly when it starts going through sparse woodland. Cross the wider path when you meet it and continue on the other side on the narrow path downhill though the trees.

8 | Near the bottom of the hill, just above the lake, you meet the wide bridleway that runs between Bury and Upton. Turn left here signed 'Bridleway to Dam and Bury'.

9 | The bridleway joins the road, the same one you crossed at the top of the hill, by these large boulders. Turn right here and take the

road down the hill signed 'Wimbleball Dam and Bury'.

10 | Turn right across the dam. At the far side of the dam turn right, over the stile and follow the grassy path above the lake.

11 | The path goes through trees above the lake, across fields then over a little bridge. Ignore the gate for the farm on the left and follow the grassy path heading off to the right.

12 | Keep following the grass path until you reach the sailing club that you pass on the left. At the gate above the sailing club turn left on the track ahead, past the children's play area on your right, up to the gate onto the main road which you passed at waypoint 2. Turn right here for the 200 metres back to the start.

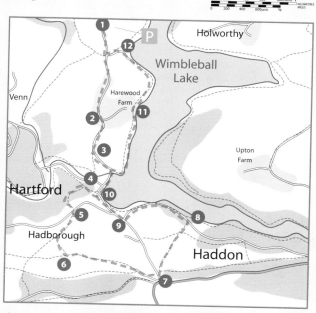

MAGIC FINGERS AT NUMBER SEVEN

No. 7 High Street, Dulverton, Somerset TA22 9HB
Tel: 01398 324457
website: www.magicfingers.co.uk

Magic Fingers at Number Seven is a successful family run business set up in 1998 with the aim of tempting customers with luxurious items, beautifully crafted by local and national designer makers.

The three creators behind Magic Fingers – Jan, Davina and Christopher – all have an art and design background.

Their styles work well together and the shop interior, and evolving displays, reflect their natural flair. "Live for colour and the seasons" they say, "celebrate life and let us help you enhance your home surroundings". They put a lot of energy is into sourcing innovative work that they feel is refreshing to the eye and works well together.

Many of their designers produce work exclusively for Magic Fingers so you can be sure you will always find true uniqueness.

They aim to provide affordable design in a relaxed and welcoming environment. A recent addition to their range is a selection of beautifully illustrated children's books that combines their love of storytelling, magic and art. Magic Fingers is open from 10am to 5pm but closed on Wednesdays and Sundays.

CAROLE KING EMPORIUM

29 High Street, Dulverton, Somerset TA22 9DJ
Tel: 01398 324692

According to the dictionary, "emporium" is derived from the Greek word for a journey and at the **Carole King Emporium** customers can indeed make a journey through a wonderful treasure trove of items from many different sources. In this stylish shop on Dulverton's main street, you'll find ladies clothing from France, beautiful Italian shoes by Riva, luxurious sheepskin boots by Ugg, Longchamp bags and English leather belts.

Also on display are a whole range of items for the home, including hand-painted furniture and mirrors, a tempting selection of fake fur or silk throws and cushions and English silver-plated tableware, goblets and candleabras. The list does not stop there

– you can find unusual doorstops, porcelain hand made witches, and sculptures and bronzes by local artists. If you are looking for an interesting gift, you will almost certainly find exactly what you want at Carole King.

🏠 historic building   📷 museum   🏛 historic site   🦢 scenic attraction   🌶 flora and fauna

General Workers Union, World War II statesman and Foreign Secretary in the postwar Labour government.

DULVERTON

12 miles S of Minehead on the B3222

RF Delderfield

Dulverton is a lively little town set in the wooded valley of the River Barle on the edge of Exmoor. Small though it is, the town boasts a suprising variety of attractions and inn recent years has come to challenge Dunster in popularity. The Exmoor National Park has an excellent Visitor Centre here, housed in what used to be the local workhouse. Close by is the Guildhall Heritage & Arts Centre (free) which has displays on Dulverton's history over the past century and

---

VANILLA JEWELLERY & LEATHER GOODS

19 High Street, Dulverton, Somerset TA22 9HB
Tel: 01398 324204   e-mail: barbaramiers@hotmail.com

In recent years the little town of Dulverton has become well-known for its wonderful range of small specialist shops. Barbara Miers established **Vanilla Jewellery and Leather Goods** in 2004 and today offers an enticing selection of quality items that includes premium jewellery, luxury handbags, leather accessories for men and women, Boccia watches and much more. Notable brands include Hearts and Crosses, beautiful glass jewellery made on Exmoor, Dower & Hall, Smith and Canova and Roberta Gandolfi handbags. Barbara has another outlet at 2 East Street, South Molton, Devon.

ASHWICK HOUSE HOTEL

Ashwick, Dulverton, Somerset TA22 9QD
Tel: 01398 323868
website: www.ashwickhouse.com

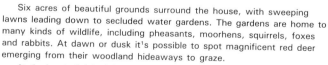

Ashwick House is unique and snuggles in glorious isolation on the south eastern edge of Exmoor National Park, high above the lush tree clad valley of the tumbling River Barle.It is a place where moorland, pasture and woodland meet. For fugitives from work and the stresses of urban life arriving at Ashwick is like stepping into another world.

Six acres of beautiful grounds surround the house, with sweeping lawns leading down to secluded water gardens. The gardens are home to many kinds of wildlife, including pheasants, moorhens, squirrels, foxes and rabbits. At dawn or dusk it's possible to spot magnificent red deer emerging from their woodland hideaways to graze.

At the heart of Ashwick House is a baronial style galleried hall furnished by the new owners with oriental pieces, which blend well with the Edwardian ambience. In winter months and chillier days its focal point is a welcoming log fire. Other reception rooms such as the library or oriental themed lounge are also available to residents.

At Ashwick, the pleasure of life are heightened by high quality cuisine, which has been traditional English but the new owners plan to enhance with a few tasteful additions to the menu introducing where it blends well, a few continental alternative flavours. Whenever possible, local fresh produce is being used.

---

 stories and anecdotes   famous people   art and craft   entertainment and sport   walks

THE CROOKED WINDOW GALLERY

7 High Street, Dunster,
Somerset TA24 6SF
Tel: 01643 821606
e-mail: info@thecrookedwindow.co.uk
website: www.thecrookedwindow.co.uk

Opening Times:
Mon-Sat 10.30am-5.30pm
Sunday variable - please enquire
Other times by appointment

The Crooked Window Gallery is situated in Dunster's picturesque High Street and is so named because the movement in its timber framed construction has caused one of the shops bay windows to become distorted and bowed. The building dates from the 15th century and is unusual for its decorative 18th century plasterwork, or 'pargeting', a feature quite untypical of this area.

The gallery is owned and run by Robert and Margaret Ricketts. Robert buys, sells, collects and lectures on antiques. You might be surprised to find an impressive collection of ancient Chinese ceramics - not normally seen outside London.

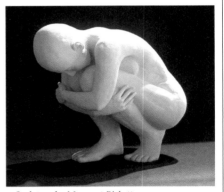

Sculpture by Margaret Ricketts

Margaret is an artist specialising in intricately detailed oil paintings of animals - especially horses, and landscapes. She also works in clay producing original ceramic sculptures.

Tang Horse

Within the atmospheric interior you will find an exciting range of jewellery in gold, silver, precious and semi-precious stones. There are quality crafts from other artists as well as interesting and unusual antique items - all eminently suitable as gifts.

 historic building   museum   historic site   scenic attraction   flora and fauna

LANCE NICHOLSON

9 High Street, Dulverton, Somerset TA22 9HB
Tel: 01398 323409   e-mail: lancenich@lancenich.f9.co.uk
website: www.lancenich.co.uk

Established in 1965, **Lance Nicholson** is now well-known nationally for its outstanding range of outdoor goods of every kind. Clothing includes the new Barbour Breathable jackets, Barbour, Le Chameau and Chris Brasher boots, jumpers, sporting ties and Barmah leather hats. Anglers will find a comprehensive range of tackle and accessories, including the shop's own West Country rods. The shop also stocks new and second-hand shotguns and rifles; walking sticks of all shapes and sizes, tractor and Land Rover mugs, Land Rover clothing, and even squirrel traps for effective pest control.

is also home to the Exmoor Photographic Archive which stages special exhibitions throughout the year. An integral p0art of the centre is Granny Baker's Cottage with its authentic Victorian kitchen. There's also a Gallery which provides a showcase for the work of local artists and craftspeople. The Centre is open from mid-April to the beginning of November.

It's a pleasure to stroll around the town with its ancient bridge, traditional hostelries, cosy tea room and family-run shops selling anything from antiquarian books to country clothing, gifts to old-fashioned fish and chips. Regular community markets offer a wide range of local crafts, while the highlights of the year in Dulverton are the Carnival, held on the first Saturday in October, and "Dulverton by Starlight" on the first Sunday in December.

DUNSTER

2 miles SE of Minehead on the A396

🏠 Dunster Castle   🏠 Dunster Working Watermill

🏠 Dunster Priory   🏠 Luttrell Arms   🏠 Dovecote

Although Dunster is one of the most popular of Exmoor's villages, this ancient settlement is also one of the least typical as it lies in the fertile valley of the River Avill. No visitor will be surprised to learn that this landscape

inspired Mrs Alexander to compose the hymn *All Things Bright and Beautiful.* The village is dominated by **Dunster Castle** standing outside the village on the top of the wooded Conygar Hill. Founded by William de Mohun on this natural promontory above the River Avill, just a few years before the Domesday Book was completed in 1089, the castle passed into the hands of the Luttrell family in 1379. It remained in that family until it was given to the National Trust in 1976 by Lt Col GWF Luttrell. The medieval castle was remodelled in 1617 by William Arnold. During the English Civil War, Dunster Castle was one of the last Royalist strongholds in the West Country to fall and here the garrison only surrendered after a siege lasting 160 days. While several Jacobean interiors have survived, the castle underwent major alterations during the latter part of the 17th century. Some of the finest features date from that period, in particular the superb plasterwork in the dining room and the magnificent balustraded main staircase with its delicately carved flora and fauna. However, the overall medieval character of the exterior of the present day castle is due to restoration work undertaken by Anthony Salvin in the 1860s, when the castle was transformed into a

Dunster Castle

by the Luttrells in the early 17th century when the village was an important cloth trading centre. Such was Dunster's influence in this trade that a type of woollen cloth, renowned for its quality and strength, bears the village's name. The nearby **Luttrell Arms**, converted from a private residence into an inn in the mid-17th century, is more than 100 years older. Distinguished by its fine 15th century porch, the inn is one of the few places in the country where the once common custom of burning the ashen faggot is still observed. On Christmas Eve, the faggot, a bundle of 12 ash branches bound with green ash bands, is burnt in the inn's great fireplace and, as each band burns through, another round of hot punch is ordered from the bar. While the ash is burning, the company sings the ancient Dunster Carol and when the faggot is finally consumed a charred remnant is taken from the embers ready to light the following year's fire.

The inn once belonged to Cleeve Abbey while the village's principal religious house, **Dunster Priory**, was an outpost of Bath Abbey. Now largely demolished, the only parts of the priory to survive are the splendid priory church and an unusual 12th century dovecote that can be seen in a nearby garden. It still contains the revolving ladder once used to reach the roosting birds. The priory church, rebuilt by the monks in a rose pink sandstone as early as 1100, is one of the most impressive of Somerset's parish churches. The church tower was added in the 15th century but its most outstanding feature is undoubtedly the fan-vaulted rood screen that extends across the nave and aisles. At 54ft it is the longest in

comfortable and opulent country mansion. The steeply terraced gardens with their striking collection of rare shrubs and subtropical plants were also laid out around this time and the castle and gardens are surrounded by a 28-acre deer park through which there are several footpaths, as well as the 'Arbutus Walk' through the National Collection of strawberry trees.

The parkland of Dunster Castle is also home to another National Trust property, **Dunster Working Watermill,** built in the 18th century on the site of a pre-Norman mill. Now restored to working order, the mill, which is run as a private business, has a shop selling mill flour, muesli and mill souvenirs and a tearoom by the riverside.

Remnants of the ancient feudal settlement that grew up in the shelter of the castle can still be seen in the village today, particularly in the wide main street. At the north end of this street stands a small octagonal building, which is the former **Yarn Market**. This was erected

England and was built in 1498 after a squabble between the priory and the townspeople. The magnificent screen served to separate the monk's choir from the parish church.

Another striking medieval survival is the 13th century **Dovecote** which has a revolving wooden ladder inside which gave access to the 500 nesting boxes and their eggs. The squabs, or fledgling doves, provided a staple element of the medieval monk's diet.

On the southern edge of the village, the ancient Gallox Bridge, a medieval packhorse bridge, spans the River Avill.

CARHAMPTON

3 miles SE of Minehead on the A39

Madam Carne

A small inland village that was the site of a Viking victory in the 9th century. Carhampton's original village church was named after St Carantoc, an early Celtic missionary from across the Bristol Channel. He is reputed to have chosen this site for his ministry by throwing his stone altar overboard and following it to the shore. The present church building, though much restored, contains a remarkable 15th century painted screen that extends across the entire church. The old inn, near the churchyard lych gate, has the date 1638 set into its cobbled floor in sheep's knuckle bones.

Each January, the residents of Carhampton re-enact the ancient custom of **wassailing the apple trees.** A toast is made to the most productive apple tree in the district and cider is poured on to its trunk in a charming ceremony that probably has pagan origins. Local folklore tells of a mysterious woman from the village, **Madam Carne**, who died in 1612 having done away with three husbands. According to legend, her ghost returned home after her funeral to prepare breakfast for the mourners.

WASHFORD

6 miles SE of Minehead on the A39

Cleeve Abbey   Tropiquaria

This village is spread out across Vallis Florida, the flowery valley dedicated to 'Our

Cleeve Abbey

*Washford, Somerset TA23 0PS Tel: 01984 640377
website: www.english-heritage.org.uk*

On 25th June 1198 the new Abbey of Cleeve was founded, dedicated to the Blessed Virgin and originally named Vallis Florida or Vale of Flowers. Since then the black death, the Dissolution of the Monasteries, destruction of the Abbey Church and use as a farmhouse, have all played a part in the 800-year history of Cleeve Abbey. Today, it survives as a haven of peace and tranquillity, one of the undiscovered jewels of Somerset boasting magnificent architecture and hidden treasures. Some of the finest cloister buildings in England can be seen including the magnificent 15th century timber roof in the refectory with its exquisite carved angels, the unique medieval wall paintings of the Painted Chamber and the heraldic tile pavements. One of the greatest pleasures however is to explore the numerous nooks and crannies, which reveal hidden carvings and paintings, from the hands of craftsmen long ago.

stories and anecdotes   famous people   art and craft   entertainment and sport   walks

Blessed Lady of the Cliff'. Washford is dominated by **Cleeve Abbey** (see panel on page 351), the only monastery in Somerset that belonged to the austere Cistercian order founded in 1198 by the Earl of Lincoln. This abbey is fortunate in that it was not allowed to fall into disrepair after the Dissolution of the Monasteries in 1539 like many great monastic houses. The cloister buildings at Cleeve were put to domestic use and they are now among the most complete in the country. Although the cruciform abbey church has been reduced to its foundations, the refectory, chapter house, monks' common room, dormitory and cloisters remain. Most impressive of all is the great hall, a magnificent building with tall windows, a wagon roof decorated with

busts of crowned angels and medieval murals, and a unique set of floor tiles with heraldic symbols. The curved dormitory staircase has particularly fine archways and mullion windows, while the combined gatehouse and almonry, the last building to be constructed before the Dissolution, makes an imposing entrance to the abbey precinct.

A short distance northeast of the village is a more recent attraction, **Tropiquaria,** a wildlife park featuring a wide range of tropical animals. There is an aquarium here as well as an aviary and visitors are offered the chance to stroke snakes, tickle tarantulas and to get in touch with their wilder side. Children can swarm over the full-size pirate ships or work off some

---

THE LYNDA COTTON GALLERY

Swain Street, Watchet, Somerset TA23 0AG
Tel: 01984 631814
website: www.thelyndacottongallery.co.uk

The Lynda Cotton Gallery is situated in the ancient harbour town of Watchet and was established over 25 years ago. From here, it is said, the Ancient Mariner set sail in the poem *The Rime of the Ancient Mariner*. It has a long and fascinating maritime history dating back to before the Viking invasions. Watchet has two excellent museums and its beaches are legendary for their rich harvest of fossils. The port has been visited by Daniel de Foe and inspired Turner to produce an engraving of the town.

The Gallery represents the best local artists whose works are permanently displayed and represent a wide spectrum of subject matter and medium, from the abstract to the representational. It also shows a large selection of period works with an emphasis on the 1850s to the 1950s and has an interesting collection of early furniture and related items, many with their origins in the West Country. When weather permits, the visitor can take delight in strolling round the sculpture garden with its fascinating collection of contemporary sculpture. Among the number of services offered are the restoration of oil paintings and the supply of bespoke period frames. The Gallery offers extensive research facilities although a prior appointment for this service is essential. Free appraisals and valuations are available on Saturdays.

The Gallery is open six days a week, Monday – Saturday from 10am.

🏛 historic building   🏛 museum   🏛 historic site   ᏫᏫ scenic attraction   🌱 flora and fauna

energy in the indoor play castle; grown-ups may be more interested in the Radio Museum.

WATCHET
7 miles SE of Minehead on the B3191

Florence Wyndham

In the 6th century, St Decuman is said to have landed here from Wales with a cow that he brought along to provide sustenance. The town's name is derived from the Welsh for 'under the hill'. Charles I was once described as wearing a waistcoat of Watchet blue, possibly taken from the very distinctive colour of the cliffs here that were worked for their alabaster. By the 10th century the Saxon port and settlement here were important enough to have been sacked by the Vikings on at least three separate occasions and Watchet today remains the only port of any significance in Somerset. During the mid-19th century thousands of tons of iron ore from the Brendon Hills were being exported through the docks each year. Unlike many similar sized ports that fell into disuse following the arrival of the railway, Watchet is now a thriving marina for yachts and boats. It was from Watchet that Coleridge's imaginary crew set sail in *The Rime of the Ancient Mariner*, the epic poem written while the poet was staying at nearby Nether Stowey.

The scale of Watchet's parish church reflects the town's long-standing importance and prosperity. It is set well back from the town centre and contains several fine tombs belonging to the Wyndham family, the local lords of the manor who did much to develop the potential of the port. There is a local story that suggests that one 16th century member of the family, **Florence Wyndham,** had to be buried twice. The day after her first funeral the church sexton went down into church vaults secretly to remove a ring from her finger. When the coffin was opened, the old woman suddenly awoke. In recent years, the town has become something of a coastal resort and one of its attractions is the small museum dedicated to local maritime history.

WILLITON
7 miles SE of Minehead on the A39/A358

Bakelite Museum

The large village of Williton was once a Saxon royal estate. During the 12th century the manor was the home of Sir Reginald FitzUrse, one of the knights who murdered Thomas à Becket. To atone for his terrible crime, Sir Reginald gave half the manor to the Knights Templar. The other half of the property remained in the FitzUrse family until the death of Sir Ralph in 1350 whereupon it was divided between his daughters. The village today is the home of the diesel locomotive workshops of the West Somerset Railway and the **Bakelite Museum**, a fascinating place providing a nostalgic look at the 'pioneer of plastics'. Housing the largest collection of vintage plastics in Britain, the museum contains thousands of quirky and rare items, including spy cameras, monstrous perming machines and even a Bakelite coffin.

MONKSILVER
8 miles SE of Minehead on the B3188

Combe Sydenham Hal   Drake's Cannonball

Nettlecombe Court   Brendon Hills

This pretty village of charming old houses and thatched cottages has, in its churchyard, the graves of Elizabeth Conibeer and her two middle-aged daughters, Anne and Sarah, who were murdered in June 1775 in the nearby hamlet of Woodford. Their tombstone bears a message to the unidentified murderer:

Inhuman wretch, whoe'er thou art
That didst commit this horrid crime,
Repent before thou dost depart
To meet thy awful Judge Divine.

Just to the south of the village is a particularly handsome manor house, **Combe Sydenham Hall,** built in the middle of the reign of Elizabeth I by George Sydenham on the site of a monastic settlement. Above the entrance, there is a Latin inscription that translates as "This door of George's is always open except to ungrateful souls". This was also the home of Elizabeth Sydenham, George's daughter, who was to become the second wife of Sir Francis Drake. After becoming engaged, Sir Francis left his fiancée to go off looting for Spanish gold. Elizabeth grew so weary waiting for her betrothed to return that she resolved to marry another gentleman. According to local stories, she was on her way to the church, when a meteorite flew out of the sky and smashed into the ground in front of her. Taking this as a sign that she should wait for Sir Francis she called off the wedding and, eventually, the couple were reunited. The meteorite, now known as **'Drake's Cannonball'**, is on display in the great hall; it is said to bring good luck to those who touch it. The 500-acre grounds around the hall have been designated a country park and they contain a working corn mill complete with waterwheel, a herb garden, a peacock house and a herd of fallow deer. The estate also incorporates a modern trout farm that stands on the site of a fully restored Tudor trout hatchery that dates from the end of the 16th century.

A mile or so to the west lies another ancient manor, **Nettlecombe Court**, once the home of the Raleigh family, relations of another great Elizabethan, seafarer Sir Walter Raleigh. Later, the manor passed by marriage to the Cornish Trevelyan family and it is now a field studies centre open only by appointment.

To the southwest of the village are the **Brendon Hills**, the upland area within the Exmoor National Park from where, in the mid-19th century, iron ore was mined in significant quantities. The ore was then carried down a steep mineral railway to the coast for shipment to the furnaces of South Wales. At one time the Ebbw Vale Company employed almost 1,000 miners here and this strictly Nonconformist concern imposed a rigorous teetotal regime on its workers. Those wanting a drink had to walk across the moor all the way to Raleigh's Cross. The company also founded a miners' settlement with a temperance hotel and three chapels that became renowned for the achievements of its choir and fife and drum band. Those walking the slopes of the hills can still see sections of the old mineral railway. A two-mile stretch of the track bed leading down to the coast at Watchet is now a pleasant footpath.

EAST QUANTOXHEAD
11 miles SE of Minehead off the A39

🏛 Court House   🏚 Trendle Ring   🏔 Beacon Hill

This is a picturesque village of thatched cottages with a mill and millpond and a handsome old manor house, **Court House**, standing on a rise overlooking the sea. The original owner's family bloodline can be traced back to the 11th century and the Domesday Book but, in the 13th century, the manor passed by marriage to the Luttrell family, who were also to become the owners of Dunster

🏛 historic building   🏛 museum   🏚 historic site   🏔 scenic attraction   🌿 flora and fauna

Castle. The manor house seen today dates from the 16th and 17th centuries and was constructed by successive generations of the same family.

From the village there is a pleasant walk to the southeast, to Kilve, where the ruins of a medieval chantry, or college of priests, can be found. From here a track can be taken from the churchyard down to a boulder-strewn beach reputed to be a favourite haunt of glats – conger eels up to 10-feet long that lie in wait among the rocks near the shore. Once known as 'St Keyna's serpents', local people used to search for them using trained 'fish dogs'.

Further to the southeast lies the village of Holford, in the Quantocks, and a track from here leads up to the large Iron Age hill fortification known as **Dowsborough Fort**. Close by are also the dramatic viewpoints **Beacon Hill** and **Bicknoller Hill** and on the latter is another Iron Age relic, a livestock enclosure known as **Trendle Ring**. This is one of many archaeological sites in this area, which lies within the Quantock Hills Site of Special Scientific Interest.

Taunton

East Quantoxhead

-  Taunton Castle
-  Somerset County Museum
-  Somerset Military Museum
-  Bath Place
-  Somerset County Cricket Museum
-  Vivary Park
-  Taunton Racecourse
-  St Mary Magdalene Church
-  Bridgwater & Taunton Canal

Despite a settlement being founded here by the Saxon King Ine in the 8th century, Taunton, the county town of Somerset, has only been its sole centre of administration since 1935. Before that date, both Ilchester and Somerton had served as the county town. By Norman times the Saxon settlement had grown to have its own Augustinian monastery, a minster and a **Castle** – an extensive structure whose purpose had always been more as an administrative centre than as a military post. However, this did not prevent the castle from being the focus of two important sieges during the English Civil War. A few years later, the infamous Judge Jeffreys sentenced over 150 followers of the Duke of Monmouth to death here during the Bloody Autumn Assizes. Even today, the judge's ghost is said to haunt the castle grounds on September nights.

The castle now houses the **Somerset County Museum**, a highly informative museum that contains a large collection of exhibits on the

 stories and anecdotes    famous people    art and craft    entertainment and sport    walks

THE BLUE BALL INN

Triscombe, Taunton, Somerset TA4 3HE
Tel: 01984 618242 Fax: 01984 618371
e-mail: rogers.gerald@btinternet.com
website: www.blueballinn.co.uk

With its thatched roof, mellow stone walls and colourful window boxes and plants, **The Blue Ball Inn** looks irresistibly inviting. This lovely old hostelry is just one of a handful of buildings in the hamlet of Triscombe at the foot of the Quantock Hills. It lies just off the A358, and is easily accessible from junction 25 of the M5, Taunton and Minehead.

The interior of the inn is as captivating as the outside. There's a wealth of old beams, oak dividers separate the tables and the bar occupies a kind of wooden barn. Owners Gerald and Sue Rogers have made the Blue Ball well-known as one of the best rural venues for dining. The award-winning restaurant offers an outstanding à la carte menu that changes for each meal. "We pride ourselves," says Gerald, "on preparing our dishes from only fresh ingredients to give our customers a memorable and unhurried dining experience, whether for lunch or an evening meal". At lunchtime, a typical menu might offer a tian of crab, gazpacho & parmesan crisp as a starter, with loin of Brendan Hills rabbit, Quantock venison sausages, or tarte tatin of tomato, goat's cheese & basil dressing amongst the main courses. For lighter appetites, ploughman's and crusty rustic rolls with a choice of fillings are also available.

The dinner menu offers an equally extensive choice, again with many dishes based on local produce – steamed wild River Fowey mussels, for example, amongst the starters; fillet of Devon-ruby beef or whole roasted Dunster plaice as main dishes. Such is the reputation of the Blue Ball's cuisine – which boasts an AA Rosette – that booking a table in advance is strongly recommended, especially at weekends. The restaurant is currently closed for food on Sunday evenings and all day on Mondays, except for Bank Holidays, though Gerald and Sue hope to open at these times for both food and drink in the very near future.

The inn also has accommodation available in two cottages which are let on a bed & breakfast basis. Stag Cottage features an inglenook fireplace with gas effect fire, plus an upstairs bathroom with separate shower and Victorian style free-standing bath.

Pheasant Cottage is equally comfortable and its amenities include an en suite shower and bath.

🏛 historic building   🏛 museum   🏛 historic site   💧 scenic attraction   🌱 flora and fauna

archaeology and natural and human history of the county. The **Somerset Military Museum** and some medieval almshouses are also to be found at the castle site. Another of the town's old buildings is still making itself useful today. Somerset's County Cricket Ground occupies part of the priory grounds that once extended down to the river. A section of the old monastic gatehouse, known as the Priory Barn, can still be seen beside the cricket ground. Now restored, this medieval stone building is home to the fascinating **Somerset County Cricket Museum**.

Soaring above the town is the exquisite 163ft-high tower of **St Mary Magdalene Church.** A church has occupied this site since at least the 12th century but the present tower was rebuilt to its original design in 1862. In order to raise the stone during this construction, a pulley system was used operated by a donkey walking down Hammet Street. When the work was completed, the builders hauled the donkey to the top of the tower so that it could admire the view it had helped to create. The main body of the church is medieval and its interior

Vivary Park, Taunton

distinguished by a host of carved saints, apostles and gilded angels floating above the congregation. The road leading to the church, Hammet Street, retains an impressive number of original Georgian houses.

Ardent shoppers will want to seek out **Bath Place,** a delightful narrow street of cottages mixed with an assortment of individual shops offering a huge range of goods and services. In medieval times when this street was owned by the Bishop of Winchester it was called

📖 stories and anecdotes   🐦 famous people   🎨 art and craft   🎭 entertainment and sport   🚶 walks

PYRLAND FARM SHOP

Cheddon Road, Taunton, Somerset TA2 7QX
Tel/Fax: 01823 334148
e-mail: pyrland@ukgateway.net

For top quality food provided with personal friendly service, it would be hard to beat **Pyrland Farm Shop** where the Read family sell their own and locally reared meats, beef, pork, lamb, free range chicken and ducks, pork sausages, lamb burgers, beef burgers and bacon. There's also an excellent selection of vegetables, most of which are grown in the Reads' own garden, along with seasonal fruit, flowers and bedding plants. And you certainly shouldn't miss out on Mary Read's delicious Aga-baked cakes, quiches, jams and preserves, all made in the farmhouse kitchen using only the best ingredients.

Swains Street and was well known for its brothels, one of the few services not on offer here today. But you can have your hair done, your body pierced, lunch or dine in a choice of restaurants, and shop for arts and crafts, jewellery, glassware, books, computer games and much more.

Like many other West Country towns and villages, Taunton was a thriving wool, and later silk, cloth-making centre during the Middle Ages. The profits earned by the medieval clothiers went into buildings. Here their wealth was used in the construction of two huge churches: St James' and St Mary's. The rest of

THE OLD MILL

Netherclay, Bishops Hull, Taunton,
Somerset TA1 5AB
Tel/Fax: 01823 289732
website: www.theoldmillbandb.co.uk

A warm welcome and hearty hospitality awaits visitors to **The Old Mill** which stands on the bank of the River Tone just two miles from Taunton town centre. Ownership of the mill in the Slipper family dates back to 1870 and although the wheels have not turned since around 1920, much of the machinery has remained untouched. The mill building has been lovingly restored to provide luxurious bed & breakfast accommodation where guests can relax and unwind amidst the wheels and cogs of a bygone era.

The feeling of peace and tranquillity is enhanced by the sound of the river flowing by. Here you can watch the endless patience of the heron waiting for his catch, or glimpse a flash of sapphire as a kingfisher streaks across the mill pond. The Old Mill has two double bedrooms: the Mill Room with its beamed ceiling and restful décor, and the charming Cottage Room with a part sloping ceiling. Both have en suite facilities and both overlook the mill pond with its 150-year-old chestnut tree. To start your day, there's an extensive breakfast menu offering choices such as salmon scramble, egg & bacon muffin, and a truly hearty corn miller's breakfast. The Old Mill holds a Five Stars with Silver Award from Visit Britain.

🏛 historic building   🏛 museum   🏛 historic site   🏞 scenic attraction   🌿 flora and fauna

the town centre is scattered with fine buildings including the timber-framed Tudor House in Fore Street. Taunton is still a thriving place with an important commercial centre, a weekly market and a busy light industrial sector that benefits from some excellent transport links with the rest of the country.

Today, the **Bridgwater and Taunton Canal** towpath has been reopened following an extensive restoration programme and it provides pleasant waterside walks along its 14 miles. A relative latecomer, the canal first opened in 1827 and it was designed to be part of an ambitious scheme to create a freight route between Exeter and Bristol to avoid the treacherous sea journey around the Cornwall peninsula. For many years, the canal was the principal means of importing coal and iron from South Wales to the inland towns of Somerset and of exporting their wool and agricultural produce to the rest of Britain.

Taunton's major open space is the extensive **Vivary Park,** located at the southern end of the High Street and approached through a magnificent pair of Victorian ornamental gates. Fully restored with lottery money in 2002, the 70-acre park is home to the Vivary Golf Course, the Taunton Bowling Club and Taunton Deane Cricket Club. Other features include tennis courts, a wildlife lake, a model boat pond, a bandstand, an ornate fountain commemorating Queen Victoria, a model train track and children's play areas.

Taunton's attractive **National Hunt Racecourse** lies on the opposite side of the motorway from the town and the combination of good facilities, excellent racing and glorious location make it one of the best country racecourses in Britain.

Around Taunton

CHEDDON FITZPAINE
3 miles N of Taunton off the A358

🦗 Hestercombe Gardens

Spreading across the south-facing lower slopes of the Quantock Hills, **Hestercombe**

Hestercombe Gardens

Cheddon Fitzpaine, near Taunton,
Somerset TA2 8LG
Tel: 01823 413923 Fax: 01823 413747
e-mail: info@hestercombegardens.com
website: www.hestercombegardens.com

Lying on the southern slopes of the Quantocks, **Hestercombe Gardens** can be found on an estate that dates back to Saxon times but from the 14th to the late 19th century it was continuously owned by one

family, the Warres. It was Coplestone Warre Bampfylde who designed and laid out the magnificent landscaped garden in the mid 18th century. In 1873, the estate was acquired by the 1st Viscount Portman and it was his grandson, the Hon Edward Portman who, in 1904, commissioned Sir Edwin Lutyens to create a new formal garden that was planted by Gertrude Jekyll. Follies abound in this wonderful place and any walk around this 40-acre garden will include lakes, temples and magnificent views.

📖 stories and anecdotes   🐦 famous people   🎨 art and craft   🎭 entertainment and sport   🥾 walks

Gardens (see panel on page 359) form part of an estate that has been in existence since Saxon times. In 1872 the estate was acquired by the 1st Viscount Portman and it was his grandson, the Hon. Edward Portman, who commissioned Sir Edwin Lutyens to create a new formal garden that was planted by Gertrude Jekyll between 1904 and 1908. Within the 40-acre site are temples, streams and lakes, formal terraces, woodlands, cascades and some glorious views. Of all the gardens designed by the legendary partnership of Lutyens and Jekyll, Herstercombe is regarded as the best preserved.

STOKE ST GREGORY
7 miles NE of Taunton off the A378

🌿 Willows & Wetlands Visitor Centre

A straggling village in the heart of the Somerset Levels, Stoke St Gregory provides an appropriate location for the **Willows and Wetlands Visitor Centre** which was established by the Coates family which has more than 170 years experience in the willow industry. Their 80 acres of willow provide the natural material for craftsmen to weave a wide variety of baskets, furniture and garden items for sale. Guided tours are available.

BURROW BRIDGE
9 miles NE of Taunton on the A361

🧺 Somerset Levels Basket & Craft Centre

🏔 Burrow Mump

This village, on the River Parrett, is home to one of several pumping stations built in Victorian times to drain the Somerset Levels. The Pumping Station is open to the public occasionally throughout the year. Burrow Bridge is also the home of the **Somerset Levels Basket and Craft Centre**, a workshop and showroom stocked with handmade basket ware.

Rising dramatically from the surrounding wetlands is the conspicuous conical hill, **Burrow Mump** (National Trust). Situated at a fording point on the River Parrett, this knoll has at its summit the picturesque remains of an unfinished chapel to St Michael begun in 1793 but for which funds ran out before its completion. Burrow Mump is situated in the heart of the low lying area known as **King's Sedge Moor**, an attractive part of the Somerset Levels drained by the Rivers Cary and Parrett. A rich area of wetland, the moor is known for its characteristic pollarded willows, whose straight shoots, or withies, have been cultivated on a substantial scale ever since the taste for wicker developed during the 19th century. The traditional craft of basket-weaving is one of Somerset's oldest commercial activities and it once employed thousands of people. Although the industry has been scaled down

Burrow Mump

over the last 150 years, it is still alive and enjoying something of a revival.

The isolated Burrow Mump is reputed to be the site of an ancient fortification belonging to King Alfred, King of Wessex. He is said to have retreated here to escape from invading Vikings. It was during his time here that he is rumoured to have sought shelter in a hut in the nearby village of Athelney. While sitting at the peasant's hearth, absorbed in his own thoughts legend has it he burnt the cakes that the housewife had been baking. Not recognising the king, the peasant boxed his ears for ruining all her hard work. In the 19th century, a stone was placed on the site recalling that in gratitude for his hospitality, King Alfred founded a monastery on the Isle of Athelney.

Just to the west of Burrow Bridge, the **Bridgwater and Taunton Canal** winds its way through some of the most attractive countryside in the Somerset Levels. The restored locks, swing bridges, engine houses and rare paddle gearing equipment add further interest to this otherwise picturesque walk. The canal also offers a variety of recreational facilities including boating, fishing and canoeing while the canal banks are alive with both bird and animal life. North Newton, one of the pretty villages along the canal, is home to the small country manor of **Maunsel House** that is occasionally open to the public. At the canal's southern end, boats have access to the River Tone via Firepool Lock in the heart of Taunton.

HATCH BEAUCHAMP
5½ miles SE of Taunton on the A358

🏠 Hatch Court

Hatch Beauchamp is a pleasant village that has managed to retain much of its rural

atmosphere despite being on the major route between Ilminster and Taunton. Its name originates from *Hache*, a Saxon word meaning gateway and this refers to the ancient forest of Neroche whose boundary was just to the north and west. The suffix comes from the Norman family who owned the local manor and whose house stood on the land now occupied by one of the finest country houses in the area, **Hatch Court**. John Collins, a rich local clothier, commissioned the Axbridge architect, Thomas Prowse, to design the house. Built of attractive honey coloured limestone the resulting magnificent Palladian mansion was completed in 1755. Among its finest features are the hall with its cantilevered stone staircase, the curved orangery with its arched floor-to-ceiling windows and the semicircular china room with its elegant display of rare porcelain and glass. There is also a fine collection of 17th and 18th century English and French furniture, 19th and 20th century paintings and a small military museum commemorating Britain's last privately raised regiment, the Princess Patricia's Canadian Light Infantry. The extensively restored grounds incorporate a walled kitchen garden, rose garden, arboretum and deer park.

PITMINSTER
3 miles S of Taunton off the B3170

🏠 Poundisford Park

Recorded as Pipeminster in the Domesday Book, although there is no evidence of a minster ever having been built here, the village does have an old church containing 16th century monuments to the Colles family. Just to the north of Pitminster is **Poundisford Park**, a small H-shaped Tudor mansion standing within a delightful, wooded deer park that once belonged to the bishops of

CUNNINGHAM'S

14-18 North Street, Wellington, Somerset TA21 8LT
Tel: 01823 661944   Fax: 01823 669549
website: www.cunninghams2.com

The motto emblazoned outside **Cunningham's** reads: "Eat –
Drink – Listen". This exciting dining and entertainment
venue was the brainchild of local artist and musician Sarah
Cunningham. Influenced from an early age by her father
who was a boogie pianist and singer, Sarah was brought
up with jazz and the blues. Her singing career hit a high
point when she worked with Ronnie Scott and Steve
Wolfe, recording three songs with these highly regarded
songwriters. Returning to Somerset, her talents shone
through fronting The White School, another classic band
featuring well-known local musicians.

Sarah first established Cunningham's restaurant and
piano diner in Taunton but has now moved to Wellington
where there is more space but the relaxed, intimate atmosphere remains the same. Sarah's
fantastic vocal talents can be enjoyed every lunchtime from noon until 4pm, and in the evening
from 7pm until late. Other renowned jazz musicians also perform from time to time. The price
includes a Cunningham's special buffet, with an à la carte menu also available, a lunchtime pizza
and tapas menu, and a carvery on Sundays. Vegetarians are catered for and wedding parties
and other private functions are welcome.

C9

4 Fore Street, Wellington, Somerset TA21 8AQ
Tel: 01884 251998

"Where Innovation Meets Tradition" is the motto of **C9**
whose full title is Cloud 9 (Worldwide Gifts) Ltd. This
amazing shop is a treasure trove of gifts and
collectables, gadgets and gizmos, toys and cards and
wraps, as well as a traditional sweet shop and an
internet café.

The shop is particularly well known for its range of
Ty Beanies and other soft toys by Jellycat and others.
The mother and daughter team of Jill and Sam Parr are
both involved with choosing and buying stock, which
helps to ensure that all ages are catered for. They live
up to their motto by keeping in touch with new trends
whilst ensuring that traditional tastes are never
neglected.

A recent addition to their stock is an extensive range
of fancy dress and accessories. The shop has been
designed to make the very best use of the long, narrow
interior with the aid of custom-built display areas, and
the colour scheme of dark blue and silver is a feature throughout. Jill and Sam have been at this
location since 2001 and have recently opened a sister establishment in Tiverton.

🏛 historic building   🏛 museum   🏛 historic site   🍃 scenic attraction   🌿 flora and fauna

Winchester. The house is renowned for its fine plasterwork ceilings and the grounds incorporate a formal garden laid out in the Tudor style.

BRADFORD-ON-TONE
4 miles SW of Taunton off the A38

🎁 Sheppy's Cider

Sheppy's Cider has been making its renowned ciders since the early 1800s and now boasts more than 200 awards, including two gold medals. Visitors can stroll through the orchards with their wide variety of apples, visit the museum for an insight into the farming of yesteryear, watch a video following the cider-maker's year, and sample the finished product in the shop. Professional guided tours are available for parties of 20 or more. Other amenities on site include a licensed tearoom, picnic area and children's play area.

WELLINGTON
6 miles SW of Taunton on the A38

🏠 Town Hall   🏠 Wellington Monument

This pleasant old market town was once an important producer of woven cloth and serge and it owes much of its prosperity to Quaker entrepreneurs and, later, the Fox banking family. Fox, Fowler and Co were the last private bank in England to issue notes and they only ceased in 1921 when they were taken over by Lloyds. The broad streets around the town centre are peppered with fine Georgian buildings, including the neoclassical **Town Hall**. At the eastern end of the town, the much altered church contains the ostentatious tomb of Sir John Popham, the judge who presided at the trial of Guy Fawkes.

To the south of the town stands the **Wellington Monument**, a 175-foot obelisk

WILLOWBROOK NURSERY & GARDEN CENTRE
West Buckland, Nr Wellington, Somerset TA21 9HX
Tel: 01823 461324
website: www.willowbrooknurseryandgardencentre.co.uk

The Grabham family - Nigel, Carol and their son Stephen - provide a friendly, personal touch at the **Willowbrook Nursery and Garden Centre**, which stands at the foot of the Blackdown Hills on the main A38 between Wellington and Taunton. The centre first opened its doors in 1990, starting off as a nursery to serve the local area. It still grows a large proportion of the plants it sells, priding itself on the range and quality; they include a wide choice of award-winning shrubs, trees, roses, perennials, climbers, alpines and seasonal bedding plants.

The garden shop is stocked with everything that the novice or professional gardener might need from seeds and feeds to pots, tools, garden gifts, fencing, sheds, summerhouses and conservatories. The Pet Shop sells small animals and birds and everything needed to keep them healthy and amused. The Aquatic Centre features coldwater and tropical fish and accessories, and the Swimming Pool Centre also has hot tubs and spas on display. Willowbrook has a café/tea room with a lawned area and picnic benches where you can sit and relax..

🎬 stories and anecdotes   🦜 famous people   🎨 art and craft   🎢 entertainment and sport   🚶 walks

erected not long after the duke's great victory at Waterloo. The foundation stone was laid in 1817 by Lord Somerville but the monument was only completed in 1854. The duke himself visited the site and the town from which he took his title only once, in 1819.

WIVELISCOMBE
9 miles W of Taunton on the B3227

🏛 Gaulden Manor

This is an ancient and isolated village where the Romans once had a fort and a quantity of 3rd and 4th century coins have been uncovered in the area. Later, in medieval times, the local manor house was used as a summer residence of the bishops of Bath and Wells. The remains, including a striking 14th century archway, have now been incorporated into a group of cottages. During World War II, the church's crypt was used to store priceless historic documents and ecclesiastical treasures brought here from other parts of Somerset that were more at risk from aerial attack.

To the northeast of Wiveliscombe, close to the village of Tolland, is the delightful **Gaulden Manor,** an estate that dates from the 12th century although the present house is largely 17th century. This is very much a lived-in house with guided tours conducted by the owner. It contains some outstanding early plasterwork, fine furniture, and many examples of embroidery by the owner's wife. The interesting gardens include a herb garden, old fashioned roses, a bog garden and a secret garden beyond the monks' fish pond. Gaulden Manor once belonged to the Turberville family whose name was adapted by Thomas Hardy for use in his novel, *Tess of the D'Urbervilles* .

To the north and west of Wiveliscombe,

THE COURTHOUSE ANTIQUES & INTERIORS

The Square, Wiveliscombe, Somerset TA4 2JT
Tel: 01984 629010 Fax: 01984 629203

The pretty little town of Wiveliscombe lies in the Vale of Taunton and is well worth seeking out in order to pay a visit to **The Courthouse Antiques & Interiors** located in the heart of the town. Owned and run by Tia and Hoss Fatemi, it occupies one of the most interesting buildings in the town, a striking 3-storey structure with pantiled walls, latticed windows and some interesting carvings above the shop front. Inside, there are 9 rooms filled with a real treasure trove of antiques and home decorating ideas. Leading names of the interior decorating world represented here include Lewis & Wood, Henry Bertrand, Scott & Coles, Voyage and James Hare Silks.

There's also an impressive range of Persian carpets, furniture, chandeliers, lights and mirrors, bed linen & quilts, original oil paintings, limited edition prints and picture frames, as well as designer jewellery, Scottish leather handbags, outdoor clothing and much more – and all at value for money prices. A recent, and popular, addition to the amenities here is a coffee shop serving light lunches, filled baguettes and delicious home-made cakes. Open Mon-Sat 9.30am-5.00pm.

🏛 historic building   🏛 museum   🏚 historic site   🍃 scenic attraction   🌿 flora and fauna

below the Brendon Hills, are two reservoirs, Wimbleball and Clatworthy, which offer excellent facilities for picnickers, anglers and water sports enthusiasts.

NORTON FITZWARREN
2 miles NW of Taunton on the B3227

Large finds of Roman pottery have been excavated in and around this village, helping to confirm that Norton Fitzwarren was the Roman settlement of Theodunum. The village's name comes from the Saxon 'north tun' (meaning north farm) and the Norman family who were given the manor here after the Conquest. Norton Fitzwarren's antiquity and former importance gave rise to the old rhyme "When Taunton was a furzy down, Norton was a market town". Today, although the village has all but been consumed by its much larger neighbour, it has still managed to retain some of its individuality.

The land around Norton Fitzwarren is damp and fertile and, for hundreds of years, cider apples have been grown here. Cider made here is now transported all over the world, but until the early 19th century cider was a beverage very much confined to Somerset and the West Country. It was the Revd Thomas Cornish, a local clergyman, who first brought cider to the attention of the rest of the nation, when he produced a drink so appetizing that it found great favour with Queen Victoria. Close to one of the largest cider breweries in the area are the remains of an early Bronze Age bank and ditch enclosure, and artefacts excavated from here can

be seen in the county museum in Taunton.

BISHOP'S LYDEARD
5 miles NW of Taunton off the A358

🦢 West Somerset Railway   🏛 St Mary's Church

🏛 Bishop Lydeard's Mill

This large village is the southern terminus of the **West Somerset Railway,** a nostalgic enterprise that recaptures the era of the branch line country railway in the days of steam. This privately operated steam railway runs to Minehead on the Bristol Channel coast and, extending for nearly 20 miles, is the longest line of its kind in the country. It was formed when British Rail's 100-year-old branch between Taunton and Minehead closed in 1971. There are ten stations along the line and services operate between Easter and the end of October. The railway's special attractions include a first class Pullman dining car and the *Flockton Flyer* locomotive which is

St Mary's Church, Bishop's Lydeard

named after the 1970s children's drama series of that name which centred on the adventures of a family running a preserved railway.

St Mary's Church has a magnificent tower built of local red stone around 1450. Fortunately, it was spared the insensitive Victorian restoration of the interior. Look out for the 'hunky punks' on the outside of the tower. Hunky punk is the local term for the carved creatures which, unlike gargoyles that carry off rainwater, serve no useful function. St Mary's has five hunky punks – the one on the south-west corner of a dragon with a stone in its mouth looks particularly menacing.

The Grade II listed **Bishops Lydeard Mill** has been painstakingly restored over many years by the Back family and is now fully working. Among the many traditional trades and crafts displayed here are a wheelwright's

shop, transported from Devon and preserved exactly as it was left on the day the owner shut up shop, and an equally authentic blacksmith's shop. Other attractions include fun interactive displays; a gift shop and Dusty Miller's tearoom.

Bridgwater

🏚 Blake Museum   🏚 Somerset Brick & Tile Museum
🔖 Carniva   🔖 Somerset Space Walk

Situated at the lowest bridging point of the River Parrett, Bridgwater is an ancient inland port and industrial town. Despite having been fortified since before the Norman Conquest, the settlement that grew up around the castle remained little more than a village until an international trade in wool, wheat and other agricultural products began to develop in the

---

CLAVELSHAY BARN RESTAURANT

Clavelshay, North Petherton, Bridgwater,
Somerset TA6 6PJ
Tel: 01278 662629
e-mail: sue.milverton@btinternet.com
website: www.clavelshaybarn.co.uk

Set on a working dairy farm on the edge of the Quantock Hills, **Clavelshay Barn Restaurant** occupies a splendid old barn which was built around 1700 and has been sympathetically converted using traditional natural materials. The interior is simple, modern and comfortable, perfect for parties, wonderful for weddings – and for memorable meals. "We are passionate about good food" say owners Sue and Bill Milverton. "Somerset has some of the best produce in the country and our menu features dishes prepared from the very best local supplies, including our own home-reared beef".

The menu changes regularly but typically includes starters such as Exmoor Blue, Spinach and Bacon Tart; and main courses like Smoked Haddock with Tower Farms Cheddar sauce and prawns, or Pheasant Pot Roast with sage, juniper, garlic, red wine and caramel sauce. There are always vegetarian dishes and all vegetables are cooked *al dente* – just ask if you prefer them cooked more. To conclude your meal, choose one of the heavenly desserts or the selection of Somerset cheeses.

🏛 historic building   🏚 museum   🏛 historic site   ⚜ scenic attraction   🌱 flora and fauna

late Middle Ages. Bridgwater grew and, at one time, it was the most important town on the coast between Bristol and Barnstaple. Although it is hard to believe now, it was the fifth busiest port in the country. The largely 14th century parish church, with its disproportionately large spire, is the only building to remain from that prosperous medieval era. The castle was dismantled after the English Civil War and the 13th century Franciscan friary and St John's Hospital disappeared long ago. Although the street layout here is still medieval, the buildings in the area between King Street and West Quay are some of the best examples of domestic Georgian architecture in the county.

Bridgwater's most famous son is the celebrated military leader, Robert Blake, who was born here in 1598. When in his 40s, Blake became an important officer in Cromwell's army and twice defended Taunton against overwhelming Royalist odds. Just a decade later, he was appointed General at Sea and went on to win a number of important battles against the Dutch and the Spanish. In so doing, he restored the nation's naval supremacy in Europe. The house in which he was born is now home to the **Blake Museum** (see panel below), which contains a three-dimensional model of the Battle of Santa Cruz, one of Blake's most famous victories, along with a collection of his personal effects. Blake was not the only military leader connected with Bridgwater. During the late 1600s, the Duke of Monmouth stayed here before his disastrous defeat at the nearby Battle of Sedgemoor. The museum suitably illustrates this decisive battle in the duke's quest for the English throne. This is also a museum of local history with a large

Blake Museum

Blake Street, Bridgwater,
Somerset TA6 3NB
Tel: 01278 456127

The Blake Museum is Bridgewater's museum of local history and archaeology, names after Robert Blake (1598-1657) Cromwell's General at Sea and who was born in Bridgewater.

The displays include archaeology from the earliest settlements in Bridgwater to the mediaeval port, and one on James, Duke of Monmouth who led an ill-fated rebellion against his uncle, King James II, in 1685. Monmouth's forces were defeated at the Battle of Sedgemoor near Westonzoyland.

The drawings and paintings of John Chubb (1746-1818), a merchant and gifted artist, provide a unique and often humorous insight into the characters of 18th Century Bridgewater. The local brick and tile industry, which employed many local people, is also illustrated here. The products made went all around the world.

The museum holds an exciting programme of exhibitions and events throughout the yearfor all the family, and has many photographs and research resources.

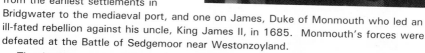

stories and anecdotes   famous people   art and craft   entertainment and sport   walks

collection of locally discovered artefacts on display that date from Neolithic times right up to World War II.

The highlight of Bridgwater's events calendar is its **Carnival** commemorating Guy Fawkes' Day. Believed to be the largest such event in the world, the celebration involves hundreds of themed 'carts', each ablaze with as many as 25,000 light bulbs, which join a procession more than

River Parrett, Bridgwater

two miles long, accompanied by various town bands. Following the procession, "squibs", or giant fireworks, are carried through the town and set alight in the High Street.

An attractive amenity of the town is the **Bridgwater and Taunton Canal** which was completed in 1827 and can still be explored on water by canoe, trail boat or narrow boat, or along the towpath on foot or by cycle. Before the construction of a canal dock, the ships arriving at Bridgwater used to tie up on both sides of the river below the town's medieval bridge. Here, too, can be seen the last remnant of the medieval castle, The Water Gate, on West Quay.

The arrival of the canal gave a great boost to local industries. The manufacture of Bridgwater glass, which had begun the previous century, expanded greatly. The river mud that caused the decline of the town's port also proved to have hidden benefits, because when baked in oblong blocks it was found to be an excellent scourer. As Bath Brick, it was used for nearly a century to clean grates and stone steps. The canal terminus, where the brickworks also stood, was finally closed in 1970 but has now been restored as a fascinating area of industrial archaeology.

More of the county's industrial heritage can be explored at the **Somerset Brick & Tile Museum** on East Quay. The last surviving kiln at the former Barham Brother's yard is a poignant reminder of the brick and tile industry which was once so important in the county. The kiln has been repaired by Somerset County Council and now provides the centrepiece of the museum.

An interesting feature on the canal is based at Mounsel Locks, about five miles south of Bridgwater. **The Somerset Space Walk** uses the 13-mile length of the canal to represent the solar system with scale models of each of the planets. The sun is placed at the locks with the inner planets nearby; Pluto can be found on the outskirts of Taunton.

Around Bridgwater

HIGHBRIDGE
6 miles N of Bridgwater on the A38

 Alstone Wildlife Park

The small coastal town of Highbridge was once a busy port on the Glastonbury Canal. Today its main visitor attraction is **Alstone Wildlife Park,** a small non-profit making, family-run park which devotes all its proceeds to the welfare and upkeep of the animals. Open daily from Easter to November, the park is home to a variety of animals including Theadore the camel, a herd of red deer, wallabies, owls, pigs, emus and ponies.

BURNHAM-ON-SEA
7 miles N of Bridgwater on the B3140

St Andrew's Church   Low Lighthouse

Brent Knoll

A traditional seaside resort as well as a thriving market town, Burnham-on-Sea has acres of sandy beach, a fine Edwardian Esplanade, a Pier Pavilion and a 15th century church that was built close by the shore. This turned out to be a not very good idea. Because of the sandy foundations, the 80ft tower of **St Andrew's Church** now leans three feet from the vertical. But the structure is apparently quite stable and has not shifted for many decades. Inside are parts of a massive altarpiece designed by Inigo Jones and carved by Grinling Gibbons. Originally installed in James II's Whitehall Palace, it survived the great fire that destroyed the palace and was re-installed in Westminster Abbey. But when the abbey was being prepared for the coronation of George IV the huge structure was deemed out of place and surplus to requirements. Somehow, the vicar of Burnham learned of its impending fate and managed to acquire it for his country church. The parts are now dispersed over various parts of the chancel.

In the early 1800s, the local curate, the Revd Davies, discovered mineral springs in the gardens of Burnham Hall. An attempt was made to turn Burnham into a spa town to rival Cheltenham and Bath. A series of buildings was erected around the springs, the most notable of them being the Bath House, now Steart House, on the Esplanade. Unfortunately, the waters were too sulphurous and stinking for most convalescents to endure and the venture fizzled out. The town would have to depend on its wide sandy beach to attract visitors.

A distinctive feature on the beach is the unique nine-legged **Low Lighthouse,** a curious square structure raised above the beach on tall stilts. An earlier lighthouse, the High Lighthouse, erected in 1750, still stands inland behind the dunes but because of the huge rise and fall of tides in the Severn estuary, its light was ineffective at low tides. Hence the need for the Low Lighthouse.

To the northeast of Burnham rises **Brent Knoll**, a conspicuous landmark that can be seen from as far away as South Wales. Before the Somerset Levels were drained, this isolated hill would almost certainly have been an island. As with many other natural features that appear out of place in the landscape, there are several stories that suggest that the knoll owes its existence to the Devil. The 445-foot summit is crowned with the remains of an Iron Age hill fort. The summit, which can be reached by footpaths beginning near the churches at East Brent and Brent Knoll, offers walkers a spectacular view out over the Bristol Channel, the Mendips and the Somerset Levels.

stories and anecdotes   famous people   art and craft   entertainment and sport   walks

E-MOOR LTD

Tel: 01458 210447   e-mail: fiona@e-moor.com   website: www.elusivecollection.com

Based in a tiny village in Somerset, this exceptional website www.elusivecollection.com features some of the UKs most brilliant designers. Everything on the site is made by hand, predominantly in Somerset. The Elusive Collection is aptly named as it brings together unique, outstanding and special products, designed and made in Britain, which would normally only be available through exclusive Galleries and Open Studios.

Shopping on holiday is always a treat! So now is the time to treat yourself and indulge your senses with some of the best shopping Somerset has to offer! And if you are visiting for a couple of weeks in September 2006, you will be able to visit the Elusive Collection as part of Somerset Arts Weeks (9th – 24th September 2006, 11.00am – 4.00pm) at Windmill House, Holcombe Lane, Moorlinch, Somerset TA7 9BX.

All year round you can see a selection of the product range at a few well chosen spots! Charlton House, Shepton Mallet, BA4 4PR, The Mount Somerset Hotel, Lower, Henlade, Taunton, TA3 5NB and Mos Food, The Crescent, Taunton, TA1 4DN. From September 2006, Number 12, Market Place, Wells, BA5 2RB.

The selection of designers from www.elusivecollection.com on display at Somerset Arts Week will be:

Mary Davis Knitwear

This well kept secret is about to break out! This range of fabulous, hand-made, felted knitwear was the inspiration for The Elusive Collection. This really is knitwear with a twist, literally in some cases. Taking a different view of texture and finish, Mary has styled a range of items that, once worn, will never be forgotten! Step out in a Mary Davis creation and be prepared for admiration and envy – then tell them where you bought it! Once worn this clothing is addictive and highly collectable! Enter into the secret of those lucky enough to live near Mary who will tell you – you can never have too many Mary Davis' outfits! And be prepared for people to stop you in the street and ask you where you bought it!

Loudware

Loudware take sympathetic shapes and add a unique touch. Using first fired biscuit ware, the designs are hand drawn and painted on using an underglazed technique. The items are then glazed and fired to give a vibrant finish.

Caroline Nicolaou

From her studio in Somerset Caroline creates beautiful ceramic jewellery. By combining different shapes, textures and glazes on individual beads she makes wonderful eye-catching necklaces and bracelets. So easy to wear and so different. Eye catching is an understatement! If you are looking for something truly original, this is the jewellery for you and an ideal holiday present!

How often have you returned from holiday wishing you had made that special purchase, or indeed, wanting to buy another, but unable to return to your holiday spot. Now you can, with www.elusivecollection.com. Join the mailing list and we will keep you informed of other venues round the country and stockists for the truly impressive English designers featured on our website.

🏚 historic building   🏛 museum   🏛 historic site   ♨ scenic attraction   🌱 flora and fauna

BREAN

11 miles N of Bridgwater off the A370

 Animal Farm Adventure Park

This elongated, mainly modern resort village is sheltered, to the north, by the 320ft high **Brean Down** (National Trust), an imposing remnant of the Mendip hills that projects out into the Bristol Channel. Another fragment can be seen in the form of the offshore island **Steep Holm**. A site of settlement, ritual and defence for thousands of years, the remains of an Iron Age coastal fort and a Roman temple have both been found on the down along with some medieval 'pillow' mounds. The tip of the promontory is dominated by the Palmerston fort of 1867, built as part of the defences to protect the Bristol Channel. There are also some 20th century gun emplacements. As well as its archaeological and geological interest, this peninsula has been designated a Site of Special Scientific Interest because of its varied habitats. Oystercatcher and dunlin can be seen along the foreshore and estuary; the scrubland is an important habitat for migrating birds such as redstart, redpoll and reed bunting; rare plants take root in the shallow and exposed soil, and the south-facing slopes are home to a variety of butterflies. Subject to one of the widest tidal ranges in Europe, the currents around the headland can be dramatic and very dangerous.

About a mile inland from Brean Sands beach, **Animal Farm Adventure Park** promises fun for all the family with a mix of domestic and rarer animals, including llamas, alpacas and emus; adventure play areas, ride-on tractors and a miniature railway.

WESTONZOYLAND

3½ miles SE of Bridgwater on the A372

🏚 Battle of Sedgemoor   🏭 Pumping Station

Just to the northwest of the village and on the southern bank of what is now the King's Sedgemoor Drain is the site of the last battle to be fought on English soil. In July 1685, the well-equipped forces of James II heavily defeated the followers of the Duke of Monmouth in the bloody **Battle of Sedgemoor**. This brought an end to the ill-fated Pitchfork Rebellion that aimed to replace the Catholic King James with the Protestant Duke of Monmouth, the illegitimate son of Charles II. Around 700 of Monmouth's followers were killed on the battlefield while several hundred survivors were rounded up and taken to Westonzoyland churchyard, where many of them were hanged. The duke himself was taken to London where, 10 days after the battle, he was executed on Tower Hill. However, it was during the infamous Judge Jeffrey's 'Bloody Assizes' that the greatest terror was inflicted on the surviving followers of the duke when well over 300 men were condemned to death. A further 600 were transported to the colonies. Today, a stark memorial marks the site of the lonely battlefield.

The village lies in the Somerset Levels and a steam-powered **Pumping Station** was built here in the 19th century to drain the water from the levels into the River Parrett. The oldest pumping station of its kind in the area, the engine on show here was in operation from 1861 until 1952. Now fully restored, it can be seen in steam at various times throughout the year. The station itself is a grade II listed building. Also on the site is a small forge, a tramway and a number of other exhibits from the steam age.

ENMORE

4 miles SW of Bridgwater off the A39

🐾 Quantock Hills   🏚 Fyne Court   🎭 Andrew Cross

To the west of Enmore the ground rises up into the **Quantock Hills**, an Area of

🎭 stories and anecdotes   🐦 famous people   ✐ art and craft   ✐ entertainment and sport   🚶 walks

Outstanding Natural Beauty that runs from near Taunton to the Bristol Channel at Quantoxhead. Rising to a high point of 1,260 feet at **Wills Neck**, this delightful area of open heath and scattered woodland supports one of the country's last remaining herds of wild red deer. The exposed hilltops are littered with Neolithic and Bronze Age remains, including around 100 burial mounds, many of which now resemble nothing more than a pile of stones. The richer soil in the south sustains arable farms and pockets of dense woodland and this varied landscape offers some magnificent walking with splendid views over the Bristol Channel, the Vale of Taunton Deane, the Brendon Hills and Exmoor. It was this glorious classical English landscape that the poets Wordsworth and Coleridge so admired while they were living in the area.

Southwest of Enmore in one of the loveliest areas on the southern Quantocks is **Fyne Court** (National Trust) which houses both the headquarters of the Somerset Wildlife Trust and a visitor centre for the Quantocks. The main house here was built in the 17th century by the Crosse family. It was largely destroyed by fire in the 1890s and the only surviving parts are the library and music room that have been converted into the visitor centre. The grounds, which incorporate a walled garden, two ponds, an arboretum and a lake, have been designated a nature reserve. The most renowned occupant of the house was **Andrew Cross**, an early-19th century scientist who was a pioneer in the field of electrical energy. Known locally as the 'thunder and lightning

man', one of Crosse's lightning conductors can still be seen on an oak tree in the grounds. Local stories tell how, during one of his electrical experiments, Crosse created tiny live insects. It was this claim that helped to inspire Mary Shelley to write her Gothic horror story, *Frankenstein*, in 1818.

NETHER STOWEY
10 miles W of Bridgwater off the A39

🏛 Stowey Court 🏛 Coleridge Cottage

🚶 Quantock Forest Trail

This attractive village of 17th and 18th century stone cottages and houses is best known for its literary connections but Nether Stowey has a much longer history. At one time, it was a small market town. A castle was built here in Norman times and the earthwork remains can be seen to the west of the village

Coleridge Cottage, Nether Stowey

centre while its substantial manor house, **Stowey Court**, stands on the eastern side of the village. The construction of the manor house was begun by Lord Audley in 1497 shortly before he joined a protest against Henry VII's taxation policy. Sadly, he was not able to see the project through to completion as he was executed soon afterwards.

In 1797, a local tanner, Tom Poole, lent a dilapidated cottage at the end of his garden to his friend, Samuel Taylor Coleridge, who stayed here for three years with his wife and child. So began Nether Stowey's association with poets and writers. It was here that Coleridge wrote most of his famous works, including *The Rime of the Ancient Mariner* and the opium-inspired *Kubla Khan*. When not writing, he would go on long walks with his friend and near neighbour William Wordsworth, who had moved close to Nether Stowey from a house in Dorset at around the same time. Other visitors to the cottage included Charles Lamb. But it was not long before Coleridge's opium addiction and his rocky marriage began to take their toll. These were not the only problems for the poet as local suspicion was growing that he and Wordsworth were French spies. The home in which the Coleridges lived for three years is now **Coleridge Cottage,** a National Trust property where mementoes of the poet are on display.

A lane leads southwest from the village to the nearby village of Over Stowey and the starting point of the Forestry Commission's **Quantock Forest Trail**, a three-mile walk lined with specially planted native and imported trees.

Ilminster

🏠 Dillington House

One of Somerset's most beguiling towns, Ilminster is perched on the side of a hill with its main street running round, rather than up and down the slope. For centuries, it stood on the main London to Exeter route; today the A303 bypasses the town allowing its special charm to be enjoyed in comparative peace.

A church was founded here by the Saxon King Ine in the 8th century and by the time of the Domesday Book in 1089, the borough had grown considerably – it was recorded as having a market and three mills. During the Middle Ages, it expanded further into a thriving wool and lace-making town. This

---

A TOUCH OF ELEGANCE

5 West Street, Ilminster, Somerset TA19 9AA
Tel/Fax: 01460 55992
e-mail: sue@atouchofelegance.org.uk
website: www.atouchofelegance.org.uk

Brimming with brilliant ideas for creating an ideal home, **A Touch of Elegance** also offers the opportunity to sit down in a comfortable friendly environment and have a one-on-one discussion about the kind of interior decoration you really want. Owner Sue Woodbury is very experienced in designing home interiors and her shop is stocked with a wide range of items from leading suppliers. There are fabrics and wallpapers from Zoffany and Nina Campbell; fabrics from Colefax & Fowler and Romo, Elstead lighting, curtain poles and accessories, and much, much more.

---

 stories and anecdotes 🐟 famous people 🎨 art and craft 🖌 entertainment and sport 🚶 walks

ILMINSTER SPECIALIST SHOPS

East & Silver Street, Ilminster, Somerset TA19 0DH

Aurea - 31 Silver Street. Tel: 01460 57761
e-mail sales@aurea.co.uk   website: www.aurea.co.uk
Aurea specialises in antique and modern furniture, fabrics and a range of unusual objects for the home and garden. These include china and glass, mirrors, lamps, rugs as well as wonderful marble/stone urns and other garden items. Aurea also provides an interior design service (est. over 20 years) offering upholstery, loose covers and hand-sewn curtains made to order.

The Amazing Dolls' House & Toy Company - 24 East Street. Tel: 01460 54328
You will be delighted when you visit The Amazing Dolls' House & Toy Company. They have a great selection of Dolls Houses - from cottages to vast Georgian mansions with thousands of miniature items, to decorate, furnish and dress them, on display in room settings. They also have a traditional toy section specialising in wooden toys. Always a friendly welcome. Open Tuesday - Saturday 9.30-5pm. Browsers are welcome.

Town & Country Hardware - Silver Street. Tel: 01460 52506
website: www.townandcountryhardware.co.uk
A family-run traditional hardware shop originally a 17th century coaching inn, it has been an ironmongers for over 100 years. Within the shop you will find an in depth selection of goods for the kitchen and around the house and garden – specialist cleaning materials, electrical appliances, ironmongery, garden furniture and picnicware all at good value prices with lots of special offers. For a different shopping experience why not pay them a visit! Open Mon-Sat, 9-5.30pm, except Thurs 9-1pm.

Bonner's - 37 Silver Street. Tel 01460 52465
e-mail:sales@bonnersthebutchers.co.uk
website: www.bonnersthebutchers.co.uk
Bonner's is a traditional family butchers and a member of Q Guild, one of only 150 in the country, who pride themselves on the quality of their meat and meat products. All the beef, lamb, pork and poultry are reared on local farms and the prize-winning sausages, faggots, burgers and cooked meat products are all prepared on the premises to Bonner's own special recipes. The delicatessen offers an excellent range of home cooked meats and an extensive choice of fresh cheeses, hors d'oeuvres, oils and vinegars.Winner of the Best Butcher in Somerset 2004/2005

Lanes Garden Shop - 17 Silver Street. Tel: 01460 57703
e-mail: lanesgardenshop@tiscali.co.uk
website: www.lanesgardenshop.co.uk
Lanes Garden Shop is owned and run by Elizabeth Ferriss whose mission is to obtain stylish, interesting and unusual ornaments for gardens and conservatories. As a qualified garden designer, Elizabeth has a sense of perspective and vision which her customers find very valuable. She is always looking for new products and is very happy to provide a personal search service for particular items. Her shop is ideally suited to those seeking a special individual look for unusual items and gifts.

🏚 historic building 🏛 museum 🏚 historic site 🗟 scenic attraction 🌿 flora and fauna

REVIVAL CRAFTS & GIFTS

24a Ditton Street, Ilminster, Somerset TA19 0BQ
Tel: 01460 53316
website: www.ilminsterchamber.org.uk

Struggling to find that unusual and distinctive gift, or something a bit out of the ordinary for yourself? **Revival Crafts and Gifts** takes the pain out of the process by stocking a dazzling range of imaginative items at sensible prices. Owner Gerd Bottom has collected a remarkable variety of pieces ranging from locally-made hand-crafted knitwear, through delicate jewellery to Fair Trade products from Asia, Africa and India. You'll also find items from a local woodturner, 3D pictures, greeting cards speciality cushions, and a choice of some 50 elegant hats for hire for all occasions.

period of prosperity is reflected in the town's unusually large parish church, whose massive multi-pinnacled tower is modelled on that of Wells Cathedral. Any walk around the old part of Ilminster will reveal a number of delightful old buildings, many constructed in golden Hamstone, including the chantry house, the old grammar school and a colonnaded market house. Another, the George Inn, proudly displays a sign proclaiming that it was first hotel that Queen Victoria stayed at, as Princess Victoria, in 1819. The future queen was on her way with her parents to Sidmouth in Devon.

On the outskirts of Ilminster is another lovely old building, the handsome part Tudor mansion, **Dillington House.** It is now owned by Somerset County Council and used as a **Residential Centre for Adult Education,** but it was originally the home of the Speke family. In the time of James II, John Speke was an officer in the Duke of Monmouth's ill-fated rebel army that landed at Lyme Regis in 1685. However, following the rebellion's disastrous defeat at the Battle of Sedgemoor, Speke was forced to flee abroad, leaving his brother, George, who had done no more than shake the Duke's hand, to face the wrath of Judge Jeffreys. The infamous 'hanging' judge

sentenced George to death, justifying his decision with the words, "His family owes a life and he shall die for his brother."

Around Ilminster

BARRINGTON
3 miles NE of Ilminster off the B3168

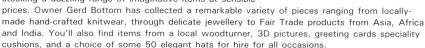 Barrington Court

To the east of the village is the beautiful National Trust-owned **Barrington Court** famous for its enchanting garden influenced by the great 20th century garden architect Gertrude Jekyll. This estate originally belonged to the Daubeney family but it passed through several hands before becoming the property of William Clifton, a wealthy London merchant, who was responsible for building the house in the mid-16th century. In 1907, the by then dilapidated Barrington Court became the first country house to be purchased by the National Trust. It was restored in the 1920s by Col AA Lyle, to whom the Trust had let the property. The garden, too, was laid out during this time in a series of themed areas including an iris garden, a lily garden, a white garden and a fragrant rose garden. Gertrude Jekyll was

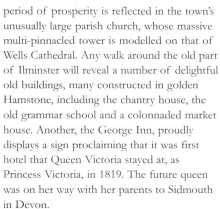

Barrington Court

Africa to confirm that Lake Victoria was, indeed, the source of the River Nile. After his epic journey, Speke returned to England a hero but, tragically, on the very morning that he was due to report his findings to the British Geographical Association he accidentally shot himself while on a partridge shoot.

This picturesque village is also the home of **Perry's Cider Mills** where the cider presses are installed in a wonderful 16th century thatched barn. If you visit in the autumn you can see the cider making in progress but the presses and an interesting collection of vintage farm tools and equipment are on view all year round. The full range of ciders, including cider brandy, is available in the shop and can be sampled from the barrel before you buy. The shop also stocks a huge range of country style pottery, stone cider jars, baskets, terracotta kitchenware, country jams and pickles and much more.

brought in to advise on the initial planting and layout and the garden remains the finest example of her work in the Trust's care. There is also an exceptionally attractive kitchen garden with apple, pear and plum trees trained along the walls that, in season, produces fruit and vegetables for the licensed restaurant that can be found here.

Just to the southeast of this pretty estate village, the remains of a medieval open-strip field system can still be made out from the air around the village of Shepton Beauchamp.

DOWLISH WAKE
2 miles SE of Ilminster off the A303 or A358

🦅 John Hanning Speke   🍐 Perry's Cider Mills

In the parish church of this attractive village can be seen the tomb of **John Hanning Speke,** the intrepid Victorian explorer who journeyed for more than 2,500 miles through

HINTON ST GEORGE
11 miles SE of Ilminster off the A356

🦅 Sir Amyas Poulett   🌿 Lower Severalls

This wonderfully unspoilt former estate village has a broad main street, thatched houses, a medieval village cross and a striking 15th century church. For centuries the village was owned by the Poulett family and it is thanks to them that Hinton St George has been left virtually untouched. The Pouletts

🏛 historic building   🏛 museum   🏛 historic site   🌣 scenic attraction   🌿 flora and fauna arrived here in the 15th century and the house that they rebuilt then, Hinton House, now forms the main structure of the present day mansion. Although this has now been converted into apartments, the building is still said to be haunted by the ghost of a young Poulett woman who died of a broken heart after her father shot dead the man with whom she was planning to elope.

Several ostentatious monuments to members of the Poulett family can be seen in the village's 15th century Church of St George. Commemorated by a superb alabaster memorial is the most famous member of the family, **Sir Amyas Poulett.** A loyal and honourable courtier of Elizabeth I, Sir Amyas fell out of favour when he declined to act on the queen's suggestion that he murder Mary, Queen of Scots who was in his custody. "A dainty and precise fellow," was the queen's scornful response to the knight's over-scrupulous behaviour.

On the last Thursday in October, called 'Punkie Night', it is traditional for Hinton children to beg for candles to put inside their intricately fashioned turnip and pumpkin lanterns. It is considered very unlucky to refuse to give a child a candle as each lantern is thought to represent the spirit of a dead person who, unless illuminated, will rise up at Hallowe'en.

Hinton seems to have a special interest in light. It was the first village in England to install gas street lighting in 1863 and recently its modern street lighting scheme received an award from the International Dark Skies Association because its street lamps minimise light pollution.

To the east of the village, **Lower Severalls** has an enchanting and original garden set in front of an 18th century Hamstone farmhouse. The garden has an informal style with profuse herbaceous borders around the house and innovative features that include a living dogwood basket, a wadi and a scented garden.

CREWKERNE
13 miles SE of Ilminster on the A30/A356

🏠 Church of St Batholomew		🏌 Windwhistle Hill	
🖼 Crewkerne & District Museum			
🌱 Clapton Court Gardens		🚶 River Parrett Trail	

Another delightful small town, noted for its antique and book shops, and the famous auction house of Lawrence's, housed in a restored linen yard. A thriving agricultural centre during Saxon times, Crewkerne even had its own mint in the decades leading up to the Norman invasion. Evidence of this ancient former market town's importance and wealth can still be seen in the magnificence of its parish **Church of St Bartholomew** built using money generated by the late medieval boom in the local wool industry. A building of minster-like proportions, this is one of the grandest of the many fine Perpendicular churches to be found in south Somerset. Unlike many other towns in Wessex, whose textile industries suffered an almost total decline in later years, Crewkerne was rejuvenated in the 18th century when the availability of locally grown flax led to an expansion in the manufacture of sailcloth and canvas webbing. Among the many thousands of sails made here were those for *HMS Victory*, Admiral Nelson's flagship at the Battle of Trafalgar. Nelson's captain in that engagement was Sir Thomas Hardy, educated at Crewkerne grammar school. Hardy's career is celebrated at the **Crewkerne and District Museum,** recently relocated in a beautifully restored 18th century house.

🎭 stories and anecdotes   🌿 famous people   🎨 art and craft   ✒ entertainment and sport   🚶 walks

THE MANOR ARMS

North Perrott, Crewkerne, Somerset TA18 7SG
Tel: 01460 72901 Fax: 01460 74055
e-mail: bookings@manorarmshotel.co.uk
website: www.manorarmshotel.co.uk

Located in the conservation village of North Perrott, **The Manor Arms** is a Grade II listed building dating back to the 16th century and full of charm and character. Overlooking the green, the inn has been lovingly restored, retaining much of its olde worlde character with its inglenook fireplace, flagstone floors, oak beams and exposed stone walls. Your hosts are Trevor and Diane Crouchen who bought the Manor Arms in early 2004 after many years of management in the hotel and hospitality trade. They have been working hard to maintain and improve upon the excellent reputation the hotel has enjoyed for many years.

The food they serve here is of exceptional quality and value for money and is possibly the main reason that so many of their guests return time and time again. The inn also carries an increasingly varying selection of real ales to complement the usual selection of beers, wines and spirits. The inn has eight en-suite bedrooms, each equipped with colour TV and tea/coffee making facilities; two of them have four-poster beds. Three rooms are on the first floor of the inn; a further five rooms are in the Olde Coach House, quietly situated behind the inn.

The economic boost provided by the flax industry was further fuelled by the development of the London to Exeter stage coach route. This led to the rebuilding of Crewkerne with elegant Georgian buildings, many of which can still be seen. The main areas, around Church and Abbey Streets, have now been designated an Area of Outstanding Architectural Interest.

To the west of Crewkerne rises the aptly named **Windwhistle Hill**, a high chalk-topped ridge from the top of which there are dramatic views on a clear day, southwards to Lyme Bay and northwards across the Somerset Levels to the mountains of South Wales. The town also lies close to the source of the River Parrett

and from here the 50-mile **River Parrett Trail** follows the river through some of the country's most ecologically sensitive and fragile areas, the Somerset Levels and Moors. Old mills, splendid churches, attractive villages and ancient monuments as well as orchards, peaceful pastureland and traditional industries such as cider-making and basket-weaving can all be found along the route.

Just a couple of miles southwest of Crewkerne, close to the village of Clapton, are the varied and interesting **Clapton Court Gardens**. Among the many beautiful features of this 10-acre garden are the formal terraces, the rose garden, the rockery and a water garden. The grounds incorporate a large wooded area containing a massive ash tree that, at over 230 years old and 28 feet in girth, is believed to be the oldest and the largest in mainland Britain. There is also a fine metasequoia that is already over 80 feet tall although it was only planted in 1950, from a seed brought back from China.

HASELBURY PLUCKNETT
14 miles SE of Ilminster on the A3066

🏛 Haselbury Bridge

This delightfully named and particularly pretty village has a large part-Norman church whose churchyard contains a series of unusual 'squeeze stones'. Just to the west of the village the lovely **Haselbury Bridge**, a medieval packhorse bridge, crosses the still young River Parrett.

CHARD
6 miles S of Ilminster on the A30

🏛 Chard Museum 🏠 Hornsbury Mill

🌱 Chard Reservoir Nature Reserve

The borough of Chard was first established in 1235 and during the Middle Ages became a prosperous wool centre with its own mayor, or portreeve, and burgesses. However, few buildings date from before 1577, when a devastating fire raged through the town and left most of it as ashes. One building that did survive the destruction was the fine Perpendicular parish church. The town was rebuilt and, today, many of these 16th and 17th century buildings remain, including the courthouse and the old grammar school. Chard also has some striking Georgian and

BARLEYMOW'S FARM SHOP

Snowdon Hill Farm, Chard, Somerset TA20 3PS
Tel: 01460 62130 Fax: 01460 61933
e-mail: barleymows@farmshop.wanadoo.co.uk
website: www.barleymowsfarmshop.com

Conveniently located beside the A30 just half a mile west of Chard, **Barleymow's Farm Shop** enjoys fabulous views across unspoilt countryside. Meat is hung and butchered on the premises in the traditional way to ensure that customers get that special Somerset flavour. The shop also stocks a wide range of "fresh from the farm" vegetables – tasty freshly dug carrots, potatoes, green vegetables and much more, and what is not grown on Barleymow's Farm is supplied by local growers.

As well as their own beef and lamb Barleymow's sells local poultry and pork, traditional Somerset faggots, delicious sausages made to their own recipes, pasties and pies, a selection of cooked meats, cheese and dairy produce and fresh free range eggs. Bread from the farm's own ovens, home-made cakes and biscuits, pickles sauces and preserves, Scrumpy cider beers and wines, along with a wide range of special frozen foods are all there to tempt you. For children, there's ice cream – and a large outdoor playing area. Barleymow's Maize Maze runs throughout the summer holiday adjacent to thier camping site.

In this family business everyone works together to run the farm and the shop, and their friendly staff look forward to your visit.

📖 stories and anecdotes 🐎 famous people ✐ art and craft ✐ entertainment and sport 🚶 walks

Victorian buildings. On the outskirts of the town the unusual round toll house, with its conical thatched roof, is a reminder of the days of stagecoaches and turnpike roads.

Chard has expanded rapidly since World War II; its population has more than doubled. Nevertheless the centre of this light industrial town still retains a pleasant village-like atmosphere that is most apparent in its broad main shopping street. At the western end of the town's High Street, housed in the attractive thatched Godworth House, is the award-winning **Chard Museum** amongst whose exhibits are displays celebrating some very inventive former residents. James Stringfellow produced the first steam-powered aeroplanes in the 1840s; James Gillingham pioneered artificial limbs a few decades later; and Margaret Bonfield was the first female British cabinet member as Minister of Labour in 1929.

To the northwest of the town is a 200-year-old corn mill, **Hornsbury Mill**, whose impressive water wheel is still in working order. It stands in five acres of beautiful informally landscaped water gardens form. The old buildings have been given a new lease of life and now incorporate a restaurant and bed & breakfast guest rooms, and also provides a popular venue for weddings, special events and conferences.

To the northeast, **Chard Reservoir Nature Reserve** is a conservation area where kingfishers, great crested grebes and other rare species of birds have made their home in and around the lake. The nature reserve also has a two-mile circular footpath that takes in rustling reed beds, broad-leaved woodland and open hay meadows.

TATWORTH
8 miles S of Ilminster off the A358

🏛 Forde Abbey

To the northeast of this village lies a meadow watered by springs that rise on its borders. This meadow is the last remaining vestige of 'common' land that was enclosed in 1819. Changes in the ownership of the land during the 1820s allowed too many farmers grazing rights on the land, and the meadow suffered from being over-stocked. Therefore, in 1832, the holders of those rights met and, calling their meeting 'Stowell Court', they auctioned off the meadow for one year and shared the proceeds. So an annual tradition was born and the Stowell Court still meets on the first Tuesday after April 6th every year. Although many more customs have been added over the years, the auction proceedings are unique. They begin when a tallow candle of precisely one inch in length is lit and they end with the last bid before the candle goes out. Today, Stowell Mead is managed as a Site of Special Scientific Interest and, as the land is not treated with fertilisers, pesticides or herbicides, it is home to many rare plants. There is no right of way across the land but it can be seen from the road.

A short distance to the southeast of Tatworth, just over the county border in Dorset, is **Forde Abbey**, founded in the 12th century by Cistercian monks after they had made an unsuccessful attempt to found an abbey in Devon. For more details, see the entry in the Dorset chapter of this book.

CRICKET ST THOMAS
9 miles S of Ilminster off the A30

🌿 Cricket St Thomas Wildlife & Leisure Park

This former estate village is now home to the

Cricket St Thomas Wildlife and Leisure Park, Today, the attractions include stables, a children's adventure fort, wildlife world and a varied assortment of theme park crowd-pleasers designed to attract the young. The central building, Cricket House, was once the family home of the great 18th century naval commander Admiral Sir Alexander Hood and, later, of the Bristol chocolate manufacturer, FJ Fry. The estate also incorporates the tiny St Thomas's Church with its impressive monument to Admiral Hood, who was later to become Viscount Bridport.

WAMBROOK
8 miles SW of Ilminster off the A30

🐾 Ferne Animal Sanctuary

Visitors interested in animal welfare will be keen to visit the **Ferne Animal Sanctuary** at Wambrook. Originally founded in 1939 by the Duchess of Hamilton and Brandon while she was living at Berwick St John near Shaftesbury, the sanctuary moved to its present position in the valley of the River Yarty in 1975. This pleasant 51-acre site incorporates a nature trail, conservation area, dragonfly pools and picnic areas.

Yeovil

🏛 Church of St John the Baptist
🏛 Museum of South Somerset

Yeovil takes its name from the River Yeo, sometimes called the River Ivel. There was a Roman settlement here but the town really began to develop in the Middle Ages when a market was established that continues to be held every Friday. Yeovil's parish **Church of St John the Baptist** is the only significant

medieval structure to survive as most of its other early buildings were destroyed by the series of fires that struck the town in the 17th century. A substantial building, with a solid-looking tower, the church dates from the late 14th century and has a surprisingly austere exterior given its exceptional number of windows. It has so many windows that it is sometimes referred to as the 'Lantern of the West'.

During the 18th century, Yeovil developed into a flourishing coaching centre due to its strategic position at the junction of several main routes. Industries such as glove-making, leather working, sailcloth making and cheese producing were established here. This rapid expansion was further fuelled by the arrival of the railway in the mid-1800s. Then, in the 1890s, James Petter, a local ironmonger and pioneer of the internal combustion engine, founded a business that went on to become one of the largest manufacturers of diesel engines in Britain. Although production was eventually transferred to the Midlands, a subsidiary set up to produce aircraft during World War I has since evolved into a helicopter plant.

Today, Yeovil retains its geographical importance and is south Somerset's largest concentration of population. It is a thriving commercial, shopping, and market town best known perhaps as the home of Westland Helicopters. Situated in Wyndham House, the **Museum of South Somerset** documents the social and industrial history of the town and surrounding area, from prehistoric times to the present. Amongst other intriguing exhibits is one that explains how a patent stove was the basis for the town's world-leading helicopter industry.

Around Yeovil

ILCHESTER
7 miles N of Yeovil off the A37

 Ilchester Museum

In Roman times, the settlement here stood at the point where the north-south route between Dorchester and the Bristol Channel crossed the Fosse Way. However, it was during the 13th century that Ilchester reached its peak as a centre of administration, agriculture and learning. Like its near neighbour Somerton, this was, for a time, the county town of Somerset. Three substantial gaols were built here, one of which remained in use until the 1840s. Another indication of this town's former status is the 13th century Ilchester Mace, England's oldest staff of office. Up until recently, the mace resided in the town hall but today a replica can be seen here, while the original mace is on display in the County Museum at Taunton.

The tiny **Ilchester Museum** is in the centre of the town, by the Market Cross, and here the story of the town from pre-Roman times to the 20th century is told through a series of exhibits that include a Roman coffin and skeleton. Ilchester was the birthplace, in around 1214, of the celebrated scholar, monk and scientist, Roger Bacon, who went on to predict the invention of the aeroplane, telescope and steam engine although he was eventually imprisoned for his outspoken ideas.

Fleet Air Arm Museum

RNAS Yeovilton, near Ilchester,
Somerset BA22 8HT
Tel: 01935 840565 Fax: 01935 842630
e-mail: info@fleetairarm.com
website: www.fleetairarm.com

The **Fleet Air Arm Museum** is one of the world's largest aviation museums and visitors can come and experience the exciting development of Britain's Flying Navy through a succession of superb exhibits. However, this is much more than just a hanger full of vintage aircraft and the highly imaginative collection on display also tells the stories of the men and women of naval aviation.

For those wishing to know just what it is like on an aircraft carrier, visitors can be 'flown' aboard the museum's own carrier where they can tour its nerve centre and experience close at hand the thrills and noises of a working flight deck. Meanwhile, through the use of touch screen interactive displays, dramatic lighting and vivid sound, the history and atmosphere of many of the museum's exhibits can be explored further. And, for those who have always wanted to experience the adrenaline rush as a pilot successfully completes his challenging mission, the Merlin Experience has been specially designed to allow visitors to act out their long held flying fantasies. Along with a children's adventure playground, a large book and souvenir shop, restaurant, airfield viewing galleries and a picnic area, this museum has much to offer visitors of all ages and interests whatever the weather.

🏛 historic building   📷 museum   🏛 historic site   🝐 scenic attraction   🐾 flora and fauna

YEOVILTON

7 miles N of Yeovil

📷 Fleet Air arm Museum

Yeovilton boasts one of the world's largest aviation museums, the **Fleet Air Arm Museum** (see panel opposite) which owns a unique collection of aircraft of which around half are on permanent display. Concorde is here along with a hangar full of fragile vintage aircraft. Visitors can 'fly' aboard the museum's own carrier; use interactive displays to explore the history and atmosphere of many of the aircraft stored here, and undertake the Merlin Experience that replicates a challenging flying mission. Other attractions include a children's adventure playground, a large book and souvenir shop, restaurant, airfield viewing galleries and a picnic area.

The River Yeo, Near Yeovilton

CHARLTON MACKRELL

9 miles N of Yeovil off the A37

🏠 Lytes Cary Manor

A couple of miles southeast of the town lies the charming manor house of **Lytes Cary Manor** (National Trust). This late medieval stone house was built by succeeding generations of the Lyte family, the best known member of which was Henry Lyte, the Elizabethan herbalist who dedicated his 1578 translation of Dodoen's *Cruydeboeck* to Queen Elizabeth "from my poore house at Lytescarie". After the family left the house in the 18th century it fell into disrepair but in 1907 it was purchased and restored by Sir

Walter Jenner, son of the famous Victorian physician. Notable features include a 14th century chapel and Tudor Great Hall. The present garden is an enchanting combination of formality and eccentricity. There is an open lawn lined with magnificent yew topiary, an orchard filled with quince, pear and apple trees and a network of enclosed paths that every now and then reveal a view of the house, a lily pond or a classical statue.

SPARKFORD

8 miles NE of Yeovil on the A359

📷 Haynes International Motor Museum

🏛 Cadbury Castle

The **Haynes International Motor Museum** **is** thought to hold the largest collection of veteran, vintage and classic cars and motorbikes in the United Kingdom. A living and working museum, it cares for more than 340 cars and bikes ranging from nostalgic classics to the super cars of today. The site contains 11 huge display halls; one of the UK's largest speedway collections; a kids' race track; adventure play area; gift shop and restaurant.

Just to the southeast of the village lies **Cadbury Castle**, a massive Iron Age hill fort first occupied more than 5,000 years ago and believed by some to be the location of King Arthur's legendary Camelot. The Romans are reputed to have carried out a massacre here in around 70AD when they put down a revolt by the ancient Britons. A major excavation in the 1960s uncovered a wealth of Roman and pre-Roman remains on the site as well as confirming that there was certainly a 6th century fortification on the hilltop. This particular discovery ties the castle in with King Arthur who, at around that time, was spearheading the Celtic British resistance against the advancing Saxons. If Cadbury Castle had been Arthur's Camelot, it would have had a timber fortification rather than the turreted stone structure of the storybooks.

This easily defended hilltop was again fortified during the reign of Ethelred the Unready in the early 11th century. The poorly-advised king established a mint here in around 1000. Most of the coinage from Cadbury was used to buy off the invading Danes in an act of appeasement that led to the term Danegeld. As a consequence, most of the surviving coins from the Cadbury mint are now to be found in the museums of Scandinavia.

The mile-long walk around Cadbury Castle's massive earthwork ramparts demonstrates the site's effectiveness as a defensive position. This allowed those at the castle to see enemy's troop movements in days gone by and it now provides spectacular panoramic views for today's visitors.

BARWICK
2 miles S of Yeovil off the A37

🏠 Barwick Park

Pronounced 'barrik', this village is home to **Barwick Park**, an estate littered with bizarre follies, arranged at the four points of the compass. The eastern folly, known as Jack the Treacle Eater, is composed of a rickety stone arch topped by a curious turreted room. According to local stories, the folly is named after a foot messenger who ran back and forth between the estate and London on a diet of nothing more than bread and treacle. The estate also possesses a curious grotto and a handsome church with a Norman font and an unusual 17th century transeptal tower.

WEST COKER
3 miles SW of Yeovil off the A30

🏠 Brympton d'Evercy Manor

Close to the village of West Coker is the magnificent **Brympton d'Evercy Manor House** dating from Norman times but with significant 16th and 17th century additions. (The house is not normally open to the public but is available for civil weddings and other functions). The superb golden Hamstone south wing was built in Jacobean times to a design by Inigo Jones. It boasts many fine internal features including the longest straight single span staircase in Britain and an unusual modern tapestry depicting an imaginary bird's eye view of the property during the 18th century. When viewed from a distance, the mansion house, the little estate church and the nearby dower house make a delightful lakeside grouping.

In the church at nearby East Coker were buried the ashes of the poet and playwright TS Eliot. This village, is where his ancestors lived before emigrating to America in the mid-1600s, and provides the title for the second of his *Four Quartets*. Its opening and closing lines are engraved on a plaque in the church:

In my beginning is my end.
In my end is my beginning.

MONTACUTE
4 miles W of Yeovil off the A3088

🏠 Montacute House   📻 TV & Radio Museum

This charming village of golden Hamstone houses and cottages is also home to the magnificent Elizabethan mansion, **Montacute House** (National Trust - see panel below), built in the 1590s for Edward Phelips, Queen Elizabeth's Master of the Rolls. The architect is believed to be William Arnold who also designed Wadham College, Oxford. There have been alterations made to the house over the centuries, most notably in the late 1700s when the west front was remodelled by the

fifth Edward Phelips. In the 19th century the fortunes of the Phelips family began to decline and the house was leased out. In the 1920s, following a succession of tenants, the house was put up for sale. A gift from Ernest Cook (the grandson of the travel agent Thomas Cook) enabled the National Trust to purchase this wonderful Elizabethan residence. Constructed of Hamstone, the house is adorned with characteristic open parapets, fluted columns, twisted pinnacles, oriel windows and carved statues. The long gallery, one of the grandest of its kind in Britain, houses a fine collection of Tudor and Jacobean portraits on permanent loan from London's National Portrait Gallery. Other noteworthy features include magnificent tapestries and samplers on display from the Goodhart Collection; the stone and stained glass screen in the great hall and Lord Curzon's bath, an Edwardian addition concealed in a bedroom cupboard. An established story tells of how Curzon, a senior Tory politician, waited at Montacute in 1923

Montacute House

Montacute, Somerset TA15 6XP
Tel: 01935 823289
e-mail: montacute@nationaltrust.org.uk
website: nationaltrust.org.uk

Built in the late 16th century for Sir Edward Phelips, Montacute glitters with many windows and is adorned with elegant chimneys, carved parapets and other Renaissance

features, including contemporary plasterwork, chimney pieces and heraldic glass. The splendid staterooms are full of fine 17th and 18th century furniture and textiles. Tudor and Elizabethan portraits, from the National Portrait Gallery are displayed in the Long Gallery, the longest of its kind in England. The House is surrounded by formal gardens with mixed borders, old roses and interesting topiary. The wider estate consists of landscaped parkland.

🎭 stories and anecdotes   🦜 famous people   🎨 art and craft   🎭 entertainment and sport   🚶 walks

for news that he was to be called to form a new government. The call never came. The house stands within a magnificent landscaped park that incorporates a walled formal garden, a fig walk, an orangery and a cedar lawn formally known as 'Pig's Wheaties's Orchard'.

Some 500 years before Montacute House was built, a controversial castle was erected on the nearby hill by Robert, Count of Mortain. The count's choice of site angered the Saxons as they believed the hill to be sacred because King Alfred had buried a fragment of Christ's cross here. In 1068, they rose up and attacked the castle in one of many unsuccessful revolts against the Norman occupation. Ironically, a subsequent Count of Mortain was found guilty of treason and forced into donating all his lands in the area to a Cluniac priory on the site now occupied by Montacute village. The castle has long since disappeared, as has the monastery, with the exception of its fine 16th century gatehouse, now a private home, and a stone dovecote.

The village is also home to the **Montacute TV and Radio Museum** where a vast collection of vintage radios, wireless receivers and TV sets, from the 1920s through to the present day, is on display. It developed from the

keepsakes hoarded by Dennis Greenham who had been in the electrical business since 1930. The huge collection of radio and TV memorabilia includes toys, books and games. There are also tearooms, gardens and a museum shop.

TINTINHULL
4 miles NW of Yeovil

🌿 Tintinhull House Garden

A couple of miles to the east of Martock is another enchanting National Trust property, **Tintinhull House Garden**, set in the grounds of an early 17th century manor house. The house itself, which is not open to the public, overlooks an attractive triangular green that forms the nucleus of the sprawling village of Tintinhull. This is home to a number of other interesting buildings: a

Tintinhull House Garden

remodelled, part-medieval rectory, Tintinhull Court; the 17th century Dower House; and St Margaret's parish church, a rare rectangular single-cell church.

Despite the age of the house, Tintinhull House Gardens were laid out between 1933 and 1961 in a series of distinctive areas, divided by walls and hedges, each with its own planting theme. There is a pool garden with a delightful pond filled with lilies and irises, a kitchen garden and a sunken garden that is cleverly designed to give the impression it has many different levels.

STOKE SUB HAMDON
5 miles NW of Yeovil off the A303

🏛 Stoke sub Hamdon Priory 🐾 Ham Hill

The eastern part of this attractive village is dominated by a fine Norman church; the western area of the village contains the remains of a late medieval priory. **Stoke sub Hamdon Priory** (National Trust) was built in the 14th and 15th centuries for the priests of the now demolished chantry chapel of St Nicholas. It was later converted into a house with a very impressive Great Hall.

South of the village rises the 400ft-high **Ham Hill** (or Hamdon Hill), the source of the beautiful honey coloured stone used in so many of the surrounding villages. This solitary limestone outcrop rises abruptly from the Somerset plain and provides breathtaking views of the surrounding countryside. A substantial hill fort, built here during the Iron Age, was subsequently overrun by the invading Romans. The new occupants built

📖 stories and anecdotes 🐦 famous people 🎨 art and craft ✍ entertainment and sport 🚶 walks

their own fortification to guard their major route, the Fosse Way, and its important intersection with the road between Dorchester and the Bristol Channel at nearby Ilchester.

It was the Romans who discovered that the hill's soft, even-grained limestone made a flexible and highly attractive building material and they used it in the construction of their villas and temples. Later, the Saxons and then the Normans came to share this high opinion of Hamstone. By the time quarrying reached its height in the 17th century, a sizeable settlement had grown up within the confines of the Iron Age fort though, today, only a solitary inn remains. A war memorial to 44 local men who died during World War I stands on the summit of Ham Hill. Now designated a country park, the combination of the view, the old earthwork ramparts and the maze of overgrown quarry workings make this an attractive place for recreation and picnics.

MARTOCK
6 miles NW of Yeovil on the B3165

🏛 Treasurer's House   🏛 Pinnacle Monument

This attractive, small town is surrounded by rich arable land and the area has long been renowned for its prosperous land-owning farmers. Martock's long-established affluence is reflected in its impressive part-13th century parish church. A former abbey church that once belonged to the monks of Mont St Michel in Normandy, the church boasts one of the finest tie-beam roofs in Somerset with almost every part of it covered in beautiful carvings.

The old part of Martock is blessed with an unusually large number of fine buildings. Amongst these can be found the **Treasurer's House** (National Trust), a small medieval

house of two stories built in the late 13th century for the Treasurer of Wells Cathedral who was also rector of Martock. Visitors can see the Great Hall, an interesting wall painting and the kitchen added to the building in the 15th century. Close by is the Old Court House, a parish building that served as the local grammar school for 200 years. To the west is Martock's 17th century Manor House, once the home of Edward Parker, who exposed the Gunpowder Plot after Guy Fawkes had warned him against attending Parliament on that fateful night.

Outside the Market House stands the **Pinnacle Monument,** an unusual structure with four sundials arranged in a square on top of its column, the whole finished with an attractive weather-vane.

EAST LAMBROOK
8 miles NW of Yeovil off the A303

🌿 East Lambrook Manor Garden

Just west of this charming hamlet is **East Lambrook Manor Garden** (see panel opposite) which was planted with endangered species by the writer and horticulturist, Margery Fish, who lived at the medieval Hamstone manor house from 1937 until her death in 1969. Her exuberant planting and deliberate lack of formality created an atmosphere of romantic tranquillity that is maintained to this day. Now Grade I listed, the garden is also the home of the National Collection of the cranesbill species of geranium. The low-lying land to the north of East Lambrook is criss-crossed by a network of drainage ditches or rhines (pronounced reens) that eventually flow into the rivers Parrett, Isle and Yeo. Originally cut in the early 19th century, the ditches are often lined with double rows of pollarded willows, a sight

🏛 historic building   🏛 museum   🏛 historic site   🌿 scenic attraction   🌿 flora and fauna

East Lambrook Manor Gardens

South Petherton, Somerset TA13 5HH
Tel: 01460 240328
website: www.eastlambrook.co.uk

The Grade I Listed garden at East Lambrook Manor is internationally recognised as the "Home of English Cottage Gardening". Packed with rare and unusual plants, visitors can wander along the crooked stone paths through a profusion of colour, scent and cottage garden style. Designed in the '50s by the horticultural icon, Margery Fish, her creation at East Lambrook was responsible for revolutionising gardening in the 20th century. She discovered many new varieties of plant, saved others from extinction and broke from the tradition of the formal design, producing a garden which is a delight and an inspiration.

Margery Fish's famous plant nursery was established in the '50s and is still open and packed with rare and unusual plants. The colour, structure and scent of the hardy perennials available will suit gardens of all sizes and locations. There is also an extensive selection of hardy geraniums available.

A newly created tiered display bed at East Lambrook Manor houses a rolling exhibition of the National Collection of geraniums, allowing visitors to view geraniums from all over the world. The collection is owned and maintained by its creator, Mr Andrew Norton.

that has come to characterise this part of Somerset. Despite having to be cleared every few years, the rhines provide a valuable natural habitat for a wide variety of bird, animal and plant life.

MUCHELNEY
12 miles NW of Yeovil off the A372

🏠 Muchelney Abbey   🏠 Midelney Manor

This village's name means 'the Great Island' and it dates from the time when this settlement rose up above the surrounding marshland, long since drained to provide excellent arable farmland. Muchelney is also the location of an impressive part-ruined Benedictine monastery thought to have been founded by King Ine of Wessex in the 8th century. This claim was, in part, confirmed

when, in the 1950s, an archaeological dig unearthed an 8th century crypt. During medieval times **Muchelney Abbey** (English Heritage) grew to emulate its great rival at Glastonbury. After the Dissolution in 1539, the buildings, dating mainly from the 15th and 16th centuries, gradually fell into disrepair. Much of its stone was removed to provide building material for the surrounding village. In spite of this, a substantial part of the original structure, including the south cloister and abbot's lodge, can still be seen today.

Opposite the parish church, which its noted for is remarkable early 17th century illuminations, stands the **Priest's House** (National Trust), a late-medieval hall house built by the abbey for the parish priest. Little has changed since the 17th century, when the

MUCHELNEY POTTERY

Muchelney, Langport, Somerset TA10 0DW
Tel: 01458 250324
website: www.johnleachpottery.co.uk

Just a mile south of the ancient village of Muchelney, John Leach, the eldest grandson of Bernard Leach, continues the family tradition at his own thatched-roofed **Muchelney Pottery**. Like his father, David Leach, and his grandfather before him, John hand-throws his distinctive stoneware pots which are then fired, in age-old fashion, using a three-chambered wood-fired kiln. The pots are practical, both microwave and dishwasher proof, and have a unique quality that comes from their warmly toasted finishes and interior glazes. No two pots are ever identical, further adding to their charm, and the range of tableware extends from jugs, casseroles and plates to bread crocks, chicken bricks and pasta pods. John's wife, Lizzie, manages the attractive Pottery Shop where a full range of the pots can be bought.

John's original signed designs, including his 'Black Mood' pots, are on display and for sale in the recently-opened John Leach Gallery adjacent to the shop. Individual pots by Nick Rees and Mark Melbourne, the other two potters in the Muchelney team, and work by invited artists and sculptors may also be bought in the gallery. Tours of the workshop can be arranged and there are usually two public kiln openings a year.

building was divided, and the interesting features to see include the Gothic doorway, the beautiful tracery windows and a massive 15th century stone fireplace. Alhough it is still a dwelling, the house is opened on a limited basis.

Just to the west of the village, near Drayton, stands the privately-owned **Midelney Manor**, originally an island manor belonging to Muchelney Abbey. A handsome manor house with architectural features from the 16th, 17th and 18th centuries, this has been in the hands of the Trevilian family since the early 1500s. The estate incorporates a heronry, a series of delightful gardens, a unique 17th century falcon's mews and woodland walks. Although the house is not normally open to the public,

there are self-catering cottages available on the estate.

LANGPORT
12 miles NW of Yeovil on the A378

🏛 Langport Gap   🏛 Stembridge Tower Mill

🏛 Langport & River Parrett Visitor Centre

The old part of this former market town stands on a rise above an ancient ford across the River Parrett. A short distance downstream from this point, the river is joined by the Rivers Isle and Yeo. Defended by an earthwork rampart during Saxon times, by 930 Langport was an important commercial centre that minted its own coins. The only surviving part of the town's defences is the East Gate incorporating a

🏛 historic building   🏛 museum   🏛 historic site   🝔 scenic attraction   🌿 flora and fauna

curious 'hanging' chapel that sits above the arch on an upper level. It is now a Masonic Lodge and rarely open to the public. The impressive tower of the church at nearby Huish Episcopi can be seen through the barrel-vaulted gateway.

During the 18th and 19th centuries, Langport flourished as a banking centre and the local independent bank, Stuckey's, became known for its impressive branches, many of which can still be seen in the surrounding towns and villages although the bank has long since been taken over by NatWest. At the time of this amalgamation in 1909, Stuckey's had more notes in circulation than any other bank in the country save for the Bank of England. Stuckey's original head office is now Langport's branch of NatWest.

Throughout history, the **Langport Gap** has been the site of a number of important military encounters. Two of the most significant occurred more than 1,000 years apart. In the 6th century, Geraint, King of the Dumnonii, was involved in a battle here while, in July 1645, the Parliamentarian victory at the Battle of Langport gave Cromwell's forces almost total control of the West Country during the English Civil War.

More about life, past and present, on the Somerset Levels and Moors can be discovered at the **Langport and River Parrett Visitor Centre** through its series of hands-on exhibits and displays. Cycles are available for hire along with suggested cycle routes.

Just to the east, at **Huish Episcopi**, one of the finest examples in the country of a late

VALENTINE ORIGINAL

Old Kelways, Langport, Somerset TA10 9SJ
Tel: 01458 253215 Fax: 01458 251992
e-mail: claire@valentineoriginal.co.uk
website: www.valentineoriginal.co.uk

For a unique shopping experience, pay a visit to **Valentine Original** in the old market town of Langport. Established by Claire Valentine, the company designs and makes original clothes in sumptuous natural fabrics. They also stock an ever-changing selection of unusual accessories, hats, jewellery and bags. They have clothes for every occasion – for business, a wedding or just for simple day-to-day comfort, with designs and fabrics to delight and inspire. Alpaca, cashmere or merino wool hand-knits co-ordinate with silk jersey or woven tweed for both style and luxury, while the made-to-measure wedding outfits with hats and hand-painted scarves to match, provide an opportunity to express your individuality.

The Valentine Original range features floaty, hand-painted silks and hand-woven matka for more formal outfits, and the shop stocks metres of silk crepes, dupions and chiffons. There's an extensive choice of original designs or Claire will create a one-off specially for you. Whatever you are looking for this season, Valentine Original will be the place to find it. The shop is open from 9.30am-4pm,

medieval Somerset tower can be found at the village's church. At its most impressive in high summer when it can be viewed through the surrounding greenery, this ornate structure is adorned with striking tracery, pinnacles and carvings. The church also has an elaborate Norman doorway, which still shows signs of the fire that destroyed much of the earlier building in the 13th century. A window in the south chapel was designed by Edward Burne-Jones, the 19th century Pre-Raphaelite.

The church at Aller, just northwest of Langport, was the scene of another historic event. It was here, in 878, that King Alfred converted Guthrum the Dane and his followers to Christianity following a battle on Salisbury Plain. The low wooded rise to the east of Aller is criss-crossed by a network of ancient country lanes which pass through some pleasant hamlets and villages including High Ham, the home of the last thatched windmill in England. Dating from 1822 and overlooking the Somerset levels, **Stembridge Tower Mill** (National Trust) continued to operate until 1910.

SOMERTON
13 miles NW of Yeovil on the B3151

🏛 Church of St Michae   ⚲ Home Gallery

This small town gave the county its name and, for 100 years between 1250 and 1350, was also its administrative centre. The prosperity this brought to the town is reflected in the fine **Church of St Michael** which was later enhanced even further by the installation of a magnificent roof. Carved by monks from

---

BJS SADDLERY

London House, New Street, Somerton, Somerset TA11 7NN
Tel/Fax: 01458 273253
e-mail: info@bjssaddlery.co.uk
website: www.bjssaddlery.co.uk

Owned and run by equine sports massage therapist Belinda Sutton, **BJS Saddlery** provides a comprehensive range of supplies for both horse and rider. "At BJS," says Belinda, "we pride ourselves on first class customer care, with the highest standards of dedication to ensure you find the products that are right for you – and your pocket." The Saddlery stocks a small selection of saddles from Rhinegold, Wintec and Thorowgood, and also deals in secondhand saddles listed on the notice board. It also offers a saddle fitting service – customers are welcome to bring in their own tack for fitting and safety checks.

Casual country clothing also occupies a large section of the shop with stockists Joules, Chukka, Horsewear and Dublin to mention a few. If you are looking for country foorwear they hold a large range for both children and adults, please visit the website for full stockist listing.

They offer a fully qualified hat and body protector fitting service, also rug cleaning and leatherwork centre.

🏛 historic building   🏛 museum   🏛 historic site   ⚲ scenic attraction   🌱 flora and fauna

Muchelney Abbey around 1500, the gloriously coffered structure is supported by tie beams on which rest pairs of Wessex wyverns, or dragons. These gradually increase in size as they near the altar, culminating in two ferocious monsters snarling across the aisle at each other.

Somerton today is a place of handsome old stone houses, shops and inns. The general atmosphere of mature prosperity is enhanced by the presence of a number of striking ancient buildings, most notably the 17th century Hext Almshouses. Broad Street leads into the picturesque market place with its distinctive covered Market Cross and Town Hall. Between 1278 and 1371, Somerton was the location of the county gaol and the meeting place of the shire courts as well as continuing to develop as a market town, reflected in the delightfully down-to-earth names of some of its streets such as Cow Square and Pig Street (now Broad Street).

Due to open in June 2006, the **Home Gallery** of the Somerset Guild of Craftsmen was formerly located in Martock. The Guild brings together craftspeople selected for the quality of design and craftsmanship in their work and the Gallery provides a showcase for work by Guild members in both traditional and contemporary styles.

Castle Cary

🏠 Round House   🏛 Castle Cary District Museum

🏠 War Memoria   🌱 Hadspen House Gardens

🎨 John Boyd Textiles

This lovely little town, surrounded by meadows and woods, has an atmosphere of mature rural calm as well as some interesting old buildings, many of them built in the local Hamstone that radiates a golden glow. There is a strikingly handsome 18th century post office, a tiny lock-up gaol called the **Round House** dating from 1779, and a splendid Market House with a magnificent 17th century colonnade. Largely constructed in 1855, the Market House is now the home of the **Castle Cary District Museum**. Perhaps the most interesting site here is the town's **War Memorial**, which stands in the middle of a pond said to be part of the old castle moat. It was used for many years as a drive-through bath for muddy horses and carts, for washing horsehair and as a convenient place for ducking scolds and witches.

Just to the west of the town at Higher Flax Mills is an interesting

Market Square, Somerton

🎭 stories and anecdotes   🕊 famous people   🎨 art and craft   🎪 entertainment and sport   🚶 walks

BLACK & WHITE FASHION AND HOME ACCESSORIES

Fore Street, Castle Cary, Somerset BA7 7BG
Tel: 01963 359190   e-mail: black.white@amserve.com
website: www.blackandwhite.org.uk

Owner Jane Milward runs **Black & White Fashion and Home Accessories**, a charming shop in the centre of Castle Cary. Her concept started with leather goods, from bags to sofas, which are still very much in evidence, but there's now much more, including a wide range of fashionable yet inexpensive co-ordinates with matching accessories such as jewellery, belts, gloves and handbags. Items for the home include unusual lighting, contemporary artwork, leather chairs, furnishings, washbags, candles – and even a selection of collars that any dog would be proud to wear.

survival from earlier days. **John Boyd Textiles** have been weavers of horsehair fabric since 1837 and are still using looms that were first installed in 1870. Horsehair was especially popular in Victorian times because of its durability, value and being easy to clean. Furniture designers such as Chippendale, Hepplewhite, Lutyens and Charles Rennie Mackintosh all used horsehair fabrics and they were also used for Empire and Biedermeier furniture. Guided tours of the mill are available by arrangement.

Also worth visiting is the beautiful **Hadspen House Gardens** situated just to the southeast

NEEDFUL THINGS

High Street, Castle Cary, Somerset BA7 7AN
Tel: 01963 351352   Fax: 01963 350353

Needful Things is a delightful double-fronted shop on the main street of an equally delightful little Somerset town. Home accessories and soft furnishings are the main stock in trade, with everything to grace and enhance a home, from beautiful furniture to exquisite fabrics and materials.

The range is impressive and customers can choose either from the displays or have something made to their own requirements from the pattern books. The shop also stocks the Sarah's Garden and Wedgwood silver plate ranges of elegant kitchen and tableware, as well as the highly effective Lampe Berger air purifiers and fragrancers.

The finishing touches are all here too, from flowers to lighting and pictures, wall mountings and window hangings, and the cards and wrapping paper make a special gift even more special. There's also a small, select range of tastefully chosen womens' clothing.

A wonderland at Christmas, when every inch is filled with festive treasures, Needful Things is a joy at any time of the year with its fabrics and colours and alluring aromas. The charming owners John and Allison Lawrence put the seal on the pleasure of a visit.

🏛 historic building   🏛 museum   🏛 historic site   ❧ scenic attraction   ❦ flora and fauna

of the town. Penelope Hobhouse, who lived at Hadspen until 1979, restored and enlarged the earlier garden and made her work here the subject of her first book *The Country Gardener.* Since 1986 the Canadian gardeners, Sandra and Nori Pope, have continued this tradition, transforming the Upper and Walled Garden with entirely new planting schemes and a bold use of colour, incorporating a quarter of a mile of old brick walls.

Around Castle Cary

BRUTON
4 miles NE of Castle Cary on the A359

🏛 Sexey's Hospital 🏛 Patwell Pump

🏛 The Dovecote

This remarkably well-preserved former clothing and ecclesiastical centre, clinging to a hillside above the River Brue, is more like a small town than a village. In the middle of the High Street is the 17th century **Sexey's Hospital** with a beautiful quadrangle providing a stunning view across the Brue valley. It has a small, candle-lit chapel with dark Jacobean oak pews and pulpit. The hospital was founded by Hugh Sexey, a courtier of Elizabeth I and James I. It still accommodates the elderly and also has a school that is one of the few state boarding schools in England.

A priory was first established at Bruton in the 11th century and although much of this has disappeared the former priory church is now the parish church. The Church of St

CLANVILLE MANOR

Clanville, Castle Cary, Somerset BA7 7PJ
Tel: 01963 350124 Fax: 01963 350719
e-mail: info@clanvillemanor.co.uk
website: www.clanvillemanor.co.uk

Just a couple of miles outside the delightful little town of Castle Cary, **Clanville Manor** offers a choice of quality bed & breakfast or self-catering accommodation. Bed & breakfast guests stay in the handsome stone farmhouse which combines 18th century elegance with 21st century comfort. There are three fully equipped en suite rooms – a double, twin and single – and guests are regaled with wonderful Aga-cooked breakfasts based on fresh local produce. The non-smoking farmhouse is for adults and children over 10, but all children are welcome in the two self-catering cottages.

The stone-built Tallet Cottage sleeps four-five people in double and bunk bedrooms. It has lots of character, a wood-burning stove and a large garden with climbing frame. Lone Oak cottage provides spacious ground floor accommodation with three bedrooms sleeping up to six guests. It has a sitting room, kitchen, shower room, large patio and enjoys country views. For both cottages, linen, towels and heating are included. During the summer months, guests have the use of an outdoor heated swimming pool. Clanville Manor is centrally situated for exploring Bath, Wells, Glastonbury and many National Trust properties.

🎬 stories and anecdotes   🕊 famous people   🎨 art and craft   🎭 entertainment and sport   🚶 walks

BILL THE BUTCHER

High Street, Bruton, Somerset BA10 0AB
Tel: 01749 812388

The only accredited Rare Breeds Butcher in Somerset, **Bill the Butcher** has been supplying quality meats since 1979. Only local meats from local farmers are used and the pork and bacon are dry cured on the premises. Owner Phil Butler also stocks a wide variety of other wholesome foods: locally grown fruit and vegetables, local cheeses, Lovington's Ice Creams, Dorset Blue soups, Yeo Valley fat-free yogurts, organic milk from Bruton, River Cottage yoghurts, Godminster eggs and, on Fridays, fresh fish from Newhaven in Sussex. Then there are the wines, Fenteman's squashes and fruit drinks, Kettle's crisps and much, much more.

Mary has a rare second tower built over the north porch in the late 1300s. The light and spacious interior is well worth a visit as it contains a number of memorials to the Berkeley family, the local lords of the manor who also owned the land on which London's Berkeley Square now stands.

Across the river from the church is the **Patwell Pump**, a curious square structure that was the parish's communal water pump and remained in use until well into the 20th century. Further downstream a 15th century packhorse bridge still serves pedestrians. However, **The Dovecote** is arguably Bruton's

BRUTON HOUSE RESTAURANT WITH ROOMS

2-4 High Street, Bruton, Somerset BA10 0AA
Tel: 01749 813395
e-mail: info@brutonhouse.co.uk
website: www.brutonhouse.co.uk

Back in 1980, the beautiful building which is Bruton House was in imminent danger of demolition. Miraculously, the grand old building was saved and it is now occupied by **Bruton House Restaurant & Rooms** which impressively combines one of the country's top restaurants and quality accommodation. The restaurant specialises in seasonal, locally sourced cuisine with separate menus for lunch and dinner. Boasting numerous awards, dining here is a memorable experience and booking is essential. A typical menu might offer Buttered Dorset Crab with foaming bisque as a starter; Loin of Clarendon Estate Venison with a thyme and juniper sauce as a main course; and poached pink rhubarb with nougat glace as a dessert. To complement your meal, there's a well-balanced wine list to choose from.

There are currently three guest bedrooms available at Bruton House, two double en-suite rooms, and one single room with a separate bathroom. The rooms have recently been refurbished, along with the guests' sitting room. There is also a terrace, which has beautiful views over to the Dovecote, St Mary's Church and some wonderful Somerset views beyond. Guests also have use of the bar downstairs, and, of course the restaurant should they wish to dine. Well-behaved dogs are always welcome, as are children. Guests are provided with a selection of morning papers and a breakfast of cereals, local yoghurts and jams, toast, tea, coffee and juices.

🏠 historic building   🏛 museum   🏛 historic site   ♤ scenic attraction   🌱 flora and fauna

GANTS MILL & GARDEN

Bruton, Somerset BA10 0DB
Tel: 01749 812393
e-mail: shingler@gantsmill.co.uk
website: www.gantsmill.co.uk

John le Gaunt, who in 1290 owned what is now **Gants Mill & Garden** would be surprised to know that the mill still bears his name. Today, the property is owned by Brian and Alison Shingler who have lived here since 1949. Brian is a 6th generation miller and on his guided tours of the mill his enthusiasm is evident both for its history and for the modern engineering wizardry that produces power from this renewable resource. Visitors can feel the barley meal coming warm out of the grindstones. As you walk around the ¾-acre garden, the sound of water is everywhere. The stream goes over waterfalls, through ponds and keeps the bog garden moist before cascading down into the river.

The lovely garden is colour themed and Alison says she is "very fierce with flowers that dare to come up the wrong colour". After a stroll around the garden, why not indulge in tea and home-made cake served in the fuchsia and begonia conservatory. And if you want to linger longer, the Shinglers offer bed & breakfast accommodation in the farmhouse or, for those who prefer self-catering, Miller's Cottage has three bedrooms sleeping up to six guests.

most distinctive building. Now roofless, it can be seen on the crest of a hill to the south of the bridge. Built in the 15th century, the dovecote is thought to have doubled as a watchtower.

WINCANTON

5 miles SE of Castle Cary off the A303

🐾 Wincanton Racecourse 🔭 Discworld Emporium

Wincanton's broad main street is flanked by substantial houses and former coaching inns, a faint echo of the era when as many as 17 coaches a day would stop here, pausing about halfway between London and the long-established naval base at Plymouth. At that time, the inns could provide lodging for scores of travellers and stabling for more than 250 horses. A former cloth-making centre, the oldest part of this attractive town stands on a draughty hillside above the River Cale. An

impressive number of fine Georgian buildings, some of which were constructed to replace earlier buildings destroyed in a fire in 1747, can be found here.

Modern day Wincanton is a peaceful light industrial town whose best known attraction, **Wincanton National Hunt Racecourse**, harks back to the days when horses were the only form of transport. Horse-racing began in the area in the 18th century and the racecourse moved to its present site to the north of the town centre in 1927. Wincanton is remembered as the course where the great *Desert Orchid* had his first race of each season during his dominance of steeple-chasing in the 1980s. For golf enthusiasts, the racecourse incorporates a challenging nine-hole pay and play course, which is open throughout the year.

Wincanton also has the distinction of being home to the only shop in the known universe

🎭 stories and anecdotes 🐦 famous people 🔭 art and craft 🐾 entertainment and sport 🥾 walks

OTTERY ANTIQUES

7 Market Place, Wincanton, Somerset BA9 9LL
Tel: 01963 34238
website: www.otteryantiques.com

Specialising in the sales of 17th, 18th and 19th century furniture and decorative items, **Ottery Antiques** have been successfully dealing in period furniture for over 20 years, they are well established and well respected within the trade and public circles, not only for their dealings in high quality items but also for their in house restoration service.

Their wide mix of stock ranges from tables to tea caddies, clocks and barometers (often local makers), pictures and prints, period brass and copper, Doulton and Staffordshire pottery and much more.

With previous clients ranging from the foreign and commonwealth office, the making of furniture for the Lord chancellors residence, to stately homes, and a list of long standing antique dealers to many private customers, your best attention is assured.

Members of LAPADA and BABAADA. If you are unable to visit their shop or workshops, samples of their stock and previous restorations can be seen on the two websites; www.otteryantiques.com or www.otteryantiques.co.uk.

---

devoted to artefacts inspired by the writings of Terry Pratchett, author of the *Discworld* novels which have sold more than 40 million copies worldwide. At **The Cunning Artificer's Discworld Emporium** devotees will find all manner of wonderful objects ranging from the Mystic Prawn Medallion to the Dibbler Pie – "A culinary delight that will act as not just a superb paperweight, but also an appetite depressant".

TEMPLECOMBE
8 miles SE of Castle Cary on the A357

🖋 Gartell Light Railway

🖼 Templecombe Railway Museum

To the east of the village is the unusual **Gartell Light Railway**, a rare two-foot gauge line that runs for around a mile through the beautiful countryside of Blackmore Vale on

the track bed of the Somerset and Dorset Railway, closed more than 30 years ago. The trains run every 15 minutes from Common Line Station, which also has a visitor centre, refreshment room and shop. The nearby **Templecombe Railway Museum** houses a fascinating collection of artefacts, photographs and models that tell the story of the nearby station, once a busy junction where some 130 railwaymen worked.

Wells

🏛 Cathedral of St Andrew   𝒫 Astronomical Clock

🏛 Bishop's Palace   🏛 Penniless Porch

🖼 Wells & Mendip Museum   🌿 Mute Swans

This ancient ecclesiastical centre derives its name from a line of springs that rise up from the base of the Mendips and deliver water at

---

🏛 historic building   🖼 museum   🏚 historic site   🌿 scenic attraction   🌿 flora and fauna the rate of some 40 gallons per second. The first church here is believed to have been founded by King Ine in around 700; the present **Cathedral of St Andrew** was begun in the 12th century. Taking more than three centuries to complete, this magnificent cathedral demonstrates the three main styles of Gothic architecture. Its 13th century west front, with more than 170 statues of saints, angels and prophets gazing down on the cathedral close, is generally acknowledged to be its crowning glory. There used to be twice as many statues, all painted in glowing colours. Following the Civil War, Puritan fanatics mutilated or destroyed as many as they could and 700 years of exposure to the Somerset weather has scoured away the colours. A few, including the central figure of Christ in His Glory, have been replaced with faithful copies.

Inside the cathedral there are many superb features including the beautiful and unique scissor arches and the great 14th century stained glass window over the high altar. However, the cathedral's most impressive sight is its 14th century **Astronomical Clock**, one of the oldest working timepieces in the world, that shows the minutes, hours and phases of the moon on separate inner and outer dials and marks the quarter hours with a lively battle between knights.

The large cathedral close is a tranquil city within a city and for centuries the ecclesiastical and civic functions of Wells have remained separate. The west front of the cathedral has an internal passage with pierced apertures and there is a theory that choirboys might have sung through these openings to give the illusion to those gathered on the

LA MAISON DU FROMAGE

14 Queen Street, Wells, Somerset BA5 2DP
Tel: 01749 679803 e-mail: lamaisondf@btinternet.com

As the name suggests, **La Maison du Fromage** offers an enticing range of cheeses. As well as old favourites such as Montgomery's Cheddar, Somerset Brie and Camembert, delicious local and organic varieties using milk and cream not just from cows but also from goats, sheep and buffalo, providing a healthy choice for all diets. Brown Cow River Cottage yogurts and cheese, Alhams organically reared buffalo cheeses, and pasturma (Romanian pastrami) are recent additions.

This stylish delicatessen, just two minutes walk from the Cathedral, also stocks a wide range of local, regional and international culinary treats. Mendip honey, local ham and bacon, freshly pressed fruit juices, a good selection of Greek and Italian olives, oils and dressings, the Nairobi coffee range, Miles teas and coffee beans from Porlock which can be ground for you while you wait. Rose Farm preserves, chutneys and marmalades make perfect gifts. Organic flours, pastas and muesli using spelt flour, which has an inedible outer husk which protects the grain on the stalk from pests and diseases thus eliminating the need for harmful chemical sprays, come from Sharpham Park near Glastonbury. Food to go - they sell an interesting range - sandwiches made daily in house with local bread, sticky cakes, including gluten-free chocolate fudge brownies, home made soup, pates, tarts, pesto, hummus, mayonnaises and dressings etc. Owners of La Maison are Mike Poole and his partner Cary Nelson.

MADDIE BROWN

*15 Market Place, Wells, Somerset BA5 2RF
& 22 Church Street, Tetbury,
Gloucestershire GL8 8JG
Tel: 0845 4304303 Fax: 01749 679459
e-mail: mail@maddiebrown.co.uk
website: www.maddiebrown.co.uk*

Maddie Brown
Gifts • Home • Interiors

Maddie Brown started in the beautiful cathedral city of Wells, Somerset. The shop is housed over two floors of an ancient building overlooking the market place. The relaxed and friendly atmosphere and wonderful presentation make it an essential destination for lovers of Emma Bridgewater Pottery, Cath Kidston, L'Occitane, Damask, Matthew Rice and DWCD.

There is also a stock of French and country style furniture and home accessories, as well as a selection of traditional children's toys.

🏠 historic building   🏛 museum   🏚 historic site   ♨ scenic attraction   🌿 flora and fauna

HARTLEY'S FGF

Glastonbury Road, Wells, Somerset BA5 1QE
Tel: 01749 671707
e-mail: matthew@poppy-farm.fsnet.co.uk
website: www.hartleysfgf.co.uk

Offering a huge selection of fine West Country foods, **Hartley's FGF** is well-established as one of the very best delicatessens in the area. There's a strong emphasis on locally-produced items such as cheeses, meats, fruit juices and local ciders. From further afield come a good selection of European and New World wines, Indian and Chinese delicacies, coffees and teas. Additional attractions include fresh breads, pastries, cakes, fruit and vegetables.

cathedral green that the then lifelike painted statues were singing.

To the south of the cathedral's cloisters is the **Bishop's Palace**, a remarkable fortified medieval building which has been the home of the bishops of Bath and Wells since 1206. The palace is enclosed by a high wall and surrounded by a moat fed by the springs that give the city its name. A pair of mute swans on the moat can often be seen at the Gatehouse, ringing a bell for food. Swans were trained to do this in the 19th century and the present pair continue the tradition, passing it on to their young.

In order to gain access to the palace from the Market Place, visitors must pass under a 13th century stone arch known as the Bishop's Eye and then cross a drawbridge that was last raised for defensive purposes in 1831. Although it is still an official residence of the Bishop of Bath and Wells, visitors can tour the palace's chapel, the 13th century Great Hall and the beautiful gardens where many of the fine trees were

planted in 1821. On the northern side of the cathedral green is the Vicar's Close, completed in 1363. This picturesque cobbled thoroughfare, built to house the cathedral choristers, is the oldest continually inhabited streets in Europe.

The cathedral green is surrounded by a high wall breached at only three castellated entrance points. One of these, the gateway into the Market Place, is known as **Penniless Porch**. It was here that the

Wells Cathedral

📖 stories and anecdotes   🐦 famous people   🎨 art and craft   🎭 entertainment and sport   🚶 walks

POTTING SHED HOLIDAY COTTAGES

Harter's Hill Cottage, Pillmoor Lane, Coxley, nr Wells, Somerset BA5 1RF
Tel: 01749 672857 Fax: 01749 679925
e-mail: info@pottingshedholidays.co.uk
website: www.pottingshedholidays.co.uk

Chris and John van Bergen have created something very special with their **Potting Shed Holiday Cottages**, six beautifully renovated self-catering properties located in Wells – one of them almost under the cathedral roof – and in Coxley village. Spiders End, dating from about 1670, provides up-to-date comforts in a setting of old world charm that includes original features such as beams, sturdy stone and a section of ancient wattle and daub walls, all carefully restored by local craftsmen using local materials. This cottage has one double and one twin bedrooms, two bathrooms, a fully equipped modern kitchen, dining room and sitting room.

The Potting Shed, originally a farmhand's shed and animal shelter, is now a cosy retreat for two with a luxurious emperor size double bed among its many attractions. Guests at the cottage have the use of a lovingly cared for garden full of interesting botanical specimens and a haven for wildlife. A new addition for 2006 is the quirky Hobbits Den in the garden which has its own garden spa.

WELLS RECLAMATION COMPANY

Wells Road, Coxley, nr Wells, Somerset BA5 1RQ
Tel: 01749 677087
e-mail: enquiries@wellsreclamation.com
website: www.wellsreclamation.com

The extraordinary collection of salvaged architectural items in the yard of **Wells Reclamation Company** is so fascinating that people come just to look around. Within the 5½ acre site of carefully laid out antiques, curios and old building materials, you may come across anything from a huge stone pineapple to stained glass windows, old telephone boxes or a spiral staircase, fireplaces and fire surrounds, baths and basins and much, much more.

Following a career in the army, Haydn Davies created this architectural treasure trove with his wife Margaret in 1985. He sees the business as a tribute to the craftsmanship and skills of those who created Britain's great architectural heritage. Although in many cases those skills have been all but lost, the fruits of their labours have been saved. Customers can benefit from the hours of research Haydn and his family have invested in amassing this wonderful collection. For anyone seeking to carry out an authentic restoration of a period property, a visit here is essential since it is almost a museum with a vast wealth of items for houses of almost any age.

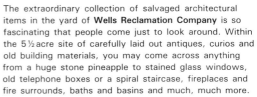
 🏛 historic building   🏛 museum   🏛 historic site   🝔 scenic attraction   🌿 flora and fauna

LITTLEWELL FARM

Coxley, Wells, Somerset BA5 1QP
Tel: 01749 677914
website: www.littlewellfarm.co.uk

Located on the A39 just one mile south of Wells, **Littlewell Farm** is a charming 18th century farmhouse offering quality bed & breakfast accommodation. The house has been refurbished to a very high standard by its owners, Elizabeth and Alan Shea, and now enjoys a four-Red

Diamonds rating from the AA. There are five guest bedrooms, four en suite and one with private bathroom, all are provided with TV and hospitality tray. Guests have the use of a comfortable TV lounge and the delightful southwest-facing gardens.

bishop allowed the city's poor to beg for money from those entering the cathedral close. Set in the pavement here is a length of brass that extends over the prodigious distance leapt by local girl Mary Rand when she set a world record for the long jump.

There is, of course, much more to Wells than its ecclesiastical buildings and heritage. A visit to the **Wells and Mendip Museum**, found near the west front of the cathedral, explains much of the history of the city and surrounding area through a collection of interesting locally found artefacts, amongst them some Roman coins and lead ingots, geological remains some 180 million years old when the Mendip Hills were a tropical paradise, and the

remains of the 'Witch' of Wookey Hole.

The city also remains a lively market centre, with a street market held every Wednesday and Saturday. For a grand view of Wells from a distance, follow the attractive footpath that starts from the Moat Walk and leads up the summit of Tor Hill.

Around Wells

STRATTON-ON-THE-FOSSE
9 miles NE of Wells on the A367

🏛 Downside Abbey

This former coal mining village is home to the famous Roman Catholic boys' public school,

RED HOUSE HOLIDAY COTTAGES

Red House Farm, Stratton on the Fosse,
nr Bath BA3 4QE
Tel: 01761 412319

Situated in the heart of the scenic Mendip Hills, **Red House Holiday Cottages** offer quality self-catering accommodation in beautifully converted former farm buildings. The luxuriously furnished cottages have one, two or four bedrooms and can sleep up to eight persons. Each cottage has a gas fire, colour TV and a comprehensively equipped kitchen. There's a separate laundry room with washing machines and tumble dryer. Owner Valerie Creed also runs a small farm shop near the site and sells local cheeses, butter, eggs, marmalade, jam and real farmhouse cider.

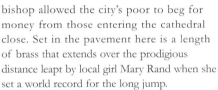

🎭 stories and anecdotes　🐦 famous people　🎨 art and craft　✏ entertainment and sport　🚶 walks

Downside Abbey, which occupies the site of a monastery founded in 1814 by a group of English Benedictines. The steady expansion of the school during the 20th century encouraged the monks to move to a new site on higher ground near the existing abbey church, an impressive building that took over 70 years to complete and numbered among its architects Sir Giles Gilbert Scott.

MIDSOMER NORTON
10 miles NE of Wells on the B3355

Radstock, Midsomer North & District Museum

The history of the area around this town is one of mining, with coal being hewn from nearby Norton Hill until as recently as the 1970s. In the churchyard of the town's parish church is a memorial to the 12 miners who were killed in an accident at Wellsway coal works in 1839. The surrounding countryside is beautiful and the sights and sounds of collieries have long since been replaced with that of open farmland. Midsomer Norton itself is a pleasant mix of old and new. There are excellent shopping facilities along with attractive Georgian buildings and a late medieval tithe barn.

At the interesting **Radstock, Midsomer North and District Museum**, housed in a converted 18th century barn, more information can be sought about the Somerset coalfield as the museum is devoted to the people of the local coal mines along with other exhibits relating to the railways, farms and schools of the area.

CAMELEY
10 miles NE of Wells off the A37

St James's Church

This attractive village is home to a church referred to by John Betjeman as "Rip Van

Winkle's Church". When the village of Cameley moved to nearby Temple Cloud in the 1700s, **St James's Church** was left alone on its low hill. Its old box pews are still in place and seem to have been custom made for their owners. Those who couldn't afford their own box could worship from the gallery along the south wall which bears the legend "for the free use of the inhabitants, 1819". A row of hat pegs was also conveniently provided. In the 1960s a remarkable series of medieval wall paintings was discovered here, under layers of whitewash. The murals are believed to have been painted between the 11th and the 17th centuries and feature such diverse images as the foot of a giant St Christopher stepping through a fish and crab infested river, a charming 14th century jester complete with harlequin costume and a rare coat of arms of Charles I.

MELLS
13 miles NE of Wells off the A362

John Horner

Mells was at one time on the easternmost limit of the lands belonging to Glastonbury Abbey. In the 15th century the Abbot of Glastonbury drew up plans to rebuild the village in the shape of a St Anthony's cross, with four arms of equal length. However, only one street, New Street, was ever completed. This architectural gem can still be seen to the south of St Andrew's parish church. While the exterior of the church is certainly imposing, the main interest lies inside where there is a remarkable collection of monuments designed by masters such as Lutyens, Gill, Munnings and Burne-Jones. One of the memorials is to Raymond, the eldest son of Herbert Asquith, the Liberal Prime Minister. Raymond was killed in the First World War. Raymond's sister was Violet Bonham Carter, whose grave is in the churchyard. Another memorial in the churchyard honours the pacifist and poet Siegfried Sassoon.

According to legend, the Abbot of Glastonbury, in an attempt to stave off Henry VIII's Dissolution of the Monasteries, dispatched his steward, **John Horner,** to London with a gift for the king consisting of a pie into which was baked the title deeds of 12 ecclesiastical manor houses. However, rather than attempting to persuade the king, Horner returned to Somerset the rightful owner of three of the manors himself. He paid a total of £2,000 for Mells, Nunnery and Leigh-upon-Mendip. This blatant act of disloyalty is, supposedly, commemorated in the nursery rhyme *Little Jack Horner* that describes how Jack 'put in his thumb and pulled out a plum'. The manor house at Mells remained in the hands of the Horner family until the early 20th century, when it passed to the Asquith family by marriage.

LULLINGTON
19 miles NE of Wells off the B3090

🏛 Orchardleigh Park

A footpath leads southwards from this peaceful riverside village to **Orchardleigh**

Park, an imposing Victorian mansion built in the mid-1800s and now a popular venue for civil weddings and conferences. In the 550 acres of parkland surrounding the house is a lake with an island on which is a small church whose churchyard contains the grave of Sir Henry Newbolt, the author of *Drake's Drum*.

SHEPTON MALLET
6 miles E of Wells on the A371

🏛 Market Cross 🏛 The Shambles

✎ Mid-Somerset Show 🐑 Pilton Manor

🏛 Tithe Barn ✎ Royal Bath & Wells Show

Situated on the banks of the River Sheppey, just to the west of Fosse Way, this old market town has been an important centre of communications since before the time of the Romans. The settlement's name is Saxon and it means, quite simply, 'sheep town'. This reveals its main commercial activity from before the Norman Conquest to the Middle Ages, when Shepton Mallet was a centre of woollen production and then weaving. The industry reached its peak in the 15th century. It was around this time that the town's most striking building, its magnificent parish church, was constructed. Other reminders of Shepton Mallet's past can be seen around its market

---

THE STRODE ARMS

West Cranmore, Shepton Mallet, Somerset BA4 4QJ
Tel: 01749 880450
website: www.fromeonline.co.uk/thestrodearms

Located close to Cranmore station on the East Somerset Steam Railway, **The Strode Arms** is a charmingly picturesque country inn with lots of charm and character. Since 2004, it has been run by Ann-Marie and Tim Gould and has become well-known for its excellent food and fine ales. Tim is the chef and his menu offers a wide selection of dishes based on local produce. Everything is home-made, including the bread, and everything is very reasonably priced. As a Wadsworths inn, the bar has beers from the Devizes Brewery and up to four real ales on tap at any one time.

🎭 stories and anecdotes   🦜 famous people   🎨 art and craft   ✎ entertainment and sport   🚶 walks

BOWLISH HOUSE HOTEL & RESTAURANT

Wells Road, Shepton Mallet, Somerset BA4 5JD
Tel: 01749 342022 Fax: 01749 345311
e-mail: enquiries@bowlishhouse.com
web: www.bowlishhouse.com

The ancient market town of Shepton Mallet is full of interesting things to see, and **Bowlish House Hotel** is an ideal base for visitors. Built in 1732 for a prosperous clothier, it was subsequently the home of generations of top brass from the local brewery. It passed into private hands in 1954 and so began its latest phase as a hotel and subsequently a restaurant. The current proprietors Jason Goy and Darren Carter are undertaking a major restoration programme on the interior of the building, creating a natural blend of Georgian architecture and colour schemes with contemporary art.

The excellent result is both stylish and charming, and the six en suite guest bedrooms combine their original splendour with modern features. The superb food is very much part of the appeal of Bowlish House. Lunch offers the choice of à la carte and set menus, while dinner is a grander affair with a seasonal two- or three-course table d'hote menu; the excellent food is enhanced by well-chosen wines and friendly, efficient service. The hotel is open to residents and non-residents for lunch, dinner, morning coffee and afternoon tea, and a function suite is available for special occasions. All rooms at the hotel are strictly non-smoking.

place where there is a 50ft **Market Cross**, dating from around 1500 and restored in Victorian times. There is also **The Shambles**, a 15th century wooden shed where meat was traded. After the Duke of Monmouth's ill-fated Pitchfork Rebellion, several of his followers were executed at the Market Cross in 1685 on the orders of the infamous Judge Jeffreys. Although it is a relatively nondescript building, Shepton Mallet's old prison, built in 1610, was thought to be so well away from the threat of enemy bombing that it was here that the Domesday Book was hidden during World War II. It was also used during that period by the US forces as a military prison.

Today, Shepton Mallet is a prosperous light industrial town that has a good selection of shopping and leisure activities. Each year the town plays host to two agricultural shows. The **Mid-Somerset Show** is in August and, late May/early June, the **Royal Bath and West Show** has a permanent showground to the southeast of the town.

To the southwest of the town lies a former residence of the abbots of Glastonbury, **Pilton Manor**, whose grounds have been planted with vines, mostly of the German Riesling variety. Visitors are encouraged to stroll around the estate and also take the opportunity of sampling the vineyard's end product. Another legacy of Glastonbury Abbey can be found at **Pilton** village where there is a great cruciform tithe barn that stands on a hill surrounded by beech and chestnut trees. Unfortunately, the barn lost its arch-braced roof when it was struck by lightning in 1963 but has since been restored.

🏠 historic building   🏛 museum   🏛 historic site   ♧ scenic attraction   🌿 flora and fauna

At Croscombe, to the west of Shepton Mallet, is a fine 15th century **Tithe Barn,** a reminder of the days when the local tenant farmers paid a proportion of the crops each year to their ecclesiastical landlords.

NUNNEY

12 miles E of Wells off the A361

 Castle

This picturesque old market town is dominated by its dramatic moated **Castle** begun in 1373 by Sir John de la Mare on his return from the French wars. Thought to have been modelled on the Bastille, the fortress consists of four solidly built towers that stand on an island formed by a stream on one side and a broad water-filled moat on the other. The castle came under attack from Parliamentarian forces during the English Civil War and, despite having a garrison of only one officer, eight men and a handful of civilian refugees, the castle held out for two days. However, the bombardment damaged the building beyond repair and it had to be abandoned, leaving the romantic ruins that can still be seen today. One of the 30-pound cannonballs that were used by Cromwell's forces can be seen in the village's 13th century church.

FROME

17 miles E of Wells off the A361

 Blue House Longleat House

The 4th largest town in Somerset, Frome is an attractive town built on steep hills with cobbled streets and boasting more listed buildings than anywhere else in Somerset.

The town developed beside the river from which it takes its name, its first recorded building being a mission station founded in

THE GOLDEN GOOSE

1 Stony Street, Frome, Somerset BA11 1BU
Tel: 01373 466681
website: www.thegoldengoose.co.uk

An eye-catching double window display tempts passers-by into **The Golden Goose,** a design-led gift shop located in a quaint cobbled street just off the high street in the heart of Frome. With many years of experience as designers, owners Mary and Tony Gibson aim to choose high-quality, well-produced gifts and are always looking for something just that little bit different to add to the stock. As a result, their friendly shop is full of beautiful things that are a delight either to give or receive. The gift wrap and ribbons they sell add the finishing touches to a special present.

The range caters for all occasions and includes toiletries and candles, gifts for babies and young children, soft toys, games and puzzles to tease the mind, Bridgwater and Gabriella Miller pottery, French wooden toys, Burts Bees natural health products and cards and books on the nice things in life. Visitors are welcome to browse at the Golden Goose which is open from 9.30am to 5.00pm, Monday to Saturday. Frome itself is well worth taking time to explore. It has more listed buildings than any other town in Somerset and is the perfect place to combine historic interest with an enjoyable shopping experience.

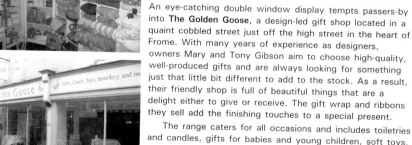

 stories and anecdotes   famous people   art and craft   entertainment and sport   walks

CAFÉ LA STRADA

13 Cheap Street, Frome, Somerset BA11 1BN
Tel: 01373 474374   Fax: 01373 454435
e-mail: cafelastrada@hotmail.com

Since it opened in 2002, **Café La Strada** has steadily grown in popularity and is now one of the liveliest Coffee bars and eating places in the area. It's owned and run by Jude Kelly who used to own the bakery next door before putting her culinary skills to even greater effect here.

The café here has a European atmosphere and there's a distinct Italian provenance in the décor and the colourful range of kitchen and tableware on sale. The Art Gallery on the 1st floor attracts artists from the area, bringing a wealth of creativity on canvas or photography - changing every calendar month.

Chocolate lovers will be drawn to the enticing display of hand-made Belgian chocolates which are sold both loose and in beautiful boxes, and few can resist sampling one of the 16 different flavours of home-made ice cream, or the wonderful varieties of fruit ices. In good weather, customers can enjoy their refreshments at tables on the pavement and enjoy watching the world go by. La Strada is fully licensed and due to popular demand will be opening a Gallery Restaurant in the summer of 2006- even more reason to pay them a visit. La Strada is open from 8.30am to 6pm, Monday to Saturday; and from 10.30am to 5pm on Sundays and Bank Holidays.

ENIGMA POTTERY

15 Vicarage Street, Frome, Somerset BA11 1PX
Tel: 01373 452079
e-mail: info@theenigmagallery.com
website: www.enigmagallery.com

Easy to find between the historic town centre and the railway station, **Enigma Pottery Studio & Gallery** is owned and run by the very talented resident ceramicists, Jenny Barton and Everton Byfield. Jenny, who spent a large part of her life on the Isle of Wight, creates thrown and press-moulded earthenware products inspired by the ocean. Everton creates hand-built, carved, burnished and smoke-fired ceramic vessels. Inspired by traditional African designs, his carving technique is a development of his passion for woodcarving. Their work, produced in their workshop in the garden, can be seen in the Main Gallery, along with that of many regular artists of quality.

There's also an on-going programme of eye-catching window exhibitions that is booked for many months ahead. Courses are available for group workshops for aspiring potters of all age groups. Between May and September, visitors can wander among the sculptures and garden pots in the secluded walled garden. Enigma, which is fully accessible to wheelchair users, is open from 10am to 5pm, Tuesday to Saturday, or by appointment.

685 by St Aldhelm, the Abbot of Malmesbury. Such was the expansion around St Aldhelm's stone Church of St John that, by the time of the Domesday Book, the settlement had a market which suggests that it was already a place of some importance. General markets still take place every Wednesday and Saturday.

Frome continued to prosper during the Middle Ages on the back of its cloth industry until competition from the woollen towns of the north in the 19th century saw the industry begin to decline. The trade in Frome died out completely in the 1960s. Since then other industries, printing in

Cheap Street, Frome

FROME MODEL CENTRE

Catherine Street, Frome, Somerset BA11 1DA
Tel: 01373 465295   Fax: 01373 451468
Opening Hours: Tue-Sat 10.00am-5.00pm
e-mail: enquiries@frome-model-centre.com
website: www.frome-model-centre.com

Probably one of the largest independent traditional model shops in the UK. Situated in the historic market town of Frome which is close to the border of Wiltshire it has easy access to the south coast and the south west. Frome Model Centre boasts over 2000 sq ft of shop floor and over 30,000 stock lines from all the major manufactures and some of the lesser known ones!

Frome Model Centre offers a wide range of services to it customers, from being a main service centre for all brands of models be it Radio Control, Model Railways or custom building. This is all taken care of by the experienced staff in a fully fitted modern workshop.

They stock every thing to do with modelling and collecting and offer a fast and friendly mail order service to any part of the country

Die-cast, model railways, kites, paint, glues, wood, plastic, brass etc. Radio control (cars/buggies/monster trucks, boats, planes, helicopters) war-hammer, plastic kits, dolls house and modelling tools. The list goes on and on so come visit and browse at your leisure.

---

 stories and anecdotes   🐿 famous people   🎨 art and craft   🖌 entertainment and sport   🚶 walks

BOLLOW HILL FARM COTTAGES

Friggle Street, Frome, Somerset BA11 5LJ
Tel: 01373 463007   Fax: 01373 463030
e-mail: bollowhillfarm@aol.com
website: www.farmhousecottages.co.uk

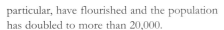

Bollow Hill Farm Cottages occupy a lovely position on top of a ridge looking across the valley. Originally they were barns on the Longleat estate but were converted into two charming cottages by owners Mark and Emma Kaye in 2000. They used local materials wherever possible – the external doors, for example, are of oak grown in Somerset. Each cottage sleeps four + in two bedrooms plus a sofa bed in the attic; each has a spacious living room combined with a comprehensively equipped kitchen. There's a TV and wood-burning stove, and French doors lead onto a patio and shared garden.

particular, have flourished and the population has doubled to more than 20,000.

Fortunately, this new growth has not spoilt the charm of the town's old centre. Best explored on foot the town's old quarter is an attractive conservation area where, amidst the interesting shops, cafés and restaurants, can be found the **Blue House**. Built in 1726 as an almshouse and a boy's school it is one of the town's numerous listed buildings. Another is the fine bridge across the River Frome, a contemporary of Bath's Pulteney Bridge dating from 1667, and unusual in having buildings along its length.

A popular excursion from Frome is to **Longleat House,** about five miles to the south and just across the county border in Wiltshire. The magnificent home of the Marquess of Bath was built by his ancestor, Sir John Thynne, in a largely symmetrical style in the 1570s. The interior is a treasure house of Old Masters, Flemish tapestries, exquisite furniture, rare books and the present Lord Bath's racy murals. The superb grounds were landscaped by Capability Brown and now contain one of the country's best-known venues for a marvellous day out. In the famous Safari Park the 'Lionsof Longleat', first introduced in 1966, have been followed

by a veritable Noah's Ark of exotic creatures, including rhinos, zebras and white tigers. The park also offers safari boat rides, a narrow-gauge railway, a children's amusement area, a garden centre, and the largest hedge maze in the world.

BALTONSBOROUGH

9 miles S of Wells off the A37

Baltonsborough was one of the 12 manors owned by Glastonbury Abbey which lies just to the northwest. In those days, the lives of the people of the village were completely governed by the monks. The permission of the abbey had to be sought before a daughter could be married, while on a man's death his chattels and beasts became the property of the abbey. St Dunstan is said to have been born here between 909 and 925 and the ancient flour mill in the village is thought to have been owned by Dunstan's father. Before entering Glastonbury Abbey, Dunstan found favour at the court of King Athelstan but, once he had given up his worldly possessions, Dunstan followed an austere regime. By setting himself apart from the abbey's other novices, Dunstan soon rose through the ranks of the religious house to become abbot, whereupon he enforced the strict Benedictine

🏛 historic building   🏚 museum   🏛 historic site   🌿 scenic attraction   🌱 flora and fauna

SOMERSET

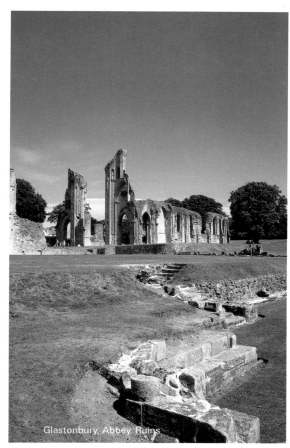

Glastonbury, Abbey Ruins

code. The wealth of Glastonbury grew under Dunstan and he also encouraged pilgrims to make their way here to see the holy relics. As well as being a great cleric and an entrepreneur, Dunstan was also an engineer. He was one of the first people to instigate the draining of the land in this area. From Glastonbury, Dunstan moved to Canterbury, where he was Archbishop until his death.

GLASTONBURY
6 miles SW of Wells on the A39

🏛 Glastonbury Abbey

🏚 Lake Village

🏛 George & Pilgrim Hotel

🏛 Somerset Rural Life Museum

⛰ Glastonbury Tor

🏵 Glastonbury Festival

Today this ancient town of myths and legends, of tales of King Arthur and the early Christians, is an attractive market town still dominated by the ruins of its abbey, which continues to attract visitors. The dramatic remains of

---

ABBEY TEA ROOMS

16 Magdalene Street, Glastonbury, Somerset BA6 9EH
Tel: 01458 832852
website: www.glastonbury.co.uk

Just across the road from the 14th century ruins of Glastonbury Abbey's great kitchen is the **Abbey Tea Rooms**, the town's 21st century equivalent. Mary Parker has been serving a selection of wholesome and appetising food here since 1989 and has made her charming old tea rooms a popular meeting place for locals and visitors alike. Along with delicious home-made cakes and scones, Mary's menu also offers freshly cooked meals based on local produce.

📖 stories and anecdotes 　 🐦 famous people 　 🎨 art and craft 　 🎭 entertainment and sport 　 🚶 walks

Glastonbury

Distance: *3.0 miles (4.8 kilometres)*

Typical time: *120 mins*

Height gain: *50 metres*

Map: *Explorer 141*

Walk: *www.walkingworld.com ID:1081*

Contributor: *Tony Brotherton*

ACCESS INFORMATION:

Park in Magdalene Street, next to Glastonbury Abbey grounds (current charge £3 all day).

DESCRIPTION:

A short tour of the town, allowing optional visits to the Abbey Ruins and Glastonbury Thorn, the Chalice Well and other points of religious interest, plus the 'obligatory pilgrimage' to Glastonbury Tor and a suggested visit to the Rural Life Museum and its tea room.

ADDITIONAL INFORMATION:

Glastonbury was the first Christian sanctuary in Great Britain and is the legendary burial-place of King Arthur. The legend of the Glastonbury Thorn and Joseph of Arimathea's visit is well-known. Chalice Well is open every day of year, 10am - 6pm or 11am - 5pm or noon - 4pm according to season. Somerset Rural Life Museum is open 10am - 5pm on Tuesday to Friday between April and October and at weekends from 2pm - 6pm; tea shop. The abbey ruins may be visited every day (except Christmas Day). Open 9:30am to 6pm (or dusk if earlier).

FEATURES:

Hills or fells, pub, toilets, museum, National Trust/NTS, wildlife, birds, flowers, great views, Butterflies, food shop, tea shop

WALK DIRECTIONS:

1 | From car park in Magdalene Street may be seen 14th Century Abbot's Kitchen in grounds of Glastonbury Abbey. Turn right along street, passing entrance to Abbey, to reach bottom of High Street. Go right to see on left, historic George & Pilgrims Hotel, founded in 1400s.

2 | Walk up High Street. Tourist Information Office is located on left, in 15th Century Tribunal: here is housed also, Lake Village Museum. Further up on left is St John's Church. This contains stained glass window

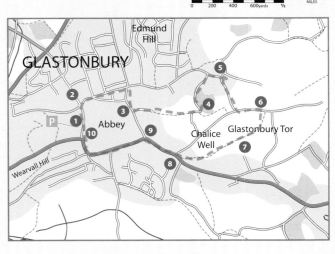

depicting Joseph of Arimathea. Carry on up High Street and turn right along Lambrook Street, as far as imposing gateway of Abbey House on right.

3 | Now turn up Dod Lane and take driveway on right signed 'Footpath to Tor', to reach squeeze-stile. Follow path uphill through fields to lane and continue ahead to see tor at bend.

4 | Turn left to follow Bulwarks Lane to end. At road (Wick Hollow) turn uphill to crossroads.

5 | Take lane to right, with tor visible ahead, to reach lane junction. Here turn left as far as footpath to Tor.

6 | Follow path into field, soon to climb past information board and squeeze-gate, through trees and onto stepped path. Path rises steeply around Tor to summit and monument. Here are superb views over surrounding countryside.

7 | Continue walk by descending Glastonbury Tor to metal gate. Take footpath running downhill to reach Well House Lane. Turn left, then right at main road to arrive at Chalice Well. Chalybeate waters of Chalice Well were considered curative.

8 | Turn right along Chilkwell Street to reach, on left at junction with Bere Lane, Somerset Rural Life Museum.

9 | To continue the walk, turn left on Bere Lane and then right downhill at crossroads to return to Magdalene Street, to visit Almshouses Chapel. The tiny chapel and garden of almshouses afford a quiet place for meditation.

10 | To complete the walk, turn left along the street, past a former pumphouse (Glastonbury was once spa-town) to return to start.

Glastonbury Abbey lie in the heart of the old town and, if the legend of Joseph of Arimathea is to be believed, this is the site of the earliest Christian foundation in the British Isles. By the Middle Ages, Glastonbury was second only to Rome as a place of Christian pilgrimage.

Joseph of Arimathea, the wealthy Jerusalem merchant who had provided a tomb for the crucified Jesus, is said to have arrived at Glastonbury in around 60AD. According to legend, while he was walking on the tor, Joseph drove his staff into the ground whereupon it took root and burst into leaf. Taking this as a sign that he should build a church, Joseph erected a simple church on the site now taken by the abbey. His staff is reputed to have grown into the celebrated Christmas-flowering Glastonbury hawthorn.

Today, the picturesque abbey ruins, with their associations with the legend of King Arthur, remain a great tourist attraction. It was Henry III who "caused search to be made for King Arthur's tomb" at Glastonbury. His workmen found it with suspiciously little difficulty. After digging down some seven feet, they unearthed a huge stone slab bearing a cross of lead. No body, however. So they continued digging another nine feet and then "found the bones of the great prince". This fortuitous find brought a further influx of sightseers to the town.

During the Middle Ages, Glastonbury Abbey was also an internationally renowned centre of learning, and scholars and pilgrims from all over Christendom, made their way here. One of the guest houses built to accommodate them is now the **George and Pilgrim Hotel.** Originally constructed in 1475, this striking building has old timber beams adorned with carved angels and an interior is guarded by a series of curious monks' death masks. Close by is another 15th century building, the handsome **Tribunal** that is home to the town's Tourist Information Centre.

Even the town's **Somerset Rural Life Museum,** which explores the life of farmers in this area during the 19th and early 20th centuries, cannot escape from the influence of the abbey. Although the museum is housed in a Victorian farmhouse, there is an impressive 14th century barn here that once belonged to Glastonbury Abbey.

To the east of the town, **Glastonbury Tor** is a dramatic hill that rises high above the surrounding Somerset Levels. The 520-feet tor has been inhabited since prehistoric times and excavations on the site have revealed evidence of Celtic, Roman and pre-Saxon occupation. Because of its unusually regular conical shape

the hill has long been associated with myth and legends and, in its time, has been identified as the Land of the Dead, the Celtic Otherworld, a Druid's temple, a magic mountain, an Arthurian hill fort, a ley line intersection and a rendezvous point for passing UFOs. Along with its mystical energy, the tor also offers magnificent panoramic views across Somerset to Wells, the Mendips, the Quantocks and the Bristol Channel. The striking tower at the summit is all that remains of the 15th century **Church of St Michael**, an offshoot of Glastonbury Abbey. Between the tor and the town lies the wooded rise of Chalice Hill, where, it is said, Joseph buried the Holy Grail, the chalice used at the Last Supper.

In recent years, a new band of pilgrims has been making their way to Glastonbury every June. The first **Glastonbury Festival** took

---

THE CRYSTALMAN
7 Northload Street, Glastonbury, Somerset BA6 9JJ
Tel: 01458 833522
www.thecrystalman.co.uk

The Crystalman is a shop of beauty and knowledge. It is also home to the world-famous gemstone of Somerset - The Mendip Potato Stone. This gem, found only in Somerset and particularly the Mendip Hills, is unique. The shop stocks it as natural pieces and exclusively as spheres, eggs, hearts and carvings (pictured right). **Mike Jackson**, who owns the Crystalman, offers his lifelong passion and knowledge, guiding and advising you toward the understanding of gems, minerals and fossils. The Crystalman in Glastonbury is a Mecca for all. Full of amazing treasures from the hidden corners of the planet. Wide varieties of stones in their natural state are stocked - carved, cut, shaped,

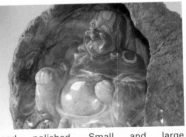

and polished. Small and large amber nuggets, as well as gold nuggets silver, ruby, sapphire, Bristol Diamonds, copal, aquamarine, jasper, rose quartz and turquoise. There are extensive varieties of minerals, stones, crystals and spheres made from semi-precious stones - from marble size up to a 15kg quartz spheres. Moldavite carvings formed from meteorite remains from millions of years ago are not to be missed. There are spheres to roll you over with pleasure. Rhodonite from Cornwall, eggs of Scottish agate, stone polishers for those pebbles picked up on the beach years ago and treasured. Extensive carvings in Whitby jet, amber, rhodochrosite, turquoise and palm nut have to be seen to be believed. The best way to know what's in store is to visit this emporium of wonder and delight!

---

 historic building   museum   historic site   scenic attraction   flora and fauna

place in 1970 and 1,500 people came; that figure has now multiplied by 100. Pop idols who have played here include Johnny Cash, David Bowie, Van Morrison, Led Zeppelin and many more. The event is now the largest open air festival in Europe.

To the northwest of the town is the site of a prehistoric **Lake Village** discovered in 1892 when it was noticed that the otherwise level fields were studded with irregular mounds. Thought to date from around 150BC, the dwellings were built on a series of tall platforms that raised them above the surrounding marshland.

STREET

7 miles SW of Wells on the A39

🏛 Friends' Meeting House   👟 Shoe Museum

The oldest part of this now sprawling town lies around the 14th century parish Church of the Holy Trinity although most of the town itself dates from the 19th century when it began to expand from a small rural village into the light industrial town of today. Much of this growth was due to one family, the Clarks. In the 1820s, the Quaker brothers, Cyrus and James Clark began to produce sheepskin slippers from the hides of local animals. Many of the town's older buildings owe their existence to the family and, in particular, there is the **Friends' Meeting House** of 1850 and the building that housed the original Millfield School. The oldest part of the Clark's factory has now been converted into a fascinating **Shoe Museum** and, although the company is one of the largest manufacturers of quality footwear in Europe, it continues to keep its headquarters

FOUR SEASONS SHEEPSKIN & LEATHER CLOTHING

105 High Street, Street, Somerset BA16 0EY
Tel: 01458 442500 Fax: 01458 447908

Located on Street's main thoroughfare, **Four Seasons Sheepskin & Leather Clothing** offers an impressive range of internationally designed sheepskin, suede and leather clothing as well as locally made products from this renowned sheepskin area. This family-owned business has earned a glowing reputation as connoisseurs of superior quality leather goods and stocks only the highest quality merchandise, provided from a knowledge and dedication to the trade, in its stores – there are two others, one in **Glastonbury** and the other in **London's Notting Hill Gate**. The range is comprehensive – everything from sheepskin and leather coats, sheepskin rugs, Morlands sheepskin slippers, to reversible sheepskin coats, Timberland footwear and luggage, kaftans and Hunter wellingtons.

There are Bridge handbags from Italy, sheepskin hats and gloves, leather sandals, laptop bags and travel cases, waxed hats and cowboy hats, waterproof Barbour jackets, Gloverall duffle coats, and a range of Musto and Toggi country clothing, not to mention the famous rocking sheep. The shop will also accept your used sheepskin or leather coat in part exchange for a new one.

📖 stories and anecdotes   🐦 famous people   🎨 art and craft   🎭 entertainment and sport   🚶 walks

AVALON MARSHES

Willows Craft Centre and Tearooms, Peat Moors Centre,
Westhay, Somerset BA6 9TT
Tel/Fax: 01458 860060   e-mail: mearesomerset@aol.com
website: www.avalonmarshes.org.uk/www.thewillows-westhay.com

The land stretching to the west of Glastonbury Tor has a character and atmosphere all its own. Lush green flowery meadows, still dark ditches, damp secret fens, shady wet fern woodlands and breeze-rippled open water fringed with rustling reedbeds all combine to make the area so unique. This is where you will find the **Avalon Marshes and Willows Craft Centre and Tearooms**, giving you the opportunity to explore the fascinating story of the ecology of the Somerset Levels and enjoy excellent freshly prepared and locally sourced food.

A series of imaginative displays describes the development of commercial peat digging, the special trades that have developed in this environment, and the measures that have been taken to conserve the area's flora and fauna.

The Avalon Marshes contain a mixture of habitats, including wet woodland, grazing marsh and fens. These habitats are being managed to encourage and protect the threatened wildlife species that exist here. The area is a stronghold for elusive otters; reedbeds are beginning to encourage rare and common wetland birds like bitterns and marsh harriers; there are beautiful marsh orchids and rare insects like the great silver diving beetle. Other species like the grey heron add greatly to the character of the wetland landscape. If you visit on a winter's day, large flocks of wintering duck can be seen and there is the dusk spectacle of millions of Starlings coming in to roost. In summer you may catch a glimpse of a hobby (bird of prey) hunting flying insects.

Informative leaflets are available detailing the varied activities within the area and providing guides to the various villages within the area. At Meare, for example, is the Abbot's Fish House which once belonged to Glastonbury Abbey and stored fish caught in the now drained Meare Pool.

Within the Avalon Marshes area are some waymarked walks and cycling paths through the area and cycles may be hired at the Peat Moors Centre; for the disabled, there is carriage driving on special routes and electric buggies

available for rides through the reserves to see the peat beds.

Another major attraction here is the excellent Willow Craft Centre which provides a showcase for a wide range of local crafts. Pottery, paintings, knitted woollen clothing and silk flower displays are just some of them, along with award-winning jams and honey from Rose Farm at Wedmore. The Centre also has a good selection of garden plants and shrubs, pots and vases, as well as fresh local free range eggs.

🏛 historic building   🏛 museum   🏛 historic site   ⚘ scenic attraction   ❦ flora and fauna

in the town and also operates the Clarks Village Shopping Outlet where 90 leading brands offer discounts of up to 60% every day.

MEARE
6½ miles SW of Wells on the B3151

🏛 Abbot's Fish House

🐾 Shapwick Heath Nature Reserve

Just to the east of this attractive village is an unusual medieval building known as the **Abbot's Fish House**. Before 1700, this isolated building stood on the edge of Meare Pool, once a substantial lake that provided nearby Glastonbury Abbey with a regular supply of freshwater fish. Before the lake was drained, this early-14th century building was used for storing fishing equipment and salting the catches.

To the southwest of Meare, in terrain scarred by years of peat extraction, is the **Shapwick Heath Nature Reserve**, which provides a safe haven for rare plants and wildlife. Parts of the Neolithic 'Sweet Track', the oldest man-made routeway in Britain, still exist beneath the wet peat. This remarkable timber track was constructed around 3800BC to cross a mile or so of reedswamp. Many artefacts have been found beside the trackway including stone axes, pots containing hazelnuts, a child's toy tomahawk and a polished jadeite axe from the Alps.

WESTHAY
8 miles SW of Wells on the B3151

📷 Peat Moors Visitor Centre

Just outside the village of Westhay is the **Peat Moors Visitor Centre**. The centre offers visitors a fascinating insight into the history and ecology of the Somerset Levels and,

through a series of imaginative displays, describes the development of commercial peat digging, the special trades that have grown up in this unique environment and the measures that have been taken to conserve the area's flora and fauna.

WOOKEY
2 miles W of Wells off the A371

🏛 Burcott Mill

A rare and historic working watermill, **Burcott Mill** has its origins in pre-Domesday times. Visitors can see stone-ground flour being hand-made and join a tour led by the miller himself. The site also has an adventure playground, country tearoom, pets and picnic area, and a pottery.

WEDMORE
7½ miles W of Wells on the B3139

🏛 Ashton Windmill

This remote village was the ancient capital of the Somerset marshes. King Alfred is said to have brought the newly baptised Danish King Guthrum to sign the Peace of Wedmore here in 878. This treaty left Wessex in Alfred's hands but gave East Anglia, East Mercia and the Kingdom of York to the Danes. The village's main street, the Borough, is lined with fine stone buildings, including a lovely old coaching inn. The parish church's spectacular Norman south doorway is thought to have been carved by the craftsmen who built Wells Cathedral.

To the northwest of the village, near Chapel Allerton, is **Ashton Windmill**. It was built in the 1700s and is now the only complete windmill left in Somerset.

WILLOW BRIDGE FARMS COUNTRY GUEST HOUSE

Godney, nr Wedmore, Somerset BA5 1RZ
Tel: 01458 835371
website: www.willowbridgefarm.co.uk

Set midway between the historic cathedral city of Wells and mystical Glastonbury Tor, **Willow Bridge Farms Country Guest House** offers top quality bed & breakfast accommodation in wonderfully peaceful surroundings. All around are peat moors and the reed beds that provide thatchers with their basic materials, as well as young withies for making willow baskets. Julie Andrews' family has been farming here for almost a century but the accommodation for guests is in a modern purpose-built single storey building which has been appointed to the very highest standards. All of the unusually spacious guest bedrooms are en suite and equipped with power showers, remote control TV/DVD, luxurious towels and bath robes, a fridge and hospitality tray.

There's excellent disabled access to all rooms and each room has a sofa that can be converted into a bed – ideal for family groups. Guests have the use of a lovely conservatory which is provided with underfloor heating. A hearty breakfast is included in the tariff while for evening meals there's a pub close by, and a good choice of other pubs and restaurants in nearby Wedmore and Glastonbury. Anglers will find good coarse and lake fishing close by, and there are also some excellent walking and cycle routes.

WOOKEY HOLE

1½ miles NW of Wells off the A371

🐾 Great Cave   🐾 Ebbor Gorge

The village, in the rolling uplands of the Mendip Hills, is a popular place with walkers, cavers and motorised sightseers who are drawn by the natural formations found here. Throughout the centuries, the carboniferous limestone core of the hills has been gradually dissolved away by the small amount of carbonic acid in rainwater. This erosion has created over 25 caverns around Wookey Hole, of which only the largest half dozen or so are open to the public. The **Great Cave** contains a rock formation known as the Witch of Wookey that casts a ghostly shadow and is associated with gruesome legends of child-eating. During prehistoric times, lions,

bears and woolly mammoths lived in the area. In a recess known as the Hyena's Den, a large cache of bones has been found, many of them showing signs of other animal's tooth marks. The river emerging from Wookey Hole, the River Axe, has been harnessed to provide power since the 15th century and the present building here was originally constructed in the early 17th century as a paper mill.

Just to the northwest lies the dramatic **Ebbor Gorge** now a National Nature Reserve managed by English Nature. There are two walks here, the shorter one suitable for wheelchairs accompanied by a strong pusher. The longer walk involves a certain amount of rock scrambling. However, the hard work is rewarded as there is a wealth of wildlife here,

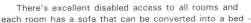

🏛 historic building   🖼 museum   🏛 historic site   🐾 scenic attraction   🌱 flora and fauna

including badger and sparrow hawk in the woodland, lesser horseshoe bats in and around the caves and buzzards flying overhead.

CHEDDAR
8 miles NW of Wells on the A371

🏛 Cheddar Gorge   🏛 Pavey's Lookout Tower

🏛 Cheddar Man Museum

This sprawling village is best known for its dramatic limestone gorge, **Cheddar Gorge** (see panel below), which extends for some two miles and is one of the most famous and most often visited of Britain's many natural attractions. It is characterised by its high vertical cliffs, from which there are outstanding views out over the Somerset Levels, the Quantock Hills and, on a clear day, across the Bristol Channel to South Wales. The National Trust owns most of the land around this magnificent ravine, which is a Site of Special Scientific Interest. Numerous rare plants grow here and it is also a haven for butterflies. A circular walk through the area takes in plantations, natural woodland and rough downland. This is a place that draws rock climbers, but the less ambitious may like to take the 274 steps of **Jacob's Ladder** that lead from the bottom of the gorge to the top of the cliffs. Here, **Pavey's Lookout Tower** offers yet more spectacular views of the surrounding area.

Cheddar Caves & Gorge

Cheddar, Somerset, BS27 3QF
Tel: 01934 742343   e-mail: caves@visitcheddar.co.uk
website: www.cheddarcaves.co.uk.

Cheddar Gorge, a place of wild and rugged beauty, is a karst limestone and calcareous grassland Nature Reserve and home to many rare plants and animals, including endangered Greater Horseshoe bats. Cheddar Caves, inhabited by our ancestors up to 40,000 years ago, were re-discovered by Messrs Gough & Cox, enterprising Victorian showmen, and are world famous for their spectacular stalactite and stalagmite decorations, whose beautiful colours are mirrored in pools of water. Easy-to-use audio-guides tell the story of the caves' formation and discovery. These caves also fired the imagination of JRR Tolkien, author of the trilogy *Lord of the Rings*, on his honeymoon visit in 1916. "The Crystal Quest", the dark-walk fantasy adventure, creates a similar world of elven magic and bold adventure underground.

The Museum of Pre-history, "Cheddar Man & the Cannibals", explores 40,000 years of British Pre-history, with demonstrations of Stone Age survival skills and beautiful cave art. Here you can discover the truth about why our *Homo sapiens* ancestors, throughout the world for most of pre-history, were cannibals.

From April to September, an open-top double-decker bus takes you on a sight-seeing tour through Cheddar Gorge, beneath rocky pinnacles rising sheer above you, the home of Peregrine falcons. There are 274 steps to reach a Lookout Tower for stunning views of this limestone countryside, then a three-mile cliff-top walk right around Britain's biggest Gorge, climbing 400ft above the road, through this internationally important Nature Reserve.

🎬 stories and anecdotes   🐦 famous people   🎨 art and craft   🎭 entertainment and sport   🚶 walks

While the gorge is undoubtedly everyone's idea of Cheddar, the village is also renowned for its caves and, of course, its cheese. Although much embellished by modern tourist paraphernalia, its two main show caves, **Gough's Cave** – an underground 'cathedral' – and the brilliantly coloured **Cox's Cave**, are worth seeing for their sheer scale and spectacular calcite formations. In 1903 an almost complete skeleton, named 'Cheddar Man', was discovered in Gough's Cave and this can be seen in the **Cheddar Man Museum,** along with cannibalised human skulls and flint tools. There are demonstrations of Stone Age survival skills and some intriguing cave art.

Back in 1726, Daniel Defoe was already singing the praises of Cheddar's most famous product. "Without all dispute," he wrote, "Cheddar is the best cheese that England affords, if not that the whole world affords." Today, in south Somerset alone, some 50 tonnes of Cheddar cheese is produced each day by nine cheese-makers. The original unpasteurised handmade farmhouse Cheddar is still produced on just two farms: Montgomery's in North Cadbury, and Keen's near Wincanton. Their round half-hundredweight cheeses are wrapped in muslin, kept for more than a year and turned regularly as they mature. The result is Cheddar cheese at its most perfect.

Since the term 'Cheddar Cheese' refers to a recipe and not a place, the cheese can be made anywhere in the world. Somerset itself is dotted with cheese manufacturers of various sizes and a number of these establishments supplement their income by offering guided tours, cheese demonstrations and catering facilities for the many visitors who come to gorge on the local speciality.

CHARTERHOUSE
9 miles NW of Wells off the B3134

🏞 Mendips 🏞 Black Down

Rising, in some places, to more than 1,000 feet above sea level, the **Mendips** form a landscape that is like no other in the region. Although hard to imagine today, lead and silver were once mined from these picturesque uplands. The Mendip lead-mining activity was centred around the remote village of Charterhouse – the last mine in the district, at Priddy, closed in 1908.

Charterhouse takes its name from a Carthusian monastery, **Witham Priory**, which owned one of the four Mendip mining sectors, or liberties. This area has been known for its mineral deposits since the Iron Age and such was its importance that the Romans declared the mines here state property within just six years of their arrival in Britain. Under their influence, silver and lead ingots, or pigs, were exported to France and to Rome, and the settlement grew into a sizable town with its own fort and amphitheatre, the remains of which can still be seen today. Centuries later, improved technology allowed the original seams to be reworked and the area is now littered with abandoned mine buildings and smelting houses.

A footpath from Charterhouse church leads up onto **Black Down** which is, at 1,067ft, the highest point in the Mendips. From here, to the northwest, the land descends down into Burrington Combe, a deep cleft said to have inspired the Reverend Augustus Toplady to write the hymn *Rock of Ages*.

AXBRIDGE
10 miles NW of Wells off the A371

🏛 King John's Hunting Lodge 🦅 Frankie Howerd

As a fortified market town, Axbridge had its

own mint during Saxon times. By the late medieval period Axbridge had developed into a prosperous wool centre that made its living processing the Mendip fleeces into woven cloth. A small town today with a delightful centre, Axbridge is now a conservation area. In its ancient market square stands an exceptional example of a half-timbered merchant's house dating from around 1500. Three storeys high and known as **King John's Hunting Lodge** (National Trust) the building was extensively restored in the early 1970s and is now home to an excellent **Local History Museum**. Although the Lodge has nothing to do with King John or hunting, its name is a reminder that the Mendip hills were once a royal hunting ground. Elsewhere in the centre of Axbridge there are many handsome Georgian shops and town houses.

About a mile west of Axbridge, near the village of Cross, is an unusual attraction. The late comedian **Frankie Howerd** lived in a cottage here for many years and his home was opened to the public at Easter 2006.

Apparently, he was a great hoarder so the cottage is full of hundreds of scripts, photographs and props, along with a pair of swords used in the film *Cleopatra,* (a gift from Richard Burton and Elizabeth Taylor), two stone cats from Laurence Olivier, and a fossilised egg presented to Frankie by the Italian government after he starred in the film *Up Pompeii.*

Bristol

🏛 Bristol Cathedral	🏰 Castle Par		
🏛 Floating Harbour	🏛 Clifton Suspension Bridge		
🏛 Bristol Industrial Museum	🐾 At Bristol		
🐦 Isambard Kingdom Brunel	🐾 Theatre Royal		
🏛 Maritime Heritage Centre	🐾 Redcliffe Caves		
🏛 Church of St Mary Radcliffe	🏛 Goldney Grotto		
🏛 British Empire & Commonwealth Museum			
🏛 John Wesley's Chapel	🐦 Bristol Zoo Gardens		
🏛 City Museum & Art Gallery			
🐦 Avon Gorge Nature Reserve			

King John's Hunting Lodge, Axbridge

Bristol was Sir John Betjeman's favourite English city. It had, he said "the finest architectural heritage of any city outside London". Today it is also one of Britain's most vibrant and stimulating cities and offers a fascinating combination of grand buildings, reverberant history and contemporary creativity.

Situated at a strategically important

🎬 stories and anecdotes   🐦 famous people   🎨 art and craft   🐾 entertainment and sport   🚶 walks bridging point at the head of the Avon gorge, Bristol was founded in Saxon times and soon became a major port and market centre. By the early 11th century, it had its own mint and was trading with other ports throughout western Europe, Wales and Ireland. The Normans quickly realised the importance of the port and, in 1067, began to build a massive stone keep. Although the castle

Bristol Docks

was all but destroyed at the end of the English Civil War, the site of the fortification remains as **Castle Park**. Situated just to the west of the castle site stands **Bristol Cathedral** founded in around 1140 by Robert Fitzhardinge as the great church of an Augustinian abbey. While the abbey no longer exists, several original Norman features, such as the chapter house, gatehouse and the east side of the abbey cloisters, remain. Following the Dissolution in 1539, Henry VIII took the unusual step of elevating the abbey church to a cathedral and, soon after, the richly-carved choir stalls were added. However, the building was not fully completed until the 19th century, when a new nave was built. Among the treasures is a pair of candlesticks donated to the cathedral in 1712 by the rescuers of Alexander Selkirk, the castaway on whom Daniel Defoe based his hero Robinson Crusoe.

During the Middle Ages, Bristol expanded as a trading centre and, at one time, it was second only to London as a seaport. Its trade was built on the export of raw wool and woollen cloth from the Mendip and Cotswold Hills and the import of wines from Spain and southwest France. It was around this time that the city's first major wharf development took place when the River Frome was diverted from its original course into a wide artificial channel now known as St Augustine's Reach. A remarkable achievement for its day, the excavation created over 500 yards of new berthing and was crucial in the city's development. Later, in the early 19th century the harbour was further increased when a semi-artificial waterway, the **Floating Harbour**, was created by diverting the course of the River Avon to the south. Another huge feat of engineering, the work took over five years to complete and was largely carried out by Napoleonic prisoners of war using only picks and shovels. Today, the main docks have moved downstream to Avonmouth and the Floating Harbour has become home to a wide assortment of pleasure and small working craft.

Much of Bristol's waterfront has now been redeveloped for recreation and down on the harbourside is **At Bristol**, the home of three spectacular attractions. **Explore** is a hands-on centre of science and discovery; **Wildwalk** takes a breathtaking journey through the natural world; and the **Imax Theatre** promises the ultimate cinematic experience. Also in the old port area is the **Bristol Industrial Museum**, which presents a fascinating record of the achievements of the city's industrial and commercial pioneers, including those with household names such as Harvey (wines and sherries), McAdam (road building), Wills (tobacco) and Fry (chocolate). Visitors can also find out about the port's history, view the aircraft and aero engines that have been made here since 1910 and inspect some of the many famous vehicles that have borne the Bristol name since Victorian times.

Another famous name, that of the engineer and inventor **Isambard Kingdom Brunel** is closely associated with the city. His graceful **Clifton Suspension Bridge** soars 200ft above the Avon gorge to the west of the city centre. Opened in 1864, five years after the death of its designer, the bridge continues to be a major route into the city and provides magnificent views over Bristol and the surrounding countryside. Brunel's mighty *ss Great Britain*, the world's first iron-hulled passenger liner was launched in 1843 and is now berthed in the harbour. Next to it is the **Maritime Heritage Centre,** dedicated to the

The British Empire & Commonwealth Museum

Station Approach, Temple Meads,
Bristol BS1 6QH
Tel: 0117 925 4980
e-mail: admin@empiremuseum.co.uk
website: www.empiremuseum.co.uk

The dramatic story of how Britain's overseas empire evolved into the modern Commonwealth is told through exciting, informative displays, using film, video, sound recordings, authentic artefacts and interactive exhibits. Sixteen galleries present 500 years of history from the perspective of both ruler and ruled, ending with a look at how Britain's colonial history continues to affect us today.

The Museum is housed inside Isambard Kingdom Brunel's 19th century railway station at Temple Meads, Bristol, the world's first purpose-built passenger railway terminus and an integral link using Brunel's railway and ships to connect the heart of the empire, London, with Britain's overseas colonies and America. Public access has now been granted to the historic railway building following its restoration.

As well as 16 permanent galleries, the Museum offers a changing series of special exhibitions, events for families, lectures and seminars. There is a full education programme, suitable for all ages and key stages from pre-school to adult learners. A rapidly growing commercial archive uniquely illustrates Britain's colonial past through film, photographs, objects, documents and sound recordings.

🕅 stories and anecdotes   🐦 famous people   🎨 art and craft   🎭 entertainment and sport   🚶 walks

history of shipbuilding in Bristol. A new exhibition, called 'The Nine Lives of IK Brunel', tells Brunel's compelling and entertaining life story, inlcuding his strengths and achievements, failures and faults. And if you arrive in the city by train from London you will have travelled along the route Brunel engineered for the Great Western Railway. He also designed every one of the bridges and stations along the way, including Bristol's Temple Meads station. Brunel was born in 1806 and to mark his bi-centenary the city has devised a year-long celebration of his life and works, including major exhibitions at the *ss Great Britain, At Bristol* and the City Museum and Art Gallery. The celebrations culminate in September 2006 with a community performance and procession at Swindon Railway Village and Works where the GWR built all its locomotives and rolling stock.

Brunel's original terminus for the GWR at Temple Meads is now home to the **British Empire and Commonwealth Museum** (see panel on page 423), which traces the history of British discovery and colonisation of foreign lands and the rich cultural legacy of the Commonwealth.

In medieval times, the city's prosperous merchants gave liberally for the building of one of the most impressive parish churches in the country. **The Church of St Mary Redcliffe** was described by Queen Elizabeth I as "the fairest, goodliest and most famous Parish Church in England". Along with its glorious exterior, the church contains monuments to Admiral Sir William Penn, whose son founded the state of Pennsylvania in the United States, and John Cabot, the maritime pioneer who in 1497 was the first non-Scandinavian European to set foot on Newfoundland. (A replica of the tiny boat,

The Matthew, in which Cabot made his perilous journey can be seen alongside Brunel's *ss Great Britain*). The sandstone beneath St Mary's church is riddled with underground passages known as the **Redcliffe Caves** and there are occasional guided tours of these unusual natural subterranean caverns.

Another ecclesiastical building of note is **John Wesley's Chapel**, the oldest Methodist building in the world. It was built in 1739 and remains completely unspoilt. Visitors can explore the preacher's rooms above the chapel, stand in Wesley's pulpit and see his preaching gown, riding whip and bed.

Elsewhere in the city are The Red Lodge, the only remaining Tudor domestic interior in Bristol; and the elegant Georgian House in Great George Street which was built in 1791. This is one of the most complete 18th century townhouses to have survived in Britain, its four floors all fully furnished and providing a fascinating insight into life at that time both above and below stairs.

The city is also home to one of the oldest theatres in the country to still be in use. The **Theatre Royal** was built in the 1760s and is the home of the famous Bristol Old Vic theatre company. Backstage tours are available.

Down by the waterfront, the **City Museum and Art Gallery** occupies a magnificent building which contains no fewer than seven art galleries as well as temporary exhibitions. It also houses important collections of minerals and fossils, eastern art, world wildlife, Egyptology, archaeology and some exceptional Chinese glass.

The land just to the west of the bridge is now the **Avon Gorge Nature Reserve** and there are some delightful walks here through Leigh Woods up to the summit of an Iron

Age hill fort. On the eastern side of the gorge an old snuff mill has been converted into an observatory whose attractions include a camera obscura. Once a genteel suburb, Clifton is now an attractive residential area of elegant Georgian terraces. Here, too, is Goldney House, now a university hall, but also the home of the unique subterranean folly, **Goldney Grotto**, which dates from the 1730s. The walls of this fantastic labyrinth, filled with spectacular rock formations, foaming cascades and a marble statue of Neptune, are covered with thousands of seashells and 'Bristol diamonds', fragments of a rare quartz found in the Avon gorge.

Clifton is also home to **Bristol Zoo Gardens** which cares for more than 400 exotic and endangered species. The summer of 2006 will see the opening of its Monkey Jungle which promises an immersive forest experience where monkeys mingle with gorillas, and visitors can enjoy close-up walk-through encounters with lemurs.

Around Bristol

CHEW MAGNA
6 miles S of Bristol on the B3130

🏠 Church House   🏛 Stanton Drew

🎎 'The Wedding'   🏛 Wansdyke

🦆 Blagdon Lake   🦆 Chew Valley Lake

Situated just to the north of Chew Valley Lake, this former wool village is a pleasant place with some handsome Georgian houses. The nucleus of the village is its three-sided green whose surrounding shops and pubs are linked by an unusual raised stone pavement. At the top of the green is the striking early-16th century **Church House** that was originally intended to be the venue for the

annual church sales and for brewing the ale and baking the bread to be sold on these occasions. The funds raised at this event were used to maintain the parish church for the coming year. These church houses, built in the 15th or early-16th centuries, were mainly confined to the counties of Somerset and Devon. Close by is the impressive parish Church of St Andrew, a testimony to the former prosperity of this village. Inside can be seen the interesting double effigy of Sir John Loe, a 15th century local squire reputed to be seven feet tall, and his wife. Behind a high wall adjacent to the churchyard stands **Chew Court**, a former summer palace of the bishops of Bath and Wells.

Just to the east of the village is **Stanton Drew**, an ancient settlement that stands beside a prehistoric site of some importance – a series of stone circles over half a mile across that were constructed by the Bronze Age

Chew Magna Parish Church

Beaker people between 2000 and 1600BC. This complex of standing stones consists of three circles, a lone stone known as Hauteville's Quoit and a large chambered burial tomb called The Cove. The stones are composed of three different types of rock; limestone, sandstone and conglomerate. They are thought to have been erected for religious, or perhaps astronomical, purposes. In common with many stone circles in western Britain, the origins of this stone circle are steeped in legend. The most widespread tale tells of a foolhardy wedding party who wanted to continue dancing into the Sabbath. At midnight, the piper refused to carry on, prompting the infuriated bride to declare that if she had to, she would get a piper from hell. At that point, another piper stepped forward to volunteer his services and the party resumed its dancing. As the music got louder and louder and the tempo faster and faster, the dancers realised, too late, that the good natured piper was the Devil himself and, when his playing reached its terrifying climax, he turned the whole party to stone. To this day, this curious group of standing stones is still known as **The Wedding.**

A couple of miles to the north of Stanton Drew, the line of the ancient **Wansdyke** runs in a roughly east-west direction around the southern fringes of Bristol. Built during the Dark Ages as a boundary line and defensive barrier against the Saxons, short sections of this great earthwork bank can still be seen, notably at Maes Knoll and along the ridge adjoining the Iron Age hill fort on Stantonbury Hill.

To the south of Chew Magna are the two reservoirs constructed to supply Bristol with fresh water but which also provide a first class recreational amenity. The smaller **Blagdon Lake** was completed in 1899 and **Chew**

Valley Lake in 1956. Together they have around 15 miles of shoreline and attract visitors from a wide area who come to fish, take part in watersports and observe the wide variety of waterfowl and other bird life that is drawn to this appealing habitat.

BARROW GURNEY
5 miles SW of Bristol on the B3130

Before the construction of the reservoirs of Blagdon and Chew Valley, Bristol's fresh water came from the three small reservoirs at Barrow Gurney. The first was opened in 1852 but within two years it developed a leak and had to be drained, causing a serious disruption to the city's water supply. Like many of the villages to the southwest of Bristol, Barrow Gurney has undergone considerable change since World War II and is now becoming a dormitory settlement for the city's commuters.

CONGRESBURY
13 miles SW of Bristol on the A370

🏛 St Congar

This sizable village, which today appears to be just another commuter town, has a long and eventful history that goes back to Roman times. Around 2,000 years ago a settlement stood here at the end of a spur of the Somerset marshes. Fragments of Roman and pre-Saxon pottery have been found on the site of the ancient hill that overlooks the present village.

The early Celtic missionary, **St Congar,** is believed to have founded an early wattle chapel at Congresbury in the 6th century. A tree bound by an iron hoop, on the eastern side of the church, is still referred to as 'St Congar's Walking Stick'. This is reputed to have grown from the saint's staff that miraculously sprouted leaves after he had thrust it into the ground outside the chapel.

CHURCH HOUSE DESIGNS

Broad Street, Congresbury, North Somerset BS49 5DG
Tel/Fax: 01934 833660
website: www.churchhousedesigns.co.uk
e-mail: robert-coles@btinternet.com

Robert and Lorraine Coles opened Church House Designs in 1986 as a showcase for Robert's bespoke furniture. Since then it has expanded into a contemporary craft gallery with an established reputation for high quality imaginative work across the spectrum of the crafts with particular emphasis on ceramics, glassware, jewellery, wood and textiles.

Reflecting the rural environment, the gallery always exhibits many animal and figurative sculptures including dogs, horses, otters, birds and hares.

Church House Designs has been selected for quality by the Crafts Council of Great Britain and is a member of the Independent Craft Galleries Association. A high spot of the gallery's year is it's lively and varied annual exhibition, which features nationally acclaimed artists. There is always an extensive display of exciting work on show by well established and up and coming artists.

Visitors are encouraged to browse at leisure from 10am to 1pm and from 2.15pm to 5pm, but closed on Wednesdays, Sundays and Bank Holidays.

CLEVEDON

15 miles SW of Bristol on the B3133

🏛 Clevedon Pier   🚶 Poet's Walk

🏛 Clevedon Court

Clevedon was developed in the late 18th and early-19th century as a resort but the lack of a railway prevented the town from expanding further and it was overtaken by Weston-super-Mare as the leading seaside town along this stretch of coast. As a result there are few of the attractions that are normally associated with a holiday resort. A notable exception is **Clevedon Pier**, a remarkably slim and elegant structure that was built in the 1860s from iron rails intended for Brunel's ill-considered South Wales Railway. When part of the pier collapsed in the 1970s, its long term future looked bleak but, following an extensive restoration programme, the pier is now the landing stage, during the summer, for large pleasure steamers such as the *Balmoral* and the *Waverley*, the only surviving sea-going paddle steamers in the world. Unusually for a holiday resort Clevedon has a **Market Hall** that was built in 1869 to provide a place for local market gardeners to sell their produce.

📖 stories and anecdotes   🕊 famous people   🎨 art and craft   🎭 entertainment and sport   🚶 walks

Yatton

Distance: *4.6 miles (7.3 kilometres)*

Typical time: *120 mins*

Height gain: *40 metres*

Map: *Explorer 154*

Walk: *www.walkingworld.com ID:1267*

Contributor: *Joy and Charles Boldero*

ACCESS INFORMATION:

Train service ring 08437 4844950. Bus service ring 0800 260 270. Free car parking at the railway station where the walk begins. Yatton is situated on the B3133 16 miles south of Bristol.

DESCRIPTION:

This walk is also along a part of the Strawberry Line track, the route goes through woodland and along tracks, over meadows and along country lanes.

ADDITIONAL INFORMATION

Waymark1: This old railway line is part of the Old Strawberry line. Now a nature reserve, short tailed field voles are found here as well as many wild flowers including the marsh marigold. Yatton station is still in use, but the main line used to serve two other junctions, the Cheddar Valley line and Clevedon line.

Waymark 2: This attractive and unusual seat was made by Yatton Junior School to celebrate the finds of the Roman remains near this spot.

Waymark 7: Cadbury Hill is a local nature reserve where green woodpeckers can be seen. The Hill fort is a scheduled ancient monument. Once a defended settlement of the Iron Age 500 BC.

FEATURES:

Pub, toilets, church, wildlife, birds, flowers, great views, butterflies, food shop

WALK DIRECTIONS:

1 | From the station car park go to barrier and along the old railway line path westwards.

2 | With the church on the far left turn left to five bar gate with, 'Batts Five Acres' on it. The path goes across the meadow. It is a permissive route. Keep to the track of sorts as it winds around going over a wide earth bridge

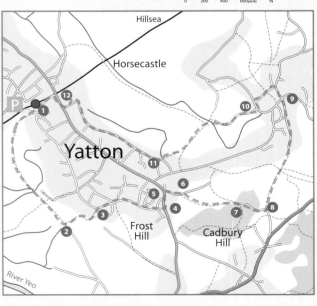

towards the farm. Climb stile on left, cross grass area.

3 | Turn right along road. At T junction turn right.

4 | At the end of Mendip Road turn left along pavement.

5 | Cross road with bus stop opposite near the bend, turn right along the 'No through road'.

6 | Turn right at white cricket notice board sign. Climb stile, cross car park and country lane. Climb stile by notice board and go diagonally left uphill over meadow. The path narrows with wood on left. Go through kissing gate, later keep to the right hand path by fence line.

7 | Go though barrier and follow path upwards. Halfway up by two trees turn left to woodland. Follow path through woodland as it goes over tree roots and boulders. Ignore paths left. Go though kissing gate. Continue along path to top. Go down left along sunken path, go through gate, it becomes a lane.

8 | Turn left at sign through iron gateway. Go down path. (this after heavy winter rain has a stream and horses use this path too, so it can be very muddy) At end it becomes a tarmac lane.

9 | At crossroads go straight ahead along High Street, with a Post Office on the right hand corner. Turn left into Chestnut Drive. Turn left at T junction.

10 | Turn right along hedged track at finger post sign to farm. Go through farmyard, cross stream and meadows, stiles, keep along meadow with houses on left. Climb stile.

11 | Turn right along road. This curves left at the No through road sign.

12 | At T junction turn right back to start of walk.

Beginning at Clevedon promenade and leading up to Church and Wain's Hills is the **Poet's Walk**, a flower-lined footpath that is said to have been popular with Victorian poets. On the top of Wain's Hill, are the remains of an Iron Age coastal fort, from which walkers can look out over the town, the Somerset Levels and the Severn Estuary.

However, it is **Clevedon Court** (National Trust), an outstanding 14th century manor house that brings most people to this town. One of the earliest surviving country houses in Britain, this house displays many of its original 14th century features still intact and incorporates a massive 12th century tower and a 13th century great hall. Once partly fortified, this imposing manor house has been the home of the Elton family since 1709. As longstanding patrons of the arts, the family invited many of the country's finest poets and writers to Clevedon in the early 1800s. These included Coleridge, Tennyson and Thackeray. It was while staying here that Thackeray fell in love with one of his host's daughters, Mrs Brookfield. He was to spend some time here seeing her and writing *Vanity Fair*. Another member of the Elton family was Arthur Hallam, a student friend of Lord Tennyson who showed great promise as a poet but who died very young. Tennyson was devastated by his friend's untimely death and sought to assuage his grief by writing the great elegiac poem *In Memoriam, AHH*, which was published in 1850.

Although the Elton family is closely associated with the arts, one member of the family in the Victorian era invented a special technique for making the type of brightly coloured pottery that was to become known as Eltonware. It was particularly popular in the

SCARLETTS SEAFRONT CAFÉ

Beach Road, Clevedon, Somerset BS21 6QU
Tel: 01275 349032

Overlooking Clevedon's Grade I Victorian Pier and enjoying grand views across the Bristol Channel from its spacious terrace, **Scarletts Seafront Café** is understandably popular because of its prime location but also because of its appetising food. Jenny, the owner, has been here for several years now and has a well-established reputation for serving value-for-money dishes. Her menu includes all day breakfasts, as many as 5 delicious soups, lunchtime meals, sandwiches and baguettes, including vegetarian options. Scarletts is open all day, 7 days a week, until 5pm. And if you feel like a stroll after your meal, the beach is just yards away.

United States. There are many fine examples on display in the house, along with a collection of rare glass from the works at Nailsea. Clevedon Court is an impressive place housing some fine treasures and is surrounded by beautiful 18th century terraced gardens. A footpath leads through nearby woodland on to a ridge overlooking the low and once marshy Gordano valley.

BANWELL

16 miles SW of Bristol on the A368

🔾 Bone Caves

This pleasant village was once the site of a

LANGFORD PET & PLANT CENTRE

Grove Nurseries, Langford Road, Lower Langford,
nr Bristol BS40 5HU
Tel/Fax: 01934 862848
e-mail: kimmers@supanet.com
website: www.thebunnybunker.com

The picturesque village of Lower Langford nestles beneath the Mendip Hills very near to Bristol Airport and it's here you will find the **Langford Pet & Plant Centre**. This small family owned business is run by Kim Standing who recently took over after having worked for two years in the shop. The Plant Centre offers personal service and advice and specialises in hanging baskets, patio tubs and container plants. Kim's personal priority is the Pet Centre. She has a wide knowledge and experience of pet care and is happy to advise on any aspect of looking after small animals. Kim will also obtain any specialist feeds and products you may need.

The centre stocks an extensive range of pet foods from producers such as Burns and autarky, along with a selection of treats and accessories "with something a little different here and there to tempt customers looking for a treat" says Kim. The centre specialises in rabbits with 12 different breeds having their home here, as well as six breeds of guinea pigs of all ages and colours. Appropriately, Lower Langford is also home to the Bristol Veterinary Hospital, one of the best and largest in the country.

🏛 historic building   🏛 museum   🏛 historic site   🔾 scenic attraction   �での flora and fauna

Saxon monastery and the parish church here is certainly ancient. Banwell Castle, on the other hand, although it looks like an authentic medieval fortress, is in fact a Victorian mansion house now converted into a hotel. Just to the west of the village, on Banwell Hill, a remarkable discovery was made in 1821. A series of caverns were found containing the remains of prehistoric animals including bison, bear and reindeer. They are now known as the **Bone Caves**.

A couple of miles north of Banwell is the village of **Puxton**, noted for its eccentric church tower that leans at such an angle that it looks as if it might topple at any moment, causing its weathercock to nosedive into the churchyard.

WESTON-SUPER-MARE
22 miles SW of Bristol on the A370

🏛 Grand Pier   🐑 Seaquarium   🔱 Sand Point

📷 North Somerset Museum   🏛 Woodspring Priory

🚂 Great Weston Train Experience   🚶 Mendip Way

📷 Helicopter Museum   🏛 Worlebury Camp

This traditional seaside resort, whose greatest asset is undoubtedly its vast expanse of sandy beach, has in recent years also developed as a centre of light industry. As late as 1811, Weston was just a fishing hamlet with just 170 residents. Within 100 years, it had grown to become the second largest town in Somerset and today has a resident population of around 70,000.

The commercial development of Weston began in the 1830s around the Knightstone, an islet joined to the shore at the northern end of the bay, and here were eventually built a large theatre and swimming baths. The arrival of the railway in 1841 stimulated the town's rapid expansion, and in 1867 a pier was built

on the headland below Worlebury Camp connecting Birnbeck Island with the mainland. Intended as a berth for steamer traffic, the pier was found to be slightly off the tourist track. Later, a more impressive pier was built nearer the town centre. Prior to serious fires in the 1930s and during World War II, it was approximately twice its current length. The **Grand Pier** now stands at the centre of an area crammed with souvenir shops, ice cream parlours, cafés and assorted attractions that are part and parcel of a British seaside resort. There are also the indoor attractions of the **Winter Gardens**, along the seafront, and the fascinating, family-friendly **North Somerset Museum**.

For anyone wishing to explore Weston on foot, the Museum Trail begins on the seafront and follows a trail of carved stones created by the artist Michael Fairfax. The **Seaquarium** has more than 30 interesting marine displays, along with feeding times and demonstrations, to amuse the whole family. The **Great Weston Train Experience** is one of the country's leading model railway exhibitions with detailed working layouts, exhibits in HO, N, Z and G scales, and further dioramas in the Model Masters shop as you enter.

An excellent viewpoint to the north of the resort is **Sand Point**, a ridge overlooking a lonely salt marsh that is home to a wide variety of wading birds. Just back from the headland is **Woodspring Priory**, a surprisingly intact medieval monastery founded in the early 13th century by a grandson of one of Thomas à Becket's murderers, William de Courtenay. The priory fell into disrepair following the Dissolution when the buildings were given over to agricultural use but the church, tower, refectory and tithe barn have all survived and the outline of the cloister can also still be made out.

At the southern end of Weston Bay, another spectacular view can be found from the clifftop site of the semi-ruined church at Uphill. This village lies at the start of the sometimes demanding **Mendip Way**, a 50-mile footpath that takes in the whole length of the Mendip Hills, including the broad vale of the Western Mendips, the high plateau of the central part and the wooded valleys in the eastern region.

Just to the southeast of the town lies Weston Airport, home to the world's largest collection of helicopters and autogyros. The only museum in Britain dedicated to rotary wing aircraft, **The Helicopter Museum** has more than 70 helicopters with exhibits ranging from single-seater autogyros to multi-passenger helicopters. Visitors can see displays on the history and development of these flying machines and a conservation hangar where the aircraft are restored. Grown-ups can take a Helicopter Experience Flight; under-12s can stage a rescue in the Lynx helicopter play area.

The area around Weston has been inhabited since prehistoric times. The wooded promontory at the northern end of Weston Bay was the site of a sizable Iron Age hill settlement known as **Worlebury Camp**. In the 1st century AD this is said to have been captured by the Romans after a bloody battle. Recent excavations, which revealed a number of skeletons showing the effects of sword damage, provided confirmation. A pleasant walk from the town centre now leads up through attractive woodland to this ancient hilltop site from where there are magnificent views out across the mouth of the River Severn to Wales.

WRAXALL

6 miles W of Bristol on the B3128

🏛 Tyntesfield   🌱 Noah's Ark Zoo Farm

One of the National Trust's most fascinating properties, **Tyntesfield** is an extraordinary Victorian Gothic Revival house that was home to four generations of the Gibbs family. The Gibbs' lived on a grand scale and spent lavishly on opulent furnishings for their magnificent mansion, including its stunning private chapel.

When the house was saved for the

Weston-Super-Mare

nation in June 2002, it needed a huge amount of conservation work which still continues with parts of the house still not open to the public. Visitors will see this work in progress but are no longer restricted to guided tours only but can wander at will through the permitted areas. Outside, there are formal gardens, an arboretum, walled garden and a working kitchen garden.

Also at Wraxall is **Noah's Ark Zoo Farm,** a hands-on real working farm with a rare collection of more than 60 types of animals including meerkats, camels, rhinos, wallabies, moneys and giraffes.

HENBURY
4 miles NW of Bristol off the A38

🏛 Blaise Castle

In her novel *Northanger Abbey,* Jane Austen described **Blaise Castle** at Henbury as "one of the finest places in England". This impressive 18th century house is set in parkland and boasts a large collection of everyday objects from times past including model trains, dolls and toy soldiers. There's also a Victorian schoolroom, picture gallery and period costumes. Within the estate grounds is Blaise Hamlet, an impossibly picturesque group of nine detached and individual stone cottages designed in a romantic rustic style by John Nash in 1809. The cottages are owned by the National Trust but are not open to the public.

Bath

🏛 Great Bath   🏛 Thermae Bath Spa
🏛 Bath Abbey   🏛 Holburne Museum of Art
🏛 Royal Crescent   🏛 Pump Room
🖉 Theatre Royal   🏛 Museum of East Asian Art

🏛 Pulteney Bridge   🏛 Assembly Rooms
🏛 Museum of Bath at Work   🏛 Bath Postal Museum
🏛 Jane Austen Centre   🏛 William Herschel Museum
🏃 Bath Skyline Walk   🌿 Prior Park Landscape Garden

Designated a World Heritage City, Bath is Britain's finest Georgian city, replete with gracious buildings of which around 5,000 are listed because of their architectural merit. Set in a sheltered valley, it is surrounded like Rome by seven hills which may have been one reason why the Romans took to it with such enthusiasm. Another important reason was, of course, its natural hot springs.

Since time immemorial over half a million gallons of water a day, at a constant temperature of 46°C, have bubbled to the surface at Bath. The ancient Celts believed the mysterious steaming spring was the domain of the goddess Sulis and they were aware of the water's healing powers long before the invasion of the Romans. However, it was the Romans who first enclosed the spring and went on to create a spectacular health resort that became known as Aquae Sulis. By the 3rd century, Bath had become so renowned that high ranking soldiers and officials were coming here from all over the Roman Empire. Public buildings and temples were constructed and the whole city was enclosed by a stone wall. By 410AD, the last remaining Roman legions had left and, within a few years, the drainage systems failed and the area returned to marshland. Ironically, the ancient baths remained hidden throughout the entire period of Bath's 18th century renaissance and were only discovered in the late 19th century. The restored Roman remains can be seen today. They centre around the **Great Bath**, a rectangular lead-lined pool standing at the centre of a complex system of buildings that

🗹 stories and anecdotes   🐿 famous people   🎨 art and craft   🖉 entertainment and sport   🏃 walks

took over 200 years to complete. It comprised a swimming pool, mineral baths and a series of chambers heated by underfloor air ducts.

One hundred yards from the Great Bath, the **Thermae Bath Spa** is scheduled to open in the summer of 2006. Visitors will be able to bathe in the natural thermal waters that the Romans enjoyed almost 2,000 years ago. There's a spectacular rooftop pool, an innovative series of steam rooms, and an extensive range of spa treatments are available.

In a city crammed with beautiful buildings, **Bath Abbey** is still outstanding. The present great church was begun in 1499, after its Norman predecessor had been destroyed by fire. Building work was halted at the time of the Dissolution in the 1540s and the church remained without a roof for 75 years. It was

not finally completed until 1901. It is now considered to be the ultimate example of English Perpendicular church architecture.

Inside, there is a memorial to Richard 'Beau' Nash, one of the people responsible for turning Bath into a fashionable Georgian spa town.

Prior to Nash's arrival in the early 18th century, Bath was a squalid place with farm animals roaming the streets within the confines of the old Roman town. Notwithstanding, the town had continued to attract small numbers of rich and aristocratic people. Eventually, the town authorities took action to improve sanitation and their initiative was rewarded, in 1702, when Queen Anne paid Bath's spa a visit. The elegant and stylish Beau Nash, who had only come to the town to earn a living as a gambler, became the Master of Ceremonies and, under his leadership, the town became a relaxing place for the elegant and fashionable of the day's high society. Among the entrepreneurs and architects who shared Nash's vision was the architect John Wood who, along with his son, designed many of the city's fine neoclassical squares and terraces. Among these is the **Royal Crescent**, John Wood the Younger's Palladian masterpiece and one of the first terraces in Britain to be built to an elliptical design. It has now been designated a World Heritage Building. Open to the public, No 1, Royal Crescent has been

Roman Baths, Bath

restored, redecorated and furnished so that it appears as it might have done when it was first built.

Bath's other 18th century founding father was Ralph Allen, an entrepreneur who made his first fortune developing an efficient postal system for the provinces and who went on to make a second as the owner of the local quarries that supplied most of the honey-coloured Bath stone to the city's Georgian building sites.

Famed for its wealth of Georgian architecture, Bath is a delightful city to wander around and marvel at the buildings. Beside the original Roman Baths is the **Pump Room**, which looks much as it did when it was completed in 1796. The **Theatre Royal** is one of Britain's oldest and most beautiful theatres and offers a year-round programme of top quality drama, opera,

dance and frequent Sunday concerts. Spanning the River Avon, in the centre of the city, is the magnificent **Pulteney Bridge**, designed by Robert Adam and inspired by Florence's Ponte Vecchio with its built-in shops.

The National Trust-owned **Assembly Rooms**, one of the places where polite 18th century society met to dance, play cards or just be seen, were severely damaged during World War II and not re-opened until 1963. They now incorporate the interesting **Museum of Costume** with a collection of more than 30,000 original items illuminating the vagaries of fashion over the last 400 years.

This is just one of the city's many excellent museums. The **Holburne Museum of Art** is housed in one of the city's finest examples of Georgian architecture and set in beautiful gardens. Originally a spa hotel, it was

OLD BANK ANTIQUES CENTRE

14-17 & 20, Walcot Buildings,
Bath BA1 6AD
Tel: 01225 469282 & 338813
e-mail: alexatmontague@aol.com
website: www.oldbankantiquescentre.com

ANTIQUES ARE THE LAST WORD IN RECYCLING.........

Situated on the London Road (A4), just ten minutes walk from Bath city centre; Old Bank Antiques Centre is now the largest retailer of antiques in this World Heritage City, but remains one of Bath's best kept secrets. Old Bank Antiques is how antiques shops used to look: a hoarder's paradise. Nineteen dealers spread through lots of showrooms in five shops, all with an ever-changing selection of good quality stock: ranging from 17th century English furniture to 1970s 'Retro' and vintage industrial.

Experienced and professional advice is always available, and there is customer parking at the rear, accessed via Bedford Street. Local deliveries are free and deliveries can be arranged anywhere in the UK or the rest of world, at cost price. We can also offer the services of our in-house furniture restorer.

Old Bank Antiques is open seven days a week including most bank holidays. 10am - 6pm weekdays & 11am – 5pm, Sundays and Bank Holidays.

📺 stories and anecdotes   🦜 famous people   ✍ art and craft   ✒ entertainment and sport   🚶 walks

converted into a museum in the early 20th
century and now contains the superb
collection of decorative and fine art put
together by Sir William Holburne in the 19th
century. Landscapes by Turner and Guardi
and portraits by Stubbs, Ramsey, Raeburn,
Zoffany and Gainborough are among its many
treasures. The **Museum of Bath at Work**
holds a fascinating collection that chronicles
the city's unique architectural evolution; the
Museum of East Asian Art displays artefacts
from China, Japan, Korea and Southeast Asia;
and the **Bath Postal Museum** illustrates 4,000
years of communication from 'clay-mail to e-
mail' and has a reconstruction of a Victorian
sorting office.

The city is synonymous with Jane Austen
and her novels and, at the **Jane Austen
Centre**, enthusiasts can learn more about the

Bath of her time and the importance of the
city to her life and works. Another famous
resident is celebrated at the **William
Herschel Museum** which occupies the mid-
Georgian house where the famous astronomer
and musician lived in the late 1700s and where
he made his discovery of the planet Uranus.

An ideal way to gather a general impression
of this magnificent city is to take the **Bath
Skyline Walk**, an eight-mile footpath,
through National Trust-owned land, taking in
some superb landscaped gardens and
woodland to the southeast of the city and
from where there are extensive views out over
Bath. The most striking feature of the skyline
is Beckford's Tower which was built for the
eccentric William Beckford in 1827. There are
yet more magnificent views of the city from
another National Trust property, **Prior Park**

SHANNON SCANDINAVIAN SHOP

68 Walcot Street, Bath, Somerset BA1 5BD
Tel: 01225 424222 Fax: 01225 426777
e-mail: sue@shannon-uk.com
website: www.shannon-uk.com

Shannon features a wide selection of Scandinavian
furniture, lighting, fabric and gifts of timeless design and
quality. The Danish furniture includes several chairs by
Hans Wegner such as the classic Wishbone, Aarne
Jacobsen's famous Egg, Swan and series 7 chairs and a
delightful assortment of small cupboards and sideboards
in oak and beech wood.

The Lamino chair upholstered in sheepskin by Yngve
Ekstrom is displayed with the elegant linen webbing
classic chairs designed by Swedish Architect Bruno
Mathson.

The Stokke movement collection includes the
upholstered Peel chair, Planet and Actulem available to
order in a choice of fabrics or leather.

The lamps and lighting are by the Danish designer Louis Poulsen and Pandul with le Klint
lampshades. Gifts and homewares include the glorious colourful designs of Marimekko fabrics
and shoulder bags, Vipp bins, Playsam toys Hoganas ceramics, iittala, glassware, Klippan
throws, Menu products and lots of Moomin mugs, plates and bowls.

The shop is open Monday to Saturday 10am until 5pm.

🏛 historic building   🏠 museum   🏛 historic site   ⚜ scenic attraction   🌱 flora and fauna

Landscape Garden which is just a 10-minute walk or short bus ride from the city centre – there is no parking at the garden itself. Within the beautiful grounds of this intimate 18th century garden are three lakes set in sweeping valleys and a famous Palladian bridge which is one of only four of its kind in the world.

Around Bath

DYRHAM
7 miles N of Bath off the A46

🏠 Dyrham Park

Set in an extensive deer park just minutes from the M4, **Dyrham Park** (National Trust) is a spectacular Baroque mansion containing a fabulous collection of 17th century furnishings, textiles, paintings and Delftware reflecting the taste for Dutch fashions at the time it was built. Visitors can wander round the park with its woodlands and formal garden, and discover how Victorian servants worked 'below stairs'.

BATHFORD
3 miles NE of Bath off the A363

🏠 Eagle House   🏠 Brown's Folly

🏛 Bathampton Down

This residential community once belonged to Bath Abbey. Among the many fine 18th century buildings to be seen here is **Eagle House**, a handsome residence that takes its name from the great stone eagle that stands with its wings outstretched on the gabled roof. On the hill above Bathford, there is a tall Italianate tower known as **Brown's Folly** built following the Napoleonic Wars to provide local craftsmen with work during the economic depression of the 1830s.

To the west lies **Bathampton** whose church

is the last resting place of Admiral Arthur Phillip, the first governor of New South Wales, who took the initial shipload of convicts out to the colony and established the settlement of Sydney. He is regarded by some as the founder of modern Australia. A chapel in the south aisle, known as the Australian Chapel, contains memorials to the admiral's family. Above the village lies **Bathampton Down**, which is crowned with an ancient hillfort that, according to some historians, was the site of the 6th century Battle of Badon in which the forces of King Arthur defeated the Saxons.

CLAVERTON
2 miles E of Bath on the A36

🏠 Claverton Manor

🏛 American Museum & Gardens

Just to the west of the village lies the 16th century country mansion, **Claverton Manor**, bought in 1764 by Ralph Allen, the quarry-owning co-founder of 18th century Bath. The mansion that Allen knew has been demolished, leaving only a series of overgrown terraces, but some of the stone from the old house was used in the construction of the new mansion on the hill above the village. It was here, in 1897, that Sir Winston Churchill is said to have given his first political speech. Claverton Manor is best known as the **American Museum and Gardens**. Founded in 1961, it is the only establishment of its kind outside the United States. The rooms of the house have been furnished to show the gradual changes in American living styles from the arrival of the Pilgrim Fathers in the 17th century to New York of the 19th century. The arboretum contains a collection of native American trees and shrubs.

🎭 stories and anecdotes   🦜 famous people   🎨 art and craft   ⏩ entertainment and sport   🚶 walks

HINTON PRIORY

3½ miles SE of Bath off the B3110

🏛 Stoney Littleton Long Barrow

All that remains of the early Carthusian monastery founded here by Ela, Countess of Salisbury, are atmospheric ruins. As in other religious houses belonging to this order, the monks occupied their own small dwellings set around the main cloister, often with a small garden attached. These communities were generally known for their reclusiveness. However, one outspoken monk from Hinton Priory, Nicholas Hopkins, achieved notoriety in Tudor times as the confessor and spiritual adviser to the 3rd Duke of Buckingham and his story is recounted by Shakespeare in *Henry VIII*. Several sections of the old priory remain, including the chapter house, parts of the guest quarters and the undercroft of the refectory.

Close by can be found one of the finest examples of a Neolithic monument in the west of England, **Stoney Littleton Long Barrow** (English Heritage), built more than 4,000 years ago. This striking multi-chambered tomb has recently been restored following vandalism and the interior can be inspected by obtaining a key from nearby Stoney Littleton Farm.

FARLEIGH HUNGERFORD

5 miles SE of Bath on the A366

🏛 Farleigh Hungerford Castle 🌿 The Peto Garden

This old fortified settlement is still overlooked by the impressive remains of **Farleigh Hungerford Castle** that stands on a rise above the River Frome to the northeast of the village. It was built by Sir Thomas Hungerford, the first Speaker of the House of Commons, on the site of an old manor house that he acquired in the late 14th century.

Legend has it that Sir Thomas failed to gain the proper permission from the Crown for his fortification and this oversight led to his downfall. The castle changed hands in the early 18th century and the incoming family saw it as a quarry for building stone rather than as a place to live. Much of the castle was left to go to ruin while the family built a new mansion on the other side of the village. Nevertheless, an impressive shell of towers and perimeter walls has survived intact, along with the castle's Chapel of St Leonard. This contains a striking 15th century mural of St George, some fine stained glass and a number of interesting monuments, including the tomb of Sir Thomas Hungerford himself.

To the north, just inside Wiltshire, is Iford Manor, home to **The Peto Garden**, a Grade I listed Italian style garden famed for its tranquil beauty. A unique hillside garden, it was the creation of architect and landscape gardener Harold Peto, who lived at the manor from 1899 until 1933.

NORTON ST PHILIP

5½ miles S of Bath on the A366

🏛 George Inn 🌿 Norwood Farm

In the 13th century, the Carthusian monks were given some land near here where they founded a Priory that was completed in 1232. The monks were also responsible for building the village's most famous landmark, the splendid **George Inn**, originally established as a house of hospitality for those visiting the priory. A wonderful fusion of medieval stonework, oriel windows and timber framing, it is still a hostelry today. The inn's timber framed upper floors were added in the 15th century when the inn doubled as a warehouse for storing the locally produced woollen cloth. In 1668, the

🏛 historic building 🏛 museum 🏛 historic site 🌿 scenic attraction 🌿 flora and fauna

CHOCOLATE ON CHOCOLATE

*Chocolate House, High Street, Rode, nr Bath,
Somerset BA11 6PA
Tel: 01373 830013
e-mail: enquiries@chocolateonchocolate.co.uk
website: iloveyoumorethanchocolate.com*

In 2003 the father and daughter team of Kerr and Flo Dunlop established **Chocolate on Chocolate** to produce top quality hand-crafted chocolates in innovative forms. Both of them are creative designers and their imaginative use of this unusual medium quickly attracted an appreciative clientele through their website and mail order service. Their chocolates are also sold in major retail outlets such as Harrods and John Lewis. They have now opened a shop right next to their factory so that visitors can see the chocolates actually being made before browsing around the huge variety of confectionery on display – at the last count there were more than 300 different designs to choose from.

The chocolates are made with the finest Belgian Callebaut chocolate. "The dark contains 53% chocolate," says Kerr, "and though this may seem fairly low, it is a delightful and manageable taste without the bitterness you would get from, say, a 70% dark chocolate. The white version contains 28% and is yummy!" The chocolates are available in gift boxes and there are always special seasonal specials at Christmas and Easter, for example, when there's a great choice of Easter eggs, ducks and bunnies.

diarist Samuel Pepys stayed here while on his way to Bath with his family and noted, "Dined well. 10 shillings." Just a short while later, the inn played host to the Duke of Monmouth, who made the George his headquarters shortly before his defeat at the Battle of Sedgemoor in 1685. According to a local story, 12 men implicated in the uprising were imprisoned here after the battle, in what is now the Dungeon Bar. They were later were taken away to be hung, drawn and quartered at the local market place.

To the north of the village, **Norwood Farm** offers an introduction to the objectives and practicalities of organic farming. A Farm Walk takes in a recycling area, explains the use

of wind turbines and provides a view of more than 30 rare and beautiful animal breeds including Saddleback pigs, Shetland ponies and Wiltshire Horn sheep. A café and farm shop on site make good use of the organic food produced on the farm.

KEYNSHAM
6½ miles NW of Bath on the A4175

🏛 Museum 🕊 Avon Valley Country Park

A former industrial centre, Keynsham is also a dormitory town for Bristol. Despite its modern appearance, it has ancient roots. During the excavations for a chocolate factory, the remains of two Roman villas were

---

📕 stories and anecdotes   🐦 famous people   🎨 art and craft   ✏ entertainment and sport   🚶 walks

discovered. These remains have since been incorporated into an interesting small **Museum** near the factory entrance. In the late 12th century an abbey was founded here, close to the River Chew, but it seems that the medieval monks were not as pious as they should have been. Eventually, they were banned from keeping sporting dogs, going out at night, employing private washerwomen and entertaining female guests in the monastery. Today, the abbey foundations lie under the bypass but the part-13th century parish church has survived and, along with being a good example of the Somerset Gothic architectural style, it contains some impressive tombs to members of the Bridges family.

Much later, two large brass mills were established at Keynsham during the town's 18th century industrial heyday, one on the River Avon and the other on the River Chew. Though production had ceased at both mills by the late 1920s, they are still impressive industrial remains.

Just to the east of Keynsham, the **Avon Valley Country Park** provides a popular day out for families. There's a large adventure playground, indoor play area, friendly animals and pets corner, falconry displays, boating lake, 1.5 mile nature trail walk, mini-steam train rides, land train rides, quad bikes, picnic and barbecue area, café and gift shop.

Cornwall

BODMIN
Shire Hall, Mount Folly Square, Bodmin,
Cornwall PL31 2DQ
Tel: 01208 76616 Fax: 01208 76616
e-mail: bodmintic@visit.org.uk

BUDE
Bude Visitor Centre, The Crescent, Bude,
Cornwall EX23 8LE
Tel: 01288 354240 Fax: 01288 355769
e-mail: budetic@visitbude.info

CAMELFORD
North Cornwall Museum, The Clease, Camelford,
Cornwall PL32 9PL
Tel: 01840 212954 Fax: 01840 212954
e-mail: manager@camelfordtic.eclipse.co.uk

FALMOUTH
11 Market Strand, Prince of Wales Pier, Falmouth,
Cornwall TR11 3DF
Tel: 01326 312300 Fax: 01326 313457
e-mail: info@falmouthtic.co.uk

FOWEY
5 South Street, Fowey, Cornwall PL23 1AR
Tel: 01726 833616 Fax: 01726 834939
e-mail: info@fowey.co.uk

HELSTON AND LIZARD PENINSULA
79 Meneage Street, Helston, Cornwall TR13 8RB
Tel: 01326 565431 Fax: 01326 572803
e-mail: info@helstontic.demon.co.uk

LAUNCESTON
Market House Arcade, Market Street, Launceston,
Cornwall PL15 8EP
Tel: 01566 772321 Fax: 01566 772322
e-mail: launcestontica@btconnect.com

LOOE
The Guildhall, Fore Street, East Looe,
Cornwall PL13 1AA
Tel: 01503 262072 Fax: 01503 265426
e-mail: looetic@btconnect.com

NEWQUAY
Municipal Offices, Marcus Hill, Newquay,
Cornwall TR7 1BD
Tel: 01637 854020 Fax: 01637 854030
e-mail: info@newquay.co.uk

PADSTOW
Red Brick Building, North Quay, Padstow,
Cornwall PL28 8AF
Tel: 01841 533449 Fax: 01841 532356
e-mail: padstowtic@btconnect.com

PENZANCE
Station Road, Penzance, Cornwall TR18 2NF
Tel: 01736 362207 Fax: 01736 363600
e-mail: pztic@penwith.gov.uk

ST AUSTELL TIC
Southbourne Road, St Austell, Cornwall PL25 4RS
Tel: 0845 094 0428 or 01726 879 500
Fax: 01726 874168
e-mail: tic@cornish-riviera.co.uk

ST IVES
The Guildhall, Street-an-Pol, St Ives,
Cornwall TR26 2DS
Tel: 01736 796297 Fax: 01736 798309
e-mail: ivtic@penwith.gov.uk

TRURO
Municipal Building, Boscawen Street, Truro,
Cornwall TR1 2NE
Tel: 01872 274555 Fax: 01872 263031
e-mail: tic@truro.gov.uk

TOURIST INFORMATION CENTRES

WADEBRIDGE
Eddystone Road, Wadebridge, Cornwall PL27 7AL
Tel: 0870 1223337 or 01208 813725
Fax: 01208 813781
e-mail: wadebridgetic@btconnect.com

Devon

AXMINSTER
The Old Courthouse, Church Street, Axminster,
Devon EX13 5AQ
Tel: 01297 34386 Fax: 01297 34386
e-mail: axminstertic@btopenworld.com

BARNSTAPLE
Museum of North Devon, The Square, Barnstaple,
Devon EX32 8LN
Tel: 01271 375000 Fax: 01271 374037
e-mail: info@staynorthdevon.co.uk

BIDEFORD
Victoria Park, The Quay, Bideford, Devon EX39 2QQ
Tel: 01237 477676 Fax: 01237 421853
e-mail: bidefordtic@torridge.gov.uk

BRAUNTON
The Bakehouse Centre, Caen Street, Braunton,
Devon EX33 1AA
Tel: 01271 816400 Fax: 01271 816947
e-mail: info@brauntontic.co.uk

BRIXHAM
The Old Market House, The Quay, Brixham,
Devon TQ5 8TB
Tel: 0870 70 70 010 or 01803 852861
Fax: 01803 852939
e-mail: holiday@torbay.gov.uk

BUDLEIGH SALTERTON
Fore Street, Budleigh Salterton, Devon EX9 6NG
Tel: 01395 445275 Fax: 01395 442208
e-mail: budleigh.tic@btconnect.com

COMBE MARTIN
Seacot, Cross Street, Combe Martin, Devon EX34 0DH
Tel: 01271 883319 Fax: 01271 883319
e-mail: mail@visitcombemartin.co.uk

CREDITON
The Old Town Hall, High Street, Crediton,
Devon EX17 3LF
Tel: 01363 772006 Fax: 01363 772006
e-mail: info@devonshireheartland.co.uk

DARTMOUTH
The Engine House, Mayor's Avenue, Dartmouth,
Devon TQ6 9YY
Tel: 01803 834224 Fax: 01803 835631
e-mail: holidays@discoverdartmouth.com

DAWLISH
The Lawn, Dawlish, Devon EX7 9PW
Tel: 01626 215665 Fax: 01626 865985
e-mail: dawtic@Teignbridge.gov.uk

EXETER
Civic Centre, Dix's Field, Exeter, Devon EX1 1RQ
Tel: 01392 265700 Fax: 01392 265260
e-mail: tic@exeter.gov.uk

EXMOUTH
Alexandra Terrace, Exmouth, Devon EX8 1NZ
Tel: 01395 222299 Fax: 01395 269911
e-mail: info@exmouthtourism.co.uk

HONITON
Lace Walk Car Park, Honiton, Devon EX14 1LT
Tel: 01404 43716 Fax: 01404 43716
e-mail: honitontic@honitontic.freeserve.co.uk

ILFRACOMBE
The Landmark, The Seafront, Ilfracombe,
Devon EX34 9BX
Tel: 01271 863001 Fax: 01271 862586
e-mail: info@ilfracombe-tourism.co.uk

TOURIST INFORMATION CENTRES

IVYBRIDGE
Ivybridge Bookshop and Information Centre, Leonards Road, Ivybridge, Devon PL21 0BS
Tel: 01752 897035 Fax: 01752 698511
e-mail: bookends.ivybridge@virgin.net

KINGSBRIDGE
The Quay, Kingsbridge, Devon TQ7 1HS
Tel: 01548 853195 Fax: 01548 854185
e-mail: advice@kingsbridgeinfo.co.uk

LYNTON AND LYNMOUTH
Town Hall, Lee Road, Lynton, Devon EX35 6BT
Tel: 0845 660 3232 or 01598 752225
Fax: 01598 752755
e-mail: info@lyntourism.co.uk

MODBURY
5 Modbury Court, Modbury, Devon PL21 0QR
Tel: 01548 830159 Fax: 01548 831371
e-mail: modburytic@lineone.net

NEWTON ABBOT
6 Bridge House, Courtenay Street, Newton Abbot, Devon TQ12 2QS
Tel: 01626 215667 Fax: 01626 337269
e-mail: natic@Teignbridge.gov.uk

OKEHAMPTON
Museum Courtyard, 3 West Street, Okehampton, Devon EX20 1HQ
Tel: 01837 53020 Fax: 01837 55225
e-mail: okehamptontic@westdevon.gov.uk

OTTERY ST MARY
10a Broad Street, Ottery St Mary, Devon EX11 1BZ
Tel: 01404 813964 Fax: 01404 813964
e-mail: info@otterytourism.org.uk

PAIGNTON
The Esplanade, Paignton, Devon TQ4 6ED
Tel: 0870 70 70 010 Fax: 01803 551959
e-mail: holiday@torbay.gov.uk

PLYMOUTH : PLYMOUTH MAYFLOWER
Plymouth Mayflower Centre, 3-5 The Barbican, Plymouth, Devon PL1 2LR
Tel: 01752 306330 Fax: 01752 306333
e-mail: barbicantic@plymouth.gov.uk

SALCOMBE
Market Street, Salcombe, Devon TQ8 8DE
Tel: 01548 843927 Fax: 01548 842736
e-mail: info@salcombeinformation.co.uk

SEATON
The Underfleet, Seaton, Devon EX12 2TB
Tel: 01297 21660 Fax: 01297 21689
e-mail: info@seatontic.freeserve.co.uk

SIDMOUTH
Ham Lane, Sidmouth, Devon EX10 8XR
Tel: 01395 516441 Fax: 01395 519333
e-mail: sidmouthtic@eclipse.co.uk

SOUTH MOLTON
1 East Street, South Molton, Devon EX36 3BU
Tel: 01769 574122 Fax: 01769 574718
e-mail: visitsouthmolton@btconnect.com

TAVISTOCK
Town Hall, Bedford Square, Tavistock, Devon PL19 0AE
Tel: 01822 612938 Fax: 01822 618389
e-mail: tavistocktic@westdevon.gov.uk

TEIGNMOUTH
The Den, Sea Front, Teignmouth, Devon TQ14 8BE
Tel: 01626 215666 Fax: 01626 778333
e-mail: teigntic@teignbridge.gov.uk

TIVERTON
Phoenix Lane, Tiverton, Devon EX16 6LU
Tel: 01884 255827 Fax: 01884 257594
e-mail: tivertontic@btconnect.com

TORQUAY
The Tourist Centre, Vaughan Parade, Torquay, Devon TQ2 5JG
Tel: 0870 70 70 010 Fax: 01803 214885
e-mail: holiday@torbay.gov.uk

TOURIST INFORMATION CENTRES

TORRINGTON
Castle Hill, South Street Car Park, Great Torrington,
Devon EX38 8AA
Tel: 01805 626140 Fax: 01805 626141
e-mail: info@great-torrington.com

TOTNES
The Town Mill, Coronation Road, Totnes,
South Devon TQ9 5DF
Tel: 01803 863168 Fax: 01803 865771
e-mail: enquire@totnesinformation.co.uk

WOOLACOMBE
The Esplanade, Woolacombe, Devon EX34 7DL
Tel: 01271 870553 Fax: 01271 870553
e-mail: info@woolacombetourism.co.uk

Dorset

BLANDFORD FORUM
1 Greyhound Yard, Blandford Forum, Dorset DT11 7EB
Tel: 01258 454770 Fax: 01258 484094
e-mail: blandfordtic@north-dorset.gov.uk

BRIDPORT
47 South Street, Bridport, Dorset DT6 3NY
Tel: 01308 424901 Fax: 01308 421060
e-mail: bridport.tic@westdorset-dc.gov.uk

CHRISTCHURCH
49 High Street, Christchurch, Dorset BH23 1AS
Tel: 01202 471780 Fax: 01202 476816
e-mail: enquiries@christchurchtourism.info

DORCHESTER
11 Antelope Walk, Dorchester, Dorset DT1 1BE
Tel: 01305 267992 Fax: 01305 266079
e-mail: dorchester.tic@westdorset-dc.gov.uk

LYME REGIS
Guildhall Cottage, Church Street, Lyme Regis,
Dorset DT7 3BS
Tel: 01297 442138 Fax: 01297 444668
e-mail: lymeregis.tic@westdorset-dc.gov.uk

POOLE
Enefco House, Poole Quay, Poole, Dorset BH15 1HJ
Tel: 01202 253253 Fax: 01202 262534
e-mail: info@poole.gov.uk

SHAFTESBURY
8 Bell Street, Shaftesbury, Dorset SP7 8AE
Tel: 01747 853514 Fax: 01747 850593
e-mail: shaftesburytic@north-dorset.gov.uk

SHERBORNE
3 Tilton Court, Digby Road, Sherborne,
Dorset DT9 3NL
Tel: 01935 815341 Fax: 01935 817210
e-mail: sherborne.tic@westdorset-dc.gov.uk

SWANAGE
The White House, Shore Road, Swanage,
Dorset BH19 1LB
Tel: 01929 422885 Fax: 01929 423423
e-mail: mail@swanage.gov.uk

WAREHAM
Holy Trinity Church, South Street, Wareham,
Dorset BH20 4LU
Tel: 01929 552740 Fax: 01929 554491
e-mail: tic@purbeck-dc.gov.uk

WEYMOUTH
The King's Statue, The Esplanade, Weymouth,
Dorset, DT4 7AN
Tel: 01305 785747 Fax: 01305 788092
e-mail: tic@weymouth.gov.uk

WIMBORNE MINSTER
29 High Street, Wimborne Minster, Dorset BH21 1HR
Tel: 01202 886116 Fax: 01202 841025
e-mail: wimbornetic@eastdorset.gov.uk

Somerset

BATH
Abbey Chambers, Abbey Church Yard, Bath BA1 1LY
Tel: 0906 711 2000 (60p per minute)
Fax: 01225 477787
e-mail: tourism@bathnes.gov.uk

TOURIST INFORMATION CENTRES

BRIDGWATER
Bridgwater House, King Square, Bridgwater,
Somerset TA6 3AR
Tel: 01278 436 438 Fax: 01278 436 480
e-mail: bridgwater.tic@sedgemoor.gov.uk

BRISTOL : HARBOURSIDE
Wildwalk @Bristol, Harbourside, Bristol BS1 5DB
Tel: 0117 946 2225 Fax: 0117 9157340
e-mail: ticharbourside@destinationbristol.co.uk

BURNHAM-ON-SEA
South Esplanade, Burnham-on-Sea, Somerset TA8 1BU
Tel: 01278 787852 Fax: 01278 781282
e-mail: burnham.tic@sedgemoor.gov.uk

CARTGATE
South Somerset TIC, A303/A3088 Cartgate Picnic Site,
Stoke-sub-Hamdon, Somerset TA14 6RA
Tel: 01935 829333 Fax: 01935 824644
e-mail: cartgate.tic@southsomerset.gov.uk

CHARD
The Guildhall, Fore Street, Chard, Somerset TA20 1PP
Tel: 01460 65710 Fax: 01460 65710
e-mail: chardtic@chard.gov.uk

CHEDDAR
The Gorge, Cheddar, Somerset BS27 3QE
Tel: 01934 744071 Fax: 01934 744614
e-mail: cheddar.tic@sedgemoor.gov.uk

FROME
The Round Tower, Justice Lane, Frome,
Somerset BA11 1BB
Tel: 01373 467271 Fax: 01373 451733
e-mail: enquiries@frometouristinfo.co.uk

GLASTONBURY
The Tribunal, 9 High Street, Glastonbury,
Somerset BA6 9DP
Tel: 01458 832954 Fax: 01458 832949
e-mail: glastonbury.tic@ukonline.co.uk

MINEHEAD
17 Friday Street, Minehead, Somerset TA24 5UB
Tel: 01643 702624 Fax: 01643 707166
e-mail: info@mineheadtic.co.uk

SHEPTON MALLET
48 High Street, Shepton Mallet, Somerset BA4 5AS
Tel: 01749 345258 Fax: 01749 345258
e-mail: sheptonmallet.tic@ukonline.co.uk

SEDGEMOOR SERVICES
Somerset Visitor Centre, Road Chef Services,
M5 Southbound, Axbridge, Somerset BS26 2UF
Tel: 01934 750833 Fax: 01934 750646
e-mail: somersetvisitorcentre@somerset.gov.uk

STREET
Clarks Village, Farm Road, Street, Somerset BA16 0BB
Tel: 01458 447384 Fax: 01458 447393
e-mail: street.tic@ukonline.co.uk

TAUNTON
The Library, Paul Street, Taunton, Somerset TA1 3XZ
Tel: 01823 336344 Fax: 01823 340308
e-mail: tauntontic@tauntondeane.gov.uk

WELLINGTON
30 Fore Street, Wellington, Somerset TA21 8AQ
Tel: 01823 663379 Fax: 01823 667279
e-mail: wellingtontic@tauntondeane.gov.uk

WELLS
Town Hall, Market Place, Wells, Somerset BA5 2RB
Tel: 01749 672552 Fax: 01749 670869
e-mail: touristinfo@wells.gov.uk

WESTON-SUPER-MARE
Beach Lawns, Weston-super-Mare, Somerset BS23 1AT
Tel: 01934 888800 Fax: 01934 641741
e-mail: westontouristinfo@n-somerset.gov.uk

YEOVIL HERITAGE & VISITOR INFORMATION CENTRE
Hendford, Yeovil, Somerset BA20 1UN
Tel: 01935 845946/7 Fax: 01935 845940
e-mail: yeoviltic@southsomerset.gov.uk

INDEX OF ADVERTISERS

INDEX OF ADVERTISERS

ACTIVITIES

ARTS AND CRAFTS

INDEX OF ADVERTISERS

INDEX OF ADVERTISERS

JEWELLERY

PLACES OF INTEREST

INDEX OF ADVERTISERS

SPECIALIST FOOD AND DRINK

Looking for more walks?

The walks in this book have been gleaned from Britain's largest online walking guide, to be found at *www.walkingworld.com*.

The site contains over 2000 walks from all over England, Scotland and Wales so there are plenty more to choose from in this book's region as well as further afield - ideal if you are taking a short break as you can plan your walks in advance. There are walks of every length and type to suit all tastes.

Want more detail for the walks in this book? Next to every walk in this book you will see a Walk ID. You can enter this ID number on Walkingworld's 'Find a Walk' page and you will be taken straight to the details of that walk

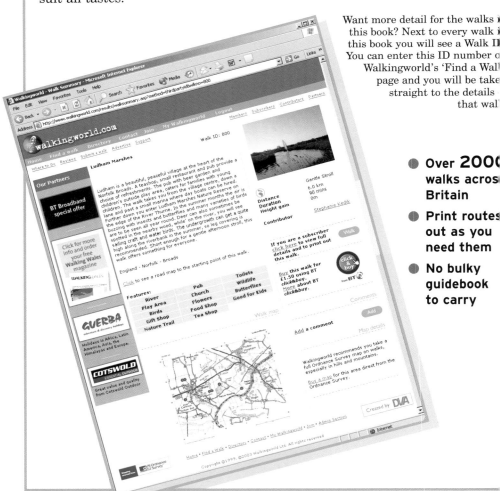

- Over **2000** walks across Britain

- Print routes out as you need them

- No bulky guidebook to carry

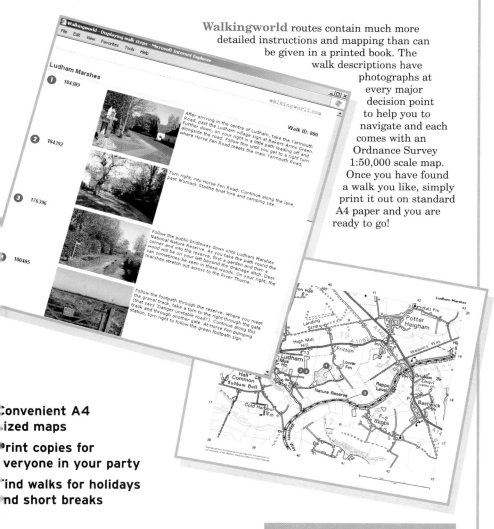

Walkingworld routes contain much more detailed instructions and mapping than can be given in a printed book. The walk descriptions have photographs at every major decision point to help you to navigate and each comes with an Ordnance Survey 1:50,000 scale map. Once you have found a walk you like, simply print it out on standard A4 paper and you are ready to go!

Convenient A4 sized maps

Print copies for everyone in your party

Find walks for holidays and short breaks

A modest annual subscription gives you access to over 2000 walks, all in Walkingworld's easy to follow format. The database of walks is growing all the time and as a subscriber you gain access to new routes as soon as they are published.

Visit the Walkingworld website at *www.walkingworld.com*

ORDER FORM

To order any of our publications just fill in the payment details below and complete the order form. For orders of less than 4 copies please add £1 per book for postage and packing. Orders over 4 copies are P & P free.

Please Complete Either:

I enclose a cheque for £ [　　　　　　] *made payable to Travel Publishing Ltd*

Or:

CARD NO: [　　　　　　　　　　]　　EXPIRY DATE: [　　　　]

SIGNATURE: [　　　　　　　　　　　]

NAME: [　　　　　　　　　　　　　]

ADDRESS: [　　　　　　　　　　　　]

TEL NO: [　　　　　　　　　　　　]

Please either send, telephone, fax or e-mail your order to:

*Travel Publishing Ltd, 7a Apollo House, Calleva Park, Aldermaston, Berkshire RG7 8TN
Tel: 0118 981 7777　Fax: 0118 940 8428　e-mail: info@travelpublishing.co.uk*

	PRICE	QUANTITY		PRICE	QUANTITY
HIDDEN PLACES REGIONAL TITLES			**COUNTRY PUBS AND INNS TITLES**		
Cornwall	£8.99	....	Cornwall	£7.99	....
Devon	£8.99	....	Devon	£7.99	....
Dorset, Hants & Isle of Wight	£8.99	....	Sussex	£7.99	....
East Anglia	£8.99	....	Yorkshire	£7.99	....
Lake District & Cumbria	£8.99	....	**COUNTRY LIVING RURAL GUIDES**		
Northumberland & Durham	£8.99	....	East Anglia	£10.99	....
Peak District and Derbyshire	£8.99	....	Heart of England	£10.99	....
Yorkshire	£8.99	....	Ireland	£10.99	....
HIDDEN PLACES NATIONAL TITLES			North East of England	£10.99	....
England	£11.99	....	North West of England	£10.99	....
Ireland	£11.99	....	Scotland	£10.99	....
Scotland	£11.99	....	South of England	£10.99	....
Wales	£11.99	....	South East of England	£10.99	....
HIDDEN INNS TITLES			Wales	£10.99	....
East Anglia	£7.99	....	West Country	£10.99	....
Heart of England	£7.99	....	**OTHER TITLES**		
South	£7.99	....	Off The Motorway	£11.99	....
South East	£7.99	....			
West Country	£7.99	....	**TOTAL QUANTITY**	[　　　　]	
			TOTAL VALUE	[　　　　]	

READER REACTION FORM

The **Travel Publishing** *research team would like to receive readers' comments on any visitor attractions or places reviewed in the book and also recommendations for suitable entries to be included in the next edition. This will help ensure that the* **Country Living** series of **Rural Guides** *continues to provide its readers with useful information on the more interesting, unusual or unique features of each attraction or place ensuring that their visit to the local area is an enjoyable and stimulating experience. To provide your comments or recommendations would you please complete the forms below and overleaf as indicated and send to:*

The Research Department, Travel Publishing Ltd, 7a Apollo House, Calleva Park, Aldermaston, Reading, RG7 8TN

YOUR NAME:

YOUR ADDRESS:

YOUR TEL NO:

Please tick as appropriate: COMMENTS ☐ RECOMMENDATION ☐

ESTABLISHMENT:

ADDRESS:

TEL NO:

CONTACT NAME:

PLEASE COMPLETE FORM OVERLEAF

READER REACTION FORM

COMMENT OR REASON FOR RECOMMENDATION:

READER REACTION FORM

The **Travel Publishing** *research team would like to receive readers' comments on any visitor attractions or places reviewed in the book and also recommendations for suitable entries to be included in the next edition. This will help ensure that the* **Country Living series of Rural Guides** *continues to provide its readers with useful information on the more interesting, unusual or unique features of each attraction or place ensuring that their visit to the local area is an enjoyable and stimulating experience. To provide your comments or recommendations would you please complete the forms below and overleaf as indicated and send to:*

The Research Department, Travel Publishing Ltd, 7a Apollo House, Calleva Park, Aldermaston, Reading, RG7 8TN

YOUR NAME:

YOUR ADDRESS:

YOUR TEL NO:

Please tick as appropriate: COMMENTS ☐   RECOMMENDATION ☐

ESTABLISHMENT:

ADDRESS:

TEL NO:

CONTACT NAME:

PLEASE COMPLETE FORM OVERLEAF

READER REACTION FORM

COMMENT OR REASON FOR RECOMMENDATION:

....

....

....

....

....

....

....

....

....

....

....

The **Travel Publishing** research team would like to receive readers' comments on any visitor attractions or places reviewed in the book and also recommendations for suitable entries to be included in the next edition. This will help ensure that the **Country Living series of Rural Guides** continues to provide its readers with useful information on the more interesting, unusual or unique features of each attraction or place ensuring that their visit to the local area is an enjoyable and stimulating experience. To provide your comments or recommendations would you please complete the forms below and overleaf as indicated and send to:

The Research Department, Travel Publishing Ltd, 7a Apollo House, Calleva Park, Aldermaston, Reading, RG7 8TN

YOUR NAME:

YOUR ADDRESS:

YOUR TEL NO:

Please tick as appropriate: COMMENTS ☐   RECOMMENDATION ☐

ESTABLISHMENT:

ADDRESS:

TEL NO:

CONTACT NAME:

PLEASE COMPLETE FORM OVERLEAF

READER REACTION FORM

COMMENT OR REASON FOR RECOMMENDATION:

READER REACTION FORM

The **Travel Publishing** *research team would like to receive readers' comments on any visitor attractions or places reviewed in the book and also recommendations for suitable entries to be included in the next edition. This will help ensure that the* **Country Living series of Rural Guides** *continues to provide its readers with useful information on the more interesting, unusual or unique features of each attraction or place ensuring that their visit to the local area is an enjoyable and stimulating experience. To provide your comments or recommendations would you please complete the forms below and overleaf as indicated and send to:*

The Research Department, Travel Publishing Ltd, 7a Apollo House, Calleva Park, Aldermaston, Reading, RG7 8TN

YOUR NAME:

YOUR ADDRESS:

YOUR TEL NO:

Please tick as appropriate: COMMENTS   RECOMMENDATION

ESTABLISHMENT:

ADDRESS:

TEL NO:

CONTACT NAME:

PLEASE COMPLETE FORM OVERLEAF

READER REACTION FORM

COMMENT OR REASON FOR RECOMMENDATION:

READER REACTION FORM

The **Travel Publishing** *research team would like to receive readers' comments on any visitor attractions or places reviewed in the book and also recommendations for suitable entries to be included in the next edition. This will help ensure that the* **Country Living series of Rural Guides** *continues to provide its readers with useful information on the more interesting, unusual or unique features of each attraction or place ensuring that their visit to the local area is an enjoyable and stimulating experience. To provide your comments or recommendations would you please complete the forms below and overleaf as indicated and send to:*

The Research Department, Travel Publishing Ltd, 7a Apollo House, Calleva Park, Aldermaston, Reading, RG7 8TN

YOUR NAME:

YOUR ADDRESS:

YOUR TEL NO:

Please tick as appropriate: COMMENTS RECOMMENDATION

ESTABLISHMENT:

ADDRESS:

TEL NO:

CONTACT NAME:

PLEASE COMPLETE FORM OVERLEAF

READER REACTION FORM

COMMENT OR REASON FOR RECOMMENDATION:

TOWNS, VILLAGES AND PLACES OF INTEREST

TOWNS, VILLAGES AND PLACES OF INTEREST

TOWNS, VILLAGES AND PLACES OF INTEREST

TOWNS, VILLAGES AND PLACES OF INTEREST

TOWNS, VILLAGES AND PLACES OF INTEREST

TOWNS, VILLAGES AND PLACES OF INTEREST

TOWNS, VILLAGES AND PLACES OF INTEREST